Social Work Practice & the Law

Lyn K. Slater, MSW, PhD, was a clinical associate professor at the Fordham University Graduate School of Social Services and adjunct professor of law at the Fordham University School of Law. She cotaught "Interdisciplinary Approaches to Child Abuse and Neglect" for graduate-level law and social work students with a practicing attorney. She was the supervising social worker at the family advocacy clinic, Fordham University School of Law for 10 years. She has presented extensively at legal education conferences regarding interprofessional practice. In previous positions, she served as director of the Child Sexual Abuse Project at Lawyers for Children (New York); and consultant, The Bronx Defenders and Legal Services of New York.

Kara R. Finck, JD, is Practice Professor of Law, Director of the Interdisciplinary Child Advocacy Clinic, and Deputy Dean for Clinical Education at the University of Pennsylvania Carey Law School. Previously, she was the managing attorney of the Family Defense Practice at The Bronx Defenders, where she created a groundbreaking interdisciplinary legal practice for parents involved in the child welfare system. Her areas of specialty include child welfare, parents' rights, and interdisciplinary practice focusing on law and social work collaboration. As a Skadden Fellow, she represented pregnant and parenting teens at The Door's Legal Services Center in New York City. She has presented on best practices in child welfare and dependency cases, the collateral consequences of child welfare involvement, and interdisciplinary collaboration. She is a graduate of Columbia Law School and Columbia College.

Marcía Hopkins, MSW, has devoted her career as a social worker to supporting child and youth clients. In her more than 13 years of experience, she has worked in gun violence prevention, in grief counseling, with seniors, and as an advocate for children and youth who are impacted by community violence, foster care, and juvenile justice and who are victims of labor and commercial sex trafficking. Throughout her career, Marcía has worked alongside stakeholders and youth leaders to engage in national policy advocacy around youth justice and child welfare reform. Marcía also serves as a social work consultant working with organizing groups, legal offices, and journalists to provide her expertise on a range of topics related to systemic reform and child welfare lived experience.

Marcía earned her master's degree in social work from Temple University. She graduated cum laude from Indiana University of Pennsylvania with a bachelor's degree in sociology. She cares deeply about social justice issues, having been affected by the child welfare system as a young child and losing her brothers to gun violence.

Social Work Practice & the Law

SECOND EDITION

LYN K. SLATER, MSW, PhD
KARA R. FINCK, JD
MARCÍA HOPKINS, MSW

SPRINGER PUBLISHING

First Springer Publishing edition 978-0-8261-1766-3 (2012)

Springer Publishing Company, LLC
902 Carnegie Center/Suite 140, Princeton, NJ 08540
www.springerpub.com
connect.springerpub.com

Acquisitions Editor: Mindy Okura-Marszycki
Production Editor: Claire Kramer
Compositor: Transforma

ISBN: 978-0-8261-0075-7
e-book ISBN: 978-0-8261-0076-4
DOI: 10.1891/9780826100764

SUPPLEMENTS:

SPRINGER PUBLISHING CONNECT™

A robust set of instructor resources designed to supplement this text is located at **http://connect.springerpub.com/content/book/978-0-8261-0076-4.** Qualifying instructors may request access by emailing **textbook@springerpub.com.**

Instructor Materials:
LMS Common Cartridge—All Instructor Resources ISBN: 978-0-8261-0079-5
Instructor's Manual ISBN: 978-0-8261-0077-1
Instructor Test Bank ISBN: 978-0-8261-5468-2
Instructor Chapter PowerPoint Slides ISBN: 978-0-8261-0078-8
Transition Guide From First to Second Edition ISBN: 978-0-8261-6216-8

25 26 27 28 / 5 4 3 2 1

Library of Congress Cataloging-in-Publication Data
Names: Slater, Lyn K., author. | Finck, Kara R., author. | Hopkins, Marcía, author.
Title: Social work practice and the law / Lyn K. Slater, MSW, PhD; Kara R. Finck, JD; Marcía Hopkins, MSW.
Description: Second edition. | New York : Springer Publishing Company, 2025. | Includes bibliographical references and index
Identifiers: LCCN 2025004893 | ISBN 9780826100757 (paperback) | ISBN 9780826100764 (ebook)
Subjects: LCSH: Social workers--Legal status, laws, etc.--United States. | Social service--United States.
Classification: LCC KF3721 .S59 2025 | DDC 344.7303/132--dc23/eng/20250212
LC record available at https://lccn.loc.gov/2025004893

Printed in the United States of America by Gasch Printing.

We would like to dedicate this book to the late Professor Ann Moynihan. She was a brilliant scholar, an inspiring teacher, a fierce advocate for justice, and a loyal friend. We were extraordinarily fortunate to have her as a mentor, and many of the thoughts and ideas presented in this book were forged during our many provocative and stimulating conversations with her.

Contents

Preface

When this book was originally published in 2012, the central premise was that the law powerfully, implicitly, and explicitly constructs and influences social work practice. Over a decade later, that premise remains as powerful as ever and provides a foundation for social workers to expand their conception of justice, advocacy, and reform. The actions and options of social workers and their clients are constantly being shaped, mandated, and regulated by law. As you will learn throughout the text, much of what social workers do is the result of some legal mandate or rule. These mandates can be products of federal, state, and local laws and regulations as well as case law where statutes and laws are applied to individual cases. In fact, the majority of state licensing laws even define the words "social work practice" and set out what activities are permissible for you to engage in by law.

Regulations create, effect, and shape the organizations where you work, how you identify who are your clients, what activities you may perform, what obligations you have to clients and, in some cases, what limits you set on how long you may work with a client. The law defines the power relationship between you and your client as can be seen in statutes that give you certain duties such as the reporting of abuse. As a profession we frequently focus on how the law places limitations on practice but this book will focus on how the law implicates and supports social work values, such as the right to confidentiality, equal opportunity, social justice, freedom from discrimination and oppression, and the balancing of intervention and control. This book presents a conceptual framework that assists the social worker in thinking about the law in a different way and applying and using the law proactively in practice.

This book will introduce you to what the authors call the implicit legal context of social work practice. The *implicit legal context* is the complex system of laws and regulations that powerfully shapes and impacts your social work practice but is frequently invisible during the course of everyday work or, at best, not consciously thought about.

You will also learn about what the authors call the *explicit legal context,* which is defined as social work practice in those overtly legal forums—courts, prisons, victim service centers, and probation and parole offices—and also known as forensic social work. We will introduce you to important reforms that are occurring in the legal system such as treatment courts and other alternatives to the adversarial system that seek to address the legal problems of clients in more holistic ways and offer many exciting opportunities for social work participation and collaboration.

It is not our goal to teach you every law that is implicated in social work practice. The volume of law is too large and changes too rapidly for us to do that effectively or inclusively. We will, however, teach you to understand how the law shapes and informs social work practice, how you might apply it to practice, and how the legal system will go about making decisions about your clients. Most importantly, you will learn the knowledge and skills necessary to access and make sense of the relevant law when you need to know it in your work with clients or as you think about your professional roles and responsibilities. Technology makes it much easier for social workers to access the law than in the past. We will not teach you about social work practice per se, but rather how to target and translate social work knowledge and practice skills you may already know for use in both implicit and explicit legal contexts. The law can change rapidly, and some of the cases that we reference may in fact be overruled by the time you are reading this book. However, the foundational skills of identifying and understanding the role of the law in your social work practice remain critical.

Finally, we will show how the law can be used to empower your client and yourself as a social worker and assist you in having effective communication with legal professionals. This book advances the idea that knowing the law will empower you to function more effectively, ethically, actively, and legally in all practice settings, not only legal arenas. This book can also be used by lawyers to understand how they can effectively access and use social workers and their knowledge base to assist them in achieving legal and nonlegal outcomes that meet the goals of their clients and that are ultimately experienced by clients as fair and just processes.

This text is written for all social workers because all social workers interface with the law, both implicitly and explicitly, in the context of everyday social work practice and life in general. Social workers that work or wish to work specifically in legal or criminal justice settings and collaborate with lawyers on a daily basis will find this book an essential resource for practice. Although written primarily for social workers, lawyers who must collaborate with the social work profession in the course of everyday work may find this book a useful resource in understanding how to more effectively enlist social work knowledge and skills to enhance their work with clients.

Written collaboratively by social workers and a lawyer, the majority of the book presents an ongoing conversation between two different professionals about a common case, *The Case of Michelle Jones,* as the vehicle through which to teach you about the law, about your own social work profession, and about the role of the legal profession in your practice. We believe that it is more effective to teach social workers about the law by starting with the social work context in which the case law or regulation will be applied. As social workers can become anxious and uncomfortable when interfacing with the law, this book will start with the familiar territory of social work issues, knowledge, language, and skills and show you how knowledge about the legal framework for practice can expand and enhance your work.

It is our hope that this method will better assist you in applying and practicing skills to help you achieve critical competence, to prepare you to effectively collaborate with other professionals in generating creative solutions to the many problems faced by low-income families, to feel competent to identify and respond to legal issues, and to respect and activate the rights of your clients. The lawyer/author will also instruct you on how to obtain legal guidance and expertise when you as a social worker do not have direct access to a lawyer.

Many of the ideas in this book are informed by evaluation research conducted by the social workers/authors that sought to identify and describe practice and educational activities that can result in more effective collaboration between social workers and lawyers, challenge and modify professional stereotypes, and provide greater feelings of empowerment and competence for social workers that work within legal forums. This book represents our belief and the contemporary view of policymakers that interprofessional dialogue and problem-solving results in more comprehensive and creative solutions for client problems and consequently the development of more effective and just laws, justice systems, and social services.

The book begins by identifying the legal needs of social work clients, with particular focus on low-income populations. We follow this with a conceptual and historical framework that provides a base for social workers from which to rethink their relationship to the law. Chapters 3, 4, and 5 provide the basic knowledge, values, skills, and ethics needed to become a critically competent practitioner including ethical differences and similarities between the two professions, an overview of both the implicit and explicit legal contexts, essential critical thinking skills, and basic skills of legal and social science research. Chapters 6 and 9 present an in-depth review of a range of civil proceedings, the path of a civil case, and stress the areas where there is an intersection between law and social work as well as identify legal decisions that often require social work knowledge. Chapters 7 and 10 cover criminal and juvenile justice proceedings, the path of a criminal and juvenile case, and the many opportunities for social work intervention with a focus on prevention. Chapter 8 deals with the basic skills and knowledge that a social worker will need to effectively participate in a trial or hearing, including such topics as witness preparation, what to expect, report writing, and expert testimony. Chapter 11 describes the many alternative venues available to traditional adversarial proceedings such as mediation, family group conferencing, and problem-solving courts.

In Chapter 12, social workers will learn about administrative law and the path of an impartial hearing, and will come to understand how administrative law is especially relevant to social work practice. Finally, Chapter 13 introduces the reader to the opportunities for collaboration on a more macro level, such as participation in class action lawsuits, civil rights litigation, and the submission of amicus briefs.

Acknowledgments

I would first and foremost like to acknowledge my incredible writing and thinking partner Kara Finck. Writing this book with her reminded me every minute what a joy it is to have a smart, funny, and creative collaborator and why I love interprofessional work. I must also acknowledge the faculty from Fordham Graduate School of Social Service and the Clinical Education Program in the School of Law who contributed to my intellectual and academic development and our thinking about social work and the law: Leah Hill, Mary Ann Forgey, Beth Schwartz, Virginia Strand, Ian Weinstein, James Cohen, and Michael Martin. I would also like to thank Dean Peter Vaughan from the Graduate School of Social Service and former Deans John Ferrick and William Treanor of the School of Law for their gracious support during my years in the clinical program. My fellow social workers in the clinical legal education world—Michelle Geller, Monica Mahan, and Lynn Barenberg—have been wonderfully encouraging and outstanding colleagues. My family as ever has been endlessly supportive, especially my partner Calvin. My greatest debt of gratitude, however, is to the many clients and students who have inspired and continue to inspire me everyday to remain passionate and committed to my incredible profession, social work.

LYN K. SLATER

I first want to thank my remarkable collaborators, Lyn and Marcía. Lyn had the original inspiration for this book and challenged and inspired me with her creativity, intellect, and commitment to the highest practice on behalf of her clients and as a scholar. Writing this book with her not only taught me to be a better lawyer, but also reminded me how rich and fulfilling interprofessional practice can be. Marcía transformed my thinking about youth engagement, strategic storytelling, and systems reform and I am so grateful that she partnered with me on this revision. I want to thank Robin Steinberg, my first mentor who created The Bronx Defenders and gave me the amazing opportunity to build a family defense practice and to work with the most talented group of advocates for parents who taught me how to be an interdisciplinary practitioner focused on collaboration, reform, and innovation. As a clinical professor, I want to thank my colleagues who have inspired me with their scholarship and insights on pedagogy, and the clinic law students and social work students whose dedication and creativity are a source of hope for the next generation of interdisciplinary advocates. Over the years, my clients have taught me how to be a better advocate and continue to inspire me with their strength, grace, and humor in the face of daily injustice. Finally, to my beloved family, Mark, Conor, and Ronan, who was a newborn when the first edition was published; thank you for your endless encouragement, patience, humor, and love.

We would both like to especially acknowledge and thank our wonderful first edition editor Jennifer Perillo, who was a fan of this book when it was only an idea, and with patience and enthusiasm supported us through the writing process. We would also like to thank Lauren Kubiak, our editor for the second edition for her support and patience in helping us navigate the revision process. We particularly wish to thank Claire Kramer for her editing, excellent support, diligence, and patience.

Kara R. Finck

I want to thank Kara Finck, who made this opportunity possible. Kara, you are a wonderful colleague and friend, and I have learned so much from you. Thank you for believing in me and trusting me. Working with you over the years, I have learned so much about legal advocacy and what it looks like to ethically and respectfully integrate social work and legal representation in ways that uplift our clients and support their decision-making. I want to thank my first mentor in the legal field, Emily Keller, who took a chance on me fresh out of graduate school while I was looking for a field placement. This led me to a wonderful career at the Juvenile Law Center. I also want to thank Jennifer Pokempner, who, without a doubt, is one of the most dedicated child welfare attorneys. Jenny, I learned so much from you that I will use forever in my career. I also want to thank Juvenile Law Center staff and Youth Advocacy Program—Paige Joki and Maura Mclnerney—at Education Law Center and the countless colleagues in the field from whom I have learned so much from and have worked alongside; you all do amazing work on behalf of children and youth. And to the youth I have worked with throughout my career, I have learned so much working alongside you. I believe in you. My best work was with you all.

To my dear friends, those with lived experience in the system and those without, I would not have been able to face my toughest times without you. You know who you are. Finally, I want to thank my family who have given me their unwavering support and my siblings and mother who experienced the failings of the child welfare systems and still persevered. All your stories, your perseverance, drive, and motivation help me to continue this work. To my father, you are our biggest supporter. To my partner Tameron, and our new sweet baby boy, Ja'Hari, you are my greatest loves.

Lastly, to my brothers, Anthony and Darryl, whose lives were taken much too young, I hope I am making you proud. To my mentor Becky Weichhand, your light is still shining down here in the field. We miss you all.

Marcía Hopkins

Instructor Resources

A robust set of instructor resources designed to supplement this text is located at **http://connect.springerpub.com/content/book/978-0-8261-0076-4**. Qualifying instructors may request access by emailing **textbook@springerpub.com**.

- **LMS Common Cartridge With All Instructor Resources**
- **Instructor's Manual**
    - Learning Objectives
    - Discussion Questions
    - Learning Activities
    - Teaching Tips
- **Instructor Test Bank** with more than 100 multiple-choice questions (including full rationales).
- **Instructor Chapter PowerPoint Slides** summarizing chapter content.

SPRINGER PUBLISHING

Visit https://connect.springerpub.com/ and look for the **"Show Supplementary"** button on the **book homepage**.

CHAPTER 1

Identifying the Legal Needs and Realizing the Rights of Social Work Clients

INTRODUCTION

This chapter introduces you to the idea that knowledge of the legal system and the development of skills to work within the legal system and with attorneys are powerful and necessary tools for effective social work practice. Knowledge of and participation in the U.S. justice system can offer social workers and clients a means to solve problems, identify and address harms, protect and realize rights, and advance personal and professional interests. This chapter introduces you to the wide range of legal and, as you will see, corresponding service needs that have been identified, and frequently remain unaddressed, for low-income clients. You will understand what some of these legal issues are, why they are frequently unaddressed, and how the legal problems are related to social work outcomes and goals.

THE INTERSECTION OF SOCIAL WORK AND THE LAW: SOCIAL SERVICE ISSUES AND SYSTEMS OF LAW

How many times do social workers come across the following scenarios: a family living in unsafe housing with an unresponsive landlord, a child who has been suspended from school, a client who has a medical emergency and cannot obtain healthcare, a parent who is not receiving income, a teenager who has been arrested for assault but who only speaks to an attorney 5 minutes before the court appearance, a veteran who is not getting benefits from the Veterans Administration, or an elder in financial trouble due to fraud?

Whether you view yourself as a clinician or a generalist practitioner, when clients have these concerns they always impact the process of social work intervention. As an example, think about how your clinical work providing trauma treatment focused on symptom management with a survivor of rape or sexual violence may be impacted if your client is unable to get the landlord to fix the lock on the door or put a light in the hallway of the apartment building. Whether the result is missed or disrupted treatment sessions, both you and your client should be aware that there are usually legal as well as nonlegal solutions that can be used to rectify the situation. The problem is that many clients, as well as the social workers who work with them, are not aware that many of these issues have a legal basis and therefore a legal solution, and that there is an appropriate system of law where the issue can be addressed.

INTRODUCTION TO SYSTEMS OF THE LAW

The United States has three systems of laws: civil, criminal, and administrative. In future chapters, we discuss the three systems in much greater depth. As an introduction, civil law is the body of law that identifies and impacts the private rights and interests of citizens and what "remedy" or solution a client may have when they are concerned about their rights. A tenant's right to safe housing conditions is considered a civil matter. Criminal law is that body of law that defines and prohibits behaviors or acts that the government believes are dangerous to the general welfare or safety of others, and establishes the punishments that are imposed when someone is convicted of a crime, including incarceration. An individual arrested for domestic abuse is facing a criminal matter. Administrative law is the body of law that governs the activities of the administrative agencies of government. A veteran not receiving benefits they are entitled to would be considered an administrative matter.

Each body of law has its own procedural laws that comprise the rules by which a court hears and determines what happens in civil, criminal, or administrative proceedings. The objectives of the rules are to ensure fair procedures and decisions. The situation already mentioned—the teenager who sees the attorney for only 5 minutes before going to trial—demonstrates a procedural legal issue as defendants in criminal proceedings can appeal their verdict on the grounds of ineffective representation by their attorney. As demonstrated by the preceding examples, social workers often have clients with legal issues that span all systems of law. Indeed, a single client of a social worker can have multiple issues implicating all the systems of law at the same time.

THE CIVIL AND ADMINISTRATIVE LEGAL NEEDS OF LOW-INCOME CLIENTS

Civil and administrative legal problems often involve basic human needs such as protection from abuse, violence and exploitation, safe and livable housing, and supplemental income such as when a person is disabled and cannot work. In order for clinical work or case management services to be effective, clients must have the very basic needs of shelter, safety, and nourishment met before there can be movement to addressing more complex concerns. The Centre for Human Rights (1994) takes the position that human needs and human rights are inseparable from each other and from social work values, ethics, and practice: "Rights corresponding to human needs have to be upheld and fostered and they embody the justification and motivation for social work action" (1994, p. 5). Social workers have an interest and a duty in seeing that the needs and rights of their clients on every level are linked together, met, and achieved.

Since 1974, the Legal Services Corporation (LSC) is the institution charged by Congress with the administration of a federally funded civil legal assistance program for those who would otherwise not be able to afford legal counsel. As part of this responsibility, the LSC collects data from states to determine the legal needs of low-income individuals and the level of legal assistance available to meet the need. The LSC has identified the difference between the level of legal assistance available and the level needed to meet the needs of low-income Americans as the "justice gap" (LSC, 2022). Researchers conducted national surveys in English and Spanish "to measure the prevalence of civil legal problems among low-income Americans and assess the extent to which low-income Americans receive the legal help necessary to resolve their civil legal problems" (LSC, 2022). The study found that 74% of low-income households faced at least one civil legal issue with over half of the survey respondents reporting that the legal issue significantly impacted their lives. The most common legal issues faced by low-income households included healthcare, housing, income maintenance, and consumer law.

Research also reports that certain groups have more legal concerns than other groups; that is, single mothers, elders, immigrants, those for whom English is not their first language, African American and Hispanic households, households composed of five or more people, and those with children (LSC, 2022).

Civil legal problems cover a range of issues and fall into the following categories: family, consumer, housing, employment, education, benefits and income, health, and immigration needs (LSC, 2022). Table 1.1 illustrates the types of civil legal problems and how they are generally categorized under the law.

As a social worker, you have probably been educated to identify and to assess many of the examples listed in Table 1.1 as social service needs. Yet research and practice clearly demonstrate that those same social service needs can just as readily be classified as legal needs. Regardless of how they are defined, solving these kinds of problems and addressing client needs are essential to fulfilling social work values and ethics such as the practice of achieving a good fit between the person and the environment, upholding and fostering human rights, and the achievement of social justice (Witkin, 1998). Legal needs and rights can be addressed in civil courts such as Family Court or in administrative proceedings such as impartial hearings that assess a claim of unfair denial of government benefits. In Chapter 4, you will learn much more about the way in which civil and administrative proceedings operate and how to conceptualize your role as a social worker and advocate in those proceedings.

However, it is imperative for social workers to also educate themselves on the significant body of research documenting that certain groups, such as African American children and families, receive disparate treatment when compared with Whites during all the decision-making points that occur in civil proceedings related to child welfare and juvenile justice (Hartley & Silva, 2007; Hill, 2007; Roberts, 2022). Awareness of this disparity will be important when listening to clients' concerns about the treatment they receive throughout their participation in civil and administrative proceedings. Each chapter will reference the ways in which systemic racism impacts the delivery of justice in legal proceedings and the role of social workers in engaging in antiracist practice on behalf of their clients and in accordance with social work ethical principles.

LEGAL NEEDS OF CLIENTS IN THE CRIMINAL JUSTICE SYSTEM

Recent data from the Federal Bureau of Investigation (FBI) reported that 10,085,207 people were arrested for a crime in 2019 (FBI, 2020). This is a 21% decrease in comparison to arrest numbers in 2010. Additionally, in comparison to 2010 data, adults arrested in 2019 totaled 6,000,327, a drop of 16%, and

Table 1.1 Types of Civil Legal Problems

Family	Consumer	Housing	Employment	Education	Income benefits	Health	Immigration
Child support	Abusive collection procedures	Failure to provide heat, hot water, and electricity or other services per the terms of the lease	Discrimination based on age, gender, disability, criminal record, religion, sexual orientation, and race	Discipline problems	Difficulty in applying and being discouraged from applying for public benefits	Access to medical and mental healthcare	Eligibility for obtaining legal permanent resident card (green card)
Custody and visitation	Oppressive contract terms	Foreclosure	Unsafe working conditions	Dangerous conditions	Unfair denial or reduction in benefits	Inability to obtain insurance or insurance disputes	Problems bringing a family member to the United States legally
Domestic violence	Identity theft	Eviction threats and conflicts with landlord	Difficulty collecting pay, overtime, and unemployment compensation	Denial of enrollment, credits, and transfer	Repayment demanded or allegation of overpayment	Refusal of provider to accept Medicare/Medicaid	Collateral consequences of immigration status on criminal and civil cases
Child welfare involvement	Utility shut-offs	Disrepair including broken locks, pests, and issues in common spaces of a building	Sexual harassment	Denial of special education and misclassification	Unfair treatment, no information on how to appeal	Difficulty obtaining advance directives or healthcare power of attorney	Eligibility for obtaining legal relief including asylum
Elder abuse	Lack of/loss of insurance	Housing discrimination	Being paid less than the minimum wage	Language access	Eligibility questions for benefits	Nursing home problems	Deportation and removal proceedings
Adoption	Bankruptcy	Public service needs such as dangerous sidewalks, abandoned buildings, hazardous and toxic waste disposal		Suspensions		Guardianship for incapacitated individuals	Lack of access to benefits and services as a result of immigration status

the number of "juvenile" (i.e., individuals under the age of 18) in 2019 totaled 428,053, a drop of 55.5% since 2010 (FBI, 2019).

State and federal prison authorities had jurisdiction over 1,230,100 persons in 2022, an increase of 2% from 2021 data (Carson, 2023). State correctional authorities presided over the jurisdiction of 1,039,500 persons sentenced to at least 1 year in prison in 2022, while the Federal Bureau of Prisons held over 146,100 persons with similar sentences in the same year (Carson, 2023). Demographic data from 2022 show that, out of all individuals imprisoned in state and federal facilities, 83,700 identified as female, which is a 5% increase in the female prison population in comparison to 2021. Across the racial divide, an estimated 32% were Black; 31% were White; 23% were Hispanic; 2% were Native American or Alaska Native; and 1% were Asian, Native Hawaiian, or Other Pacific Islander (Carson, 2023).

The legal needs of clients in the criminal justice system are pressing and profound at every stage of their interaction with the system because of the high stakes involved, particularly for men and women of color (Glaze & Maruschak, 2008). From 2022 data, the estimated rate of incarceration for Black persons was 911 per 100,000 U.S. residents, Native Americans or Alaska Natives was 801 per 100,000 residents, and Hispanic persons was 426 per 100,000, in comparison to White persons at 188 per 100,000 residents (Carson, 2023). On any given day, 2.7 million children have a parent serving time in prison or jail, and more than 5.2 million children identify with having had a parent incarcerated at some point during their lives (The Sentencing Project, 2021). Numerous studies report racial disparities exist at every decision-making point of the criminal justice process; prearrest, arrest, pretrial prosecutorial discretion, during trial, and sentencing with similar findings reported for youth in the juvenile justice system (Hartney & Vuong, 2009; The Sentencing Project, 2010).

Table 1.2 presents the range of legal problems that can be experienced by low-income individuals before and throughout their involvement in the criminal justice system. Many of the legal matters identified in Table 1.2 can also be thought of as social service needs. Assisting a family you are working with to prepare for the incarceration of a loved one or provider implicates a number of legal decisions to be made, rights to uphold, and visiting arrangements, and ways for incarcerated parents to remain involved in the lives of their children. If a child is incarcerated, the Legal Information for Families Today (2010) will help with arrangements for parents to stay involved with the child. Helping a client advocate for a child in jail who may need mental health treatment but is denied access may be another instance of a legal right and social service need. This may also include working with the child's legal team to present findings to the court on why a child may be better served in the community, and voicing the dangers child prisons have on children's mental and physical health, specifically for children with unique and special needs. Social workers also have a key role to play in advocating against the overall damning effects of imprisonment on children, including shackling children, solitary confinement, harsh restraints, and the imminent risk of abuse. Working with a youth or adult who has reentered the community and wishes to continue or pursue education or vocational training as a way of remaining free of the system but does not initially have access to

Table 1.2 Types of Criminal Legal Problems

Prearrest	Arrest	Pretrial	Trial	Sentencing	Incarceration	Reentry
Racial profiling	False and coerced confessions	Pleading guilty for fear of more penalty	Ineffective assistance of counsel	Mitigation assessment	Appeals of conviction or sentence	Fines as a result of a criminal conviction
Illegal search and seizure	Immigration consequences based solely on the arrest	Employment problems including job suspension pending resolution of the case	Eyewitness error	Making legal arrangements for care and custody of children	Custody and visitation	Restriction from employment and licenses
Improper detention	Child welfare involvement	Competence to stand trial	Inappropriate use of informants	Immigration and deportation	Child support	Eviction from public housing
Harassment and police brutality	Child custody concerns	Temporary orders of protection excluding person from home, children, or family	Unethical police or prosecutorial conduct	Lack of judicial discretion in sentencing	Administrative hearings on the use of psychotropic medication and commitment to psychiatric facilities	Inability to vote
Threat of involving child welfare officials	Impact on public housing	Lack of access to meaningful legal representation	Jury bias		Filing of complaints about treatment and access to medical and mental healthcare	Inability to access student loan programs
					Restraint and pregnancy	
					Marriage or divorce	Reunification with children in foster care
					Sexual abuse and harassment	

funding can be a problem faced by many social workers. We see again how issues we might initially define as social service outcomes also have a corresponding legal component.

Once arrested, the most pressing legal need low-income individuals have is access to an effective attorney who can ensure that the client receives a robust defense, that their rights are protected, and violations prior to and during the arrest process are remedied. Unlike many civil legal issues, clients who enter the criminal justice system have a constitutional right to a lawyer. The Sixth Amendment to the U.S. Constitution establishes the right of federal criminal defendants to counsel, a right that was extended by the U.S. Supreme Court to defendants in state and local criminal prosecutions because of the "obvious truth" that a fair trial and a defendant's right to due process could not be guaranteed without an attorney (*Gideon v. Wainwright*, 1963).

A publicly funded attorney or a public defender office represents 80% of low-income defendants (National Right to Counsel Committee, 2009). Numerous reports have documented the inadequacies of low-income defense services (American Bar Association Standing Committee on Legal Aid and Indigent Defendants, 2004). These problems continue with underfunded public defender systems and a lack of remedies for clients who face ineffective assistance of counsel, leading scholars to label a national crisis in the right to counsel in criminal cases (Backus & Marcus, 2018). Due to lack of resources, systemic racism, and other factors that increase the overcriminalization of behaviors due to "tough on crime" policies on the part of state and local governments, and the increasing complexity of criminal law, public defenders are forced to carry large caseloads, in some instances 100 clients at a time, making it nearly impossible to effectively defend and represent their clients (National Right to Counsel Committee, 2009). Additionally, defense attorneys often lack funding for access to experts, social workers, investigators, and interpreters, which are critical to an effective defense.

Many of the clients who are represented by public defenders are charged with serious crimes, which have significant consequences including extended periods of incarceration and, in some states, capital punishment. These cases raise the issue of wrongful convictions, which are reported by organizations such as The Innocence Project (www.innocenceproject.org) and the Death Penalty Information Center (www.deathpenaltyinfo.org). There have been 375 postconviction DNA exonerations in the United States as of 2020 (Innocence Project, 2024). The average length of time served by those exonerated is 16 years. Of the 375 individuals, 58% were African American, and 33% were White (Innocence Project, 2024). Since 1973, there have been 197 individuals serving time on death row who have been wrongly convicted and exonerated. Of those individuals, 107 were African American, 68 were White, and 19 were Hispanic (Death Penalty Information Center, 2004). Research has also shown that wrongful conviction and imprisonment can cause serious psychological consequences (Grounds, 2004). As noted by Ruesink and Free (2005), very few studies have been done on the wrongful conviction of women. These statistics demonstrate the undeniable need for social workers to incorporate an understanding of the criminal legal system when working with impacted individuals and families if the goal is to provide meaningful and individualized advocacy.

LEGAL NEEDS OF VICTIMS OF CRIME

On September 30, 2022, 46% of all persons in federal prison were serving time for a drug offense and 43% were serving time for a public order offense. Of the 1,021,300 persons in state or federal prison at year end 2021, 63% were serving sentences for a violent offense, 13% for a property crime, 13% for a drug offense, and 11% for a public order offense (Carson, 2023).

Social workers in the course of their work will confront the effects or secondary adversities associated with the aftermath of being a victim of crime. These outcomes can include physical and mental health concerns and loss of employment, income, and property. In 2007, for crimes both reported and not reported, the economic cost to victims was $16 billion (Rand & Truman, 2010). Studies show that there is an increased risk for future mental health problems when one is a victim of crime (Kilpatrick & Acierno, 2003).

With the advent of state and federal legislation that has expanded the rights of victims of crime, social workers who are knowledgeable about the rights of victims can advise and assist clients in obtaining benefits, such as compensation for medical injuries or lost wages; protection, such as a police escort to and from court; safe housing or simply help the client advocate for a speedy trial when the legal proceedings are delayed; and effects on your client's ability to move forward and return to stability or work on other important goals or concerns that need to be addressed in their lives.

Another reason for social workers to know how to identify and activate victims' legal rights and their right to benefits are the data indicating that certain vulnerable groups who are frequent clients of social workers (e.g., the elderly, the developmentally disabled, the mentally ill, and youth) are victimized at greater rates than the general population and are at greater risk of victimization (Rand & Harrell, 2009; Rand & Truman, 2010). Race, age, and gender are also implicated when looking at who are the victims of violent crimes with Black males and those younger than 20 years of age having the highest rates of victimization (Rand & Truman, 2010). More recently, there has been an increase in the number of hate crimes involving racial, religious, sexual orientation, ethnicity or national origin, and disability bias against many of the groups social workers traditionally work with and advocate for, such as immigrants, gays, lesbians, and the transgendered (U.S. Department of Justice, 2009). More specifically, recent data from the UCLA Williams Institute School of Law show that transgender women and men are victimized at alarming rates. Transgender individuals are four times more likely to experience violent victimization, including rape, sexual assault, aggravated and simple assault in comparison to cisgender people with more than half of victimizations not reported to police (Flores et al., 2021). Additionally, in more recent years, there has been public outcry and data on the increase in police brutality at the hands of police. Specifically, the killing of 46- year-old George Floyd on May 25th, 2020, by police that shocked the nation, garnered national attention, and incited civil rights protests across the country. His death, among others including Breyonna Taylor, an African American female medical worker who was shot and killed in March of 2020 during a botched raid on her apartment, and the 2025 beating to death of prisoner Robert Brooks by correction officers, also raised bigger concerns around racial discrimination and victimization from police on people of color.

INCREASING NUMBER OF UNREPRESENTED INDIVIDUALS IN THE LEGAL SYSTEM

Studies that identify and report on the unmet legal needs of low-income individuals in both the civil and criminal justice systems also report high numbers of clients who are representing themselves, particularly in civil courts where one in two requests for help to legal services offices are turned away (LSC, 2022). In the criminal system, clients are more frequently unrepresented when they are trying to appeal their verdicts or sentences and when addressing family matters or medical and mental health needs while incarcerated. Individuals involved in the criminal system also have unmet legal needs that confront them when they are released from prison and seeking to obtain housing, healthcare, and employment.

Clients who represent themselves are also referred to as "pro se" litigants. Studies conducted across the country have reported increasing numbers of self-represented clients and also forecast that this trend will continue and greatly impact on the fair and unbiased administration of justice in the long term (Office of the Deputy Chief Administrative Judge for Justice Initiatives, 2005). A study in Virginia conducted by the National Center for State Courts detailed the prevalence of self-represented litigants, finding that the majority of civil cases included at least one unrepresented party, and low income litigants were less likely to have representation (Strickland, Graves, & Schauffler, 2017). A similar study in Wisconsin found that as many as 70% of family cases involved a client who was not represented (Wisconsin Pro Se Working Group, 2000). For housing cases where an individual risks eviction, national data show that landlords are represented in 80% of cases compared to tenants who have legal representation in 3% (Buenaventura, & Heaton, 2025). A number of factors have been found to result in this trend including decreases in funding for legal services for low-income clients, an increased desire on the part of clients to want to know the law and participate in their legal matters, and the rising cost of legal representation (LSC, 2009).

Findings from an analysis of data collected through the distribution of a survey to pro se litigants in New York City Family and Housing Courts report that 83% of the respondents identified as African American, Hispanic, or Asian with less education and income than New York City residents as a whole, believed they could not afford an attorney, and were involved in very critical cases such as evictions, domestic violence, child custody, guardianship, support, and paternity (American Bar Association Coalition for Justice 2010; Office of the Deputy Chief Administrative Judge for Justice Initiatives, 2005).

Both the increasing number and the characteristics of unrepresented clients pose significant implications for the administration and realization of justice, particularly for disadvantaged and "at-risk" groups—groups social workers are ethically required to advocate for and serve (National Association of Social Workers [NASW], 2021). Many clients acting on their own behalf may not be informed about the law or proper procedures and may have language and literacy challenges that create enormous demands on court staff and create court delays or misunderstandings about the kinds of legal problems clients have or the solutions clients are requesting. In a recent study of housing litigants facing eviction, researchers found that renters who were unrepresented in proceedings were more likely to be evicted, whereas represented parties remained in their homes 90% of the time when they were in private housing and 80% of the time when they were in public housing (Hasvold & Regenbogen, 2017). In addition, this situation creates ethical dilemmas for judges who must remain impartial and unbiased yet must do everything in their power to provide clients with a fair hearing (Office of the Deputy Chief Administrative Judge for Justice Initiatives, 2005). Given these kinds of cases, clients may also be in crisis or experiencing traumatic stress in ways that further interfere in the level of cognitive and social functioning required for effective advocacy in court.

WHY CLIENTS DO NOT ALWAYS ACCESS AND VIEW THE LEGAL SYSTEM AS HELPFUL

It is important for social workers to understand the reasons why the legal needs of clients go unaddressed and why clients do not enforce their rights. Low-income individuals only reached out to seek legal help in regard to 19% of their legal problems, and oftentimes when the problem seemed more explicitly legal (LSC, 2022). Reasons for not addressing legal concerns at the client level are complex and may include a lack of knowledge about their legal rights and entitlements; lack of access to legal professionals or a belief that a legal professional would not be able to help with a civil legal issue; low literacy; physical or mental disability; isolation; apprehension about the courts and legal system; sense of stigma; and self and others' prior experiences with the legal system that discouraged participation (LS, 2009, 2022). These reasons suggest that clients believe there are both social and psychological costs associated with accessing and enforcing their rights and entitlements (Hernanaz et al., 2004).

Clients in the state surveys also expressed that enforcing the rights and benefits they were entitled to was just "too much hassle" (LSC, 2009). This speaks to "transaction costs" and refers to modes of operation in government agencies such as intrusive policies and procedures, disrespectful interactions that clients endure, stigma, and the administrative obstacles they face as they attempt to activate their legal rights and entitlements (Lens & Vorsanger, 2005; Weiss-Gal & Gal, 2009). Social workers are sometimes part of the reason that clients do not access the legal system or understand its potential to remedy wrongs, enforce rights, and ensure entitlements. Social service providers' lack of knowledge that a client's problem could be solved legally, and therefore did not connect the client to legal resources, is identified as one of the reasons clients do not access legal services (LSC 2009). This is a crucial point because low-income clients are far more likely to have interactions with community and social service providers than legal services.

In a study conducted by Braye and Preston-Shoot (2006) that investigated what service users expected from their social workers with regard to legal knowledge and skills, the authors report that clients want and need their social workers to know the law and to know how to interact effectively with the legal system. A persistent complaint identified by clients was that social workers claimed to know the law but actually did not, the results being that clients were misinformed. Further, clients note that social workers' lack of knowledge about the law made them less effective and credible when the social workers engaged in legal proceedings (Braye & Preston-Shoot, 2006). At the same time, clients wanted social workers to think proactively and positively about the law, so that social workers could use the law to empower themselves and the client and promote access to resources. To achieve this end, social workers must have knowledge of a wider range of laws, statutes, and regulations and develop a more critical perspective on the role of law in society and the pervasive ways in which it affects the lives of social work clients (Braye & Preston-Shoot, 2006).

Social workers have an ethical responsibility to address client reasons for not activating their rights as well as to provide clients with information and assistance in realizing their rights because the NASW Code of Ethics explicitly tells social workers to "strive to ensure access to needed information, services and resources" as a way of obtaining social justice (NASW, 2021, p. 5). Part of effective case advocacy and a robust social work practice that seeks to promote a client's access to services, entitlements, and other social rights is to "provide clients with information on rights, coaching them so they can effectively exercise their rights and participating in forums to further clients' rights or to reverse decisions made relating to those rights" (Weiss-Gal & Gal, 2009, p. 270).

Many social workers also meet clients in crisis, a time when thinking about legal solutions and implications may not be a priority for the service user or for the social worker. However, a lack of immediate attention to these important legal needs may result in serious trouble for the client later on. In an article by Letiecq et al. (2008) that addresses the challenges that occur when a grandparent takes custody of a grandchild, the authors describe the difficulty caregivers face having to learn about the legal system on their own at the same time they are in the midst of family crisis and trauma. In order to assume the most fundamental parenting duties such as enrolling their grandchild in school or giving approval for a medical procedure, grandparents must have legal custody, which involves going to court (Glass & Huneycutt, 2002). In such a scenario, not paying prompt attention to a legal issue can cause secondary adversity if the grandparents' report enduring financial difficulties and almost losing their home because of having to pay out of pocket for their grandchildren's medical care. In this instance, the grandparents were not told about the kinds of financial assistance they were legally entitled to by the social service providers they were working with (Letiecq et al., 2008).

As this scenario suggests, studies conducted in the United States, Canada, and Israel indicate that social workers' participation in case advocacy is limited (Hardina, 1995; Koren & Doron, 2005; Teare & Sheafor, 1995).

WHY SOCIAL WORKERS DO NOT ALWAYS ACCESS AND VIEW THE LEGAL SYSTEM AS HELPFUL

Social workers have been identified in many reports on access to legal services as being a part of the reason low-income individuals do not activate their rights, but social workers have also been identified as being important players in the solutions being proposed to help close the "justice gap" (LSC, 2009; Legal Services NYC, 2009). Other professional groups, including lawyers, are inviting the social work profession to collaborate with them in the project of giving clients access to justice and realizing the fulfillment of their civil and human rights.

In this chapter, we identified that literally millions of individuals who potentially engage with social workers are enmeshed in the legal system in some way and may avoid enforcing their legal rights and benefits. We also established that there exists documented evidence of discrimination, oppression, and unequal access to justice based on race and class. It is clear from the NASW Code of Ethics that social workers have a moral and ethical obligation to address this social injustice. The Preamble to the Code of Ethics clearly states that the primary mission of the social work profession "is to enhance human well-being and help meet the basic human needs of all people, with particular attention to the needs and empowerment of people who are vulnerable, oppressed, and living in poverty" (NASW, 2021, p. 1). The Code provides further instruction that social workers must address discrimination: "Social workers should act to prevent and eliminate domination of, exploitation of, and discrimination against any person, group, or class" (NASW, 2021, Section 6.04). We as social workers have been invited to engage with the legal system and legal professionals to participate in initiatives that advance the goal of achieving social justice. Our ethical mandate is clear. The question then becomes what are some of the reasons and barriers that can explain the social work profession's reluctance to engage with the law?

Various social work commentators have identified the contradictory, yet complementary relationship of social work and the law (Healy, 2009; Madden, 2000; Weiss-Gal & Gal, 2009). The impact of the legal system on the lives of clients has greatly expanded in recent years and because of this trend, the U.S. legal system is an arena where many social work client issues are sorted out, competing interests are addressed, and policy decisions have been made. Yet some authors suggest that little has been done by the profession to address the problems within the justice system (Madden, 2000; Mitchell & Lynch, 2003; Reamer, 2004; Van Wormer, 2009).

The perception of some social work commentators is that despite the enormous impact and control the legal system has on social work practice, the profession acts more often as passive collaborators (rather than aggressive advocates) when it comes to the law and that social workers more often take on the role of enforcing existing statutes rather than recognizing the inadequacies and injustices within the legal system and acting to change them (Madden, 2000; Mitchell & Lynch, 2003). Social workers have been reluctant to study the basis of the law as it relates to their work or to think of it as a tool that can advance the achievement of their objectives in working with clients (Doron et al., 2010).

In fairness to social workers, there have been a number of structural impediments that interfere in their ability to perform case advocacy activities or to see the law in a positive way. Perhaps the most important reason is the lack of attention to the law and human rights in social work education (Doron et al., 2010; Kopels & Gustavsson, 1996; Madden, 2000; Steen & Mathiesen, 2005). In most U.S. schools of social work, courses in social work and the law are offered only as electives, and despite exhortations to infuse legal content throughout the social work curriculum, there has been no systematic attempt to do so (Kopels & Gustavsson, 1996; Madden, 2000).

This lack of a systemic approach is in contrast to the United Kingdom where specific guidance on law content is required and provided by the qualifying body for social work education for England, Scotland, Wales, and Northern Ireland (Central Council for Education and Training in Social Work, 1995). Social work educators in the United Kingdom have developed an evidence-based body of knowledge that describes and evaluates teaching and learning methods designed to arm social work students with the knowledge, values, and skills necessary to actively use the law in support of practice (Braye et al., 2005).

It is also much more common in the United States when legal content is introduced in social work courses and texts for the law to be presented as somewhat oppositional to social work values, focusing much more attention on restricting and limiting social work practice than on the ways the law can be accessed for promoting rights and achieving social justice (Preston-Shoot, 2001). There is generally much more focus on content related to liability, malpractice, and ethical conflicts than on content that views the law as a proactive tool for empowered practice and teaches social workers how to use the law to counteract discrimination and support ethical values.

It is also suggested that organizational obstacles can affect a social worker's attitude toward, and ability to engage in, case advocacy activities. In fact some social workers have either faced or feared sanctions from their agency when they devoted time to case advocacy activities (Weiss-Gal & Gal, 2009). It has also been argued that social workers may face conflicts between their duties to clients and loyalty to employing agencies, thus interfering in their ability to prioritize client rights (Hardina, 1995).

Another potential reason social workers are reluctant to engage with the law and legal systems is the widely held stereotypes about the challenges of working with lawyers. There are very few studies that exist that investigate collaboration between lawyers and social workers and studies that do exist are over two decades old. Much of the research looked at how attitudes of members of the legal profession and how attitudes of social workers contributed to conflict between the two professions. These attitudes translated into widely held stereotypes such as "lawyers are too analytical" and "social workers are too emotional" (Fogelson, 1970; Sloane, 1967; Weil, 1982). Other studies looked at the division of roles and responsibilities as causing competition and conflict between social workers and lawyers (Fogelson, 1970; Russell, 1988). As is the case with many other professional groups, differences in professional culture and how one is socialized during professional education have also been found to contribute to conflict and problems in collaboration for lawyers and social workers (Hall, 2005; Russell, 1988; Taylor, 2006).

Recently, there has been a number of studies suggesting that, much like clients, social workers' actual experience with the courts and the legal system discourages participation and causes workers to challenge the legitimacy of those institutions (Ellett & Steib, 2005; Faller et al., 2009; Greeno et al., 2013; Vandervort et al., 2008). These studies focused on public and private child welfare social workers and caseworkers that are in a situation where they must interact frequently with courts and judges who exercise a high degree of control and scrutiny over their work. Ellett and Steib (2005) observed in their study that at times the demeanor of judges to caseworkers "seemed unnecessarily disrespectful and harsh" (Ellett & Steib, 2005, p. 344), "courts (judges, parent's attorneys and ADAs) tended to treat caseworkers as functionaries who were expected to provide documentation and services" (Ellett & Steib, 2005, p. 345) and "although problems in legal representation were widely acknowledged they were more readily attributed to workload or inability to compensate attorneys at a higher level than was the case with caseworkers" (Ellett & Steib, 2005, p. 348). With caseworkers the tendency was to blame performance problems on lack of competence or a lack of interest. It was found, however, that many of the social workers and caseworkers observed during the study appeared not to understand the legal system, nor know how to write well-documented and relevant court reports, nor demonstrate the ability to effectively testify in court (Ellett & Steib, 2005).

Faller et al. (2009) studied the level of comfort with court proceedings among child welfare workers at the time they began their employment and then again 6 months after employment. An increase in the level of comfort with court proceedings at 6 months was associated with being male, being White, having an MSW, and working for a private versus public agency (Faller et al., 2009). Perhaps the most troubling finding in this study was the decrease in comfort level of professionals of color with court proceedings after 6 months. The authors voiced the concern that given the overrepresentation of minority children in the child welfare system, a lack of comfort on the part of a large number of the professionals charged to advocate for families may be indirectly related to disparate outcomes for children of color in the child welfare system (Faller et al., 2009). More recently, scholars have noted the impact of the overrepresentation of Black children in the foster care system on the practice of Black child welfare caseworkers and the importance of antiracist policies for Black caseworkers (Cantey et al., 2020).

Evidence from the studies cited and arguments presented from some social work educators suggest the need for the Council on Social Work Education to require the development of courses that consider social work's interface with the legal system, teach the knowledge and skills for social workers to be confident and empowered actors within the legal system, and make this a curriculum requirement for all MSW programs (Ellett & Steib, 2005). Incorporating the study of legal systems and collaboration with lawyers as part of the social work curriculum is in line with renewed calls for interdisciplinary education especially at the graduate level (Christian et al., 2020).

MEETING THE LEGAL NEEDS OF LOW-INCOME CLIENTS: WHAT SOLUTIONS ARE BEING PROPOSED AND HOW THE SOCIAL WORK PROFESSION CAN PARTICIPATE

The reports that document the lack of access to justice experienced by low-income individuals and the increasing numbers of pro se litigants advocate for increased funding and use of pro bono or volunteer legal services as a direct method of decreasing the "justice gap." As you learned in the section of this chapter that addressed the legal needs of low-income criminal defendants, one reason preventing the effective representation of a client is that their lawyer often does not have access to professional expertise or support personnel. Social workers can respond to this need by offering pro bono services to legal aid offices to assist in client defense, to conduct home visits and evaluations, and can also offer their services to courts so that the social worker can be assigned to assist attorneys in their representation of clients. In both civil and criminal matters, social worker can provide critical assistance to clients navigating the legal system and in need of mitigation, social services, evaluations, and resources. Social work professors and experienced practitioners in areas such as clinical social work, social welfare policy, and social work practice can volunteer to testify as expert witnesses in a range of cases such as identifying best practice and proper procedure in child welfare cases or summarizing the research base about a particular topic such as the impact of exposure to community violence and risk of juvenile delinquency.

Another way the profession can be involved is to not only produce research that documents the effects of the law and legal policy on practice, but to understand the role that social workers can play in the various legal systems as a knowledge broker (Madden & Wayne, 2003). In this role social workers are aware of their power to introduce social science and empirical research into the decision-making processes across all systems of law. Social workers can bring social science research to the attention of lawyers and judges and introduce evidence-based practice as a framework to be used for the development of legal policies, programs, and decisions.

Pragmatically, given the current economic situation, the reports also suggest that the greatest impact can be made through collaborative advocacy projects with social service organizations (LSC, 2009, 2022; Legal Services NYC, 2009). Across the country there are two types of collaborative initiatives that are of interest to social workers. The first intervention involves providing legal training and support to nonlawyer professionals such as social workers, teachers, clergy, and medical personnel. This "indirect" service can greatly expand the number of clients who receive legal information, materials, referrals, and who can be assisted in identifying a problem as a legal issue. Social workers working in community-based agencies can proactively reach out to legal service providers to arrange training for themselves and their clients as well as network with self-help community organizations.

The second kind of collaborative intervention involves legal service providers teaming up with other agencies and professions to think more broadly about expanding the number and kinds of solutions to the multiple and complex problems faced by low-income individuals and families. The goal of collaboration is to provide a "holistic solution" by offering clients a mix of legal and nonlegal services in one location. This is potentially the most exciting and valuable way social workers could target their knowledge and skills and participate in a long-term solution for closing the justice gap. An example of this holistic practice demonstrated improved outcomes for children in abuse and neglect proceedings when parents accused of abuse or neglect are represented by interdisciplinary holistic teams of lawyers, social workers and parent advocates (Gerber et al., 2020). Other professions are beginning to make the connection between a state of health and wellness and the importance of accessing the legal system to intervene in environmental conditions that both cause and effect disparate health, mental health, economic, social, and educational outcomes for different groups of clients (Walter-McCabe, 2019). An example of this movement is the medical–legal partnerships (MLPs) model. MLPs train healthcare providers such as doctors, nurses, and social workers to understand the social causes of their patients' health concerns and identify those patients whose stressors may be ameliorated or resolved by legal intervention (www.medical-legalpartnership.org). Poor housing conditions, food and energy insecurity, and educational and employment factors are just a few examples of nonmedical problems that present significant barriers to health. MLPs address these issues in the healthcare setting rather than referring the client out. Early process and outcome studies showed improved client health outcomes, lower levels of client stress, higher uptake of benefits and entitlements, decreased avoidance of medical care because of concern with cost, improved clinical workforce skills, and cost benefits to the medical institution (Teufel et al., 2009; Weintraub et al., 2010).

The ecological theories underlying collaborative, multidisciplinary programs that focus on intervention at the level of the client's environment and on prevention should be a familiar and comfortable framework for social workers. Social workers have the values, knowledge, and skills to effectively participate in interdisciplinary collaborations and to organize and become leaders in collaborative service delivery. The following chapters present the knowledge, values, and skills you need to collaborate with legal professionals and your clients in ways that address client needs and client rights. You will learn to appreciate how the activation of client rights can be a critical tool for advancing and realizing a strength-based, empowering social work practice that moves beyond disparate outcomes and meets the medical, mental, social, educational, and economic needs of all people in an equal and socially just way.

REFERENCES

American Bar Association Coalition for Justice. (2010). *Report on the survey of judges on the impact of the economic downturn on representation in the courts.* https://legalaidresearch.org/wp-content/uploads/2020/02/aba-coalition-justice-survey-judges-2010.pdf

American Bar Association, Standing Committee on Legal Aid and Indigent Defendants. (2004). *Gideon's broken promise: America's continuing quest for equal justice.* https://www.in.gov/ccaa/files/ABAGideonsBrokenPromise.pdf

Backus, M. S., & Marcus, P. (2018). The right to counsel in criminal cases: Still a national crisis? *George Washington Law Review*, *86*, 1564–1603. https://ssrn.com/abstract=3541332

Braye, S., Preston-Shoot, M., & Johns, R. (2005). Law in social work teaching: Reviewing the evidence on teaching, learning and assessment. *Social Work Education, 24*(5), 547–563.

Braye, S., & Preston-Shoot, M. (2006). Broadening the vision: Law teaching, social work and civil society. *International Social Work, 49*(3), 376–389.

Buenaventura, M., & Heaton, P. (2025). Forced out?: Civil legal access and housing stability. *Fordham Urban Law Journal, 52*(3), 697–753.

Cantey, N., Smith, L., Sorrells, S., Kelly, D., Jones, C., & Burrus, D. (2020). Navigating racism in the child welfare system: The impact on black children, families, and practitioners, *Child Welfare, 100*(2), 163–184. https://www.jstor.org/stable/48663461

Carson, E. (2023). *Prisoners 2021: Statistical tables.* https://bjs.ojp.gov/sites/g/files/xyckuh236/files/media/document/p21st.pdf

Central Council for Education and Training in Social Work. (1995). *Assuring quality in the diploma in social work-1, rules and requirements for the DipSW.* London.

Centre for Human Rights. (1994). *Human rights and social work: A manual for schools of social work and the social work profession.* Professional Training Series No. 1. Retrieved from: Office of the High Commission on Human Rights, United Nations website, http://www.ohchr.org/Documents/Publications/training1en.pdf

Christian, C., Finck, K., Connolly, C., Jaffee, S., Greeson, J., Garcia, A., Carlough, S., & Watts, C. (2020). Tear down those walls: The future of graduate education in child and family advocacy. *International Journal on Child Maltreatment: Research, Policy and Practice, 3*, 307–315. https://doi.org/10.1007/s42448-020-00057-3

Death Penalty Information Center. (2004). *Innocence and the crisis in the American death penalty.* http://www.deathpenaltyinfo.org/innocence-and-crisis-american-death-penalty

Doron, I., Karpel, M., & Or-Chen, K. (2010). Social workers attitudes towards the law: An Israeli perspective. *International Journal of Social Work, 19*(1), 95–103. https://doi.org/10.1111/j.1468-2397.2009.00640.x

Ellett, A. J., & Steib, S. D. (2005). Child welfare and the courts: A statewide study with implications for professional development, practice and change. *Research on Social Work Practice, 15*(5), 339–352. https://doi.org/10.1177/1049731505276680

Faller, K. C., Grabarek, M., & Vandervort, F. (2009). Child welfare workers go to court: The impact of race, gender and education on the comfort with legal issues. *Children and Youth Services Review, 31*, 972–977. https://doi.org/10.1016/j.childyouth.2009.04.010

Federal Bureau of Investigation. (2020). *Uniform crime report: crime in the United States, 2019.* https://ucr.fbi.gov/crime-in-the-u.s/2019/crime-in-the-u.s.-2019

Federal Bureau of Investigation. (2024). *2023 hate crime statistics annual report.* https://www.justice.gov/hatecrimes/hate-crime-statistics

Flores, A., Meer, I., Langton, L., & Herman, J. (2021). Gender identity disparities in criminal victimization: National Crime Victimization Survey, 2017–2018. *American Journal of Public Health, 111*(4), 726–729. https://doi.org/10.2105/AJPH.2020.306099

Fogelson, F. (1970). How social workers perceive lawyers. *Social Casework, 51*, 95–101. https://doi.org/10.1177/104438947005100205

Gerber, G., Guggenheim, M., Pang, Y., Ross, T., Mayevskaya, Y., Jacobs, S., & Pecora, P. (2020). Understanding the effects of an interdisciplinary approach to parental representation in child welfare. *Children and Youth Services Review, 116*, 105163. https://doi.org/10.1016/j.childyouth.2020.105163

Gideon v. Wainwright. 372 U.S. 335 (1963).

Glass, C. J., & Huneycutt, T. L. (2002). Grandparents raising grandchildren: The courts, custody, and educational implications. *Educational Gerontology, 28*, 237–251. https://doi.org/10.1080/036012702753542535

Glaze, L., & Maruschak, L (2008). *Parents in prison and their minor children.* Bureau of Justice Statistics. https://bjs.ojp.gov/content/pub/pdf/pptmc.pdf

Greeno, E., Bright, C., & Rozeff, L. (2013). Lessons from the courtroom: Perspectives from child welfare attorneys and supervisors. *Children and Youth Services Review, 35*(9), 1618–1624. https://doi.org/10.1016/j.childyouth.2013.06.015

Grounds, A. (2004). Psychological consequences of wrongful conviction and imprisonment. *Canadian Journal of Criminology and Criminal Justice, 46*(2), 165–182. https://www.ojp.gov/ncjrs/virtual-library/abstracts/psychological-consequences-wrongful-conviction-and-imprisonment

Hall, P. (2005). Interprofessional teamwork: Professional cultures as barriers. *Journal of Interprofessional Care, 19*(Suppl. 1), 188–196. https://www.ojp.gov/ncjrs/virtual-library/abstracts/psychological-consequences-wrongful-conviction-and-imprisonment

Hardina, D. (1995). Do Canadian social workers practice advocacy? *Journal of Community Practice*, *2*(3), 97–121. https://doi.org/10.1300/J125v02n03_05

Hartley, C., & Silva, F. (2007). *And justice for some: Differential treatment of youth of color in the justice system.* National Council on Crime and Delinquency.

Hartney, C., & Vuong, L. (2009). *Created equal: Racial and ethnic disparities in the U.S. criminal justice system.* National Council on Crime and Delinquency. Retrieved from the National Council on Crime and Delinquency website: http://www.nccd-crc.org/nccd/pdf/CreatedEqualReport2009.pdf

Hasvold, A., & Regenbogen, J. (2017). *Facing eviction alone: A study of evictions, Denver, CO, 2014–2016.* http://cclponline.org/wp-content/uploads/2017/10/Facing-Eviction-Alone-9-11-17_revised.pdf

Healy, L. M. (2009). Exploring the history of social work as a human rights profession. *International Social Work*, *51*(6), 735–748. https://doi.org/10.1177/0020872808095247

Hernanaz, V., Malherbet, F., & Pellizzari, M. (2004). *Take-up of welfare benefits in OECD countries: A review of the evidence (JT00159470).* Organization of Economic Cooperation and Development. https://www.oecd.org/en/publications/take-up-of-welfare-benefits-in-oecd-countries_525815265414.html

Hill, R. B. (2007). *An analysis of racial/ethnic disproportionality and disparity at the national, state and county levels.* Casey-CSSP Alliance for Racial. Equity in Child Welfare. Retrieved from the Center for the Study of Social Policy website, https://assets.aecf.org/m/resourcedoc/aecf-AnalysisofRacialEthnicDisproportionality-2007.pdf

Innocence Project. (2024). *DNA exonerations in the United States (1989–2020).* https://innocenceproject.org/dna-exonerations-in-the-united-states/

Kilpatrick, D., & Acierno, R. (2003). Mental health needs of crime victims: Epidemiology and outcomes. *Journal of Traumatic Stress*, *16*(2), 119–132. https://doi.org/10.1023/A:1022891005388

Kopels, S., & Gustavsson, N. S. (1996). Infusing legal issues into curriculum. *Journal of Social Work Education*, *36*(1), 115–125. https://doi.org/10.1080/10437797.1996.10672289

Koren, C., & Doron, I. (2005). Being a social worker in homes for the aged: The real, the ideal and the gaps between. *Journal of Gerontological Social Work*, *44*(3/4), 95–114.

Legal Services Corporation. (2009). *Documenting the justice gap in America: The current unmet civil legal needs of low-income Americans.* https://lsc-live.app.box.com/s/5d2ivjp22w29p9pco5rz9fz6nkj0co0p

Legal Information for Families Today. (2010). *Preparing for the incarceration of a loved one.* http://www.liftonline.org/guides/pdf/guide_120.pdf

Legal Services Corporation. (2022). *The justice gap: The unmet civil legal needs of low-income Americans.* https://lsc-live.app.box.com/s/xl2v2uraiotbbzrhuwtjlgi0emp3myzl

Legal Services NYC. (2009). *New Yorkers in crisis.* http://www.legalservicesnyc.org/storage/lsny/PDFs/new_yorkers_in_crisis.pdf

Lens, V., & Vorsanger, S. E. (2005). Complaining after claiming: Fair hearings after welfare reform. *Social Service Review*, *79*, 430–453. https://doi.org/10.1086/430892

Letiecq, B. L., Bailey, S. J., & Porterfield, F. (2008). "We have no rights, we get no help": The legal and policy dilemmas facing grandparent caregivers. *Journal of Family Issues*, *29*(8), 995–1012. https://doi.org/10.1177/0192513X08316545

Madden, R. G. (2000). Legal content in social work education: Preparing students for interprofessional practice. *Journal of Teaching in Social Work*, *20*(1/2), 3–17. https://doi.org/10.1300/J067v20n01_02

Madden, R. G., & Wayne, R. H. (2003). Social work and the law: A therapeutic jurisprudence perspective. *Social Work*, *48*(3), 338–347. https://doi.org/10.1093/sw/48.3.338

Mitchell, J., & Lynch, R. S. (2003). Beyond the rhetoric of social and economic justice: Redeeming the social work advocacy role. *Race, Gender & Class*, *10*(2), 8–26. http://www.jstor.org/stable/41675070

National Association of Social Workers. (2021). *Code of ethics of the National Association of Social Workers*. Author.

National Right to Counsel Committee. (2009). *Justice denied: America's continuing neglect of our constitutional right to counsel*. https://www.opensocietyfoundations.org/publications/justice-denied-americas-continuing-neglect-our-constitutional-right-counsel#publications_download

Office of the Deputy Administrative Judge for Justice Initiatives. (2005). *Self-represented litigants: Characteristics, needs and services*. Retrieved from the website of New York State Unified Court System. http://www.nycourts.gov/reports/AJJI_SelfRep06.pdf

Preston-Shoot, M. (2001). Regulating the road of good intentions: Observations on the relationship between policy, regulations and practice in social work. *Practice*, *13*(4), 5–20. https://doi.org/10.1080/09503150108411523

Rand, M. R., & Harrell, E. (2009). *Crime against people with disabilities, 2007. Bureau of Justice Statistics Special Report (NCJ 227814)*. U.S. Department of Justice, Bureau of Statistics. Retrieved from: Bureau of Justice Statistics website, http://bjs.ojp.usdoj.gov/content/pub/pdf/capd07.pdf

Rand, M. R., & Truman, J. (2010). *Criminal victimization, 2009. Bureau of Justice Statistics Bulletin (NCJ231327)*. U.S. Department of Justice, Bureau of Justice Statistics. Retrieved from: Bureau of Justice Statistics website, http://bjs.ojp.usdoj.gov/content/pub/pdf/cv09.pdf

Reamer, F. G. (2004). Social work and criminal justice: The uneasy alliance. *Journal of Religion & Spirituality in Social Work*, *23*(1/2), 213–231. https://doi.org/10.1300/J377v23n01_12

Roberts, D. (2022). *Torn apart: How the child welfare system destroys black families and how abolition can build a safer world*. Basic Books.

Ruesink, M., & Free, M. D. (2005). Wrongful convictions among women: An exploratory study of a neglected topic. *Women & Criminal Justice*, *16*(4), 1–23. https://doi.org/10.1300/J012v16n04_01

Russell, R. (1988). Role perceptions of attorneys and caseworkers in child abuse cases in juvenile court. *Child Welfare*, *67*, 205–216. https://pubmed.ncbi.nlm.nih.gov/3396441/

The Sentencing Project. (2010). *Disproportionate minority contact fact sheet*. http://sentencingproject.org/doc/publications/publications/jj_DMCfactsheet.pdf

The Sentencing Project. (2021). *Parents in prison*. https://www.sentencingproject.org/policy-brief/parents-in-prison/

Sloane, H. (1967). Relationship of law and social work. *Social Work*, *12*, 86–92. https://www.jstor.org/stable/23710171

Steen, J. A., & Mathiesen, S. G. (2005). Human rights education: Is social work behind the curve? *Journal of Teaching in Social Work*, *2*(3), 141–154. https://doi.org/10.1300/J067v25n03_09

Strickland, S., Graves, S., & Schauffler, R. (2017). *Virginia self-represented litigant study: outcomes of civil cases in general district court, juvenile & domestic relations court and circuit court*. https://ncsc.contentdm.oclc.org/digital/collection/accessfair/id/810

Taylor, S. (2006). Educating future practitioners of social work and law: Exploring the origins of interprofessional misunderstanding. *Children and Youth Services Review*, *28*, 638–653. https://doi.org/10.1016/j.childyouth.2005.06.006

Teare, R. J., & Sheafor, B. W. (1995). *Practice-sensitive social work education: An empirical analysis of social work practice and practitioners*. Council on Social Work Education.

Teufel, J., Brown, S., Thorne, W., Goffinet, D., & Clemmons, L. (2009). Process and outcome evaluation of a assistance and health care community partnership. *Health Promotions Practice*, *10*(3), 378–385. https://www.jstor.org/stable/26736922

Van Wormer, K. (2009). Restorative justice as social justice for victims of gendered violence: A standpoint feminist perspective. *Social Work*, *54*(2), 107–116. https://doi.org/10.1093/sw/54.2.107

Vandervort, F. E., Gonzalez, R. P., & Faller, K. C. (2008). Legal ethics and high child welfare worker turnover: An unexplored connection. *Children and Youth Services Review*, *30*, 546–563. https://doi.org/10.1016/j.childyouth.2007.10.016

Walter-McCabe, H. (2019). Social work as an important collaborator in transdisciplinary public health law: Why does it matter and where does it fit? *Saint Louis University Journal of Health Law & Policy*, *13*, 77. https://scholarship.law.slu.edu/jhlp/vol13/iss1/8

Weil, M. (1982, September). Research on issues in collaboration between social workers and lawyers. *Social Service Review*, *56*, 393–405. https://doi.org/10.1086/644022

Weintraub, D., Rodgers, M. A., Botcheva, L., Loeb, A., Knight, R., Ortega, K., Heymach, B., Sandel, M., & Huffman, L. (2010). Pilot study of medical-legal partnership to address social and legal needs of patients. *Journal of Health Care for the Poor and Underserved*, *21*, 157–168. https://doi.org/10.1353/hpu.0.0311

Weiss-Gal, I., & Gal, J. (2009). Realizing rights in social work. *Social Service Review*, *83*(2), 267–291. https://doi.org/10.1086/599982

Wisconsin Court System, Wisconsin Pro Se Working Group. (2000). *Meeting the challenge of self-represented litigants in Wisconsin*. http://www.wicourts.gov/about/pubs/supreme/docs/prosereport.pdf

Witkin, S. L. (1998). Human rights and social work. *Social Work*, *43*, 197–201. https://doi.org/10.1093/sw/43.3.197

CHAPTER 2

A Conceptual and Historical Framework for Using the Law in Social Work Practice

INTRODUCTION

This chapter lays out the arguments from social work commentators and academics on the importance of developing critical competence and collaborative skills with legal systems and lawyers as part of their education, experiential learning, and professional practice. This chapter also presents an overview of conceptual frameworks and current models of collaborative law reform that are available for social workers to use in thinking about and developing a role for the law in their social work practice and a role for the social work profession in law reform initiatives. Not surprisingly, you will also learn that many of the collaborative, evidence-based, and alternative justice models that are being advanced are identical to innovations developed by social workers in the early history of our profession. The interdisciplinary and data-driven vision of these early initiatives can serve as a reminder of social work's historical leadership in this field and offer us a model that will inspire the social work profession to renewed leadership and action.

DEVELOPING A CONCEPTUAL FRAMEWORK TO THINK ABOUT SOCIAL WORK PRACTICE AND THE LAW

Social work services are often called upon when there is a failure on the part of the justice system or the administration of the law to accomplish its stated purpose. One of the founders of social work education described the inception of social work as a result of the widespread and unanimous agreement that the organization of the courts needed radical reconstruction, and, while great bodies of substantive law were able to adjust themselves to changing social needs, the administration of the law was seriously retarded, making the administration of justice a travesty on those in distress (Breckinridge, 1934).

There are several social work scholars who continue to advocate that social workers must become more active in their attempts to challenge, influence, and use the law in a proactive way. In this view, the law is seen as an instrument through which to realize human and civil rights, fight discrimination, advance social justice, achieve positive therapeutic aims, and develop fair and just processes and procedures (Ashford & Holschuh, 2006; Lynch & Mitchell, 1995; Madden & Wayne, 2003; Van Wormer, 2009).

One common theme among all the authors of this textbook is the identification of the need for a conceptual framework that can help structure social workers' analyses of legal issues and give guidance about the kind of involvement they should have in the legal system. Each of the authors identifies and describes a particular theoretical framework and corresponding law reform as examples of how to think about and structure social work engagement and practice with the law and legal systems. The authors of this text believe that when taken as a whole, these perspectives provide social workers with a comprehensive framework through which to view the interaction between social work and the law and to think about and expand their role as actors interacting with the legal system.

Therapeutic Jurisprudence

Madden and Wayne (2003) suggest that the concept of therapeutic jurisprudence may be a starting point for social workers to begin to consider how, when, and why social workers might take a more proactive stance toward the law. Therapeutic jurisprudence focuses on whether the legal rule or practice contributes to the psychological and physical well-being of the individual (Wexler, 2000). This perspective advances the idea that procedures, processes, legal actors, nonlegal actors (including social workers when they are playing a role in the legal system), and the rule of law can have therapeutic, antitherapeutic, even harmful, consequences even if the intent of the law and the actors applying it may be positive. Therapeutic jurisprudence is another way of assessing the relationship of one aspect of the environment—the legal system— with an individual, family, group, or community and as such is a good fit with social work values, knowledge, and skills (Madden & Wayne, 2003). Legal scholars have also recognized the continued impact of therapeutic jurisprudence in crafting laws and legal systems that work to promote even greater therapeutic impact (Spencer, 2014).

Proponents of therapeutic jurisprudence have not embraced a single normative framework for determining what is therapeutic in any given context. Brooks and Ronen (2005) propose that the values, principles, concepts, and methods of social work offer a normative framework for therapeutic jurisprudence that is both compatible with and enhances the practice of law. Social work and therapeutic jurisprudence have a focus on client well-being and social work offers many strategies and methods designed to promote the welfare of clients and allow for the actual *practice* of therapeutic jurisprudence (Brooks, 2005; Brooks & Ronen, 2005).

Therapeutic jurisprudence has been used as a conceptual framework to study and analyze the effects of a specific law such as the "Don't Ask, Don't Tell" legislation mandating that gay individuals may serve in the military but cannot disclose their sexual orientation and those in interaction with them may not ask about sexual orientation. When the law is viewed through a lens of psychological harm, a therapeutic jurisprudence perspective suggests that in actual practice the law has served to increase feelings of isolation and marginalization of gay soldiers and effects their social relationships and family interactions on many levels including psychologically and economically (Kavanagh, 1995; Westcott & Sawyer, 2007). More recently, scholars have noted the impact of a therapeutic jurisprudence lens on immigration policy, which was criticized for promoting fear and trauma in immigrants and their families as a result of increased deportations and forced family separations (Yamada, 2019).

Findings from studies such as these could be and are used by a number of disciplines—law, psychology, and social work—to collaboratively advocate for law reform. Madden and Wayne (2003) also suggest that therapeutic jurisprudence as a concept supports interprofessional collaboration because it is not a legal theory but rather a common conceptual framework about the law and legal systems that crosses professional silos and boundaries. In addition to law reform, some practitioners are beginning to look more closely at legal structures and processes and how they might be changed in ways that can prevent and reduce negative psychological and social effects for clients (Perlin, 2019).

Preventive Law

Related to therapeutic jurisprudence, and characterized as a method of obtaining the goals of therapeutic jurisprudence, is preventive law (Madden & Wayne, 2003). Some authors characterize preventive law as the tool through which to realize the *practice* of the *theory* of therapeutic jurisprudence (Doron & Gal, 2006; Stolle, 1996). Preventive law in the broadest terms seeks to prevent legal problems and court involvement and advocates for the use of alternative methods to the adversarial process, such as mediation, conferencing, and alternative dispute resolution. Preventive law practitioners seek to reduce risk of legal involvement as well as attempt to address the underlying problems that create the chance of involvement with the courts and the legal system and strive to consider a client's psychological and physical well-being (Doron & Gal, 2006).

Preventive law has been likened to preventive medicine in that the strategy of preventing illness is less costly that treating the illness. This concept has been applied to legal issues in that preventing legal disputes is less costly than litigation (Stolle, 1996). Legal documents such as advance directives and living wills used in working with elders are examples of preventive legal tools whose content and implementation are determined by an individual's choice at a time when they are capable of making a choice and thus avoiding legal disputes that may arise if they become impaired (Doron & Gal, 2006). Medical–legal partnership models of legal service delivery are also based in preventive law with a focus on moving away from crisis-oriented lawyering to preventive lawyering to address underlying legal issues that impact health and well-being (Curran, 2014).

The preventive focus of this legal reform movement has also led to the development of what are called "problem-solving courts." Examples of problem-solving courts are drug treatment courts, youth courts, mental health courts, and domestic violence courts. The central purpose of specialized courts is to intervene in such a way that while still holding the individual accountable for their crime, the underlying causes of the legal problem are assessed and addressed by an interdisciplinary and community-based group of professionals and self-help organizations. The judge and the court oversee the implementation and monitoring of the treatment plan. Problem-solving courts are thought to be effective in preventing future legal system involvement and improved client condition outcomes.

Another example is the development of veteran courts. Veteran courts were designed to reduce the criminal activity associated with the high rates of posttraumatic stress disorder (PTSD) experienced by veterans as a result of combat in Iraq and Afghanistan. Veteran Treatment Court, as described by All Rise, seeks to divert eligible veteran defendants with substance dependency and/or mental illness, who are charged with felony or misdemeanor nonviolent criminal offenses, to a specialized criminal court (www.allrise.org). Intake workers, many times social workers, use evidence-based screening and assessment to determine who meets the criteria for participation in the intervention.

After assessment, the veterans voluntarily participate in a judicially supervised treatment plan that a team of court staff, veteran healthcare professionals, veteran peer mentors, and mental health professionals develop collaboratively with the veteran. There are regular court hearings where treatment plans are reassessed and evaluated, incentives and praise are offered to reward the completion of treatment plan elements, and sanctions for nonadherence are handed down (http://nadcp.org). Many veterans have their charges dismissed on successful completion of the program and others are ensured of receiving a sentence that does not involve jail time or incarceration upon finishing the program.

Social work focuses on strength-based practice and identifying protective factors and coping abilities that mitigate the effects of social problems on their clients. Increasingly, these skills and methods are being targeted toward a greater focus on prevention (Hawkins et al., 2010). Many social workers know that clients who have chronic substance use and mental health problems often have involvement at various levels in the legal system, whether in civil court for abuse or neglect or in criminal court for a related crime. Preventive law models can be accessed as an adjunct and support to individual treatment and recovery because they are aimed at addressing the root cause of the system involvement and interrupting the traditional path of a court case.

Procedural Justice

Ashford and Holschuh (2006) suggest that while the concept of therapeutic jurisprudence is consistent with many values of the social work profession, it does not go far enough as a conceptual framework. The authors point out that the focus of therapeutic jurisprudence is on outcomes and gives no real assistance in offering a theoretical perspective about how the law can be effective in achieving therapeutic results (Ashford & Holschuh, 2006).

The missing component of therapeutic jurisprudence is that it does not incorporate issues of justice and fairness that are realized in the procedures and interpersonal relations through which the law is administered and legal decision-making occurs (Ashford & Holschuh, 2006). Ashford and Holschuh (2006) use the example of how early outcome studies of drug courts revealed that having a judge in the role of case manager contributed to differences in treatment engagement and retention as opposed to other traditional case managers. However, the authors note that none of the studies identified how the relationship with the judge or any of the other procedures associated with drug courts, such as sanctions, contributed to or influenced the outcome (Ashford & Holschuh, 2006). The authors advance the position that social workers adopt procedural justice as a framework to investigate justice and fairness concerns and the use of social science to inform legal decision-makers about how consumers perceive the fairness of legal procedures and processes (Ashford & Holschuh, 2006).

Procedural justice is a concept that has been developed and studied in the field of social psychology (Tyler, 1990). The study of procedural justice has focused on understanding the perceptions of consumers about whether or not service outcomes were perceived as fair, whether or not the decision-making processes were perceived to be fair regardless of outcome, and finally what the role is that procedures, processes, and actors play in conveying relational information to the consumer about their value and worth as a person.

Social workers and social science knowledge can play a key role in designing procedures that comport with principles of fairness as well as report the experiences clients have when they are in interaction with the legal system. Studies have shown that even when consumers do not achieve their desired outcome, if they feel the decision-making process was fair and that they were treated with respect they accept the decision. Lens and Vorsanger (2005) studied clients who appealed public benefits decisions and found that the opportunity to speak, having their views considered by an impartial decision-maker acting in good faith, and being treated with respect were identified as manifestations of fairness even in the cases where they lost the hearing or did not receive the outcome they were hoping for. Research also suggests that despite zealous advocacy and access to legal counsel, there are still significant racial disparities in both criminal and civil legal and court proceedings. Research findings show that an estimated 20% of people currently incarcerated (23 million) in the United States are awaiting trial and have not been convicted of any crime; they are often living in poverty with a disproportionate number of individuals identifying as Black and Latino (National Academies of Sciences, Engineering, and Medicine [NASEM], 2021). Additional research shows continued disparities in pretrial detention, with Black individuals less likely to have the ability to make cash bail, to spend more time in pretrial detention, and to be subject to increased systemic harms (NASEM, 2021). Further research also shows significant disparities and monetary sanctions, including fines and fees associated with court hearings, prosecution, and defense. Studies conducted by the Innocence Project, show significant racial disparities in wrongful convictions and exonerations, with Black people seven times more likely to be wrongfully convicted of murder than White people. Black exonerees are also more likely to spend more time incarcerated before exoneration (NASEM, 2021). Despite changes in due process, the expanding access to counsel, and criminal reform, more work must be done to address the significant racial and gender disparities that exist at both the front and back end of the system. Both lawyers and social workers have critical roles to play in not only addressing racial disparities when they arise but working to develop preventive methods and analyzing legal theories that challenge institutional racism before it happens to their clients. Some researchers have advocated the position that the treatment people receive from authorities represents another kind of justice; that is, "interactional justice" or how individual actors treat people as they are subjected to various decision-making processes (Ashford & Holschuh, 2006). In her analysis of public benefit hearings, Lens (2009) suggested that requesting hearings to contest public benefit decisions serve as a substitute for the personal attention lacking in the worker–client relationship in the typical welfare office. Fagan and Tyler (2005) found in their study of the legal socialization process of children and adolescents that negative attitudes toward the legitimacy of the law were influenced and created by negative experiences with legal actors. Procedural justice theory has also been explored in the context of policing policy, interactions with police, and compliance with the law (Nagin & Telep, 2020). In Chapter 1, we reported studies on the retention of child welfare workers that found a relationship between negative and disrespectful treatment by court personnel and child welfare workers leaving their jobs. All the studies reviewed report that many workers both perceived and received relational messages that conveyed attitudes of disrespect, low worth, and incompetence by other professionals and the courts (Ellett & Steib, 2005; Faller et al., 2009; Vandervort et al., 2008). These outcomes have further negative effects when we look at research that reports staff turnover has been found to be associated with poor outcomes for children and families involved in the child welfare system (Glisson & Hemmelgarn, 1998). Other studies on child welfare retention look at the significant number of Black social workers employed by child welfare systems, their roles in mandated reporting, and child removal rates for Black families, also as a contributing factor for the ever transitioning and high turnover in social services (Cantey et al., 2020). Specifically, research shows that there is a large number of Black social workers working for child serving systems, while Black children are overwhelmingly overrepresented in the child welfare system. Black social workers, similar to their White counterparts, are also more likely to subjectively report that they believe Black children are at higher risk of harm and more likely to substantiate Black families for maltreatment (Cantey et al., 2020). Unfortunately, research shows the complicated nature and impact on Black and Brown social workers when they play critical roles in the child removal process, particularly when the children they serve are from the same racial and ethnic background. Procedural and interactional justice perspectives offer a framework to better understand and respond to the experience reported by the child welfare workers and observed by researchers (Ellett & Steib, 2005). Preventive law would prescribe a collaborative problem-solving approach involving judges, lawyers, workers, and social work researchers and educators, to develop interventions and interactions to decrease secondary stress and racial disparities, in addition to increasing the sense of efficacy felt by workers during interaction with the court and to ultimately have better outcomes for children and families by reducing turnover, burnout, and job stress.

Procedural justice research also suggests that there is another possible route to effective social regulation besides punitive outcomes and punishment (Tyler, 1990; Tyler & Huo, 2002). This route involves recognizing the importance of just procedures and treating people with respect throughout all stages of a legal proceeding or interaction with a government official. Procedural justice is not only important for those who break rules and laws, but the provision of, or lack of, procedural justice in how systems respond to victims of crime also influence the crime reporting behavior of victims (Ruback et al., 2008). When people are treated fairly and respectfully, they view law and legal authorities as more legitimate and entitled to be obeyed and accessed. As a result, people become self-regulating, taking on the personal responsibility for following social rules. This approach has been labeled as a process-based model of regulation (Tyler, 2003, 2006).

Restorative Justice

The restorative justice movement builds upon the concepts of procedural and interactional justice and attempts to develop a conception of justice that is personal rather than an abstract and impersonal construct (Van Ness, 2004). This movement began in response to an increasingly punitive criminal justice system and attempts to change the focus of the system response away from law or rule breaking to a focus on harm to the victim, the community, and the offender that occurs when a crime is committed. It also transforms the relationship among individuals, families, and government in responding to crime (Van Ness & Crocke, 2003).

The theoretical tradition that organizes the practice of restorative justice is known as peacemaking criminology (Pepinsky, 1995; Wheeldon, 2009). The theory stems from the belief that responding to crime with punitive and repressive measures is substituting one form of societal violence for another. Solutions to crime would be better focused on prevention, reconciliation through mediation and alternative dispute resolution, and reintegration back into the community once crime has occurred (Wheeldon, 2009).

Under this analysis, justice is understood as repairing the harms with the offender taking responsibility to repair the damage and is involved in a process where the victim, offender, and other community members address the personal and interpersonal consequences of rule breaking. This is achieved through the development of personal relationships that will not only make amends to the victim but will also reengage and reintegrate the offender back into the community. It is hoped that through participation in the process, the offenders will develop empathy for the victims and regret what they have done (Van Wormer, 2006, 2009). It is believed that if the offender has feelings of shame about their action, accepts responsibility, and sincerely offers apology to the victim and community, their sense of dignity will be restored. While the feelings of the victim are paramount, disapproval of the bad conduct of the offender is combined with respect for the person who committed the crime (Tyler, 2006).

Both the victim and offender are able to bring family, friends, and community members to restorative justice convenings. The objective is to identify and amplify the social connection that people feel toward their family and community. The goal in reconnecting the offender to their community is to encourage and increase feelings of responsibility that will enhance commitment to self-regulation of actions and this in turn serves a preventive function with regard to future rule breaking (Tyler, 2006). There are some studies which suggest that for some types of crime, participation in restorative justice processes can lead to greater law-abiding behavior in the future (Nugent et al., 2004; Poulson, 2003).

The structures in which restorative justice concepts are applied are victim–offender mediation, family group conferencing, healing circles, and community mediation (Van Ness, 2004; Van Wormer, 2006, 2009). Trained facilitators usually conduct victim–offender mediation and family group conferencing; in some situations, the facilitators are social workers. Many communities also have engaged in their own restorative practices, with states having implemented pilot programs offering diversion and restorative justice, which have often resulted in increased victim satisfaction (Smith et al., 2022). For example, Native communities often engage in peacemaking circles and other indigenous practices that support communities and restore harm. Schools are also often involved in engaging children and youth and their families in school-based restorative justice programs (Smith et al., 2022). Many social workers working in child welfare are familiar with family group conferencing as a tool of restorative justice (Connolly, 2009). Some clinicians treating family violence by implementing a family systemic approach are using restorative justice processes as an adjunct to therapy (McNevin, 2010).

A major argument to be made is that restorative justice is a form of social justice as it seeks to provide a balance of power among people who have varying degrees of it. It is also compatible with a more solution-based and less problem-focused social work response. An important distinction between alternative dispute resolution or more formal mediation processes sometimes used in the legal system and restorative justice processes is that the parties are not seen as equals with a dispute to be negotiated but rather a victim and offender and not disputants (Van Wormer, 2006).

Abolition

Abolition refers to the movement to deconstruct and abolish unjust and oppressive laws, systems, and policies alongside repairing the harms caused by those institutions (Cullors, 2019). Abolition has been presented as a tool for reforming both the carceral state and the child welfare system, often referred to as the family regulation system (Roberts, 2022).

Social work commentators have noted the role of social workers in perpetuating the carceral state and argued for social work to embrace anticarceral social work models (Jacobs et al., 2021). Throughout history there have been various topics and issues challenged by scholars and activists fighting for the abolition of harmful, oppressive systems and federal policies like slavery. Today, many social work scholars and others are reexamining the carceral state and outlining the effects of family surveillance, mass incarceration, and the criminalization of poverty and mental health, and calling for full abolition of existing institutions like the family regulation system or "child welfare" system and the prison system. Today's family regulatory systems, including the prison system, use methods of carceral and criminal punishment that can be traced back to chattel slavery— the first existence of police was during slave patrols and Jim Crow, enforcing racial subjugation by inflicting harm and carrying out inhumane racist policies, practices, and terror on Black people (Roberts, 2021). Additionally, state-funded family regulatory programs and systems rely too heavily on surveillance, overreporting, and on child removal rates, instead of family reunification and intervention services that address the often complex needs and/or economic needs of families (Roberts, 2021). Research shows that more than half of Black children will have experienced the child welfare system at some point in their lives. Indigenous children are also overrepresented in the child welfare system (Roberts, 2021). Despite significant wins to reduce racial disparities and to decrease the number of children in both systems, both the child welfare and prison systems continue to overuse and, at times, abuse their control by using punishment and harm that mostly affects Black, Brown, Indigenous, and migrant children and their families.

Justice System Advocacy as the Route to Realizing Racial Justice

In the first two chapters, we have presented, identified, and discussed the need for social workers to incorporate an understanding of the impact of legal system interactions on their clients and to attend to the actual experiences, psychological consequences, and the perceptions of justice and fairness reported by their clients. This understanding is crucial to the enactment of social work's historic mission of advocacy for the disenfranchised and for he achievement of social justice. What is missing from the discussion is a way to specifically acknowledge and address the indisputable evidence that clients of color are more likely to be involved with the legal system, more likely to experience biased decision-making during every phase of the legal process, and as well experience more negative outcomes and consequences than Whites during interactions with the legal system and legal actors.

Lynch and Mitchell (1995) have long advocated for social workers to understand the power of the legal system that, in their view, does not consistently and specifically recognize the equality of all persons. The authors suggest that the judicial system is, and can be, an arena for social action, particularly for addressing racism and oppression. The authors reinforce and remind social workers of the ethical duty to address discrimination and emphasize that in order to effectively discharge their advocacy role, social workers must be *informed* advocates (Lynch & Mitchell, 1995). Without knowledge of the U.S. legal system, laws, legal practitioners, and legal process and procedure it is further suggested that social justice as practiced by social workers is little more than rhetoric (Mitchell & Lynch, 2003). The "teeth" of the law are necessary to make social justice a reality and rights are only as good as the extent to which they are realized. Social workers can only "empower" clients if they are aware of the rights and benefits clients are entitled to and that allow clients to claim their power as citizens.

Much of the commentary about racial justice and the legal system focuses on the racial and ethnic disproportionality and disparity that occurs in the criminal justice and child welfare systems. There is an extensive body of research, some presented in Chapter 1, that continues to document the racial and ethnic disparity that occurs in every human service system: healthcare, mental healthcare, education, special education, housing, and employment (Alliance for Health Reforms, 2006; Farkas, 2003; Flores et al., 2005; Halliday, 2000; Holley & VanVleet, 2006). As we have presented, the systems that social workers may identify primarily as helping systems or service systems are created and administered by law and, because of this fact, the authors of this book suggest that the arenas of civil and administrative law are important vehicles through which discrimination and oppression can be addressed, as well as advocacy opportunities that can advance the achievement of a social justice that is also racial justice.

As an example of how to achieve racial justice when social work practice is legally informed, Mitchell and Lynch (2007) describe a programming model for the reunification of low-income African American fathers with their children that includes a component that addresses the underlying legal barriers found to impede reunification as the program was being implemented. The authors point out that most programs designed to increase responsible parenthood for low-income men focus only on the emotional or economic barriers to responsible fatherhood (Mitchell & Lynch, 2007).

On the basis of data collected during the program-monitoring phase of a demonstration project, Mitchell and Lynch (2007) identified a significant number of legally related variables that created barriers for the participants, the majority of whom were African American men. These include consumer issues, divorce, child support, custody, domestic violence, housing, employment, benefits, and criminal histories that make it impossible to obtain employment, safe housing, or public benefits (Mitchell & Lynch, 2007).

As a result of these findings, the program expanded to include a partnership with lawyers and several courts, and added a forensic legal and social work assessment component to the program. There were positive outcomes reported by participants with regard to reunification with their children; the courts were better able to process and address the multiple needs of the participants because they were represented; and the benefits from transdisciplinary practice between social workers and the legal system were seen to contribute to increased efficiency of governmental organizations and an increased profile for forensic social work in the community (Mitchell & Lynch, 2007).

RETURNING TO OUR ROOTS: SOCIAL WORK, LAW, EVIDENCE, AND INTERDISCIPLINARY COLLABORATION

The conceptual frameworks presented in this book are not new or original for the profession of social work. In fact, an empowered, interdisciplinary, evidence-based, and preventive approach to thinking about and using the law was first developed at Hull House, the settlement house in Chicago founded by Jane Addams. Addams and her colleagues used the law to achieve social work values and goals, studied the impact of laws and procedures on various groups, researched and assessed the fairness of administrative rules, and used the social science they produced to argue for and create alternative legal venues as well as address discrimination (Shields et al., 2023).

Sociology and criminology scholars advance the idea that many of the early theoretical frameworks and research methods used for the development of crime and delinquency policies, usually attributed to male scholars in both fields, were actually based on the research and practice of Jane Addams and the other women scholars who lived and worked at Hull House (Deegan, 1990; Frey, 2007; McGuire, 2004; Moyer, 2003).

Jane Addams won the Nobel Peace Prize for her work in human and civil rights and was a cofounder of the American Civil Liberties Union as well as the National Association for the Advancement of Colored People (NAACP). Addams served on numerous committees related to the legal system such as the Committee on Crime and Immigration for the American Institute of Criminal Law and Criminology, president of the National Conference of Charities and Corrections, National Advisory Board for the World's Court League, and League for the Abolition of Capital Punishment (Frey, 2007).

Interestingly, a number of women residents of Hull House, usually identified as social workers, were also trained as lawyers. Florence Kelley studied law at Northwestern University where she completed her law degree after being denied admittance to the University of Chicago Law School based on her gender. Julia Lathrop studied and read the law while working in her father's law office and passed the state bar. Sophonisba Breckinridge not only read law in her father's law office but was also the first woman to be admitted to the bar in Kentucky. Her examination was so brilliant that she received unanimous approval from the bar committee and later was the first woman inducted into Coif, an honorary legal society (Abbott, 1948). Breckinridge was later the first woman to be awarded a doctorate in law from the University of Chicago.

Therapeutic Jurisprudence

The women residents and neighbors of Hull House effectively used legal channels to intervene at the municipal, state, and eventually the federal level. In relation to the principles of therapeutic jurisprudence, the most significant aspect of their work is that all their analyses began at the micro level of practice—that is, how the law, or the absence of law, affected the individual. They conducted detailed empirical research into neighborhood conditions, gathered individual-level narratives, and studied the effect of the environment, including the legal environment, on the physical, psychological, and social well-being of the neighbors the residents engaged with.

As an example, in 1911, Sophonisba Breckinridge and Edith Abbott wrote an article detailing their research on social conditions in a section of Chicago that combines photographs, maps, verbal descriptions, interviews, physical measurements of room size and number of windows, statistical profiles of ethnicity and occupation, and an analysis of housing law and codes to present a multidimensional account of life in a desperately poor area (Breckinridge & Abbott, 1911). The research demonstrated numerous violations of existing laws and the presence of unsanitary, hazardous, and toxic conditions. The authors linked those conditions to infant mortality and poor health outcomes. In this instance, the findings revealed not only that new laws needed to be written but also that current laws were not being enforced equally. The authors suggest that this lack of enforcement rose to the level of "criminal neglect" and used their data to make recommendations for law reform and achieved administrative reform in the structuring of existing governmental agencies (Breckinridge & Abbott, 1911).

Another stunning example of what we now call therapeutic jurisprudence is the work done by Florence Kelley and Josephine Goldmark on the historic Supreme Court case *Muller v. Oregon* (1908) that addressed the physical, psychological, and social impact of long working hours on women and children. Louis Brandeis, later to become a Supreme Court Justice himself, argued the case in front of the Court but Kelley and Goldmark wrote the legal brief (McGuire, 2004).

The brief contained social science evidence collected from the United States, England, and other industrialized countries, interviews, and personal narratives and documented the effect of long workdays on women, their children, their health, and their communities. The case marked the first time that social science was used in a legal forum, established the precedent of using social science data in legal decision-making, and made the case for the necessity for a law rather than merely arguing constitutionality (Boyd, 2008).

This style of legal brief is also known as a "Brandeis Brief" and has been used in subsequent Supreme Court cases such as *Brown v. Board of Education* (1954) (McGuire, 2004). Social workers such as Kelley, Goldmark, and Molly Dewson continued to work with and write briefs using social science evidence for progressive lawyers such as Brandeis and Felix Frankfurter (later to become the Chief Justice of the Supreme Court) on a variety of issues related to health and labor, including the case for a minimum wage (McGuire, 2004).

Preventive Law

Much of the work these social work pioneers did could be characterized as preventive law in that they viewed the law as a major intervention and tool that could be employed in the prevention of conditions such as infant mortality, crime and delinquency, child abuse and neglect, and poor health outcomes for adults and children due to unsafe and unsanitary living and working conditions. Jane Addams was frequently called upon to mediate various disputes between families, groups, and communities in Chicago (Knight, 2010; Shields, 2003).

As a pragmatist, Addams believed firmly in the values of compromise and negotiation. Within her local neighborhood, in addition to language barriers, many of the immigrants from Europe brought long-standing hostilities between regions and groups that made mediation a necessity (Shields, 2003). She also mediated disputes between parents and children, eventually establishing the Labor Museum specifically for the purpose of restoring and balancing power relationships between immigrant parents and their more Americanized children who perceived their parents lacking the power to adjust themselves to American standards. The Labor Museum, through showcasing the skills of the older community, attempted to make a connection between the past and present as a way of restoring the balance of power between the young and the old (Jackson, 2001).

Addams saw herself and Hull House as mediator and opposed the kind of dualistic thinking that creates disputes. She brought this perspective into her work negotiating labor disputes:

> The settlement may be of value if it can take a larger and steadier view than is always possible to the workingman, smarting under a sense of wrong; of the capitalist, seeking only to "quiet down." It is possible to recall them both to a sense of the larger development. (Addams, 1895, p. 196)

The settlement also developed alternative structures both to *address and to prevent* social problems and used the law as a tool in the achievement of these goals. In Chapter 1, you were introduced to a current preventive law intervention known as medical–legal partnerships (MLPs) that address the social determinants of poor health outcomes. In 1867, a woman physician named Alice Hamilton came to live and work at Hull House and with other residents set up the first well-baby clinic in the country as a way to prevent infant mortality. Because of her deep trust and respect for the immigrants' experience she began to study previously undocumented reports of environmental hazards in the workplace and their effects on physical health (Fee & Brown, 2001). She pioneered the use of qualitative research methods such as interviews of subjects as part of medical research and was the first physician because of her work with social workers to tie social conditions to physical health (Moye, 1986).

During the typhoid epidemic of 1902, Dr. Hamilton traced the carrier of the disease to flies that surrounded open and undrained privies. Along with her colleagues, she persuaded the Board of Health to address the issue and the result was subsequent changes in health codes and regulations (Moye, 1986). Hamilton then noted that the health problems of many of the immigrant poor were due to unsafe conditions and noxious chemicals, especially lead dust, to which they were being exposed in the course of their employment. Her work, along with her Hull House colleagues, led to the passage of the first occupational health law in the country in 1911.

Another example of the early use of preventive law was the development of the juvenile court. In 1892, when the campaign began to establish a juvenile court, when children broke the law, they were subject to the same laws and procedures as adults. Children were both jailed and sent to prison with adults. The offenses of children were tried under the same laws and courts. Julia Lathrop, along with the Chicago Woman's Club and the Chicago Bar Association, secured legislation for this separation and the first juvenile court system in the country was created (Stivers, 2002). She also helped set up a psychiatric clinic to help rehabilitate young offenders and raised money to pay the salaries of the first probation officer. Julia Lathrop became the first chairperson of the Juvenile Court Committee; a working-class Hull House resident, Alzina Stevens, became the court's first probation officer. From the start, a research arm was attached to the court so that it could be continuously evaluated as well as to further study and address the causes of delinquency (Frey, 2007).

Procedural Justice

The very purpose of the establishment of the juvenile court was to address procedural justice concerns about the way juveniles were being treated in the adult criminal justice system. The juvenile court and the development of probation and parole were all designed to create a transition from a system that was experienced punitively by those involved in it, to one that would assist with the reincorporation of the offender back into the neighborhood, family, and community (Frey, 2007). It was believed that being treated in a more cooperative manner would prevent further crime, similar to the process-based model of regulation suggested by today's social psychologists (Tyler, 2003, 2006).

In 1893, Julia Lathrop was appointed head of the Illinois State Board of Charities, responsible for overseeing all the state institutions for the poor, elderly, and mentally ill who, at that time were frequently housed in the same institution (Stivers, 2002). Julia Lathrop believed, as did the other scholars of Hull House, that social science evidence—both collecting it and publishing it—was the key to changing policies and regulations. Lathrop was a pioneer in the use of descriptive and detailed narratives to describe the processes and procedures of institutions and organizations from the service recipient's experience.

Similar to the work of Alice Hamilton, the narratives of those impacted by the conditions were privileged and through careful listening, the Hull House researchers presented both qualitative and quantitative documentation of institutional practices and policies that were inhumane and unfair. Lathrop applied this analysis to numerous topics such as the treatment and care of mentally ill inmates to how charity was distributed (Stivers, 2002). This evidence was then used to sway public opinion and to change laws and administrative rules about how organizations should be administered.

Based on her research, Lathrop found and described how institutional rules and regulations had tangible consequences for the vulnerable people disciplined by them (Stivers, 2002). In her work honoring Julia Lathrop, Addams (1935) notes:

> What distressed Julia Lathrop most ... was the regulation which separated an old couple, sending the husband into the men's side, the wife into the women's side. It allowed them to see each other once a week with the heavy netting of a screen between them through which, if not too deaf to hear or too feeble to shout, they might communicate with each other for half an hour ... Such a state of mind affords one more example of the danger of administering any human situation upon theory uncorrected by constant experience. (Addams, 1935, pp. 70–71)

Restorative Justice

Recently, sociologists have been creating a scholarship that documents the ways that Jane Addams and her colleagues at Hull House actually theorized and practiced peacemaking criminology and restorative justice (Frey, 2007). As we discussed earlier in this chapter, peacemaking criminology and restorative justice focus on how inequality and power impact how crime or lawbreaking is viewed and responded to, and advocates a more restorative and rehabilitative approach rather than one that is oppressive and retributive. Addams believed that crime was a symptom of social maladjustment and this perspective refutes criminologists from her day suggesting that crime was inherent in the individual or a product of biology (Frey, 2007). She suggests that crime should be addressed on the community or local level because there are more powerful forces of interpersonal social control than larger structures that allow anonymity (Frey, 2007). She advocates that effective responses to crime should include collaboration among multiple sources such as family, community, and local institutions such as education and social services (Frey, 2007). This theoretical perspective foreshadows the rationale underpinning the many community-level courts and restorative justice programs that are proliferating in the United States today.

Addams also felt strongly that a response to crime that included violence and repressive force would result only in more violence and criminal activity. This view is expressly articulated in an article that Addams wrote denouncing lynching (Addams, 1901). Her major argument, presented by using historical analysis, was that the use of violence results in more violence and that lynching was a waste of human life and capacity that could only result in social division and further antagonism (Hamington, 2005). In Addam's view, violence was the least effective method of teaching self-control (Addams, 1901).

Foreshadowing and articulating the key principles of what we currently call victim–offender mediation, Breckinridge (1934) explained to social work students:

> Sound casework requires that what is done to the person punished should have for its purpose the gain of the person punished as well as the security of the community. Those forms of punishment which express a contempt for the victim are therefore always scrutinized with grave doubt by the social worker. (Breckinridge, 1934, p. 402)

Racial Justice

Jane Addams and the women who lived at Hull House also studied and addressed the inequities faced by Black men, women, and children but this writing is less well known (Hamington, 2005). Some scholarship has highlighted the work done at Hull House that sought to address race relations and illuminated the important personal and professional relationships that Jane Addams maintained throughout her lifetime with W. E. B. DuBois and Ida B. Wells (Deegan, 2002; Lengermann & Niebrugge-Brantley, 1998). Ida B. Wells called her "the greatest woman in America" in her autobiography (Lengermann & Niebrugge-Brantley, 1998, p. 259). Addams also maintained working relationships with other Black clubwomen including Mary Church Terrell, Mary R. Talbert, and Josephine St. Pierre Ruffin (Apthecker, 1977).

Jane Addams worked with Ida B. Wells to stop the *Chicago Tribune* from publishing a series of articles that advocated for racial segregation in the public schools. Addams headed a delegation of White supporters to the *Tribune* and effectively stopped the series of articles (Hamington, 2005). Addams and Wells later joined forces with W. E. B. DuBois in 1908 to issue a call to action against lynching, convict lease systems, disenfranchisement, and segregation (Apthecker, 1977). The following year the NAACP was founded.

As Sophinisba Breckinridge and Edith Abbott continued their investigations into the social conditions of Chicago they began to uncover for the first time the conditions under which Black families were living. Along with one of the first Black social work students, Birdye Haynes, they documented that the most conspicuously dilapidated sections were where Blacks were living (Stehno, 1988). A study undertaken of juvenile court records in 1899 and 1905 found a disproportionate number of Black children involved with the court and what they called an "unduly large" number of Black girls being sent to the girls' reformatory (Stehno, 1988, p. 488). The women used these findings to advocate for the development of public child welfare services, establish new child welfare policy and law, and the development of legal standards of care for Black dependent children (Stehno, 1988).

Grace Abbott wrote a series of books on immigration using her signature method of combining individual narratives, statistics, and legislative and legal analyses. Abbott was responsible for producing one of the most comprehensive analyses of the Mexican immigrants and their encounters with the criminal justice system. The report was published in 1931 as a result of her work for the National Commission on Law Observance and Enforcement (Deegan, 1991).

A final example is the work of Florence Kelley addressing what we would identify today as "institutional or structural racism." The Institute for Race Relations defines institutional racism as "racism that which, covertly or overtly, resides in the policies, procedures, operations and culture of public or private institutions—reinforcing individual prejudices and being reinforced by them in turn" (CARF, 1998). In a call to action to address the issue of institutional racism, the National Association of Social Workers (NASW) identifies examples of how in the current time the profession may perpetuate institutional racism (NASW, 2007). The first reason given in the self-assessment is that "support is given to policies and practices without analysis of the racial effect or worse" (NASW, 2007, p. 12). Once again, the founders of our profession can provide modern-day social workers with inspiration about how to use the law as a way to address inequities our profession may unwontedly reproduce such as institutional racism or violations of civil rights. The following example shows the way Florence Kelley analyzed the law to assess for discrimination.

Florence Kelley, who was a Board member of the NAACP, had the reputation of being wary of details in legislation, and when it came to bills involving the provision of federal monies for education or social welfare she was especially rigorous. Athey (1971), in an article that outlines the work Florence Kelley did in the service of Black equality, reports "Mrs. Kelley carefully screened each measure to ferret out methods by which discrimination was intended or might be practiced" (p. 252).

In her analysis of the Sterling-Towner education bill (which she referred to as the "Sterling Discrimination Bill"), Kelley assessed that the bill was crafted to reproduce patterns of discrimination in the South (Athey, 1971). She identified unequal expenditures for the education of Black children in 15 states in the South and the District of Columbia and found six sections that would "legalize discrimination against public education for Negroes" (Athey, 1971, p. 253).

The Integration of Law and Social Work in Social Work Education

Because Julia Lathrop, Sophinisba Breckinridge, and Grace and Edith Abbott were also heavily involved in the development of social work education, many of the books and articles they wrote about the intersection of social work and the laws were used as classroom texts and readings.

Social Work and the Courts (1934), authored by Sophinisba Breckinridge, documents how the law shapes and effects the definitions of social problems and how to solve them. Unlike most of the social work and law textbooks today where laws and legal structures are merely surveyed, Breckinridge laid out the existing implicit and explicit legal frameworks but then went on to critique them from a social work and social justice perspective offering suggestions for social work advocacy and activism for changing laws and the judicial system. By writing the book in this way she was teaching social work students to become critical consumers of the law.

In the preface, justifying the writing of the book, Breckinridge identifies what she calls the deficiencies of judicial administration such as the costs of counsel, the expense of litigation, and delays in the timely administration of justice (Breckinridge, 1934). Her book is designed to illustrate for social workers these deficiencies. The book also critiques the philosophy underlying criminal law of that time and advocates a more rehabilitative approach while also acknowledging the need to protect constitutional rights: "The violation of the constitutional rights of even the weakest and most degraded members of the community must be recognized as threatening the liberty of all and as being inconsistent with principles of sound social work" (Breckinridge, 1934, p. 5).

The arguments for a proactive, knowledge-based, and problem-solving approach to the law made by the authors in the preface of this book are remarkably like those made by Breckinridge (1934) in the introduction to her text and course, "Social Work and the Courts." Her words seem a fitting close to this chapter:

> That a better understanding of the legal habit of thought and of the judicial organization is as essential for intelligent cooperation of social workers with the courts is as true as that a reasonable understanding of the hospital is

necessary for sound cooperation of social workers with physicians in cases of physical or mental illness. It is a bridge across the professional gap that separates the social worker from the lawyer that a course of this kind is designed. The documents should be supplemented by continuously edited bibliographies and by the formulation of problems to be attacked by the students in the light of the immediate jurisdiction and special interest of the student. (Breckinridge, 1934, p. 7)

REFERENCES

Abbott, E. (1948). Sophonisba Preston Breckinridge over the years. *The Social Service Review*, *22*(4), 417–423. https://doi.org/10.1086/637031

Addams, J. (1901). Respect for law. In B. Apthecker (Ed.), *Lynching and rape: An exchange of view* (p. 23). American Institute for Marxist Studies (Reprinted from *The Independent*, 53, p. 9).

Addams, J. (1935). *My friend Julia Lathrop*. Macmillan.

Addams, J. (Ed.). (1895). *Hull House maps and papers*. Crowell.

Alliance for Health Reforms. (2006). *Racial and ethnic disparities in health care*. https://www.allhealthpolicy.org/wp-content/uploads/2017/03/pub_38.pdf

Ashford, J. B., & Holschuh, J. (2006). Fairness issues in law and mental health: Directions for social work research. *Journal of Sociology and Social Welfare*, *XXXIII*(4), 151–172. https://doi.org/10.15453/0191-5096.3208

Athey, L. (1971). Florence Kelley and the quest for Negro equality. *The Journal of Negro History*, *LVI*(4), 249–261. https://doi.org/10.2307/2716966

Boyd, A. (2008). *Paying the precious price of equality:* Muller v. Oregon *and the conflict protective legislation*. Unpublished manuscript.

Breckinridge, S. P. (1934). *Social work and the courts: Select documents*. University of Chicago Press.

Breckinridge, S. P., & Abbott, E. (1911). Housing conditions in Chicago, III: Back of the yards. *American Journal of Sociology*, *16*(4), 433–468. https://doi.org/10.1086/211908

Brooks, S. L. (2005). Practicing (and teaching) therapeutic jurisprudence: Importing social work principles and techniques into clinical legal education. *St. Thomas Law Review*, *17*, 513–530. https://ssrn.com/abstract=3587913

Brooks, S. L., & Ronen, Y. (2005). The notion of interdependence and its implications for child and family policy. *Journal of Feminist Family Therapy*, *17*, 513–530. https://doi.org/10.1300/J086v17n03_02

Brown v. Board of Education, 347 U.S. 483 (1954).

Cantey, N. I., Smith, L. W., Sorrells, S. F., Kelly, D., Jones, C., & Burrus, D. (2022). Navigating racism in the child welfare system: The impact on Black children, families, and practitioners [Special issue]. *Child Welfare*, *100*(2), 163–184. https://www.jstor.org/stable/48663461

CARF. (1998). *What is institutional racism?* https://irr.org.uk/article/what-is-institutional-racism/

Connolly, M. (2009). Family group conferencing in child welfare: The fit with restorative justice. *Contemporary Justice Review*, *12*(3), 309–319. https://doi.org/10.1080/10282580903105822

Cullors, P. (2019). Abolition and reparations: history of resistance, transformative justice, accountability. *Harvard Law Review*, *132*(6), 1684–1694.

Curran, M. (2014). Preventative law: Interdisciplinary lessons from medical–legal partnership. *N.Y.U. Review of Law & Social Change*, *38*, 595–606.

Deegan, M. J. (1990). *Jane Addams and the men of The Chicago School, 1892–1918*. Transaction Books.

Deegan, M. J. (1991). Jane Addams (1860–1935). In M. J. Deegan (Ed.), *Women in sociology: A bio-bibliographical sourcebook* (pp. 37–44). Greenwood Press.

Deegan, M. J. (2002). *Race, Hull House, and the University of Chicago: A new conscience against ancient evils.* Praeger.

Doron, I., & Gal, I. (2006). The emergence of legal prevention in old age: Findings from an Israeli exploratory study. *Journal of Cross-Cultural Gerontology, 21*, 41–53. https://doi.org/10.1007/s10823-006-9016-0

Ellett, A. J., & Steib, S. D. (2005). Child welfare and the courts: A statewide study with implications for professional development, practice and change. *Research on Social Work Practice, 15*(5), 339–352. https://doi.org/10.1177/1049731505276680

Fagan, J., & Tyler, T. R. (2005). Legal socialization of children and adolescents. *Social Justice Research, 18*(3), 217–242. https://doi.org/10.1007/s11211-005-6823-3

Faller, K. C., Grabarek, M., & Vandervort, F. (2009). Child welfare workers go to court: The impact of race, gender and education on the comfort with legal issues. *Children and Youth Services Review, 31*, 972–977. https://doi.org/10.1016/j.childyouth.2009.04.010

Farkas, G. (2003). Racial disparities and discrimination in education: What do we know, how do we know it, and what do we need to know? *Teachers College Record, 105*(6), 1119–1146. https://doi.org/10.1111/1467-9620.00279

Fee, E., & Brown, T. M. (2001). Alice Hamilton: Settlement physician, occupational health pioneer. *American Journal of Public Health, 91*(11), 1767. https://doi.org/10.2105/AJPH.91.11.1767

Flores, G., Olson, L., & Tomany-Korman, S. C. (2005). Racial and ethnic disparities in early childhood health and health care. *Pediatrics, 115*, 183–193. https://doi.org/10.1542/peds.2004-1474

Frey, C. D. (2007). *Jane Addams on peace, crime, and religion: The beginnings of a modern day peacemaking criminology.* Doctoral dissertation. Available from ProQuest Dissertations & Theses database. (UMI No. 3273921).

Glisson, C., & Hemmelgarn, A. (1998). The effects of organizational climate and inter-organisational coordination on the quality and outcomes of children's service system. *Child Abuse and Neglect, 22*(5), 401–421. https://doi.org/10.1016/S0145-2134(98)00005-2

Halliday, S. (2000). Institutional racism in bureaucratic decision-making: A case study in the administration of homelessness law. *Journal of Law and Society, 27*(3), 449–471. https://doi.org/10.1111/1467-6478.00163

Hamington, M. (2005). Public pragmatism: Jane Addams and Ida B. Wells on lynching. *Journal of Speculative Philosophy, 19*(2), 167–174. https://doi.org/10.2307/jspecphil.19.2.0167

Hawkins, J. D., Shapiro, V. B., & Fagan, A. A. (2010). Moving toward effective community prevention practices: Opportunities for social work education. *Research on Social Work Practice, 20*(5), 518–527. https://doi.org/10.1177/1049731509359919

Holley, L. C., & VanVleet, R. K. (2006). Racism and classism in the youth justice system: Perspectives of youth and staff. *Journal of Poverty, 10*(1), 45–67. https://doi.org/10.1300/J134v10n01_03

Jackson, S. (2001). *Lines of activity: Performance, historiography, and Hull House domesticity.* University of Michigan Press.

Jacobs, L. A., Kim, M. E., Whitfield, D. L., Gartner, R. E., Panichelli, M., Kattari, S. K., Downey, M. M., McQueen, S. S., & Mountz, S. E. (2021). Defund the police: Moving towards an anti-carceral social work. *Journal of Progressive Human Services, 32*, 37-DD. https://doi.org/10.1080/10428232.2020.1852865

Kavanagh, K. (1995). Don't ask, don't tell: Deception required, disclosure denied. *Psychology, Public Policy, and Law, 1*(1), 142–160. https://doi.org/10.1037/1076-8971.1.1.142

Knight, L. W. (2010). *Spirit in action: Jane Addams.* W.W. Norton & Company, Inc.

Lengermann, P. M., & Niebrugge-Brantley, J. (1998). *The women founders: Sociology and social theory, 1830–1930.* McGraw-Hill.

Lens, V., & Vorsanger, S. E. (2005). Complaining after claiming: Fair hearings after welfare reform. *Social Service Review, 79*, 430–453. https://doi.org/10.1086/430892

Lynch, R. S., & Mitchell, J. (1995). Justice system advocacy: A must for NASW and the social work community. *Social Work, 40*(1), 9–12. https://doi.org/10.1093/sw/40.1.9

Madden, R. G., & Wayne, R. H. (2003). Social work and the law: A therapeutic jurisprudence perspective. *Social Work, 48*(3), 338–347. https://doi.org/10.1093/sw/48.3.338

McGuire, J. (2004). From the courts to the state legislatures: Social justice feminism, labor legislation, and the 1920s. *Labor History, 45*(2), 225–246. https://doi.org/10.1080/0023656042000217264

McNevin, E. (2010). Applied restorative justice system as a complement to systemic family therapy: Theory and practice implications for families experiencing intrafamilial adolescent sibling incest. *The Australian and New Zealand Journal of Family Therapy, 31*(1), 60–72. https://doi.org/10.1375/anft.31.1.60

Mitchell, J., & Lynch, R. S. (2003). Beyond the rhetoric of social and economic justice: Redeeming the social work advocacy role. *Race, Gender & Class, 10*(2), 8–26. http://www.jstor.org/stable/41675070

Mitchell, J., & Lynch, R. S. (2007). Re-uniting low-income African American fathers with their children: A transdisciplinary model to address the legal conundrums embedded in the social challenges. *Race, Gender & Class, 14*(1–2), 236–252. http://www.jstor.org/stable/41675207

Moye, W. T. (1986, June). BLS and Alice Hamilton: Pioneers in industrial health. *Monthly Labor Review*, 24–27.

Moyer, I. M. (2003). Jane Addams: Pioneer in criminology. *Women & Criminal Justice, 14*(2/3), 1–14. https://doi.org/10.1300/J012v14n02_01

Nagin, D., & Telep, C. (2020). Procedural justice and legal compliance. *Criminology & Public Policy, 19*(3), 761. https://doi.org/10.1111/1745-9133.12499

National Academies of Sciences, Engineering, and Medicine. (2021). *Reducing racial inequalities in criminal justice: Data, courts, and systems of supervision: Proceedings of a workshop—in brief.* Washington, DC: The National Academies Press. https://doi.org/10.17226/26192.

National Association of Social Workers. (2007). *Institutional racism and the social work profession: A call to action.* https://ncwwi.org/files/Cultural_Responsiveness__Disproportionality/Institutional_Racism_and_the_Social_Work_Profession.pdf

Nugent, W., Williams, M., & Umbreit, M. S. (2004). Participation in victim-offender mediation and the severity of re-offense: A meta-analysis. *Research in Social Work Practice, 14*, 408. https://doi.org/10.1177/1049731504265831

Pepinsky, H. (1995). Peacemaking primer. *Peace and Conflict Studies, 2*(2), 32–53. http://doi.org/10.46743/1082-7307/1995.1380

Perlin, M. L. (2019). Dignity and therapeutic jurisprudence: How we can best end shame and humiliation. In C. Chowdhury & M. Britton (Eds.), *Human dignity: Practices, discourses, and transformations 113* (p. 10). Human Dignity Press. http://doi.org/10.2139/ssrn.3502587

Poulson, B. (2003). A third voice: A review of empirical research on the psychological outcomes of restorative justice. *Utah Law Review, 1*, 167–204. https://www.academia.edu/5108819/Poulson_2003_A_third_voice_A_review_of_empirical_research_on_the_psychological_outcomes_of_restorative_justice

Roberts, D. (2021). Strengthened bonds: Abolishing the child welfare system and re-envisioning child well-being: How I became a family policing abolitionist. *Columbia Journal of Race and Law, 11*(3), 455–470. https://scholarship.law.upenn.edu/cgi/viewcontent.cgi?article=3891&context=faculty_scholarship

Roberts, D. (2022). *Torn apart: How the child welfare system destroys Black families and how abolition can build a safer world*, Basic Books.

Ruback, B. R., Cares, A. C., & Hoskins, S. N. (2008). Crime victims' perceptions of restitution: The importance of payment and understanding. *Violence and Victims, 23*(6), 697–710. https://doi.org/10.1891/0886-6708.23.6.697

Shields, P. M. (2003). The community of inquiry: Classical pragmatism and public administration. *Administration & Society, 35*(5), 510–538. https://doi.org/10.1177/0095399703256160

Shields, P., Hamington, M., & Soeters, J. (2023). *On the maturation of Addams studies: A figure of vital intellectual and practical significance, the Oxford handbook of Jane Addams.* Oxford University Press.

Smith, L. E., Mozaffar, N. S., Feierman, J., Parker, L., NeMoyer, A., Goldstein, N. E., Spennce, J. M. H., Thompson, M. C., & Jenkins, V. L. (2022). *Reimagining restitution: New approaches to support youth and communities.* Juvenile Law Cente. https://jlc.org/sites/default/files/attachments/2022-07/JLC-Reimagining-Restitution.pdf

Spencer, P. (2014). From alternative to new normal: Therapeutic jurisprudence in the mainstream. *Alternative Law Journal, 39*, 4. https://doi.org/10.1177/1037969X1403900404

Stehno, S. M. (1988). Public responsibility for dependent Black children: The advocacy of Edith Abbott and Sophonisba Breckinridge. *The Social Service Review, 62*(3), 485–503. https://doi.org/10.1086/644562

Stivers, C. (2002). Unfreezing the progressive era: The story of Julia Lathrop. *Administrative Theory & Praxis, 24*(3), 537–554. https://doi.org/10.1080/10841806.2002.11029374

Stolle, D. P. (1996). Professional responsibility in elder law: A synthesis of preventive law and therapeutic jurisprudence. *Behavioral Sciences and the Law, 14*, 459–478. https://doi.org/10.1002/(SICI)1099-0798(199623)14:4<459::AID-BSL257>3.0.CO;2-V

Tyler, T. R. (1990). *Why people obey the law.* New Haven: Yale University.

Tyler, T. R. (2003). Procedural justice, legitimacy, and the effective rule of law. In M. Tonry (Ed.), *Crime and justice* (Vol. 30, pp. 431–505). University of Chicago Press.

Tyler, T. R. (2006). Restorative justice and procedural justice: Dealing with rule breaking. *Journal of Social Issues, 62*(2), 307–326. https://doi.org/10.1111/j.1540-4560.2006.00452.x

Tyler, T. R., & Huo, Y. J. (2002). *Trust in the law: Encouraging public cooperation with the police and courts.* Russell-Sage Foundation.

Van Ness, D. (2004). Justice that restores: From impersonal to personal justice. *Journal of Religion and Spirituality in Social Work, 23*(1/2), 93–109. https://doi.org/10.1300/J377v23n01_06

Van Ness, D., & Crocke, C. (2003*). Restorative justice: Definitions, principles, values and goals.* PFI Centre for Justice and Reconciliation.

Van Wormer, K. (2006). The case for restorative justice. *The Journal of Teaching in Social Work, 26*(3), 57–69. https://doi.org/10.1300/J067v26n03_04

Van Wormer, K. (2009). Restorative justice as social justice for victims of gendered violence: A standpoint feminist perspective. *Social Work, 54*(2), 107–116. https://doi.org/10.1093/sw/54.2.107

Vandervort, F. E., Gonzalez, R. P., & Faller, K. C. (2008). Legal ethics and high child welfare worker turnover: An unexplored connection. *Children and Youth Services Review, 30*, 546–563. https://doi.org/10.1016/j.childyouth.2007.10.016

Westcott, K., & Sawyer, R. (2007). Silent sacrifices: The impact of "don't ask don't tell" on lesbian and gay military families. *Duke Journal of Gender Law and Policy, 14*, 1121–1142. https://scholarship.law.duke.edu/djglp/vol14/iss2/10

Wexler, B. (2000). Therapeutic jurisprudence: An overview. *Thomas M. Cooley Law Review, 17*,125–134. https://papers.ssrn.com/sol3/papers.cfm?abstract_id=256658

Wheeldon, J. (2009). Finding common ground: Restorative justice and its theoretical construction(s). *Contemporary Justice Review, 12*(1), 91–100. https://doi.org/10.1080/10282580802681774

Yamada, D. (2019). On anger, shock, fear, and trauma: Therapeutic jurisprudence as a response to dignity denials in public policy. *International Journal of Law and Psychiatry, 63*, 35. https://doi.org/10.1016/j.ijlp.2018.06.009

CHAPTER 3

Roles and Ethics

INTRODUCTION

In this chapter, we introduce you to a family who will serve as a case study to begin to discuss the roles that social workers may play when working with clients who are also interacting with the legal system. The case study also illustrates how to implement the theory and practices espoused in this book into your everyday practice as a social worker, either in the implicit or explicit legal context. The legal and social service issues faced in the case study are representative of cases that the authors have handled in their practice and provide an opportunity to explore the roles, responsibilities, and best practices of a social worker. In the first instance, we consider how relationships implicate ethical duties and discuss professional values, differences, and tensions between the professionals and their ethical implications. We provide you with some examples of how other social work and legal practitioners have resolved these dilemmas so that collaboration could occur. In this chapter, you will look at your own ethical code in more depth, as well as become familiar with the ethical code of the lawyers with whom you are collaborating.

INTRODUCTION TO THE CASE STUDY

A case study is used throughout the text to illustrate the interface between social work and the law. By presenting the case from the perspective of social workers practicing in different roles, we hope to demonstrate the many ways that social workers can effectively collaborate with legal professionals. You will see how social workers in settings as different as a substance abuse treatment agency and a legal services office can work with attorneys to advocate for Ms. Jones and her family in implicit and explicit legal contexts. In this chapter, the case is used to introduce you to the ethical considerations that flow from the various roles and collaborative relationships between social workers and attorneys.

> Michelle Jones is a 22-year-old woman who has a 7-day-old infant just removed by Child Protective Services (CPS). Ms. Jones was told by a CPS caseworker to come to Family Court. When Ms. Jones arrives at Family Court, she is assigned an attorney. The attorney learns that Ms. Jones was released from the hospital the day before, but her son

(*continued*)

(CONTINUED)

Matthew remains in the hospital at the request of CPS, pending a decision from the Family Court judge of whether the newborn is released to Ms. Jones's care or placed in a foster home. When Ms. Jones gave birth, she tested positive for drugs and admitted to the hospital social worker that she used drugs while she was pregnant. Matthew weighed 7 pounds, 9 ounces and was born 2 weeks early. He tested positive for drugs at birth and was classified as a healthy baby boy. The attorney learns from the petition filed in Family Court that the allegations against Ms. Jones include a history of abusing drugs, failing to complete a substance abuse treatment program, and a recent arrest for possession of drugs while she was pregnant.

Throughout this chapter, keep in mind these basic facts of the case as a starting point for our analysis of the possibilities for collaboration between attorneys and social workers and the various roles that a social worker might have in relation to Ms. Jones and her son. Additionally, the case study will allow us to explore the ethical issues raised in the collaboration between social workers and lawyers and in social work practice in both the implicit and explicit legal contexts. We will reference the case study as an opportunity to reflect on how you apply the ethical principles, social work roles, and social work theory in your practice with clients in a variety of roles and settings. The first step, then, is to identify the different ways in which lawyers and social workers can collaborate.

WHEN AND HOW DO SOCIAL WORKERS WORK WITH CLIENTS' LAWYERS?

As you learned in Chapter 1, there are many situations that will arise in your work where the social problems faced by your client may need to be resolved jointly by a lawyer and social worker. Because many of the problems clients face are ill-defined and complex, it is logical to apply interdisciplinary advocacy to problem-solving and service delivery. Even from the few facts in our case study, we can already identify that Ms. Jones is interacting within two different legal systems: civil and criminal. She is involved with a hospital and a CPS agency, must deal with past allegations, and may currently have a substance use problem. Her newborn son is in the custody of CPS and a court appearance to determine her custody is imminent. As a social worker, you can already identify several complex and intertwined legal and social issues. A number of Ms. Jones's rights are implicated, including her right to privacy during her medical care and consent to drug testing, as well as her right to have an immediate hearing in a Civil Court to evaluate the decision to remove her child and to determine if he can be returned to her care. If she cannot afford to have an attorney, she has a right to have one assigned to her case to help her prepare for the Criminal

Court hearing. In some states, she also has the right to an attorney appointed to represent her in the Family Court case. Finally, once Ms. Jones becomes involved with a government agency such as CPS, the court may mandate that she be assigned to the Department of Probation or a substance abuse treatment program. In addition, there are a multitude of other regulations that are triggered, affecting what services she must get, their required time frames, and how these services will be delivered to her and her son, implicating administrative and procedural bodies of law.

In addition to your role as a social worker with Ms. Jones, there are many potential ways you may be called upon to collaborate with attorneys or, as we propose in this book, that you may want to initiate collaboration with a lawyer. In fact, if you are assigned as Ms. Jones's child protective caseworker, you may need to collaborate with her substance abuse treatment provider, the hospital social worker, or a clinician providing mental health treatment. Therefore, it is a good idea to anticipate and prepare for your interaction with the legal system and to think about the ways you might effectively collaborate with attorneys to protect the rights of your client and to make decisions proactively about how you as a social worker will interact with a court or a lawyer. It is also important to also consider your role with the court and legal system, and the ways in which working for CPS, the Department of Human Services, or even the substance treatment provider may impede on your relationship with Ms. Jones and the ways in which you are able to advocate on her behalf. Your role can change once you know where to refer a client when they present to you with a legal matter, sometimes serving as a consultant for an attorney, being called to testify, or being employed in a legal services office, a prison, or a court. Yet, regardless of the specific role, an understanding of the legal system will enhance your ability to advocate for your client as they face challenging legal and social issues.

Social Work Roles When Addressing a Client's Legal Issues and Working With Lawyers

Before you begin to collaborate with other disciplines and professionals, it is incumbent on you as the social worker to identify the role you play with your client. Different roles in relation to the work you perform, especially with an attorney, implicate different interpretations of your ethical responsibilities. In interprofessional work, it is crucial that there is a clear identification of what role you as a social worker will play in a particular case and your client. It is not enough to say that you will "do" social work or simply "be" the social worker. Clarity about the role is critical for understanding the social worker's role in relation to the other professionals and in relation to the client. The following section describes some of the possible roles that social workers can play on behalf of clients in collaboration with attorneys and legal professionals.

Social Worker as Member of a Legal Team in an Interdisciplinary Law Firm or Legal Services Organization

In this role, a social worker acts as a member of an interdisciplinary team that includes a social worker, an attorney, and sometimes other members such as paralegals, lay advocates, and private consultants such as a psychiatrist or a psychologist. Within this model, the social worker and attorney are employed by the same law firm or legal services organization and work together on all aspects of the legal representation. Therefore, in our case study, Ms. Jones is the client for both the lawyer and the social worker for the purpose of providing her with holistic legal representation both in and out of court. The lawyer and social worker would function as a team in all aspects of her legal defense in both the Criminal Court and Family Court cases. There is a higher degree of collaboration, which requires communication about roles, goals, and ethical guidelines.

In the case of Michelle Jones, a number of social needs that coexist with her legal needs are immediately evident. Based on the little information presented thus far about the case, you can begin to identify several tasks that a social worker could potentially perform as part of Ms. Jones's legal team. The social worker has the expertise to screen and identify whether or not Ms. Jones is dependent on or abusing substances so that she could be referred to the appropriate treatment. A clinical social worker may also screen for other conditions, such as posttraumatic stress disorder (PTSD) or depression, which have been associated with women's substance abuse. Case management tasks such as assessing whether Ms. Jones has access to employment, education, housing, parenting support, and income and identifying who in her life can function as a support system would also be key concerns because they relate to her ability to care for and support a child. The level of stress related to the client's legal difficulties and the temporary removal of her child may also impact her ability to actively participate in her defense and would be significant information that a social worker could and should provide to Ms. Jones's attorney to assist in effective representation and counseling of their client.

Social Worker as Employee of a Multiservice Agency That Provides Both Legal and Social Services

In this role, a social worker may provide social services independent of a concurrent legal matter and the client can access social services and legal services independently. Under this model a social worker working in one part of the agency may also be asked to collaborate or consult with an attorney in another part of the agency. For example, the social worker may be providing counseling to Ms. Jones and decide to refer her to the agency attorney for assistance with her legal case. Conversely Ms. Jones may have contacted the agency to get legal representation and after the initial screening, the attorney felt that Ms. Jones's legal interests would be better served if she had access to social service resources, such as financial assistance, education and employment counseling, housing, substance abuse treatment, counseling, and parenting support services. Regardless of who originated the referral, it would be important for the social worker and attorney to meet and decide how much, if at all, they would be collaborating and what are the ethical responsibilities while collaborating on behalf of a shared client. As we discuss later, this conversation can include explicit discussions about how information is shared between the professionals, what counseling is provided to the client, and what the goals of each professional's intervention are in the case.

Social Worker Who Is Appointed by the Court (Non–Child Protective Services or Child Welfare Agency)

In this role, the social worker functions as a consultant who is appointed by the court to assist a lawyer in representing a client at the lawyer's request. For Ms. Jones, the court-appointed attorney could request the assistance of a social worker from the Family Court judge. This is often available when the court-appointed lawyer is not part of a larger legal services organization or firm and therefore must engage the services of a social worker on a case-by-case basis. A social worker is appointed by the judge to assist the attorney in the representation of the client. Even though the judge appointed the social worker, the social worker is working with the attorney for Ms. Jones's representation and not on behalf of the court. To clarify, the social worker in this instance may be appointed and paid for by the court or city agency but has the same ethical duties of confidentiality and advocacy as social workers embedded in legal services organizations and law firms. As we identified earlier, there may be a number of functions you might play in this role: some functions identified by the attorney and some functions you yourself may identify yourself as a professional social worker. In another situation you might be on a panel of clinicians that a judge can call upon to make an independent evaluation of a client for the court. For example, in the case of Ms. Jones the Judge may request an independent evaluation of Ms. Jones's capacity to parent. In this role, your client would not be Ms. Jones, as your social work services were retained by the court with the limited role of conducting an evaluation.

Social Worker as Employee of the Court

In this role you would be employed by the state or state agency and assigned to work within the court system, often in a problem-solving court focused on family, substance abuse, domestic violence, and mental illness. Social workers in this role will conduct assessments, refer litigants to services, and evaluate and monitor service and treatment plans. For Ms. Jones, a social worker employed by the drug court would be responsible for conducting the initial eligibility assessment and developing a treatment plan for Ms. Jones. The drug court social worker may also provide regular updates to the court and all parties in the case on Ms. Jones's progress in treatment. In this scenario, the social worker is an employee of the court and not equivalent to a social worker collaborating with the client's attorney.

Social Worker as Hired Consultant

In this role, the social worker functions as a private practitioner who can be hired by an individual attorney or law firm as a consultant, evaluator, or expert witness in a case. When operating in this role, the social worker effectively becomes a member of the legal team. Often, the terms of the consultant agreement with the social worker will dictate the expectations surrounding confidentiality, role, and communication with the legal team.

In the case of Michelle Jones, social workers could be involved in a variety of ways under this model. An attorney for Ms. Jones's Family Court may seek a social worker to testify on substance abuse and the relation to parenting capacity.

A social worker could potentially be assigned to work with the lawyer advocating for Ms. Jones in both her criminal case and her civil case. In that example, the social worker would focus on assessing Ms. Jones's needs in both court forums, advocating for appropriate services and for the client's rights. Additionally, the social worker may function as a bridge between the family defense attorney and the criminal defense attorney, ensuring that the legal counseling and case strategy are not at odds.

Additional Collaborative Social Work Roles in the Case Study

A social worker may also work with the attorney who is assigned to represent Ms. Jones's newborn son, generally called the law guardian or attorney for the child, ensuring that the infant receives any necessary services. Depending on the specific state's laws regarding the obligations of attorneys for children, the social worker may also help decide what is in the best interests of the child. The child protective caseworker or their supervisor may be a social worker trained in investigating allegations of abuse and neglect and facilitating meetings to determine treatment and service plans for families. In this case, the child protective caseworker would be assessing the level of risk of harm to Ms. Jones's son and a beginning assessment of what services may reduce the risk of harm to promote reunification.

Social Workers in a Social Service or Mental Health Agency

A social worker may also be employed in any of the human service agencies with which Ms. Jones may already be engaged will engage as a result of her involvement with the child welfare system and Criminal Courts. This could include a substance abuse treatment program, a mental health clinic, a benefits program, a foster care agency, or a healthcare setting. While the social worker would not be working for the attorney in this model, the attorney may collaborate or engage with the social worker to access information about the client's treatment, needs, and options in the legal case. Additionally, the attorney could request that a social worker in this scenario participate in court hearings either by preparing written reports or providing live testimony to the court.

For example, after consultation with their client to obtain consent to disclose information, a proactive and legally informed social worker assisting Ms. Jones in a substance abuse program may want to contact her attorney to address the issue of visitation, given concerns about developmental and attachment consequences and the relational bond because of their separation at this delicate time of the infant's development. A legally informed social worker might also want to alert the attorney that Ms. Jones is in treatment. Similarly, a proactive social worker may want to advise the attorney that they could be available to assist in preparing for the hearing that will evaluate the decision to remove the infant, or that they would like to know the legal issues and consequences for their client before agreeing to participate in a child safety or family group conference.

As a proactive and legally informed social worker in any of these roles, you might also ask Ms. Jones if she received anything in writing that documents her legal rights and responsibilities while she is involved with CPS and Family Court, or her rights as a medical patient as far as consent to drug testing while in the hospital. If not, you can assist her to request these documents from her caseworker, attorney, or the hospital so you can be sure that she understands what should or should not happen with her and her son or what requirements she will be expected to meet.

A critically competent social worker would also be thinking about how they could use their knowledge about the legal issues Ms. Jones faces in determining how to respond if required to testify in court, including what information they would share, what would be in their report, and what part of their case record might be relevant or not. As part of this reflection, the social worker would be especially mindful about their notes ensuring that the notes do not include unrelated information, baseless conclusions, personal opinions, or theories that might imperil their client's rights. Moreover, the social worker should write notes and build testimony from a strengths-based perspective to limit bias, and to avoid stigmatizing or stereotypical statements based on judgment. A strengths-based approach in social work sees each client as individuals with strengths, adversities, and the capacity for change. Instead of beginning with "weaknesses," using this model social workers should critically underscore factors that may have contributed to the challenges a client is facing, including the effects on their coping skills, and work to identify consistent and adequate treatment and resources that can decrease and/or eliminate these challenges over time (Venkat, 2017). For example, in the case of Ms. Jones, a social worker may testify about building on Ms. Jones capacity for change and suggest opportunity for connections to services, like drug treatment, trauma therapy, and parenting support. A strengths-based perspective would also underscore the impetus that connections to these critical and specialized services could have a significant impact on improving Ms. Jones's health and lowering the risk of safety concerns for Ms. Jones's son.

ETHICS OF INTERDISCIPLINARY PRACTICE

The ethical codes and licensing requirements of both the legal and social work professions are implicated when a social worker interacts with the legal system. This is especially the case when a social worker and attorney work collaboratively on a case. Increasingly, research suggests that the conflicts and difficulties experienced by social workers while collaborating with attorneys can be traced to a lack of knowledge and misunderstanding about the ethical responsibilities of both professions (Anderson et al., 2007; Vandervort et al., 2008).

There are many issues of disclosure and confidentiality that must be considered carefully and discussed among the professional collaborators. It is critical that these issues are explicitly discussed, even in long-running collaborations, to ensure that the ethical mandates of each profession are clear. For example, a *represented party* is defined as an individual who is a part of the legal case and is represented by an attorney in that same case. An attorney may not speak directly to an individual that they know to be represented by another counsel. The attorney must direct all communication through that party's attorney, as opposed to the party or client themselves. Therefore, a social worker employed by a social service agency or local community-based organization would be able to speak to any lawyer—the defendant's counsel or an attorney for the city child welfare agency—as long as the client signed a release permitting that disclosure of information. However, a social worker in a legal services office representing one of the parties in the legal case may be prohibited from speaking to anyone who was a represented party in the case without consent from that party's attorney.

In Family Court, this would mean if a social worker working with Ms. Jones wanted to speak or meet with Ms. Jones's child, the social worker would need permission to do so from the child advocate attorney. Likewise, the CPS worker should not question Ms. Jones about legal issues without her attorney present or without the attorney's expressed permission to do so. It also may mean that the social worker working for Ms. Jones and her attorney could not speak with the CPS caseworker without getting permission from the attorney who represents the "state" or the child protective agency. The child protective caseworker in this instance may be considered a represented party because they have a lawyer in court and are responsible for initially bringing the charges of neglect in Family Court. While seasoned practitioners know that these rules are often ignored especially in high volume practices such as Family Court and Criminal Court, it does not negate the ethical rule or diminish the importance of clients' rights for protection from an abuse of power when represented by counsel.

National Association of Social Workers' Code of Ethics: The Social Worker's Ethical Code

The introduction to the Code of Ethics exhorts us to remember that the Code is not a set of rules that must be followed but rather principles and guidelines within which social workers, as individuals, make professional decisions. The Code's introduction raises three points that are critical for interdisciplinary practitioners to remember: The Code recognizes (a) that applications of the Code must be considered in the context in which the Code is being applied; (b) that there is a possibility of conflicts among the Code's values and principles; and (c) that deciding which application may be more important is an individual decision made by the social worker (National Association of Social Workers [NASW], 2021). As scholars have noted in recent years, "social workers have developed comprehensive ethical standards to guide practitioners and decision-making frameworks that are useful when practitioners face difficult ethical dilemmas" (Reamer, 2013).

Code of Professional Responsibility: The Attorney's Ethical Code

The Code of Professional Responsibility sets out the rules governing how attorneys work on behalf of clients, whether the client is an individual, group, corporation, or government entity. The Code of Professional Responsibility binds all attorneys who represent clients, regardless of whether they are paid by the client, assigned by the court, or retained as pro bono or free counsel. The Code has a broad view of the attorney–client relationship with its mandate of zealous representation, but it also specifies the limits to that relationship, in particular the boundaries of confidentiality and disclosure.

Each state adopts its own professional rules of conduct that attorneys licensed to practice in that particular state are bound to follow. However, the basic tenets have been laid out by the American Bar Association (ABA) in the Model Rules of Professional Conduct (2024). All states with the exception of California have adopted the format and major content of the Model Rules (www.americanbar.org). California revised their ethical code in 2018 to more closely align with the Model Rules, but there are still some distinct differences for California practitioners. We will discuss some of the major sections of the Model Rules of Professional Conduct as they relate to the principles expressed in the NASW Code of Ethics and interprofessional collaboration. Of course, it is always good practice to determine what the specific state's rule of conduct is whenever there is a question as to the collaboration's impact on the social worker's or attorney's ethical code.

Licensing of the Social Work Profession

All states have licensing, certification, or registration requirements regarding social work practice and the use of "social worker" or "clinical social worker" as a professional title. Standards for licensing vary by state, but most states require passing a standardized examination and completion of an accredited social work undergraduate or graduate program. Licensing can be obtained at the bachelor's and master's levels. Most states require 2 years of post-master's, supervised clinical practice, and in some cases an examination, to be licensed as a clinical social worker. Some states also have an advanced generalist practice license. There are also states that have requirements for continuing education credits, while others do not.

Many states reference and require adherence to the NASW Code of Ethics as a requirement for licensure, although the degree of adherence to the Code will differ from state to state. Each state also identify standards of unprofessional conduct that can result in the loss of a license and possible legal penalties. The Code is generally used as a standard against which the behaviors and actions of social workers are viewed even when adherence is not required by law. The Code also identifies the difference between peer review of ethical conduct, a situation where the profession monitors itself, and legal or judicial processes when a social worker is violating a law or regulation. The most recent update to the NASW Code of Ethics was in 2021, which provided updated language on the significance of professional self-care, revisions to the cultural competence standard, and other amendments under the Code: Purpose of the NASW Code of Ethics, ethical principles (namely, the Value of Integrity), and cultural competence (NASW, 2021). It is important to know that a violation of the NASW Code of Ethics does not automatically mean that there will be legal consequences or that you will be legally liable. NASW has a peer-review process that allows the organization to give counsel and review the actions of its members within the profession of social work. Decisions that implicate legal liability can only be made within a legal or judicial hearing (NASW, 2021). As you can see, it is imperative to check the licensing requirements for your individual state and to understand when you are legally required to adhere to the Code as well as to clearly know the legal duties and obligations that your state attaches to your license and how the new updated changes will affect your licensure.

Licensing of the Profession of Law

Attorneys are licensed through the state in which the attorney wishes to practice law. Whether the attorney is a recent graduate of law school or has been practicing for some time, a lawyer is not licensed to practice law in a state unless they have been admitted to that state's bar or received a waiver to practice in the state for a limited period of time. Admission generally entails passing the state bar exam and the Multistate Professional Responsibility Exam (MPRE). Even if a law graduate passes both exams, they also need to be approved by a state committee on character and fitness. Once you have been admitted to a state's bar, an attorney can practice in any state or local courthouse in that jurisdiction. For practice in federal courts, whether at the trial level (generally referred to as the district court) or for appellate proceedings in the Circuit Court of Appeals or Supreme Court, an attorney must be admitted to the specific federal court. As a result of this licensing structure, attorneys are often members of multiple state and federal bars.

As part of the process of remaining certified to practice law in a state or federal jurisdiction, attorneys are required to complete mandatory continuing legal education (CLE) programs. In most states, newly admitted attorneys are required to complete more CLE hours than experienced attorneys. In New York, for example, attorneys who have been practicing for 2 years or less are required to complete 16 hours of CLE including 3 hours that are devoted to ethics and professionalism in each of their first 2 years of practice, whereas experienced attorneys must complete 24 hours in each biennial reporting period (N.Y. Codes, Rules & Reg. title 22 § 1500.12, 1200.22, 1998). Generally, the CLE programs fall into the following four categories: ethics and professionalism, skills, professional practice, and law practice management. CLE courses can be helpful for social workers practicing in legal fields as they tend to include basic introductions to different fields of law and advocacy strategies. Often social workers will present at CLE courses so that attorneys can gain knowledge in social work's assessment, services, and crisis intervention.

State bars, which license attorneys to practice in their specific state, are also responsible for maintaining a disciplinary committee to handle complaints against attorneys. Clients or other interested persons can file complaints if they believe that an attorney has failed to carry out their professional and ethical duties toward a client. Generally, the committee reviews whether an attorney has complied with the standard set forth in that state's rules of professional conduct. A disciplinary committee can take one of the following actions in response to a disciplinary complaint: dismiss the complaint as without any merit or refer the complaint to a trained mediation professional. The disciplinary committee can also refer the complaint to a court to recommend a private or public sanction. In the most serious instances, suspension or removal of a lawyer's license to practice law is an option available to the state bar.

THE ETHICAL LANDSCAPE OF COLLABORATION: KEY QUESTIONS

Historically, there are two major ethical tensions that are identified in the literature on social worker and attorney collaboration. These are the questions surrounding mandated reporting responsibilities of social workers and the perceived tension between a lawyer's duty of "zealous advocacy" and the social worker's attention to the broader interests of society (Anderson et al., 2007; Vandervort et al., 2008).

These questions can and should be explored by a direct reading of the professional ethical codes and laws to which each profession is bound. The following discussion of some of the major tenets of the social workers' and attorneys' codes will demonstrate how there is substantial common ground that can be found between the ethics of the professions. We will focus on the relationship of the client to the professional and the issues surrounding confidentiality as examples of this overlap in complementary ethical duties.

WHO IS YOUR CLIENT?

Conflicts of interests and the question of who can be considered a client are areas where the standards for social workers and attorneys are quite different. The Code of Ethics allows social workers to work with people who have relationships with each other, for example, a husband and wife or a child and a parent, whereas the attorney's code does not. There may be conflicts of interest depending on the appointment of the social worker—that is, if a social worker is appointed by the state as part of a CPS case or a social worker is teaming with a parent's separate counsel. The reason is that, as previously s mentioned, each social worker must follow specific guidelines around representing each client independently regardless of the relationship between both parties.

Social Worker Standards

The code does provide that the social worker "be alert to and avoid" any potential conflicts between the parties with whom they are working and take reasonable steps to minimize them (NASW, 2021, Section 1.06). The social worker must attempt to protect the interests of all parties to the relationship, even if that may mean terminating with and referring one of the clients to someone else. In the case of Michelle Jones, we can easily identify a potential conflict that might emerge for a social worker between the interests of Ms. Jones and those of her infant son, making it difficult to have an impartial judgment and to prevent any interference in professional decision-making.

A social worker has an ethical duty to determine whether they can fairly exercise impartial judgment and professional discretion on behalf of all their clients. Although social workers often identify this skill as being self-aware, often there are not formal processes in practice to ensure compliance with this ethical standard. Minimally the Code requires that a social worker inform their client of any potential or actual conflicts and the steps that will be taken by the social worker to resolve the conflict in a way that "makes the client's interests primary and protect client interests to the greatest extent possible" (NASW, 2021, Section 1.06 [a]).

The social worker working with Ms. Jones should have a conversation with her that clarifies what responsibility the social worker has toward both her and her son and how the social worker will attempt to anticipate or to minimize potential conflict. If you are the social worker working in a foster care agency, you will be working with Ms. Jones, her son, and the foster parents. Ethically the Code requires that you inform each client of what role you will play and what responsibilities are owed to each of the parties (NASW, 2021, Section 1.06 [d]). This is also important to explain to the attorneys who are representing the CPS agency, Ms. Jones, and her son. The conversation should include why you may share certain information, under what circumstances you can make decisions, and how and why you can protect yourself and your client. Being clear about what you as a social worker need to do to meet your ethical responsibilities is critical to successful interprofessional collaboration with all professions, not just lawyers. It is also the foundation for being able to work with Ms. Jones whether she is your client or not.

Attorney Standards

Attorneys are prohibited from representing clients when there are actual or potential conflicts of interest. A conflict of interest occurs when the attorney's representation of one client has the potential to be adverse to another client's representation or interest (ABA, 2024, Rule 1.7). Therefore, the lawyer must determine at the beginning of the attorney–client relationship whether there are any conflicts with current or former clients.

You should note that *conflict* is also defined as the *potential* for a conflict even if the conflict has not arisen yet. In either situation, an attorney is prohibited from taking a case where representation of the client would be limited by the representation of another client. For example, if the family court case alleged that both Ms. Jones and the child's father were neglectful, one attorney could not represent both parents, even if they are planning parenting and living together. This is because there is the potential for the parents to have different and conflicting interests at any point in the case. Similarly, an attorney who previously represented the father in a criminal case could not now represent Ms. Jones in the Family Court case against the father. For the attorney to advocate zealously for the client, the attorney cannot be constrained by another client's goal or competing interests.

WHO DECIDES: THE CLIENT OR THE PROFESSIONAL?

Central to the relationship between lawyers and social workers is the question of who makes the decisions in the professional relationship: clients or professionals? This question can be heightened by interdisciplinary collaboration when there may be multiple and potentially conflicting perspectives from the professional on counseling, case strategy or litigation goals. Additionally, your role as the social worker and the attorney's role, especially with respect to children and vulnerable adults, may also determine whether you are following the client's directed interests or the best interests of the client as determined by the professional in their role. In cases involving the representation of children and vulnerable adults, it is important to ascertain whether the local law requires an attorney to be directed by the client or to represent the best interests of the client, often referred to as a substitution of judgment for client-directed representation.

Social Worker Standards for Client Self-Determination and Informed Consent

Many times when reading the Code of Ethics, there is confusion on the part of social workers between standards of practice and values. The NASW Code states that social workers focus on individual well-being in a social context and the well-being of society. The Code states that for the social worker, the clients' interests are primary and there are only limited times when the loyalty owed to clients is trumped by responsibility to the larger society. The example used in the Code is when the social worker has a legal obligation such as mandated reporting (NASW, 2021, Section 1.01). The vagueness of the words "responsibility to the larger society" can be made clearer by looking at the standards of practice of the ethical code, which gives more specific direction about who decides and those circumstances when client decision-making ought to be limited for the welfare of others or the larger community.

Several standards in the Code provide some guidance about the question of who decides for social workers. Two central ideas are implicated in this discussion: client self-determination and informed consent. In Section 1.02 of the Code, social workers are exhorted not just to respect a client's right to decide but also to promote the right of clients to self-determination. This right is central to all social work values, and we note that it is identified in the Code as a "right." The standard of practice gives social workers discretion about the decision when the right might be limited when they use the word "may" rather than "must" or "shall" (NASW, 2021, Section 1.02).

The Code suggests that a social worker may limit a client's right to self-determination only when, in the social worker's professional judgment, there is a serious, imminent, and foreseeable risk to the client themselves or others because of a potential decision a client is making. The standard of serious, foreseeable, and imminent risk is a very high bar to meet and because this professional judgment is also implicated in the discussion of confidentiality it will be further addressed later in this chapter.

The Code also instructs social workers that they may provide services only in the context of a professional relationship based on "valid informed consent" (NASW, 2021, Section 1.03 [a]). In "plain English" or a language the client can understand, the social worker must explain what the services are and should only provide services when there is informed consent. As part of this requirement, the Code also specifies that when clients are not literate or have difficulty understanding, the social worker must take active steps to make sure that the client understands, including arranging for a qualified interpreter or translator (NASW, 2021, Section 1.03 [b]).

To be in ethical compliance social workers must expressly state what the services are, why they are being recommended, any risks and benefits related to the service, the time frame that will be covered by the client consent, and a client's right to withdraw or refuse the service at any time (NASW, 2021, Section 1.03 [a]). Developing and implementing evidence-informed social work practice will equip you to give a truly informed consent process and make it far more likely you will be practicing in a way that meets ethical standards as well as social work values including that of competence.

The Code does not provide specific guidance on the issue of informed consent for the treatment of children,which often poses many ethical challenges and confusion for social work students and social workers. Unless a parent's rights have been terminated or there is a custody order from a court limiting the parent's rights to consent, a parent generally retains their rights to consent on behalf of their child. In regard to parents who have never been married, the mother has the right to consent to services unless the father's name is on the birth certificate, or he has obtained a decree of paternity issued by a court. In the event of divorce or separation, the rights of the parents to consent are found in the final divorce agreement or in a court order regarding custody of the children (Bogie, 2001).

Once again, we advise the reader of the need to become familiar with your state laws and regulations because states can have very different regulations and laws covering the same issues. Some states allow minors to give informed consent if they have reached a certain age or under certain conditions. For example, in California, a minor over the age of 12 can consent to mental health counseling and treatment, but still requires parental consent for any psychotropic medication (Cal. Fam. Code § 6924[b]). We will cover in greater depth the knowledge and skills you need to access the law in your particular state or jurisdiction in Chapter 5.

Attorney Standards for Client Self-Determination and Informed Consent

The Code of Professional Responsibility underscores one of the most important overlaps between legal and social work practice. Attorneys are ethically bound to provide competent representation to their clients, but they are also bound by how the client defines the goals and objectives of the representation. Under their Model Rules of Professional Conduct, an attorney must abide by the client's wishes in all matters of representation including when to accept a settlement in a civil case or a plea agreement in a criminal case. Lawyers are bound by professional ethical codes to follow a client's decision when it comes to the goals of the legal representation (ABA, 2024, Rule 1.2). To understand this mandate, an example from Ms. Jones's case is illustrative. If Ms. Jones informed her attorney that she wanted to settle the family court case, thereby potentially prolonging the time that her son spent in foster care, the attorney must abide by her decision even if the attorney believes that she can achieve a more favorable legal outcome by proceeding to trial. Of course, the attorney has an obligation to counsel the client on the various potential outcomes in a legal case, but ultimately the decision is up to the client.

WHEN MAY LIMITS BE PUT ON A CLIENT'S RIGHT TO DECIDE?

The issue of whether a client has the capacity to provide informed consent or to exert their right to self-determination is a professional judgment that social workers and attorneys are sometimes called upon to make.

Social Work Standards Relating to Client Capacity

The social worker must make a decision about whether or not the client's mental status or age and level of cognitive and emotional development interfere with a client's ability to make decisions about their case or causes them to pursue a course of action that will result in serious, foreseeable, and imminent harm to themselves or others (NASW, 2021, Section 1.03 [c]). Sometimes the terms "capacity" and "competence" are used interchangeably, but "capacity" here will refer to a clinical judgment and "competence" refers to a legal judgment. The Code also provides some guidance on how a social worker should proceed once they have made the decision that a client does not have capacity.

An important consideration here, for which the Code does not give guidance, is how a social worker should go about determining whether a client lacks capacity to exercise their right to client self-determination and whether they have the ability to give an informed consent. The Code provides information on how to proceed once you as a professional have made the decision about capacity but is not of much assistance in determining what process you should use or how you might go about making that assessment.

Briefly, the social worker will need to assess whether the client is able to communicate a choice, understand the relevant information in regard to the particular issue or decision, appreciate the situation they are in and its consequences, and be able to evaluate and reason about different options (Appelbaum, 2007). A more comprehensive process for assessing the competence or capacity of a client for both legal and clinical purposes will be covered in greater depth in Chapter 9.

The Code offers guidance on the steps to take once you have determined that a client lacks the capacity to make decisions for themselves particularly with regard to obtaining informed consent (NASW, 2021, Section 1.03 [c]). It is incumbent upon the social worker once they have determined that a client lacks capacity that they do everything they can to safeguard the rights and interests of their client. Even if you have determined that your client lacks the capacity to understand ethical practice demands, you must continue to find ways to inform and obtain guidance from your client that is consistent with what they can understand, as well as find a responsible third party to give permission and consent. The social worker then has a responsibility to fully inform the third party as they would their client and make sure that party acts in the best interest of the social worker's client (NASW, 2021, Section 1.03 [c])

Frequently clients are mandated to receive service and as a result they feel that there are no choices involved and that they must accept the service recommended. In the case of Michelle Jones, she could be ordered to attend substance abuse treatment, parenting classes, and/or counseling whether she wishes to or not as part of the conditions or plan to have her son returned to her care. In the case of mandated services, the Code advises social workers to provide information about the extent and nature of the services and the extent of the client's rights to refuse services (NASW, 2021, Section 1.03 [d]). The same evidence-based, transparent, and analytic counseling process is recommended for use with mandated clients and in, fact, the very process itself may assist the client in moving toward a more voluntary acceptance of services.

Attorney Standards Relating to Client Capacity

When there is an issue as to capacity or the client's ability to make decisions in their case, the attorney can only seek to take protective action if there is a substantial risk of harm, either physical or financial (ABA, 2024, Rule 1.14[b]). In some instances, the attorney will be required to seek the assistance of a counselor or the appointment of a guardian ad litem, conservator, or guardian to serve as additional protection for the client's interests when the attorney believes that the client does not have the capacity to protect their own interests (ABA, 2024, Rule 1.14[b]). The latter three roles are only appropriate when the lawyer believes that protective action is necessary to protect the client from physical, financial, or other harm. A guardian ad litem or guardian would be responsible for representing the best interests of the client to the court that are distinguished from their self-directed interests and may conflict directly with the stated interests of the client. This rule is an example of when the process of determining client capacity is vague and the expertise of a social worker in assessing the client's capacity could be a valuable role in the attorney–social worker collaboration. One can envision a scenario in Ms. Jones's case where the social worker, after interviewing Ms. Jones, believes that there may be an issue of capacity that renders her incapable of understanding the legal counsel and placing her physical and legal interests at risk. In that scenario, the attorney and social worker can consult and collaborate on the assessment and the next steps to ensure that Ms. Jones's physical and legal interests are protected.

WHAT INFORMATION MUST BE KEPT PRIVATE AND CONFIDENTIAL?

The other major tenet of both professions' Codes is the mandate of privacy and confidentiality between the professional and the client. Again, there are similarities in both ethical codes' insistence that confidentiality is a fundamental tenet of the professional relationship. It is important for social workers to know that standards of confidentiality and privacy are implicated in both the Code of Ethics but also in state licensing laws under descriptions of professional conduct, and for specific groups such as clients with a mental health diagnosis or a diagnosis of HIV, in state statutes.

Social Work Standards on Privacy and Confidentiality

The social worker's Code begins with the expectation of confidentiality but then lays out when a social worker should disclose, how much to disclose, and how to discuss informed consent and disclosure with the client during this process. A client's right to privacy and confidentiality is both an ethical and a legal right. As mentioned, the keeping of confidences and client privacy is always a legal requirement of having a professional social work license.

When social workers work with clients, they should only ask for the information they need to provide the service being requested or to conduct an assessment. Prior to receiving confidential information from your client, social workers should discuss with their client all the potential circumstances that may arise where the social worker may be called upon to disclose confidential information about the client. There are times such as the reporting of child abuse or neglect, elder abuse, or potential harm to another that you will be legally required to break your client's confidences. This is a conversation you must ethically have throughout the course of your work with clients and when taking any action to disclose information without consent.

Once you receive information from the client, it is confidential and must be kept private and protected. From here on in, information can only be shared with the express and—most often—written consent of the client or if you are legally required to do so (NASW, 2021, Section 1.07 [a] [b]). Prior to your disclosure, it is also advisable to inform clients whenever you intend to disclose confidential information and the potential consequences of doing so. This applies whether social workers disclose confidential information based on legal requirement or client consent (NASW, 2021, Section 1.07 [d]).

As mentioned in our earlier discussion about conflicts of interests, social workers are frequently involved in providing services to related parties. Social workers provide services to more than one client at the same time such as families, couples, parents, children, and groups. When this is the case, social workers are instructed to institute a process that would inform each party of the rights and limits to their privacy, clarify each individual's right to confidentiality and the limits on that confidentiality, seek to achieve consensus on how the social worker will protect the confidentiality of information shared by each of the parties, and reiterate that they cannot guarantee that all involved parties will honor such agreements. When working in an agency that has policies about the sharing of information, the social worker must inform all clients of what those policies are (NASW, 2021, Section 1.07 [e, f, g]).

Earlier in this chapter, we identified a few different professionals who could potentially ask the social worker for information about the client Ms. Jones. It is important that you understand and can articulate your ethical duties regarding confidentiality to your client but also to other professionals who may not understand the ethical mandates surrounding disclosure in social work. You should be thoughtful about discussing these issues with your client and obtaining an informed consent about whom you are providing information to and how that information may be used in your client's legal proceedings.

It is important to know that you are under no legal obligation to give information about your client to any lawyer or other professional unless they have obtained a legal subpoena or consent from your client. A subpoena can be from an attorney or from a court and may be approved and ordered by a Judge. The subpoena generally orders that the recipient provide records or testimony to the court. It is important to remember that subpoenas can be challenged as improper, especially if you believe that the other party is not entitled to the confidential information. As a professional, you can question both the need, scope, and purpose of the disclosure and, if in your professional judgment you believe it can cause harm to your client, the Code directs you as the social worker to request the court to withdraw the order or narrowly limit it (NASW, 2021, Section 1.07 [h]).

For example, it may be that during your evaluation of Ms. Jones there is a disclosure of a long history of substance abuse. However, she is currently in treatment and not using substances. During supervised visits, you have also observed that she has good parenting skills and the ability to respond empathetically to the nonverbal cues of her infant. You receive a subpoena requesting the entire case record of your client and you are unsure how the information about her early history may be used. Upon further consideration of the subpoena, you are in fact concerned that this history may justify the prolonged removal of Ms. Jones's son, even though she has been progressing well in treatment and her attachment with her son is strong. You may request that the order be withdrawn or that it be limited to the parts of your case record that are relevant to Ms. Jones's current parenting abilities, substance use, and participation in treatment. It is important to engage in a critical analysis of any request for disclosing confidential information to ensure that you are maintaining your obligation to your client.

WHEN MUST CONFIDENTIALITY BE BROKEN?

The Code of Ethics gives the social worker some guidance about when a social worker should break client confidentiality. The general expectation that social workers will keep all information confidential does not apply when disclosure is necessary to prevent serious, foreseeable, and imminent harm to the client or to other identifiable person(s). It is in this standard that legal and ethical requirements coincide in that the harm is of a very serious nature and is identifiable by the professional and not merely speculative. In all instances, social workers should disclose the least amount of confidential information necessary to achieve the desired purpose; only information that is directly relevant to the purpose for which the disclosure is made should be revealed. This section addresses those times when a social worker must breach client confidences.

Social Work Standards Relating to Breaching Confidentiality

The first limit on client confidentiality is the mandated reporting law that imposes a mandatory duty on social workers to report suspected child abuse and neglect to child protective authorities, or abuse and neglect of vulnerable elders or developmentally disabled adults. You should access and read the mandated reporting statutes for your state to find out what and when you must report, under what circumstances, and what is considered to be reportable child and adult abuse and neglect in your state. Such laws do not always require lawyers to make these reports although this varies by state and the role a lawyer may play depends on who is their client. We will be discussing mandated reporting in greater length in Chapter 6.

The second instance where confidentiality may be breached by a social worker is known as a "duty to warn." Unlike mandated reporting, which stems from a statutory duty or law, the "duty to warn" or the requirement that social workers have a duty to warn a third party of potential danger from their client, even when they find out about this during confidential communication, is the result of a court decision. In *Tarasoff v. The Regents of the State of California* (1976), the Supreme Court of California found that a therapist does have a "duty to warn" under certain circumstances and may be sued for damages if they fail to do so. It is important to know that the case only applies to California because this is a state court decision. Other jurisdictions have followed the lead of the California court, but others have not.

Herbert and Young (2003) reported that, at the time of their review, that there are 27 states following the *Tarasoff decision* and about half of those imposed a mandatory duty to warn, although the conditions under which to report vary widely. Another 10 jurisdictions give psychotherapists permission to warn without explicitly imposing a duty to warn. One state, Virginia, flatly rejects the *Tarasoff decision,* at least in the outpatient context. The remaining 14 jurisdictions have no definitive law on the issue. It is important that you check the opinions of the courts and the laws in your state to determine if you are bound by the duty to warn, in which case you must reveal client confidences. The NASW Code of Ethics states you may break a client confidence if in your professional judgment the client presents a serious, imminent, and foreseeable harm to others (NASW, 2021, Section 1.07 [c]). NASW guidance in 2017 reported on 22 states that had a duty to warn with other states either having no statutory language addressing a social worker's obligation to warn or a standard that gives permission for a social worker to warn. Given the variance in state statutes, it is imperative that social workers consult the law in their respective jurisdictions.

Attorney Standards Relating to Breaching Confidentiality

Attorneys are bound to maintain all client confidences by their state's Code of Professional Responsibility. It is one of the fundamental tenets of the attorney–client relationship and is the foundation for establishing trust with a client. The ethical code for attorneys clearly mandates that lawyers may not reveal information about the client unless they are provided with informed consent (ABA, 2024, Rule 1.6). This means that the lawyer is strictly prohibited from disclosing any information that the client provides unless the client has previously authorized the disclosure or the content of the information falls into one of the few exceptions to attorney–client confidentiality that are laid out in the state-specific rules and typically include preventing serious harm or the client committing a crime (ABA, 2024, Rule 1.6[b]).

In any of these situations, the lawyer may reveal information to the extent necessary to alleviate the risk of severe harm or criminal activity. It is important to note that the Code does not require attorney to reveal the information but does allow the attorney to do so ethically in one of the circumstances mentioned.

However, the attorney is still limited by confidentiality and may only reveal the related and relevant information and not all of the information received during the course of representing the client. This is a critical difference between social work practice and legal practice, because some attorneys are not mandated reporters with a responsibility for reporting a reasonable suspicion of abuse or neglect. The information would have to give rise to a reasonable belief of impending death or serious bodily injury, but even in that situation disclosure of the confidential information is not mandated. Therefore, if Ms. Jones revealed to her attorney that she was still using drugs even though the infant was home in her care, the attorney is barred from revealing that information to any third party without receiving Ms. Jones's explicit consent.

HOW SHOULD WE COLLABORATE?

Social Worker Standards

Social work is a highly collaborative profession, and social workers frequently work in settings that are not primarily social work staffed. The settings are commonly referred to as "host" agencies. Because of this dynamic, the Code offers some guidance, giving, for example, the social worker working in legal settings an incentive to both collaborate and to have conversations with employers about ethics and values. The Code suggests that it is almost inevitable that social workers' ethical responsibilities may conflict both with agency or organizational policies and relevant laws or regulations (NASW, 2021, Section 3.09 [c] [d]).

The Code focuses on the process that the social worker should initiate to attempt to resolve any issues in a way that is consistent with their ethical principles. The Code always supports proactive social worker–initiated problem-solving and negotiations. Social workers should not be passive when it comes to informing their employers about their ethical responsibilities, informing employers when their policy and practice may not adhere to the standards promulgated in the Code, or when the regulations interfere with their ethical practice (NASW, 2021, Section 2.03 [a] [b]).

The Code supports interdisciplinary collaboration and suggests that when it comes to collaborations that support and enhance client well-being, social workers should actively contribute their values, knowledge, and skills. Again, the Code advocates that the social worker proactively sets up a discussion where the ethical rules and responsibilities of each profession are clearly articulated and agreed upon. In the event of a conflict, the social worker should make every effort to resolve the conflict in a way that supports client well-being (NASW, 2021, Section 1.06 [a]).

Attorney Standards

When someone who is not licensed to practice law is working with a lawyer, the ethical code provides some guidance for the attorney's supervision of the nonlawyer. For example, if working with a social worker, the attorney's rule states that the attorney is expected to supervise their work and ensure that they are meeting the professional code (ABA, 2024, Rule 5.3). Therefore, one of the first issues would be whether the social worker's professional code was in any way incompatible with the lawyer's code. This is not a simply academic matter since the Model Rules continue to state that a lawyer can be held responsible for the social worker's conduct, which would be in violation of the code if undertaken by an attorney (ABA, 2024, Rule 5.3[c][2]).

WHAT RESOURCES ARE AVAILABLE WHEN WE HAVE AN ETHICAL CONFLICT?

Mandated reporting and the duty to warn are two areas where tensions can arise in interdisciplinary collaboration. A social worker has a responsibility to reveal client confidences and legally report a suspicion of abuse or neglect of children, and sometimes elders and other vulnerable adults pursuant to mandated reporting law. In states where attorneys are not considered to be mandated reporters, their ethical responsibility is to protect client confidences, which prohibits them from revealing confidential information even if it relates to the potential abuse or neglect of children and elders.

The NASW website (www.socialworkers.org) has resources on legal and ethical issues confronting social workers in practice in interdisciplinary settings. Another helpful source for determining the interplay between an attorney's responsibility of confidentiality and a social worker's mandated reporting requirements is the opinion of your state's bar association. In many cases, the state bar association will issue an advisory opinion on specific ethics provisions and questions raised by practitioners. While those opinions are purely advisory and not law, they are helpful for guiding the interprofessional collaboration in your state and ensuring that you are identifying the correct issues to discuss.

Another source of information is interdisciplinary law clinics that are working with both social work and law students. There are well-established interdisciplinary clinics at the University of Pennsylvania Carey Law School, Fordham University, Stanford Law School, Boston College, University of Chicago, Northwestern University, University of Nevada, Michigan State University, University of Maryland, and Rutgers University, to name a few. Academics in those settings have developed protocols and papers that address both the process and outcomes they have developed to address the ethical concerns surrounding collaboration and are frequently very open to consulting with outside professionals about these issues. There are also many legal organizations that have social workers on staff and have successfully resolved these issues such as The Bronx Defenders and Lawyers for Children in New York City, Children's Law Project at Legal Assistance Foundation of Metropolitan Chicago, and Bet Tzedek Legal Services in California.

The following section describes the various ways that social workers and lawyers from around the country have resolved these ethical tensions. As you will see, these solutions represent a broad spectrum and are certainly context dependent as are all cases in practice. In this book we are not advocating that social workers working with attorneys choose any of the following solutions. Instead, we want to present you with the information from the Code of Ethics and the Code of Professional Responsibility and discuss some ways social workers have resolved these tensions. How you as a social worker decide is up to you as an individual in consultation with your supervisor and interdisciplinary partners. It should be an informed and educated decision based upon your reading of the Code, the licensing requirements of your state, and your prioritizing of social work values.

HOW COLLABORATING SOCIAL WORKERS AND LAWYERS HAVE RESOLVED THESE QUESTIONS

Unfortunately, there are no clear guidelines for social workers or attorneys about how to resolve the issue when there is a conflict between the attorney and the social worker with regard to mandated reporting and disclosure of confidential information. There are no reported judicial opinions that directly address this question and provide clear guidance, and the opinions issued by the state bar associations and ethics committees are not always clear and are sometimes contradictory. You should also be familiar with any opinions from bar associations, attorneys general, or ethics committees in your state. Bar opinions can be obtained by going to the website of your state bar association. This is an area where once again social workers are advised to be proactive and to address the issue with the attorney and anticipate any potential conflicts

As we noted, the Code of Ethics gives social workers the freedom to think about the context in which the principles are applied, the organizational setting in which they are employed, the duty owed to an employer, and their contribution to identifying the ethical responsibilities of interdisciplinary teams. The Code also acknowledges that at times there may be conflicts among the values in the Code itself and that the decision about what values take precedence is a judgment made by the individual social worker.

Social workers who work in a wide variety of legal settings have contributed to the formation of policies about ethical responsibilities when working with lawyers and in legal settings after they have gone through a process of identifying their values and priorities as an ethical professional. Several authors have contributed to the discussions around this issue and we encourage social workers to review this issue more thoroughly in the literature if an ethical issue arises (Anderson et al., 2007; St. Joan & Salomonsen-Sautel, 2001). The following section reviews how various social workers and lawyers have attempted to resolve these questions given the constraints of no clear guidelines.

Social Workers Are Employees of the Law Office and Follow the Rules of Professional Responsibility of the Attorneys

Under this analysis, because the social worker is viewed as an employee of the law firm, anything that is said to a social worker is subject to the same confidentiality requirements as the attorney. Therefore, the social worker that works in a law office is also bound by the attorney–client privilege. Social workers in the explicit legal context working directly with attorneys on cases should affirmatively discuss the attorney's expectations around mandated reporting and their practice with regard to social workers on the legal team. In some instances, a social worker on a legal team will be hired as "nonlawyer assistants" who would be under the attorney's supervision and responsibility under the Model Rules of Professional Conduct to ensure that nonlawyers working on behalf of the attorney "conform their conduct to the rules" (Rule 5.3). In that scenario, neither the lawyer nor the social worker as an employee of the attorney may disclose otherwise confidential information. This scenario still involves tension for the social worker between two mandated duties that can be particularly key in those jurisdictions where attorneys are not mandated reporters. Another concern is that some states list in their regulations which employees may be covered by attorney–client privilege and do not include social workers, whereas other states do not list specifically who is covered.

The Social Worker as Consultant

Under this model the social worker is hired by the attorney to assist in the preparation of the legal defense for a client by providing expert testimony, research, jury selection advice, and other tasks that are directly related to the preparation of the legal case. Because the social worker is not providing direct services to the client but rather assisting the attorney in the representation of the client, social workers in this scenario are believed to be covered by attorney–client privilege.

Confidentiality Walls

The approach of erecting confidentiality walls limits the social worker's access to protected client information. The lawyer may screen the client for any potential child abuse issues before referring a client to the social worker. The client and attorney create a shadow file into which information about child abuse and neglect may go to prevent that information from being accessed by the social worker (St. Joan & Salomonsen-Sautel, 2001). As the social worker does not have access to this information, they therefore would not be under an obligation to disclose the information pursuant to mandated reporting laws. A social worker may still find a need to make a report if they receive information directly from the client, but the initial screening by the lawyer limits this possibility. A social worker who is hired as a consultant by an attorney for the express purpose of providing services to the client would need to function under this model given that social workers would still retain their mandated reporting duties. It would also be critical to ensure that both the attorney and the social worker discuss how the confidentiality wall will be discussed with the client so that the client is fully informed as to the limits of confidentiality for each professional, where those overlap, and where they are different.

Informed Consent and Transparency Around the Limits of Confidentiality

In this model, the social worker identifies the times that information can and should be kept confidential and has a clear conversation with the client. The social worker discusses when they are legally obligated to breach client confidentiality. The client is also informed that if they have any doubts about what may happen if they share this information with the social worker or whether the information that they share falls under the confidentiality exception, they should request to speak with the attorney privately. This involves the clients clearly understanding the roles and ethical and legal duties of all the professionals involved in their case.

The social worker and the attorney would draft an agreement detailing the client's consent to disclose any confidential information and the process for determining what information, if any, would be disclosed and when. The counseling function of the social worker is precisely to point out to the client all the pros and cons including that of disclosure. The client should have a full discussion of pros and cons of making a report and the consequences thereof.

Advisory Opinions by the Local Bar Association or Disciplinary Committee

A lawyer working on behalf of the social worker's organization or on behalf of the legal services office can seek an ethics opinion from the local bar association to determine whether a particular situation violates the legal Code of Ethics. As noted earlier, ethical opinions from your local state bar can be particularly helpful in resolving these tensions in interdisciplinary collaboration.

Long-Term Radical Solutions

As the professions increasingly engage in collaborative practice, there are renewed calls to reform the ethical codes of all professions and relevant laws to assist professionals in the ability to respond ethically within this changing context of professional practice. Additionally, reforming or abolishing mandated reporting laws has been proposed to promote greater access to justice and services, with the specific reform of exempting social workers in legal settings from mandated reporting requirements.

PROMOTING INTERDISCIPLINARY CONVERSATIONS ABOUT ETHICS AND PROFESSIONAL RESPONSIBILITY

In the experience of the authors of this textbook, many of what seem to be irresolvable conflicts at first glance can be negotiated successfully in ways where both professionals feel comfortable that their concerns are addressed ethically and professionally. We have found that if parties believe in the value of their collaborative work as a benefit to the client and there is a sincere wish to collaborate, then issues related to working together can be and are usually successfully resolved. The following are some guidelines we have developed in the course of our work with law clinics and interprofessional legal organizations that we believe are critical to a satisfying and mutually respectful working relationship.

1. Collaborate among clients and social workers—often and ongoing—as professionals. Realize that collaboration is constantly evolving through the course of the representation and the collaborative relationship.
2. Interprofessional conversation is one in which all members, and most

importantly the client, are encouraged to voice their concerns. Passivity and internalized oppression are not acceptable. Everyone is encouraged to defend their convictions, raise questions about policies and actions, and be equally responsible for the client outcome, including the client. Social workers working in host settings sometimes feel reticent about clearly expressing views that may be different than that of the predominant profession. It is imperative that all participants encourage full expression of all concerns. To achieve this, it is critical for there to be an explicit discussion of the presence of power dynamics and the processes that will be used to ensure that everyone in the collaborative relationship is able to share their perspective. All perspectives should continue to underscore the best outcome for the client, and not be grounded in bias judgments based on political perspectives or personal views of a client's past history.

3. Challenge the meaning of language by going directly to the "source" of the knowledge you and your attorney collaborator "think" you have. This means having a copy of both the Code of Ethics and the Code of Professional Responsibility in front of you when you begin to discuss ethics. "Going to the source" implies that preparing for conversation means researching, accessing, and knowing the individual state licensing laws as well as any legal limits on client confidentiality.
4. Understand that professional ethics often implies much balancing and discretion for the professionals interpreting them. Some states require adherence to the professional Code of Ethics as a licensing requirement for social workers, while others do not. Attorneys must abide by their state's Code of Ethics and professional responsibility to practice law in that state. Some attorneys are mandated reporters.
5. Put the involvement and goals of the client at the forefront. One strategy for ensuring this principle is to always inquire whether a proposed solution or plan of action serves the client's goal before proceeding with the decision.
6. Have consistent and reliable work structures to facilitate regular conversations and to get advice and assistance including interprofessional supervisory conferences, third-party independent reviewers, and the identification of ethics experts in schools of social work and law. Given the often crisis nature of social work practice, this is extremely important and is often best scheduled at the beginning of the case to ensure space for reflection and critical conversations.

PREPARING TO COLLABORATE: A CONVERSATION BETWEEN A SOCIAL WORKER AND LAWYER ABOUT WORKING TOGETHER FOR MICHELLE JONES

At the beginning of any collaborative professional relationship, it is important to lay out the foundations of the partnership and the division of roles before meeting with the client. This will ensure that you can thoroughly describe your role to the client and delineate it when appropriate from the attorney's role.

The following reflects what may be the first conversation between the court-appointed attorney and court-appointed social worker in Ms. Jones's case, illustrates how to apply the preceding guidelines to practice, and shows how two professionals may discuss ethics.

After the interview with Ms. Jones, the attorney decides to request that a social worker be appointed to work with Ms. Jones on her legal case. The attorney has provided the social worker with the information from the beginning of the chapter, including the allegations against Ms. Jones that are contained in the legal petition filed in Family Court.

Attorney: Why do I want to work with a social worker on this case, and what do I see as the role of the social worker with Ms. Jones?

When I first read the petition, I am immediately concerned about the state of my client because she has just given birth and there are allegations of substance abuse. I believe that a social worker could be helpful in conducting a clinical assessment and providing recommendations and counseling for the substance abuse allegations. While I take all the allegations in the petition as only a starting point for my analysis of Ms. Jones's case, I am concerned that the criminal case means that there may be a longer history of substance abuse.

Finally, it is not clear to me what the impact of prenatal substance abuse is on a newborn. I can envision wanting more information on substance abuse exposure during pregnancy, infant development, and mother–infant bonding. Additionally, I am curious as to whether she knew that she was being tested for drugs and what consent she provided for that testing. Considering all of these issues, I want the social worker to play a critical role both in counseling the client and determining the legal strategy collaboratively with me.

The first step would be for us to meet with Ms. Jones together and explain why we feel it is important for her to have a social worker working with her lawyer on the legal case and secure her agreement with her plan. Once Ms. Jones agrees to the social worker's participation, I would want the social worker to assess Ms. Jones's current emotional state and to assist in gathering a more complete history of her pregnancy and alleged substance abuse, and identify if there has been a history of Ms. Jones seeking assistance for substance use.

Second, I want the social worker to help gather collateral information from any service providers that Ms. Jones has worked with previously and any relatives who could help care for her son. Finally, I hope that the social worker can play a role in counseling Ms. Jones about her options at the beginning of this case.

Social Worker: What do I think I can add to this case, and how can I help the attorney in achieving the client's goals?

There are several potential roles that a social worker can play in this case. Initially it would be best for me to proceed in the role of "social worker as advocate for the client." I will be hired as a consultant for the purpose of providing social work advocacy for your client and assist you in protecting and advocating for the rights of the client. In this role, a social worker can assist the attorney in investigating the facts that are alleged in the petition; for example, that Ms. Jones has a long history of substance abuse and that she has never completed substance abuse treatment. I know from experience that many times facts in a legal petition are not always accurate.

The second function I, the social worker, could perform is to assess the level of stress and the emotional state of Ms. Jones and determine if and how that may impact her ability to assist and participate in her legal representation as well as making her vulnerable for relapse if she does have a substance abuse problem. I can assist the client in identifying her coping mechanisms and provide short-term crisis intervention counseling. In addition, I may also want to know if there were any significant life events that may have caused Ms. Jones to become introduced to substances, to use them for coping, and/or if any significant life events may have contributed to relapse. These details are often significant when supporting clients with substance use, and also to provide a full holistic view of the client.

The third task that can be performed is to assess Ms. Jones's use of substances and to recommend and refer her to an appropriate treatment program if warranted. I can also provide information to the attorney regarding the developmental needs of Ms. Jones's son and what kind of visitation plan needs to be put in place that will respond to those needs and facilitate parent–child bonding.

Finally, an assessment can be made of Ms. Jones's capacity to parent, including her housing, income status, and support system. As part of our informed consent process, I the social worker would explain why these assessments are crucial to her effective legal representation as well as for her emotional and social well-being. I would explore the pros and cons of her participation as well as potential outcomes for her and her child. We would also inform Ms. Jones that in the event of any subsequent work, we will meet with her to renegotiate and explain our reasons for requiring other information or requesting her participation in services.

Attorney: To think about the ways that I can most effectively use your expertise in Ms. Jones's case, could you tell me about your training and experience as a social worker?

For example, do you have any specialized knowledge in the field of child welfare law or substance abuse? Are you aware of any programs—community-based organizations, service providers, or treatment programs—in the area? Do you have relationships with service providers, and do you feel qualified to explain to the client and me the specifics of different treatment programs and services? Finally, I am interested in learning more about the effects of prenatal substance abuse on infants and mother–infant bonding. Do you have any experience in this area? Do you know how to research this issue?

Social Worker: I am a licensed clinical social worker and have worked as a social worker for 10 years, primarily with low-income families who are involved with the child welfare system. Because I became aware of the large amount of child protection cases in which substance abuse is implicated, I obtained my certification as a certified substance abuse counselor (CSAC) 2 years ago. I received advanced clinical training at a family therapy institute. I have been working with attorneys and as a court-appointed social worker for the last 5 years and am a member of the National Organization of Forensic Social Work.

Although I am a clinical social worker, I focus on all system levels of a client's life and do not see problems residing solely in the individual client. I address environmental causes for client problems in my work as well. I see myself as an advocate for client rights. I also adhere to "evidence-based practice," which means I keep current with the research in my field, particularly regarding what kind of interventions are effective with the child welfare population.

I noticed that Ms. Jones has a criminal case as well. Do you have the expertise to represent her in that case, too? What has been your experience collaborating with social workers in the preparation and presentation of a child neglect case?

Attorney: My area of practice is family law, and I work in an office where there are also criminal defense attorneys. While I have never handled a criminal law case, I am knowledgeable about the procedures and basics of a criminal case. I will certainly consult with Ms. Jones's criminal defense attorney to make sure that our efforts in Family Court do not negatively impact her criminal case. I have collaborated with social workers on other child neglect cases, most recently having a social worker from a substance abuse treatment agency testify about my client's treatment program, efforts at rehabilitation, and relapse. I have also worked with social workers who have not testified in Family Court but have provided ongoing support to clients who must testify in their case or who need referrals for services to address some of the issues in their legal case.

Social Worker: I think this can be a great collaboration. We are both experienced, and this seems like a case where there will be real value for the client and her son that can happen by us working together on her behalf.

Let's discuss the way we will handle the ethical issues that may come up during the case. What do our state laws and ethics opinions say about how I should proceed in the event of a conflict or a concern about harm to the client's self or others or the issue of mandated reporting?

Attorney: After reading some of the bar opinions in other states and the law in this state, my interpretation is that you are also bound by my ethical obligation with regard to confidentiality and client self-determination as a consultant on this legal case because I have hired you with the express purpose of helping me defend Ms. Jones. As you know, I am bound to protect attorney–client privilege and keep everything relayed to me by Ms. Jones in the strictest of confidences unless she expressly allows me to release the information to outside parties, including the court and CPS agency. I believe that this principle is especially important at the beginning of a relationship with a client in establishing trust and hopefully allowing Ms. Jones to be as forthcoming as possible with us in our interviews. Therefore, I would want you to relay the same standard of confidentiality to Ms. Jones.

I would anticipate discussing the issues of confidentiality, mandated reporting, client self-determination, and conflicts with you now at the beginning of our relationship. However, I would also expect that these discussions would continue throughout the case as any potential conflicts with those duties we have discussed arise.

Social Worker: I agree. I have also read the NASW discussion of the legal and ethical issues in social worker–lawyer collaborations. Regarding client self-determination, many of my colleagues have suggested that we will have a conflict because attorneys will "do whatever their client wants no matter what." I wanted to get your thoughts on that and to share with you some of the ways my code addresses client self-determination.

Attorney: While you are right that my code requires me to follow my client's wishes in the case, I also have a duty to counsel my client about the pros and cons of each decision throughout her case. This counseling can include a frank discussion of what the consequences of some choices may be. I also have a duty to make sure that my client's decisions in the case are informed, and I cannot be certain that they are informed decisions unless I have fully and thoroughly counseled my client. Of course, if my client tells me that they are going to do something illegal or lie to the court, I have an overriding obligation as an attorney to counsel them against those actions and potentially end the representation of that client as a result, or be in a position where I have to make the court aware of the misrepresentation or illegal conduct.

Social Worker: That puts us in much closer agreement, as social workers are ethically obligated to respect the right of client self-determination, make sure they are fully informed and counseled about the risks and benefits of their decisions. Only when I believe there is serious, foreseeable, or imminent harm can I restrict their right to self-determination.

One concern that I would like to raise is the possibility that a conflict may arise for me between the interests of my client and those of her infant son as I proceed with my investigation of the facts. There are two ways my ethical code can help me in thinking about this and the first is that Ms. Jones has a right to self-determination and her interests are primary unless I as a professional can see that there is a serious, foreseeable, and imminent harm to her infant or herself through the course of action she wishes to take. Because Ms. Jones is in a vulnerable state as a mother who has just delivered a child who was then removed, postpartum depression is a concern. If I believe that Ms. Jones may harm herself, her right to confidentiality could be implicated and the same standard of serious, foreseeable, and imminent harm is applied in this case as well. This means that some harm will happen now, not in the future or not because I believe there is a potential risk of harm.

The second action I can take is to speak with Ms. Jones and you as the attorney about these possible conflicts regarding confidentiality and client self-determination and how I would respond in the event that these conflicts occur. Prior to taking any action I would inform and consult with both you the attorney and the client Ms. Jones.

Attorney: I think that we are closer in agreement to our obligations regarding confidentiality than I initially thought. If I believed that Ms. Jones was going to cause serious physical harm to herself or her child, I am covered under my Code if I choose to reveal that limited information. I have a short memorandum of law that summarizes the laws and ethical opinions in our state for collaboration between attorneys and social workers who are appointed by the Court to assist attorneys working with parents. We can work from that document.

Another way we can address your concern is to include a provision in our representation agreement with Ms. Jones that advises her to speak first with her attorney about any information that may raise this conflict. We will have to make sure that we inform Ms. Jones of this provision and provide her with an example of information that could potentially trigger a social worker's responsibility to report.

Social Worker: That feels right for me. Let's discuss some of the logistics of working together. Will you make yourself available to explain the law or legal procedures to me if I need to know them as part of my work on this case?

I know that you have a large caseload, but I would like to request that we set up regular phone or in-person meetings to share information, identify strategies, and try to anticipate any potential obstacles as we are moving forward. Ideally, we would include Ms. Jones in these conversations.

Attorney: I am happy to make myself available to answer questions about the laws and processes in Ms. Jones's case. I can also provide you with some very helpful overviews of the laws and processes in Family Courts that have been prepared by other legal services offices. I think it is a good idea to have regularly scheduled meetings with Ms. Jones, and I would suggest that we meet separately before each of those meetings. While we should certainly meet with each other and with Ms. Jones prior to any court date, I would like to have a biweekly check-in by phone or in person on Ms. Jones's case.

Next Steps

After the meeting with the social worker, the attorney drafts the client representation agreement with the provisions that address possible tensions in the collaboration including what the team decided about how to address potential conflicts, limits to confidentiality, and mandated reporting requirements. The agreement also includes the roles and responsibilities of the attorney, the social worker, and Ms. Jones. The attorney reviews the draft representation agreement with the social worker, and a meeting is scheduled for the social worker, attorney, and Ms. Jones to discuss and explain the representation agreement and the next steps in her legal agreement. During this meeting, Ms. Jones signs the representation agreement, and the team is ready to proceed.

REFERENCES

American Bar Association. (2024). *Model rules of professional conduct.* https://www.americanbar.org/groups/professional_responsibility/publications/model_rules_of_professional_conduct/model_rules_of_professional_conduct_table_of_contents/

Anderson, A. L., Barenberg, L., Paul, R., & Tremblay, P. R. (2007). Professional ethics in interdisciplinary collaboratives: Zeal, paternalism and mandated reporting. *Clinical Law Review, 13*, 659.

Appelbaum, P. S. (2007). Clinical practice. Assessment of patients' competence to consent to treatment. *New England Journal of Medicine, 357*(18), 1834–1849. https://www.nejm.org/doi/full/10.1056/NEJMcp074045

Bogie, M. (2001). *Child custody and consent to treatment.* NASW Assurance Services 1(10). Retrieved from http://www.naswassurance.org

Cal. Fam. Code § 6924(b).

Herbert, P. B., & Young, K. A. (2003). Tarasoff at twenty-five. *Focus, 1*, 376–381. https://doi.org/10.1176/foc.1.4.376

N.Y. Codes, Rules & Reg. title 22 § 1500.12, 1200.22 (1998).

National Association of Social Workers. (2021). *Code of ethics of the National Association of Social Workers.* Author.

Reamer, F. (2013). Ethics and values. In *Encyclopedia of Social Work* (6th ed.). Columbia University Press.

St. Joan, J., & Salomonsen-Sautel, S. (2001). The clinic as laboratory: Lessons from the first year of collecting social research in an interdisciplinary domestic violence clinic. *Loyola Law Review, 47*(1), 317–358.

Tarasoff v. Regents of the University of California, 17 Cal. 3d 425 (Cal. 1976)

Vandervort, F. E., Gonzalez, R. P., & Faller, K. C. (2008). Legal ethics and high child welfare worker turnover: An unexplored connection. *Children and Youth Services Review, 30*, 546–563. https://doi.org/10.1016/j.childyouth.2007.10.016

Venkat, R. P. (2017). Strengths-based approach in social work: A distinct ethical advantage. *International Journal of Innovation, Creativity and Change, 3*, 97–114.

CHAPTER 4

The Implicit and Explicit Context of Social Work Practice

INTRODUCTION

This chapter describes the implicit and explicit legal contexts of social work practice. Our premise is that the legal system operates implicitly and explicitly in clients' lives and in social work practice consistently. While most social workers are familiar to some extent with the explicit legal system of courts and judicial hearings, the implicit legal context of laws and systems regularly defines the rules, responsibilities, and entitlements for your clients. You will learn how these laws and regulations exist at the federal, state, and local levels and how court cases become case law with the same effect as laws. We describe the ways in which knowledge of the implicit context can be used by social workers to advocate and to create opportunities for clients even if you are not working in explicitly legal settings. In order to understand the explicit legal context, you will be introduced to the U.S. judicial system with all of its courts, other legal decision-making forums, and the processes and pathways involved in each of these forums. This chapter also describes forensic social work, a practice that occurs within contexts that are defined as specifically legal such as courts, prisons, law offices, forensic hospitals, and juvenile justice settings. We continue to reference *The Case of Michelle Jones* in order to illustrate the myriad ways for social workers to play a critical role in assisting clients with identifying and resolving legal issues.

LOCATING THE IMPLICIT LEGAL CONTEXT: LAWS, REGULATIONS, AND POLICIES

The implicit legal context of social work practice refers to the laws, regulations, and court decisions that govern and regulate clients' everyday lives. This context is implicit precisely because it shapes clients' rights, responsibilities, and entitlements but is often invisible or unknown to an individual. Through an understanding of the implicit legal context of clients' lives, social workers are in a better position to improve their practice by being aware of and providing critical information, advocating for clients, and ensuring that legal needs are identified and addressed.

Laws are made at the federal, state, and local levels. Federal laws are applicable to all states, and must be followed by the courts and in all state and local practices. Federal laws have a great impact on state and local systems, as evidenced by federal laws concerning education or welfare laws. Federal laws cover a wide range of issues, including discrimination, consumer protection, federal funding, and commerce, to name just a few. However, there are many areas that are not covered by federal law and are left to states and local municipalities to govern.

One of the most common examples of this relegation to states is the power to regulate families, including laws governing the child welfare system, marriage, custody, and divorce. State laws are passed by state legislators and only apply to that specific state, while local jurisdictions can pass rules and regulations that cover everything from traffic codes to how a local school department is organized. Most states and local jurisdictions, particularly larger cities, maintain detailed websites where you can access the specific language of laws, rules, and regulations. States now have websites with information on the structure of the local government, laws and regulations, and agency departments. For example, you can access the California State Constitution at www.ca.gov and determine whether there are pending bills in the Illinois legislature at www.illinois.gov. Federal legislation is easily accessible and searchable at www.congress.gov where you can search for the text of pending bills, enacted legislation, and committee reports. These websites can be an important resource for locating the law, regulation, or department at issue in a client's case.

In order to illustrate how laws impact clients' lives, we first return to *The Case of Michelle Jones*. You will see how the implicit legal context shapes Ms. Jones's ability to enroll and fully participate in a drug treatment program. Additionally, you will see the interplay among federal, state, and local laws and regulations in the context of welfare laws that determine Ms. Jones's eligibility for treatment and services. Finally, the authors hope you will recognize the opportunities for a social worker with knowledge of the implicit legal context to advocate for Ms. Jones's goals.

Most importantly, it is crucial to recognize that Ms. Jones's ability to apply for public assistance, the process by which she applies, and the requirements for continuing to receive assistance are governed by local laws and regulations. As we show you in the next section of this chapter, the process of applying for public assistance requires that applicants provide multiple sources of identification, documentation of need, and eligibility.

Public Assistance and *The Case of Michelle Jones*: An Example of the Implicit Context of the Law

As the substance abuse counselor working with Ms. Jones, you conducted a thorough assessment when she first entered the outpatient program to address her use of substances. This assessment included a review of her education and employment history, in addition to reviewing her healthcare and source of income. You learned that Ms. Jones went to public schools but did not graduate from high school, finishing only her junior year. When she entered the outpatient program, she was receiving public assistance and participating in a work-readiness program as part of her eligibility for receiving the entitlement. The work-readiness program required her to attend a number of eligibility appointments, provide documents, and participate in training programs. She was also living in subsidized public housing with a relative. Ms. Jones was regularly participating in group and individual counseling after waiting 2 months to be assigned a counselor. One day you learn that Ms. Jones's case is at risk of being closed because she begins to attend less frequently and you have a harder time reaching her. The agency supervisor raises concerns that Ms. Jones is not complying with the requirements of the program and therefore will be terminated.

As you can see from the case study, the social worker in a substance abuse treatment center is faced with a number of implicit legal issues when working with Ms. Jones. Ms. Jones is involved not only with the public welfare system as her source of income and healthcare, but also with the public housing system. Therefore, in addition to addressing Ms. Jones's substance abuse issues, the social worker has to take into account her current involvement with public benefits and public housing systems since both systems directly impact her ability to continue with ongoing treatment. If the goal of the substance abuse social worker's intervention is to assist Ms. Jones in participating fully in the treatment program, then it is imperative to have a better understanding of the impact of those additional implicit legal contexts in her client's life.

A survey of welfare law and policy will demonstrate how the underlying laws, regulations, and case law play out in Ms. Jones's life. Welfare laws and their corresponding policies were initially created by the federal legislature. A federal law must be passed by both the House of Representatives and the Senate, the two sectors of the legislative branch of our government, before being signed by the president in the executive branch. The current federal law, Temporary Assistance for Needy Families Act which was enacted in 1996 (TANF), provides money from the federal government in a block grant. This means that states accepting the grant can determine, within general guidelines, the specific procedures for distributing the money to individuals and families. Once the states have received the federal money for welfare, they are charged with creating agencies and regulations to implement the welfare practice and policy within the state. As you can imagine, the regulations must cover eligibility requirements, processing guidelines, and review processes among other administrative systems. While the federal government sets out some general guidelines that must be followed in order to receive the money, individual states can determine the specific eligibility requirements and processes for individuals to access welfare benefits. For example, in Illinois you can apply for cash assistance or welfare if you fall under the eligibility criteria defined in part by the federal law which include that the applicant is a U.S. citizen, pregnant or with children under the age of 19 who live with you, and are a resident of Illinois (www.dhs.state.il.us). In California, the welfare program, called CalWorks, requires that all recipients receive work assistance and training as a condition of receiving aid (www.cdss.ca.gov). In light of the differences from state to state that can impact your client's ability to access and receive services, best practice is to check your state and local government websites to determine the specific policies in your state.

Once the federal government has dispersed the money and the state has implemented the local program, individuals retain their rights to challenge local practices or the federal guidelines through litigation. It is important for your practice to understand the role of the court system in interpreting laws and regulations. While the federal law sets out the funding structure and basic eligibility criteria for states to receive funding for welfare programs, the state is ultimately responsible for administering the program and dispersing the funds. As a result, both federal and state laws are implicated in the public welfare process and when clients access benefits.

A good example of the overlap between federal law, state practice, and client's rights is the seminal Supreme Court case of *Goldberg v. Kelly* (1970). In this case, a welfare recipient sued the State of New York on behalf of himself and other New York welfare recipients, claiming that the state's process for denying benefits was a violation of his federal constitutional right to due process because he was not given notice of the denial or an opportunity to contest the decision. The Supreme Court determined that the federal constitutional right to due process of law under the Fourteenth Amendment mandated that welfare recipients be provided with an opportunity to contest the state's decision to deny them benefits by having a hearing where they could present evidence and cross-examine witnesses. For Ms. Jones, this would mean an administrative hearing, often referred to as a fair hearing, to determine if her budget was improperly decreased and whether or not benefits were rightfully denied. At the fair hearing, she would be entitled to review evidence provided by the government agency and also present her own evidence to prove her case. You will learn much more about the administrative hearing process later on in this chapter when we review the explicit legal context of administrative review and how understanding this process as her social worker would inform and improve your advocacy on her behalf.

The Impact of Welfare's Implicit Legal Context on Ms. Jones

The hypothetical situation of benefits being improperly denied in the case study is realistic because research tells us that in close to half of public benefit cases that receive sanctions, the sanctions are imposed erroneously (Lens, 2005). Supporting much of the evidence we presented in Chapter 1, research has also found that almost half of the recipients did not realize they were sanctioned or why they were sanctioned because they did not understand the complicated rules and regulations related to their benefits (Hasenfeld et al., 2004).

The first way a rights- and needs-oriented social worker could respond is to make sure that Ms. Jones has an understanding of why her benefits were cut off. The second action would be to let Ms. Jones know that if she does not understand or disagrees with the decision, she can request an administrative review or hearing. In an article looking at the use of hearings to address issues with public benefit claims, Lens (2005) reports very low rates of appeals but very high success rates in cases where the client does appeal which supports research indicating there is a high rate of error by public welfare caseworkers in applying sanctions and rules. Unfortunately, due to the sometimes vague nature of the law, public welfare agencies can misinterpret the laws that qualify people for federal or state benefits, resulting in a lapse or denial of critical services that can sometimes lead to further extenuating circumstances for clients who should have received those services.

Since welfare reform, applying for or receiving public benefits results in significant implications for the privacy of clients who are poor, like Ms. Jones, some states and counties have instituted aggressive home visiting policies, some triggered by simply applying for public benefits (Gustafson, 2009).

Additional requirements such as having your child vaccinated, monitoring the school attendance of children in the home, reporting a new boyfriend, and not being eligible for benefits for additional children born while on welfare are examples of some individual state rules that could impact Ms. Jones.

Ms. Jones is required by federal law to be fingerprinted and photographed, and any law enforcement agency can have unlimited access to public benefit records without any basis for suspecting her of committing a crime. Once the client's information is entered in the system it is automatically checked for any outstanding warrants or drug offenses. In many states, if a client on public benefits has been convicted of a drug charge they are subject to a lifetime ban on receiving benefits (Gustafson, 2009). So, if Ms. Jones is convicted in her criminal case involving possession of a drug, she will not be eligible to collect welfare and may lose her ability to access and live in public housing. Ironically, even though welfare-work programs offer substance abuse treatment as part of their programming there is an inherent disincentive for clients to reveal they may be involved in using illegal substances (Gustafson, 2009).

In *The Case of Michelle Jones*, the social worker should be concerned about how the implicit legal context affects her ability to continue in treatment, as well as the potential criminal justice issue. Ms. Jones has been arrested and charged for possession of a controlled substance and will be processed through Criminal Court. Being sanctioned or having a lifetime ban on welfare can have critical implications for her Family Court case as it relates to Ms. Jones's ability to obtain income and housing, crucial to reunification with her child. A criminal conviction can also make it extremely difficult for Ms. Jones to obtain employment making it almost impossible for her to access adequate income to support herself and her child, a stressor that can contribute to relapse during her recovery from substance abuse. Ms. Jones's criminal defense lawyer may not be aware of the ramifications of a criminal conviction for Ms. Jones and her relationship with her child. Having home visits conducted by public benefit workers who are mandated reporters could trigger additional child protective investigations if there were other children at home or even law enforcement actions if any evidence of suspected illegal activity was observed (Raz, 2020).

As you can see, the implicit legal context of the welfare system alone can trigger invisible interactions between systems, such as law enforcement and public assistance, and can implicate a number of rights, responsibilities, and entitlements for clients. Whether or not you agree with the policies and rules the federal government, state, or locality impose on the distribution of public benefits, at the very least, ethical social workers should be aware of the many implications this implicit context has on their clients' lives and treatment outcomes and their own ability to deliver critical services needed to achieve social service goals and outcomes. When those laws and regulations are not followed—either by the individual or the government—your practice switches from consideration of the implicit context to the explicit context of the judicial system of review and enforcement.

As was pointed out in Chapter 1, social workers are often in a position where consumers come to them for advice or when they have a problem. Many of the clients are overwhelmed and have difficulty even knowing what rights, protections, and entitlements they may have, never mind understanding how to enforce them. Clients often are also baffled about processes and procedures and may not understand legal rights and responsibilities they have as they move through the judicial system. Knowing the implicit legal system will assist you in identifying if an issue is a legal issue and advocating for the client. Knowing about the explicit legal system will allow you to assist clients with understanding processes and procedures as well as the ways legal decisions are made and, most importantly, the seriousness of what is at stake for the client and their family.

LOCATING THE EXPLICIT PRACTICE: THE JUDICIAL SYSTEM AND COURTS

The explicit legal context of social work practice refers to when clients have legal issues that are being addressed or could be addressed in a civil, criminal, or administrative forum. As we discussed in Chapter 1, there are three bodies of law—civil, criminal, and administrative—with separate judicial review systems, most commonly referred to as courts. Understanding the explicit legal context, as well as the legal ramifications of the activities in which you are engaged as a social worker, is critical to fulfilling your ethical mandate to protect the rights of your client and to advance social justice. Therefore, it is essential as a social worker that you are familiar with legal decision-making forums and the pathway of your client's case when they are involved in the legal system.

Throughout the process there are many roles a social worker may play and many actions that could be taken to facilitate the process for your client, or to intervene on behalf of a client and their family. Often, there are enormous psychological burdens imposed on clients and their families as they move through the court system. Most frequently, when clients become involved in the judicial system, they are in crisis. Having to become familiar with a complex and sometimes intimidating system simultaneously is often an impossible task. By knowing the explicit legal system, social workers can play a crucial role in advancing the cause of justice and assisting clients in understanding how to meet their legal needs more effectively and lower the degree of distress usually associated with legal proceedings. In order to do so, social workers require a solid understanding of the various legal proceedings and decision-making forums in which they and their clients may find themselves. When you understand the explicit legal context, you will also feel more empowered and confident in the performance of your practice whenever you are interacting with attorneys and within these legal and judicial forums.

Legal Forums and Judicial Decision-Making Processes

Whether the legal context is implicit or explicit in your practice as a social worker, it is highly likely you will find yourself or your client interacting in some way with one of the multiple legal forums. The next section introduces you to the various forums where legal decisions are made, what questions are being decided, and the general path of a case. It is important to remember that social work knowledge and skills can be applied at every stage of the process.

Courts are defined both by what types of cases they can decide, what decisions can be made at the conclusion of the cases, and where they are located. The types of cases are generally divided into three categories: criminal, civil, and administrative. The following section describes the basic path of a case in each of these forums with case examples involving Ms. Jones and her family to illustrate the similarities and differences in each court.

First and foremost, courts are permitted to make certain decisions depending on whether the court is a trial or appellate court. The trial court is where a case begins, whether it is civil or criminal, and the court will conduct a trial to determine whether or not there is sufficient evidence to make a decision. Once the trial court has made a decision, an individual, sometimes referred to as a party to the case or a litigant, can appeal the trial court's decision to an appellate court. The appellate court will not hold another trial but instead will review the evidence presented at trial and the legal decisions made by the trial judge to determine whether or not there were legal errors. If the appellate court determines that there was legal error, they can decide to reverse the trial court's decision and rule in favor of the other litigant, or they can send the case back to the trial court to rehear the case often with guidelines for the appropriate interpretation or application of the relevant laws and procedures in the case. Finally, a litigant can appeal to the highest appellate court, generally referred to as the Supreme Court of a state or of the United States, for the final review of whether or not there was a legal error in the decision of the case.

Courts at the federal level include the U.S. Supreme Court, Circuit Courts, which are divided among the states to hear appeals from trial courts, and the Federal District Courts that decide trials in both civil and criminal matters involving federal laws. Federal courts are generally not permitted to review state laws, unless the argument in the case is that a particular state law violates federal law, including the U.S. Constitution. State courts include both civil and criminal trial courts that determine whether state or local laws have been violated. Appellate Courts are responsible for hearing cases that have finished at the trial level to determine whether there were any legal errors. In some instances, Appellate Courts can hear certain specific questions of law during the pendency of a trial. For example in New York State, a case can be tried in a local Family Court, appealed to an Appellate Division Court, and ultimately reviewed by the New York Court of Appeals, the highest court in New York State. Additionally, Ms. Jones is able to appeal a decision to remove her child from her care on an emergency basis even though her case did not reach a resolution. The preceding sections provide an overview of each of the three courts.

Criminal Court

Criminal Courts handle all cases where an individual is charged with a crime and faces the possibility of incarceration. Criminal cases range from minor infractions such as trespassing to more serious crimes including robbery, possession of a weapon, and assault. While state laws generally govern Criminal Courts, there are a number of protections provided to both defendants and victims of crimes that are codified in federal law and the federal courts' interpretation of the U.S. Constitution. States are required to follow and ensure that the federal protections are available in state Criminal Courts.

A Criminal Court case is initiated by an arrest, when the police formally detain an individual because they believe that the individual has committed a crime. Once an individual is arrested, the police may question them but they must first provide them with a reminder of their rights during a criminal investigation. This practice stems directly from the Supreme Court case, *Miranda v. Arizona* (1966), which determined that police must provide criminal suspects with specific warnings including their right to remain silent and to consult with an attorney in order to protect the Constitution's Fifth Amendment right against self-incrimination.

A criminal case is formally initiated when a complaint or petition is filed in Criminal Court. This is the formal legal document that lists the charges against the defendant and the basis for those charges, including statements or observations from a victim, complaining witness, or police officer. After the criminal complaint is filed, the defendant is arraigned and formally charged in Criminal Court where an attorney can be appointed for the first time, regardless of whether the defendant can afford to hire an attorney. This is another legal right that stems from a Supreme Court decision in *Gideon v. Wainwright* (1963), where the Supreme Court held that the U.S. Constitution's guarantee of a fair trial required that individuals who were not able to afford an attorney to defend them in a criminal case be provided with a defense attorney.

A defendant can be released from detention, with or without bail, or the judge can order that the defendant remain in jail pending the outcome of the criminal trial. The next steps in the case depend on your client's role in the case as the defendant, victim, or witness. For the attorneys, next steps could include gathering evidence, making legal motions to exclude evidence gathered by the police, and entering into potential plea negotiations to resolve the criminal case without going to trial. If there is a criminal trial, a judge will preside over the trial including selecting a jury if the case is going to be decided by a jury trial. A trial concludes when the defendant is found guilty or not guilty of some or all of the charges against them in the criminal complaint. For example, if Ms. Jones was charged with both possession of illegal drugs and selling illegal drugs, she may only be found guilty of the possession charge after her trial if there were not sufficient evidence to prove beyond a reasonable doubt that she was guilty of selling the drugs.

Civil Court

Civil cases are distinguished from criminal cases in that, with a couple of notable exceptions, a Civil Court does not have the power to incarcerate a party. One exception is when juveniles are detained in delinquency proceedings which are civil proceedings. Civil matters can be divided generally into two categories: civil cases where the government or a government agency is the initiating actor, and civil cases between two private parties, whether they are individuals, groups, or corporations. As a reminder, only the government can initiate a criminal case against an individual. Civil cases where the government is the initiating actor include child protection matters, juvenile delinquency cases, civil commitment, and public housing issues. Child protection cases are civil cases but are initiated and filed by the local child welfare agency against a parent or caregiver. Juvenile delinquency cases are considered civil, even though the court generally retains the power to detain a young person. Additionally, cases involving civil commitment can be brought by a government or public entity in a Civil Court. Civil commitment is a notable exception to the general rule for civil cases, as individuals can be committed to psychiatric facilities against their wishes. Other examples that are relevant for social workers include appeals from administrative hearings including special education issues.

When the government or a government agency is the initiating actor, the case begins when the government agency files a petition detailing the allegations against the individual. For example, with Ms. Jones, the child welfare agency filed a petition alleging that she had neglected her infant son by abusing drugs. The petition, similar to the complaint, has to list the specific law that is alleged to have been violated and also the basis for that belief including statements from witnesses or records. Depending on the type of allegations and the laws implicated, the civil case will be heard by a judge sitting in a Family Court, Housing Court, or general Civil Court sometimes referred to as Supreme Court or Civil Court.

Once a petition has been filed, the process is like the Criminal Court process because the person being charged with a violation of the law has the opportunity to review the evidence that the government has gathered against them, conduct their own investigation, and file legal motions. Both sides will participate in settlement negotiations, and a successful settlement would mean that the court either dismisses the case or enters an order that is agreed to by all the parties to the case. If the case goes to trial, then the judge or a jury will determine whether the government agency has met its legal burden in proving the allegations or if the defense has prevailed. Depending on the type of case and the specific state, a judge or a jury will decide your client's case. In many civil cases, the judge acts as the fact finder at the trial and determines whether the government agency has proven their case.

Additionally, in certain cases, the trial will be bifurcated or have two parts. Generally, the first part of the case is a trial on the merits of the allegations in the petition and the second part of the case determines what orders the court will enforce. In cases such as Ms. Jones's Family Court matter, the first trial would be a fact-finding process to determine whether the government agency can prove the allegations of neglect in the petition. The second hearing would be the disposition, when the Family Court is authorized to enter an order determining where the child resides and what services Ms. Jones is ordered to complete.

It is important to remember that in civil cases, unlike criminal cases, the individual cannot be incarcerated because of their alleged or proven violation of the law. The Civil Court, however, does have extensive powers to impose fines, penalties, and orders for clients to engage in mandated services. If a client fails to follow or is alleged to be in noncompliance with a court order, the court can hold them in contempt for violating a court order. While a final order of the court can only be made after there has been a decision on the petition, the court does have broad powers to enter temporary or interim orders that it believes are necessary.

Civil Court as a Forum for Practice: When an Individual Is the Initiating Actor

A civil case may also be brought by one party—an individual, group, or corporation—against another party for a violation of the law. In these matters, the outcome could be an order of the court prohibiting or allowing a party to do something or a monetary award of damages for illegal actions. Civil cases that are not filed by the government include the following: custody and visitation cases, housing cases between a tenant and a private landlord, family offense cases where one relative or partner seeks an order of protection against another relative, and small claims matters. Guardianship (over persons), conservatorship (over finances), child support, consumer protection, product liability, credit card fraud/debt, bankruptcy, mortgage and debt actions, and civil rights actions are all examples of civil cases brought by individuals, groups, or an organization. As an individual or group, you can also sue a government party including the state, city, or a government agency. The range of civil cases is extremely broad and encompasses many substantive areas of the law. However, the general path of a case is similar regardless of the specific nature of the civil action.

As with the civil cases filed by the government, the legal case is initiated when a petition is filed alleging that another party violated the law and the petitioner is seeking relief from the court. For example, the father of Ms. Jones's son could seek physical custody of Matthew by suing Ms. Jones in civil court alleging that she is not caring properly for their son. In his petition for custody, he would request that the court make an order granting custody to him based on all the reasons why he believes it would be in Matthew's best interest for his father to have physical and legal custody. Likewise, an employee could sue their employer in federal court if they believed that they were discriminated against because of their gender or disability. The employee would file a discrimination suit against the employer listing the basis for the allegations and making a request for relief, potentially money damages.

Once the petition is filed, the opposing party has the opportunity to file a formal response in court responding to the allegations in the petition and potentially raising additional allegations against the petitioner. The case will generally proceed with a discovery period during which both sides are able to gather evidence through various mechanisms prescribed by the law. That process generally leads to settlement discussions, based on an attorney's review of the evidence in the case and the strength of their relative positions. If no settlement is reached, a trial is conducted, and a prevailing party is determined based on the standard set forth in the specific law governing the case. For example, Matthew's father could allege that Ms. Jones's substance abuse impacts her ability to provide for their son's care and Ms. Jones could potentially respond that she is in a drug treatment program and her son's physical and emotional health have not been impacted by the substance abuse program.

In future chapters, we will discuss these kinds of cases and the implications for social work practice in much greater detail. However, there are countless social work functions that are applicable in both civil court contexts including child custody evaluations, adoption assessments, visitation risk assessments, grandparent visitation evaluations, mediation of parental conflicts about children, therapeutic supervised visitation, personal injury evaluations, assessment of emotional factors in sexual harassment and discrimination cases, worker's compensation evaluations, and civil competency evaluations. The range of opportunities for social workers to engage with the legal system on behalf of individuals or groups is significant.

Administrative Proceedings as a Forum for Practice

Administrative proceedings are brought by government agencies under the specific regulations and laws for that agency. An individual can also instigate administrative proceedings against a government agency. The process during which agency and government decisions are reviewed or contested is called the impartial hearing process or a fair hearing. While the decision-making process can and most likely will vary from agency to agency and state to state, there are basic tenets of administrative law that will help you navigate these agency systems on behalf of your client. As we discussed earlier, there are multiple occasions where clients will interact with state and federal agencies and may need to assert their rights in reference to the agency's decision-making.

Individuals apply for benefits from government agencies such as public housing, immigration status, disability benefits, or special education services. The right to a judicial review or fair hearing is generally triggered when an individual wishes to challenge the action or inaction of an agency. This action or inaction could include being wholly denied a benefit or being provided with only partial benefits. For example, Ms. Jones would be able to request a fair hearing to review the welfare agency's decision to provide her with emergency food stamps, but to deny her cash assistance. Generally, the client must request the fair hearing within a certain amount of time after they receive notice of the agency's decision. If you do not formally request the fair hearing within the prescribed time limit, you may lose your right to challenge the agency's decision.

The administrative hearings are presided over by hearing officers or judges who are able to make interim orders before the case goes to a fair hearing. These interim orders can include benefits continuing until the decision. Prior to a fair hearing, the agency generally has a responsibility to provide your client with documents related to their hearing, and your client should engage in their own evidence gathering.

If a case does not settle before the fair hearing, then the agency produces evidence of why its action was legal and your client produces evidence of why the action was not legal under the regulation or law at the hearing. As always, evidence can be testimony from a live witness or records. The hearing officer determines whether the agency followed regulations and the law. In some instances, states allow individuals and agencies to appeal to a civil court if they do not agree with the decision made by the hearing officer. Social workers can assist clients in identifying and obtaining evidence that will be persuasive in the fair hearing and might even be in a position to testify on behalf of a client depending on the subject of the fair hearing.

While the administrative forums vary from state to state and even from agency to agency, it is important for social workers to understand the process of requesting and preserving a client's right to hearing. It is also critical to know what notice is required for clients so that you can advise as to the clients' rights and responsibilities if they were or were not provided with notice. Additionally, administrative hearings are one of the few areas where social workers, as nonlegal advocates, are allowed to represent clients in hearings. As you will learn in Chapter 8, this can be an especially powerful tool for social workers in advocating for clients and ensuring that client goals are met.

Alternative Venues as a Forum for Practice

As you learned in Chapter 2, the preventive law and therapeutic jurisprudence movements have been critical in reforming the adversarial aspects of the judicial system when cases involve substance abuse, mental illness, and domestic violence. However, before an alternative venue can be considered, a case must be filed in civil or Criminal Court to begin the formal court process. Depending on the allegations in the petition or the complaint, an alternative venue may be available for the parties.

For example, if the criminal complaint alleges drug possession, a defendant may be eligible for drug court. This may be an option that a social worker would discuss with Ms. Jones versus participating in a criminal trial. However, if the complaint includes a physical assault charge or there is a prior history of convictions for drug possession, the defendant may be deemed ineligible for the alternative venue. In most instances, the program conducts its own admission process, which usually requires meeting with program staff and determining whether the eligibility criteria are met. In some alternative venues, certain issues or types of cases such as mental illness may be excluded from participation.

If the alternative venue requires that the client waive their right to a trial and proceed quickly to an admission, then the client will make an admission to the petition or complaint at the beginning of the process. Prior to making this decision, the client should be advised by an attorney of all the possible consequences including, as already discussed, the potential impact on benefit and entitlements. Most alternative venues will have a regular schedule of court appearances that all parties will be required to attend and at which detailed reports will be provided to the court. In a drug treatment court, for example, the client will engage in treatment with an approved outside service provider who will make regular reports to the court on the client's progress. The social worker working with Ms. Jones in the substance abuse treatment program will be an essential part of this process even though the court does not employ the worker. In many instances, the program social worker is testifying at the status updates and making recommendations about the length of the program and type of treatment. Upon successful completion of the program, the court case will end and the client will have fulfilled their obligation to complete the program.

System Intervention as a Form of Legal Practice

Up to this point, the cases we have been discussing generally involve individual clients and litigants. However, the law has a rich history of intervening in systemic injustice through large-scale impact litigation. The most important example of the law's ability to reform systems is the class action case. *Cass action* is defined as a case brought against another party such as a government agency or corporation on behalf of a number of plaintiffs. That group of plaintiffs bring a legal action and allege harm because of the actions or inactions of the government or corporation that are referred to in the case as the respondent.

The first step in filing a class action is to determine the issue and law that is being violated and whether the violation is one that impacts a number of individuals in the same unjust or illegal way. Once the legal issue has been identified, the plaintiffs must be found by identifying who is impacted by the illegal policy or practice and determining whether they are willing to participate in the class action lawsuit. The petition is filed alleging the illegal policy and practice and setting forth the reasons why the lawsuit is a class action on behalf of a number of plaintiffs. Like other civil cases, inclusive laws of discovery or evidence gathering govern class actions. Parties are allowed to subpoena records and documentary evidence. In addition, parties can conduct depositions where sworn testimony is taken from a witness in front of both parties but without a judge present. This part of the case process is integral for determining the relative strengths of the plaintiff's case and the respondent's case. As you might imagine, the information garnered during the discovery phase of a case often informs settlement discussions and decision-making.

A trial is when the petitioner presents all its evidence through records or live witnesses, including the testimony of the named plaintiffs. The respondent has the right to cross-examine the witnesses and present its own evidence and defense to the charges in the petition. At the end of the trial, the court or jury will make a decision, which will impact all of the class plaintiffs who were involved in the litigation.

The Appellate Review Process

The appellate process occurs once a decision has been made at the trial level. For civil cases, the decision could be the final determination of custody or a finding of neglect against a parent. In a criminal case, the decision would be that the defendant is found guilty after a trial. In those instances where the court conducted a trial or a hearing, the parties generally have the right to appeal the decision to a different court. In many cases, the appellate court will review the trial court's decision and determine that there were legal errors made during the process of the trial or in the ultimate decision.

After the court has issued an order or decision, a party can file an appeal to have an appellate court review that decision. In some cases, a party has a right to appeal the decision. However, some cases require permission from the Appellate Court to appeal the decision or order. Additionally, most states have laws that govern how long a party has to file an appeal once a trial court has made a final decision. The party appealing the order cannot present new evidence in the appeal and has to rely on the record established in front of the trial judge. The record consists of everything that the attorneys, parties, witnesses, and judge said throughout the trial. Once the party seeking review of the trial court has filed their papers, the opposition has the opportunity to file response papers detailing why the trial court did not err or why the matter should not be overturned. In some instances, the Appellate Court will hear oral arguments on the case in addition to reviewing the written papers. During the oral arguments, a panel of judges, generally anywhere from three to five or up to nine judges, will question the attorneys about the legal arguments and merits of the appeal.

The Appellate Court decides the case and issues a written decision. If all the judges agree, then the decision is unanimous. If there are judges who do not agree, then they can write a concurring opinion or a dissenting opinion. The only opinion that matters for the parties is the majority opinion, which can agree with the trial court, overturn the trial court's decision, or send the case back to the trial court for a new trial.

Legislative Advocacy and the Path of a Law

While class actions are one example where the law can be changed for many individuals, legislative testimony is another opportunity to influence and reform the law. Social workers have historically played an important role in influencing important social welfare legislation by providing legislative testimony and lobbying legislators on behalf of their clients. Whether a social worker prepares an issue statement that is provided to legislators working on a subcommittee or testifies in front of the legislature on why a specific bill is critical, social workers can play an important role in bringing critical social justice and social welfare issues to the forefront of the legislative debate. As an example, a social worker who has experience working with mothers in substance abuse treatment programs such as Ms. Jones would be able to provide testimony to legislators at the local, state, and federal levels about research on harm reduction and infant attachment in support of a bill encouraging infants to remain in their mother's care during the course of treatment.

AFFILIATED LEGAL INSTITUTIONS

There are several institutions that are affiliated with the judicial and court systems. The state and federal governments legally sanction these agencies in order to provide services throughout the judicial process. In some states where there is privatization, the state will contract out some of these services to private corporations. Some agencies, like probation and child protection, provide services throughout all phases of the court process such as investigation and disposition. Other agencies are primarily focused on carrying out and monitoring sentences, dispositions, and court orders such as state departments of corrections. Any social worker, no matter what their practice context or the population they serve, will have occasion to interact with one or more of these institutions during their career as a professional social worker.

Child and Adult Protective Services

Child and Adult Protective Services are generally part of state agencies that provide human services for children and families and that are responsible for overseeing and setting policies and regulations for the reporting, investigation, referral, service provision including foster care services, and monitoring of cases of abuse and neglect for children and vulnerable adults such as the elderly and the developmentally disabled. It is important to note that while Child and Adult Protective Services aim to protect those most vulnerable, social workers must be aware of discrepancies in reporting, including overreporting of certain communities, racial and economic disparities within the reporting, and regulatory processes that significantly impact families who are most vulnerable.

Juvenile Justice Services

Juvenile justice services are also usually part of state agencies providing human services for children and families. Juvenile justice agencies provide a range of services throughout the intervention, supervision, and rehabilitation phases of client interaction within the juvenile justice system. Juvenile justice services can be secure or nonsecure detention facilities and programs, home detention monitoring, observation and assessment, secure residential and correctional facilities, work camps, diversion services, community programs, educational programs, and case management. Despite its aim to rehabilitate children, the juvenile justice system has been shown to also cause significant harm with many facilities across the country cited for a lack of oversight, with children experiencing neglect and abusive practices (Mendel, 2015). It is important for the social worker as an advocate to seek out alternatives for children that are evidence based, and other community-based alternatives that support their physical and emotional well-being.

Forensic and State Psychiatric Hospitals

Forensic hospitals serve those individuals who have been committed by civil or criminal court for treatment, often on an involuntary basis. Most of the time, but not always, the hospitals are part of state offices of mental health. Increasingly, public and private hospitals offer forensic services on an outpatient basis. Criminal Court services may include treatment on the basis of referral for incompetence to stand trial, not guilty by reason of insanity, competent to stand trial but needs treatment while the trial is happening, and temporary commitment from community-based mental health treatment facilities pending a rehearing on commitment. Forensic hospitals also provide postsentencing services such as transfer from prisons for mental health reasons, inpatient treatment for an individual as a condition of parole, and services for a mentally disordered parolee returned from community care.

Civil Court commitments can include temporary conservatorship over an individual's finances, permanent conservatorship based on a grave disability, time-limited involuntary commitment based on dangerousness, and postparole extension of commitment to additional time. These kinds of services, usually provided for by a multidisciplinary team, include assessment and recommendations about competency to stand trial, risk assessment, motivation to engage in treatment, diagnosis and recommendations for dispositional services, and assessment of sex offenders.

Probation Services

Probation departments are responsible for preparing a written report concerning a defendant's background and the circumstances surrounding the offense and supervising defendants sentenced to probation. Probation is a sentence ordered by a judge, usually instead of, but sometimes in addition to, serving time in jail. It allows the convicted person to live in the community for a specified period of time, sometimes under the supervision of a probation officer. Its services to the community include recommending sanctions to the court, enforcing court orders, incarcerating delinquents, assisting victims, and providing corrective assistance to individuals in conflict with the law. The equivalent of about one in every 45 adults was under community supervision at midyear 2009.

Among offenders supervised in the community, probationers (4,270,917) represented the majority (84%) of this population (Glaze, 2010). By the end of 2021, it was reported that over 3.74 million adults were under community supervision representing one adult for every 69 resident, which was the lowest rate in over three decades (Kaeble, 2024).

The probation department usually supports both adult and juvenile courts. In 2009, there were 2.11 million arrests of persons under the age of 18. Of those adjudicated, or found to have committed the crime, 34% of delinquents were placed on formal probation (Livsey, 2009). Probation can be used by juvenile justice agencies to achieve different purposes and during different decision points throughout the life of a case. Probation can serve as a "sentence" once adjudicated or as a way to divert a youngster out of the court system. Sometimes it can be used as a monitoring device and a preventive measure. Unlike the adult system where there are clear limits, the term of probation may be for a specified period of time or are open-ended. Review hearings are held to monitor the juvenile's progress and to hear reports from probation staff. Social workers in community-based programs working with juveniles may be asked by a probation officer to prepare a report for these hearings. A juvenile's case can be closed if they are successful at meeting all the conditions of their probation.

Jails

A jail is used by local jurisdictions such as counties and cities to confine people for short periods of time. There are approximately 3,600 jails in the United States. As of midyear 2009, 767,620 inmates were held in custody of county and city jail authorities (Minton, 2010). Jails are most often run by sheriffs and/or local governments and are designed to hold individuals awaiting trial or serving short sentences. Typically they are intended to hold persons for less than 1 year. Jails are typically located within the county where the individual was arrested. A person who is being held in custody before a trial will be held at a local jail. Jails are also a place for people who have been convicted of relatively minor crimes.

Juvenile Detention and Residential Centers

A youth detention center, also known as a juvenile detention center, is a secure residential facility for young people awaiting court hearings or placement in long-term care facilities and programs. In 2007, there were 81,000 juveniles in all types of residential centers: secure and nonsecure, public or private, long- or short-term (Sickmund, 2010). In October 2021, the Office of Juvenile Justice and Delinquency Prevention reported 24,894 youth in residential placements. In comparison, there has been a significant decline in the number of juveniles, age 17 or younger, housed in adult jails and prisons from a high of over 10,000 in 2008 to a low of over 2,000 in 2021 (Zeng et al., 2023).

Prisons

A prison, or penitentiary, is used to house individuals who have been convicted of a crime for periods of much longer duration than those held in jails.

State governments and the Federal Bureau of Prisons (FBOP) operate prisons. Defendants who are convicted of state crimes will serve their time in a state prison; those convicted of a federal crime will serve their sentence in a federal prison. A state or federal prison could be very far away from a convicted person's home and family. There are only about 100 federal prisons, detention centers, and correctional institutions in the United States. In 2024, there were over 158,000 individuals incarcerated in federal prisons and 130 federal prisons across the country.

Parole

With many crimes, sentencing has a maximum limit to how long someone may remain in prison or jail. Sometimes when clients demonstrate "good behavior" that sentence length can be shortened and the rest of the time can be served on parole as long as there is no serious opposition to an early release. The decision to grant parole is the responsibility, in a majority of states, of a board of parole or commission. The parole board has the power not only to decide about parole but to impose limits or restrictions while someone is on parole. If someone does not comply or breaks one of the conditions they can be found "in violation" of their parole and have to return to prison. In midyear 2009, there were 828,169 adult men and women on parole (Glaze, 2010). Research has found that the number of individuals on parole and probation continues to decline with one in 69 adults on probation or parole at the end of 2021 (Pew Charitable Trust, 2024).

Juvenile aftercare is similar to adult parole. Following release from a secure or nonsecure juvenile detention institution, the juvenile is often ordered to a period of aftercare or parole. During this period, the juvenile is under supervision of the court or the juvenile corrections department. If the juvenile does not follow the conditions of aftercare, they may be recommitted to the same facility or to another facility. Conditions can include requirements for attending programming and school and would be important to understand for any social workers partnering with clients coming out of juvenile detention.

THE EXPLICIT LEGAL CONTEXT OF FORENSIC SOCIAL WORK

Social work practice where the legal issues and laws, regulations, statutes, processes, and procedures are usually explicit is called forensic social work. As reported in Maschi et al. (2009), there are many definitions of forensic social work ranging from the very specific (i.e., the intersection of mental health and the law), to the general (i.e., the interface between the human services and legal systems). A broader definition includes social work practice that is in any way related to legal issues and litigation, both criminal and civil. Child custody issues involving separation, divorce, neglect, termination of parental rights, the implications of child and spouse abuse, juvenile and adult justice services, corrections, and mandated treatment all fall under this definition.

For the purposes of this book, forensic social work is defined as a specialized social work practice that occurs in explicitly legal and criminal justice contexts such as courts, prisons, jails, forensic hospitals, probation and parole offices, and juvenile justice settings. We make this distinction because of our belief that the application of social work knowledge and skills to questions and issues relating to law and legal systems, including administrative venues, should be an integral part of everyday social work practice and so we recognize forensic social work as a specialized practice.

The National Organization of Forensic Social Workers (NOFSW) is a professional organization representing forensic social workers. In order to be a member, you must have requisite education, training, and experience in forensic social work. The organization has also promulgated an ethical code specifically addressing forensic social work practice including ethics for forensic social workers with regard to lawyer consultations, transdisciplinary practice, confidentiality, and privilege (NOFSW, 2020). The values of the organization that shape the practice are clearly stated as "uphold[ing] the dignity and worth of every person involved with legal systems throughout the world" (NOFSW, 2020, p. 2). Part of the Code calls for the forensic social work practitioner to conduct pro bono work on behalf of indigent clients. The Code covers ethical responsibilities to clients, colleagues, employers, and society within a forensic or explicit legal context. Information about the journal, conferences, and specialized training for forensic social workers is also available on their website (http://nofsw.org).

There are a number of roles social workers play in the explicit legal context, both in courts as well as in affiliated institutions. In subsequent chapters you will learn more specifically what these roles entail and the beginning knowledge and skills to carry out the tasks and responsibilities for each. The following list suggests some of the many exciting possibilities open to our profession in the explicit legal context of social work practice:

- social worker in a police department
- social worker in a public defender's office
- social worker in a prosecutor's office
- social worker as forensic expert
- social worker in a victim services agency
- social worker in a forensic hospital
- social worker as probation or parole officer
- social worker as correctional treatment specialist
- social worker as mitigation specialist
- social worker in a reentry program

Thus far, we have suggested that proactive, legally informed social work practice requires an ability to access the law on the federal, state, and local levels. We have also at times referred to court cases as a source of law. We have also identified evidence-informed social work practice as an essential element in both the implicit and explicit forums of practice. The following chapter introduces you to the basic skills needed to conduct both legal and social science research to further your advocacy in any of the roles listed and others to be referenced in later chapters.

REFERENCES

Gideon v. Wainwright, 372 U.S. 365 (1963).

Glaze, L. E. (2010). *Bureau of Justice Statistics Bulletin, correctional populations in the United States, 2009 (NCJ 231681).* U.S. Department of Justice. Retrieved from: Bureau of Justice Statistics website, http://bjs.ojp.usdoj.gov/content/pub/pdf/cpus09.pdf

Goldberg v. Kelly, 397 U.S. 254 (1970).

Gustafson, K. (2009). The criminalization of poverty. *The Journal of Criminal Law and Criminology, 99*(3), 643–716. https://papers.ssrn.com/sol3/papers.cfm?abstract_id=1401107

Hasenfeld, Y., Ghose, T. J., & Larson, K. (2004). The logic of sanctioning welfare recipients: An empirical assessment. *Social Service Review, 78*(2), 304–319. https://doi.org/10.1086/382771

Kaeble, D. (2024). *Annual probation survey and annual parole survey.* Bureau of Justice Statistics. https://bjs.ojp.gov/data-collection/annual-probation-survey-and-annual-parole-survey

Lens, V. (2005). Advocacy and argumentation in the public arena: A guide for social workers. *Social Work, 50*(3), 231–238. https://doi.org/10.1093/sw/50.3.231

Livsey, S. (June, 2009). Juvenile delinquency probation caseload, 2005. *OJJDP Fact Sheet* (NCJ224536). Washington DC: U.S Department of Justice, Bureau of Justice Programs, Office of Juvenile Justice and Delinquency Prevention. https://www.ojp.gov/pdffiles1/ojjdp/224536.pdf

Maschi, T., Bradley, C., & Ward, K. (Eds.). (2009). *Forensic social work: Psychosocial and legal issues in diverse practice settings.* Springer Publishing Company.

Mendel, R. (2015). *Maltreatment of youth in U.S. juvenile corrections facilities: An update.* Annie E Casey Foundation. https://assets.aecf.org/m/resourcedoc/aecf-maltreatmentyouthus
corrections-2015.pdf

Minton, T. D. (2010, March). *Jail inmates at midyear 2009; statistical tables (NCJ 230122).* U.S. Department of Justice. Office of Justice Programs. Bureau of Justice Statistics. Retrieved from: Bureau of Justice Statistics website, http://bjs.ojp.usdoj.gov/content/pub/pdf/jim09st.pdf

Miranda v. Arizona, 384 U.S. 436 (1966).

National Organization of Forensic Social Workers. (2020). *Specialty guidelines for values and ethics.* https://www.nofsw.org/_files/ugd/f468b9_20e60b0830ed4a51808154902b7e9f20.pdf

Pew Charitable Trust. (2024). *Number of U.S. adults on probation or parole continues to decline.* https://www.pew.org/en/research-and-analysis/articles/2023/12/14/number-of-us-adults-on-probation-or-parole-continues-to-decline

Raz, M. (2020). *Abusive policies: How the American child welfare system lost its way.* University of North Carolina Press.

Sickmund, M. (2010). *Juveniles in residential placements 1997–2008. OJJDP fact sheet (NCJ 229397).* U.S. Department of Justice, Office of Justice Programs, Office of Juvenile Justice and Delinquency Prevention. Retrieved from: National Criminal Justice Reference Center, http://www.ncjrs.gov/pdffiles1/ojjdp/229379.pdf

Zeng, Z., Carson, A., & Kluckow, R. (2023). *Juveniles incarcerated in U.S. adult jails and prisons 2002–2021.* https://bjs.ojp.gov/document/jiusajp0221.pdf

CHAPTER 5

Social Work Functions, Knowledge, and Skills in the Legal Context

INTRODUCTION

This chapter identifies some of the tasks and functions social workers may be called upon to perform in both the implicit and explicit legal context. In this chapter you are introduced to the concepts of ecological assessment and holistic lawyering as complementary frameworks with which to approach evidence-informed practice when working within implicit and explicit legal contexts. You will learn how to identify and access relevant law and social science and apply them to your practice. You will also learn how to develop answerable questions to research as well as ways to assess your decision-making process for bias and errors. Additionally, this chapter focuses on how to share your professional knowledge with other professionals and how to identify intersections between the law and social work to support collaborative practice. Using case examples, this chapter presents an initial interprofessional, collaborative analysis of how to begin to think about a client's legal issues.

FUNCTIONS OF SOCIAL WORKERS WITHIN THE LEGAL CONTEXT

This section presents an overview of some of the functions of social workers when they are interacting with the legal context and working with legal professionals such as judges and attorneys. The use of evidence-informed practice and the theoretical lens of person-in-environment provides the framework that informs how you will perform these functions in the implicit and explicit legal context. You will learn in future chapters much more about the specifics of these functions in different venues such as civil, criminal, and administrative proceedings. For this chapter, however, we want to focus on how you begin to define your role and your practice when there is a legal context, which we believe exists in almost all instances whether you are working with an individual client, family, community, or organization.

One of the first questions about role will be the degree of direct client contact when a social worker is working with an attorney or in a legal setting. As you learned in the preceding chapter, there can be very strategic reasons why attorneys and social workers may want to limit the amount and type of contact that social workers have with the client. This situation may occur more frequently in multiservice agencies and while working as a private consultant with an attorney.

Many of the skills that social workers already have—such as summarizing research, giving and receiving information, engaging, educating, mediating, advocating, assessing, problem-solving, referring, monitoring, and evaluating—will be critical in the effective performance of the following functions. What social workers may not know is how to apply this social work knowledge and skills specifically to an explicit legal context. As you will see, many of the functions a social worker will be called upon to perform in a legal context are familiar activities. By knowing about the implicit and explicit legal contexts you will be able to adapt and target the knowledge and skills you already have and use them more effectively and strategically when your client has a legal issue or is involved in a legal system. Using evidence-based practice (EBP), critical thinking skills, and legally informed assessment will prepare you to be articulate, credible, and persuasive when communicating the results of your work to legal professionals.

Functions That Do Not Involve Contact With Clients

Sometimes the social work profession diminishes work that does not involve direct client contact. However, there are many important functions social workers can provide with minimal client contact that are equally as valuable to a client and result in a positive legal outcome as is providing these services directly to a client. In addition, these indirect functions are the ways that the profession of social work can exert an influence on the shaping, development, and reform of legal policies, programs, and procedures. Some examples of social work functions with minimal to no client contact include the following:

- finding resources and navigating systems
- providing education and information on social work or mental health and social justice issues
- conducting informal assessments such as being asked to conduct case record reviews
- participating in social science research, review, and interpretation
- providing consultation, education, or training to criminal justice, juvenile justice, child welfare system personnel, correctional system personnel, legislators, law enforcement personnel, attorneys, law students, and members of the public
- developing and reshaping policy, advocacy, activism, organizing, and program development

Functions Involving More Direct Contact With Clients

There will be times when the social work function involves more direct contact with clients. It is important that you identify your ethical and legal responsibilities regarding confidentiality and reporting requirements when you are working directly with a client. With direct client contact, you want to be clear about the role that you are playing and the importance of distinguishing between when you are in an advocacy role and when you are in an impartial role. Functions that involve direct client contact include the following:

- conducting initial screening of clients for social service needs
- interviewing clients jointly with attorneys or alone as part of a case
- preparing preliminary assessments and work plans for services and support

- assessing for rights or procedural violations and discriminatory practices in collaboration with an attorney
- providing clinical and treatment assessments, including conducting appropriate diagnoses, and/or developing treatment plans as needed according to a client's holistic needs
- assessing clinical needs, including referring clients for mental health or physical health services, and/or other services based on need and underlying conditions, and advocating for criminal and juvenile justice populations
- diagnosing or making recommendations about mental status, children's best interests, unique or critical needs, including capability or inability to testify
- advocating for parents and children impacted by the child welfare system
- assessing, planning, and engaging in advocacy for appropriate services resulting from an evidence-informed assessment and determining a culturally coherent case plan tailored to the specific client need and that addresses the legal issues in question
- managing the client's case;
- creating, implementing, and evaluating service plans on a long- term and short-term basis
- educating and counseling the client
- managing case recording and file management
- preparing the client to testify before any kind of hearing and preparing the client for court
- educating, counseling, and collaborating with client family members and other stakeholders to achieve the client's goals
- intervening when there might be short-term crises
- using, when possible, negotiation and settlement when it may be a potential route to obtaining a client's needs or wishes

Functions During Case Investigation and Trial Preparation

Another very specific function of the social worker is to assist the lawyer in carrying out an independent and thorough investigation that will help the client and the attorney to prepare an effective and evidence-based case in court. This includes but is not limited to the following social work functions:

- interviewing all involved professionals and relevant family members;
- obtaining and evaluating case records;
- identifying the need for professional reports from others, identifying potential experts for those reports, and evaluating professional reports pursuant to expert practice guidelines for the specific profession;
- identifying, interviewing, and preparing other witnesses;
- identifying and preparing an expert witness;
- testifying as an expert; and
- assessing for rights violations and discriminatory practices in addition to other legal and social service needs that may have an impact on the client's goals or ability to participate fully in the case.

The following sections of this chapter introduce you to a theoretical framework that can provide initial guidance on how to proceed when you are carrying out the social work functions already described. You will also learn about the importance of developing critical thinking skills and becoming an evidence-based practitioner to carry out these functions credibly and professionally.

A THEORETICAL APPROACH TO COLLABORATIVE, EVIDENCE-INFORMED PRACTICE CONSISTENT WITH CURRENT LAW REFORM EFFORTS

The approach to practice advocated in this book begins with the idea that many problems faced by families and children are complex, occur within the micro- and macrolevels and within the legal and regulatory systems, and need to be addressed on multiple levels by a number of different professions. Without an accurate and comprehensive assessment of the social and interpersonal problems faced by individuals when they are interacting with the implicit or explicit legal contexts, it is unlikely that the problem, if viewed only as legal, will be solved or prevented from recurring.

Conversely many client problems that come to you as a social work issue may be resolved more effectively and efficiently through legal processes and the legal remedies that a person may be entitled to. Because of the obstacles identified in Chapter 1, social workers many times fail to consider the impact, both positive and negative, of the legal environment on the individual client or family, or even on themselves as a social worker. Social workers need to remember that as a profession, our most defining characteristic has been our focus on the person-in-environment. In social work history, a focus on the legal environment has been identified as a powerful tool that can assist us to achieve justice, or, in the absence of a critical analysis of laws and legal institutions, can be experienced as harmful and discriminatory by the populations we serve.

This comprehensive approach to social work practice stems from ecological theory and views individuals as being involved in continuous transactions with their environments. Both the person and the environment are modified during this process. This theoretical approach is concerned with growth as well as the potential for growth and development, and with the properties of the environment that support or fail to support the individual. In this view, social workers need to develop a set of environmental interventions and a set of interventions targeted to the transaction between the individual and their environment. This view is compatible with many of the concepts identified in a rights-based approach to programming for social workers (Ife, 2008). Rights-based programming identifies the government institutions, the individuals and public and private sector organizations, such as those responsible to make sure that individual rights are realized and enacted are viewed in transaction with those who bear the rights. The responsible parties have a duty to create the conditions that advance the ability of those individuals having rights to fulfill them, including supporting people when they are trying to achieve their rights. Those individuals with rights are expected to demand them. In this view, social workers are considered to have a duty to always have a rights-based approach to their practice and to use courts to achieve justice and equality (Lynch & Mitchell, 1995).

In a very practical example, Duncan et al. (2003) use an ecological approach to teach social workers about the wider legal frameworks that affect all aspects of the social and individual worlds of children. They suggest it as a way to think about how to use and critique the law to help social workers expand the options for services to children and address issues of discrimination and exclusion.

The ecological perspective informed many of the legal reform theories that you read about in Chapter 2, such as therapeutic jurisprudence and preventive law, and was the underlying theory for the early social workers you learned about in that chapter. However, some commentators suggest that sometimes a focus on more therapeutic processes may dilute some of the legal rights and protections that a client may have (National Drug Court Institute, 2003). As those responsible for making sure the rights of clients are protected, social workers must be the professionals who ensure that any specialized or therapeutic processes do not compromise the legal rights of their clients. The legal and ethical issues associated with specialized treatment courts will be elaborated in Chapter 11.

The theory of holistic lawyering provides an excellent corollary for the ecological perspective not only in the explicit legal context, but also for interdisciplinary work in the implicit legal context. Holistic lawyering refers to the theory of legal practice where interdisciplinary work and community presence are paramount to the lawyer's representation of a client as a whole, instead of as a single legal case or issue. As one of the founders of holistic lawyering Robin Steinberg noted, "Working compassionately with indigent clients means seeing firsthand that the problems and challenges they face stretch farther than the confines of the criminal cases before them" (2006, p. 626). Therefore, the legal practice switches from a limited focus on the particular legal case at hand to a holistic approach to the issues and challenges that brought the client into contact with the legal system in the first place.

Under this view, an interdisciplinary, holistic practice between social workers and attorneys is essential to ensuring that clients receive client-centered practice addressing their legal and social service needs in tandem. The model, originated by public defenders such as The Bronx Defenders in New York, has grown to include assessing and addressing the host of collateral consequences from a Criminal Court or legal case in housing, immigration, child welfare, and public benefits. The model focuses on collaborative, interprofessional work between lawyers experienced in civil and criminal cases and social workers. The application of holistic lawyering is best described by the Center for Holistic Defense, recently created by The Bronx Defenders (www.bronxdefenders.org/holistic-defense/center-for-holistic-defense/).

In both the ecological and holistic view, the common perspective is that client problems are frequently interconnected and nested together in such a way that focusing on a single issue will not result in effective or lasting solutions. Problems stem from interactions at the societal, community, family, and individual levels. As was previously identified in *The Case of Michelle Jones*, Ms. Jones's ability to engage in her substance abuse treatment program is directly impacted by her legal proceedings in both the Criminal Court and Family Court, in addition to her ongoing ability to be enrolled in the program that is tied to the legal status of her public benefits. To assess Ms. Jones's problems, a skilled social worker must be able to identify the issues that Ms. Jones is confronting on both a legal and social service level, and the different legal forums and systems implicated by those issues. A social worker will not only take responsibility for assessing whether Ms. Jones is informed of all her rights but will also provide the conditions of support, such as access to information or an attorney that would allow her to actually realize and demand her rights. A rights-based social worker will also be knowledgeable about the role that oppression may play in the client's problem and the mechanisms in the law that promote or mitigate disparity in decision-making processes and outcomes.

When individual cases are worked on, the perspectives implicated by the ecological and holistic view will assist you to identify and build upon the interconnectedness of issues that face your clients. It is also important in social work to analyze a variety of theories and practices, specifically because your work across disciplines and fields may overlap with the legal systems in a variety of ways. While ecological and holistic theories are key to focusing on the strengths of the individual, other critical theories, such as Structural Social Work Theory, assess ways in which societal structures inflict harm and oppression on individuals and groups often already most marginalized. This theory underscores the need for social workers to empower communities and to collaborate on developing solutions that address structural oppression (Carrillo & Grady, 2018). More recent theories, such as Anti-Oppressive Theory, challenge social workers to take a view from a variety of methods grounded in anti-oppressive social work practice, social justice, activism, and organizing (Baines & Kia, 2022). Both methods focus on moving away from methods in social work that pathologize individuals on the basis of their responses to their oppression. Instead, they identify opportunities for collective healing within communities, provide empowerment, and push for critical solutions that address systemic and structural and institutional change.

THE IMPORTANCE OF USING EVIDENCE-INFORMED PRACTICE AND CRITICAL THINKING IN LEGAL SITUATIONS

In the authors' experience, one of the most challenging situations for social workers interacting with lawyers or the legal system is the way that knowledge and professional decision-making is made "public" or transparent and is critiqued and challenged. Social workers are not often called upon publicly to justify or support their professional decision-making during regular social work practice. When challenged it is usually within the private context of supervision or a client meeting. Sometimes social workers perceive challenges to their decision-making in court or by attorneys as "disrespect" or not being given professional status by others. Social workers may not see themselves in the position of challenging the actions of legal professionals, even when there have been reports by other lawyers that indicate substandard practice with vulnerable clients (American Bar Association, 2009; National Right to Counsel Committee, 2009). Both attorneys and social workers should hold each other accountable for a practice that rises to the level of what clients are legally and ethically entitled to expect.

In a legal situation you will always be asked what you have relied on to come to your professional assessments and you must be able to explain how your work relates to the legal question at hand. It is not enough to say that the client is "depressed." You will be asked how you know that, what specific behaviors indicate that your assessment is accurate, and what criteria you used to come to your judgment. If you relied on a report by a psychiatrist to support your conclusion, you will be asked if you evaluated the report for adherence to well-accepted professional standards and guidelines. If this is in the context of a custody evaluation, you will be asked how depression is relevant to parenting capacity.

The important thing to understand in this instance is that this type of questioning is not personal nor about you as a social worker. Lawyers are systematically trained during their education to critique knowledge claims and to focus on facts and evidence. One way to be prepared for this kind of situation is to become an evidence-informed and self-critiquing practitioner. This is consistent with a larger trend in our profession toward increasing advocacy for and use of evidence-based assessment and practice in social work generally, not just in legal settings.

In social work, most agree that evidence-informed or EBP is the process of creating an answerable question based on a client or organizational need, locating the best available evidence to answer the question, evaluating the quality of the evidence as well as its applicability, applying the evidence, and evaluating the effectiveness and efficiency of the solution (Gibbs & Gambrill, 2002; Thyer, 2004).

EBP is a process in which the practitioner combines well-researched interventions and studies on the reliability and validity of assessment measures with clinical experience, ethics, client preferences, and culture to guide and inform the delivery of treatments and services. An important component of EBP is to continuously evaluate one's performance and effectiveness in carrying out the process of identifying and implementing the intervention. Currently, an important focus for scholars in the field of forensic social work is to develop knowledge and skills for evidence-based assessment and EBP in forensic settings. It is predicted that the future of forensic social work will be grounded in EBP (Springer & Roberts, 2007).

Increasingly, the term EBP is entering into the discourse of the implicit and explicit legal contexts. For example, in the case of *Malenchik v. State of Indiana* (2010), the Indiana Supreme Court supported the use of EBP in sentencing decisions. Indiana's highest court noted that "evidence-based assessment instruments can be significant sources of valuable information for judicial consideration in deciding whether to suspend all or part of a sentence, how to design a probation program for the offender, whether to assign an offender to alternative treatment facilities or programs, and other such corollary sentencing matters." In federal legislation that seeks to achieve equality and educational justice for all children such as the No Child Left Behind Act (2001) and Individuals with Disabilities Education Act (IDEA; 1990), evidence-based methods of education are required, including for school social work practice. EBP is also increasingly being used in juvenile justice, probation, and corrections and in shaping regulations, policies, and administrative procedures (Scott & Steinberg, 2008; Serin, 2003; Woodward, 2009).

It is important for legally informed and rights-based social workers to include another level of analysis in the decision about choosing evidence-informed interventions and treatments: the idea that many program practices are driven by laws and when practices become driven by research, they must be consistent with underlying legal principles and laws (VanNostrand, 2007). In an example of applying EBP to the field of pretrial services, VanNostrand (2007) uses the term Legal and Evidence-based Practices (LEBP) to refer to evidence-based pretrial practice that is consistent with legal principles such as the presumption of innocence. Under this analysis, a social worker would not refer a client to an evidence-based intervention that required an admission of guilt or responsibility, even if the intervention addressed a client problem and was found to have good outcomes. Rather, social workers would either adapt or advocate for adaptation and study of the EBP in such a way that it would not compromise the legal rights of the client. This approach may also address concerns of some social workers about the widespread acceptance of EBP by the social work profession. For the purposes of this book, we propose using VanNostrand's (2007) term LEBP as a conceptual framework to be used beyond pretrial services to conceptualize rights-based practice and EBP. It is important to note that while EBP is a critical method in the field for connecting clients to key EBPs, critiques of EBP include limitations on the number of practices evaluated at one time, the complexity and time-consuming nature of research evaluations, variations in methods, and the exclusion of other critical beneficial practices that have not yet be evaluated and thus are excluded from EBP.

Social workers are required to take two semesters of research and therefore have the knowledge and skills to competently assess and summarize relevant research and EBP for use in legal settings. Social workers also learn research skills to evaluate practice interventions. Social workers in their many roles in criminal and civil proceedings are in an excellent position to disseminate EBP into legal systems. They can do this through submitting reports that are based on, and cite, evidence and research; through testimony as an expert witness; using and describing evidence-based assessment guideline; collaboration with attorneys during the preparation of affidavits, briefs, and written depositions, all of which are legal documents filed before a case goes to trial to advance a particular legal argument or strategy.

Social workers can also advance EBP by developing and evaluating problem-solving courts and alternate dispute resolution formats, not only for outcomes but also for consumer perceptions of fairness and justice. Finally, social workers can collaborate with community-based legal providers to evaluate program models. Through effective collaboration with attorneys, social workers can assess and adapt EBPs to be compliant with legal principles and laws. This will also increase the likelihood that EBPs will be disseminated in explicitly legal forums.

CRITICAL THINKING AND THE IDENTIFICATION OF BIAS IN PROFESSIONAL DECISION-MAKING

The exercise of sound professional judgment and the effective carrying out of many of the previously identified functions require the ability to think critically. One way of developing critical thinking skills is to become knowledgeable about how we think and what conditions can influence our thinking processes when we are developing and making professional decisions. Frequently professional decisions are decontextualized and little or no attention is given to how one comes to a determination and what factors in the environment can effect that determination (Azar & Goff, 2007; Horwath, 2007). There are many institutional pressures that exist for both lawyers and social workers that may impact their decision-making. As examples, in heavily burdened courts, a defense attorney may feel pressured to have their client accept a plea, or in family court, a social worker may pressure a client to accept a service that the client does not agree with in order to appear cooperative to the court. Rarely are these processes acknowledged or addressed, and this results in biased decision-making in both civil and criminal courts (Azar & Goff, 2007; Oldfather, 2007). In a study of how social workers make decisions in child protection contexts, Horwath (2007) found that variables at the personal, professional, organizational, and community level all exerted an influence on decision-making including how the social worker believed other professions viewed their practice.

One recommendation is for professionals to learn how to identify bias in their professional decision-making and attempt to correct errors in thinking (Munro, 2008; Oldfather, 2007). Another recommendation is for social work researchers to use the evidence base on bias and decision-making to study and identify how disproportionate and disparate outcomes in justice systems occur (Wells et al., 2009).

How human beings process information and make meaning of experience is called social information processing. Schemas are mental representations that are stored in our memory and become a filter through which we organize our experiences (Azar & Goff, 2007). Schemas influence what we notice, how we interpret information, and how we shape our response to and evaluation of situations we are presented with during our professional and personal lives. Schemas are formed by experiences with one's own family, interactions with individuals, encounters with institutional settings, professional education and training, and the media (Azar & Goff, 2007). If schemas are not complex enough or are rigid or contain bias, the result can be biased data-gathering processes, a premature end to the decision-making process, or misinterpretation or misperception in response to what you are seeing or being told by others (Azar & Goff, 2007). This can then result in discrimination.

Particularly in environments that are crisis oriented where emotions are high, or in situations where professionals have excessive caseloads and little supports, contextual stress from the environment can narrow cognitive processing and increase the possibility of error (Ferguson, 2010). Researchers have begun to apply these concepts in legal settings as a way of explaining how transactions with the legal system can be differentially experienced and how the intent of statutes is not always carried out in an even-handed way (Azar & Goff, 2007; Oldfather, 2007).

Methods of Challenging Bias in Professional Decision-Making

Interprofessional collaboration and the use of EBP and assessment are two ways that one can check and adjust for the presence of cognitive bias in decision-making during the assessment phase. As was discussed earlier, by evidence-informed practice we mean practice that is based on one's professional knowledge base, not only one's personal experience or moral values, and in this instance conforms to legal principle and laws. For social workers this means knowing how to access, evaluate, and use evidence-based professional knowledge; for lawyers this means always using the law to support your decision-making. By having conversations together, social workers and lawyers can identify and advance the principles of LEBP.

Interprofessional conversations among and between diverse professionals can increase our capacity to perceive information in more complex and flexible ways. Social workers have an important worldview to bring to lawyers, as do lawyers to social workers. Slater (2007), in an evaluation study of an interdisciplinary clinical education curriculum, found that law and social work students report an expanded repertoire of professional skills and world views that they attributed to working and learning with a different profession. Law students report that being exposed to social work students assisted them with seeing the complexity and interrelatedness of client issues, gave them a more complex understanding of client behaviors, and assisted them in being better able to address client emotions. Social work students report that being exposed to law students taught them how to break down problems into steps and prioritize better, to use research to set a foundation for problem-solving, and to be more comfortable challenging the knowledge of others.

There are two important aspects to identifying cognitive bias during interprofessional work. The first is identifying your own cognitive schema that may be operating either about the person or the problem you are addressing, and then identifying the assumptions that are contained in your schema, and seeking out tools, evaluations, and feedback from supervisors and colleagues. The second is to identify and address the presence of assumptions that others may be operating under when it comes to how they are thinking about your client and the problem your client may have. Asking ourselves and others to be clear about what theories and assumptions we are operating under, assessing their validity, and determining whether they are based on scientific or legal knowledge or "gut" instinct can also have secondary gains such as addressing the racial bias that occurs during legal processes and decision-making (Azar & Goff, 2007). Up to this point, we have not identified the race or ethnicity of Michelle Jones but given the facts of the case, where you might live and work, media portrayals of single mothers, and your own positionality, we can all assume we may have preconceived notions and different assumptions about her race.

APPLYING OUR KNOWLEDGE AND SKILLS: PROFESSIONALS INVESTIGATE THEIR ASSUMPTIONS ABOUT MICHELLE JONES

Often, attorneys and social workers assume that they can assess what their client's goals are based on minimal information. It would be important for both the social worker and the lawyer to identify what they think they know about substance use, prenatal substance use, the potential harm to the child, the hospital regulations, and the process for testing mothers and babies, as well as preconceived ideas of how a mother should act in this situation. The professional assumptions for both the attorney and the social worker are also based on their past experiences with similar cases or issues and often the legal history of the client. It is critical for both professionals to identify what aspects of their assessment and analysis are evidence informed and what aspects are assumptions and/or preconceived notions of Ms. Jones based on the facts of her case.

The following section is an example of how professionals can begin to identify cognitive schemas and assumptions that underlie assessments and decisions they may make about clients, their problems, and what to do about them. By identifying what they really do not know, professionals can turn assumptions into research questions. Professionals can then use their knowledge of the law and social science to critically evaluate what they think they know about a client or a client's problem as a way of challenging assumptions and applying critical thinking skills.

Another benefit to this exercise is that other professionals such as judges or child protection workers may also have assumptions about your client based on cognitive schemas that are operating on an unconscious level or stem from a shared institutional culture. Identifying your own assumptions and using research, facts, and evidence to challenge them will also set you up to more effectively challenge the assumptions of others if they emerge as impacting your client and the legal decision-making process. It will, of course, also allow you to see what assumptions and schemas you may have based on professional experience that are valid or not and are most applicable to your case.

We continue with *The Case of Michelle Jones* and read about some of the perceptions and assumptions an attorney and a social worker have identified that they have or may have about their client. Each professional will illustrate the process of turning their assumptions into researchable questions that can then help evaluate the validity of the assumptions they have identified.

Attorney's Perspective

Attorneys may come to the case with varying views depending on their own personal experiences; Ms. Jones's age, race, history of legal trouble; whether they believe they can win the case; if Ms. Jones is a paying client or if she was appointed counsel; and the number of cases similar to Ms. Jones's that an attorney has previously handled. It may be difficult to imagine that Ms. Jones would not want her baby to be back with her and even more difficult to envision that she would refuse to enter a drug treatment program if that is what it would take to have her infant returned to her care. Both these statements are grounded in assumptions and not in understanding of Ms. Jones as a parent and the impact of substances on individuals. With a focus on her legal rights, the attorney might enter the interview with a strong sense of Ms. Jones's right to request an immediate hearing to have her baby returned to her care. However, they would not know whether the client was prepared to testify in court, have her infant at home, or accept the terms and conditions most likely to be set by the court.

Additionally, the attorney may believe that the only program available to treat drug abuse is a residential program, or that such a program would never allow an infant to reside with his mother in the program. An attorney may also believe that drug use is more serious and harmful both to Ms. Jones and her infant. In those moments, it is good practice to gather information on resources that may be available to Ms. Jones and the impact of various resources on parents with substance use by working with experts with more information on the issue. Additionally, it is important to question the underlying assumptions in your own practice that are leading you to a sense of knowing your client's goal.

A critical method to challenge these assumptions is to review research and case law around supporting mothers in situations similar to Ms. Jones's and formulating research questions based on the respective professional's knowledge.

Attorney's Questions for Using the Law to Challenge Assumptions

- What is the standard for neglect regarding prenatal substance abuse? What evidence is necessary to prove neglect and how does that relate to the evidence noted in the petition and the evidence provided by the county agency?
- Is there a different legal standard for risk when determining if a child should be placed in foster care or outside of their parent's care?
- How has harm to an infant because of prenatal drug use been dealt with in the case law, and specifically in your current state or county?
- Are there different degrees of harm? If so, what are the possible levels of impairment?
- How does prenatal substance abuse impact an infant's health and development?
- What are the short-term consequences of drug exposure in terms of degree of harm to the child? What are the long-term consequences? Can any of those be remedied?
- Does the law distinguish between the use of different drugs; for example, marijuana versus cocaine? This includes understanding the differences in potential charges in Criminal Court against your client depending on the law around the use of different substances and quantities, and around minors in your state.
- What are the laws around consent for testing a pregnant woman in the hospital or testing an infant, and was Ms. Jones afforded those rights?

Social Worker's Perspective

The social worker might enter the interview with many preconceived ideas about the case. Some of these may come from personal experience, professional training, values and ideology, and even the media. Based on these factors several ideas may immediately come to mind. One social worker may feel that they have a conflict because they feel they must do what is in "the best interest" of the infant and therefore Ms. Jones's needs may be secondary. Another social worker may feel that the best way to take care of a child's interests is to meet the needs of that child's parent. A clinically oriented social worker may immediately focus on the possibility of postpartum depression, while a generalist practitioner may immediately focus on the kind of support system that is available to Ms. Jones. A feminist social worker may want to explore the role that interpersonal violence, oppression, and trauma have played in Ms. Jones's use of substances. A social worker focused on social justice may want to focus on a combination of solutions including one that would decrease or eliminate the likelihood of Ms. Jones being separated from her child, and limiting the legal ramifications possible for Ms. Jones. It would be critical, then, for the social worker to work in collaboration with the attorney to address the increased harm to Ms. Jones and her child if

Ms. Jones is criminalized and/or at risk of a termination of parental rights. The point here is that there are many variables that will affect what a social worker may focus on and what kind of information and data they collect about a client or a problem.

If the social worker is honest and self-aware, and unaware of the complexities and challenges of substance use and co-occurring disorders, they may need to acknowledge that they may have judgments and limitations on understanding of why and how a mother could abuse drugs while pregnant. The social worker may also automatically assume that there will be negative effects for the child because of prenatal exposure to substances because in general practice this is taken as a given. Therefore, the social worker may think that prenatal substance abuse is automatically child abuse or neglect. The social worker may also question why Ms. Jones did not immediately seek treatment when her child was removed so she could be reunited with her child.

As with the attorney it is important for the social worker to check their understanding of how they know what they think they know and to identify when they may need to seek additional knowledge for themselves from other professionals. In *The Case of Michelle Jones*, a social worker might consult with both an attorney and a medical professional who has expertise in dealing with substance exposed infants. Preparing questions for research as well as for conversations with other professionals will not only assist the social worker in correcting for bias in problem identification and solution, but will also result in more productive interprofessional conversations. In this case several questions are implicated.

Social Worker's Questions for Using Social Science to Challenge Assumptions

- What do we know about substance use during pregnancy and the decision to seek treatment?
- What is the immediate and long-term impact of prenatal substance abuse on an infant's development?
- Are there specific impacts related to drug use during pregnancy? Are all exposed infants impacted?
- What is the relationship between the kind of substance and its impact on development?
- What is the relationship between the duration and degree of use of the substance during pregnancy and its impact on development? What protective factors mediate impact on development? What risk factors mediate impact on development?
- Is having a positive toxicology at birth automatically child abuse and neglect under the law in my state?
- What is the policy within the hospital for testing mothers and babies for substance use, and are there any potential rights of Ms. Jones that were violated by the hospital?
- Under the law does it matter if a mother is in substance abuse treatment if their infant tests positive for substances at birth?
- Did the hospital previously connect Ms. Jones to the hospital social worker for resources and support? If so what was the outcome of that connection?

HOW TO ACCESS SOCIAL SCIENCE KNOWLEDGE

Sources of Research

Research reports can be found in peer-reviewed journals, on government-sponsored websites such as Substance Abuse and Mental Health Services Administration (SAMHSA) and the National Institute of Health and Mental Health, and on websites specifically developed to collect and disseminate EBP such as the Campbell Collaboration, the California Clearinghouse for EBP in Child Welfare, and the Cochrane Library, which consists of a collection of systematic reviews. The Campbell Collaboration also prepares, maintains, and disseminates systematic reviews of research related to social work, psychology, education, and criminology as well as policy evaluations related to each of the previously mentioned fields. The Cochrane Library gives free access to summaries of systematic reviews.

A systematic review uses a very rigorous and specific method that identifies, evaluates, and synthesizes relevant studies in a body of research. A meta-analysis is a kind of systematic review that applies quantitative research methods to assess a body of research. The benefit of systematic reviews and meta-analyses are that they assess the level of consistency across studies and reduce the amount of literature a busy professional may have to read. Many schools of social work have library pages specifically geared toward EBP with descriptions and links to important resources.

There are hundreds of peer-reviewed academic journals. Many peer-reviewed academic journals provide a free table of contents e-mail service that allows you to keep up to date with what is being published. Journals that are relevant to your areas of practice or touch on issues that may occur during your practice can be identified. Journals that relate specifically to interdisciplinary practice in legal settings include *Journal of Forensic Social Work, American Journal of Forensic Psychology, Law and Psychology Review, Psychology Public Policy, Law and Criminal Justice & Behavior,* and *Law and Human Behavior.* For research in *The Case of Michelle Jones,* there are a number of peer-reviewed journals that address substance abuse during pregnancy such as the *American Journal of Drug and Alcohol Abuse, Journal of the American Medical Association* and the *Journal of Substance Abuse Treatment.* Journals that specifically address substance abuse and child welfare include *Child Abuse and Neglect, Child Welfare,* and *Children and Youth Services Review.*

There are several selected databases and indexes that are useful for conducting literature reviews. The social services abstracts provide bibliographic coverage of current research focused on social work, human services, social welfare, social policy, and community development. PsycINFO contains summaries and citations of journal articles, book chapters, books, and technical reports all in the field of psychology. PubMed is the U.S. National Library of Medicine's web-searchable MEDLINE database that includes journals dealing with biomedical research. Academic Search Premier, EBSCOHost, and ProQuest are all large, general databases that cover a variety of disciplines.

Research reports have been ranked according to method in terms of their ability to reliably and directly inform practice. The methods are usually presented in a hierarchy with systematic review and meta-analyses as the most reliable, and then moving down from randomized controlled trials, controlled studies without randomization, cohort or case-controlled analytic studies, multiple time series, preexperimental group studies, surveys, qualitative studies, opinions of respected authorities based on clinical experience, descriptive studies, and case reports or reports of expert committees. It is important to note that despite this hierarchy, if evidence is lacking at the highest levels of reliability, the practitioner can still obtain guidance from qualitative studies if this is in fact the best available evidence (McNeece & Thyer, 2004).

Skills for Conducting Research in the Social Sciences

There are several key skills related to accessing research for the purpose of EBP. These include asking an answerable question, conducting literature searches, and critically appraising literature. Social work students have probably learned how to do this as an assignment for their research classes when asked to complete a literature review. It is very helpful when reviewing the literature or investigating questions such as, "Does drug use during pregnancy impact infant and child development?" or "What are the effects of drug use during pregnancy on infant development?" to write a brief literature review for use in a legal proceeding, which can be in the form of a memo to an attorney. An example of a short memo summarizing the research the social worker finds about a specific question is included at the end of this chapter.

ACCESSING LEGAL KNOWLEDGE

Whenever you work on a legal case, it is important to begin your research by accessing the source of the law in question. There may be multiple sources for the law because your client's case implicates state laws and local regulations. It is important to understand what type of legal case your client has and where you should look to research those issues. As you remember from Chapter 4, laws are created at many levels of government including federal, state, and local.

A federal law would be applicable in every state and would primarily be at issue in a case heard in federal court. A state law is applicable only within the given state. For example, family law and the law of abuse and neglect are defined by state statutes which can differ from state to state. It is critical to understand how the state defines neglect or abuse under the law. This is why it is important for you to check your local state law as there are often significant differences among states. For example, as you will learn later in this chapter, in New York State a positive toxicology at birth may or may not be sufficient to determine that a mother neglected her infant. However, in Minnesota, substance abuse during pregnancy is considered not only to be child abuse under their local family law statutes, but also a ground for civil commitment (Dailard & Nash, 2000). In South Carolina, not only is substance abuse during pregnancy a basis for child abuse but also grounds for criminal child abuse in Criminal Court (Dailard & Nash, 2000).

Finally, local municipalities including cities, towns, and counties can promulgate regulations to govern how agencies and other government officials are responsible for providing services and conducting business. In Ms. Jones's case, the specific regulations for the child protective agency govern, among other things, how the caseworkers conduct their investigation, what services are available for families, and how the caseworkers record their efforts and investigation. Therefore, a first step in any legal research must always be consulting the specific laws and regulations in your state.

You can easily identify the source of law when your client has legal papers or documents. Ms. Jones was provided with petitions in Criminal Court and Family Court that specifically state the law in question. The New York State law of abuse or neglect is cited as N.Y. Fam. Crt. Act § 1012(f)(i)(B) (1962). Therefore, you would need to access Article 10 of the Family Court Act, which has all the laws of abuse and neglect and then reference the specific section discussing abuse and neglect as a result of substance abuse in § 1012(f)(i)(B). If Ms. Jones lived in a different state, you would need to access the law of neglect in that state. As noted earlier, states have different laws regarding what is neglect, including whether prenatal substance abuse raises the level of child neglect under the law. For example, in California a specific criminal law—Cal. Penal Code, § 11165.13 (2009)—states that a positive toxicology at birth is not in and of itself a basis for making a report and clarifying that any report is properly made to the child welfare agency and not the police, Cal. Penal Code, § 11165.13 (2009). However, according to Alabama Code § 26-15-3.2 (2023), substance abuse during pregnancy can not only lead to a child welfare investigation but also to a criminal child abuse case for chemically endangering the fetus (Alabama Code § 26-15-3.2, 2023).

In addition to being referenced in most legal papers including complaints and petitions, the source of the law is also referred to in most administrative documents your client might be given, such as a denial of benefits or notification about an indicated case of child abuse or neglect. Under most administrative regulations, agencies are required to notify clients of the specific law or regulation that is being implemented to provide, alter, or deny public benefits. As you will learn in Chapter 12, federal law requires that clients be provided with adequate notice, which includes a description of the regulations enacted in their case. Once you know which regulation is at issue, you can easily access the text of the regulation as most state and federal administrative agencies have websites listing their regulations. As a result, it is critical to ask clients to maintain and share any legal documents that they receive so that you can review them, share them with the client's attorney if you are working collaboratively, or advise the client to seek legal representation if needed.

After an attorney determines the specific law in question, the next step in the legal analysis is to review the relevant case law or prior decisions in similar cases. While many laws are written clearly, other laws may have vague language. One of the major functions of a court is to interpret the law to resolve conflicting interpretations and ambiguity. Therefore, attorneys refer to case law or decisions that other courts have made with regard to the specific law in question. The first search would be for cases on the same issue and law that have been decided in the same geographic area or jurisdiction as the client's case. For example, if Ms. Jones's Family Court case was in the Bronx then an attorney would research cases that have been decided in the Bronx Family Court (the trial court), First Appellate Division (the first level for an individual to appeal a trial court's decision), and New York Court of Appeals (the highest court in New York State and the final level to appeal a decision of the trial court and/or appellate division). Although cases in other states or jurisdictions may be helpful in understanding the legal issue or proposing a particular legal theory to support a client's case, case law from other states and jurisdictions may not have any impact on the case in your court because it is a different state's law or jurisdiction's precedence.

When a judge issues a decision in a case, it can be rendered in writing or orally from the bench. If a decision is written, it can be published and made available to the public. Many courts, including all federal courts and all the highest state courts, have all of their decisions rendered in writing and published immediately. Lower trial courts, including family courts and criminal courts, may only have decisions published if the judge or involved parties request publication.

Most attorneys these days use web-based databases including Westlaw and Lexis/Nexis to conduct legal research and to identify case law and precedence. These databases are comprehensive and include laws, regulations, and written decisions from judges at the local, state, and federal levels. Additionally, the databases contain scholarly articles written for law reviews and journals, and treatises covering specific subject matter. You can often access a state or local municipality's laws through an internet-based search; many academic institutions or governments make those laws and regulations readily available to the public.

IDENTIFYING THE INTERSECTION OF SOCIAL WORK AND THE LAW IN A CASE: USING PROFESSIONAL KNOWLEDGE TO INFORM COLLABORATIVE PRACTICE

When working in the explicit legal context and partnering with an attorney, it is usually best to begin your discussion of a shared case by understanding the legal issues implicated by the case. Once a social worker has a clear understanding of the legal issues to be decided, there can be more clarity and direction in how to develop both a research and assessment plan. Knowing what legal questions will be asked and decided will also help determine what information the attorney and the client may need from the social worker to assist in developing and preparing for the case.

The Attorney's Research Plan in Ms. Jones's Case

When beginning research on Ms. Jones's legal issues, an attorney practicing in Family Court might start by conducting a search of the applicable case law to determine whether Ms. Jones has any defenses to the allegations. As discussed earlier, web-based legal search engines such as Westlaw and Lexis/Nexis compile all of the published and sometimes unpublished decisions from courts at the trial and appellate levels, in addition to statutes, regulations, and commentaries from legal scholars, including treatises and law review articles. For Ms. Jones's case, an initial search should include the most salient facts from the petition. Therefore, you would include the terms "substance abuse," "neglect," "positive toxicology," "Family Court," "imminent risk," and "impairment."

Once the search is completed, there would be a number of cases sorted either by their relevance to your search terms or the date. An attorney would review the cases found through the search and determine whether the fact pattern or decision in the case is applicable to the particular fact pattern and legal issue in Ms. Jones's case. While it is most helpful to find cases that support Ms. Jones's legal strategy, the attorney would also take note of any cases that go against the defense theory so that those cases could be distinguished. *Distinguishing a case* is when an attorney argues that the case and its decision are not applicable because the facts of the case are different or distinguishable.

Often, attorneys who practice in one forum such as Family Court or Criminal Court will have research memos that cover the law and case law for a particular issue, such as parental substance abuse and neglect or possession of drugs. It is helpful to review any existing research or case law memos first, in order to get a more comprehensive summary of the current law and interpretation of the cases. For example, a Family or Dependency Court practitioner might have a legal memo on the law of neglect with regard to parental substance abuse. The legal memo would lay out the text of any relevant laws and summarize cases which have interpreted the law. While it is helpful to consult these memos for a summary, it is critical to conduct additional research to capture any new decisions or developments in the law. A sample legal memorandum is attached for your review at the end of this chapter.

Using the basic information and question at issue in Ms. Jones's case, a research plan would focus on gathering cases that interpret the New York law of neglect and substance abuse, specifically with regard to prenatal exposure to drugs. After conducting a search for cases in New York, you would find a number of cases that address the issue of a parent's drug abuse, but one case decided by the Court of Appeals in New York, *Matter of Nassau County Department of Social Services o/b/o Dante M. v. Denise J.* (1995), is particularly relevant to Ms. Jones's case for a number of reasons. First, the *Dante M.* case is from the highest New York appellate court, the Court of Appeals, which means that it is binding law in all of New York State. You know that the case is from the highest court both from the citation that lists the specific court, and also from the text of the decision, which states the court's name. In cases from a lower Appellate Court or trial court, the year that that case was decided would be preceded by the specific court; for example, 3rd Dept. 2018 or Fam. Ct. N.Y. Co. 2020. The case is also relevant to our research because the main question is whether a positive toxicology result at birth is sufficient to find that a parent neglected a child. As you know from the facts of Ms. Jones's case, this is one of the main allegations at issue in her Family Court case.

When reading the decision in relevant cases, generally an attorney focuses on two aspects: the reasoning behind the court's ultimate decision and the particular facts of the case. The reasoning behind the court's decision, or holding, is important because it demonstrates how the law was interpreted and the factors that the court considered when rendering its decision. The particular facts in the case are important because an attorney can argue that the case is applicable or not to their client's case depending on whether the facts are similar or different.

Generally, a court begins its decision either by reciting the specific facts of the case at hand or by stating the issue at hand and the court's ultimate decision. In the *Dante M.* case the court begins its decision by stating that "[t]he issue before the Court is whether a finding of neglect as to a newborn and the newborn's older sibling may be based solely on the newborn's positive toxicology for a controlled substance. We conclude that more than a positive toxicology is generally required for a neglect determination" (p. 76). For Ms. Jones's case then, we know that we need to discover what more is needed to determine neglect according to the court's decision. For that analysis, we would review the specific facts of the case in *Dante M.* that are listed immediately following the court's holding.

In *Dante M.*, both the mother and her infant son tested positive for cocaine at birth and a petition alleging neglect was brought in Family Court. The infant was removed from his mother's care and placed with his older sister. At the fact-finding hearing on the allegations in the petition, the child welfare agency presented the following evidence: two medical reports regarding the positive toxicology for the mother and the infant, evidence about the mother's prior history of substance abuse, and an admission from the mother that she "may have smoked a cigarette containing cocaine, while she was pregnant with Dante, at a Halloween party" (p. 77). There was also evidence that the baby was born premature with a low birth weight. The mother's attorney presented evidence from two experts, who testified to the following:

> [Mother] provided a clean, well-ordered environment for her children, that [mother] interacted appropriately with her children and that four random urine samples taken from [mother] tested negative for controlled substances.
>
> The experts opined that the appellant had not been a regular user of controlled substances since the latter half of the 1980s. The experts testified that [mother] was voluntarily receiving counseling at a general education and support program run by Family Service Association (p. 77).

The fact pattern in the *Dante M.* case is similar to the facts in Ms. Jones's case as there was a positive toxicology when Ms. Jones gave birth and an admission from her of prior use of drugs. Therefore, one of the first factual questions would be what specific substances were reported in the test and whether the test was consented to by Ms. Jones. Furthermore, while the mother in *Dante M.* had older children who were in care, Ms. Jones has no prior history with the child welfare agency or Family Court. However, there is an allegation that Ms. Jones has a criminal case involving drugs. Either way the court in *Dante M.* determined that "[r]elying solely on a positive toxicology result for a neglect determination fails to make the necessary causative connection to all the surrounding circumstances that may or may not produce impairment of imminent risk of impairment in a newborn child" (p. 79).

Ultimately, though, the court found that there was a causative connection between the mother's drug use and the impairment to the child because the infant required extended medical care after birth and follow-up care at a high-risk clinic. Additionally, the court concluded that the mother's prior history of involvement with the child welfare system with her older children who were placed in foster care because of her drug abuse and the testimony from two witnesses who observed her on drugs while pregnant was sufficient to make the causal connection between the mother's conduct and the infant's impairment.

Another step in researching the legal issues in Ms. Jones's Family Court case is to identify the specific law that she is alleged to have broken. In this case, she is alleged to have neglected her son by abusing drugs, pursuant to a specific provision of the Family Court Act. That law states that:

> A neglected child means a child <18 years of age whose physical mental or emotional condition has been impaired or is in imminent danger of becoming impaired as a result of the failure of his parent … to exercise a minimum degree of care … by misusing a drug or drugs … provided however that where the respondent is voluntarily and regularly participating in a rehabilitative program, evidence that the respondent has repeatedly misused a drug or drugs … shall not establish that the child is a neglected child in the absence of evidence establishing that the child's physical, mental or emotional condition has been impaired or is in imminent danger of becoming impaired. (N.Y. Fam. Crt. Act § 1012[f][i][B], 1962)

As you can see from the text of the law, the first section relates to Ms. Jones's case because the parent's drug use has to put the child at risk of or actually harmed. That impairment is defined with regard to the child's physical, mental, or emotional condition. The *Dante M.* case specifically discussed this statute and the definition of impairment to a child by referencing the text of the statute and the Practice Commentaries to the law. Additionally, the law includes a specific provision for parents who are in a substance abuse treatment program. That section clarifies that if the parent is "regularly and voluntarily" in a treatment program, then there needs to be additional evidence of impairment to the child's physical, mental, or emotional condition. For Ms. Jones's case then, upon reading the statute, we know that abusing drugs can be considered neglect if there is impairment or risk of impairment to the child. However, we also know that if she was participating in a treatment program, then there is a strong probability of requiring additional evidence of impairment.

From our review of the case law, research memo, and statute, a legal strategy begins to emerge. Ms. Jones's defense could be that there was no impairment or risk of impairment based on her prenatal substance abuse, which is only evidenced from the positive toxicology at Matthew's birth. Additionally, Ms. Jones may be able to defend against the allegations of neglect if she was enrolled in a treatment program.

Certainly, the attorney would need to consult the social worker in order to answer questions that are implicated by the potential legal strategy. Tellingly, the court noted in *Dante M.* in a footnote that "expert testimony would be particularly helpful in cases such as these, where medical records must be interpreted, especially when a question exists as to whether a newborn exhibited drug withdrawal symptoms after birth" (p. 77, fn. 4).

The Social Worker's Research Plan in Ms. Jones's Case

The social worker will most likely have several questions that they identify as areas for research as well as questions that are being asked by the attorney. Based on the reading of the law and the case law, it appears that there is a central question needing to be answered from both legal and a social work perspectives and that is, "What impact does drug use have during pregnancy and on the current and longer-term development of the child?" A social worker would also want to know the answer to this question as a way to know what important questions regarding Ms. Jones's prenatal history and the child's current condition need to be asked, not only for legal purposes but also for the planning of services. This information will assist the social worker in determining what kinds of services Ms. Jones may need as preventive measures to ensure access to her child or, if there are effects from drug use during pregnancy, how they might be mitigated. If the social worker finds that the research is inconclusive this is also important information to know from a client advocacy perspective because, unless there are other compelling reasons creating danger to the child, Ms. Jones should not be separated from her child.

A central aspect of the attorney's case is figuring out whether Michelle Jones's use of drugs during her pregnancy resulted in "impairment" or risk of impairment" to her newborn son. Impairment is thought by the law to relate to harm to the child's physical, mental, or emotional condition. Therefore, a social worker would want to specifically look at research that assesses whether or not there is a negative impact resulting from drug use during pregnancy on a child's cognition, growth, and general development.

The social worker would initially want to see if there are any systematic reviews, meta-analyses, and literature reviews on this question. Once the literature was accessed, the social worker would want to identify the limitations of the research, including identifying the demographics of those included in the sample and whether the research can be analogized to their client. For example, much of the research on the impact of substance abuse is done on women who use cocaine during pregnancy. If Ms. Jones had a positive toxicology for marijuana, much of that past research may not be relevant although there is the additional disclosure of cocaine use. Additionally, many states have changed their laws around marijuana use within the criminal code, with multiple states legalizing marijuana for medicinal use versus recreational use, and also allowing for legal medical marijuana cards. This does not mean the use of marijuana has also changed in states' child welfare statutes and underscores the importance of having familiarity with the law of your jurisdiction (Rogers, 2023). It would be important to review this new information and the process in which medical providers and or other provider agencies may be responding to marijuana use in maternal health, and also any changes in the criminal code around the use of marijuana for the case. Once the social worker has reviewed the research they can summarize the findings in the form of a short memo. The memo the social worker completed for this case can be found at the end of this chapter (Short Research Memo Exemplar: What is the Impact of Marijuana Use During Pregnancy on Immediate and Long-Term Child Development?).

The second aspect of the legal case is addressing whether Ms. Jones was in treatment or conversely why she might not have obtained treatment. Obtaining research findings about this question will not only assist the legal strategy but will assist the social worker (and others) in deconstructing any cognitive schema they may have about why women abuse substances during pregnancy as well as to assist the social worker in understanding what might be contributing to Ms. Jones's reluctance to seek treatment for her substance use. A rights-based or legal and evidence-based practitioner would also look to the literature with an eye toward how the literature on women seeking treatment during pregnancy and legal implications may overlap. A cursory review will tell us that research shows that pregnant women are often afraid to seek both treatment for their substance use as well as prenatal care because of fear of losing custody of their child or other children who may live at home (Jessup et al., 2003). As we reported earlier, fears of police involvement or the loss of benefits may also interfere. We have also learned that in some states using substances during pregnancy automatically results in a finding of abuse and neglect. There are some states that have attempted to make prenatal substance use a criminal offense.

What is disconcerting about these findings is that there is also research that shows when substance-using women receive prenatal care and treatment, the birth outcomes and prognosis for their infants is more positive than when women do not access care (Brown et al., 2004; Kim & Krall, 2006). It is important that we assess legal costs or barriers to treatment compliance before we assume that a client is simply "resistant" or does not care about the well-being of the child, and that we educate others who may also make that assumption such as judges or other legal professionals.

Interdisciplinary Practice and Sharing Our Research

The best practice for sharing the research is for the practitioners to provide their respective research memos to each other prior to meeting in person. The authors want to stress that the exemplars provided in this chapter are by no means being put forth as exhaustive or at the level of more extensive legal memos and social science literature reviews. These exemplars are to be used to have beginning conversations about the issues in a case, to make it practical to use legal and EBP in actual practice, and may be used to identify questions that need to be asked of experts or more experienced practitioners. In addition, the research memo examples provide a starting point and framework for social workers to memorialize their research and begin interdisciplinary conversations.

At the initial meeting between professionals, they can discuss any questions that the research raised and brainstorm the next steps for working with the client. For example, the attorney and social worker in Ms. Jones's case would exchange their legal memos and literature reviews prior to the meeting.

At the meeting, the social worker might ask for clarification on how impairment is defined in the law. The attorney might want to know more about the short- and long-term consequences of prenatal substance abuse. Through the discussion of these questions and the research, the practitioners begin to develop their initial strategy in Ms. Jones's case. The social worker will come away with targeted information to guide the focus of the client assessment and conversations with other professionals.

As you will learn in the next chapter, this research and initial strategy will also form the foundation for the next meeting with Ms. Jones during her civil proceedings.

We anticipate that busy practitioners will not be able to write lengthy research memos for every case or have the luxury of meeting. However, our experience in practice has shown us that similar issues arise for clients time and again. For example, in a practice that frequently represents parents in child protection matters there is a good chance that, like the case of Michelle Jones, you may be called on to represent women who may have used substances during pregnancy. If you are a school social worker, it is highly likely that you will participate in impartial hearings where parents of children with autism are requesting evidence-based teaching methods. Writing a memo about the evidence-base for the assessment and treatment of autism and the legal basis for the use of EBP in special education will allow you to evaluate the quality of assessment and service that is being provided by others as a way of advocating for and protecting the rights of your clients during the counseling and hearing process. Therefore, a skilled and competent practitioner would continually compile and update their research on individual issues that come up most frequently in practice.

In addition, it is always good practice to seek out research support from colleagues and other practitioners who may have already dealt with an issue that is new to your practice. Periodic meetings and training to update professional knowledge bases can also address this need. In fact, this is a way for social workers to actively participate in the education and training of lawyers and judges. Lawyers can also present to social workers updates regarding case law, regulatory changes, or other issues that impact their collaborative practice in explicit contexts as well as those impacting social work practice in the implicit context.

Legal Research Memo Exemplar

Issue Presented: Does substance use during pregnancy fall under the definition of abuse or neglect in New York State?

Short Answer: Substance abuse during pregnancy as the only evidence of neglect is not enough to sustain a cause of action under New York law. The petitioner must present additional evidence of neglect and impairment to the child, and there are potential defenses available.

Long Answer

Definition of a Neglected Child: First, we must look to the definition of a neglected child under N.Y. law to determine whether substance abuse during pregnancy is abuse or neglect in New York State. Pursuant to the N.Y. State Family Court Act § 1012(f) a neglected child is someone who is under the age of 18 and "(i) whose physical, mental or emotional condition has been impaired or is in imminent danger of becoming impaired as a result of the failure of his parent or other person legally responsible for his care to exercise

(*continued*)

Legal Research Memo Exemplar (Continued)

a minimum degree of care ... in providing the child with proper supervision or guardianship, by unreasonably inflicting or allowing to be inflicted harm, or a substantial risk thereof, including the infliction of excessive corporal punishment; or by misusing a drug or drugs ... provided, however, that where the respondent is voluntarily and regularly participating in a rehabilitative program, evidence that the respondent has repeatedly misused a drug or drugs or alcoholic beverages to the extent that he loss self-control of his actions shall not establish that the child is a neglected child in the absence of evidence establishing that the child's physical, mental or emotional condition has been impaired or is in imminent danger of becoming impaired as set forth in paragraph (i) of this subdivision. (N.Y. Fam. Crt. Act § 1012[f][i][B], 1962)

The law defines a drug under this section as "any substance defined as a controlled substance in § 3306 of the public health law" (N.Y. Fam. Crt. Act § 1012 [d], 1962). A respondent's misuse of legal prescription drugs, as well as the use of illegal drugs such as heroin and cocaine, can constitute neglect. Therefore, exposing the fetus to drugs may be a form of abuse or neglect under New York State law, if doing so demonstrably harmed the baby or created a "substantial risk" or an "imminent danger" of serious harm. However, this would only become an issue under the law once the child is born. Additionally, the 2021 law legalizing the use of cannabis included a specific provision that cannabis use was not a basis for alleging or finding neglect, per the N.Y. Marijuana Regulation and Taxation Act (2021).

In an appellate case, *In Re Jessica Y. Y.*, 258 A.D.2d 743 (3rd Dept. 1999), the child was born without any health issues or positive toxicology, so the only evidence presented was of the parent's past history of alcohol and drug abuse and failure to complete a parenting program. In this case, the parent's prenatal conduct alone could not be the basis of a neglect finding in the absence of evidence showing that the child was harmed or placed at imminent risk of harm by the parent's actions.

Additionally, a positive toxicology alone is not sufficient to sustain a cause of action for neglect against a parent. See *Matter of Nassau County Department of Social Services o/b/o Dante M. v. Denise J.*, 661 N.E.2d 138 (1995). The reasoning for this decision is that a positive toxicology for a controlled substance generally does not in and of itself prove that a child has been physically, mentally, or emotionally impaired, or is in imminent danger of being impaired, as required by the definition of a neglected child. In the Dante case, the Court of Appeals held that "relying solely on a positive toxicology result for a neglect determination failed to make the necessary causative connection to all the surrounding circumstances that may or may not produce impairment or imminent risk of impairment in the newborn child."

Based on that decision from New York's highest court, we must look at other factors and evidence of potential neglect when determining whether a child is a neglected child under the law. Other cases provide guidance for the types of evidence that would support a finding of neglect including an admission by the respondent of substance abuse or other evidence in conjunction with a positive toxicology for a controlled substance if that evidence demonstrates or allows an inference to be made that the respondent continued to use drugs after the birth of the child. In the case, *Matter of Theresa J.*, 158 A.D.2d 364 (1st Dept. 1990), the Court held that testing positive for cocaine, making an admission to drug use, the proximity of the parent's drug use to the premature birth, and the respondent's willingness to enter a substance abuse treatment program established that the child was a neglected child. In another case from the First Department, the Court determined that there was sufficient evidence of neglect based on an assessment by the caseworker of the parent's drug use. See *In Re Jocelyn S.*, 30 A.D.3d 273 (1st Dept. 2006). However, the Court determined that "a newborn's positive toxicology for marijuana along with the mother's admission to prior marijuana use are insufficient to support a finding of neglect because the test result coupled with the admission, fail to establish that the baby or the baby's older siblings were physically, mentally or emotionally impaired or placed in imminent danger of becoming impaired." See *In the Matter of Smith Jones Children*, 950 N.Y.S.2d 491, (N.Y. Fam. Ct. 2012).

Of course, if there is evidence of physical impairment to the child in addition to a positive toxicology at birth, this is sufficient to sustain a neglect cause of action against a parent. The petitioner has "the burden of proving such actual impairment by a preponderance of the evidence and may introduce hospital records to show what, if any, detrimental effects were suffered by the children as a result of their mothers' use of drugs during pregnancy." (See *Matter of Stefanel Tyesha G.*, 157 A.D.2d at 329 (1990).

Finally, if harm to the child is proven, other persons and parents who were in the household including fathers may be found to have neglected the child if they failed to take any action to protect the child during the pregnancy. This was the case where a finding of neglect was entered against the infant's father because he failed to take action or protective steps when the mother abused drugs during her pregnancy. See *Matter of K. Children*, 253 A.D.2d 764 (2nd Dept. 1998).

SHORT RESEARCH MEMO

What Is the Impact of Drug Use, Including Marijuana, During Pregnancy on Immediate and Long-Term Child Development?

The research on the impact of substance abuse during pregnancy generally has a number of limitations associated with the methodology and conclusions (Kim & Krall, 2006). The most the research can say is that for some children, under some circumstances of exposure and dependent on the type of substance, frequency of use, timing of use, and dosage, there may be some subtle neurobiological effects that in interaction with environmental variables can impact child development. For marijuana specifically, systematic reviews of the literature now demonstrate that use of marijuana during pregnancy does not on its own impair cognitive functioning, despite persistent public perception of the harms and public policy focus (Torres et al., 2020).

It is frequently difficult to isolate the impact of a particular substance on the development of the infant because of the presence of many other variables that can also exert an effect. For example, the fetus may be simultaneously exposed to other substances as well as a lack of prenatal care or poor nutrition during pregnancy. Research has found that mothers who used illegal drugs during pregnancy were also more likely to have used greater amounts of alcohol and tobacco as well and were less likely to receive prenatal care than mothers who did not use illegal substances during pregnancy (Shankaran et al., 2004).

In addition, other variables such as the type of substance, amount of exposure, frequency of use, and timing of exposure can all play a part in creating impact (Singer et al., 2004). The research also reports multiple individual, family, and environmental factors—such as nutritional status, extent of prenatal care, neglect or abuse, socioeconomic conditions, and maternal level of education—that can also impact the development of the child and make it difficult to determine the direct impact of prenatal drug use on the child (Covington et al., 2002). It has also been found that even when there are biological vulnerabilities that may result from substance exposure such as low birth weight or small head size, some negative outcomes in exposed children can be ameliorated by supportive home environments and quality parenting (Frank et al., 2001, 2005). The conclusion of most researchers is that some neurobiological vulnerability may exist and, in combination with environmental factors, may influence child development.

Historically, the overall literature has been critiqued for lack of consistency of research method, measurements of substance use, limitations due to the use of self-report measures, lack of longitudinal studies, and use of samples that are primarily African American women from low-income backgrounds at urban hospitals, which puts into question generalizing the findings to other populations. In addition, because of all the attention to the "crack epidemic" in the 1980s much of the research is focused on the effect of cocaine use during pregnancy (Kim & Krall, 2006).

The impact of marijuana use during the course of pregnancy on the infant appear to be considerably moderated by a number of other risk factors with some evidence suggesting very limited effects, if any, on fetal growth and central nervous system functioning (Fried & Smith, 2001). Not all exposed children are affected, similar to results found among cocaine-exposed children. In a review of the literature, Fried and Smith (2001) report there have only been two longitudinal cohort studies with very different sample characteristics (the Maternal Health Practices and Child Development Study—University of Pittsburgh, a high-risk cohort of a low socioeconomic population, and the Ottawa Prenatal Prospective Study, a lower risk cohort of White middle class population) that have followed marijuana-exposed infants beyond early school age. The authors extensively draw on these two studies to critique and evaluate research on the impact of marijuana use during pregnancy on growth, cognitive development, and behavior. Since that time, studies have failed to find a relationship between prenatal marijuana exposure and fetal growth. Instead, studies have found that Black patients who are pregnant have a higher likelihood of being tested for drugs than other races regardless of substance use (Jarlenski et al., 2023).

A recent review of research studying the immediate and long-term effects of cannabis use during pregnancy noted the limitations of the scientific data on whether cannabis use on its own caused adverse effects in infants and children, but cautioned that there was enough evidence to warrant concern about the impact on infant development (Ryan et al., 2018). Earlier studies show a decrease in head circumference at 9 to 12 years of age (Fried et al., 1998). In regard to marijuana use specifically, some research has shown that some babies born to women who used marijuana during their pregnancies display altered responses to visual stimuli, increased tremulousness, and a high-pitched cry, which could indicate problems with neurological development (Lester & Dreher, 1989). In school, some marijuana-exposed children at age 6 to 12 were more likely to show gaps in problem-solving skills, memory, and the ability to remain attentive (Fried et al., 1992). During testing of 9- to 12-year-olds, both longitudinal studies found poorer visual spatial reasoning ability and planning, impulse control, and difficulty with sustained attention among those children exposed during pregnancy (Fried & Smith, 2001). There are however no studies to suggest that marijuana exposure during pregnancy impacts IQ and the impact on language is mediated by environment and maternal characteristics (Fried & Smith, 2001; Lewis et al., 2004). Researchers noted at that time that more research is needed to disentangle the drug-specific factors from the environmental ones (Schempf & Strobino, 2008). That need for additional research was echoed in a recent review of the impact of prenatal marijuana use and neurodevelopmental outcomes in children (Thompson et al., 2022).

In summary, the research is not conclusive and EBP would not support a determination that a positive toxicology for marijuana on its own as evidence of impairment to the infant.

REFERENCES

Alabama Code 26-15-3.2 (2023).

American Bar Association, The Michigan State Court, Child Welfare Services Division. (2009). *Legal representation for parents in child welfare proceedings: A performance-based analysis of Michigan practice.* https://bettercarenetwork.org/sites/default/files/2020-10/michigan_parent_representation_report.pdf

Azar, S. T., & Goff, P. A. (2007). Can science help Solomon? Child maltreatment cases and the potential for racial and ethic bias in decision-making. *St. John's Law Review, 81*, 533–573. https://scholarship.law.stjohns.edu/lawreview/vol81/iss3/3/

Baines, D., & Kia, H. (2022). *Anti-oppressive social work practice theory: Activist social justice social work.* https://doi.org/10.1007/978-981-16-3059-0_10-1

Brown, J. V., Bakeman, R., Coles, C. D., Platzman, K. A., & Lynch, M. E. (2004). Prenatal cocaine exposure: A comparison of 2-year-old children in parental and nonparental care. *Child Development, 75*(4), 1282–1295. https://doi.org/10.1111/j.1467-8624.2004.00739.x

Cal. Penal Code, § 11165.13 (2009).

Carrillo, A., & O'Grady, C. (2018). Using structural social work theory to drive anti-oppressive practice with Latino immigrants. *Advances in Social Work, 18*, 704–726. https://doi.org/10.18060/21663

Covington, C. Y., Nordstrom-Klee, B., Ager, J., Sokol, R., & Delaney-Black, V. (2002). Birth to age 7 growth of children prenatally exposed to drugs: A prospective cohort study. *Neurotoxicology and Teratology, 24*, 489–496. https://doi.org/10.1016/s0892-0362(02)00233-7

Dailard, C., & Nash, E. (2000). State responses to substance abuse among pregnant women. *Guttmacher Report on Public Policy, 3*(6), 1–9.

Duncan, T., Piper, C., & Warren-Adamson, C. (2003). Running rings round law? An ecological approach to teaching law for child-centered practice. *Social Work Education, 22*(5), 493–503. https://doi.org/10.1080/0261547032000126434

Ferguson, H. (2010). Walks, home visits and atmospheres: Risk and the everyday practices and mobilities of social work and child protection. *The British Journal of Social Work, 40*(4), 1100–1117.

Frank, D. A., Augustyn, M., Knight, W. G., Pell, T., & Zuckerman, B. (2001). Growth, development, and behavior in early childhood following prenatal cocaine exposure: A systematic review. *JAMA, 285*(12), 1613–1625. https://doi.org/10.1001/jama.285.12.1613

Frank, D. A., Rose-Jacobs, R., Beeghly, M., Wilbur, M., Bellinger, D., & Cabral, H. (2005). Level of prenatal exposure and 48-month IQ: Importance of preschool enrichment. *Neurotoxicology and Teratology, 27*(1), 15–28. https://doi.org/10.1016/j.ntt.2004.09.003

Fried, P. A., Watkinson, B., & Gray, R. (1992). A follow-up study of attentional behavior in 6-year-old children exposed prenatally to marihuana, cigarettes and alcohol. *Neurotoxicology and Teratology, 14*, 299–311. https://doi.org/10.1016/0892-0362(92)90036-A

Fried, P. A., & Smith, A. M. (2001). A literature review of the consequences of prenatal marihuana exposure: An emerging theme of a deficiency in aspects of executive function. *Neurotoxicology and Teratology, 23*, 1–11. https://doi.org/10.1016/s0892-0362(00)00119-7

Fried, P. A., Watkinson, B., & Gray, R. (1998). Differential effects on cognitive functioning in 9- to 12-year olds prenatally exposed to cigarettes and marihuana. *Neurotoxicology and Teratology, 20*, 293–306. https://doi.org/10.1016/s0892-0362(97)00091-3

Gibbs, L. E., & Gambrill, E. (2002). Evidence-based practice: Counterarguments to objections. *Research on Social Work Practice, 12*, 452–476. https://doi.org/10.1177/104973150 2012003007

Horwath, J. (2007). The missing assessment domain: Personal, professional and organizational factors influencing professional judgment when identifying and referring child neglect. *British Journal of Social Work, 37*, 1285–1303. https://doi.org/10.1093/bjsw/bcl029

Ife, J. (2008). *Human rights and social work: Towards rights-based practice.* Cambridge University Press.

In Re Jessica Y. Y., 258 A.D.2d 743 (N.Y. 3rd Dept. 1999).

In Re Jocelyn S., 30 A.D.3d 273 (N.Y. 1st Dept. 2006).

Jarlenski, M., Shroff, J., Terplan, M., Roberts, S. C. M., Brown-Podgorski, B., & Krans, E. E. (2023). Association of race with urine toxicology testing among pregnant patients during labor and delivery. *JAMA Health Forum, 4*(4), e230441. https://doi.org/10.1001 /jamahealthforum.2023.0441

Jessup, M., Humphreys, J., Brindis, L., & Lee, K. (2003). Extrinsic barriers to substance abuse treatment among pregnant drug dependent women. *Journal of Drug Issues, 33*(2), 285–304. https://doi.org/10.1177/002204260303300202

Kim, J., & Krall, J. (2006). *Literature review: Effects of prenatal substance exposure on infant and early childhood outcomes.* National Abandoned Infants Assistance Resource Center, University of California at Berkeley.

Lester, B., & Dreher, B. M. (1989). Effects of marijuana use during pregnancy on newborn cry. *Child Development, 60*, 765–771. https://doi.org/10.2307/1131016

Lewis, B. A., Singer, L. T., Short, E. J., Minnes, S., Arendt, R., Weishampel, P., Klein, N., & Min, M. O. (2004). Four-year language outcomes of children exposed to cocaine in-utero. *Neurotoxicology and Teratology, 26*, 617–627. https://doi.org/10.1016/j.ntt.2004.06.007

Lynch, R. S., & Mitchell, J. (1995). Justice system advocacy: A must for NASW and the social work community. *Social Work, 40*(1), 9–12. https://doi.org/10.1093/sw/40.1.9

Malenchik v. State of Indiana, 928 N.E.2d 564 (Ind. 2010). https://scholarship.law.marquette .edu/facpub/60

Matter of K. Children, 253 A.D.2d 764 (N.Y. 2d Dept 1998).

Matter of Nassau County Department of Social Services o/b/o Dante M. v. Denise J., 661 N.E.2d 138 (N.Y. 1995).

Matter of Smith Jones Children, 950 N.Y.S.2d 491 (N.Y. Fam. Ct. 2012).

Matter of Stefanel Tyesha G., 157 A.D.2d 322 (N.Y. App. Div. 1990).

McNeece, C. A., & Thyer, B. A. (2004). Evidence based practice and social work. *Journal of Evidence Based Social Work*, *1*(1), 5–23. https://doi.org/10.1300/J394v01n01_02
Munro, E. (2008). *Effective child protection*. Sage.
N.Y. Fam. Crt. Act § 1012(d) (1962).
N.Y. Fam. Crt. Act § 1012(f)(i)(B) (1962).
N.Y. Marijuana Regulation and Taxation Act (2021).
National Drug Court Institute. (2003). *Critical issues for defense attorneys in drug court*. https://allrise.org/wp-content/uploads/2023/09/Monograph-Critical-Issues-F_WEB.pdf
National Right to Counsel Committee. (2009). *Justice denied: America's continuing neglect of our constitutional right to counsel*. https://www.opensocietyfoundations.org/uploads/52165620-3308-4802-9a58-ce8b4c00a31d/justice_20090511.pdf
Oldfather, C. M. (2007). Heuristics, bias and criminal defendants. *Marquette Law Review*, *91*, 249. https://scholarship.law.marquette.edu/facpub/60
Rogers, L. S. (2023). *The evidence—and lack thereof—about cannabis*. Johns Hopkins: Bloomberg School of Public Health. https://publichealth.jhu.edu/2023/risks-and-benefits-of-legalized-cannabis
Ryan, S. A., Ammerman, S. D., O'Connor, M. E., Committee on Substance Use and Prevention, Section on Breastfeeding, Gonzalez, L., Patrick, S. W., Quigley, J., Walker, L. R., Meek, J. Y., Johnston, M., Stellwagen, L., Thomas, J., & Ware, J. (2018). Marijuana use during pregnancy and breastfeeding: Implications for neonatal and childhood outcomes. *Pediatrics*, *142*(3), e20181889. https://doi.org/10.1542/peds.2018-1889
Schempf, A. H., & Strobino, D. M. (2008). Illicit drug use and adverse birth outcomes: Is it drugs or context? *Journal of Urban Health*, *85*(6), 858–873. https://doi.org/10.1007/s11524-008-9315-6
Scott, E. S., & Steinberg, L. (2008). *Rethinking juvenile justice*. Harvard University Press.
Serin, R. C. (2003). Expanding the "what works" agenda for effective corrections: The role of correctional staff. *International Community Corrections Association Monograph*, *8*(2), 36.
Shankaran, S., Das, A., Bauer, C. R., Bada, H. S., Lester, B., Wright, L. L., & Smeriglio, V. (2004). Association between patterns of maternal substance use and infant birth weight, length, and head circumference. *Pediatrics*, *114*(2), 226–234. https://doi.org/10.1542/peds.114.2.e226
Singer, L. T., Arendt, R., Minnes, S., Farkas, K., Salvator, A., & Kirchner, H. L. et al. (2002). Cognitive and motor outcomes of cocaine-exposed infants. *JAMA*, *287*(15), 1952–1960. https://doi.org/10.1001/jama.287.15.1952
Slater, L. K. (2007). "Practicing in slow motion": The development and assessment of an interprofessional clinical education curriculum for law and social work students. Doctoral dissertation. Available from ProQuest Dissertations & Theses database (UMI No. 3283610).
Springer, D. W., & Roberts, A. (Eds.). (2007). *Handbook of forensic mental health with victims and offenders: Assessment, treatment, and research*. Springer Publishing.
Steinberg, R. (2006). Beyond lawyering: How holistic representation makes for good policy, better lawyers and more satisfied clients. *N.Y.U. Review of Law & Social Change*, *30*, 625–635. https://socialchangenyu.com/review/beyond-lawyering-how-holistic-representation-makes-for-good-policy-better-lawyers-and-more-satisfied-clients/
Thompson, M., Vila, M., Wang, L., Thabane, L., & Shea, A. K. (2022, October 27). Prenatal cannabis use and its impact on offspring neuro-behavioural outcomes: A systematic review. *Paediatrics & Child Health*, *28*(1), 8–16. https://doi.org/10.1093/pch/pxac079
Thyer, B. A. (2004). What is evidence-based practice? *Brief Treatment and Crisis Intervention*, *4*, 167–176. https://doi.org/10.1093/brief-treatment/mhh013
Torres, C. A., Medina-Kirchner, C., O'Malley, K. Y., & Hart, C. L. (2020, May 8). Totality of the evidence suggests prenatal cannabis exposure does not lead to cognitive impairments: A systematic and critical review. *Frontiers in Psychology*, *11*, 816. https://doi.org/10.3389/fpsyg.2020.00816

VanNostrand, M. (2007). *Legal and evidence-based practices: Applications of legal principles, laws, and research to the field of pretrial services.* Crime and Justice Institute & National Institute of Corrections.

Wells, S. J., Merritt, L. M., & Briggs, H. E. (2009). Bias, racism and evidence-based practice: The case for more focused development of the child welfare evidence base. *Children and Youth Services Review, 31*, 1160–1171. https://doi.org/10.1016/j.childyouth.2009.09.002

Woodward, W. (2009, February). *Evidence-based policy and practice in offender re-entry.* Presented at Re-entry in the State of Connecticut: Partners in Progress. https://portal.ct.gov/-/media/opm/cjppd-main/cjppd/cjresearch/forecastresearchworkgroup/partnersinprogress/04evidencebasedpolicypracticeoffenderreentrypdf.pdf?rev=2470a5b489ed42dbbe9dc51c17de3284&hash=C76D0B690774E6143BA6976CD1C1A32A

CHAPTER 6

Civil Proceedings, Players, and the Client

INTRODUCTION

In this chapter we introduce you to the procedures and types of cases in civil proceedings, focusing on two types of civil cases that are frequently confronted by social workers and that involve many of the best practices identified in this book for practice in the implicit and explicit legal context. Returning to our case scenario for Ms. Jones, we examine how a civil case begins including the role of a government agency in investigating and filing a case and the role of social workers as mandated reporters who may be called upon to report suspected maltreatment. It is critical for social workers to understand the process clients go through when there is a report of suspected maltreatment and how that report may or may not be linked to future civil court actions against the client. As part of learning about civil proceedings, we focus on identifying critical questions for your first collaborative interview with a client in a Civil Court setting if you are a forensic social worker. We use the concept of relevance as a framework to assist you in identifying the key issues that are of immediate concern for a social worker, a lawyer, a court, and, as always, your client. You will begin to see in greater depth the intersection of law and social work in this forum of practice. The case of Ms. Jones will be used to illustrate the social work practices and theories discussed in each chapter, highlighting the explicit and implicit legal context for clients.

MANDATED REPORTING AND INVESTIGATIONS OF SUSPECTED MALTREATMENT OF CHILDREN, ELDERS, AND OTHERS

Ms. Jones's journey to a civil case in Family Court began with someone making a report of suspected child abuse or neglect to a state child protective or law enforcement agency. All 50 states have laws and policies that specify procedures for making and responding to reports of child abuse and neglect. The federal Child Abuse and Prevention Treatment Act of 1974 provides a foundation for states to define what conduct qualifies as abuse or neglect. Generally, states define suspected child abuse and neglect as encompassing physical abuse, emotional abuse, sexual abuse, and neglect. Any individual can make a report of suspected child abuse and neglect to the state-based agency responsible for coordinating reports, generally referred to as the State Central Registry. Reporters generally do not have to identify themselves, unless they fall under the category of individuals mandated to report suspicions of child abuse and neglect and are protected from any civil or criminal liability as long as the report was made in good faith or when the reporter has a sincere intent to act fairly.

An example of one state's mandating reporting statute is Fla. Stat. Ann. ch. 39, § 39.201(1)(a) (2010), where the law states that:

> Any person who knows, or has reasonable cause to suspect, that a child is abused, abandoned, or neglected by a parent, legal custodian, caregiver, or other person responsible for the child's welfare . . . or that a child is in need of supervision and care and has no parent, legal custodian, or responsible adult relative immediately known and available to provide supervision and care shall report such knowledge or suspicion to the department.

In addition to laws requiring reporting of suspected maltreatment against children, there are a substantial number of states that have laws requiring social workers to report elder abuse or abuse of any vulnerable adult, such as the developmentally disabled (Bergeron & Gray, 2003). For example, Idaho defines a vulnerable adult in the Idaho Code Ann. ch. 53, § 39-5302 (dd) (2010) as:

> "Vulnerable adult" means an adult who is unable to protect himself from maltreatment because of: (i) A mental, physical, or developmental disability; (ii) A degenerative brain disease; (iii) An inability to communicate or implement decisions regarding his person; or (iv) Other infirmities of aging in an older adult.

There are several categories of law involving mandated reporting of domestic violence that affect social workers, particularly hospital or medical social workers. The categories are: (a) laws that specifically require injuries caused by domestic violence or abuse to be reported; (b) laws that require injuries caused by non-accidental or intentional conduct to be reported; (c) laws that require injuries caused by criminal conduct to be reported; and (d) reporting requirements relating to other crimes or injuries that may impact victims of domestic violence or abuse (Scalzo, 2006). In Colorado, for example, a healthcare professional is required to either inform law enforcement or provide the victim with a referral to a victim's advocate or services to address domestic violence as given in Colo. Rev. Stat. § 12-240-139(1)(a)(VI) (2010). Therefore, it is important that you become familiar with the laws and statutes in your state that define what is child abuse, neglect, vulnerable adult abuse; which persons are considered to be mandated reporters; what and how you are required to report abuse; and what response the state must make once a report has been received. Most states have a toll-free number for reports to be made by individuals and mandated reporters. All states allow reports to be made orally, but some states require that a mandated reporter follow up an oral report with a written report. Most states also specify what information must be contained in a report, including the basis for making the report and the mandated reporter's contact information. Most states also have training programs for professionals who are mandated reporters.

The Child Welfare Information Gateway maintains a searchable database of all state laws relevant to child welfare (www.childwelfare.gov) and is a helpful resource to access your state's mandated reporting laws for child abuse and neglect. Usually, a person must report when, during the course of their professional duties, they suspect or have reason to believe that a child or a vulnerable adult has been abused or neglected. It is important, and often required, that you identify yourself when making a report if you are a mandated reporter because this can assist those investigating the allegation.

State statutes and laws also specify professions whose members are mandated by law to report child and vulnerable adult abuse, neglect, and maltreatment. In some states, attorneys are mandated reporters if they are working with children. In most states, though, the attorney-client privilege has been affirmed, and an attorney would not be able to make a report against their client without violating their ethical code to maintain confidentiality. Social workers are typically mandated reporters, especially if they are licensed by the state. For most states, many other professionals fall under the category of mandated reporters such as teachers, nurses, and doctors. However, there is a robust and ongoing debate about whether social workers working with attorneys are subject to mandated reporting laws or are bound to maintain the same the attorney-client confidentiality that would prevent disclosure. In addition, mandated reporting laws are frequently updated and have changed in various states over the years, most notably Pennsylvania, in ways that have broadened or limited categories of mandated reporters. For these reasons, it is important to review state statutes and seek guidance from your office and other professionals to clarify if any attorneys and social workers in your state are subject to mandated reporting laws and when there are exceptions to the rule.

Once a report is made, the statutes and policies of all states specify procedures and timelines for the initial response required by local child and adult protective agencies. When the agency receives the report, it is screened to make sure that it contains evidence of actions that meet the statutory definition of abuse and neglect in that state. Therefore it is not enough to know just the mandated reporting law in your state, but you must also know what actions the law states as meeting the standard of child and vulnerable adult abuse and neglect. Reports that do not meet the legal standards should be screened out and not referred to the local child or adult protective agency. Reports should be ethically made and legally based with facts and observed behaviors documented in alignment with your state's laws on abuse and neglect to ensure that the report meets the mandated reporting standard and is appropriate for investigation.

Investigating Reports of Suspected Maltreatment

Reports that are accepted for investigation are sent to the local child and adult protective agency for cases involving children and to another government agency for cases involving vulnerable adults and seniors. Depending on the report of suspected maltreatment, a report may also be referred to the district attorney to commence a criminal investigation. In the most serious cases, child or adult protective services staff, the police, or a multidisciplinary team composed of both, as well as medical professionals, may conduct investigations. In less serious cases, the child protective caseworker generally conducts the investigation. In recent years, because of reports of trauma that victims of interpersonal violence experienced during the investigation and prosecution process, multidisciplinary centers that include police, protective service caseworkers, district attorneys, medical, mental health, and victim advocate professionals meet in a central location to investigate, conduct joint interviews, make decisions about how to proceed in a case, develop a treatment plan, and monitor the prosecution of the case. The research conducted by the National Child Advocacy Center suggests there are a number of benefits to this approach including more immediate follow-up to reports; more efficient medical and mental health referrals; reduction in the number of victim interviews; increased successful prosecutions; and more consistent support for victims and their families (http://nationalcac.org).

The purpose of the investigation, traditionally, is to determine if a child or adult has been harmed or is at risk of harm, to reduce the risk of abuse and increase the safety of the child or adult, and to determine the need for services to support the family. During child and adult protective service interventions, safety and risk assessments are often conducted by the investigative caseworker to determine how safe children and vulnerable adults are in their environments as well as the level of risk for future harm. At the end of an investigation the allegation may be "indicated" or "substantiated," which means that the investigating agency found the allegation of abuse or neglect to be credible, or it may be deemed "unsubstantiated" or "not indicated," meaning the allegation did not have merit or was not found to be credible.

If the allegations involve less serious abuse, a dual track investigation or differential response is an alternate form of investigation used to determine the type of investigation required based on the allegations in the initial report. Dual track investigations are used for less serious reports with minimal safety concerns. Families can generally refuse to participate in the investigation and the requirement of supportive services is voluntary for families. The dual track system is a response to the widespread belief that child welfare investigations were too adversarial and not tailored to the individual needs of the families and children. Rather than focusing on an investigation of specific reports of abuse or neglect, the child welfare agency conducts an assessment to provide supportive services to the family (Child Welfare Information Gateway, 2008). For example, in Delaware, a report is classified as either for "family assessment and services" or investigation under Del. Code tit. 16, § 906(b) (9) (2007). If a family in Delaware refuses the services suggested by the child welfare agency, the case—in fact any case involving potential criminal offenses—can still be referred for investigation. Only those cases that are concluded as "services required" are entered into the state's child welfare registry. You can reference the dual track legislation in your state by accessing the local regulations or reviewing a clearinghouse of state statutes such as the National Conference of State Legislatures (www.ncsl.org).

Indicated or substantiated allegations of neglect and abuse have long-term effects for parents, and it is important that social workers understand the consequences of a report even if a case is never brought in Family Court and a child is never removed from a parent's care. If a report against a parent has been substantiated at the agency level or a judge makes a finding of abuse and neglect in the course of civil case in Family Court, the parent or caregiver's name remains on the State Central Registry for many years, in some states until the youngest child of that person is 28 years old. Certain kinds of employers have access to those records when determining whether to hire an applicant as do agencies investigating whether a client may adopt a child or become a foster parent. The most serious implication, particularly for women, is that in many cases this will impact any job that requires work around children or vulnerable adults such as teacher's assistant, home care attendant, or, even with a college or advanced degree, a counselor, teacher, social worker, or day care worker. Often referred to as the collateral consequences of mandated reporting, placement on the registry can have a serious economic impact on clients.

What social workers may not know is that even when a judge dismisses a case, or Child Protective Services (CPS) withdraws the case, the indicated report will still be on file and your client must affirmatively request that it be removed. In some states, there are administrative proceedings that your client can request to seal child protective records by employers under certain circumstances. This process is covered in further detail in Chapters 9 and 12. It is critical for clients seeking to have the report expunged from the registry to be aware of notifications from the state agency and their rights to contest the report within a certain amount of time. Social workers must be aware that a judge dismissing a case or the agency determining not to proceed does not necessarily or automatically remove the client's name from the registry.

During an investigation, investigators and attorneys from child and adult protective services may seek to petition the court to order the family to participate in a safety plan or to remove a child or adult from their home for their safety. There is no requirement that a child or adult protective investigation ultimately results in a court case, and many cases can resolve with services or without any continued involvement from the child or adult protective agency at all. The investigation can also lead to criminal charges of child or vulnerable adult abuse and neglect, in which the alleged perpetrator of abuse or neglect may also be prosecuted in criminal court.

THE RIGHTS OF PARENTS AND CHILDREN DURING AN INVESTIGATION

Many parents and children may not know what, if any, rights that they have during the investigation process, regardless of the model used by the state child protective agency. For example, can a child welfare caseworker interview a child without the parent's consent? Can the child welfare caseworker perform a body check to determine whether there are any marks or bruises on a child? Is a parent required to allow a child welfare caseworker to come into their home? Can a parent refuse to answer a child welfare caseworker's question? What confidentiality or privacy provisions govern the interactions between families and child welfare investigators? Does a child have a right to be protected from abuse? Do children have rights during the investigation phase? Do the parents or children have a right to an attorney during the investigation? Each state will differ on the answers to these questions; however, under both state law and in practice, there are general principles that apply across the board. Generally, a child welfare investigator does not require a warrant to enter the child's home and investigate the allegations in the report. The investigator can speak with the children who are present in the home and assess various risk factors by observing the home and effectively conducting a search of the home for evidence of abuse or neglect. A warrant is unnecessary because the investigation is civil and not criminal as it would be if conducted by law enforcement. Therefore, a parent does have the right to refuse entry to their home without a warrant from a court. Parents also have the right to notice of the report that was made against them and the subsequent investigation, although not necessarily of the source if the report was made anonymously. As another protection, the investigations are generally time limited (between 30 and 60 days) and require that the parent be notified in writing of the child welfare agency's conclusion regarding the investigation.

The rights of parents and children to refuse to participate in an investigation vary from state to state. For example, in New Mexico, a parent has the right to refuse to participate with the investigation by not speaking to the caseworker or disclosing documents, codified in the statute as their basic right not to be "compelled to appear at any conference, to produce any papers or to visit any place" (N.M. Stat. Ann. ch. 32A, § 32A-4-4[B], 1978). However, the parent cannot interfere with the investigation or limit access to the child (N.M. Stat. Ann. ch. 32A, § 30-6-4, 1978). Finally, parents have the right to communicate in their own language and have relevant documents translated into their native language. As a result, child protective staff should use language assistance lines or translators when working with non-English–speaking families.

The rights of children during an investigation are less clear in part because the United States has not ratified the U.N. Convention on the Rights of the Child, which includes a provision that a child has the right to be free from all forms of violence (www.unicef.org). Depending on the individual states, children may be subject to questioning from multiple investigators, medical examinations, and photographs.

A case in Oregon addressed the issue of children's rights during an investigation. In *Camreta v. Greene* (2009), a U.S. Court of Appeals found that a child's right includes freedom from unreasonable search and seizure. The facts of this case addressed a 2-hour interview at a child's school by a child protective caseworker and a sheriff with a visible gun. Unfortunately, when the decision was appealed, the Supreme Court declined to resolve the Fourth Amendment question about whether the child's right to be free from an unreasonable search and seizure was violated. Many organizations including National Association of Social Workers (NASW) filed amicus briefs supporting the overturning of this decision. The NASW brief argued that the requirement imposed by the Appeals court that the child protective agency had to show reasonable cause or get parental consent to interview a child at school goes against the legislative intent of child protection laws (NASW Brief, 2010).

However, on the other side of the issue, many children's rights advocates have long been concerned about the degree of trauma experienced by children during investigation and prosecution particularly in child abuse cases. Because of these concerns, child advocacy centers, described earlier in this chapter, were developed. In fact, to address these continuing concerns, Congress passed the Children's Justice Act of 1986, which provides funds to states to improve the investigation, prosecution, and judicial handling of cases of child abuse and neglect, particularly child sexual abuse and exploitation, in a manner that limits additional trauma to the child victim. One example of a resource for attorneys and social workers who wish to minimize trauma and address the needs of children during investigation and removal can be found at the Center for Improvement of Child and Family Services at Portland State University School of Social Work website (www.pdx.edu/center-child-family/reducing-trauma-children).

Applying Our Knowledge to the Investigation of Ms. Jones

In *The Case of Michelle Jones,* we know that a mandated reporter in the hospital—possibly a doctor, nurse, or social worker—made a report of suspected child neglect. The mandated reporter may under the state law be required to make an automatic report when there is a positive toxicology at birth. The mandated reporter may have interviewed Ms. Jones in the hospital, and it would be important to know what Ms. Jones relayed to that mandated reporter and also whether the mandated reporter referred Ms. Jones to any services. Regardless of whether a case is filed in family court as a result of the report, Ms. Jones would be entitled to know the status of the investigation and any conclusions reached by the child welfare agency about her family. Furthermore, Ms. Jones would be entitled to request copies of her case record, which in some states would include detailed progress notes regarding the investigation. Additionally, there would be a set period during which the investigation should be concluded and a decision made on the report.

Social workers in the implicit and explicit legal context would want to consider the following questions at the beginning of a child abuse or neglect investigation:

- What information or notices do you have about the pending investigation?
- What do you understand to be the scope of the investigation?
- What records do you have from the parent's pregnancy, prenatal care, treatment plan, and any other related services?
- What do you understand to be the process for the investigation? What do you think that you have to do and what do you think that the agency investigating has to do?
- What is your goal for the investigation? What do you want as an outcome?

CASES IN CIVIL COURT INVOLVING CHILDREN AND VULNERABLE ADULTS

Civil courts can handle a wide range of issues related to children and the protection of vulnerable adults. As you will see, it is up to each state to decide where and in what kind of court these issues are heard. These civil courts may have different names in different states; for example, family court, Children's Court, Dependency Court, Surrogates Court, Probate Court, Orphans Court or Supreme Court Civil Division. Most states have a website that identifies how the court system is organized and which civil matters are heard in each court. Specialized civil courts such as Drug Treatment Courts and Mediation Programs will also be listed. You can access your individual state court systems at their specific websites or via the National Center for State Courts, which has a listing of all state court websites (www.ncsc.org). As an example of the path of a civil case, we now review what happens when a case of alleged child abuse or neglect is referred to a Family of Dependency Court. As a general matter, cases in civil court always begin with a filing from the petitioner who will be an individual, entity, or a government agency that contains the allegations against the respondent and the basis in fact for those allegations. Once a petition has been filed, each court will determine the next steps required before proceeding to a civil trial on the matter. In some states, parties will be required to go through a mediation process to see if they can resolve the matter without going to trial. Often parties will have a discovery schedule set so that each side is able to review the evidence that will be presented at trial and seek to gather new evidence through depositions, subpoenas, and other discovery methods. It is important for social workers to understand the steps of the legal process in civil courts so that you can best advise clients about the potential outcomes of each step and how to advocate for their goals accordingly.

Who Are the Players in a Civil Court Case?

One of the most important aspects of understanding the path of a civil case for the client is understanding the players and their roles. While this section discusses the players in a civil proceeding where child abuse and neglect are alleged, it is critical for social workers to identify the stakeholders in any civil proceeding and to understand the stakeholder's role in the case. There are numerous sources for this information including the aforementioned court websites that describe specific courts. Additionally, participating as a court observer is another strategy for understanding your client's civil case and the various stakeholders and decision-makers in the matter. Although cases involving children are often closed to the public, social workers should understand the importance of supporting clients and observing colleague's cases as a way of gaining a better understanding of the civil court practice. Observing the ways that others advocate for clients in court can help the social worker get a deeper understanding of the case as perceived by all parties in the court, as well as their client's goals and feelings about their choices.

Government Child Welfare Agency Caseworkers

In Family Court, Ms. Jones will have a number of court stakeholders and professionals involved in her civil neglect case. Initially, Ms. Jones had contact with the caseworker employed by the city's child welfare agency who investigated the situation. Generally, this employee is responsible for investigating reports of abuse or neglect on behalf of the jurisdiction. In many jurisdictions, this child welfare caseworker provides all of the information to the city or county attorney in order to file the petition alleging abuse or neglect in Family or Dependency

Court. This means that Ms. Jones's statements to the investigative caseworker can be used in a petition alleging abuse and neglect against her.

The primary role of the child protective caseworker is to investigate allegations of abuse or neglect. When the worker receives a report of abuse or neglect, they are responsible for determining if there are facts that support the allegation and whether the allegation is founded. If the allegations are considered valid, the worker will make an initial service treatment plan for the parent and child. In some jurisdictions the worker will implement the plan themselves; in other jurisdictions the worker will refer the family and child to another agency to carry out the plan. The worker is also responsible for representing the position of the CPS agency during court proceedings and providing testimony, both through written and oral reports to the court.

Attorneys for the Government Agency

Once a case has been filed in Family Court, an attorney for the city or county will prosecute the matter by representing the local child welfare or children and youth agency in Court. This may be the same attorney for the government that drafted the initial petition alleging abuse and neglect. The attorney for the government, often referred to as the solicitor or agency attorney, is responsible for proving the case in Family Court and representing the agency's position. A case alleging abuse and neglect against a parent or where a child has been removed from their parent's care can only be initiated by a government agency. This contrasts with private civil custody actions which are initiated by private individuals against a parent or custodian, and do not involve a government agency as the petitioner.

The primary role of the attorney representing CPS is to safeguard the legal interests of the agency and to represent the CPS worker in presenting the legal case against a parent who has been alleged to have abused or neglected their child. On behalf of the city or local agency, the attorney for CPS will attempt to prove the allegations and ensure that the goals for the family and child, determined by the worker and agency, are being met. They are equivalent to the prosecuting attorney in a criminal case. For example, in Ms. Jones's case, the attorney representing CPS would have met with the investigative caseworker to write out the petition alleging abuse and neglect.

Attorneys for Parent(s)

The primary role of the parent's attorney is to protect the legal interests of the parent and to defend against the allegations of abuse and neglect. Attorneys for parents are generally guided by the legal foundation that parents have a right to family integrity and privacy with regard to their children absent a demonstration by the state that there is harm or risk of harm to the children. Therefore, a parent's attorney will want to ensure that a parent receives due process of law before their right to family integrity, in other words custody of their children free from state interference, is infringed upon. To do this effectively, the parent's attorney will have to do an independent and thorough investigation of the case against their client. This process may include interviewing the client and relatives, obtaining and reviewing records, and consulting with their own expert witnesses including doctors or psychiatrists. The attorney is an advocate for the client and makes sure that the parent understands their legal rights and has information about what will happen in court and why. The attorney for the parent will also advocate for services that are beneficial for their client and challenge those that the client believes are not important in solving the problem. The lawyer for the parent will also monitor and evaluate the treatment plan that is presented by the CPS workers.

As noted earlier, states differ as to whether counsel is mandated for parents in abuse and neglect or termination of parental rights cases. As a result, the systems and models for legal representation of parents vary from state to state. In some states, solo practitioners who are paid on an hourly basis by the state are assigned to represent parents. In other states, there are organizations or groups that represent parents in civil cases either through private funding or state funding. In recent years, there has been a trend toward interdisciplinary institutional models specializing in parent representation such as The Bronx Defenders Family Defense Project in New York (www.bronxdefenders.org), Center for Family Representation in New York (www.cfrny.org), and the Parents Representation Program in Washington State (www.opd.wa.gov). The Washington Office of Public Defense has published evaluation results (Courtney & Hook, 2012) and standards for social work practice when representing parents (Washington State Office of Public Defense, 2008).

Depending on the state where Ms. Jones lives, she may have a defense attorney appointed by the court to defend her against the charges of neglect if she is unable to hire a private attorney. Unlike in criminal court when an individual faces the risk of incarceration, the U.S. Supreme Court has held that a parent does not have a right to an attorney in a termination of parental rights case even though they could lose all parental rights to their child (*Lassiter v. Department of Social Services*, 1981). As a result, while most states provide counsel to indigent parents in family or dependency court at some point during the case as a result of state law right to counsel statutes, some states such as Wisconsin and Nevada give the court discretion on whether to appoint counsel to parents accused of abuse or neglect. Children who are the subject of abuse or neglect cases in civil court may also have a qualified right to an attorney or guardian ad litem in abuse and neglect cases depending on the state law. In contrast, parties in custody cases are generally not provided with counsel if they are not able to afford an attorney. Additionally, legal services organizations that provide pro bono or reduced fee representation for parents in custody matters are limited. A helpful resource for the assignment of counsel in civil proceedings is the National Coalition for a Civil Right to Counsel which tracks cases and legislation regarding the appointment of counsel in civil proceedings including abuse and neglect cases, housing, benefits, custody, and divorce (www.civilrighttocounsel.org).

The Role of the Child's Attorney or Advocate

The primary role of the attorney for the child is to protect the legal rights and interests of the child. Like the parent's attorney, the lawyer for the child must conduct an independent assessment of the case and advocate for the wishes of the child, depending on the child's age, even when the attorney may not agree.

The child's attorney must independently evaluate and assess the treatment plan presented by CPS, make recommendations for services or visitation plans, and make sure the child's position is presented to the court. In the role of advocate, the child's attorney assists the child in understanding their legal rights, explains the roles of other participants, and as well explains what decisions are being made by the judge.

As mentioned earlier, the child who is the subject of the abuse and neglect proceeding is provided with an attorney or representative in every state. The Child Abuse and Prevention Treatment Act of 1974 is a federal law that provides money to states to fund their local child welfare programs and requires the states to provide an attorney or representative to the child who is the subject of an abuse or neglect case. Therefore, a child would be represented by either an attorney or lay person serving as guardian ad litem. In some jurisdictions, an attorney or representative is bound to represent the wishes of the child client depending on their age and competency. In other jurisdictions, the legal representative for the child may be able to substitute their own judgment about the child client's goals. It is important for social workers working with attorneys and representatives to understand whether that legal professional is required to follow their client's directives or to substitute judgment on behalf of their client regardless of the age or competency of the child client.

In some jurisdictions children are also appointed an advocate by the court, either in addition to the attorney for the child or, as mentioned previously, as the sole representative for the child in the court proceeding. The purpose of this advocate is to decide what is best for the child. Court-appointed special advocates (CASAs) also conduct an independent assessment that attends to all the significant aspects of a child's life: social, emotional, physical, educational, and recreational. The CASA, usually a trained volunteer from the community who is not required to be an attorney, will make an independent judgment of what they believe is best for the child, even if the child may disagree. Their job is to protect the child during the court proceedings, monitor the implementation of the CPS plan, and advocate for what is best for the child when they feel it is necessary. Several states publish standards of practice for guardians ad litem, for example, Maine (www.courts.state.me.us) and Connecticut (www.jud.ct.gov).

When social workers are working with families involved in the child welfare system, they may hear concerns from clients regarding the quality of their legal representation and sometimes social workers even have concerns about this issue themselves. Several reports by states and organizations have found the quality of representation for both parents and children to be uneven and that representatives are frequently unprepared (Taylor, 2009).

Many lawyers have expressed concern and have advocated for better standards of casework practice in child protection cases through class action lawsuits. Justice-oriented social workers should be equally concerned with the quality and level of child and parent legal representation during dependency proceedings. It is important that social workers familiarize themselves and their clients with the American Bar Association's Standards of Practice for lawyers representing parents (American Bar Association, 2006) and children in abuse and neglect cases

American Bar Association (1996), as well as Standards of Practice for Attorneys Representing Child Welfare Agencies (American Bar Association (2004; www.abanet.org). Similar to practice guidelines that relate to clinical practice, these standards of practice will give you and your client an understanding of what they should expect from the attorney representing them.

Civil Court Judge

A civil court judge is responsible for overseeing and ruling on civil cases including when there are allegations of abuse or neglect of a child and requests for custody and visitation. Generally, the judge conducts bench trials, meaning that the judge listens to the evidence presented by all sides and determines whether there is enough evidence to find abuse or neglect. This is in contrast to other criminal and civil cases where the evidence at trial is heard by a jury who makes the final decision. The judge in an abuse or neglect proceeding has the authority to make a finding after a hearing as to whether or not the parent abused or neglected the child, the placement of the child, and the return of the child to their parent's care. The judge may also order services for both the parent and the child. In Ms. Jones's case, then, the judge will determine after a hearing on the petition whether there is sufficient evidence to prove that Ms. Jones neglected her infant by abusing drugs at the adjudication and then decide what is in the child's best interest at the dispositional hearing. At the dispositional hearing, the judge has broad authority to order services for Ms. Jones and her infant and to make the final decision on where the infant will reside during the case. The judge can also issue orders of protection in favor of one of the parents or in favor of the child, barring another parent or person from having any or limited contact with them. Finally, the judge can make orders regarding the type, frequency, and level of supervision for visitation and contact with the child.

Starting a Civil Case: The Petition

In any civil case, the first step in the process is the filing of a petition which includes the names of the petitioner and the respondents, the claims that are being made against the respondent, and the basis or evidence for those claims. In a case alleging abuse and neglect of children, once a report is made, the CPA determines whether there is enough basis in their investigation to file a petition in Family Court alleging neglect or abuse.

There are other civil matters where social workers can initiate legal action such as guardianship or commitment petitions for mental health and substance abuse treatment (Saltzman & Furman, 1999). Increasingly, as more social workers enter the field of geriatric social work, knowing both the circumstances about when to file for guardianship and the process involved in filing will be a critical tool for effective and just social work practice and advocacy. In emergency situations, adult and vulnerable adult protection workers can file petitions to compel services or for removal if the court believes the vulnerable adult is not competent to consent to services. For example, Chapter 5101, Sections 5101.67–5101.68 of the Ohio Rev. Code (2020) permits a filing of a petition to protect a vulnerable adult. Clients who are the subjects of these proceedings should also receive notice of the petition as well as a written copy. You will learn more about the assessment process for guardianship, civil commitment and risk assessment, custody, and termination of parental rights in Chapter 9.

Once a petition is filed in civil court, the parent or individual must be served or given notice of the petition and the pending court action against them. This is because any individual who is the subject of a civil proceeding has the right to be notified of the court proceeding and to respond to the allegations in the petition. Generally, this process is referred to as "serving" or providing notice to the parent in the case and, in most jurisdictions, the parent must be notified in writing and also be provided with a copy of the petition which lists the allegations against them and specific laws implicated. Each state will have its own rules of how the notice must be given to parents, including the substance of the notice and timeframes for providing notice. For example, if Ms. Jones had not appeared in court on the first court date when the petition was filed, the judge would have most likely ordered that the child welfare agency serve her with a copy of the petition and a summons or an order of the court to appear on the case within 3 days under N.Y. Fam. Crt. Act art. 10, § 1035 (2024). The judge may also require the petitioner to demonstrate how they attempted to locate and to provide notice to Ms. Jones of the pending case and the date for the first court hearing. As a rights-based social worker, you will want to make sure that your client is aware of their right to be notified of any civil cases against them in a timely manner and to be present in court for all court appearances.

Reading Formal Legal Documents

Reading legal documents is a significant part of interdisciplinary practice for social workers in both the implicit and explicit legal context. Furthermore, as a rights based social worker, you want to be comfortable with reading legal documents that clients may bring to you seeking clarification or assistance. In all instances, legal cases will include a range of formal legal documents that should be provided to clients and ideally explained in full to clients by their attorney or legal team. Given the lack of access to justice discussed in prior chapters, it is not unusual for clients to bring to you legal documents that they do not understand, may not be in their preferred language, and have not been explained to them.

One of the most important legal documents is the petition that initiates the legal case. The petition contains critical pieces of information for both the attorney and the social worker to guide their advocacy on the case. (see Exhibit 6.1). It is important to understand that an attorney and social worker may emphasize and think differently about the information contained in the petition. It is also important to remember that the petition is only the first piece of information in a case, since the petition contains allegations against a party and generally does not include any mitigating or strength-based evidence. Therefore, it is important to view the petition as a starting point for your investigation and practice as opposed to a recitation of facts which have been established or proven in court. In other words, the petition does not necessarily include facts which have been proven to be true but rather allegations against an individual which the petitioner seeks to prove in court. As an exercise in interdisciplinary practice, we review the petition in Ms. Jones's case and the different professional emphases after reading the petition. The dialogue between the attorney and social worker after reading the petition models the nature of interdisciplinary practice with both professionals

Exhibit 6.1

FAMILY COURT OF THE STATE OF NEW YORK
CITY OF NEW YORK, COUNTY OF MANHATTAN

--X

In the Matter of:

BABY BOY JONES Docket No: NN-5555/20XX

A Child Under Eighteen Years

Of Age Alleged to be Neglected by Petition: Neglect Case

MICHELLE JONES

--X

NOTICE: IF YOUR CHILD REMAINS IN FOSTER CARE FOR FIFTEEN OF THE MOST RECENT 24 MONTHS THE AGENCY MAY BE REQUIRED BY LAW TO FILE A PETITION TO TERMINATE YOUR PARENTAL RIGHTS AND MAY FILE BEFORE THE END OF THE 15-MONTH PERIOD.

The undersigned respectfully petitions the following:

1. Petitioner, John N. Charge, Commissioner of the Child Welfare Administration, is authorized under the law pursuant to Article 10 of the Family Court Act to file this petition.
2. BABY BOY JONES is a male child under the age of eighteen who was born on 4/16/20XX and is under one year old.
3. BABY BOY JONES currently resides in the hospital of New York Health pending this Court's determination of placement.
4. The father of the child is or is alleged to be unknown. The date of birth of the father is unknown. The mother of the child is MICHELLE JONES who resides at 555 Stewart Avenue, New York, NY 100XX. The mother's date of birth is (3/30/20XX).
5. BABY BOY JONES is a child <18 years of age whose physical, mental, or emotional condition has been impaired or is in danger of becoming impaired as a result of the failure of his mother, MICHELLE JONES, to exercise a minimum degree of care in providing him with proper supervision or guardianship by misusing a drug or drugs and not voluntarily and regularly participating in a rehabilitative program pursuant to Family Court Act Section 10212(f)(i)(B) because
   a. On April 16, 20XX, a social worker from New York Health hospital reported to the State Central Registry that MICHELLE JONES and BABY BOY JONES tested positive for drugs at the time that the child was born.
   b. On April 16, 2024, MICHELLE JONES admitted to a caseworker from the Child Welfare Agency that she had smoked marijuana throughout her pregnancy and that she is not currently enrolled in a drug treatment program.
   c. On April 16, 2024, MICHELLE JONES admitted that she had been arrested and charged in Manhattan Criminal Court with a substance abuse offense involving cocaine.
   d. On April 16, 2024, a caseworker from the Child Welfare Agency reported that Ms. Jones has a history of substance abuse including abusing crack cocaine.

Wherefore, the child, BABY BOY JONES, is a neglected child or is at risk of becoming a neglected child.

Dated: 4/17/20XX

John N. Charge, Petitioner

foregrounding their expertise while also raising questions for the other professional to help inform their professional strategy. The next sections also focus on the critical legal issues from the petition to isolate the research questions and advocacy strategies that a social worker in this matter would produce.

Attorney's Perspective: The primary allegation in this case is neglect because of substance abuse while Ms. Jones was pregnant and an alleged refusal to engage in a substance abuse treatment program. I am immediately concerned about the admission to substance abuse alleged in the petition, and the positive toxicology test at birth which may not have been fully consented to by our client. I am also concerned because there is a pending criminal case and I need more information to understand the charges, status of the case, and possibility that Ms. Jones might be facing incarceration or probation.

Social Worker's Perspective: The biographical information tells me that Ms. Jones has recently given birth to her only son. I would be concerned about her postpartum medical condition and mental status, particularly with the additional trauma of having a child removed. It is also noted that the father of the child is unknown and this would trigger questions about the presence and degree of social support in Ms. Jones's life. I would of course be concerned about the issue of past, present, and future substance use and what "refusal to engage" in a treatment program actually means.

Attorney's Perspective: Section 3 of the Petition states that the infant has been removed from Ms. Jones's care and is remaining in the temporary custody of the child welfare agency pending a judge's determination at the first court appearance. Therefore, I know that Ms. Jones has the right to request an immediate hearing for her child to be returned to her care and for the petitioning agency to demonstrate that there is imminent risk to her child. In order to think about how to counsel Ms. Jones about her right to request that hearing, I would want to know from the social worker and the client whether there are services or collateral supports that could alleviate the imminent risk to the infant which will be persuasive evidence for the court. I would also be thinking about the potential evidence that the child protective agency might have to support their claim of imminent risk including reports from the hospital and investigative staff. Most importantly, I would want to know what Ms. Jones wants and what she thinks will be best for her and her son.

Social Worker's Perspective: I would be concerned about the infant remaining in the hospital without a primary caretaker and what impact this may have on the child's development. If it is not possible for the baby to be returned to Ms. Jones's care, I would want to make sure that she is allowed to visit with her son, and advocate for how often and for how long she is visiting with her infant son. Additionally, I would want to understand whether she is nursing or there are upcoming medical appointments that would be important for her to attend as his mother.

Attorney's Perspective: In strategizing for the first meeting, I know that the infant has been removed and is very young. I would be concerned about when my client last saw her son and would begin thinking about what visitation schedule could be put in place if the court determines that the infant cannot be in Ms. Jones's care after the initial appearance.

Social Worker's Perspective: I immediately noticed the fact that both mother and child tested positive for marijuana. I would notice that the mother and baby did not test positive for crack cocaine although it was alleged in the petition. I would want to know more about the degree, frequency, and nature of Ms. Jones's use of any controlled substances. I would want to know more about the circumstances of the birth, such as the infant's birth weight and **A**ppearance, **P**ulse, **G**rimace, **A**ctivity, and **R**espirations (APGAR) score (a test given at 1 and 5 minutes after birth to assess the general health of a newborn).

Attorney's Perspective: The fact that the infant did not have medical complications is a possible defense because there was no harm or risk of harm to the health of the infant. I want Ms. Jones to know that a positive toxicology at birth is not enough under New York law for her child to be removed from her care or considered neglect under the law. I would be interested in hearing the social worker's understanding of risk in a newborn solely from prenatal exposure to substances and whether there is any research linking cannabis use during pregnancy with any impairment or harm to infant development. I would also be wary of the allegations regarding other drug use in light of the recent test, which only resulted in a positive toxicology for marijuana.

Social Worker's Perspective: What is the link between the use of drugs during pregnancy and child health and developmental outcomes? Even though there were no medical complications at birth that are referenced in the petition, is there still a risk of harm to the infant? I would want to conduct some research to determine the answers to those questions and make sure that Ms. Jones was not being unfairly targeted for drug testing because of her race.

PRACTICING IN THE EXPLICIT LEGAL CONTEXT

A social worker in the explicit legal context might be working directly with the attorney representing Ms. Jones in the Family Court proceeding. The attorney and social worker would collaborate on the case, ideally from the inception of the matter which is when the petition is filed. Therefore, two of the most important sections of the petition are the allegations of neglect and the description of whether the child was removed on an emergency basis from Ms. Jones. Both sections implicate critical statutes that the social worker on Ms. Jones's case should be comfortable referencing and discussing. First, as we discussed in Chapter 5, the drug abuse allegations direct us toward the definition of neglect in the local jurisdictions. For the purposes of the discussion, we will be using the statute from New York that we examined in Chapter 5.

In most every jurisdiction, the local child welfare agency has the power to remove children from their parent's care before going to court and without the parent's consent if the investigative caseworker determines that there is an emergency situation. For example, if a caseworker observed a parent physically abusing a child and causing serious physical harm, the caseworker would be authorized to remove the child immediately from the parent's care without seeking an order of removal from a Family Court Judge. In New York under N.Y. Fam. Crt. Act art. 10, § 1024(a)(i)-(ii) (2024), a caseworker can legally remove a child if "such person has reasonable cause to believe that the child is in such circumstance or condition that his continuing in said place of residence or in the care and custody of the parent . . . presents an imminent danger to the child's life or health" or "there is no time enough to apply for an order" from the court. In cases of vulnerable adults and elders, some states including Fla. Ann. Stat. ch. 415, § 415.1051(2) (2023), allow emergency entry into the home and emergency removal when there is "reasonable cause to believe that a vulnerable adult is suffering from abuse or neglect that presents a risk of death or serious physical injury to the vulnerable adult and that the vulnerable adult lacks the capacity to consent to emergency protective services."

In Ms. Jones's case, the petition makes clear that the caseworker believed there was an emergency situation and consequently removed the infant. One can infer from the petition's allegations that the evidence of imminent risk includes the infant's age and the allegation of ongoing substance abuse potentially evidenced by the positive toxicology, alleged disclosure to the hospital social worker, and the assertion that Ms. Jones is not currently in a treatment program. A rights based social worker would be aware of a client's right to challenge an emergency removal and the law surrounding emergency removals requiring that there be an imminent risk to the child's safety.

Once a child has been removed from their parent's care, a case must be filed in family court and the parent is entitled to a judge reviewing whether the emergency removal complied with the law. The first issue for the judge to resolve is whether or not the child will remain in the temporary care and custody of the child welfare agency. Although the agency has the authority to remove the child on an emergency basis, the law requires that a court review the removal by the next court date (N.Y. Fam. Crt. Act § 1027 [a][i], 2024). At the first appearance, the court has a legal obligation to determine whether the removal remains necessary as mandated by N.Y. Fam. Crt. Act art. 10, § 1027, 2024). Parents also have the right to request that the court hold a hearing to determine whether their child should remain out of their care pending the ultimate resolution of the abuse or neglect case (N.Y. Fam. Crt. Act art. 10, § 1028, 2024). The court is guided by the law's standard that a child should not be removed unless there is imminent risk to that child's life or health. While a parent may understand that they have a right to request that their children be immediately returned to their care, the parent might not understand that the court will look at whether there is imminent risk to the children. In many cases, the parent might mistakenly believe that the child welfare agency determines whether their children remain out of their care when actually it is the judge who hears evidence and arguments from all parties. As such, it is critical that the client be made aware of the judge's power to preside over any hearing and will ultimately decide where and with whom the children will reside. Additionally, it is critical that the client understands what will be considered evidence of imminent risk to the child. In Ms. Jones's case, a social worker can play a significant role in assisting with the legal counseling for Ms. Jones and to help her identify her goals, share information with the attorney, gather evidence to support her, and plan for a hearing or next steps in her case.

While much of our discussion so far has been about the role and responsibility of Ms. Jones in the case, it is important to remember that under the law, the child welfare agency has obligations under the law to prevent family separation and promote reunification if a child has been removed. The services that the child protective agency offers to the parent to prevent a child from entering foster care or to facilitate the return of a child who is in foster care are generally referred to as *making reasonable or diligent efforts.* Throughout the family court case, the court also has the obligation to determine what, if any, reasonable or diligent efforts have to be made by the child welfare agency. Laws in all states require the provision of services that will assist families in remedying the conditions that brought the child and family into the child welfare system. The statutes in most states, however, use a broad definition of what constitutes reasonable efforts. Some commonly used terms associated with reasonable efforts include "family reunification," "family preservation," "family support," and "preventive services." A social worker familiar with this requirement would take a critical eye not only to the services offered to Ms. Jones and her infant after the removal but also to what was offered at the hospital to prevent the removal, including during the investigation phase. In some jurisdictions there are programs that allow for family assessment and diversion which means that Ms. Jones should have been offered services prior to the removal of her son.

It is important to note that there are specific instances when reasonable efforts are not required by the child welfare agency. The Adoption and Safe Families Act (ASFA, 1997), a federal law, requires that states receiving federal funds for state child welfare programs promulgate laws that shorten the length of stay in foster care. One method of achieving this, as stated in the law, requires that agencies file to terminate a parent's parental rights if the child has been in foster care continuously for 15 of the last 22 months. The agency is required to make reasonable efforts during this time period to reunify the family which can include the provision of services. However, the agency can forego reasonable efforts to preserve or reunify the family when the court has determined that the parent has subjected the child to aggravated circumstances, as defined by state law. The definition of aggravated circumstances may include, but need not be limited to, abandonment, torture, chronic abuse, and sexual abuse. The laws in all states, the District of Columbia, and Puerto Rico are substantially in compliance with these requirements under the federal law. In addition, several states and Puerto Rico provide one or more additional grounds for not making reasonable efforts. Therefore, it is important that you research both the grounds in your state for what constitutes reasonable efforts to reunify and prevent foster care, as well as the circumstances when it is permissible for the agency not to make reasonable efforts.

Interdisciplinary Practice at the First Court Appearance

When the attorney and social worker meet Ms. Jones in family court, it is her first appearance before a family court judge. Up until this point, the family court has not had any interactions or appearances involving Ms. Jones. The judge will only have the petition drafted by the child welfare agency and any information that Ms. Jones's legal team provides during the first appearance in court from which to decide where and with whom her son will reside. As noted earlier, the first issue for the judge to resolve is whether the child will remain in the temporary care and custody of the child welfare agency and a determination of whether there is imminent risk to his life or health.

As you recall, the petition stated that the child protective agency had removed the child on an emergency basis. Under the law, the child protective agency must file a petition in court by the next business day (N.Y. Fam. Crt. Act § 1027 [a][i], 2024). According to that timeline, 1 day after the infant was born a report of neglect was made. The child protective caseworker came to the hospital to investigate the case and determine whether to remove the infant from Ms. Jones's care. If the caseworker decided to remove the infant on a Friday, the case most likely would not be heard in family court until Monday. At this point, the infant is now 6 days old. The infant has remained in the hospital, and it is unclear what if any visitation Ms. Jones has had with her son since he was born and the report was made.

In order to determine where the baby will reside, the judge will need to address two important issues: Was and is there still imminent risk to the infant's life or health, and did CPS made reasonable efforts to provide services that could have avoided removing the child? The most important issue for the judge to resolve is whether the child will remain in the temporary care and custody of the child welfare agency, which is undoubtedly the most important issue for Ms. Jones as well. These central concerns and legal decisions provide a framework for the social worker to begin to think about and to plan for the first contact with Ms. Jones which may be in court.

In addition to the initial court appearance, 45 states currently use some kind of family conferencing process for families entering the child protection system. These conferences have different names depending on jurisdiction but essentially precede a judicial hearing within 48 hours. CPS workers and most often a supervisor convene the conference, and parents are invited to bring family, friends, other advocates, or service providers to determine if there are other options to foster placement or to make sure placement is with a relative or friend and is in the child's community. In most instances, attorneys are not invited to these conferences although social workers are invited even if they are working in collaboration with an attorney (Casey Family Services, 2009). You will learn more about the different kinds of conferences that are often a part of the legal process and the role of the social worker in these extrajudicial conferences in Chapter 11.

PRACTICING IN THE IMPLICIT LEGAL CONTEXT

The legal process and decision-making during the beginning of a civil case are also important for you to know about and understand when you are working in the implicit legal context. Consider the scenario where you are a social worker employed in a community-based housing and social service assistance program. You have been working with Ms. Jones to obtain housing once her child is born. In the last few sessions, she had started to open up about other issues in her life such as past abusive experiences and her use of marijuana when feeling stressed. Ms. Jones had been considering starting a treatment program to address these issues, including her substance use. You were pleased with how your work has progressed, and had created a plan for obtaining housing once her infant was born. At some point closer to her due date, Ms. Jones began to miss appointments with you and failed to return your calls. You hypothesized that she might be in "denial" or that she was showing "resistance" because she had previously been receptive to a service plan. You considered that there was a significant life event or challenge that Ms. Jones was facing that may have contributed to why she unexpectedly began to withdraw from services. How might understanding the legal context of her current environment change the way you might think about her behavior? How would knowledge of her current legal case change your assessment of her needs? How might knowing what she is experiencing in the legal context assist you in reengaging Ms. Jones in the process and what kinds of concrete supports and services might you provide? What information might you provide that is relevant to her legal situation? How might your knowledge of her legal situation impact the level of urgency you might feel for her to obtain housing? What might you have to add as her advocate at a safety planning conference? What do you need to know about a parent's rights during an investigation and after a removal and how that knowledge might assist you in restoring your therapeutic alliance with your client? How might a client's knowledge of their rights heighten their feelings of safety and security? Certainly, one of the first steps in incorporating legal knowledge into your practice in the implicit legal context is to consider these questions when working with clients and beginning the process of ascertaining a legal case's impact on your client.

THE INITIAL MEETING WITH THE CLIENT IN A CIVIL CASE

Oftentimes, the initial meeting with a client in a civil case will be in the heightened environment of court on the day of the first hearing. However, in some cases, the client may know their first court appearance in a civil matter in advance and the interdisciplinary team will have more time to meet with the client and prepare for the first appearance. In either instance, it is critical for social workers to understand the perspective taken by an attorney during the first meeting with the client and to think through, in an interdisciplinary manner, the social work perspective supporting the work of the lawyer advocating for the client. Although it may seem obvious, the initial meeting is critical for setting the stage with a client about your role as the social worker in a legal case and the expectations for the professional relationship with the client. This section summarizes the considerations for both the attorney and the social worker during the first meeting.

Attorney Considerations

The initial meeting with the client is an opportunity for the attorney to establish trust and rapport at a moment of crisis and uncertainty for the client. In the case of Ms. Jones, the attorney would want to review the petition's allegations with Ms. Jones and obtain some basic information. Most importantly, the attorney would have an eye toward the upcoming court appearance and would likely provide information to Ms. Jones about the other parties in the courtroom and the decisions that the court would be making at this time. Ms. Jones should know from the outset that the legal team works on her behalf to accomplish her goals. Clearly identifying the roles played by the attorney and the social worker, and reiterating that the legal team works for her and not the child protective agency, the court, or any other agency, can often most effectively communicate this. One of the most effective ways of communicating roles is to delineate the rule of confidentiality for the client so that the client understands that the legal team is bound by attorney/client privilege, whereas other stakeholders in her case are not and may be mandated to report suspicions of neglect or abuse.

Social Worker Perspective

It is very important that the social worker understands the role they are playing in a government-initiated civil proceeding. In the case of Michelle Jones, a social worker could be the child protective caseworker who made the decision to remove Ms. Jones's son. A social worker could also be employed by the child's attorney or law guardian and in that role, you would be concerned about obtaining information about what might be best for the well-being of Ms. Jones's son. There are also alternative problem-solving courts in family court, many related to substance abuse and as we know from the research, a very large majority of child protective cases, perhaps as much as 80%, involve substance abuse allegations (Smith et al., 2005). You might be employed by the court to assess the appropriateness of Ms. Jones for referral to a special court. You might also be working with children or adult victims of abuse who have been referred for treatment. Finally, and for purposes of this discussion, you could also be employed or appointed by the court to assist Ms. Jones's attorney with her representation.

The role you play will influence what information you may need to obtain, who you may speak to, and the level of trust you may expect from the client. Regardless of your role, you will need to know the legal questions to be decided and use your interviewing skills to obtain the best possible information for the judge to make an informed decision about the legal question at hand or for those professionals in the role of advocates to use in their representation of the client. The principles of honesty, transparency, respect, and identification of one's potential biases all apply to the practice of interviewing in legal situations.

In this case, regardless of role, the social worker will be dealing with the very sensitive and difficult issue of a child, here a newborn infant, being removed from their parent. The stakes attached to this issue are high for everyone involved. One way to think about approaching this task, regardless of role, is to remember that the judge is the person who has the power to decide and that your job is to conduct an assessment that will give the judge factual, relevant, and useful information that will assist them in this decision-making.

Additionally, it is important to understand the provisions of confidentiality and to recognize the other professionals involved in the case and whether the same confidentiality provisions bind them. For example, once a petition is filed, the client should only speak to the attorney who is assigned to their case or retained to be their attorney. Any other attorney—for the child welfare agency or the child—is not allowed to speak to the client since they are a represented party in a pending legal case pursuant to their ethical guidelines for attorneys. This does not apply, however, to the CPS caseworker, who is not an attorney and who, in the vast majority of jurisdictions, is still allowed and expected to speak directly to your client about the substance of the case. Additionally, the child protective caseworker is not under any obligation to keep your client's information confidential and in fact has a professional obligation to report and record all of their interactions with your client to the child protective agency and attorney. As you might imagine, this may be a complicated setting for Ms. Jones as she decides who she should confide in and trust throughout a stressful and potentially overwhelming process.

One of the difficulties for the social worker involved in legal cases is that there are generally time limits applied to your ability to collect information and develop rapport. The client may be guarded and self-protective, and many times appropriately so. You are most likely meeting your client for the first time at the first court date or initial hearing. This means that the primary source of information will be your client and skilled and focused interviewing is critical for competence in this arena, particularly for forensic social workers. There are several significant limitations and considerations when interviewing children, victims of violence, and those with learning or developmental difficulties. Those considerations are covered in more depth in Chapter 8. For this chapter, we use an interview with a competent adult as our example.

A social worker who is called on to make an assessment at this point in the process will need to know the following: (a) risk and protective factors found to be associated or correlated with neglect, particularly when a parent is using substances, (b) what the research tell us about prenatal maternal use of drugs and the subsequent effects on the newborn, (c) how to assess for substance use and substance abuse, (d) what services have been found to be effective for treatment of drug use, (e) what services or interventions have been found to reduce risk for children when their parents use or abuse substances both prenatally and subsequent to the birth, (f) potential effects of removal on the infant and the mother, and (g) knowledge about child development and trauma.

Another key function of the social worker would be to contextualize the experience for both Ms. Jones and her infant for the attorney to inform any arguments to the court. The challenge is how to present the situation faced by Ms. Jones and her infant so that the very real effects of this important decision are central to the argument. For example, what is it like for Ms. Jones to be still feeling the physical effects of childbirth but not have access to her baby or even possibly understand what has happened to her and how it happened? What is the experience of a newborn that has been separated from his mother? The social worker can provide invaluable assistance by gathering information and research to provide this context and to inform the lawyer's arguments on behalf of Ms. Jones.

Considerations for Both Professionals

It is important to note that the initial interview can frequently be hindered because the goals of the attorney and the goals of the client are not the same. For example, Ms. Jones is most likely primarily concerned with knowing the outcome of the court appearance, whereas the attorney has to gather some essential information about their client's background while also informing the client of what will happen in court and their rights under the law. It can be difficult, to say the least, to reconcile these competing goals. The attorney cannot provide any assurance about the outcome of the court appearance without first obtaining information to assess the merits of the petition. In many instances, a social worker assisting the attorney in the initial interview will have tools to help redirect the conversation so that the most important information can be conveyed to the client, but also to make sure that the client's questions are answered to the extent possible.

Once the CPS decides to remove a child from a parent's care, the first hearing available to a parent is with a judge to determine whether the child can be immediately returned to the parent's care. In most jurisdictions, this hearing can happen on the very first day in family court or soon thereafter. As we discussed earlier in Chapter 6, the court's inquiry must focus on any imminent risk to the child's life or health and whether there are services that could ameliorate the identified risk to the child.

At this preliminary hearing, the burden of proof rests on the child protective agency, which must present evidence supporting that the child is at imminent risk if the child remains with the parent. The child protective caseworker will testify to their investigation of the family, discussions with collateral sources including other service providers and relatives, and the results of any family team conference convened by the caseworker. Other witnesses to the alleged neglect or abuse can testify as well to demonstrate that the child remains at imminent risk. Finally, the child protective agency can present documents and records from hospitals, service providers, schools, and caseworker records as well.

The attorney for the parent can present their own witnesses and records to support that the child is not at imminent risk. This evidence can include services and support that can be put in place or are already in place to alleviate risk. The attorney for the child can also present their own witnesses and records, depending on the position that they are taking with regard to the potential placement of their client. As noted earlier, the family court proceeding is presided over by the judge who also serves as the finder of fact. Therefore, the judge hears all the evidence and then determines whether the child will be temporarily placed in foster care or returned to the care of the parents. The pretrial hearing is not a hearing or trial on the allegations in the petition, but limited to whether the child can be returned to their parent's care. Therefore, the court is not making a finding of abuse or neglect at this hearing, but solely determining the placement of the child to ensure there is no risk of harm. Typically, a court is not able to order a parent to undergo any evaluations or participate in any services until there has been a finding of abuse or neglect. However, if a court decides to return a child to their parent's care prior to the fact finding on the allegations in the petition, the judge can place conditions on that order including, for example, participation in services, random drug testing, or cooperation with the child welfare agency.

The initial meeting is an opportunity to discover crucial information that is not found in the legal documents. In many cases, the only information that the attorney has when first meeting a client is biased and incomplete. The petition in Ms. Jones's case does not include any mitigating evidence and consists solely of allegations of neglect. In addition to knowing the client's reaction to the allegations, the attorney must obtain considerable information about Ms. Jones's family, background, medical situation, and substance abuse. Ideally, a degree of trust will have been established through the discussion of confidentiality and zealous advocacy so that the client is receptive to answering intimate questions.

This information gathering begins the process of developing a legal strategy with your client that will guide the next steps.

INTERVIEWING THE CLIENT: WHAT ARE THE LEGAL ISSUES AND IMPLICATIONS FOR DEVELOPING INTERVIEW QUESTIONS?

The following example illustrates how an attorney and a social worker would attempt to begin explaining their roles, gaining the client's trust and gathering critical information to advocate for their case. For the purposes of this scenario, we proceed with the understanding that the social worker is employed by the legal services office working directly with the attorney on the legal case and therefore not subject to mandated reporter requirements:

Attorney: As your attorney, I am responsible for representing you in this case. This means that I will be your advocate in court and will make sure that the judge has all the information that you want the judge to have in your case. It also means that I will defend you against any allegations that the child welfare agency makes and will fight to get your child home with you if that is what you want. I do not work for the court, the judge, CPS, or the child's attorney. I work for you. While everything that you say to me is confidential, that is not the case for anyone else that you speak with in this case. What you say to the judge, caseworker, or foster parent is not confidential and can and most likely will be relayed to the child welfare agency or the judge. I hope that you feel comfortable speaking openly with me, since that will help me represent you in this case.

Again, as your attorney, everything you say to me is confidential because I am representing you and as a lawyer am required to keep your information confidential. This means that I am required to keep everything you tell me in confidence unless you give me permission to disclose it. If I believe that there is information that will help your case, we will talk about disclosing that to the other attorneys and the judge. If I believe that there is information that could harm your case, we will talk about why I believe you should not reveal that information to anyone other than your legal team.

Social Worker: As the social worker who works with your attorney, I also work just for you, not for the judge or for CPS. I will work with you, and with your attorney, to identify services and resources you will need to achieve the outcome you want in court. I will help your attorney with your defense by making sure that the assessments of other professionals are accurate and are based on the appropriate professional standards. Our job is to make sure that the story you tell us about what happened and about your experience gets told in court. It is important for you to tell me honestly what are your challenges and what you may be struggling with so that we can make a plan together to help address them. It is also important for you to share with us your understanding of what happened with your case and your knowledge of the allegations and reports. This is important so we know the information shared with you, how it was shared, and your full understanding. As your social worker in this case, I will also keep what you tell me confidential and will only speak to others with your permission. If I feel that you are doing something that could put you or someone else at risk, I will speak with you about that directly and share that with your attorney.

As we discussed in Chapter 5, prior to the interview with the client there needs to be a conversation with the attorney where you share your research and where you collaboratively identify the key issues that will be addressed in the current proceeding. A social worker does not need to wait for an attorney to initiate this meeting. In fact, a busy attorney will appreciate a meeting with a focused and informed agenda that can assist in preparing them and the client for the upcoming proceedings. The attorney can help you know the standards the judge will be using to make their decision. This will then assist you in developing questions that are targeted to obtain information that will be helpful in advocating for your client as well as being better able to explain the relevance of your questions to your client. By explaining the relevance of each question to the legal matter you are giving the client important information about the legal process and balancing the interview between getting information from your client and giving information to your client.

In Chapter 5, the attorney and the social worker for Ms. Jones identified those areas where the law and social science intersected. The attorney and the social worker focused their research and developed memos that reported on what they found. A central aspect of the attorney's case is figuring out whether Ms. Jones's use of drugs during her pregnancy resulted in "impairment" or "risk of impairment" to her newborn son. The second aspect of the legal case is addressing whether Ms. Jones was in treatment or conversely why she might not have obtained treatment. The attorney and the social worker can use their respective research memos to explain to each other—and most importantly to the client—why they are asking particular questions. It will be helpful for you to refer to the legal research memo exemplar and the social science short research memo so you can see how other professionals used them in developing their collaborative interview plan.

The following section presents a guide for developing interview questions for the attorney and social worker to begin gathering critical information, build trust with your client, and develop an advocacy strategy in partnership with your client. Because there are several issues in our sample case, the guide uses the petition to help organize the structure of the questions for both professionals. Additionally, we return to our concept of relevance to help identify clearly the basis for the question which should always guide your practice with clients.

Gathering Information About the Allegations of Child Neglect

1. Allegation of Substance Abuse

A. Substance Use History

Sample Questions:

The petition states that CPS is alleging that you have a history of untreated drug abuse. It is important to understand that information on this issue is critical for us to be able to address the allegations. It is also important to know that we do not and will not judge your behavior or history. If you can share this information with us, we will be able to work together on a plan to respond to the petition's allegations.

Can you please tell us if you have used drugs before? If you have used, how long you have used drugs and what kinds of drugs? How do you think that this has impacted your everyday life? Have you ever enrolled in a drug treatment program? The child protective agency has also claimed that you never completed a drug program even though you had been referred to one. What do you think of that claim? Can you tell us about how and when you were referred to a program? Have you ever had any other treatment for drug use? If so, where and what form of treatment did you undergo? If not, can you share with us why you decided not to enter a treatment program? Did you or do you have concerns about entering treatment? If you stopped treatment, what was the reason? How do you feel your use is affecting you now, and what do you want to do about it? What do you think would be best for you and best for your family? Please also share and include any challenges or reservations you have?

Relevance: Why You Are Asking—Attorney

In New York State, a child is not considered to be a neglected child under the law unless the parent failed to use a minimum degree of care because of their drug use. Additionally, if a parent is engaged in a drug rehabilitation program, then drug use alone is not sufficient proof of neglect. However, proof that a parent repeatedly misused a drug would be enough for the court to find that a child is neglected. With this legal foundation in mind, the attorney would want to inquire further about Ms. Jones's admission to the caseworker of cocaine and marijuana use. Given that this is the main allegation in the petition, it would be critical to determine what if any evidence the petitioner might have on this issue. Did she tell the hospital social worker that she used the drugs once or frequently? Is there any evidence such as drug tests that corroborate the allegation that she is a repeated drug user? Is there any proof that the caseworker or any other provider made a referral for her to a drug treatment program?

Relevance: Why You Are Asking—Social Worker

It is important for the social worker to understand whether and if Ms. Jones has a substance abuse history and how this may impact both her ability to participate in her legal defense as well as how it may affect her capacity to parent. If Ms. Jones does have a problem with substance abuse, knowing the type of substance, frequency of use, and the circumstances under which she uses substances will be important in determining what kinds of services and treatment she may need, if any. Also, it will be important for the social worker to know from both a legal and clinical perspective what barriers may exist to participation in treatment so these may be addressed if treatment is mandated or entered into on a voluntary basis, as well as to explain why treatment was disrupted. The social worker would also be thinking about how the research reveals that pregnancy and childbirth is a time where there is a high degree of motivation to stop use of drugs. Again, gaining information about the father as a potential support or resource is important to explore regarding expanding client options.

B. Prenatal Use History

Sample Questions:

What did you share with the hospital social worker about using drugs? What else did you tell her about when you use drugs? Can you tell me how often you used marijuana? Cocaine? When you used drugs, how much did you use and how frequently? Were there certain times during the pregnancy you used more than others? Can you remember the months of the pregnancy? Did something triggered the use? Were you under any significant stress during your pregnancy? Can you explain what some of those stressors were, including if they were internal or external, physical stress and so forth?

Did you receive prenatal care? Do you feel like you were able to get access to food and nourishment while you were pregnant? Did you feel like you were able to eat and care for yourself for the full duration of your pregnancy? At any point where you referred for resources or connections from the hospital or other agencies? Can you share what they were or if you were able to access them? Did you use any other substances, or drink alcohol during your pregnancy? Was the father of the baby involved during the pregnancy? Were there any other programs or services that helped you during your pregnancy?

Relevance: Why You Are Asking—Attorney

The attorney will need to know whether there were other mandated reporters, such as doctors and nurses, interacting with her and observing her during her pregnancy. Additionally, it is helpful to know what steps Ms. Jones took to protect, prepare for, and care for her child during her pregnancy and after birth. Because the child is so young, it is reasonable to consider prenatal care as evidence of her ability to parent. The attorney representing Ms. Jones will always view her case with an eye to potential legal defenses in court. For example, the attorney might argue that the risk to the infant was greatly decreased by Ms. Jones's participation in regular prenatal care where the health of her baby was frequently monitored. Knowing that the law requires that Ms. Jones exercise a minimum degree of care toward her child, the attorney would want to know the level of involvement that Ms. Jones had with any healthcare providers during her pregnancy in addition to any other programs or services that would support her and the baby's health and stability.

Relevance: Why You Are Asking—Social Worker

At this point in the case, a social worker would have begun to research the literature on whether prenatal substance use always results in harm to the child. Frequency and severity, as well as timing of use during gestation can all impact whether or not there will be impairment. In addition, we know that other conditions such as poor nutrition, maternal stress, and lack of prenatal care can also impact a child's development. If Ms. Jones did seek out prenatal care during her pregnancy, this could be seen as a protective factor when it comes to assessing the risk of potential neglect. We also know, that in terms of risk of neglect, that the type of substance also matters with use of some substances being more likely to result in neglect (Cash & Wilke, 2003).

C. Testing at Birth

Sample Questions:

So, let us start with the allegation that your drug use is placing your baby at risk of harm. The CPS worker has stated that you told the hospital social worker that you used marijuana and cocaine during your pregnancy. Can you tell us about the conversation you had with the hospital social worker? Did the conversation take place before or after you and your baby were tested?

Did you know that you were being tested? Did anyone explain to you that you would be tested for drugs and what might happen with the results? Did you give consent to test you and your child—either in writing or orally—to a nurse or hospital staff member? Did you understand fully what you were consenting to? Do you have any of your records from the hospital? Did you ask for any of your records and were you offered any of your records?

Relevance: Why You Are Asking—Attorney

The attorney wants to understand whether Ms. Jones's rights were violated during her hospital stay, including her right to full information and the requirement for her voluntary and informed consent for any medical tests. The attorney might be concerned that the hospital has a pattern and practice of testing for drugs based on the age and race of the mother and that this practice is more widespread than Ms. Jones's case. The attorney would want to know what other witnesses might say about Ms. Jones's admissions. It will also be critical evidence to review the hospital records for what was documented about her admissions of use and what, if any, services were offered.

Relevance: Why You Are Asking—Social Worker

The social worker would want to ask Ms. Jones more about her conversation with the hospital social worker and see if her disclosures were a manifestation of her desire to engage in treatment. This would suggest protective action regarding her new baby. Additionally, the social worker would want to know whether the hospital social worker provided Ms. Jones with the relevant information when gaining her consent and making the report.

D. Criminal Case

Sample Questions:

The CPS has also reported you were arrested while pregnant for possession of drugs. Can you tell us more about this? What were the circumstances of the arrest? Were you arrested while you were pregnant? Were you held in jail for any period? Were you with the child's father during this time? When were you arrested? Who is your lawyer? Do you know how to contact them and when is the last time you were able to talk to that lawyer? Do you know what the charge was? Have you ever been arrested before? Have you ever been convicted of a crime? Do you know when your next court date is? Do you know if you are being charged and what your full charges are? Would you be willing to give me permission to speak with your criminal defense lawyer?

Relevance: Why You Are Asking—Attorney

It will be critical for the attorney in family court to understand what Ms. Jones is facing in criminal court and to reach out to her criminal attorney as well. It is also helpful for the attorney to get a better sense of Ms. Jones's awareness of her legal issues and her ability to comprehend the two pending cases. The petition informs us that Ms. Jones was arrested and charged with a drug crime. However, it does not tell us the status of her case.

Relevance: Why You Are Asking—Social Worker

The social worker would be interested in knowing the circumstances of the arrest as well as the timing of the event in relation to the pregnancy. Additionally, the level of stress involved, such as being held in jail during pregnancy, could have an impact on the development of the child as well as the anxiety level of the mother, also related to potential risk of neglect by substance using mothers. The social worker would also be interested whether the criminal court case has mandated any programs or services.

2. *Allegation of Impairment or Risk of Impairment*

A. Positive Toxicology

Sample Questions:

The petition states that your son was born with a positive toxicology at birth. Do you understand what this means? To your knowledge, did he have any health problems? Did he require any special medical interventions? Do you know if he has been eating? Has he been gaining weight? Is he on any special medication? Did you ever get tested before for drugs when you were pregnant? Do you know the results of those tests? Were you provided with any information from the hospital about your son's health or any next steps in his medical care?

Relevance: Why You Are Asking—Attorney

The attorney will want to know whether there is any immediate harm or risk of harm from the alleged substance abuse. Additionally, the attorney will want to know whether there are other drug tests, which might show that the positive test at birth was an isolated incidence. Additionally, if Ms. Jones was tested throughout her pregnancy, there is potential evidence of the level of substance abuse and concerns raised as a result of her drug use.

Relevance: Why You Are Asking—Social Worker

This information is critical regarding determining the potential impact on child development, as we know that timing and frequency of use have an impact on child development. Additionally, this information will help the social worker identify potential health issues for Ms. Jones and her son that may impact the development of a plan of services and supports.

B. Medical Status of Infant

Sample Questions:

Did your son's pediatrician in the hospital tell you anything about his physical condition or whether there were any medical concerns about your son? Did you have a vaginal or cesarean delivery? Was the baby's father present? Did you deliver around your due date, or did you deliver early? Do you remember what the APGAR score was for your son? What was his weight at birth? Do you remember the sound of his cry? If you could describe it, how would you say it sounded? Was your baby easily startled? Do you remember if the baby was shaking? How would you describe your son after he was born?

Relevance: Why You Are Asking—Attorney

The attorney wants to have a better understanding of the actual harm or risk of harm for the child. Therefore, the attorney will include questions that look at the other tests for the baby's health and well-being. To understand the other results, the attorney will want to know the context of these tests by inquiring whether Ms. Jones faced any additional medical issues during her labor which would impact the baby's test results.

Relevance: Why You Are Asking—Social Worker

Based on what the social worker found in the research regarding the impact of drug use during pregnancy, it would be important to explore whether there were effects on the growth of the child and whether the markers of potential problems with neurological development were present. Conversely, a normal birth weight and delivery that was not premature could indicate a lack of impairment, and a potential defense to the petition. It would be important for the team to know what claims may be raised from the medical history, and the client's perception of her son's health and well-being.

C. Interaction With Her Infant Son During Hospital Stay

Sample Questions:

Can you tell us about Matthew? What kind of baby do you feel he is? Who would you say he looks like? How much contact did you have with Matthew while you were still in the hospital? Were you able to feed him on your own, and what method of feeding did you use? Were you able to change him? Did you have any friends or family who visited and observed Matthew in the hospital with you? Did the baby's father or other relatives visit? What if anything did the nurses tell you about Matthew when he wasn't with you and was in the nursery? Was he easy to comfort when you held him? How did you take care of him in the hospital? When were you last able to see him, and how often have you seen him since you gave birth? How are you feeling about visitation and being about to spend time with Matthew?

Relevance: Why You Are Asking—Attorney

The attorney will focus on presenting evidence to the court that Ms. Jones is fit to parent her infant. The attorney would want to show that Ms. Jones cared appropriately for the infant while they were in the hospital, understood the infant's needs, and began the process of bonding with the infant. This information may also be included in the hospital records but would be critical to obtain from Ms. Jones who may have to testify to her caregiving in the hospital if there is an emergency hearing to return Matthew to her care.

Relevance: Why You Are Asking—Social Worker

The condition and temperament of the infant relates to the question of impairment or risk of impairment. These questions also begin to assess parenting capacity and the presence of supportive, protective factors in relation to risk of neglect and harm to the child.

3. *Removal*

A. Circumstances of Removal

Sample Questions:

Who told you that Matthew was being removed? When were you told? What was your response? Did you attempt to leave the hospital with your son? Do you know if your son was medically ready to be discharged? Did you offer any family members to help take care of your son? Who have you spoken to since? Have you been told about where he is? Have you been allowed to visit? When was the last time that you saw him and how long were you able to visit with him?

Relevance: Why You Are Asking—Attorney

The attorney must evaluate whether there would be more harm to the infant being removed from his mother's care than remaining in her care with services to make an argument for the child's return. Therefore, the attorney would want to know the circumstances of the removal and whether Ms. Jones has seen her son since the removal. Additionally, the attorney wants to know what the visitation has been like and begin to formulate an argument for frequent and meaningful visitation between Ms. Jones and Matthew, if the hearing to return the child is not successful. An example of an argument would be that the removal is more harmful to Matthew during this critically important time in infant development and especially if Ms. Jones is appropriately bonding with her son and perhaps if she is breastfeeding as well.

Relevance: Why You Are Asking—Social Worker

The removal of a child is a severely traumatic event for a parent and a child regardless of the circumstances necessitating the removal. Particularly for parents who are among communities most marginalized, those who have a history of trauma or who have been in the foster care system themselves, removal can trigger a host of symptoms including anxiety and depression, and at times relapse. It will be important to assist the client in managing the strong emotions and reactions they will have to their infant being removed. These reactions can influence how they respond to CPS workers during the investigation and even how they present to a judge. Knowing Ms. Jones's reaction and feelings to this event and helping her manage her response allow the social worker to assist Ms. Jones with her presentation during the CPS investigation and during the upcoming hearing. It is also important from a developmental perspective that Ms. Jones has very frequent contact with her infant son, and this may be an advocacy issue for the attorney and social worker.

B. Assessment of Reasonable Efforts by Agency

Sample Questions:

Has CPS spoken to you about any services or programs that would allow you to keep Matthew with you? Have they referred you to any programs for drug treatment? Have they asked you about any relatives who might be willing to care for Matthew? Have they asked you who the baby's father is? What other questions have they asked you? Have you had a visit with your baby? Did CPS observe the visit and how you interacted with your baby? What would you want to have in place to help you if Matthew came home to your care?

Relevance: Why You Are Asking—Attorney

The attorney will assess whether the agency exercised the required reasonable efforts prior to removing Ms. Jones's son to avoid having the child placed in foster care. Additionally, the attorney would want to understand what services the client was willing to participate in and also what services were seen as necessary to the child protective agency. This will allow the attorney to start developing cross-examination questions for the child protective agency caseworker and potential recommendations to the judge about what orders can be put in place to reunite Ms. Jones with her son safely.

Relevance: Why You Are Asking—Social Worker

The social worker would be interested in evaluating the kind of assessment that was done by CPS and whether there was any assessment specifically related to parenting capacity. The social worker would also want to know what type of risk assessment instrument CPS is using: consensus based or actuarial. Frequently, there is an assumption that substance use will automatically mean a parent will neglect their child, and it would be important for the social worker to identify those assumptions for the attorney to identify potential lines of questioning on cross examination of the CPS caseworker.

C. Postremoval Functioning

Sample Questions:

How are you feeling physically? How are you feeling emotionally on a scale of 1 to 10? Are you feeling depressed anxious? Are there things you have access to or are doing to help you cope during this period? Who is supporting you? Do you feel safe? Are there friends or relatives in your immediate environment that are using drugs? How are you feeling regarding your usage or sobriety?

Relevance: Why You Are Asking—Attorney

The attorney needs to assess Ms. Jones's emotional status to determine whether she should testify at the hearing and also if additional short-term supports might be necessary. Also, the attorney would want to know about relatives and friends since the law in New York favors placing children with their relatives over strangers.

Relevance: Why You Are Asking—Social Worker

The social worker is doing a brief assessment to determine what services and support Ms. Jones may need immediately. Ms. Jones's physical and emotional status is important information relating to her current capacity to parent as well as her ability to recover from substance use. If a client is actively in a rehabilitation program, it is important to note that relapse is a part of recovery and must be explored during a traumatic event with the client or with the client in drug treatment. Additionally, Ms. Jones has recently delivered a child and based on subsequent events may be at risk for postpartum depression. The issue is not whether Ms. Jones is depressed; the issue is whether she is managing her depression in a proactive way that minimizes the impact of depression on her capacity to parent. Other protective factors such as social support are also important to explore.

4. *Current Level of Functioning and Risk Assessment*

A. Plan for Care of Self and Child

Sample Questions:

What was your plan when you and Matthew were discharged from the hospital? Where would you live? Who would live with you? What would you do to support Matthew? What items did you have to prepare for Matthew's arrival? What do you still need for your son? What was your plan for Matthew's medical care? Do you have family members and friends who are able to help? What about Matthew's father? How were you preparing to care for your baby? Have you ever cared for a baby before? What did you already know and what were you hoping to learn about caring for an infant? Why do you want Matthew to come home with you?

Relevance: Why You Are Asking—Attorney

The attorney needs to present evidence that the child would not be at risk if returned to Ms. Jones's care. One of the ways of accomplishing this legal goal is to present evidence that Ms. Jones has prepared to care for the baby, including having provisions, information, and a support network. Additionally, it would be important for the attorney to present the reasons why Ms. Jones wishes to have Matthew home with her and prove her love for her son.

Relevance: Why You Are Asking—Social Worker

Again, the social worker is making an immediate assessment of whether Ms. Jones has the ability to provide a "minimal degree of care" for herself and her infant. The social worker is also beginning to assess Ms. Jones's knowledge of child development and whether she has the information necessary to respond to the needs of her infant. Lack of information about child development and developmentally inappropriate expectations of infants and children is a risk factor for child neglect. Although the social worker in this instance is in the role of client advocate, an important aspect of advocacy is to understand if the risk factors that CPS will be assessing are present to any degree in your case so that you can develop an immediate safety plan that targets risk factors and increases protective factors.

B. Safety Plan for Child in the Event of Relapse

Sample Questions:

What are some of the circumstances that preceded your use of substances in the past? Would you be willing to make a list of some of the warning signs that indicate you might use again? If your infant is returned to you and you relapse, what is your plan to keep him safe and to make sure he receives care? Is there anyone who can be available to come and get your child when you begin to notice the warning signs? Are there any other family members or friends who can be involved in monitoring the plan or reminding you when they see some of the warning signs?

Relevance: Why You Are Asking—Attorney

Proactively, the attorney would want to know other risk factors that might be present for Ms. Jones so that they can be minimized.

Relevance: Why You Are Asking—Social Worker

Parents, significant others, children if they are old enough, and extended families should develop a written safety plan which identifies warning signs of relapse. It is good practice to develop this plan and make sure it specifies who will take what steps to ensure the children's safety if these warning signs occur. This is a proactive way to meet the concerns of the court and CPS. We know that even when in treatment, relapses during early recovery are common and it is best practice to be prepared for this eventuality. This plan can also address concerns about risk of harm and the ability to provide a minimum degree of care.

5. *Discussion of Potential Outcomes After the Initial Court Appearance*

A. Reunification

Sample Discussion and Questions:

As we mentioned before, the judge will hold a hearing to determine whether Matthew will be returned to your care. At the hearing, the judge will hear testimony from the caseworker and read any reports that are submitted from the agency. Those reports will probably include the results from the toxicology tests and may also include other medical reports. We have the opportunity to present evidence also and can share the plans that you had to take care of Matthew in your home, the services that you were already working with, and the prenatal care that you received. If you decided that you wanted to enter an outpatient treatment program, we could also present the judge with evidence documenting that you have entered treatment. Once the hearing is concluded, the judge will make a decision. One outcome is that the judge could return Matthew to your care and require you participate in services. These services could include drug treatment, parenting skills training, child abuse, and neglect prevention programs that could take place in your home. These services will be part of a court order and if you fail to do the services, that can be used against you in court.

If you were able to have services in your home, which services might be helpful for you? For example, some programs have nurses who will assist you in learning more about child development and caring for a newborn as well as taking care of yourself. What are the issues that are most troubling to you and for which you wish immediate help?

Relevance: Why You Are Asking—Attorney

The attorney is thinking both in the short-term and long-term framework for Ms. Jones. In the short term, the goal may be to have the hearing so that Ms. Jones's child can return to her care. However in the long term, the attorney wants to ensure that the home situation is stable so as to prevent the child from going back into care. In either situation, the attorney wants to explore what services are amenable to Ms. Jones so that she knows her preferences when discussing any potential court orders. It is also important for Ms. Jones to understand the process in the hearing so that she will know what to expect in the courtroom and how she can be best prepared for the hearing.

Relevance: Why You Are Asking—Social Worker

In their review of the evaluation literature of substance abuse treatment for parents involved in the child welfare system, Osterling and Austin (2006) report that home visiting programs by a nurse who also provided support and linkages to concrete services had many positive outcomes in relation to child development and further involvement in the child welfare or criminal justice system. When mothers were able to retain custody of their children while participating in outpatient substance abuse programs, they were more likely to complete the program, less depressed, and more likely to abstain (Osterling & Austin, 2006). With this knowledge, the social worker would want to explore whether Ms. Jones would be amenable to this program and whether it would provide helpful supports to her.

B. Mother Child Treatment Program

Sample Discussion and Questions:

Another decision could be that the Judge orders that Matthew live with you in a residential mother/child drug treatment program. However, you should know that there are frequently waiting lists for those kinds of programs, and his return would most likely be on the condition that you maintain compliance and participation in the program. What do you think about that option? What concerns would you have about that option? What would appeal to you about being in a program with Matthew? What questions do you have about that option?

Relevance: Why You Are Asking—Attorney

If the judge credits the testimonies of the child welfare caseworker and hospital social worker of ongoing substance abuse, the attorney may advise the client that a mother/child drug treatment program would be the only acceptable placement for the judge to consider in returning the child to Ms. Jones's care. In that instance, there would be a court order mandating that the child remains in care with his mother at the treatment program. The attorney has an obligation to make sure that Ms. Jones fully understands the terms and conditions of that outcome, including the consequences of leaving the program with or without the child and violating the court's order. Additionally, the attorney may counsel on this option if Ms. Jones does not have stable housing available because the mother/child program would provide a place for the family to reside safely and with supports in place.

Relevance: Why You Are Asking—Social Worker

The client should know that there have been very positive results reported by residential programs that meet the needs of both mothers and their children, particularly children who are born with positive toxicology. In a review of the evaluation literature, Osterling and Austin (2006) report that in programs where women live with their children they are much more likely to complete treatment, are less depressed, have increased likelihood of employment, less chance of criminal justice involvement, and greater self-esteem. Clark (2001) reports that children in residential care with their mother also had improved developmental screenings, were healthier and did better in school than children who were not treated with parents.

C. Placement in Foster Care

Sample Discussion and Questions:

Another possible outcome is that the judge could continue Matthew's placement in foster care and order the CPS agency to investigate your relatives as possible kinship foster parents. This is likely if the judge decides that your drug use continues to pose a risk to Matthew and you do not have a safe environment to care for him. Do you have any family supporting you? Are there any close friends that are able to help you? If Matthew had to live with a relative for some time, who would you want that to be? What do you know about their background? Have you talked to them about potentially taking care of your son? What are your concerns about having a relative as a potential caregiver for your son?

Relevance: Why You Are Asking—Attorney

Under N.Y. Fam. Crt. Act art. 10 § 1027 (b)(1) (2024), there is a statutory preference for children who are placed in foster care to live with relatives or family friends in kinship foster homes. In fact, the judge can order that the local child welfare agency "commence an investigation of the home of such relative or other suitable person within 24 hours and thereafter expedite approval or certification of such relative or other suitable person, if qualified, as a foster parent" pursuant to the same section of the Family Court Act. Many states have specific laws and policies that make it easier for relatives to become kinship care providers. For a review of state statutes that lay out the policies for kinship care and what benefits and supports kinship foster parents are entitled to, social workers can consult the state statute database maintained by the Child Welfare Information Gateway at https://www.childwelfare.gov/resources/states-territories-tribes/. An attorney would want to know about the client's relationship with family members who may be put forward as options for kinship foster care to ensure that they will be supportive of Ms. Jones's efforts to regain custody of her son.

Relevance: Why You Are Asking—Social Worker

Parents are often much more comfortable when their child is placed in the care of someone they know and trust. It is also easier for the parent to remain in communication with the child when placement is with a relative or a friend. It has also been found that children placed in kinship care experience more placement stability and have fewer behavior problems (Conway & Hutson, 2007). Children in kinship homes are less likely to reenter care after they've gone home or been adopted, and are three to four times less likely to be maltreated than children in traditional foster homes (Hurley, 2008). The social worker would want to work with Ms. Jones to identify relatives that she is comfortable with and assist her in having those conversations with relatives.

D. Counseling About Options and Identifying Your Client's Goals and Compromise Positions

Sample Discussion and Questions:

It is important that we know what your goal is and what you are willing to accept as an outcome. What is your goal for this hearing? Do you want Matthew returned to your care? If he is not able to return to your home, where would you want him to live? Who would you want to take care of him and why? What is most important to you and what do you not want to happen?

Relevance: Why You Are Asking—Attorney

It is critical for the attorney to understand the client's primary goal but also to identify what they are willing to compromise on and not willing to compromise on. This allows the attorney to identify potential compromise positions and ideally negotiate an outcome that is closest to their client's goals.

Relevance: Why You Are Asking—Social Worker

It is critical for the social worker to understand Ms. Jones's goals and what she is willing to accept. There are many more questions a competent social worker would want to ask to complete a comprehensive assessment of the needs and rights of their client. For women who have a substance abuse concern, it is important to address the many concrete needs, including mental health, medical care, housing education, employment, and legal needs while simultaneously providing substance abuse treatment. However, as we pointed out in the beginning of this section, you are interviewing and meeting your client for the first time before a preliminary, or removal hearing. Asking focused and targeted questions that will address the legal issues being decided will be critical to develop because you have a very limited time to access information and prepare your case. The social worker will have time after the preliminary hearing to set up meetings with their client in more comfortable and less crisis-oriented circumstances.

AFTER THE INTERVIEW: NEW FACTS AND NEW QUESTIONS IN THE CASE OF MS. JONES

After interviewing Ms. Jones, the attorney and social worker learn that she is 20 years old and this is her first child. The father of the baby has not been involved in her life for the last month, and she did not put his name on Matthew's birth certificate. She does not remember the nurses or doctors telling her that she was being tested for drugs, but she signed a number of forms when she came in to give birth. The hospital social worker told her that Matthew would most likely go into foster care because he had drugs in his system. The child welfare caseworker came to visit her in the hospital and asked her if she would enroll in a drug treatment program but did not clarify whether her son could be with her in the program. Ms. Jones told the caseworker that she would do whatever they asked as long as she was able to stay with her baby. She attempted to breastfeed Matthew but was told by the nursing staff that she could not because the marijuana was still in her system. She tells the team that she stopped using cocaine when she found out she was pregnant, but she smoked a couple of joints in the last months of her pregnancy. She has been living with her aunt who has a teenage son who is no longer living with her. Ms. Jones was arrested for trying to sell cocaine and is represented by a public defender. She started working with a local community-based organization after her arrest and met weekly with a counselor to talk about her drug use, relationship history, and growing up in foster care herself. The counselor convinced her to enroll in a drug treatment program, which she attended for a couple of months, but stopped attending when she got arrested. While she is answering the team's questions, she often breaks down and cries uncontrollably. She repeatedly asks the team when she will be able to see her baby and if she will be able to bring him home with her. She states that she has bought a crib, blankets, bottles, and clothes for the baby that are all at home. She has not seen Matthew in over 4 days because the hospital refused to let her be with the baby in the nursery over the weekend. She is adamant that she wants her son home with her and that she will be able to take care of him and keep him safe. She does not want him in foster care, especially since she was raised in the system herself.

REFERENCES

Adoption and Safe Families Act of 1997, 42 U.S.C. §1305 (1997).

American Bar Association. (1996). *Standards of practice for lawyers who represent children in abuse and neglect cases.* https://www.americanbar.org/content/dam/aba/administrative/child_law/repstandwhole.pdf

American Bar Association. (2004). *Standards of practice for lawyers representing child welfare agencies.* https://www.mncourts.gov/mncourtsgov/media/scao_library/CJI/ABA_Standards_for_Agency_Representation.pdf

American Bar Association. (2006). *Standards of practice for attorneys representing parents in abuse and neglect cases.* https://www.americanbar.org/content/dam/aba/administrative/child_law/aba-parent-rep-stds.pdf

Bergeron, L. R., & Gray, B. (2003). Ethical dilemmas of reporting suspected elder abuse. *Social Work, 48*(1), 96–105. https://doi.org/10.1093/sw/48.1.96

Camreta v. Greene, 563 U.S. 692 (2009).

Casey Family Services. (2009). *Family teaming: Comparing approaches.* https://www.pdx.edu/center-child-family/sites/centerchildfamily.web.wdt.pdx.edu/files/2020-07/FGC-family-teaming.pdf

Cash, S. J., & Wilke, D. J. (2003). An ecological model of maternal substance abuse and child neglect: Issues, analyses, and recommendations. *American Journal of Orthopsychiatry, 73*(4), 392–404. https://doi.org/10.1037/0002-9432.73.4.392

Child Abuse and Prevention Treatment Act of 1974, Pub. L. No. 93-247, 88 Stat. 5 (1974).

Child Welfare Information Gateway. (2008). D*ifferential response to reports of child abuse and neglect.* U.S. Department of Health and Human Services. https://www.govinfo.gov/content/pkg/GOVPUB-HE23_1200-PURL-gpo84530/pdf/GOVPUB-HE23_1200-PURL-gpo84530.pdf.

Clark, H. W. (2001). Residential substance abuse treatment for pregnant and postpartum women and their children: Treatment and policy implications. *Child Welfare, 80*(2), 179–198.

Colo. Rev. Stat. § 12-240-139(1)(a)(VI) (2010).

Conway, T., & Hutson, R. Q. (2007). *Is kinship good for kids?* Center for Law and Social Policy. https://www.clasp.org/sites/default/files/public/resources-and-publications/files/0347.pdf

Courtney, M. & Hook, J. (2012) Evaluation of the impact of enhanced parental legal representation on the timing of permanency outcomes for children in foster care. *Children and Youth Services Review, 34*(7), 1337–1343. https://doi.org/10.1016/j.childyouth.2012.03.016

Del. Code tit. 16, § 906(b) (9) (2007).

Fla. Ann. Stat. ch. 39, § 39.201(1)(a) (2010).

Fla. Ann. Stat. ch. 415, § 415.1051(2) (2023).

Hurley, K. (2008). Preserving family ties: after a long decline, kinship care becomes more common. *Child Welfare Watch, 15*, 8–13.

Idaho Code Ann. ch. 53, § 39–5302(dd)(10) (2010).

Lassiter v. Department of Social Services, 452 U.S. 18 (1981).

National Association of Social Workers as Amici Curiae in Support of Petitioners, Camreta v. Greene, 588 F.3d 1011 [09-1454, 09-1478], 2010.

N.M. Stat. Ann. ch. 32A, § 30-6-4 (1978).

N.M. Stat. Ann. ch. 32A, § 32A-4-4(B) (1978).

N.Y. Family Crt. Act, art. 10, § 1024(a)(i)–(ii) (2024).

N.Y. Fam. Crt. Act § 1027 (a)(i) (2024).

N.Y. Fam. Crt. Act, art. 10, § 1027 (2024).

N.Y. Fam. Crt. Act art. 10, § 1028 (2024).

N.Y. Fam. Court Act art. 10, § 1035 (2024).

N.Y. Fam. Crt. Act § 1027 (a)(i) (2024).
N.Y. Fam. Crt. Act art. 10 § 1027 (b)(1) (2024).
Ohio Rev. Code, c.5101, §§ 5101.67–5101.68.
Osterling, K. L., & Austin, M. J. (2006). Substance abuse interventions for parents involved in the child welfare system: Evidence and implications. *Journal of Evidence-Based Social Work*, *5*(1–2), 157–189. https://doi.org/10.1300/J394v05n01_07
Saltzman, A., & Furman, D. (1999). *Law in social work practice*. Nelson-Hall.
Scalzo, T. P. (2006). *Reporting requirement for competent adult victims of domestic violence*. National Center for the Prosecution of Violence Against Women, American Prosecutors Research Institute.
Smith, B., Elstein, S. G., & Klain, E. J. (2005). *Parental substance abuse, child protection and ASFA: Implication for policy makers and practitioners. Substance abuse policy research program ID #048783*. American Bar Association.
Taylor, L. (2009). *The unfulfilled promise: The right to counsel for parents and children in child welfare proceedings*. American Bar Association Center on Children and the Law.
Washington State Office of Public Defense. (2008). *Social worker practice standards*. https://opd.wa.gov/sites/default/files/2023-08/0062-2008_PRP_SW_Standards.pdf

CHAPTER 7

Criminal Proceedings, Stakeholders, and the Client

INTRODUCTION

In this chapter, we provide you with an overview of criminal court proceedings and your role as a social worker in the explicit context of criminal case representation and the implicit context when your clients are involved in the criminal justice system. You will learn about the processes that trigger a criminal case and what legal rights your client has during that process. We introduce you to the juvenile justice system, which handles cases involving youth who are accused of criminal activity. If you are a social worker in the implicit context such as working in a mental health clinic or community-based social service office, it is key to understand the process that clients go through when they come in contact with legal systems such as the juvenile or criminal justice system and what you can do to assist the client. You will also learn about the rights available when your client is a victim of crime. Finally, we identify important questions for your first collaborative interview with a client in a Criminal Court setting if you are a forensic social worker. We again use the concept of relevance as a framework to assist you in identifying the key issues that are of immediate concern for the social worker, lawyer, court, and always and most importantly, your client.

ARREST AND ARRAIGNMENT

There are many steps that happen before your client's case is filed in Criminal Court. It is important that you understand what happens to your client before a criminal case is filed, whether your client is charged with a crime or is the victim of a crime. Criminal cases all begin with the arrest of an individual who may then be formally charged with a crime. In every state, the police have the power to arrest individuals that they believe are in the process of committing or have committed a crime. In the legal context this is called "probable cause." These arrests can take place with or without an arrest warrant, which is an order from a Criminal Court judge authorizing an arrest. For example, an individual can be arrested on the street if a law enforcement officer believes there to be probable cause, and the individual would then be charged with a felony or misdemeanor crime. Arrests can take place in any range of places including a person's home or workplace. It is possible for someone to be arrested but not be charged with any criminal activity which is when a prosecutor declines to prosecute. The police also have the right to stop an individual in public to request information, but the individual in turn has the right to refuse to answer any questions and walk away.

However, if the police have what is referred to as a reasonable suspicion that an individual is carrying a weapon, then the police officer can conduct a pat down search of that individual (*Illinois v. Wardlow*, 2000).

An arrest is generally defined as when an individual is taken into custody by the police, and is not free to leave at their own will. Individuals have a number of rights during the arrest and interrogation processes, which have been laid out in the seminal Supreme Court case *Miranda v. Arizona* (1966). Those rights include police informing every individual when arrested that they have the right to remain silent, that anything they say can be used against them in Criminal Court, that they have the right to an attorney who can be present during the police questioning, and that if they cannot afford an attorney then one will be appointed to them by the court. The Fifth Amendment to the U.S. Constitution also provides that a suspect or criminal defendant can remain silent during police questioning and that silence cannot be held against the defendant in Criminal Curt. There are a number of national and state-specific resources for locating an individual's rights with respect to the police and the Criminal Court system. For example, the American Civil Liberties Union (ACLU, 2024) publishes a "Know Your Rights If …" series, outlining an individual's rights when stopped by police or immigration officers. In Pennsylvania, researchers have created a comprehensive video project describing the criminal justice process from arrest to possible incarceration (Institute on Disabilities, 2021). A resource such as this can be particularly helpful for individuals more comfortable with videotaped informational material as opposed to written material. It is helpful to identify organizations that focus on the rights of adults and juveniles when interacting with law enforcement and the criminal justice system, as they generally have considerable resources that describe client's rights and responsibilities during the process, as well as fact sheets and materials that you can share with your clients.

Stakeholders and Their Roles in the Criminal Justice System

Social workers interact with a number of different professionals when a client has a case in the criminal justice system. If you are a social worker providing nonlegal services to your client, it is critical that you understand what is happening legally for your client, where your services may intersect or impact the legal case, what role you may potentially play, and that other professionals at some future point may contact and communicate with you in connection with your client's criminal case. If you are a social worker providing legal services to your client, your work may be significantly linked to the Criminal Court process and require that you have multiple interactions with stakeholders who are part of the Criminal Court process and criminal justice system.

Understanding the roles of the different professionals in a Criminal Court case is essential to understanding the process that leads up to filing a criminal case. The roles played by those professionals can differ depending on the relation to the client's legal rights and responsibilities. As discussed in Chapter 3, where you learned about ethics and communication, it is critical for you to identify the roles played by various professionals and, depending on your role, the implications for the kind of relationship you and your client may have with each professional.

Social workers can also play a critical part in educating and counseling clients about the different systems and the importance of working with their attorney to understand their options, to enforce their rights, and to play an integral role in developing their legal strategy.

In our case example, Ms. Jones would encounter many different professionals throughout both of her cases in Family Court and Criminal Court. She meets the police at arrest and then court officers who run the courthouse when she is processed during arraignment, which is the first court appearance after an arrest. At arraignment, Ms. Jones will meet her court-appointed defense attorney if she is not able to afford her own counsel. She may also meet with a probation officer. The defense attorney will interview her before she meets with the Criminal Court judge, who ultimately has the power to decide whether Ms. Jones stays in jail that day by setting the terms of her bail or releases her without bail. During the first appearance before the Criminal Court judge, Ms. Jones will also meet the prosecutor, often referred to as the assistant district attorney, who is the city or county attorney responsible for prosecuting the criminal case on behalf of the jurisdiction. Given the number of players in the criminal court system, one of the first steps in helping clients through this process is your own understanding of the various professional roles in the legal system which are listed in the following.

Criminal Court Judge

The overarching role of a judge in a criminal matter is to preside over the legal proceeding and make sure there is a fair trial that comports with the law and is conducted in an orderly process. In a criminal case, the judge will assess the evidence presented by both sides to make sure it was legally obtained and determine what evidence is allowed into the trial. If there is a jury trial, the judge will also give instructions to the jury about the law or other standards that are relevant to the particular case and important for the jury to understand as part of their deliberations. In bench trials (i.e., no jury), the judge will assess the facts and evidence presented and come to a legal decision about the particular case determining guilt or innocence. If a defendant admits to the allegations in the criminal complaint or settles the case with a plea agreement, the judge will determine whether the admission or plea is legally acceptable, ensuring that the plea was informed and voluntarily made by the defendant. Throughout the criminal case, the judge can also make orders for evidence to be produced or for the defendant to stay away or refrain from contacting the victim. Finally, if the defendant is convicted of a crime, the judge will decide the sentence whether a trial by jury or a bench trial.

Prosecuting Attorney in Criminal Court

The role of the prosecuting attorney is to review all the evidence against an individual accused of committing a crime and, with the help of the police, victims of crime, and other witnesses, build a case against that person. Prosecuting attorneys are in charge of bringing criminal charges against individuals and presenting evidence that they believe should result in a conviction. They typically work under the jurisdiction of the city or county's district attorney. In

Ms. Jones's case, the district attorney's office would work with the police officers that arrested Ms. Jones to gather evidence to support the charge of her possession of drugs. The prosecutor would present that evidence at trial through witnesses that testify and documents or records that are entered into evidence, and would recommend a sentence for Ms. Jones that could be community service, a drug treatment program, or a period of incarceration. The prosecuting attorney would also negotiate with the defense attorney to determine whether there are any settlement options available to Ms. Jones. In most cases, the settlement offers may require Ms. Jones to make an admission of guilt.

Criminal Defense Attorney

The role of the criminal defense attorney is to represent the legal rights and interests of the criminal defendant and to ensure that the defendant receives due process of law including a fair trial. As part of that job, the defense attorney will evaluate the case that the prosecuting attorney is presenting by reviewing the evidence and determining the relative merits and weaknesses of the prosecution's case. A defense attorney will conduct their own investigation of the allegations and work on creating a defense to the alleged criminal behavior. Even when a client tells the defense attorney that they are guilty, a defense attorney will do everything possible to make sure that the client is not convicted of the crime that the client is charged with or receives the best possible legal outcome in their case. As we discussed earlier, the criminal defense attorney is required to maintain the client's confidentiality as part of the attorney–client relationship. The defense attorney is also ethically required to advocate zealously for the client in all aspects of their defense.

As a social worker for a client on a criminal matter, you can assume that the client has a criminal defense attorney because defendants in Criminal Court are entitled to an attorney regardless of whether or not the defendant can afford to hire an attorney. In *Gideon v. Wainwright* (1963), the U.S. Supreme Court concluded that the possibility of incarceration and the loss of an individual's freedom meant that every criminal defendant had the right to an attorney in a criminal proceeding, even if they could not afford to hire an attorney themselves. As a result, Criminal Courts can appoint a public defender or legal aid attorney to represent a client when the court determines that the client is unable to pay for their own legal representation. In some states, the state, county, or city reimburses private attorneys when the court appoints them to a client. In larger states like New York and Illinois, there is a robust system of public defenders and institutional providers where organizations provide court-appointed representation to poor clients. Many states, including New York, have both systems in place. It is important to remember that the attorney in Ms. Jones's case will represent her at every appearance in Criminal Court from arraignment through trials and sentencing, and will provide her with substantial advice and counsel about her legal options in the criminal case. However, as you learned in Chapter 1, there are serious concerns about the quality of representation for indigent defendants, in part because of the reduced funding and high caseloads of public defender programs. Part of advocating for your client is to familiarize yourself with the expectations for criminal defense attorneys published by the American Bar Association

(2017) (www.abanet.org) and the National Association of Criminal Defense Lawyers (n.d., http://www.nacdl.org).

Probation Officer in Criminal Court

When probation officers are assigned to do pretrial investigations, supervise pretrial diversion programs, and make bail recommendations, they are called pretrial service officers. The probation officer conducts presentencing investigations, gathering and verifying information about your client and the alleged offense. The role of the probation officer can also include investigating and supervising clients found guilty whom the court has conditionally released to the community on probation or parole. The probation officer compiles a report, reviews statutes and sentencing guidelines, and makes a recommendation to the court. The recommendation may include conditions, such as participating in a substance abuse treatment program, that are mandatory.

The probation officer is also responsible for supervising the individual on probation when released to the community. The individual will be assigned to a probation officer who will then complete an assessment that will result in rehabilitation goals. The probation officer will then monitor the individual to ensure compliance with the plan and to continually assess the level of risk that may be posed to the community. For clients who are working with probation officers, this monitoring often includes weekly meetings, attending all of their appointments with you, or submitting to drug tests.

The Victim Advocate in Criminal Court

Victim advocates are professionals, many times social workers, who are trained to support victims of crime. Victim advocates may be employed by the police, the district attorney, courts, or community-based not-for-profits. Many states and counties have offices of the victim advocates which can be helpful in locating information on victim's rights, restitution, and victim services organizations. For example, the Pennsylvania Office of the Victim Advocate is responsible for the state programming supporting victim's rights, services, and restorative justice programs (Pennsylvania Office of the Victim Advocate, 2024). Some organizations also use volunteers in the role of victim advocates. Victim advocates generally provide a range of services, such as crisis intervention, advocacy, information about rights and the working of the system, assisting with safety planning, assisting with the development of written or verbal impact statements that illuminate the effects of the crime on the many facets of the victim's life, intervening with employers on behalf of victims, and generally providing support to the victim throughout the legal process including addressing issues such as testimony and confidentiality of victims' addresses (National Center for Victims of Crime, 2008).

Levels of Criminal Law and Locating Your State's Criminal Code

Criminal law is made at the state level, and most states make distinctions between the seriousness of a crime by having felony level and misdemeanor level crimes. A felony is defined as a more serious crime where the potential incarceration period if convicted of the crime would be more than a year. A misdemeanor is defined as a less serious crime where if convicted, the sentence would be a year or less of incarceration. In many states, there are also violations, known mostly as quality-of-life crimes, including loitering, public drunkenness, or disturbing the peace. In most such instances, when charged with a violation, the individual is not charged with a crime and therefore cannot be imprisoned as a result. It is important to locate your particular state's criminal or penal code, so that you know what the exact wording of the charges means. Most every state or state legislature has a website that includes the full text of their state criminal code. The federal criminal justice system involves cases where a violation of federal criminal law is alleged and there are important differences from the state criminal justice system in the terms of the roles of stakeholders, criminal procedure, use of magistrate judges, and requirement of a grand jury. For the purposes of this section, we focus on state criminal justice systems.

The Path of a Criminal Case: Arrest and Filing of the Criminal Complaint

In addition to understanding the stakeholders and their roles in the criminal justice system, it is important for social workers to know the path of a criminal case and the process that a client will go through if they are impacted by the criminal justice system either as a defendant, victim, witness, or family member. In our case example, Ms. Jones was most likely arrested on the street for illegal possession of drugs, in this case cocaine and marijuana. When she was arrested, the police brought her to the precinct where she was booked, which is the formal process of filing a case against Ms. Jones. While she was at the precinct, she was fingerprinted and searched thoroughly. Any property on Ms. Jones was taken away and might be used as evidence against her if the police believe the property was used to commit the crime (e.g., money or drug-related property). Ms. Jones was questioned by police officers or detectives about the alleged crime and possibly about other criminal activity. If the police suspect that Ms. Jones was working with other people to sell or use drugs, the police would most likely question her about them as well. As you learned earlier, the police are required to inform Ms. Jones of her rights during this process, but any statements Ms. Jones makes after being read her rights can be used in court.

Throughout this process, the police file reports about the alleged criminal activity including any statements made by Ms. Jones or other witnesses. After Ms. Jones was booked, she was transferred from the local police precinct to the Criminal Court where the Criminal Court judge heard her case for the first time. In most jurisdictions, this process is known as an *arraignment* and it is the first time that Ms. Jones would have a lawyer appointed to represent her, if she was not able to hire a private attorney.

By the time that Ms. Jones entered the courtroom, a prosecutor—often referred to as the assistant district attorney (ADA)—would have spent time reviewing the police reports and speaking to the police officers who first arrested Ms. Jones to begin the process of formally charging Ms. Jones with a crime or crimes. In order for the case to proceed, the ADA had to file a formal charging document, sometimes referred to as an information that states the specific charges against a defendant, including the laws the defendant allegedly violated and the basis for that belief. This is an important document since it contains a significant amount of information, including the level of crime that has been charged. The complaint or information will indicate all of the charges against the defendant; the specific statute or penal code that is alleged to have been broken; whether the law is a felony, misdemeanor, or violation; the date, time, and location of the alleged criminal activity; and the basis for the complaint, including statements from victims, police officers, or the defendant themselves. Although states and cities differ in the format of this legal document, the basic information contained in a complaint is the same and will include the following information:

- the name and date of birth of the defendant or defendants if multiple individuals are being charged at the same time
- the jurisdiction for the case which includes the court and county
- the statement from a police officer or other law enforcement official including the date, time and location of the alleged offense
- the specific criminal statutes that are alleged to have been violated by the defendant including the statute number and the title of the statute
- the reasons or grounds for the allegations

There is always the possibility that the ADA reviewing the police records may determine that the initial charge for which the client was arrested and booked at the police station is not appropriate. Ultimately, although the police officer will make a recommendation about the charge, the ADA who writes the complaint determines the severity and specifics of the charge because it is a legal decision. The reason is that the ADA is the lawyer responsible for drafting the information or criminal complaint and ensuring that it is legally sufficient, meaning that it details all of the elements of the crime. For example, the police may initially arrest Ms. Jones both for possession of drugs and selling drugs. However, upon review of the evidence and statements of the police, the ADA may determine that Ms. Jones can only be charged with possession, a less serious crime than selling.

Arraignment

The arraignment is the first court appearance after an individual has been charged with a crime. At the arraignment, the defendant will hear the list of criminal charges against them and the potential penalties that are associated with those charges if the defendant is found guilty. In addition to the reading of the specific charges against a defendant, there are three main parts of the arraignment appearance: the assignment of counsel, an entering of a plea, and a decision on release of the defendant. At the arraignment, the Criminal Court judge will advise the defendant of their right to have counsel assigned to their case if they cannot afford an attorney and will order that counsel be assigned if requested. The judge will also ask the defendant, through their attorney, whether they wish to plead guilty or not guilty to the charges in the criminal complaint against them. While most defendants enter a plea of not guilty at arraignments especially when the allegations are more serious, some attorneys will counsel clients to enter a plea of guilty at arraignments for less serious crimes, such as petty offenses and violations, so that the case is disposed of or ended more quickly. If the case is more serious and there are felony charges, the judge will first need to hold a preliminary hearing to determine if there is sufficient evidence to proceed given the severity of the charges and resultant punishment if the defendant is found guilty. If there is sufficient evidence to proceed, often referred to as probable cause, then the case will be set for trial which will likely take place in front of a different judge unless the defendant pleads guilty beforehand. Finally, if the prosecution is requesting that the defendant remain incarcerated, then the judge will determine whether or not to set bail in the case.

The purpose of setting bail in a case is to ensure that a defendant returns to court and is present for the court proceedings. This is why many states have agencies whose sole responsibility is to interview defendants prior to the arraignment with regard to their housing, employment, and family and community supports, and to make recommendations about bail. The theory is that a defendant is more likely to return to court if they have community ties and other indicators of stability. As will be noted later, this is an area where social workers working with attorneys can be particularly helpful in eliciting information about a client's community ties or stability to argue in favor of having a defendant released from custody.

As you can imagine, it is much better for the client and the client's case if they are released pending the outcome of the criminal case. Being released without having to pay any money is referred to as being released on your own recognizance. Research has found that financial terms of bail have resulted in disparate outcomes due to a person's financial status and it has been demonstrated that this results in discrimination against Black and Hispanic defendants at the point of the bail decision and continuing through future decision-making. Studies have shown that Black and Hispanic defendants are less likely than White defendants to meet the financial conditions for bail and thus result in a much greater likelihood of pretrial detention (VanNostrand, 2007). Additionally, research shows that young Black men are 50% more likely to be detained than their White counterparts (Vera Institute of Justice, 2024). There are also secondary adversities related to pretrial detention such as disruptions to family and caregiving relationships, employment, education, and the ability to prepare an adequate defense. Finally, research shows that clients who are detained prior to trial are more likely to plead guilty and to receive more severe sentences if convicted (Tartaro & Sedelmaier, 2009). In New York State, bail reform legislation, which included a mandate that judges set the least restrictive option that will ensure a defendant's appearance in court, was passed in 2019 and resulted in a 35% decrease of the pretrial jail population (Kim et al., 2022). Rights-based, proactive social work advocacy is therefore essential at this juncture.

Judges consider a variety of factors when determining if they will set bail and at what amount an individual may be required to pay in order to leave jail. A Criminal Court judge might consider whether there is a prior criminal record, the severity of the alleged crime, community and family ties, and the likelihood that the defendant will return to court for the next court appearance. As mentioned, bail reform efforts nationally have expanded the court's discretion in some jurisdictions to consider the impact of detention on the individual's life and to select the least restrictive option. Social workers are experts at assessing the transaction between people and their environments, whether working in the implicit or explicit context and can contribute important information to both advocates and decision-makers in the bail determination process given these recent reforms. If the judge sets a money bail, then the client or their family must pay a certain amount of money to be held in case the client fails to appear in court on the next court date. If the judge does not set bail, then the individual is either released on their own recognizance (ROR) or held in jail until the next court date.

Temporary Orders of Protection

Depending on the charge, the judge may issue an order of protection, which is a court order forbidding the criminal defendant from having contact with the victim or victims identified in the complaint. In many cases, this could include prohibiting the defendant from going near the victim's home, place of work, or school. It can also include an order forbidding the defendant from contacting the victim in person or over the phone or requesting that a third party contact the victim on their behalf.

At times, an individual's child will be the subject of an order of protection, particularly if the child was present when the parent was arrested or the allegations include a crime against the child. Because the case is in the beginning and has not gone to trial yet, the order of protection is generally only in effect until the next court date and is therefore referred to as a temporary order of protection. Once a case has gone to trial or is settled, a judge can enter a final order of protection, which can last for as many as 5 to 10 years in some jurisdictions.

Grand Jury Process

In some states, including New York, North Carolina, and Massachusetts, the grand jury process is used to determine whether the prosecution has enough evidence or probable cause to bring a case against a defendant. The grand jury is generally comprised of anywhere from 11 to 23 individuals who sit on the grand jury for an extended amount of time and hear cases. The purpose of the grand jury is not to determine guilt or innocence, but rather to determine whether there is sufficient evidence to bring charges against a defendant. For example, in New York, a grand jury of 23 individuals is convened to determine whether or not an individual can be charged with a felony (New York State Unified Court System, 2009). The grand jury listens to the testimony of witnesses brought by the prosecutor and determines whether there is sufficient evidence to charge the individual with the felony or, in other words, to indict the defendant. If the grand jury does not believe that there is sufficient evidence then the case is dismissed and there is no indictment. If the grand jury finds that there is sufficient evidence, then the case proceeds to a criminal trial.

The prosecutor is the only attorney allowed to present witnesses and evidence in the grand jury proceedings. A judge is available to assist with questions of law, but the prosecutor instructs the grand jury members on the law and conducts all of the questioning of the witnesses. It is important to remember that victims of crime and witnesses are often called to testify at grand jury proceedings about the alleged criminal activity. The witnesses are not subject to cross-examination from the defense attorney, as they would be at a jury trial or bench trial once a defendant has been indicted. Social workers can play a key role in preparing victims of crime to testify in the grand jury and can assist prosecuting attorneys in eliciting the necessary testimony. More detailed information on how to effectively prepare victims to testify is covered in Chapter 8.

The Rights of Criminal Defendants During the Criminal Proceeding

In addition to the rights that individuals have prior to and during an arrest, defendants in Criminal Court are afforded a number of critical legal rights. The bulk of these rights are contained in the Sixth Amendment to the U.S. Constitution, which states the following:

> In all criminal prosecutions, the accused shall enjoy the right to a speedy and public trial, by an impartial jury of the state and district wherein the crime shall have been committed, which district shall have been previously ascertained by law, and to be informed of the nature and cause of the accusation; to be confronted with the witnesses against him; to have compulsory process for obtaining witnesses in his favor, and to have the assistance of counsel for his defense. (U.S. Const. amend VI)

As you can see, the Sixth Amendment guarantees criminal defendants a number of legal rights that apply whether the defendant is being tried in state or federal Criminal Court. Additionally, these rights apply whether the defendant is charged with a felony or a misdemeanor. The first right is the right to a speedy trial, which means that the prosecuting attorney cannot delay bringing charges against a defendant. The right to a jury trial is specific to Criminal Court, and requires that the defendant be permitted to have a jury decide whether the prosecution has met their burden of proof at trial. Additionally, the Criminal Court jury has to be impartial and there are various procedural rules that protect a defendant's right to an impartial jury of their peers. The prosecutor and the defense attorney select the jurors by interviewing potential jury members during a process called "voir dire" (to speak the truth) to see whether they have any bias or prejudice that would impact their decision-making during the trial.

The defendant has a right to due process of law in the Criminal Court proceeding, which includes the right to cross-examine any witnesses called by the prosecution, to present their own defense, and to be represented by counsel to assist in the legal case even if the defendant cannot afford to hire an attorney on their own. For immigrant clients who are defendants in criminal matters, the Supreme Court determined in *Padilla v. Kentucky* (2010) that a defense attorney must inform a noncitizen criminal defendant of the possibility of deportation as a result of pleading guilty to a crime. In that case, a lawful permanent resident was not advised that his guilty plea to drug charges would render him automatically deportable. Fundamentally, defendants have the right to a fair trial that encompasses all of the rights mentioned and the general rules that govern how the judge rules and presides over a trial.

JUVENILE JUSTICE

Juvenile justice refers to the system for handling cases when minors commit what would be considered criminal or illegal offenses. This is an area of the legal system where there is a critical need for rights-based social workers to be informed and proactive to prevent clients' entry into the juvenile justice system and to advocate for and assist youth and their families impacted by the system. There is considerable racial disparity in the treatment, decision-making, and outcomes for the youth involved, and social workers can bring a critical and rights based focus to practice in the juvenile justice sphere.

In 2021, there were 437,000 juvenile cases nationally which represented the lowest number of cases for all offense types since 2005 (Hockenberry & Puzzanchera, 2024). The juvenile justice proceeding is a hybrid proceeding that has some elements and rights of adult criminal proceedings and some elements and rights of civil child welfare proceedings. Because of the increasing level of punitive treatment of juveniles, such as being tried as an adult for certain crimes, we have decided to address juvenile justice by describing the early phases of criminal proceedings. For youth impacted by the juvenile justice system, the experience can feel similar to that of a criminal defendant in an adult case, especially given the possibility that a juvenile court will place a youth in detention.

In some jurisdictions, the same court that hears civil child welfare cases, called Dependency court or Family Court, also handles juvenile delinquency cases. While states differ on the purpose and goals of juvenile courts, many states include language that encompasses balanced and restorative justice, in particular the three goals of "public safety, individual accountability to victims and the community, and development of skills to help offenders live law-abiding and productive lives" (Snyder & Sickmund, 2006).

There are two types of juvenile offenses: status offenses and delinquency offenses. A status offense is when a juvenile breaks a law that is only against the law because of the juvenile's age. Examples would be running away from home, truancy, being out of the control of their parents, or underage drinking. Status offenders are sometime called persons in need of supervision (PINS) or child in need of supervision (CHINS). When a youth is charged with delinquency, it is because they have committed an offense that if the youth were an adult would be considered a crime. Delinquency offenders are sometimes called juvenile delinquents or JDs.

In general, police officers are authorized to temporarily detain juveniles for investigation purposes to issue a citation, to arrest them, or to safeguard them, for example if they have run away from home. Individual states will have various statutes and regulations that describe these specific processes. Like adults, juveniles can be arrested for a misdemeanor or a felony. The same laws and rights during arrest and interrogation for adults that you read about earlier in this chapter also apply to juveniles with the exception that juveniles cannot be detained with adult offenders. The police are also required to notify the parent or guardian of the youth and, if under a certain age, parents must be present during the questioning of the child by the police or if the child decides to waive any of their rights.

As is the case in the adult criminal justice system, Black children are arrested at significantly higher rates than White youth, and even more concerning, for all types of crime (Arya & Augarten, 2008). For example, if a White youth and a Black youth vandalize a property, the youth of color is twice as likely to get arrested than the White youth. In regard to drug and person-related crimes, Black children are four times more likely to be arrested than White children (Arya & Augarten, 2008). More recent statistics demonstrate that Black youth have 13 times the case rate for juvenile delinquency matters than White or Hispanic youth (Hockenberry & Puzzanchera, 2024). Additionally, research has also found disparate juvenile court outcomes for disabled youth (Mallet, 2009).

Juvenile courts differ from state to state in their individual processes, but generally juvenile courts accept cases from law enforcement and other parties including schools, parents, and probation officers. As is the case in Civil and Criminal court, a petition or a complaint must be filed with the court and there will be an initial hearing where the youth will be read the charges against them, their right to an attorney, a determination on whether they can be released, and scheduling of a trial date. Similar to adult criminal defendants, all states have laws requiring the court to hold a hearing on the detention within a short time period, usually 24 hours. Additionally, juveniles have the right to an attorney if they are not able to afford one because of the Supreme Court decision in *In re Gault* (1967). One difference between adult and juvenile processes at this point is that juveniles do not have a constitutional right to bail when they are incarcerated pretrial, although there are some states, such as Colorado and West Virginia, that allow children to post bond at the point of pretrial incarceration (Steinhardt, 2006).The court will hold a trial and if the youth is found guilty, a dispositional hearing will be called aimed at determining what can be ordered to rehabilitate the youth. This is another area where social workers can play a significant role in contributing to the court's understanding of the youth's needs by conducting assessments, identifying resources, and working with family and partners to support the youth. Your state or local court website will usually post the procedures and sometimes the forms needed to file a petition if you are a school social worker or working with a parent and need to file a petition.

Many cases of juvenile offenders, particularly PINS and CHINS cases, are diverted to alternative programs before ever coming to Juvenile Court. Social workers frequently staff programs and agencies that provide screening and referral services also called diversion programs. Unfortunately the disparate treatment of children based on race is also evident at this crucial decision-making point; that is, whether a child will enter the system at all. White children are twice as likely to be diverted, and Black children are twice as likely to be detained (Arya & Augarten, 2008). A more recent study conducted by the Annie E. Casey Foundation over a 3-year span of juvenile detention found that Black children are 10 times more likely to be detained than their White peers, while postpandemic and prepandemic studies showed Black youth were six times more likely to be detained (Annie E. Casey Foundation, 2023). These decisions, and flaws in the system create serious short- and long-term implications for Black youth. Despite a serious decline in youth incarceration (down by 75% from 2000 through 2002 even when accounting for offenses and other factors), racial disparities continue to exist at every stage of the process (Rovner, 2024). Researchers found that youth who were arrested and detained for minor crimes were seven times more likely to be arrested and incarcerated as adults than youth who had been diverted from the juvenile justice system (Gatti et al., 2009). Youth in detention are at much higher risk of abuse, injury, and suicide (Children's Defense Fund, 2007). Other long-term affects of youth incarceration and detention placement include that detained youth are less likely to complete their high school education, gain employment and have increased risk for developing mental health needs as a result of their detainment (Annie E. Casey Foundation, 2014).

For particular crimes, juveniles may be tried as adults. States have enacted significant reforms in light of advocacy to treat children as children in these proceedings. In 2018, New York reformed state laws raising the age for criminal responsibility to 18 so that the state was no longer one of only two states which automatically charged 16- and 17-year-old minors as adults in criminal proceedings. North Carolina, the other state, reformed its laws in 2019. You can access the age limits for Juvenile Court in your state by referencing the federal Office of Juvenile Justice and Delinquency Prevention's website (https://ojjdp.ojp.gov/statistical-briefing-book/structure_process/faqs/qa04102). It is important to understand the lower age limit for delinquency cases as well as the upper age limit. Most times individual Juvenile Court judges have the discretion to waive Juvenile Court jurisdiction and transfer the case to Criminal Court. In some instances both criminal and juvenile courts can share original jurisdiction. An individual prosecutor has the discretion to transfer the case to Criminal Court. Advocates for youth should be aware that in many states there are some circumstances where a case can be transferred back to Juvenile Court from Criminal Court, sometimes called a *reverse*. Under certain circumstances, identified by state statute, certain juveniles can petition for a reverse back to family court. There are other circumstances in which a youth must be transferred to adult court pursuant to mandatory transfer laws. Mandatory transfer requires that after establishing probable cause and confirmation of a youth's age that the youth be transferred to Criminal Court. Within mandatory transfer laws, there is an additional provision referred to as a statutory exclusion that requires that if a youth committed a certain type of crime, then their case must be heard in criminal court (Evans, 2018).

It is also important to know that many states have what is called "*once an adult always an adult*" provisions which mean that once a youth has been convicted as an adult they must be prosecuted in Criminal Court for any subsequent offenses (Redding, 2010).

Some research at the individual state level indicates that minority youth are "waived" into the adult system at far greater rates than Whites (Banks et al., 2009). It is important to know whether a teenage client will be charged in Criminal Court or Juvenile Court, as the procedures, options, and consequences can differ.

For those cases that are referred to Juvenile Court, the court can order that a juvenile be held in a secure detention facility pending the outcome of their trial. The Juvenile Justice Delinquency Prevention and Protection Act (1974), which was reauthorized and amended in the Juvenile Justice Reform Act (2018), makes distinctions between secure and nonsecure detention and most state statutes and/or regulations define what secure and nonsecure mean. "Secure" generally means a residential facility that is specifically constructed and has features designed to physically restrict the movements and activities of the youth placed there. Social workers in this context must be aware that there are significant harms to this type of youth detention which have been documented over the past decades including abuse and maltreatment and significant decrease in educational and career outcomes for detained youth (Mendel, 2023). There have been numerous reports and state-specific investigations documenting the poor conditions youth experience while housed in juvenile detention (Children's Defense Fund 2007; Parent et al., 1994). These conditions include serious overcrowding, violence, lack of ability to participate in meaningful educational programming, and a lack of specialized programs to treat chronic problems associated with delinquent behavior such as substance abuse and histories of trauma (Austin et al., 2005).

The disparate treatment of Black children is again evidenced at this decision point in the juvenile justice system. Children of color make up at least 75% of the detention population and Black youth are twice as likely to be detained as White youth (Arya & Augarten, 2008). Although detention is meant to be used for serious crimes where there is a real risk of danger to the community or of flight, fairly large percentages of youth are in detention for property or drug-related crimes, are status offenders, or are charged with violations of probation (Sickmund et al., 2008).

In 1993, the Annie E. Casey Foundation initiated the Juvenile Detention Alternative Initiative (JDAI) with the objectives of reducing unnecessary or inappropriate secure confinement of children, reducing crowding and improving conditions for children in secure detention facilities, encourage the development of nonsecure alternatives to secure juvenile confinement, and discourage failures to appear in court and subsequent delinquent behavior (Steinhardt, 2006, p. 5). A major part of this initiative is to develop evidence-informed risk-assessment tools and address racial disparity through evidence-informed decision-making. JDAI has expanded nationally to include sites engaged in evidence-based programming to reduce the reliance on detention for juveniles.

Because juveniles can be both temporarily detained and ultimately ordered by the judge to remain in detention, the Supreme Court ruled in *In re Gault* (1967) that juveniles have the same right to notice of the proceedings against them, to question and cross-examine any witnesses against them, to be provided with an attorney, and to invoke their right against self-incrimination. Juveniles also have the right to have their parent or guardian present throughout all phases of Juvenile Court. Despite this requirement, as discussed in Chapter 1, many juveniles lack effective representation when detained. A study of youth detained in Ohio found that attorneys were appointed for detention hearings in a small number of jurisdictions, that when appointed it was not in a timely manner without time to meet with the youth prior to the hearing, and that many youth waived their right to counsel at this point in the process (American Bar Association Juvenile Justice Center, National Juvenile Defender Center, & Central Juveniles Defender Center, 2003).

Additionally, juveniles have the right to a trial before a judge on the allegations and the Supreme Court held in *In re Winship* (1970) that a juvenile is entitled to a fair trial where the prosecution had to prove their case beyond a reasonable doubt, as opposed to any lower standard of proof. Generally juvenile courts are run more informally than adult Criminal Courts and the professionals have more discretion in making decisions about what happens to the juvenile during the dispositional phase.

Once there is an adjudication, the judge can enter a dispositional order based on reports from probation or the juvenile's attorney that include continued detention, residential care, aftercare services, or probation monitoring. Although the decision-making standard during the trial for juveniles is the same as adult Criminal Court, during the dispositional phase the decision-making standard that is used to determine the best plan for the juvenile is "best interest of the child." You will learn more about the dispositional phase in Chapter 9.

When Your Client Is a Victim of Crime

If your client is a victim of a crime, you should know that the federal government and most state governments have passed laws to establish victim's rights during the arrest and arraignment process and during subsequent criminal justice proceedings (National Center for Victims of Crime, 2002). Like most of the laws we have been discussing, statutes pertaining to victim's rights depend on the jurisdiction—state, federal, or tribal government. Your state government website, the National Center for Victims of Crime (www.victimlaw.info), and the National Crime Victim Law Institute (2006, http://legacy.lclark.edu) are all good sources to help you find the law in your jurisdiction. Many district attorney office websites have information and materials for victims of crime as well.

In general, most of the states afford victims the right to be treated with dignity, respect, and sensitivity by law enforcement and other personnel and to be informed of their rights and the services available to them (National Center for Victims of Crime, 2008). In some states, advising a victim of their rights is the responsibility of the investigating police officer. Respecting these rights are particularly important when a victim is reporting a crime as they may be injured or psychologically traumatized. If you are a social worker working in the implicit context and your client has been a victim of a crime, it will be important that you discuss and remind your client of their rights repeatedly because they may not be able to take in or understand their rights at the time of their victimization due to shock, trauma, and physiological arousal.

Once the police have made an arrest, victims in most states have the right to receive notice about the arrest and arraignment of the defendant, bail and pretrial proceedings, dismissal of charges, and plea negotiations (Kilpatrick et al., 1998). In many states such as North Dakota, under Section 12.1–34.02 of the N.D. Crim. Code (2010), victims have the right to speak with prosecutors prior to plea agreements under the state law governing fair treatment standards for victims. In other states, such as Missouri, a victim has the option to address the court verbally or provide a written statement before the plea is entered (Mo. Rev. Stat., § 557.041, 2013). It is important to know the law in your state because in some cases, victims' rights are automatically activated but in other cases, victims must take steps such as written requests or contacting various agencies such as the court, district attorney's office, or probation in order to have their rights as a victim of crime activated.

Another important right for the victim at this stage of the process is that, in many states, the victim has the right to apply for compensation for medical or psychological expenses as well as lost income due to being a victim of a crime (National Center for Victims of Crime, 2002). However, research has shown that victims of crime drastically underuse the victim compensation system: The number of applications represents fewer that 5% of all victimizations (Alvidrez et al., 2008). Special classes of victims such as the young, homeless, less-educated adults, and members of an ethnic minority were found to be less likely to file claims without very active assistance. Similar to the research presented in Chapter 1 regarding the reasons clients do not activate their legal rights, victims did not receive information about their right to file a claim, as well as assistance in filing from their service providers (Alvidrez et al., 2008). Social workers for victims of crimes can play an important role in educating victims about their rights during the process and helping them activate those rights and benefits if available. Additionally, rights-based social workers should understand that within the legal system clients may have experienced both victimization and engagement in criminal activity, making cases more complex and sensitive. In other words, clients can be both victims of crime and perpetrators of crime. Specifically for youth in delinquency proceedings, this can be more complicated depending on the type of crime, severity, age of the victim(s), and jurisdiction. It is imperative for a social worker to work with the client's attorney to understand the complexities and the role that a client may have played in a particular act. Social workers may be uniquely qualified to provide additional information on whether the client experienced victimization. An example of this complexity is a client who may have been trafficked and therefore would be considered both a victim of trafficking and alleged perpetrator of illegal activity as a result of the force and coercion of their trafficker.

The Special Case of Immigrant Victims

Federal legislation has addressed the unique needs of immigrant victims of domestic violence to self-petition for citizenship in the Violence Against Women Act (VAWA) (1994) and for immigrant victims of crime in the Victims of Trafficking and Violence Protection Act (VTVPA; 2000, 2008). The VTVPA created two new visa categories for immigrant victims of crimes, the U visa and the T visa. The goal of this legislation is to encourage immigrants who are victims of serious crime both to feel freer in reporting the crime as well as to increase cooperation with law enforcement during the investigation and prosecution of these crimes (Immigrant Rights Clinic of Stanford Law School, 2012).

To qualify for a U visa under the law in VTVPA, an immigrant must: (a) prove that they have suffered "substantial physical or mental abuse" as a result of one of the following forms of criminal activity: rape, torture, trafficking, incest, domestic violence, sexual assault, abusive sexual contact, prostitution, sexual exploitation, female genital mutilation, being held hostage, peonage, involuntary servitude, slave trade, kidnapping, abduction, unlawful criminal restraint, false imprisonment, blackmail, extortion, manslaughter, murder, felonious assault, witness tampering, obstruction of justice, perjury, attempted perjury, conspiracy, or solicitation to commit any of the previously mentioned crimes; (b) show that they possess information concerning criminal activity; and (c) provide certification from a federal, state, or local law enforcement official, prosecutor, or judge stating that the U-visa applicant is being, has been, or is likely to be helpful to the investigation or prosecution of the criminal activity. It should be noted that this list of crimes is not comprehensive and social workers working with immigrant victims of crime should access the full law to determine whether this legal remedy is available to their client (U.S. Citizen and Immigration Service; www.uscis.gov).

To address crime for which immigrants are more likely to be targeted, VTVPA authorizes the T visa for victims of severe human trafficking. VTVPA defines severe trafficking as the following:

> (A) Sex trafficking in which a commercial sex act is induced by force, fraud, or in which the person induced to perform such act has not yet attained 18 years of age; or (B) the recruitment, harboring, transportation, provision, or obtaining of a person for labor or services, through the use of force, fraud, or coercion for the purpose of subjection to involuntary servitude, peonage, debt bondage, or slavery. (VTVPA § 103[8])

The T visa provides a trafficking victim with the legal means to prevent their own deportation. To be eligible for a T visa, the immigrant applicant must prove that they: (a) are a victim of a severe form of trafficking; (b) are physically present in the United States; (c) complied with any reasonable request for assistance in the investigation or prosecution of acts of trafficking; and (d) would suffer extreme hardship involving unusual and severe harm if deported (VTVPA § 1513 [b] [3]).

In a reauthorization of VTVPA, the law was amended to include a special status for immigrant juveniles placed under state custody by a family or dependency court because of abuse or neglect. This is referred to as special immigrant juvenile status and is an additional remedy for immigrant youth who are in foster care or with one parent to achieve permanency and legal status. There is an additional requirement that the Family or Dependency Court find that "reunification with one or both of the immigrant's parents is not viable due to abuse, neglect, abandonment, or a similar basis found under State law," which requires the immigrant youth to obtain an order from a custody or dependency state court before applying for the immigration classification as a Special Immigrant Juvenile from the U.S. Citizenship and Immigration Services (Immigration and Naturalization Act, § 101[a][27][J]).

Initial Impact of Crime on Victims: What Social Workers Need to Know

Research about a victim's ability to cope with a crime tells us that depending on certain factors, not all victims will respond the same way (Danis, 2006a, 2006b). For example, if a person has been a victim of a crime before, this can increase the degree of trauma a person experiences when the person is a victim of a subsequent crime. A history of mental health issues can also increase the level of trauma experienced, particularly posttraumatic stress disorder (PTSD) or major depression. Additionally victims of violent crime are more likely than victims of property crime to experience increased trauma, as will victims who have little social support or have had negative experiences with the criminal justice system (Danis, 2006a, 2006b).

Research has also shown that most victims experience some short-term impact that usually resolves within 1 to 3 months after the crime has taken place. In some cases, depending on the factors already mentioned, there might also be a longer-term impact. It is important for social workers to know that how the helping system and the criminal justice system respond can impact whether or not there will be long-term impact for victims of crime (Menard, 2002). Short-term reactions may include feelings of shock, terror, anxiety, feeling helpless and out of control, concern with safety of self and family members, physiological arousal, concern about not being believed, and flashbacks and preoccupation with the crime itself. These feeling states can also affect cognitive functioning and memory and have implications for interviewing and providing services for crime victims. Allowing the victim to tell their narrative in their own words, asking simple questions, repeating questions, reassuring the victim that their reactions are normal, assessing body language, and repeating information about what will happen and victims' rights will assist the victim in the expression of emotions and in telling what happened to them (Danis, 2006a, 2006b). This is an area where peer support and peer advocates can be particularly effective and helpful.

The most important short-term interventions are to address any immediate medical problems; to mobilize a client's support system; to give the client control over as many decisions as possible; to reassure the victim that any reactions they are having are normal; to provide safety planning; to accompany the client to the police station to report the crime and during the investigation; and to explain to the client what comes next in regard to forensic examinations, the investigation, and what will happen to the offender after arrest (Danis, 2006a, 2006b). Information about a victim's rights needs to be repeated throughout the process and social workers should provide psychoeducation about what symptoms they may normally expect in the aftermath of victimization (Danis, 2006a, 2006b).

POSSIBLE ROLES AND FUNCTIONS OF THE SOCIAL WORKER

Social workers, whether in the implicit or explicit context of practice, can play a crucial role in the pretrial phase of criminal or juvenile cases. Social workers who focus on clients' rights know that there is substantial research documenting racial and ethnic disparities in the decisions to release an offender on bail or to detain them. As you read in the section of this chapter about juvenile justice, this disparity also applies to juveniles during pretrial detention decision-making. Blacks are more likely to be detained pretrial than Whites (Freiburger et al., 2010). The decision to detain is a critical one because research has shown that whether or not an offender is detained prior to trial has an important impact on later court processing decisions such as sentencing and length of sentencing (Tartaro & Sedelmaier, 2009). Risk factors for juvenile defendants when they are detained have also been detailed earlier in the chapter.

In adult criminal and juvenile cases, the court or representing attorneys may ask a social worker to make an assessment of whether or not a client should be released from jail and allowed to return to the community to await trial. The social worker may also be asked to recommend programs and supports that may be critical for the client, or to provide testimony as to the client's release, which may influence the court's decision. Social workers in the role of pretrial probation officer may be requested by both the adult and Juvenile Courts, to conduct an investigation, write a report, and make a recommendation about continued incarceration or detention of a juvenile. Social workers working in Juvenile Court may be asked to screen a juvenile for the purpose of diversion into a community-based program and if needed, to assess and recommend family-based supports. A social worker's assessment of a client's ties to family and the community, as well as risk assessment, can provide the judge with important information to assist in making the decision about bail or, in the case of a juvenile, continued detention.

A social worker assigned to work with a client's attorney as an advocate could also secure programs or services that will strengthen the argument supporting the client's release from jail or detention at arraignment. Additionally, with the advent of problem-solving courts for juvenile mental health, adult mental health, substance abuse, and domestic violence cases, a social worker may be called upon to make a recommendation about diverting a client into one of these alternative arenas. Finally, you may be working with the district attorney's office or in a social service agency in the role of victim advocate.

If you are a social worker working with the client in the implicit legal context, you can make sure the client and, in the case of a child, their parents or guardians, are educated about the process and discuss with the client whether or not you have information that might be helpful to the client that can be shared with the attorney. In the case of juveniles, it is also important to understand the process in which the youth was arrested and detained and whether the youth understood their rights and the consequences of pleading guilty or not guilty. As mentioned, there are additional protections in place for minors to decrease the risk of coercion and false confessions in interrogations, and to ensure that children with disabilities or unique needs understand the court process and their right to legal representation.

In the event your client is a victim of crime, you could assist the client in developing questions they may want to ask the district attorney and putting those into writing. You could also educate the victim about their right to speak or provide a written statement prior to a plea or sentencing, and provide support and guidance for drafting that statement. You could also explore the impact of Criminal Court involvement as either a victim or an offender on the client's relationships, finances, education, health, mental health, employment, or other significant life areas and develop intervention plans that minimize risk and enhance protective factors.

The Importance of Clearly Defining Your Role

Identifying your role in relation to the client and clearly understanding for whom you are preparing a report or providing information and toward what purpose are the first steps for any social worker in this process. We again stress the importance of confidentiality in this setting regarding who you may speak with and the implications for your ethical responsibilities in Chapter 3.

If the attorney who represents Ms. Jones employs you, your assessment will be tailored toward advocating and obtaining the outcome that Ms. Jones, your client, has identified to her legal team. This would be the same posture for attorneys and legal service offices that represent juveniles and employ social workers on staff to assist with client advocacy. If you are employed by the court, your report will be more objective and neutral and will need to balance the interests of the client, both adult and juvenile, with the potential risk to the community if the client is released, as well as the likelihood that the client will return for any future court appearances. When handling diversion to a problem-solving court or a community-based alternative to incarceration program, you would additionally assess the youth's or adult's willingness to participate in treatment, motivation to change, and eligibility for the diversion. If you are a victim advocate, your job is to advocate for the victim and where you work may have implications for your ability to keep certain information confidential. For example, if a police department employs you, information that the client gives you may be used in the criminal investigations. A victim's right to privacy during counseling is an area that is covered in federal and state statutes that elaborate the rights of victims.

INTERVIEWING THE CLIENT: THE PRETRIAL INTERVIEW

The process of collecting information is the first step to think about when beginning an assessment and recommendation about bail or detention. This will involve obtaining some essential background information and, depending on your role, conversations with the prosecutor or the defense attorney. The process will also include interviewing the defendant and speaking with other sources of information if time permits. It is very important to identify any assumptions or schemas you may have about the client that may bias your interview and impede your identification of relevant sources of information. The next section presents an overview of some of the key issues that need to be addressed during this phase of practice and at this point in a criminal or juvenile proceeding. It is important that you keep in mind that the ultimate decision-maker in this scenario is the judge. Your job as a social worker in certain roles is to provide the most accurate, relevant, and evidence-based information to the decision-maker. The judge will decide about whether or not to grant bail, detain a youth, or to release the client to the community.

Setting and Special Circumstances of the Pretrial Interview

If you are working with the defense attorney, at the time of arraignment, it is likely that your interview with the client will take place in a holding area at the court that offers little or no opportunity for privacy. By the time the person meets you, they will have been arrested, held at a police precinct, and brought to court. There is evidence to suggest that some defendants experience this as an extremely traumatic event, the impact of which should be considered in light of the individual's prior trauma. In the example of Ms. Jones who was arrested for drug possession, we know from research about women who use substances that there is a relationship between substance use disorders and past traumatic experiences (Grella & Greenwell, 2007). We also know that men and women entering jails and prisons have considerable histories of trauma prior to incarceration (Glaze & James, 2006). The implications for interviewing in this context are the same as for interviewing victims of crime. Your client may be triggered and physiologically stimulated. The client may have difficulty remembering what happened and giving a coherent description, history, or information. Most likely the person you are interviewing will be tired, stressed, upset, and in crisis.

In some circumstances the individual may not speak English or another language commonly spoken in the criminal justice system. For hearing-impaired individuals, they may not have been able to communicate at all with the police or the other court personnel. You can imagine the level of crisis that will be compounded by significant confusion as a result of these language and communication barriers.

For Ms. Jones where the offense involves the possession of a controlled substance, there is the possibility that she may have an active and ongoing substance use disorder and has been without access to the substance for a number of hours. Depending on the level of use, she may be suffering from withdrawal symptoms. In addition, in the role of forensic social worker or probation officer, you will have to collect information during a very short time period without real opportunities to develop a rapport with Ms. Jones, as you might in other circumstances. Additionally, if Ms. Jones is a new client for your practice, you will not have knowledge of her baseline functioning prior to this crisis, which can make an accurate assessment more difficult. Ms. Jones may be very resistant to giving any information that might be potentially used against her in a criminal proceeding. These conditions present special challenges for a social worker tasked with interviewing the client and gathering critical information that may be needed within a short time frame or may be part of a longer relationship-building process and intervention.

One of the first steps to take is acknowledging the limitations of the setting and the impact that they will have on your ability to interview and gather information. Conveying an understanding of the person's need to protect themselves in this context, addressing confidentiality, your role, and being as discreet as possible given the circumstances, is an essential place to begin. Identifying yourself and who employs you is important and you should make an extra effort to obtain feedback from the client that indicates the client is clear about your role. As mentioned earlier in the chapter, there are a number of actors in this system and it can be confusing to clients what roles individuals play. You should also clearly explain the rules of confidentiality that you have to follow in your given role in relationship to the client. In each instance, it will be important to gauge the client's understanding of the information that you have shared with them about your role, next steps, and confidentiality. This can be done by allowing space for the client to ask questions and also by asking the client to share with you what they understand your role and next steps to be so that you can check for comprehension along the way in an interview.

A high level of transparency is required in this situation and it is critical to explain to the client why you are asking the questions that you are asking and how they relate to the legal decisions being made. We call this concept relevance and use it throughout the book to assist us in providing a direction for conversations you might have with clients during investigation and assessment and when you are developing intervention plans within legal settings. Additionally, in criminal and juvenile cases, it is also important to determine that the client understands the specific charges against them and the particular legal issue for arraignment, in addition to the role that the lawyers play and who will be making the decision. Although the client was most likely told this information by their attorney, important information should be repeated and clarified because stress and crisis interferes with cognitive functioning and cognitive retention.

In Ms. Jones's situation, the two primary legal decisions for the arraignment are whether or not Ms. Jones will be released from jail and whether she will participate in any specialized court. Given that the allegations make reference to drugs, it is possible that Ms. Jones would be referred to a drug treatment court. If Ms. Jones were 14 years old rather than an adult, the decisions would be the following: should her case be diverted out of the system completely, should she be transferred to adult Criminal Court, should her case be diverted to a juvenile substance abuse court, should she remain detained, what is the level of detention (secure or nonsecure), and, in some states, should she be allowed to post bail. In many states, the decision to transfer a criminal case to a specialized court or alternative venue is made on the first appearance; in other states it is later in the process so you will want to understand the local practice and laws governing this decision in your state. The next sections discuss the role of evidence-based practice (EBP) in a pretrial setting for criminal and juvenile cases, and the various roles and practices that social workers may fill in that process.

Pretrial Legal Evidence-Based Practice for Adults

Evidence-based pretrial practice is defined as "interventions and practices that are consistent with the pretrial legal foundation, applicable laws, and methods research has proven to be effective in decreasing failures to appear in court and danger to the community during the pretrial stage" (VanNostrand, 2007, p. 12). The pretrial investigation is the mechanism for relaying the necessary information to judicial officers so that they can make the most appropriate pretrial release/detention decision. Components of a pretrial investigation should include an interview with the defendant; verification of specified information; a local, state and national criminal history record; an objective assessment of risk of failure to appear and danger to the community; and a recommendation for terms and conditions of bail. The two primary components of a pretrial investigation that are supported by EBP are the risk assessment and bail recommendation. The National Association of Pretrial Service Agencies (NAPSA) has released practice guidelines and standards for pretrial investigations and pretrial supervision (NAPSA, 2004).

The purpose of a pretrial risk-assessment instrument is to identify the likelihood of failure to appear and the danger to the community posed by a defendant during the pretrial stage. A pretrial risk-assessment instrument should use research-based objective criteria to identify the likelihood of failure to appear in court and danger to the community. Pretrial risk-assessment research has identified common factors that are good predictors of court appearance and/or danger to the community as follows: current charge(s), outstanding warrants at time of arrest, pending charges at time of arrest, active community supervision at time of arrest (e.g., pretrial, probation, parole), history of criminal convictions, history of failure to appear, history of violence, residence stability, employment stability, community ties, and history of substance abuse (VanNostrand, 2007). There are also pretrial risk assessments that have been developed for use with specific populations such as defendants charged with a sex crime (Muller, 2009). Scholars have critiqued pretrial risk assessment tools especially as they are increasingly being used as alternatives to cash bail as not objective and evidence based but subject to racial and socioeconomic bias (McCoy, 2023).

Pretrial Legal Evidence-Based Practice for Juveniles

As discussed earlier in this chapter, the Annie E. Casey Foundation has been partnering with states and localities to achieve the goal of detention reform. A central aspect of this initiative is to develop, evaluate, test, and validate evidence-based risk-assessment screening tools that can reduce the amount of individual discretion and determine which arrested youth should be diverted, detained securely, detained nonsecurely, or released. The risk-assessment instruments, similar to those developed for adults, develop criteria that are based on specific and empirically validated detention-related risk factors. It is also the hope of the initiative that by following these principles the kind of discretion that can result in biased decision-making and racial disparity will be minimized. The risk-assessment instruments are locally designed but most are all-point instruments or those that assign points for various risk factors (Steinhardt, 2006, p. 5). When you are evaluating a risk-assessment instrument that may have been used to assess your client, whether adult or juvenile, the instrument should be objective (based on research not personal opinion); uniform in that the same instrument should be applied equally to all arrestees; legally based; and is focused on the only question to be answered; that is, will the person reoffend prior to trial and will they appear (Steinhardt, 2006).

Most juvenile risk assessments concur that the most significant predictor of risk is the criminal history risk scores of the youth. Usually, offenses are ranked by seriousness and level of violence against other persons. Criminal history risk is usually measured by looking at the age at first offense, misdemeanors, felonies, weapon referrals, against-person misdemeanors, against-person felonies, prior detention orders, prior dispositions to state detention facilities, and outstanding warrants. Status offenses and, in some cases, technical violations of probation do not get points (Washington State Institute for Public Policy [WSIPP], 1998).

Risk-assessment instruments for juveniles, like those for adults, have identified other variables that may mitigate risk and, even in the case of a moderately serious criminal history, lower risk. These include what is referred to as social history risk. Categories of social history risk have been identified at the level of personal, school, family, and peer (WSIPP, 1998). For example, in New York City, researchers found that school attendance and whether the juvenile expected someone to show up at the appearance in conjunction with criminal history either lowered or increased risk (Phillips, 2007). Examples of risk factors along the social history continuum are: gender (males have higher risk of detentions), victim of child abuse or neglect, history of substance abuse, history of foster care, current level of parental control, and being expelled from school. In essence, the social history risk factors are the child version of the extent and quality of community ties but on a more developmentally appropriate level. The Annie E. Casey Foundation (www.aecf.org) and the Juvenile Detention Alternative Initiative (www.jdaihelpdesk.org) post examples of various state and local risk-assessment instruments on the internet. Similar to adult risk assessment tools, researchers have noted the racial and socioeconomic bias in the risk and needs assessments conducted in the juvenile justice system (St. John et al., 2020).

Suicide Risk: An Important Caveat

Pretrial risk assessment instruments for adults and children do not assess suicide risk because the primary purpose of the instrument is to identify risk of harm to the community or others and risk of flight or nonappearance. Although some status offenders are detained for purposes of self-protection, conditions in detention facilities often increase the risk of suicide and self-injury. One national study estimated that more than 11,000 juveniles engage in more than 17,000 incidents of suicidal behavior in juvenile facilities each year (Parent et al., 1994). In 2014, it was reported that "incarcerated youth die by suicide at a rate two to three times higher than that of youth in the general population" (Abram et al., 2014). Thirty-seven percent of all suicides occurred in detention centers. Suicides occurred within the first 4 months of detention and of those, 40% occurred within the first 72 hours. More than 69.9% of suicides were committed by those detained for a nonviolent offense (Hayes, 2009).

Suicide was the single leading cause of death by unnatural causes in adult local jails. Suicide accounted for 29% of all jail deaths between 2000 and 2007 (Noonan, 2010). The majority of suicides (64%) occurred during the first month of incarceration and of those, at least half occurred during the first week (Mumola, 2005). If a client is being detained in a small jail they are six times more likely to commit suicide than a client being detained in a larger jail (Noonan, 2010).

Given these statistics for both adults and youth, social workers practicing in a legal and evidence-informed manner would make sure that any client being considered for detention or currently detained is screened for risk of suicide an, based on that screening, immediately receives necessary services. This approach is supported by the law as juveniles in detention have a constitutional right to adequate basic care, medical care, and protection from harm. Adults in jails also have an Eighth Amendment right to "adequate" mental health treatment and, as a matter of policy many, but not all, jails provide mental health services to defendants while they are in confinement (Glaze & James, 2006). Social workers are trained to perform general suicide-risk assessments and should identify additional risk factors for the population they are working with in order to perform a contextually relevant assessment.

The Pretrial Interview in Ms. Jones's Case

In this section, we will discuss the role of a forensic social worker in a collaborative relationship with the attorney whose role is to advocate for Ms. Jones. Although our case example of Ms. Jones involves an adult, many of the practices and concepts discussed throughout the text would apply if she was a juvenile involved in a delinquency proceeding. While we will focus on her as an adult in a criminal justice setting, social workers in a juvenile delinquency setting can adapt the same principles of relevance in age-appropriate and trauma informed practices for youth.

When crafting an interview plan between the attorney and forensic social worker, you must always return to the concept of relevance—what is at issue in the immediate proceeding; what information must be gathered from the client in order to advocate for the client and what information must be provided to the client in order to counsel her and determine her goals. The initial joint meeting must gather information in order to make an argument for Ms. Jones to be released from jail. Additionally, the attorney and forensic social worker must counsel Ms. Jones on participating in a drug treatment court if that option has been made available to her. Finally, the attorney and social worker need to inform Ms. Jones of what will happen in court today and any additional steps or follow up that is planned.

Keeping in mind all of the special circumstances surrounding any kind of interview at arraignments, the attorney and social worker should begin by determining who will begin the interview and the order of subjects to be covered. Since you will generally be constrained to a limited amount of time, the advocates should also determine the relative priority of those subjects. A description of the role of the attorney and social worker is critical and should include a discussion of confidentiality between the advocates and the client. Before conducting the interview, make sure the following steps are taken:

- Formulating a clear explanation of your role, who you work for and the purpose of the interview
- Clarifying your own understanding of the charges so that you can assess the client's understanding of the charges and the question or decision you are being asked to provide information about which guides your interview
- Discussing confidentiality and the limits on information that will or will not be released and to whom

As we discussed earlier, depending on the severity of the charge and the client's history of involvement in the criminal justice system, the judge can determine one of three outcomes: releasing the client on their own recognizance, setting bail at a certain amount (only in some states for juveniles) or denying bail entirely. Generally, judges consider the recommendations of the prosecuting attorney as to what type of bail should be set and arguments from the defense attorney about the client's community ties and likelihood of appearing in Criminal Court for future court dates. In some jurisdictions, a neutral court-based agency may interview clients to determine their risk of flight. In these interviews, the agency worker questions the client about employment, income, housing stability, family ties, and prior history of arrest and incarceration. In order for the defense attorney to make a strong argument for release or a relatively low bail amount, it is important for attorneys and social workers working with defense attorneys to question Ms. Jones about all of those issues as well. Probation officers usually conduct assessments prior to the detention hearing for juveniles.

Ms. Jones may be able to participate in a Drug Court program and the social worker and attorney should assess whether this legal venue would better meet Ms. Jones's legal and social service goals and needs. Traditionally, a Drug Court program requires the client to make an admission to the alleged crime in exchange for assistance in gaining treatment and ultimately a reduced sentence or a dismissal of the criminal case. Many Drug Courts focus on first time offenders or clients who have not previously attended inpatient programs. Other Drug Court models bar clients with extensive substance abuse histories or mental health issues from participating. It is important to be familiar with the eligibility criteria in your court so that you can appropriately assess and counsel the client. Motivational interviewing is a helpful technique to use during interviewing and counseling about alternative venues as that facilitates client readiness for change. You will learn more detailed information about alternatives to traditional courts in Chapter 11.

Evidence-based pretrial practice also advocates the use of motivational interviewing as an effective information-gathering method during the pretrial phase to reduce the level of defensiveness and establish rapport quickly. Motivational interviewing is a technique many social workers are familiar with, can be used with adults or youth, and is usually covered in many foundation year practice texts. Motivational interviewing in pretrial services may be a beneficial technique for staff during supervision when attempting to enhance motivation for compliance with conditions, court appearance, and a reduction in danger to the community.

As always, care should be taken by social workers to ensure motivational interviewing techniques are used in such a way that the pretrial legal principles, specifically the presumption of innocence and the right against self-incrimination, are honored. This means that throughout the pretrial phase any interventions that require an admission of guilt or ownership of responsibility should not be recommended or should be modified to address the legal rights of the client. For example, many cognitive behavioral interventions such as anger management require an admission to the alleged conduct as part of the treatment. These interventions should be adapted to protect the legal rights of clients during the pretrial phase.

The same principles and standards of LEBP used with adults should also be applied to juveniles. Any instrument as well as intervention plans to address risk should incorporate all of the rights juveniles are afforded during the pretrial process. Services and conversations should be amended to respect the juvenile's right not to incriminate themselves prior to their hearing and the presumption of innocence.

Background information can begin to assist you in knowing about the seriousness and circumstances of the current offense, the pattern of any prior offenses, whether at this point in the proceeding there is information about any outstanding matters you may have to address, and any requests from the judge. You should obtain the following information prior to beginning your assessment:

- the date the final report is due to the court
- name of the defendant, contact information, address, and employment information;
- copy of the complaint
- the current or outstanding matters such as warrants or fines involving this client
- previous convictions involving this client
- other reports ordered, such as drug tests or psychiatric examinations

The key issues that must be addressed at this point in the process are the person's offending behavior, their personal and social circumstances, and their suitability for the various options the court has to consider, such as remand or release related both to risk of flight as well as risk of harm to the community. Generally, you will gather data and information about the following areas of the client's life: income, employment, family relationships, community relationships, education and training, housing, physical and mental health, substance abuse, and interview with the client's permission of collateral sources.

Another key question is the person's attitude toward and explanation for the crime as well as perceptions regarding the seriousness of the behavior. In addition, you would want to note any discrepancies between the report from the defendant and the available information about the crime. You would also want to know how the person feels about the crime and whether there is any expression of remorse or concern. Asking if the person sees any patterns in their behavior and actually thinks about their behavior prior to acting are also important topics to cover.

When you are attempting to interview a person about their personal and social circumstances you are attempting to place their behavior in context. Understanding a client's family relationships is also important because family members are frequently those who would be arranging for bail and can be greatly affected by the arrest of the family member. This information will give you some sense of why the person has become involved in the criminal justice system and what needs to change in order to prevent or reduce future offending. Finally, a key assessment question is to determine the extent to which the person is or could be motivated to try and change their behavior as well as take responsibility by attending future court appearances.

Keep in mind that if you are not working with the client's defense attorney, you may be prohibited from asking the client questions regarding the alleged criminal activity that is the subject of this proceeding. If you are working with the client's defense attorney, you would want to explain in detail the information that you believe is relevant to the bail assessment and identify any information that the criminal defense attorney may not want you to share at this stage with the court, so as not to unintentionally impact your client's legal strategy.

If you are a social worker who works in the community and have been providing services such as counseling or substance abuse treatment and your client has been motivated and participatory, then you may want to discuss with your client how this information may be helpful to those gathering information related to the decision to grant bail. After obtaining the client's consent, you can provide this information to the client's attorney or probation officer.

To illustrate the concept of relevance, the following list of sample questions and their relevance to the legal issue in question at the first appearance in Criminal Court could be included at a joint interview at arraignments.

Income and Employment

Sample Questions

How do you support yourself? Have you ever been employed? How long have you been employed and what is your role at your job? Are you currently receiving any benefits to help support yourself or your child? Do you have any upcoming appointments about your benefits that you may miss if you are detained? How would you like to address your absence with your employer? Who else do you support?

Relevance

Obtaining information about income and employment is important as both a possible explanation for the crime as well as capacity to pay a financial penalty, and indicates some level of stability. It is important for the social worker to determine if the client is currently receiving benefits as a criminal conviction can impact entitlements. It is also important to know if the client has any upcoming appointments so that sanctions are not automatically applied that would create hardship for the client's family. The client may also need assistance in deciding whether and how to communicate with their employer regarding the arrest. Also, the information from these questions will assist the attorney in being able to explain to the client any risk to current employment posed by arrest, plea, or conviction. Income is also one of the risk-assessment categories in evidence-based pretrial services.

Family Relationships

Sample Questions

Do you have any children you need to make arrangements for? In the case of Ms. Jones, the answer would be yes as she has an infant son. Do you have any family members or friends who can help you? Is there anyone would is currently with the child or could provide support in the event that you are away for any amount of time? Are any of these family members or friends able to post bail for you if necessary? Are any of these family members or friends able to serve as a reference or a support? What is your relationship like with these family members and friends? Do you have any concerns about the effect of your arrest on family members, or child(ren)? Do you know if there is a family history of mental disorder or substance abuse or family history of suicide or exposure to family member suicide (suicide-risk assessment)?

Relevance

Understanding the social connections of the defendant is important as both a possible contribution for offending, such as increased family tension or disruption, as well as the degree of active support and involvement to assist the client in changing their behavior and chances of making bail. In the case of parents, a social worker may be in the position of assisting the client to make arrangements for the care of their children for a short period, or, in the case of longer periods of incarceration, assisting with legal custody or guardianship arrangements. Clients who are parents may be apprehensive and show concerns around custody of their child during this conversation. Therefore, it is important for social workers to approach this topic with sensitivity and practicality, and engage in a process of weighing the pros and cons with the client. The best scenario would be to avoid having the child placed with the child welfare agency, unless the parent lacks support, or if it is deemed that the child must be removed from the parent's care. Social workers may provide support and, with the client's permission, information to concerned family and friends. Social workers can also work with the defendant to develop plans to minimize the impact of the arrest on family members by proactively addressing issues such as income, housing, and the care of children, also potentially avoiding child protection involvement. Family and relational ties and responsibilities such as parenting are also considered in some risk-assessment instruments.

Education and Training

Sample Questions

It is important for the social worker to assess how to approach these conversations and limit any bias, as individuals with various levels of education and backgrounds encounter the criminal system for different reasons. What is the last grade or level of education you have completed? If applicable, have you ever attended school or a training program? Are you currently enrolled in any kind of education, including college, or a training program? Depending on how the client answers the previous questions, the social worker or attorney should assess whether it is necessary to ask a client how they might rate their reading and writing skills? Do you want to engage in an educational or vocational program? Is there any support you need during the interviews, including language and/or reviewing documentations and court orders? It is important to note that regardless of education level, many individuals have a hard time understanding legal systems and court proceedings. It is important to always repeat and review these concepts with your client after each hearing and whenever a decision is about to be or has been made by the court.

Relevance

Understanding the person's educational background is an important part of identifying strengths that can be expanded, or limitations that could be addressed through learning opportunities to improve employment prospects. It is also important to assess the level of literacy the person has attained to make sure they can comprehend legal documents they may be given or explanations about what is happening to them during legal proceedings.

Housing

Sample Questions

Where do you live? Who do you live with? Do you own the home you live in or rent? Do you live in public or transitional housing? Does anyone else help pay your rent? Are you the person on the lease or is it someone else? In the event that your housing is not permanent, is there anyone else you can stay with? How long do you think you could stay there? What would your plan be if you were unhoused?

Relevance

Understanding a defendant's living situation is important as both an explanation for the crime, as homelessness or housing instability increases instability, and increases risk of offending, which will be a key factor in determining whether to release the person on bail. Also as mentioned in Chapter 4, criminal justice involvement can affect the ability to continue to live in public housing.

Physical or Mental Health

Sample Questions

How would you describe your health generally? Do you have any illnesses or medical conditions? If yes, how are you feeling now? Do you have any health issues that we should know about? Are you on any medication? Are you receiving prenatal care? Have you had any complications in the pregnancy? Have you ever been treated or seen by a psychiatrist or psychologist? Are you currently under the care of a psychiatrist or psychologist? Do you take any medications prescribed for you by a psychiatrist or psychologist? Have you missed any medications since you have been detained?

Relevance

It is important to understand whether there is a medical condition or disability with which the person has had to contend that could affect their understanding and participation in the legal process, as well as offer some insight into the offending behavior. In regard to mental health it is important to establish whether the person is receiving treatment for any psychological condition, has been diagnosed with a learning disability or brain damage, and there has been any recent experience of trauma. Identifying any risk of harm to others or to themselves is another key function of the interview. Asking about depression, any prior suicide attempts or experiences of violence and abuse are part of that assessment. A social worker may also need to advocate for medical or mental health treatment while in jail or access to necessary medications for conditions such as diabetes, high blood pressure, or depression. The level of a person's cognitive and psychological functioning as it relates to their ability to understand the nature of the charges against them, participate and assist in their defense, and have the capacity to make important decisions about their case need to be assessed at this point.

Substance Abuse

Sample Questions

Have you ever used drugs? If yes, what drugs do you use? What drugs have you used? Have you ever been in a treatment program? Was the program inpatient or outpatient? Did you complete the program? Why do you think it was helpful or not helpful? Do you think that you have a substance abuse problem? Would you be interested in getting treatment? What do you think the best treatment would be?

Relevance

These questions are important because substance abuse and misuse are frequently associated with criminal behavior and if the offense specifically relates to a drug-related crime, it will be important to address this in regard to the consideration of possible options. As you might imagine given the subject matter, it can be helpful to reiterate the terms of confidentiality in this section as disclosing substance abuse may be difficult for some clients. Parents particularly may be frightened that a disclosure of substance abuse will necessarily result in their child being removed from their care. It is important to assess if the client is using drugs as well as selling drugs. Substance use is an evidence-based risk factor for both pretrial risk assessment and suicide-risk assessment. If the client agrees to voluntarily accept and participate in treatment this may be used as an argument to release the client on bail or on their own recognizance, as well as during settlement negotiations.

Collateral Sources

Sample Questions

Is there anyone that you want us to contact for you? Are there any organizations, programs, or other supports that you work with now that could provide letters of support for you? Is there anyone else that we should reach out to for more information or support for your case? Do we have your permission to speak with them about your services? Do we have permission to speak with them about this case? Is there anything that you do not want us to share with these other sources?

Relevance

Talking to collateral sources, such as family members, physical and mental health treatment providers, employers, and others who may be involved in the client's life, can be used as way of confirming information. Sources can also provide information the client may not think of because of the circumstances of the interview or their level of distress at being incarcerated. Key to the question at hand is the source's ability to support the person as well as provide resources or the availability of resources. The other point to consider is the level of responsibility that the client has for the care or well-being of others such as children or spouses. This relates to the question of whether or not the individual has ties to the community that would lower their risk.

Making a Recommendation to the Court on Behalf of Ms. Jones

In interviewing the defendant, the most critical task would be to assess where your client stands on the indicators of risk outlined in the previous sections on adults and juveniles. As you can see through the prior questions relating to background information, you are evaluating risk when you are asking about outstanding warrants, prior convictions, and a copy of the complaint to assess type of crime. Even if you are in the role of advocate for the defendant or youth, it is critical to do a risk assessment to know what issues the court will be concerned about and developing a postrelease plan that will specifically target and address these risk factors.

After conducting the interview with Ms. Jones, the social worker assesses each of the evidence-based risk factors relevant to pretrial decision-making. On the protective side, Ms. Jones does not have any outstanding warrants, no other pending charges, and has never been arrested before. She has no documented history of violence. In addition, Ms. Jones is about to become a parent and is far along in her pregnancy. She has been receiving ongoing prenatal care from her physician and has regular appointments scheduled in the next weeks. Continued access to prenatal care is an important advocacy issue for both the social worker and the attorney. Ms. Jones also has demonstrated her willingness and ability to use the resources and supports provided by her community through her participation in a community-based social service agency and a substance abuse treatment program.

On the side of risk, Ms. Jones is currently living with a relative, her aunt, but has only been in that home for the last 2 months. She is currently unemployed and collecting public assistance. Finally, she has a self-disclosed history of substance use, but she is currently in treatment as well as working with a social worker in a community-based agency who is helping her obtain permanent housing and benefits. Overall, the assessment of risk about the two most pressing pretrial questions—the likelihood of failure for her to return to court and danger to the community—is low.

In regard to context-relevant suicide risk, Ms. Jones is a woman and 56% less likely to commit suicide if she were detained than if she were a male (Mumola, 2005). Ms. Jones is older than 18 but much younger than 55. Although we have not identified her race, if she is not White for purposes of this assessment and has not committed a violent crime, a suicide risk assessment would suggest that she is not at context-relevant risk of suicide. In regard to the mental health risk factors for suicide, on the side of negative risk Ms. Jones does not have a family history of suicide, has never attempted suicide, nor was exposed to a suicide. She is appropriately sad, but not depressed. Possible risk factors for Ms. Jones include a history of family violence, a possible diagnosis of posttraumatic stress disorder (PTSD), and a possible substance abuse problem. So, in regard to a mental health assessment, there may be some risk and that should be addressed in your recommended plan for Ms. Jones. It is important to check with the defense attorney to ascertain the effect of any potential suicide risk on the client's legal case, in addition to the risk of any other disclosures in the recommendation.

In order to address the risk factors and minimize their impact on the court's decision-making, the social worker would want to obtain the following documents as evidence in support of a release on her own recognizance: written confirmation from Ms. Jones's aunt that Ms. Jones is living in her home and can continue to live in her home, a statement from the substance use treatment provider that Ms. Jones is enrolled in treatment and will continue in treatment, and a statement from the community-based social worker that Ms. Jones is working on obtaining a stable income and housing and attends meetings regularly.

The attorney would argue to the judge that Ms. Jones should be released based on the information in the aforementioned documents. Keeping in mind that bail is not meant to be punitive, the attorney might begin by noting that Ms. Jones is currently in her third trimester of pregnancy and regularly receives prenatal care at the community clinic. It would be important to note that Ms. Jones, while unemployed, is working with the local community-based organization on securing her own housing and receiving voluntary services including drug treatment. Additionally, the attorney would state that she resides with her aunt and would bring the judge's attention to the aunt or any other family members who are present in the courtroom at arraignment. The attorney would want to emphasize that this is Ms. Jones's first arrest and she has no prior involvement in the criminal justice system. Therefore, according to the risk factors identified for returning to court, Ms. Jones presents to the court with a very low level of risk of flight.

NEXT STEPS WITH MS. JONES'S CRIMINAL PROCEEDING

After arraignment, Ms. Jones should be released from Criminal Court on her own recognizance based on the social worker's assessment and the attorney's advocacy in arguing for release to the judge. One potential outcome is that she is required to come back to Criminal Court in approximately 6 weeks when the attorneys will discuss possible resolutions or preparation to go to trial. Of course we know from our case example that Ms. Jones will give birth to her son and subsequently be charged with neglect in Family Court in the intervening weeks and before she is required to be back in Criminal Court for the next appearance. In Chapter 10, we discuss in more depth what role a social worker may play during pretrial conferencing, plea bargaining, and pretrial investigation. We also cover the role of a social worker if the criminal case proceeds to a trial and results in sentencing, incarceration, and postincarceration advocacy.

REFERENCES

Abram, K., Choe, J., Washburn, J., Teplin, L., King, D., Dulcan, M., & Bassett, E. (2014). *Suicidal thoughts and behaviors among detained youth (July 2014)*. OJJDP Juvenile Justice Bulletin. Office of Juvenile Justice and Delinquency Prevention.

Alvidrez, J., Shumway, M., Boccellari, A., Green, J. D., Kelly, V., & Merrill, G. (2008). Reduction of state victim compensation disparities in disadvantaged crime victims through active outreach and assistance: A randomized trial. *American Journal of Public Health*, *98*(5), 882–888. https://do.org/10.2105/AJPH.2007.113639

American Bar Association. (2017). *ABA Standards for Criminal Justice: Providing Defense Services*. ABA. https://www.americanbar.org/groups/criminal_justice/resources/standards/defense-function/

American Bar Association Juvenile Justice Center, National Juvenile Defender Center, & Central Juveniles Defender Center. (2003). *Justice cut short: An assessment of access to counsel and quality of representation in delinquency proceedings in Ohio.* https://www.defendyouthrights.org/document/justice-cut-short-an-assessment-of-access-to-counsel-and-quality-of-representation-in-delinquency-proceedings-in-ohio-2003/

American Civil Liberties Union. (2024). *Know your rights: Stopped by the police.* https://www.aclu.org/know-your-rights/stopped-by-police?redirect=drug-law-reform-immigrants-rights-racial-justice%2Fknow-your-rights-what-do-if-you

Annie E. Casey Foundation. (2014). *Juvenile detention alternatives initiative progress report.* www.aecf.org

Annie E. Casey Foundation. (2023). *Changing course in youth detention: Reversing widening gaps by race and place.* www.aecf.org

Arya, N., & Augarten, I. (2008). *Critical condition: African-American youth in the justice system. Policy brief, race and ethnicity volume 2.* Campaign for Youth Justice. https://www.campaignforyouthjustice.org/images/policybriefs/race/criticalcondition/CFYJPB_CriticalCondition.pdf

Austin, J., Johnson, K. D., & Weltzer, R. (2005). *Alternatives to the secure detention and confinement of juvenile offenders* (NCJ 208804). OJJDP Juvenile Justice Practices Series. U.S. Department of Justice, Office of Justice Programs, Office of Juvenile Justice and Delinquency Prevention. Retrieved from National Criminal Justice Resource Service: http://www.ncjrs.gov/pdffiles1/ojjdp/208804.pdf

Banks, L., Hatcher, S., & Risler, E. (2009). Youth in the adult system: The legislative waiver. In T. Maschi, C. Bradley, & K. Ward (Eds.), *Collaborative forensic practice: A social work justice systems approach* (pp. 289–297). Springer Publishing Company.

Children's Defense Fund. (2007). *America's cradle to prison pipeline.* https://www.childrensdefense.org/resources/cradle-to-prison-pipeline-2007-full-report/

Danis, F. S. (2006a). OVC *bulletin victim assistance and the profession of social work.* Office for Victims of Crime, U.S. Department of Justice, Washington, DC. http://ovc.ncjrs.gov/Publications.aspx?SeriesID=39

Danis, F. S. (2006b). *Victims of crime: A social work response, building skills to strengthen survivors* (NCJ 212962). Office for Victims of Crime, U.S. Department of Justice. Retrieved from: Office of Victims for Crime website: http://ovc.ncjrs.gov/Publications.aspx?TopicID=77

Evans, B. (2018). *The impact of mandatory transfer and statutory exclusion statues.* The Campaign for the Fair Sentencing of Youth. https://www.campaignforyouthjustice.org/images/factsheets/Mandatory_Transfer_FINAL_1.pdf

Freiburger, T. L., Marcum, C. D., & Pierce, M. B. (2010). The impact of race on pretrial decisions. *American Journal of Criminal Justice, 35*(1–2), 76–86. https://doi.org/10.1007/s12103-009-9069-z

Gatti, U., Tremblay, R. E., & Frank Vitaro, F. (2009). Iatrogenic effect of juvenile justice. *Journal of Child Psychology and Psychiatry, 50*(8), 991–998.

Glaze, L. E., & James, D. (2006). *Mental health problems of prison and jail inmates* (NCJ 213600). U.S. Department of Justice, Bureau of Justice Statistics. Retrieved from: Bureau of Justice Statistics website. http://bjs.ojp.usdoj.gov/index.cfm?ty=pbdetail&iid=789

Grella, C. E., & Greenwell, L. (2007). Treatment needs and completion of community-based aftercare among substance-abusing women offenders. *Women's Health Issues, 17*(4), 244–255. https://doi.org/10.1016/j.whi.2006.11.005

Hayes, L. M. (2009). OJJDP *Juvenile Justice Bulletin: Characteristics of juvenile suicide in confinement* (NCJ 2144340). U.S. Department of Justice, Bureau of Justice Programs, Office of Juvenile Justice and Delinquency Prevention. https://www.ojp.gov/pdffiles1/ojjdp/214434.pdf

Hockenberry, S., & Puzzanchera, C. (2024). *Juvenile court statistics.* National Center for Juvenile Justice. https://ojjdp.ojp.gov/library/publications/juvenile-court-statistics-2021

Illinois v. Wardlow, 528 U.S. 119 (2000).
Immigrant Rights Clinic of Stanford Law School. (2012). *Getting a U-Visa: Immigration help for victims of crime.* https://www.ilrc.org/sites/default/files/resources/proseuvisamanual_english.pdf
Immigration and Naturalization Act, § 101(a)(27)(J).
In re Gault, 387 U.S. 1 (1967).
In re Winship, 397 U.S. 358 (1970).
Institute on Disabilities. (2021). *Under arrest: Understanding the criminal justice system in Pennsylvania.* https://disabilities.temple.edu/justice/under-arrest
Juvenile Justice Delinquency Prevention and Protection Act of 1974, Pub. L. No. 93-415, 88 Stat. 1109 (1974).
Kilpatrick, D. G., Beatty, D., & Howley, S. S. (1998, December). *Rights of crime victims does legal protection make a difference? Research in brief* (NCJ173839). National Institute of Justice.
Kim, J., Green, C., Boldin, A., Hood, Q., & Purkayastha, S. (2022). *A year of unprecedented change: How bail reform and COVID-19 reshaped court practices in five New York counties.* https://www.vera.org/downloads/publications/a-year-of-unprecedented-change-bail-reform-covid-19-five-new-york-counties.pdf
Mallet, C. A. (2009). Disparate juvenile court outcomes for disabled delinquent youth: A social work call to action. *Child & Adolescent Social Work Journal, 26*, 197–207. https://doi.org/10.1007/s10560-009-0168-y
McCoy, E. (2023). *The risks of pretrial risk assessment tools: Policy considerations for Michigan.* https://stpp.fordschool.umich.edu/sites/stpp/files/2023-05/Risk%20Assessment%20Policy%20Brief%20Final%205.2.23.pdf
Menard, S. (2002). *Short- and long-term consequences of adolescent victimization. Youth Violence Research Bulletin* (NCJ191219). U.S. Department of Justice, Bureau of Justice Programs, Office of Juvenile Justice and Delinquency Prevention. http://www.ncjrs.gov/html/ojjdp/yv_2002_2_1/contents.html
Mendel, R. (2023). *Why youth incarceration fails: An updated review of the evidence.* The Sentencing Project. https://www.sentencingproject.org/reports/why-youth-incarceration-fails-an-updated-review-of-the-evidence/
Miranda v. Arizona, 384 U.S. 436 (1966).
Mo. Rev. Stat., § 557.041 (2013).
Muller, J. (2009). Implementing pretrial services risk assessment with a sex offense defendant population. *Federal Probation, 73*(2), 45–47. https://www.uscourts.gov/sites/default/files/73_2_6_0.pdf
Mumola, C. (2005, April). *Suicide and homicide in state prisons and local jails. bureau of justice statistics special report* (NCJ 210036). U.S. Department of Justice, Office of Justice Programs, Bureau of Justice Statistics. http://bjs.ojp.usdoj.gov/content/pub/pdf/shsplj.pdf
N.D. Crim. Code, c.12.1-34, § 12.1-34.02.
National Association of Criminal Defense Lawyers. (n.d.). *Standards for indigent defense.* http://www.nacdl.org/public.nsf/DefenseUpdates/Standards?OpenDocument
National Association of Pretrial Service Agencies. (2004). *Standards on pretrial release.* http://www.napsa.org/publications/2004napsastandards.pdf
National Center for Victims of Crime. (2002). *Crime victims rights.* http://www.ncvc.org/ncvc/AGP.Net/Components/documentViewer/Download.aspxnz?DocumentID=45732
National Center for Victims of Crime. (2008). *Victim impact statements.* http://www.ncvc.org/ncvc/AGP.Net/Components/documentViewer/Download.aspxnz?DocumentID=45721
National Crime Victim Law Institute. (2006). *A review of the American Bar Association's guidelines for fair treatment of crime victims and witnesses.* http://www.lclark.edu/live/files/6450-a-review-of-abas-guidelines-for-fair-treatment-of

New York State Unified Court System. (2009). *Grand juror's handbook.* https://www.nyjuror.gov/pdfs/hb_Grand.pdf

Noonan, M. (2010). *Special report deaths in custody reporting program: Mortality in local jails, 2000–2007* (NCJ 222988). U.S. Department of Justice, Bureau of Justice Statistics. https://bjs.ojp.gov/content/pub/pdf/mlj07.pdf

Parent, D., Leiter, V., Kennedy, S., Livens, L., Wentworth, D., & Wilcox, S. (1994). *Conditions of confinement: Juvenile detention and corrections facilities* (NCJ145793). U.S. Department of Justice, Office of Justice Programs, Office of Juvenile Justice and Delinquency Prevention. http://www.ojjdp.gov/publications/dc_facilities.html

Pennsylvania Office of the Victim Advocate. (2024). *Office of the victim advocate.* https://www.pa.gov/en/agencies/ova.html

Phillips, M. (2007). *Bail, detention, and nonfelony case outcomes.* New York, NY: Criminal Justice Agency, Inc. htttp://www.cjareports.org/reports/detention. pdf

Redding, R. (2010). Juvenile transfer laws: An effective deterrent to delinquency? *ODJJDP Juvenile Justice Bulletin* (NCJ220595). Washington DC: U.S. Department of Justice, Bureau of Justice Programs, Office of Juvenile Justice and Delinquency Prevention. National Criminal Justice Resource Center, http://www.ncjrs.gov/pdffiles1/ojjdp/220595.pdf

Rovner, J. (2024). *Youth justice by the numbers.* https://www.sentencingproject.org/policy-brief/youth-justice-by-the-numbers/

Sickmund, M., Sladly, T. J., Kang, W., & Puzzanchera, C. (2008). *Easy access to the census of juveniles in residential placement.* Office of Juvenile Justice and Delinquency Prevention. http://ojjdp.ncjrs.gov/ojstatbb/ezacjrp/asp/display.asp

St. John, V., Murphy, K., & Liberman, A. (2020). *Recommendations for addressing racial bias in risk and needs assessment in the juvenile justice system.* https://cms.childtrends.org/wp-content/uploads/2020/01/Duke-Risk-Assessment-FAQ_ChildTrends_Jan2020-1.pdf

Steinhardt, D. (2006). *A practice guide to juvenile detention reform: Juvenile detention risk assessment.* Annie E. Casey Foundation. http://www.aecf.org/upload/PublicationFiles/JJ3622H5038.pdf

Snyder, H.N., & Sickmund, M. (2006). *Juvenile offenders and victims national report* (NCJ212906). Washington, D.C: U.S. Department of Justice: Office of Justice Programs, Office of Juvenile Justice and Delinquency Prevention. http://www.ojjdp.gov/ojstatbb/nr2006/downloads/NR2006.pdf

Tartaro, C., & Sedelmaier, C. (2009). A tale of two counties: The impact of pre-trial release, race and ethnicity on sentencing decisions. *Criminal Justice Studies*, *22*(2), 203–221. https://doi.org/10.1080/14786010902975507

U.S. Department of the Attorney General. (2024). *Steps in the criminal process.* https://www.justice.gov/usao/justice-101/steps-federal-criminal-process

VanNostrand, M. (2007). *Legal and evidence-based practices: Applications of legal principles, laws, and research to the field of pretrial services.* Crime and Justice Institute & National Institute of Corrections. https://www.dcjs.virginia.gov/sites/dcjs.virginia.gov/files/publications/corrrections/legal-and-evidence-based-practices-application-legal-principles-laws-and-research-field-pretrial.pdf

Vera Institute of Justice. (2024). *Bail reform.* https://www.vera.org/ending-mass-incarceration/criminalization-racial-disparities/bail-reform

Victims of Trafficking and Violence Prevention Act. (2000, 2008). Pub. L. No. 106-386, 114 Stat. 1464.

Violence Against Women Act of 1994, Pub. L. No. 103-322, 108 Stat. 1796 (1994).

Washington State Institute for Public Policy. (1998). *Validation of the Washington state juvenile court assessment: Interim report.* http://www.wsipp.wa.gov/rptfiles/98-11-1201.pdf

CHAPTER 8

Trials and Hearings: General Knowledge and Skills for Civil and Criminal Proceedings

INTRODUCTION

In this chapter, you are introduced to the general knowledge and skills that are needed to prepare your client and yourself for empowered participation during legal proceedings. First, you are introduced to the variety of roles social workers may play during trials and hearings. Regardless of the specific role, there are a number of competencies that must be mastered for the effective performance of these roles. These competencies include preparing to participate in a trial or hearing, identifying different types of testimony, defining basic legal terms, knowing what evidence is permissible depending on the forum, preparing the client to testify, writing court reports, testifying as fact or expert witness, evaluating reports and documents for use at trial, and ethical concerns raised at trial. By the end of this chapter, you should be more comfortable when, during the course of your social work practice, you are faced with the prospect of participating in a legal proceeding.

SOCIAL WORK ROLES AND SKILLS DURING TRIALS AND HEARINGS

This chapter describes how to prepare for the proceedings that you will be introduced to in Chapters 9, 10, and 12. Preparing reports or testimony for hearings and trials, whether in civil, criminal, or administrative proceedings, all involve the same set of skills and principles. The activities most frequently involved for social workers include functioning as a fact or expert witness, preparing yourself and others for testimony and trial, writing reports and evaluations, identifying experts, assisting attorneys to develop questions to examine experts, evaluating and assessing records and reports by other professionals, assisting and supporting the client throughout the process and giving them information about the process, and assisting attorneys in effective interviewing and questioning of special populations such as children, elders, and victims of violent crimes. As always, when you are asked to carry out these activities, it is very important to be clear about what role you are playing during a trial or hearing, who is your client, and who has hired you because that will inform your practice and ethical considerations.

Depending on your role, there are implications about who you may speak to, what role you play with the client and other stakeholders, what you can testify about or evidence you can present, and most significantly, implications for client confidentiality. Many times social workers, particularly those that have functioned in the role of therapist for the client, are unwilling participants in hearings and trials. Conducting therapy and testifying in court are two different roles requiring different sets of skills and have implications for your relationship with the client. These issues are discussed more fully later in the section that addresses ethical concerns that may come up for the social worker during the hearing and trial phase of a case. Regardless of what role you play, a thorough understanding of the legal context you are operating in is essential and will make your involvement in a trial less anxiety provoking (Stein, 2004). The following are some of the roles a social worker may play during the hearing and trial process.

Social Worker as Fact Witness

A social worker is frequently in a position where they have to testify during a hearing or trial about an issue relevant to their social work practice with a client. The general definition of a witness is someone who has observed or knows something that is relevant to the trial. There are generally two types of witnesses: a *lay witness* and an *expert witness.* A lay witness is someone who has observed an event relevant to a trial. Lay witnesses are sometimes called *fact or material witnesses.* A fact witness can only testify to something they directly observed and cannot offer an opinion. It is also important to understand that a lay witness cannot respond to a hypothetical question or offer interpretations of the facts, which is distinguished from permissible testimony for an expert witness (Bernstein & Hartsell, 2005). A social worker who is testifying as a fact or lay witness can say that a client said they were hearing voices on three different occasions during an appointment, but the social worker cannot say that the client has a mental illness because that would qualify as an opinion, which, depending on the social worker's training, may not be within their practice and would only be permissible if called as an expert witness.

In the case of Ms. Jones, if you are the community-based social service worker, you may be called as a fact witness to describe how often Ms. Jones came in for services, what the services were, and whether she followed through on any assigned tasks. Even though you know that Ms. Jones has used substances because she disclosed this to you, in this role you cannot be asked your opinion about whether or not she has a substance use disorder. If an attorney asks you to give your opinion in that way during testimony as a fact witness, you should answer that you are not qualified to give an opinion about whether or not Ms. Jones has a substance abuse disorder. If you exceed your knowledge in testifying, your responses can be struck from the record, meaning that what you say is not admitted into evidence and therefore not considered in the judge's or jury's decision. Even if you believe that you are qualified to give that opinion or you have strong beliefs about that conclusion or opinion, it is not appropriate to testify to that conclusion as a fact witness.

You can enhance your effectiveness as a fact witness and avoid cross-examination pitfalls by understanding how your testimony and the evidence presented through your testimony will be used to answer a legal question or to prove a legal claim. Many times social workers are testifying as fact witnesses and are not apprised of why they are being asked to testify, what information they are supposed to be giving, and how it relates to the legal questions. Social workers who do not know the basis for their testimony will be unprepared, not know how to organize their information, what information and facts are actually relevant, and which are more vulnerable when it comes to making errors during cross-examination.

It is important to know that your testimony during a trial or hearing is being used as evidence to prove or disprove something or, as we learned in Chapter 6, support the lawyer's "theory" of their case. Each lawyer will have a different theory depending on the interests of their client and their position in the case. During your preparation meeting with the attorney who is calling you as witness, you can ask what the alternative "theories" may be so you can more effectively prepare for cross-examination. Testimony is also used to give the trier of fact—a judge or jury—information that will assist them in becoming clearer about or expanding their understanding of the issue at hand. Preparation that includes thorough conversations with the attorney detailing the goals, relevance, and potential pitfalls of your testimony will provide a strong foundation for testifying in court.

When you are testifying, the attorney who called you to testify will be trying to get information from you that supports their "theory" of the case. For example, if you are the community-based social worker working with Ms. Jones, her attorney may call you as a fact witness in her civil neglect trial where custody of her son is at issue. Her attorney would most likely want to ask you about how often she came to the program and how she was attempting to access services to stabilize her living situation as a way to show Ms. Jones exercised a "minimum degree of care" for her child. If you are testifying in the role of Ms. Jones's substance abuse counselor, her attorney will want to get information about how often she participated in services and the level of her participation in your counseling sessions. The attorney in that instance would ask many more questions about Ms. Jones's participation prior to leaving treatment to demonstrate that she was actively involved in the treatment program and to argue to the court that the treatment program was a reasonable effort and therefore Ms. Jones should be allowed to reunify with her son. The attorney representing the child welfare agency however might focus on how many sessions Ms. Jones missed, how often she relapsed, what substances she was tested for, how often she failed the drug tests, and additional questions to demonstrate neglect and a theory that Ms. Jones is not willing to engage in drug treatment. Depending on what her son Matthew's lawyer or guardian ad litem believe is in his best interest, Matthew's attorney might question if you have any knowledge of whether Ms. Jones was also receiving prenatal care during the time she was in treatment and whether she discussed any plans for his birth and care with you as part of the program. As you can see in the case example for Ms. Jones, each attorney's "theory" of the case informs their line of questioning to a witness.

If you are the child protective caseworker and you are called to testify at the removal hearing we discussed in Chapter 6, you may be cross-examined by Ms. Jones's attorney about how you made your assessment of risk and whether you provided "reasonable efforts" to avoid placement. It is important that during your testimony as a fact witness that you give specific dates and times, and relate the facts to the legal issue you are being asked to shed light on. If you are the Child Protective Services (CPS) worker being asked to testify about "reasonable efforts," it is much more effective when you are testifying to say "I attempted on three occasions, date and time 1, date and time 2, and date and time 3 to arrange a home visit with Ms. Jones's aunt to assess the potential living situation as an alternative to placement but the aunt did not respond to phone messages" than to just say, "I tried to contact the aunt but could not get in touch with her." As a general matter, testimony will be more helpful if there is more specificity and detail, and avoids general conclusions or baseless statements.

Social Worker as Expert Witness

A social worker may also be called as an *expert witness.* An expert witness is someone who has the knowledge to help explain the evidence to a judge or jury. The U.S. Supreme Court gave social workers legal status as expert witnesses in *Jaffee v. Redmond* (1996). The court granted social workers the same status as other mental health professionals including psychotherapists and stated that because of the similarities in mental health practice the same best practice standards could be applied to all mental health professions (Sarnoff, 2004). Social workers regularly testify as experts in criminal, civil, and larger class-action lawsuits in both state and federal courts.

In a Supreme Court Case in New York, *People v. R.R.* (2005) regarding whether or not a social worker should be qualified as an expert witness, the court stated that the determination of who is an expert depends "far more on the professional involved and the thoroughness of his or her evaluation, rather than his or her discipline. . . . Clinical social workers are uniquely suited to assist the courts as forensic experts because they have particular competence in assessing the impact of a person's mental and physical condition on his or her social functioning, a key element in rendering forensic mental health assessments and opinions." This suggests recognition of social work's particular and unique perspective on the person and environment.

Unlike a fact witness, an expert witness can offer an opinion, draw conclusions, and respond to hypothetical questions (Bernstein & Hartsell, 2005). The court relies on expert witnesses to provide critical evidence when there is a need to explain complex information, draw conclusions, and interpret data. Expert witnesses are often hired by one of the parties to the case to support their "theory" of the case. Expert witnesses usually have specialized education, training, and experience related to a specific phenomenon; for example, sexual abuse, the credibility of children's testimony, the effect of a developmental delay on a person's cognitive functioning, or evaluating families as part of a custody dispute. Social workers frequently testify as expert witnesses in custody and visitation evaluations, termination of parental rights, child sexual abuse, domestic violence, and juvenile justice cases. Social work experts have also testified in death penalty and education cases and about victimization and trauma, competence to stand trial and substance abuse (Sarnoff, 2004; Siegel, 2008). Increasingly, with the advent of a specific clinical license for social workers that allows them to make mental health diagnoses and provide mental health treatment and the availability of more cross-profession evidence-based assessment tools, the types of cases in which social workers may perform forensic evaluations and testify as expert witnesses have expanded. Social workers can be authorized to conduct forensic evaluations and provide expert testimony explicitly through state statutes and administrative regulations. In Nevada, Utah, Tennessee, North Carolina, South Carolina, and Washington as examples, social workers are explicitly allowed to be certified as forensic evaluators (Siegel, 2008).

Another way social workers can be authorized to testify as experts is at the discretion of trial court judges. Usually the judge will base their decision on whether the social worker has the appropriate qualifications, knowledge, and skills; the appropriateness of testimony about the subject at hand; and whether a sufficient factual basis exists to support the testimony (Ashford, 2009). Judges have qualified social workers as experts on other mental health issues such as the presence of a mental disorder as a predicate for involuntary civil commitment.

In our case example, the attorneys representing each of the parties—Ms. Jones, Matthew, and the child welfare agency—may want to retain social workers as expert witnesses to support their various defenses or theories. The law guardian representing Matthew may request a mental health evaluation, a substance abuse assessment, and a parenting capacity evaluation in addition to the CPS report. The attorney representing Ms. Jones may want to try and qualify the substance abuse counselor as an expert on substance abuse. This would be likely as the substance abuse counsellor has a licensed clinical social worker (LCSW) with 8 years of experience in treatment programs and a certification in substance abuse treatment. The attorney would instruct the social worker in this context to provide testimony about the frequency and likelihood of relapse during early recovery, why women who are using substances do not seek medical care or treatment during pregnancy, and how substance use may or may not effect parenting capacity.

While the previous cases all involved social workers testifying about a specific client or individual that is personally known to them, social work experts can also testify in cases where they do not have a personal relationship with the individual involved in the case (Saltzman & Furman, 1999). Social work experts can also testify about standards of care and best practices in their field and can offer testimony about whether or not an agency has followed "best practice" in the case in question (Stein, 2004). So, in our case example, a social work expert in the field of substance abuse treatment who has never met Ms. Jones, could be called to present research on the most effective treatment for both mothers and children when there is prenatal substance use or why many women do not obtain treatment while they are pregnant. Social work expert witnesses can also review and evaluate whether or not an evaluator or another social worker followed evidence-informed and valid protocols when making an assessment.

For ethical reasons, social workers should always strive for neutrality regardless of who retains you, and you should be clear with whoever retains you that that is the case. In other words, your testimony as an expert witness is based on your assessment and is not swayed by the position of the attorney or client that retains you as an expert witness. Experts, regardless of who hires them, should always be independent, and social workers must be equally mindful of their specific ethical obligations with regard to competence, confidentiality, and conflicts of interest (Reamer, 2018). In fact, Ashford (2009) suggests that social workers that have a forensic practice should only obtain 20% of their income from conducting forensic evaluations as a way to mitigate potential charges of being biased or what is colloquially known as a "hired gun." Ethical considerations in regard to being an expert witness or evaluator are discussed later in the chapter.

Social Worker as Advocate and Consultant to Attorneys

Social workers frequently work in organizations with attorneys and help them prepare for a case in a variety of ways including their advocacy role and fact witness. Other times social workers may be hired as a consultant by a defense attorney or prosecutor to assist them in preparing a case and support their positions. In these situations, testimony is often viewed more for advocacy purposes and is often not considered to be "neutral." Having role clarity is exceptionally important in this instance and as a consultant you should never perform as an expert witness on the same case.

Most times, an attorney will have the primary responsibility for preparing a client to present testimony during a hearing or trial. However, in many instances clients also need to be psychologically prepared for the experience. Social workers can function as advocates for defendants, respondents, or victims throughout legal proceedings. In organizations where social workers work with attorneys, whether a prosecutor's office or a legal defense practice, a key aspect of their job is assisting clients to productively address the emotions that may come up during a court proceeding and when testifying. There are certain types of vulnerable witnesses, such as children or developmentally disabled persons, that may present challenges for some attorneys and social workers can be helpful in offering information about development and communication skills, such as identifying the most effective methods to elicit information from a victim of violence. In each of these instances, social workers who are trained in trauma-informed interviewing and counseling can bring critical skills and perspectives to the process of preparing a client or witness to testify credibly and successfully. We discuss the special needs of vulnerable witnesses later in this chapter.

Social workers can also assist clients to prepare for forensic evaluations by other mental health professionals by making sure the client understands their rights and responsibilities regarding informed consent and confidentiality, as well as being clear about who will have access to court reports. The social worker should ask the attorney whether other parties, including the client's attorney or social worker, are allowed to be present during any of the forensic evaluations. The social worker can assist the client in preparing documents or records that clients have been requested to bring to the evaluation and to encourage the client to ask questions about anything they may not understand such as the use of particular tests and measurements. Clients in this situation frequently have feelings of mistrust about clinicians, doubts about their usefulness, and fears about what they will find out or say in court. Helping the client to identify any concerns and encouraging them to have an open discussion with the evaluator will help clients appear less angry and guarded and lower the risk of their behaviors being misinterpreted.

Social workers can also identify potential witnesses and meet with them to assist the attorney in assessing what kind of witness the person may be and whether or not they can handle the stress of testifying. Referring back to our practice in Chapter 5 for interdisciplinary research, after completing the brief research memo on the effect of prenatal marijuana use on child development, a social worker could recommend that testimony from a developmental pediatrician would be important in the case. In this instance, the attorney could use questions pulled from the social worker's review of the research during the preparation of the pediatrician's testimony.

As important as it is to prepare clients to testify and if possible to support them during their testimony, social workers can and should be available to meet with the client after the proceeding to debrief the experience and offer support (Bernstein & Hartsell, 2005). For many clients, whether they are victims, defendants, or respondents, sitting in a court and hearing and seeing their life pulled and picked apart in such a visible and public way is a demoralizing, stressful, and upsetting experience. Many times clients have to publicly contain very difficult feelings of anger, humiliation, shame, revenge, fear, and physiological arousal during these proceedings. Clients are constrained by legal rules, procedures, and questioning by attorneys in regard to how they are allowed to tell their stories. The complexity of client lives and narratives is frequently lost or subjugated to the legal argument and theory. As discussed in Chapter 5, individual actors in the legal system have schemas or frameworks through which they hear and interpret client narratives. Biased and racist schemas such as "welfare mom" or "crack babies" or "super predators" promulgated by the media can result in schemas that find their way into courts and decision-making. Rights-based and socially just social workers have a critical responsibility and opportunity during their own testimony and when assisting lawyers and clients to prepare testimony, to find, create, and expand opportunities for clients to tell their story and re-story the biased schemas that may emerge in legal decision-making forums (Schroeder et al., 2005).

Social workers who work with attorneys and who are not testifying can also offer valuable insights and observations by debriefing what occurred in the courtroom during hearings and trials with the lawyer. An attorney may be focused on cross-examining a witness, and a social worker can be observing and taking notes about how the judge and jury might be responding. Social workers can offer suggestions on strategy based on these observations and how to approach certain personalities in the courtroom, or how to present certain information that may address perceived bias about your client. Social workers can also assist attorneys during the trial proceedings by making attorneys aware of any needs of the client for services or court action during the course of the proceeding.

SOCIAL WORKER AS GUARDIAN AD LITEM AND GUARDIANS

In many jurisdictions, a guardian ad litem (GAL) is appointed to cases that are in litigation where the court wishes special attention to be paid to what is best for the children involved in the case. As you learned in Chapter 6, guardians are also appointed in cases where adults have been found to lack capacity to make decisions about themselves or their property. Cases involving children typically include adoptions, termination of parental rights, and contested custody and visitation. Adults who may be appointed a GAL include elders and mentally ill and developmentally disabled persons.

Typically GALs are appointed by the court and have completed a special training program. In some jurisdictions GALs can receive payment and in some instances, particularly those involving payment, a background in social work or a related field is a requirement. The training for a GAL generally involves understanding the particular needs of the client population, the court process, and the resources to support the child or vulnerable adult.

Typically, a GAL will be presented with an issue or concern the court or any of the parties wish to be investigated, and will be asked to prepare a written report to be presented to the court. The GAL in all cases is charged with presenting information and making a recommendation that is in the "best interests" of the person or child. Therefore, under a standard that is somewhat ambiguous, the GAL has considerable discretion. The National Association of Social Workers (NASW) Code of Ethics states in Section 1.4 "when social workers act on behalf of clients who lack the capacity to make informed decisions, social workers should take reasonable steps to safeguard the interests and rights of those clients" (2021, p. 14). We believe that using the strategies presented in Chapter 5 for identifying and addressing bias through interdisciplinary conversations and evidence-informed practice become even more critical when you are in the position of having to make a decision for someone else and will help you to meet the reasonable steps and standard of the ethical code. For example, the GAL assigned to represent Matthew, Ms. Jones's son, may have some of the biases we described in Chapter 5. Having a conversation with Matthew's pediatrician regarding their observations of the child's condition during the first week of life would be essential to challenge an automatic assumption that the child may be neurologically impaired. The same skills and tasks of any other kind of witness in the preparation of testimony are implicated when you are in the role of GAL if you wish to meet your ethical responsibility.

SOCIAL WORKER AS REPRESENTATIVE OF THE COURT

Social workers may be employed or assigned by a court to evaluate clients and produce reports that can provide information to assist the judge and jury in their decision-making. This role involves evaluation or investigation, writing a report, and presenting the report to the court. In Chapter 6, we discussed the role of the pretrial services officer and the roles and tasks of social workers working with adults, juveniles, and victims of crimes. During the trial and hearing phase in Criminal Court, probation officers are frequently required to investigate and present a presentencing evaluation and make recommendations to the court after a person has been convicted and the trial is in the sentencing phase. Probation officers may also make progress reports to the court if the person is under pretrial supervision. In civil proceedings, social workers may be on a panel of experts that the court can draw from to conduct an evaluation or give a report. In our case example, the judge in Ms. Jones's case has the discretion to order an independent mental health evaluation for her, even if the attorneys representing all the parties have hired their own evaluators or have decided not to request an evaluation. Some other examples are mental health professionals who specialize in the evaluation of sexual abuse, sex offenders, posttraumatic stress disorder (PTSD), and child custody. In this case, being perceived as neutral and fair by all of the parties is crucial to your success as a witness because the court hired you and the court is supposed to be neutral and impartial at all times.

CRITICAL LEGAL TERMS FOR SOCIAL WORKERS

Pro Se

Pro se (on one's own behalf) refers to a client who is not represented by an attorney during the legal proceeding and is therefore representing themselves. In many civil cases, where parties are not guaranteed the right to counsel as they are in criminal cases, litigants may appear pro se to argue their case without assistance from an attorney. For example, Ms. Jones may appear pro se if Matthew's father filed a custody complaint seeking full legal and physical custody because there is no guaranteed right to counsel if you can't afford an attorney in a custody proceeding. In some cases, litigants might refuse to have an attorney appointed to their case because they prefer to represent themselves in the proceeding. Very often, individuals who have been convicted of a crime will appeal the Criminal Court decision pro se because is no guarantee of counsel at the appellate stage. As we discussed in Chapter 1, pro se litigants are often considered to be at a disadvantage in the legal proceeding as they do not have legal training and yet are still required to participate fully in the proceeding, including examining witnesses and presenting evidence. A study of state court judges in 2010 found that 62% of the judges believed that appearing pro se had a negative impact on the litigant's case (American Bar Association [ABA], Coalition for Justice, 2010). Most state and federal courts have resources available in the courthouse or online for pro se litigants. In addition, many community-based organizations work with local courts to provide support and counseling to pro se litigants, including social work services in many instances.

Social workers working in the implicit context should always determine whether a client is representing themselves in a legal case and whether they are able to access an attorney or legal services office for full representation or brief advice and counseling. A social worker working in the implicit context can assist individuals appearing pro se in legal proceedings by connecting them to legal help resources online and in the court systems, and in some cases by assisting the client in locating an attorney from a legal services office. Social workers can also assist pro se clients in obtaining and organizing necessary documents and forms. Although not legal requirements, the social worker can prepare a pro se client psychologically for the process and make sure the client knows their right to an interpreter if they do not speak English or are hearing impaired.

Subpoena

A *subpoena* is defined as an order from the court demanding that you appear in court to testify or turn over records to the court. A judge or an attorney who is a party to the case can sign a subpoena. If you refuse to appear in court or to produce documents after being subpoenaed, the court can issue a fine or other punishment for not complying with the order. The NASW (2021) Code of Ethics in Section 1.07 (c) "Privacy and Confidentiality" when discussing disclosure reminds us that in any instance, social workers should "disclose the least amount of confidential information necessary to achieve the desired purpose; only information that is directly relevant to the purpose for which the disclosure is made should be revealed."

Additionally, the NASW (2021) Code of Ethics requires that when a social worker has been ordered by a court or other legally authorized body to disclose confidential or privileged information without the client's consent and the social worker believes that that disclosure "could cause harm to the client, social workers should request that the court withdraw the order or limit the order as narrowly as possible or maintain the records under seal, unavailable for public inspection" (NASW 2021, Section,1.07 [j]).

As the foregoing illustrates, it is important to read the subpoena carefully to determine what testimony or records are specifically sought and identifies what parts of the record are relevant so that the social worker is prepared and accordingly limits what they say. If the subpoena does not have explicit information you can call the attorney who asked the court to issue it and get more specific information. The legally informed social worker will understand the reason why they are being called to testify, as well as the legal basis for what they will be asked to testify about, and can advocate more effectively to limit their testimony when this may create harm for the client.

Discovery

Discovery is the process of evidence gathering that occurs before a case goes to trial, and is sometimes referred to a pretrial discovery. This evidence gathering can include records, statements, and sworn testimony. There are rules that govern what evidence can be discovered or requested by the various parties and whether or not an attorney has to share that potential evidence with the opposing side. For example, in Criminal Court, the prosecutor must disclose any evidence that would tend toward mitigating the defendant's guilt or establishing their innocence because of the Supreme Court ruling in *Brady v. Maryland* (1963). In civil cases, the general rules of discovery provide for inclusive sharing of evidence among all of the parties, and attorneys generally initiate the discovery process by filing legal papers such as notice of discovery and inspection to request all documents relevant to the case that are in the parties' control or may be submitted at trial. If you are going to testify, it is important to let the attorney who called you as a witness know what documents you are relying on for your testimony well in advance as these documents need to be listed and submitted to the parties prior to the start of the trial so that advocates may effectively prepare. Again, it is important for social workers in the implicit context to remember that, depending on the agency where they work, records and reports otherwise maintained as confidential may be subject to discovery in litigation.

Depositions

As part of the discovery process before trial, any party to the legal proceeding can use depositions to gather evidence and information. A *deposition* is when an attorney outside of the court and the formal trial questions a party or witness. The deposition is still considered to be sworn testimony and can be used to impeach or attack the credibility of a witness later testifying in court. Depositions are frequently done in attorneys' offices and are recorded by a court reporter so that there is an official transcript of the questioning.

Motions and Affidavits

Motions are written legal documents filed in court and presented to the judge, arguing for a specific remedy or outcome. For example, the defense attorney in a civil proceeding could file a motion for summary judgment arguing that even if the judge took everything in the petition to be true, it is still not sufficient to make a cause of action that a law was violated. Motions contain legal arguments that reference relevant laws and case decisions. In addition, motions often contain *affidavits*, which are written statements from individuals that are sworn to and notarized. For example, in Ms. Jones's case, a social worker from the treatment program could sign an affidavit that states she supports Ms. Jones having increased visitation with her son because of her progress in treatment. The social worker would collaborate with the attorney about the content of the affidavit and ultimately the signed affidavit would be the same as the sworn testimony of the social worker in court. The written motion to modify the court's visitation order from supervised once a week to unsupervised visitation twice a week would be supported by the social worker's affidavit describing Ms. Jones's success in treatment.

A rights-based, legally informed social worker working in the implicit context would know that Ms. Jones has an attorney and would ask whether or not she was meeting with her attorney in between court dates to prepare, that she has a case in civil court, and that the proceeding is to determine child neglect and her custody of her child. The social worker would also know that there could be motions filed prior to an actual decision to address issues of concern to the client that cannot wait until the actual trial or hearing, such as the frequency of supervision. The social worker would feel quite comfortable reaching out to an attorney and offering information such as writing an affidavit that would facilitate this request if their client wanted and needed them to.

Burden of Proof

The *burden of proof* or *standard of proof* refers to the requirement that the plaintiff in a civil case or the prosecution in a criminal case prove their case. In other words, the plaintiff or prosecution must demonstrate through their own witnesses and evidence that they have met their burden of proving the allegations against the respondent or defendant. In a criminal case, the prosecutor bears the burden of proving that the defendant is guilty of the alleged criminal conduct "beyond a reasonable doubt." This means that the jurors or judge must find a defendant guilty only if they are certain that the defendant committed the alleged crime or if any doubt that they have can be considered unreasonable. As you can imagine, this is a very high standard of proof and is often explained to clients as a juror or judge being 99.9% certain that the defendant committed the crime. However, in *civil cases*, the plaintiff bears the burden of showing that the allegations in the petition are demonstrated through "clear and convincing evidence" or a "preponderance of evidence." Clear and convincing evidence is a lower standard of proof than beyond a reasonable doubt, but is a higher standard of proof than preponderance of the evidence. In civil cases, with the preponderance of the evidence standard, attorneys often explain to clients that the judge or jury must believe that more likely than not the allegations are true.

Jury Selection

Before a *jury trial* begins, the parties must select the jurors from a large number of individuals who have been called for potential jury duty. When attorneys question jurors about their beliefs, backgrounds, or their ability to be unbiased in reviewing the evidence in the case before them, it is referred to as *voir dire*. Attorneys are able to ask for a juror to be stricken from the jury "for cause" if there is evidence that the juror has a bias in the proceeding; for example, if the juror was related to one of the parties or previously worked for the same company. Attorneys can also use peremptory challenges, or challenges where they are not required to state a reason or cause for their challenge to the judge, to have a potential juror removed from the jury panel. Each state has different regulations on how many peremptory challenges are provided to each side. The Supreme Court ruled in *Batson v. Kentucky* (1986) that race cannot be the basis for using a peremptory challenge to remove a juror and in *J.E.B. v. Alabama* (1994) that gender is similarly prohibited as a basis for striking a juror.

The Opening Statement

The *opening statement* is delivered by all parties in the case and is the first opportunity for the attorneys to tell the jurors and judge about the trial. The opening statement focuses on the evidence that will be presented at trial and each side argues how the evidence will support their theory of the case. In criminal cases, opening statements can be critical opportunities for the defense to humanize their client and present an alternate story or "theory" to the prosecution's allegations. As discussed, contextual knowledge and facts about the client narrative provided by the social worker can assist the attorney in this task of telling an alternative client story. In some civil proceedings where there is no jury trial, attorneys will not make opening statements and will simply proceed to the direct examination of the first witness.

Direct Examination

The *direct examination* is when an attorney calls a witness to the stand to testify on behalf of their client. It is, put simply, the presentation of the facts of the case. In a civil case alleging that someone was negligent, the plaintiff who was injured would testify on direct examination to the facts of how the injury occurred. In Ms. Jones's case, the child welfare case worker would testify on direct examination to the facts of the investigation into Ms. Jones's alleged neglect, including any conversations with Ms. Jones or any observations of Ms. Jones and her son. As you can imagine, the success of the direct examination depends significantly on the ability of the witness to appear credible or believable.

Cross-Examination

If the direct examination is the method of laying out the facts of the case in the strongest possible manner, then *cross-examination* is the process by which attorneys attempt to show the weaknesses or gaps in their opponent's case. The weaknesses could include trying to cast doubt on the credibility of the witness, highlighting important facts that have been left out, or demonstrating that the witness is biased. For example, the defense attorney for Ms. Jones could cross-examine the child welfare caseworker to elicit testimony that Ms. Jones was in fact in a substance abuse program throughout her pregnancy, did receive prenatal care, and had made adequate preparations for her son. That line of cross-examination would support the defense's position that Ms. Jones was not neglectful and in fact, did meet the minimum degree of care required under the law.

Throughout the trial, attorneys will make *objections* to testimony and records that are being offered as evidence. Generally, attorneys make objections by interrupting a witness or the opposing counsel by declaring "Objection" and then stating the legal basis for the objection. Objections can be made for a variety of reasons, but at heart the concern is whether or not the proposed evidence or testimony is admissible at trial.

The most common objection at trial is to *hearsay* statements. Hearsay refers to statements that were not made by the witness who is testifying. In other words, a hearsay statement would be a witness testifying to what someone else said. The laws of evidence favor testimony from the actual source and not a second-hand source, as would be the case if a witness testified to what someone else said. This is to be distinguished from a witness testifying to what someone else did in their presence, which would not be considered a hearsay statement but an observation.

The laws governing admissibility of evidence vary from state to state and depend in large part on the type of proceeding. For example, in a civil case such as Ms. Jones's Family Court matter, hearsay may be admissible during some of the hearings including the dispositional hearing. However, in her criminal case, hearsay statements would not be admissible unless they fell into one of the exceptions to the hearsay rule. Exceptions to the hearsay rule include any statements that would be considered an admission by Ms. Jones or any statements that Ms. Jones made to a medical professional when seeking treatment.

Exhibits

Exhibits are submitted at trial to help the fact-finder, either the judge or the jury, make a decision in the case. Generally, exhibits fall into one of the following four categories: (a) real evidence which is a tangible object; (b) demonstrative evidence that represents the object including photographs, maps, or models; (c) writings, which are documents bearing a particular legal significance such as a contract or will; and (d) records that have been maintained including business records from hospitals, schools, or companies (Mauet, 1996). So, for example, in the criminal trial in Ms. Jones's case, a prosecutor will introduce the drugs that the police found in Ms. Jones's possession in addition to an exhibit that documents the results of the drugs being tested and confirmed as cocaine. In the civil neglect proceeding, the attorney who represents Matthew may introduce his medical records from the hospital to argue that he was healthy upon birth and suffered no injury or harm from his mother's alleged drug abuse.

Expert Witness

Expert witnesses are frequently used at trial to explain more complicated theories or facts to the judge and jury. In recent years, expert witnesses have become commonplace in trials involving medical malpractice or criminal trials seeking to introduce DNA evidence. In order for the expert testimony to be considered admissible, it has to pass a test to determine whether or not the testimony and methodology was relevant and reliable. The judge ultimately decides whether the expert testimony will be admitted and attorneys will often challenge an expert witness's qualifications on their resume or the methodology used when coming to their ultimate conclusion on a case. As we discussed earlier, social workers may be called as expert witnesses in a number of situations.

The Supreme Court decided the guidelines for admitting expert evidence and what can be considered a scientific method in *Daubert v. Merrell Dow Pharmaceuticals* (1993), focusing on the reliability of the evidence and the judge's role to exclude any evidence that is not based on reliable data or methods. The standard was adopted in Rule 702 of the Federal Rules of Evidence, which states the following:

> If scientific, technical, or other specialized knowledge will assist the trier of fact to understand the evidence or to determine a fact in issue, a witness qualified as an expert by knowledge, skill, experience, training, or education, may testify thereto in the form of an opinion or otherwise, if (1) the testimony is based upon sufficient facts or data, (2) the testimony is the product of reliable principles and methods, and (3) the witness has applied the principles and methods reliably to the facts of the case.

As far as social workers testifying as expert witnesses, the standard of what can be considered expert testimony is the same for civil and criminal cases. Under *Daubert v. Merrell Dow Pharmaceuticals*, the judge will consider a variety of factors when evaluating if the testimony can be considered expert testimony including the following: Has the technique or theory that the expert used been tested for validity? Has the technique or theory been subject to peer review or publication in academic or professional journals? What is the determined or potential rate of error with the methodology used? and Is the theory or technique employed by the potential expert witness generally accepted by the scientific community? During research courses, social workers learn many of these skills including how to read and critique a research article which will allow you to testify credibly as an expert.

Closing Statement

When all of the evidence has been presented and all of the witnesses have finished their testimony, the attorneys will make *closing statements.* The closing statement is the last opportunity for the attorneys to communicate to the jury or judge their theory of the case and how the evidence supports that theory. The closing statement may also highlight gaps in the other side's case and call witnesses' credibility into question. After the closing statement, the judge may provide instructions on the law to the jury. However, if the judge is the fact-finder, the judge may render a decision immediately from the bench, or may wait to render a decision in writing.

GENERAL CONSIDERATIONS FOR WITNESS PREPARATION

The main task of a witness, whether client, fact witness, or expert witness, is to present information to assist a judge or jury to come to an informed conclusion about the matter that is the subject of the proceeding. Saltzman and Furman (1999) suggest that "good" evidence is evidence that is "admissible, credible and persuasive" (Saltzman & Furman, 1999, p. 62). Judges and jurors are influenced by the assessment they make of a witness's appearance and dress, nonverbal behaviors, how they speak, the quality of their written reports and evaluations, attitude, and demeanor. This is confirmed in the studies discussed in Chapter 1, where researchers found that many times child protective caseworkers who may have a masters in social work appeared to not understand the legal system, know how to write well-documented and relevant court reports, or demonstrate the ability to effectively testify in court, which resulted in perceptions of incompetence by other professionals (Ellett & Steib, 2005).

As a social worker testifying in a case, you will be a credible witness if you have done a competent job as a legally evidence-based social worker prior to being called to court. As we have discussed throughout this book, if you identify your assumptions and biases, challenge them through interdisciplinary conversations and the use of your research skills, know and target your information to the legal questions at hand, and use legal and evidence-based practice (LEBP) to support your recommendations, you will be fully prepared to be perceived as a competent, credible, and effective witness. This may seem self-explanatory but sometimes, because social workers have large caseloads, documentation requirements, and are pressed for time, they do not proofread their work or pay attention to small details. We cannot stress enough the importance of submitting written work to the court that is neat, well organized, and free of spelling and grammatical errors.

Much of the information that you have already learned in this book should make you feel competent and less anxious about testifying during a court or hearing. You have already been introduced to the roles of others you will meet during this experience and you understand the basic processes and structures of the court for various forums. Additionally you know what outcomes can be expected and how social work knowledge can assist the judge or jury during the process of analyzing and interpreting facts and information.

Being a competent and evidence-based practitioner prior to testifying and understanding the legal context will assist you in projecting a professional and confident demeanor, and this in turn will go a long way toward the judge and/or jury perceiving you as credible. Researchers found that when social work students working with law students utilized research, targeted their knowledge in ways that helped the legal process move forward, and assisted the law students in better understanding the client, the perception of social worker competence on the part of law students increased (Slater, 2007). Social work students' feelings of confidence also increased. Once social workers demonstrated their credibility at this level they were able to exercise more influence and direction related to cases than social work students who used more generalized social work terminology and saw social work practice as something separate from the legal context of the work (Slater, 2007).

PREPARATION PRIOR TO THE COURT APPEARANCE

Generally you will find out when you or your client will be testifying through the attorney for the client or the attorney who is calling you to testify. As mentioned this could be done formally through a summons or subpoena, or informally through a telephone call or written correspondence. You should always try to meet with the attorney who called you before the trial. Not only is it their responsibility to prepare you and the client to give testimony but you can be proactive and suggest that the attorney asks you certain questions that from your perspective will produce important information or explanations for the judge and/or jury to hear. This will be possible because you have familiarized yourself with the legal questions you will be providing evidence about.

Speaking with the attorney prior to testifying is critical whether you are working with an attorney or separately employed by an outside agency so that you are fully aware of what you will be expected to testify about and what you should expect on cross-examination. At this meeting, the attorney can also advise you about the process and rules for testifying, including that once you have begun testifying in a case, you are not allowed to discuss that testimony with anyone, including the attorney and your client, until you finish your testimony.

If an attorney suggests meeting immediately before the trial on the day of the trial, the social worker should express their preference to meet prior to the court date. Social workers can reference the ABA Standards of Practice that we identified in Chapters 6 and 7. For example, if you are a child protective caseworker you should be aware that the ABA Standards of Practice for Lawyers Representing Child Welfare Agencies recommend preparing all witnesses and the client, in addition to requesting notes and documents from the caseworker prior to any hearing or testimony. Because we know social workers and attorneys are very busy, social workers should be well prepared for the meeting and have very specific rather than general questions to present to the attorney so that the time will be well spent. Of course, if an attorney sets aside time to meet with a social worker who is testifying as a fact or expert witness, the social worker should ensure that they are available for the entire duration of the meeting and have prepared their questions, documents, and record review, and have identified any other concerns in advance.

You should make sure in advance that you know the exact location of the court, who you will need to check in with when you arrive outside of the courtroom, and what time you should be at court. Always give yourself additional time, as many courts require you to go through a metal detector and have your bag searched unless you are an employee of the court or have a special identification card. The time you are given will usually be the time the hearing is scheduled to begin, not necessarily the time you or the client will be called as a witness. You should confirm with the attorney whether the time is considered a "time certain," which means it will begin at that exact time, or a general call which means that the case may be called anytime after the listed time.

When you are a witness you must remain outside the courtroom until you are called in order to protect your testimony from being influenced by other people who are testifying or anything you may hear in the courtroom. If you are there in the capacity of an expert witness, the projection of neutrality means that you do not communicate with or otherwise engage with any of the people you have evaluated, even if you were able to develop a comfortable rapport for evaluation purposes. It goes without saying that you should dress professionally as it will enhance your credibility and put you on par with other professionals in the courtroom, even if you are testifying in a limited way as a fact witness.

It is important to know that once you enter the courthouse, you are being observed by attorneys, court officers, and clients and thus should not speak about your case to anyone except the attorney you are working with or your client. Additionally, you want to conduct yourself professionally in the waiting room until you are called to testify and be sure to remind your client of the importance of this if they are waiting with you for any portion of time. Any conversations you have with attorneys or clients should be conducted in private, such as an attorney meeting room, as most conversations in advance of a court hearing will likely include confidential material. Depending on where you live, you and your client may have to wait for several hours to testify so be prepared by bringing reading material or work with you to court.

Clients should be counseled to dress in a way that does not reinforce stereotypes or biases that decision-makers may hold about an individual's social positions such as race, class, gender, or sexual orientation. This is often a challenging counseling issue for social workers as it places them in a situation where some social workers feel they are promoting the status quo and biases, compromising a client's identity, and placing the burden of the problem on the client rather than on the attorney or social worker to challenge the stereotypes in the public forum. One way to address this with a client is to acknowledge the stereotypes and discuss the pros and cons of various ways to approach the situation.

You can also ask the client what the most important characteristics they want the judge, jury, or other legal actors to know about them and to think about how their personal presentation can assist them in achieving that objective. For example in the case of Ms. Jones, if she wanted the judge to know she is a "good" parent, how could her personal appearance and presentation assist her in projecting that? Identifying the characteristics that people associate with competent parenting would then result in identifying ways that could be communicated nonverbally. For example, most people believe that parents need to have some level of organizational skills to function competently to address the multiplicity of children's needs. Assisting Ms. Jones to have a notebook with important papers such as medical information, birth certificate, names, addresses, and phone numbers of all medical and social service providers and any important documentation such as training completion or a lease will support advocacy in demonstrating her skills. When asked a very specific question, Ms. Jones will know exactly where the answer is and have access to her and her son's records. Encouraging Ms. Jones to take notes so she can remember what went on during the proceeding could also be a strategy for demonstrating to the court her engagement and commitment to parenting, and underscoring the critical role that she plays in the proceeding and empowering her in that role.

As mentioned earlier in this chapter, coming to court and having to testify is a very stressful and emotional experience for clients regardless if they are a defendant, respondent, or a victim. Sometimes a client may lose control, raise their voice, and be chastised by the court, heightening the feelings of powerlessness and humiliation that one feels in this situation. Helping the client to anticipate some of the emotional triggers that may come up during testimony and teaching some cognitive behavioral techniques such as breathing, relaxation techniques, and self-talk prior to the court date can be effective tools for both the client and the social worker to employ. Role playing and practicing prior to the court date are also effective trial preparation techniques. If not testifying, social workers can provide physical and emotional support by being in the courtroom with the client; even if the social worker is not in the courtroom the social worker should make sure the client has time after the proceeding to sit down and process the situation and gain some closure before rushing off to work or parenting or other important responsibilities. Additionally, social workers in the courtroom can help the client identify questions from the court appearance and work with the attorney to ensure that the client understands what happened in court, what happens next, and what if anything they are required to do as part of a court order. Social workers working in implicit legal contexts that are aware their client will be testifying in a legal proceeding can also help their clients psychologically prepare and debrief the experience.

WHAT HAPPENS WHEN YOU TESTIFY

When the court is ready for a witness to testify, the court officer or another member of the court's staff will call you into the courtroom. You will be asked to state your name and professional affiliation and your relationship to the case. Then you will be asked to take an oath stating that you will tell the truth when presenting testimony, also called "swearing in." There is usually a special chair for the witness generally located to the right or left of the judge, facing the tables where the attorneys and involved parties sit throughout the trial. The first person to question the witness will be the attorney who called you or your client as a witness. As you learned earlier in the chapter, questioning by the attorney who called you as a witness is called direct examination. If you are testifying as an expert there will be more detailed questions about your professional education and training as well as any research or scholarship you have produced in order to qualify you as an expert.

When being asked questions while testifying, if you do not know something like a specific date, it is best practice not to guess or estimate, but rather to make clear that you do not know the answer to the question or would need to look at your records in order to clarify a specific point. Another strategy for testimony is to take responsibility for your work and your testimony by starting your answer with "I." Bernstein and Hartsell (2005) suggest that the use of "we" makes the witness less credible and looks as if they do not want to assume full responsibility for their work. Social workers are generally socialized to be collaborative and may frequently find themselves saying "we" do it this way or this is the procedure "we" use.

Always make sure you understand the question being asked of you and remember that you will not be penalized for saying, "I don't know" or "I don't remember." In fact, when done thoughtfully, deliberately, and nonevasively, this admission can make you look more credible. Another tendency that social workers have that may influence testimony is their desire to be helpful (Bernstein & Hartsell, 2005). No matter how much you think it will explain the situation or shed light on it, do not volunteer information unless you are asked about it. If you can answer with a yes or no, do so. If the attorney wants to know more they will ask another question (Bernstein & Hartsell, 2005). If you are unsure what is being asked, you should ask the attorney to clarify their question or make clear that you do not understand what the attorney is asking you to answer.

Direct examination is followed by cross-examination conducted by the lawyer for the opposing side. In some instances there may be a number of parties, each represented by an attorney, who will all have the opportunity to cross-examine you. For example in the civil neglect case of Ms. Jones, if you are the substance abuse counselor and Ms. Jones's attorney asked you to testify, you can be cross-examined by the child welfare agency attorney and the attorney or GAL assigned to represent the child. In Ms. Jones's criminal case, you could be called by the defense attorney for Ms. Jones to testify in her defense and be cross-examined by the prosecutor who is trying to prove that Ms. Jones is guilty of the alleged crimes.

Cross-examination is probably the most stressful part of testifying for social workers and other witnesses because the objective is to discredit your testimony or your credibility as a professional. It is easy to feel personally attacked and difficult to handle the strong emotions that may come up when we feel that our work or professional competence is being attacked.

The best way to manage cross-examination is to be exceptionally well prepared by rereading all material you will be referring to, asking the attorney who called you to help you anticipate what may come up on cross-examination, and presenting the information you have in a neutral and calm way. Avoid any perception of advocacy as this may elicit the perception that you are biased and emotionally involved, thus not credible (Bernstein & Hartsell, 2005). You can research or ask the attorney you are working with to provide you with the names of cases where social work testimony has been found not to be credible or where workers have overreached the limits of their professional knowledge base. It is often enlightening to read the facts of the case and see why the judge thought the social worker's testimony was flawed so you can avoid making the same kinds of errors in your testimony. If you are frequently testifying as an expert witness you should make sure you are very familiar with the cases that discredit certain kinds of testimony or procedures used for assessment in the area you are working in.

Another important tip is to listen very carefully to the question being asked by the attorney. You are always able to ask that the question be repeated if you do not understand it or need more time to formulate an answer and provide the minimal amount of information needed to answer. It is important to remember that the job of the attorney who called you as a witness is also to ensure that you are able to give your testimony in full. Wait for a brief moment after cross-examination questions are asked in case the attorney that called you decides to object to the question. The judge will decide whether or not you have to answer the question based on the objection and the judge's interpretation of the law of that objection. If the judge responds "sustained," you do not have to answer the question as the judge agrees that the question is not permissible; if the response is "overruled," you do have to answer the question. As a general rule, do not attempt to argue or to defend your work and try to answer as neutrally as possible by keeping control of your emotions. Remember that after the cross-examination, the lawyer who called you to testify will have another opportunity, called redirect examination, to question you. It may help in handling your emotions to know that you will have a chance to explain your testimony. It is important to have the same demeanor toward all the attorneys who are questioning you, even when you feel under attack. Projecting the attitude of someone who is helpful and concerned toward all attorneys will establish your professionalism and increase your credibility with judges and juries.

Cross-examination is particularly difficult for clients who, as discussed, may already feel in a very defensive position because they are the subject of the proceeding or their behavior and decisions are being questioned and scrutinized in some way. Assisting the client in contacting the attorney in advance and ensuring that there be an adequate time to prepare the client to give testimony is important in your role as a rights-based social worker whether working in the implicit or the explicit legal context. Social workers can play a role in making sure that attorneys are preparing clients to testify in ways that are trauma informed and focus the testimony in the client's voice and agency.

There are certain classes of victims, offenders, witnesses, respondents, and plaintiffs about whom there may be a number of stereotypes and biases. These groups include children and adolescents; learning disabled and cognitively impaired individuals; the elderly; victims of interpersonal violence such as rape, date rape, and domestic violence; and people of different races and cultures who are disproportionately impacted by legal processes and systems; as well as particular kinds of defendants such as sex offenders.

Social workers, whether working only with the client or with an attorney, have an important educative role to play as professionals when vulnerable clients are involved in legal proceedings. Social workers have knowledge about human development across the lifespan, the process of aging, learning disabilities, the assessment of cognitive functioning, the impact of trauma on physical functioning and psychological or cognitive functioning; and the impact of institutional racism, oppression, and discrimination on human well-being. Conveying this knowledge to your client's lawyer will allow them to be better advocates in court by instructing judges and juries about the special needs of these populations during trials and hearings and by presenting disconfirming information to the court regarding any bias and schemas that may be operating about their client.

Cognitive Interviewing as Preparation for Testimony

Information obtained from client interviews is critical because information of good quality and quantity essentially guides the direction of an investigation and case preparation. Quality information from client interviews will generate other avenues of exploration and lines of investigation (Milne & Bull, 2006). However, even for trained social workers, obtaining information in a way that maximizes quality and quantity is a specialized task and not as easy as it first appears.

Research suggests that the cognitive interview is an effective method for reducing suggestibility; can be used with children, adults, older adults, and people who are cognitively impaired; and results in increases in both the amount of information recalled and the accuracy of what is recalled (Fisher et al., 2002). Based on psychological principles of memory, general cognition, social dynamics, and communication, the cognitive interview was developed as a tool for professionals to conduct "forensically sound" investigations that would stand up to cross-examination in court (Fisher et al., 2002).

Many of the techniques involved in cognitive interviewing such as asking open-ended questions, probing for details, allowing clients to give a free narrative, are also characteristics of effective social work interviewing skills that are generally taught in foundation year. The practice of cognitive interviewing is beyond the scope of this text, but the principles and practices involved are important to raise in the context of social work practice in legal settings. Certainly if you are frequently conducting investigative interviews with children and adults you will want to access and study the literature on suggestibility as it pertains to children, the learning impaired, and elderly clients. There is also a large evaluation literature on cognitive interviewing (Bull, 2010). Experts also recommend that conducting and videotaping multiple cognitive interviews and critiquing them with supervision is a necessary aspect of training in cognitive interviewing (Lamb et al., 2008).

Usually cognitive interviews follow a designated sequence that is designed to maximize the techniques being used. The typical sequence is as follows: introduction and rapport building, open-ended narrative, probing, review, and close (Bull, 2010). The purpose of the introduction and the rapport building stages is to let the client know what will be happening and to establish the ground rules of communication during the interview. These usually include avoiding guessing, correcting the interviewer if they say something wrong, and needing to provide very detailed information.

The second phase, or eliciting a free narrative, means facilitating a description of the event using the client's own words. This is achieved through the use of open-ended questions. Certain types of questions—leading, yes-and-no, and why questions—should be avoided during this phase as well as any exploration of feelings. Instructing witnesses to focus on sensory elements of the narrative, such as smells, colors of clothing, or season of the year, and having a witness describe and think about events in different ways are strategies that can be used during this phase (Fisher et al., 2002).

The third phase or probing phase is clarifying important terms and descriptions of events and identifying and exploring any inconsistencies that may have come up in the free narrative. In the review stage, the interviewer reviews the information that has been obtained during the interview and obtains feedback from the client about the level of accuracy. Finally, during closing, the interviewer would want the client to leave the interview with positive feelings so that in the event that they need to be reinterviewed or remember something that did not come up that the client would feel positively about contacting the interviewer (Bull, 2010).

Increasingly, forensic evaluators are video- or audiotaping investigative interviews in order to document client answers as well as to show that the investigator is not using leading or suggestive techniques of questioning that has been associated with witness and child suggestibility. It is critical when using video or audio equipment that you explain why and how it is being used to both adults and children, who will see or hear the tape, and get written permission from the adult to use the equipment (Bull, 2010; Fisher et al., 2002). Tapes should be kept in a secure place where confidentiality is ensured and these arrangements should be relayed to the client.

Children as Witnesses

Preconceived biases about the credibility and suggestibility of child witnesses are common in the legal system, whether from judges, jurors, or attorneys. Despite this bias, children can be very effective witnesses. Most challenges to children's testimony raised by defense lawyers during trial are frequently related to interviewer bias and poor interviewing. Research conducted on children's memory and suggestibility generally concludes that children can be accurate witnesses under certain conditions, but inaccurate under other circumstances. This research has also identified a list of variables that impact quality and quantity of children's testimony: child age and individual differences, social circumstances, and interviewer and interview characteristics (Perry et al., 2013). Children's performance has been found to be highly variable, so it remains difficult to assess which children are reliable witnesses (Dickinson et al., 2005). However, as previously mentioned, the use of cognitive interviewing techniques has been found to be effective with children age 7 and older (Fisher et al., 2002).

There are several process elements to preparing a child to testify: preparing the child, preparing and educating caregivers, and assisting the attorney to understand the child's level of cognitive functioning. A social worker must first obtain information in order to understand a child's cognitive ability, language capacities, experience of time, and level of abstract thinking. Being able to understand and explain this to a lawyer is crucial because research shows that a child's credibility and performance as a witness depend on whether the prosecutor asks age and developmentally appropriate questions (Cashmore & Bussey, 1996).

Equally important is for the child to have some orientation to the context and who the players are, just as it has been for you as a social worker. In many courts there are special programs for child witnesses where the child will go to the courtroom, be introduced to other players such as a judge or a court officer, and where age appropriate pamphlets or coloring books about the process are distributed to the child.

In many states, processes that make it easier for children to testify such as allowing the presence of a support person, using child-sized chairs, letting the child sit on the parent or guardian's lap, or permitting testimony in the judge's chambers have been instituted. Some states have even adopted procedures in which a child may be able to testify via closed-circuit television or videotaped depositions so that the child does not have to be in the courtroom. This is a highly contested issue in criminal cases because of the right of the defendant to face their accusers in court that you learned about in Chapter 7. Again you will want to check your local jurisdiction and relevant case law to determine what accommodations may be allowed for child witnesses. As a social worker, you may be asking for these accommodations yourself or empowering the caregivers to advocate for their child.

As a general rule working with child witnesses, questions should be kept short and basic, avoid abstract concepts, and always placed in context. Placing a series of questions in context for a child witness will assist then in shifting focus when moving on to another topic. For example, "I am going to ask you some questions about what was happening before your dad took out the knife," or "Now I am going to ask you some questions about what happened after the lady ran away." It is also important to know that children need more time to think about questions, to try and remember events, and to put information into words (Milne & Bull, 2006).

Elders as Witnesses

There are a variety of ways in which elderly people can become involved in the justice system and they face challenges in each of these areas. First, when they testify in court they may be viewed through the lens of ageist bias and stereotypes related to memory and cognitive functioning. Being older does not necessarily mean the witness has an impaired memory, but some jurors may have biased opinions about elderly people that affect their decisions (Gaydon & Miller, 2007).

Research shows that when compared to college students, elders are somewhat more suggestible. As is the case with children, this does not mean that elders cannot be good witnesses but rather they must be interviewed in ways that do not include leading questions or suggestions from the interviewer. When properly questioned, elders can give accurate descriptions and details of events similar to younger adults. Elderly witnesses have been shown to do poorly under cross-examination, and a lawyer may want to avoid putting an elder witness on the stand because of the chance that jurors will not believe them (Mueller-Johnson & Ceci, 2004). When elderly witnesses must testify, lawyers should take extra time to prepare elders for examination and cross-examination. Other decision-making points where rights-based social workers may need to advocate for elders are during arrest and prosecution when an elder is a victim because they may not be viewed as a reliable witness. Also social workers can advocate when elders receive smaller monetary awards during civil cases because of shorter life expectancies and that do not take into account surviving dependents (Gaydon & Miller, 2007).

Learning Disabled or Cognitively Impaired Individuals as Witnesses

As we read in Chapter 1, people with learning disabilities or cognitive impairments are likely to be at greater risk of having crimes committed against them. The Bureau of Justice Statistics reports that almost 40% of individuals incarcerated in jails and prisons never completed a high school education, and 36.5% of those defendants report having a learning disability (James and Glaze, 2006). The ability to provide a detailed and accurate statement during investigation and testimony is important to successfully prosecute and defend clients with learning disabilities.

Similar to the other populations we have been discussing, research has shown that clients with learning disabilities or cognitive impairment are a very diverse group and research says that members of this group can give accurate testimony, again related to the conditions of the questioning and the characteristics of the interviewer (Bull, 2010). As with other vulnerable witnesses, this population may become less reliable when subjected to aggressive and coercive investigative and cross-examination techniques (Milne & Bull, 2006). Social workers who work with learning disabled or cognitively impaired clients can assist the client's advocate in giving the judge information about the effect of aggressive and coercive questioning on the reliability of testimony for this population so the judge may feel more confident to intervene (Kebbell et al., 2001). Like other vulnerable witnesses clients with a learning disability will need more time to think about and answer questions, remember what they are being asked about, and how to communicate the answer to the question.

Victims and Witnesses of Violence

Part of a social worker's or attorney's role as advocate is to both know and be able to identify the most common types of bias that research has found to be associated with victims of interpersonal violence. Part of this role is to eliminate as many of these biases as possible by preparing testimony that will effectively address and challenge the bias of the judge or jury. Victims—ironically, similar to defendants or respondents—will also have to endure public scrutiny and challenges to their credibility and have intimate and painful details of their experience presented in court (Miller, 2008).

Jurors and decision-makers will look to see if the victim is a responsible person and whether or not they hold any responsibility for the crime occurring. One way to address this is to develop questions that elaborate the victim's role as a mother, worker, sister, grandmother—in other words, as a responsible member of society. Second, it can be persuasive to keep the focus on the defendant's actions, not the victim's. In Chapter 7, we learned that victims of crime can have both long- and short-term physical, cognitive, emotional, and behavioral responses to being a victim of a crime (Miller, 2008). These symptoms can impact how well a client can remember and communicate a narrative and the level of emotion they are able to express. Symptoms such as "numbing" or disassociation commonly associated with trauma can reduce the victim's credibility in court as most individuals expect victims to cry or show some emotion.

Advocacy by a social worker, either as an expert witness to explain the client's presentation clinically or with the prosecutor to protect the victim, is often necessary. Orth (2002) suggests that the criminal court proceeding itself can result in secondary victimization in crime victims. Working closely with any treating clinicians and engaging them in assisting the victim to psychologically prepare for court will be important. Many of the cognitive behavioral techniques that are part of evidence-informed trauma treatment can be used to prepare the client for the court experience (Miller, 2008).

PREPARING FOR COURT AS A PROFESSIONAL SOCIAL WORKER

If you have been asked to testify and/or prepare a court report it is very important that you review any relevant records or progress notes and develop a timeline to refresh your memory about important details and dates. This is especially important for fact witnesses because often you will have to testify to important dates and events. Even if you think you know the information, the stress and anxiety of testifying may cause you to forget. Preparation, no matter how focused or limited your testimony may be, is essential.

Timelines and Data Collection

One of the most effective ways to prepare your testimony, whether you are a fact or expert witness but especially for a fact witness, is to develop a timeline of all the important events and facts relevant to your case. The first step is to understand exactly what you are covering in your testimony. Are you being asked to identify the observable facts that indicate "imminent risk of harm" during a civil removal hearing? Are you being asked to testify that the child protective agency did provide reasonable efforts to avoid placement of Ms. Jones's baby? As you know, each of those issues involves a statute and whether the standard indicated in the statute was met (imminent risk) or was complied with (reasonable efforts). This allows you to be clear and clearly identify the events, when they occurred, and how they relate to the legal issue that you are testifying about.

Another example might be if you were testifying as a fact witness at Ms. Jones's bail hearing. You would be providing facts about dates and events that would indicate Ms. Jones does have stable housing or employment because you understand the relationship of those facts to pretrial risk and the decision to release or detain and what that decision is based on. You would not present irrelevant observations you may have made such as Ms. Jones is irritable or underweight because these facts have nothing to do with risk of her not appearing for her trial.

While developing a timeline, you can also indicate next to the event and date which statute, standard, or requirement the event refers to as a way of being prepared and being able to cite and reference the standard while you are testifying. This will make you come across as exceptionally competent and convey your understanding of the legal issues, thus increasing your credibility. Making a timeline will also allow you to see where there may be gaps in your knowledge and where you may need to investigate further. This is very important if you have been hired as a consultant for the purpose of helping an attorney prepare a case for trial.

Timelines can be developed as a result of interviews you have conducted, review of evaluations, reports from other professionals, and review of case records relevant to the case. Developing a timeline may also show you the impact of certain events on the case you may be presenting. If we were to make a timeline for Ms. Jones's civil neglect case we may want to begin the timeline prior to the onset of her pregnancy. We would want to include any dates she received prenatal care, when she started substance abuse treatment, and when she began to work with the social worker on housing and public assistance. We would want to include the date she was arrested, the date of her arraignment and bail hearing, the date she was denied benefits, the date she gave birth, the date of the report about abuse and neglect, when the investigation occurred, and so on, and any other significant events or stressors that could impact her substance use or factors that could impact the development of her infant in utero.

Developing a timeline is the first step in developing a client narrative and is in many ways similar to taking a social work history. The way to adapt this skill to legal settings is to include specific dates and times and always keep in mind the relevance of events to the legal issue the client is facing. Timelines allow us to tell a client story in a more holistic way and often show connections and explanations for events that at first do not seem related to each other. Using our case example again, a timeline could show that Ms. Jones was in treatment for substance use until that treatment was disrupted by the loss of benefits or during her incarceration after arrest. A timeline could show that Ms. Jones applied for services but there was a waiting list of 6 months. The timing of the arrest and temporary incarceration could have occurred the week before giving birth, creating a stressful event that could have given rise to a relapse. It has often been our experience that developing a detailed and rich timeline from interviews with your clients, court documents, case records, reports and evaluations, and interviews with collateral sources frequently tell a story that is often very different than that contained in a complaint or a petition.

You should be mindful that any documents that you bring to a trial as a witness may be subject to examination and review by any of the attorneys in the case.

As with most topics we are presenting, identifying your role and whom you are working for is critical to understanding the guidelines and limits to confidentiality when you are called to testify as a fact witness. To illustrate, if you are a child protection caseworker, the attorney for the child or the attorney for the parent may request to review any case notes or progress reports that you have prepared while working with the family. In many cases, the attorney for the child and the attorney for the parent may have already received these documents through the discovery process before trial. Therefore, you should expect that the other attorneys would have thoroughly reviewed those records in anticipation of the trial and your testimony.

Meeting With the Attorney

When the attorney reviews the case notes and records, they will be looking for discrepancies or inconsistencies in your file. Therefore, it is good practice to bring the case record, notes, and your timeline to the meeting with the attorney who is calling you as a witness so that you and the attorney can brainstorm how to handle any inconsistencies or discrepancies in advance of the trial. For attorneys, this is a regular aspect of preparing a witness to testify and should not be interpreted by the social worker as a comment on their practice. In fact, it can be very empowering if the social worker proactively reviews their case file prior to the meeting and identifies and raises inconsistencies themselves. Even though you are not testifying as an expert, it can enhance your professionalism if you bring a copy of your resume to your meeting with the attorney.

Preparation for the Expert Witness

During the early years of your social work career, you will usually be in the role of fact witness. Later, as you gain experience, continue your education, obtain a clinical license, and develop areas of expertise you may be asked to testify as an expert witness. As an expert witness you may engage in activities such as assessment and evaluation, report writing, and interviewing that you are already skilled in as a social worker. However, additional preparation for an expert witness must include knowledge of the most current research and expert practice guidelines for the question you are being asked to provide testimony about, as well as details regarding the level of professional experience you have assessing the matter at hand. An expert witness can critically evaluate existing research and practice, identify competing and alternative hypotheses, and be transparent about any bias that may influence their judgment or perception about a case.

As a result, you should expect that the other attorneys in the case will request your notes and records, which could include any evaluations, copies of raw data from structured assessment tools, scales or psychological tests, in addition to summaries of results. Finally, in order to be qualified as an expert, the attorney who is calling you to testify will have to provide a copy of your curriculum vitae to the other parties as well as the court. Those documents are always accessible to the other party so that they can prepare their cross-examination in advance.

It is important to know and research reasons why social work expert testimony has been disqualified in previous cases. Some general themes have been lack of reliability of methodology and conclusions, the theory or technique was not subjected to peer review and publication, the technique or theory was not generally accepted in the mental health community, and the expert witness went beyond the scope of their knowledge.

Again, we stress that if you have followed the suggestions presented in Chapter 5 regarding how to identify and address bias and present evidence-informed information within legal contexts, you will be better prepared to face challenges to your testimony. Knowing what the statutes and case law allow you as a social work expert to testify about in your specific state is important research to do prior to making the transition to social work expert.

WRITING EVALUATIONS AND REPORTS

The most important first step when you are in a position where you must prepare a report for the court is to be absolutely clear why the case has been referred to you and what question or questions you have been asked to provide information about. Saltzman and Furman (1999) characterize social work court reports as informal or formal.

Informal reports are those that a social worker might develop as a way to assist them to prepare for testimony or to give an update to the court on how a case is progressing. Often, informal reports are not taken seriously by social workers and so they may not adequately prepare or be thoughtful about what to say, why they are saying it, the impact it will have on the eventual legal outcome, the impact it may have on any immediate court action, what the client knows or does not know about what is being reported, the impact of the report on the client's life, how the client and others may hear and perceive the report, and the effect of the report on the worker's relationship with the client. Even though your report is informal it is still being given in the context of a legal proceeding, is related to a legal issue requirement, and thus should receive thoughtful preparation.

A more formal report is a report that is based on statutes and must contain certain information that will indicate the statute has been complied with or the content is determined by law (Saltzman & Furman, 1999). Some courts will provide a form or have a specified format for these types of report to both remind the evaluator of statutory requirements and provide documentation that they were met. An example of a formal report is the evaluation you will prepare as an expert witness. General guidelines for writing reports should be similar to guidelines for producing any piece of professional research writing: It should be factual, objective, supported by data, and supported by the literature; incorporates different methods of collecting data for triangulation; addresses competing hypotheses; and proofread and professionally presented as a way of maximizing the credibility of the writer. A meaningful report should be easy to read and user friendly so use simple language and avoid the use of professional jargon (Oberlander-Condie, 2003).

An evaluation report is both a clinical and a forensic document, the primary purpose of which is to describe and interpret relevant data that speak to an issue or question the court needs more specialized information about in order to answer (Oberlander-Condie, 2003). The process of creating a report requires good writing and analytic skills. Above all, the social worker should attempt to make the report meaningful to the decision-maker by presenting relevant and useful information and not suggesting for the judge what the decision should be. Always remember that your role is not to tell the judge what to do, but rather to give the judge information that is necessary to answer the legal question at hand.

In Chapter 6, you learned how to conduct an investigation for a civil removal hearing that was related to legal questions including what rises to the level of "imminent risk of harm" or a statutorily required standard. In Chapter 7, you learned how to identify and collect data and what to include in pretrial risk assessments for adults and juveniles. As you saw in the previous chapters, the question being decided, or the referral question, gives you the framework with which to proceed with data collection, interpretation, analysis, and report writing when you are being used as an expert or asked to do an investigation for the court. For example, if you are being asked to evaluate a parent in a child abuse and neglect case, simply making a diagnosis that the parent has PTSD will not in and of itself be of assistance. In that kind of proceeding there would need to be a connection of the diagnosis to how the condition and current functioning create limitations on parenting capacity, the parent's ability to be protective and carry out the essential functions of parenting, and whether or not the condition if untreated may contribute to an increased risk of child abuse or neglect. A fair report would also address how the symptoms and functioning could be improved. A quality evaluation report provides useful data to facilitate decisions of legal strategy that must be made by attorneys and judicial decisions made by the court (Grisso, 1986).

A competent report integrates and interprets the data in light of the original referral question. Many times social workers will be asked or directed by attorneys or the court to conduct "an assessment of the client" or "do a mental health evaluation." Social work assessment can be incredibly comprehensive as our profession draws on many theories of human behavior and has a comprehensive view of persons and environment. There are many models of social work assessment and hundreds of assessment instruments and scales. Social workers should always request from the referral source a more specific description of the referral question, the purpose of the referral, and the legal issue for which the evaluation report is being used. This will result in your report being targeted and useful to the decision-makers. Ethically it makes it easier for you to make choices about what information should or should not be contained in the report and therefore comply with the ethical codes concerning confidentiality and disclosure.

It is critical that you craft an outline, based on the referral question at the beginning of your report writing. Ideally, as noted in Chapters 6 and 7, this should be done prior to assessment. Some basics that should be covered in a good report include: the circumstances of the referral and referral question, how informed consent was obtained, a detailed listing of the sources of data used to formulate the report, results of data collection, analysis and interpretation, summary, and conclusion. Examples of how to list data relied on is to include the names, dates, time, and duration of each interview conducted; names, dates and duration of any observations; the names of assessment instruments used and date administered; and what documents or records you reviewed with dates of review (Oberlander-Condie, 2003).

The next section is your analysis and includes organizing your findings, identifying the data you relied on which is both supporting and contradicting, articulating the process you went through to ensure the reliability of the data you are using, identifying alternative hypotheses, how you investigated them and came to conclusions, and finally a summary and recommendations if requested by the court (Oberlander-Condie, 2003).

The other topic to address is to identify anything that could have influenced the process of data collection (Oberlander-Condie, 2003). For example, you may have observed a visit between a parent and young child that could only be scheduled during the child's regular nap time and the child was irritable or having tantrums. The influence of the timing of the visit must be mentioned in relation to any interpretation of the behavior so as to place that observation in its appropriate context.

As mentioned earlier in this chapter, when interviewing children the question of suggestibility will often arise. Knowing the literature that identifies interviewing conditions that increase child suggestibility and documenting your methods of avoiding them during your interview are critical to avoiding claims of suggestibility in response to your report. In cases where you do not video- or audiotape interviews with children, you should keep verbatim documentation of each question you asked the child and verbatim documentation of their response to each question.

Current research and theory about the question asked is the basis for data interpretation and analysis. For example, in Chapter 7, the question you were being asked to provide information about was, "Is this client at risk for not appearing for trial?" As we learned there are currently evidence-informed standards being used in the assessment of risk for juveniles and adults. Knowing the standard then gives you a framework to discuss your findings in a targeted way. To the extent possible you should use direct quotes and direct references to the data you relied on. So, if you were writing a risk assessment of Michelle Jones, you would support your conclusion of low risk by citing the scores that Ms. Jones received when you administered the risk-assessment instrument. You would also add direct quotes relating to any drug testing and the dates and times from meetings with her substance abuse counselor that you pulled after reading the case file from the substance abuse program to explain how the higher risk score Ms. Jones received on substance abuse is mitigated.

You should also know that attorneys frequently reference and use published critiques of psychological and psychiatric methodology as well as critiques of evaluation instruments to prepare for cross-examination. For example, in preparation for any testimony at the bail hearing for Ms. Jones, you would make sure that you had read about the validation process for any instrument you used and limitations associated with the instrument. An example would be in regard to the development of juvenile risk-assessment instruments and knowing what design approach was used to develop the instrument. Detention risk-assessment instruments can be developed using statistical prediction methodology or using a stakeholder consensus approach (Steinhardt, 2006). You should be prepared to discuss the pros and cons of each method to prepare for challenges during cross-examination.

As we suggested in Chapter 5, writing brief summaries of the literature on issues or conditions you frequently encounter in your work, identifying and collecting expert practice guidelines, identifying and collecting meta-analyses and published reviews of research on relevant topics, as well as bookmarking websites that track current reports, and keeping these documents on file and updating periodically will save the time of doing this as you are writing each individual report. If you are called to testify on best practices rather than to evaluate a specific person or family, knowing the evaluation literature, for example, on outcomes of parenting skills–training will be important for you to review and update prior to testimony.

EVALUATING REPORTS, RECORDS, AND EVALUATIONS

Even if you are not at the point of being an expert, you can still assist the attorney by providing them with meta-analyses and expert and best practice guidelines that can be used to evaluate the quality of reports and evaluations that are part of a trial. Many professional associations such as the American Psychological Association (www.apa.org) and the Academy of Child and Adolescent Psychiatry (www.aacap.org) publish both expert practice and ethical guidelines that are easily accessible and informative. Similar to the ABA Standards for Attorneys, NASW publishes standards of social work practice. Just as we have been suggesting that a good advocate should access the standards of practice for attorneys that work with their clients, social workers consulting with attorneys should also assist attorneys in accessing standards of social work practice to evaluate the performance of the social workers working with their client. In Ms. Jones's case, a social work advocate would want to access the NASW Standards of Social Work Practice for Clients with Substance Use Disorders, Standards of Social Work Practice in Child Welfare, and Standards of Social Work Practice in Health Care Settings. Those standards can be used as the foundation for evaluating the actions and recommendations of the child welfare agency social worker. Good advocates for clients always monitor, evaluate, and critique their own profession's performance as well as the other professions working with their client.

The first challenge in reading and evaluating case records is that there is frequently an enormous amount of information in the records for a client's case. Therefore, it is important that you have a clear framework through which to interpret what you are seeing and what information you may be seeking in the records. Again, having clarity about the "theory" or the arguments the attorney is making on behalf of the client and what facts need to be "proved" or "disproved" will make your review more targeted and productive. Knowing the "theory" of the other attorneys will also help you identify information from the records that other advocates may use to argue their case.

We suggest that you and the attorney identify key legal issues and themes and develop a content analysis protocol or form that identifies key legal issues and where facts about them can be found in the record or report. Identifying the dates allows you to easily incorporate these facts into your timeline. To use our example of a CPS social worker preparing for a civil removal hearing, the CPS worker understands that part of their testimony will be to show that their agency complied with the statute and made "reasonable efforts to avoid placement."

The worker in reviewing the case record can pull dates and events that demonstrate the standard was met. For example, a summary of a child safety conference where alternative arrangements were discussed or the worker's efforts to get Ms. Jones enrolled in substance abuse treatment can all be evidence that the agency was in compliance. The social worker working with Ms. Jones would review the record with an eye toward demonstrating the agency did not meet the standard and might look at how often Ms. Jones was contacted prior to the hearing. Another standard relevant to the removal hearing is whether Ms. Jones's child was and is in "imminent risk of harm." The social worker working with the law guardian for Matthew would review the record to see how this assessment was made, what facts the CPS worker relied on, and whether or not any risk-assessment instrument was used, and if so, was used properly.

The second challenge related to reading records and case files is that although you want to be looking for legally relevant data and facts, you do not want to be so focused that you overlook important information that you, the client, and the attorney had not previously identified or knew existed. Many times an overlooked yet very important fact or event is buried in a record or old report in a case file. It is also important that you do not look only for confirmatory facts to support your legal theory or your hypothesis about what happened with your client. This will leave you very unprepared to address challenges from other advocates, who will be looking for information to disprove your theory.

It is important for all social workers to properly document their work, but particularly so if there is any potential for interaction with the legal system. In court, if the event is not documented in the record it did not occur, even if it did and you just did not have time to enter it. Being a rights-based and legally informed practitioner will assist you in knowing what information is essential for case file documentation, protect you in the event your case file is subpoenaed, support your live testimony on the stand, and enhance your credibility.

ETHICAL ISSUES

It should go without saying that ethical social work practice means not only that your client should be aware that you are testifying but also know very clearly what you will be testifying about and what other attorneys may be seeing in the client's case record or in the report you have prepared. It has been our experience that there are occasions when the first time a client learns about a recommendation that is being made by a professional about them is in open court. This betrayal creates tremendous disruption not only to the working alliance of the professional and the client but also may impact the client's willingness to engage or participate in services that may be essential to a successful resolution of their legal and social services issues.

There are several important ethical considerations that are implicated when you have been subpoenaed to give testimony and/or retained as an expert

(Reamer, 2018). As we have repeatedly stressed, these depend on what role you are playing and who has hired you. You should always consult the NASW Code of Ethics. The National Organization of Forensic Social Work (2020) has a Code of Ethics and can be accessed online.

The first ethical issue is the issue of competence. Both the NASW Code (1.04) and the NOFSW Code (2020, Canon 1) address the issue of competence. When being retained as an expert or a consultant you should always decline to accept a referral to conduct an evaluation or provide information to the court about an area of practice that is beyond your expertise. You should possess the qualifications, education, training, and experience to perform the duties of forensic social work competently (NOFSW Code of Ethics, 2020, Canon 1).

The second ethical issue is that of dual relationships and conflicts of interest. When a client's social worker or therapist is asked to participate in a client's legal relationship, they are being asked to have a dual relationship with their client because the objectives of legal proceedings are very different than clinical work and are potentially opposed. Sometimes as a treating clinician you may be asked to testify and give your expert opinion by the attorney for your client. Most ethical codes advise against participating in dual relationships unless they cannot be avoided such as you receiving a subpoena. The NASW Code of Ethics (2021) states "social workers should not engage in dual or multiple relationships with clients in which there is a risk of exploitation or potential harm to the client" (1.06c). The Code defines dual relationships as "… hen social workers relate to clients in more than one relationship, whether professional, social, or business. Dual or multiple relationships can occur simultaneously or consecutively." If there is some reason or condition that means you cannot be completely impartial, even if the person is not your client, you should also decline the referral. This is considered to be a conflict of interest because it may interfere in the exercise of your professional discretion and is addressed in Section 1.6 of the NASW Code (2021) and Canon 22 in the NOFSW Code (2020).

Informed consent and confidentiality are important in legal situations not only ethically but to also protect the social worker from liability. Social workers in legal settings have an additional duty to "ascertain the limits of confidentiality and if and/or how attorney-client privilege may be affected" (NOFSW, 2020).

An informed consent for an evaluation should include any situation where the evaluator is required by state law to breach confidentiality without a client's written consent such as mandated reporting of child and elder abuse and neglect and the "duty to warn" requirements. When doing an evaluation for a client's attorney or the court, the client must be advised in writing that they will see and have access to the report and advised of the risks if you are compelled to provide testimony about confidential information you learn about in the course of the evaluation. Clients, of course, always have the right to refuse to participate and must be advised of the pros and cons of this decision. In some states, what you must tell the client about informed consent is contained in state statutes and regulations.

Telling the client who you are, what your credentials are, why the evaluation was ordered or requested, how the evaluations relate to their legal case, and ensuring that a client understands all of this is essential to performing ethically. No matter who is requesting information from you, it is ethically and legally defensible to release records or confidential information only with written consent from the client or under a court order (Bernstein & Hartsell, 2005).

In the next two chapters, we will be narrowing our focus to what occurs next during the path of civil government and actor-initiated proceedings and criminal proceedings. There will be many opportunities to see how the skills you learned in this chapter will be specifically applied in each of the forums of legal practice.

REFERENCES

American Bar Association, Coalition for Justice. (2010). *Report on the survey of judges on the impact of the economic downturn on representation in the courts.* https://legalaidresearch.org/wp-content/uploads/2020/02/aba-coalition-justice-survey-judges-2010.pdf

Ashford, J. B. (2009). Forensic social work. In A. R. Roberts & J. Watkins (Eds.), *Social workers' desk reference* (p. 910). Oxford University Press.

Batson v. Kentucky, 476 U.S. 79 (1986).

Bernstein, B. E., & Hartsell, T. L. (2005). *The portable guide to testifying in court.* Wiley.

Brady v. Maryland, 373 U.S. 83 (1963).

Bull, R. (2010). The investigative interviewing of children and other vulnerable witnesses: Psychological research and working/professional practice. *Legal and Criminological Psychology, 15*, 5–23. https://doi.org/10.1348/014466509X440160

Cashmore, J., & Bussey, K. (1996). Judicial views of child witness competence. Special Issue on Children's Capacities in Legal Contexts. *Law and Human Behavior, 20*, 313–334.

Daubert v. Merrell Dow Pharmaceuticals, 509 U.S. 579 (1993).

Dickinson, J. J., Poole, D. A., & Laimon, R. L. (2005). Children's recall and testimony. In N. Brewer & K. Williams (Eds.), *Psychology & law: An empirical perspective* (pp. 151–176). Guilford.

Ellett, A. J., & Steib, S. D. (2005). Child welfare and the courts: A statewide study with implications for professional development, practice and change. *Research on Social Work Practice, 15*(5), 339–352. https://doi.org/10.1177/104973150527668

Fisher, R. P., Brennan, K. H., & McCauley, M. R. (2002). The cognitive interview method to enhance eyewitness recall. In M. Eisen, G. Goodman, & J. Quas (Eds.), *Memory and suggestibility in the forensic interview* (pp. 265–286). Erlbaum.

Gaydon, L. B., & Miller, M. K. (2007). Elders in the justice system: How the system treats elders in trials, during imprisonment, and on death row. *Behavioral Sciences and the Law, 25*, 677–699. https://doi.org/10.1002/bsl.781

Grisso, T. (1986). *Evaluating competencies: Forensic assessments and instruments.* Plenum.

J.E.B. v. Alabama, 511 U.S. 127 (1994).

Jaffee v. Redmond (1996).

James, D., & Glaze, L. (2006). *Mental health problems of prison and jail inmates.* https://bjs.ojp.gov/content/pub/pdf/mhppji.pdf

Kebbell, M. R., Hatton, C., Johnson, S. D., & O'Kelly, C. M. E. (2001). People with learning disabilities as witnesses in court: What questions should lawyers ask? *British Journal of Learning Disabilities, 29*, 98–102. https://doi.org/10.1046/j.1354-4187.2001.00138.x

Lamb, M. E., Hershkowitz, I., Orbach, Y., & Esplin, P. W. (2008). *Tell me what happened: Structured investigative interviews of child victims and witnesses.* Wiley.

Lassiter v. Department of Social Services. 452 U.S. 18 (1981).

Mauet, T. (1996). *Trial techniques* (4th ed.). Boston: Little, Brown and Company.

Miller, L. (2008). *Counseling crime victims—practical strategies for mental health professionals.* Springer Publishing Company.

Milne, R., & Bull, R. (2006). Interviewing victims, including children and people with intellectual disabilities. In M. Kebbell & G. Davies (Eds.), *Practical psychology for forensic investigations* (pp. 7–23). Wiley.

Mueller-Johnson, K., & Ceci, S. J. (2004). Memory and suggestibility in older adults: Live event participation and repeated interview. *Applied Cognitive Psychology, 18*(8), 1109–1127. https://doi.org/10.1002/acp.1078

National Organization of Forensic Social Work. (2020). *Specialty guidelines for values and ethics.* https://www.nofsw.org/_files/ugd/f468b9_20e60b0830ed4a51808154902b7e9f20.pdf

National Association of Social Workers. (2021). *Code of ethics of the National Association of Social Workers.* Author.

Oberlander-Condie, L. (2003). *Parenting evaluations for the court: Care and protection matters.* Kluwer.

Orth, U. (2002). Secondary victimization of crime victims by criminal proceedings. *Social Justice Research, 15*(4), 313–325. https://doi.org/10.1023/A:1021210323461

People v. R.R., 807 N.Y.S.2d 516 (Sup. Ct. 2005).

Perry, S. P., York, C. S., Block, S. D., Johnson, H. M., & Bottoms, B. L. (2013). Children: As witnesses. In A. Jamieson & A. Moenssens (Eds.), *Wiley encyclopedia of forensic sciences* (2nd ed.). Wiley. https://doi.org/10.1002/9780470061589.fsa235.pub2

Reamer, F. (2018). Social workers as expert witnesses: Ethical considerations. *Journal of the American Academy of Matrimonial Lawyers, 30*, 437–453. https://aaml.org/wp-content/uploads/MAT204_9.pdf

Saltzman, A., & Furman, D. (1999). *Law in social work practice.* Nelson-Hall.

Sarnoff, S. (2004). Social workers and the witness role in ethical and legal perspective. *Journal of Social Work Ethics and Values, 1*(1), 30–44. http://www.socialworker.com/jswve/content/view/10//

Schroeder, J., Chaisson, R., & Pogue, R. (2005). Restorying the defendant's life: Using narrative to revise juror viewpoint in capital cases. *Journal of Ethnic & Cultural Diversity in Social Work, 14*(1/2), 1–26. https://doi.org/10.1300/J051v14n01_01

Siegel, D. M. (2008). The growing admissibility of expert testimony by clinical social workers on competence to stand trial. *Social Work, 53*(2), 153–163. https://doi.org/10.1093/sw/53.2.153

Slater, L. K. (2007). "Practicing in slow motion": The development and assessment of an interprofessional clinical education curriculum for law and social work students. Doctoral dissertation. Available from ProQuest Dissertations & Theses database. (UMI No. 3283610.).

Stein, T. J. (2004). *The role of law in social work practice and administration.* Columbia University Press.

Steinhardt, D. (2006). *A practice guide to juvenile detention reform: Juvenile detention risk assessment.* Annie E. Casey Foundation. www.aecf.org/upload/PublicationFiles/JJ3622H5038.pdf

CHAPTER 9

The Intersection of Law and Social Work in Civil Proceedings

INTRODUCTION

In this chapter we look at the next steps in a civil proceeding initiated by the government or individual private actors. You will learn about a range of civil proceedings where the objective of the proceeding is the protection of a vulnerable child or adult because those are most often the cases involving social workers in the explicit and implicit legal context. We also focus on issues that can affect individuals and families and that may require legal resolution such as divorce, custody, visitation, paternity, child support, guardianship of children, adoption, landlord/tenant disputes, public housing eviction, and civil rights and discrimination. You are introduced to the legal standards used in decision-making and the range of potential outcomes and remedies that may follow a trial. By knowing how to access and identify the legal standards used by the court in coming to a decision, you will learn how to use social work knowledge strategically to facilitate decision-making and support the litigation of a civil case that seeks to protect others while being mindful of their rights and protections. You will also be better able to assist and refer for targeted legal consultation those clients who are representing themselves in civil proceedings or do not have an attorney.

As we have noted throughout the text, we are not advocating that you understand the legal standard in order for you to act like a lawyer or advise your clients legally. It is critical that social workers in both the implicit and explicit context of the law remember the boundaries of their profession and practice. We are advocating that you know about the legal standards so you can have productive and focused conversations with attorneys and how to target your assessment and data collection as a way of giving the court more useful and relevant information in your capacity as a social worker. We are advocating that your knowledge of legal procedure and practice allows you to develop your social work practice more strategically and holistically to assist clients in reaching their goals through legal and nonlegal means.

GOVERNMENT- AND INDIVIDUAL-INITIATED CIVIL CASES: COMMON RIGHTS AND PROCEDURES

There are a variety of different civil cases that can be initiated by the government or individuals about which social workers in the implicit or explicit legal context should be knowledgeable. While the substantive law of each case differs depending on the type of case, there are many similarities in how cases are handled in civil proceedings. As is always the case, it is important to consult your local court rules and state laws and regulations when working with a client who has a civil case. The local rules and statutes will help you understand the procedure to be followed, the standards and burden of proof that must be met for proving a civil case, and any specific rights that your client has during the proceeding.

At the beginning of most state statutes, there is generally a section on definitions. This section can be very helpful for social workers to review because it lays out exactly what the law means when it says, for example, "vulnerable adult" or "abused child," or "capacity to consent." Many times social workers may use the same term but have a very different definition or meaning than that which is codified in the law. It is our experience that this lack of a common definition or conceptual framework is often the root of conflict between lawyers and social workers. We need to check the meaning of the "language" we are using with each other and to ensure that critically competent social workers know that when they are "visiting" in legal forums, part of being competent is to learn the "language." Learning the language allows social workers to communicate more effectively and have their recommendations heard. It is also key to learn the language so that you are working realistically with your client in accordance with the current law and processes and advocating to achieve the best outcome for your client.

Similar to each of these proceedings having its own body of substantive law, each of these proceedings has its own body of practice knowledge and social science literature. It is important for social workers to be familiar with the literature relevant to the legal issue being decided by using the process and procedure you learned in Chapter 5 regarding targeting your research by understanding what decisions are being made in court. Social workers should also be able to easily "translate" their professional language for legal decision-makers so it can be understood and used to craft more holistic and fully informed outcomes and plans.

It is also important to remember that there is case law at the state and federal levels that relate to many of the issues that will be addressed in this chapter. State court websites frequently have links by topic to recent and relevant cases in your state. You can also ask the lawyer who you are working with or consulting for to let you know about any important cases that pertain to the interpretation of the legal standard or the burden of proof the state or other party must meet in the particular civil proceeding in which you or your client is involved. Particularly important would be those cases that speak to the testimony of social workers or mental health professionals. Depending on the social worker's profession, it may also be pertinent to review precedents from case law and expert witness testimony from various professionals on the issue. This research can help identify arguments and defenses in cases similar to your client's case.

As mentioned, an excellent beginning resource for obtaining information about civil proceedings is the National Center for State Courts (www.ncsc.org). This website contains links to all the state court websites and has a chart for each state identifying the names of all the courts in each state and what kinds of matters they hear. Once you are on your state court system site, most have links to court rules and state regulations for each of the courts listed. For those social workers who interact with Tribal Justice systems, an excellent resource is the

Tribal Law and Policy Institute (www.tribal-institute.org). This site includes a link to tribal courts and individual tribe regulations and procedures.

Court rules will cover a wide range of topics including whether a proceeding is open to the public, whether there may be a jury trial, what must be contained in petitions and notices, the procedure to file a motion, how testimony may be presented, whether there are requirements to attend mediation or other dispute resolution processes before trial, and even the conduct that is expected in court. State and tribal court websites often have forms and instructions posted on their websites, such as petitions, motions, and sample notices.

There are basic rights that clients have in all civil proceedings, regardless of whether the matter involves housing, civil rights, custody, or other civil law areas, or whether the specific court is called Family or Superior Court. These rights revolve in large part around the procedures that must be followed in civil cases, so that all litigants are provided with a fair and just proceeding. One of the most important procedural rights in a civil case is that the party that is being sued must be provided with formal notice of the proceeding. *Notice* is generally achieved through a summons issued by the judge for a party to appear in court, and can also be achieved through personal service when an individual has to hand deliver the summons or legal filing in person to the respondent or through publication of the proceedings in local newspapers. Additionally, every party who is being sued has the right to know what the allegations or claims are against them and to answer those claims formally to the court. This means that parties have the right to receive and review copies of any of the legal papers filed in court detailing the allegations against them and the request for relief or court orders.

The initial allegations and claims are contained, as you know from Chapter 6, in the *petition* and the response filed by the opposing side is referred to as the *answer*. It is at this juncture that you would apply the knowledge and skills you learned about preparing yourself and the client for court. You would review the information in the petition and think about how that would shape your assessment, intervention, and advocacy role. In most of the civil proceedings we discuss, there are regulations or court rules that require certain information be included in the notice and in the petition. For example, some states may require that a petition for guardianship for an incapacitated adult identify what alternatives to guardianship have been explored prior to filing the petition and an explanation of the functional level of the person for whom guardianship is being sought.

While the specifics of what evidence can be obtained may vary in each substantive area, civil cases generally allow for expansive discovery. As you know, *discovery* is the process by which both parties gain information about the case through record gathering, depositions, and other forms of investigation. This discovery process could include deposing or taking testimony in advance of trial, a social worker, or subpoenaing the clinical records of a social worker in a treatment facility. Here you would use the skills you learned in Chapter 8 in order to evaluate the validity of reports by other professionals, help the attorney decide who should testify or not (including the client), prepare questions for the attorney, or prepare yourself or your client to testify.

While there may be settlement offers, the parties have the right to proceed to trial either in front of a jury or a judge depending on the substantive area. In some areas, the parties can select whether they wish for their case to be decided by a jury of their peers or by the judge. At trial, the parties have the right to present both testimonial and documentary evidence to prove their case, and the opposing side has the right to cross-examine any adverse witnesses.

Finally, the parties have the right to be represented by an attorney or to represent themselves. However, there is no uniform right to counsel in civil cases as there is in criminal proceedings. Therefore, a client may have the right to have an attorney in a civil matter, but will not be provided with an attorney by the government if unable to afford an attorney on their own. Throughout the rest of this chapter, we will reference whether states provide a guaranteed right to counsel in the specific civil proceeding, such as dependency cases where there is an allegation of abuse or neglect.

There are also common and corresponding skills for social workers during these proceedings, such as preparing to testify, preparing a client for court proceedings, writing and presenting reports, and responding to subpoenas. We recommend that you review the general knowledge and skills just presented in Chapter 8 and identify, as you read this chapter, how the knowledge and skills might be utilized and implemented in each of the following kinds of civil proceedings.

CHILD AND VULNERABLE ADULT PROTECTION PROCEEDINGS

The use of legal evidence-informed practice in these types of proceedings is crucial because, although protective in nature and motivation, they often also involve wide professional discretion, the possibility of significant restrictions of rights and the ability to make decisions, and the potential to substantially limit the self-determination of your client. An important task for the social worker to acknowledge as part of understanding civil proceedings that are protective in nature, is the acceptance of the fact that in most of the following proceedings there may be competing interests and tensions among the parties that a social worker is frequently called upon to balance.

In many protective proceedings, social workers may be working with an entire family, one of whom may have committed an act of abuse against a child or an adult. In a guardianship or commitment hearing, a social worker may again be working with an entire family each of whom may hold very different positions on how the matter should be resolved. Identifying that the law often requires a balancing between the rights of the individuals, families, and the duties of the state is an important aspect of case analysis and formulation for a social worker interfacing with protective proceedings for vulnerable adults and children. Knowing what the law says about the rights and interests of all the parties is important for social workers because they are often put in the position of having to balance the values of autonomy and protection (Donovan & Regehr, 2010). Another common and important value when it comes to child and adult protection cases is that of "least restrictive" circumstances. This means that any protective decision be one that imposes the least amount of restrictions on the rights and freedoms of the individual including freedom of movement in regard to placement or living arrangements.

Regardless of the specific type of protective proceeding, there are three general areas for research and knowledge that are implicated for social workers: (a) the identification of risk and protective factors related to the identified harm or danger, (b) engagement or lack of participation in treatment or services to mitigate harm or danger, and (c) the assessment of capacity and decision-making ability. These three themes are implicated throughout all of the following protective proceedings and provide a targeted framework for the legal and social science research a social worker may need to access when involved in protective proceedings. Because many of these proceedings have serious liberty interests at stake, social workers should be familiar with evidence-based practices that are known to be effective for the treatment of abuse and neglect, domestic violence, elder abuse, serious mental illness, and substance abuse so that there will be a reduction in harm and risk of harm, and protection of a client's liberty interest.

A social worker may be a fact witness, an expert witness, or an advocate in protective proceedings. It is important for social workers to remember that in protective proceedings the mere fact that an individual has a diagnosis, such as substance dependence or schizophrenia, is not enough to show that abuse or neglect occurred or that a person is incompetent or a danger to self or others. As seen in our case example, Ms. Jones's disclosed substance abuse is not sufficient on its own to prove that her son is a neglected child under the law. A legal evidence-based social worker, as a result of their assessment, will be able to show a causal path between the symptoms related to the diagnosis; how those symptoms or behaviors impact capacity whether it be parenting or functional capacity; how the person's incapacity creates a harm or risk of harm to self and others; be able to specify what the harm or risk is; and what treatment or services the person needs to be engaged to mitigate the danger or risk of harm. In assessing risk and harm in cases regarding mental health and substance use, it is also imperative to take a harm reduction approach and include an assessment of the impact of separation on parents. Specifically, if Ms. Jones is separated from her child, an understanding of both issues of withdrawal and relapse as a part of recovery throughout the social worker's assessment would be required. Additionally, identifying key strengths like Ms. Jones's willingness to attend treatment, the services available through treatment, and other tangible supports like supportive housing and trauma therapy should be explored.

If you do this level of assessment and analysis when you are working on these kinds of cases, you will have done much to ensure all of the parties have a fair and just decision-making process, and decisions and plans will be made that clearly identify what protective factors mitigate the risk and what can be done to increase capacity and lower risk. By doing so, you are protecting a person's rights in a knowledgeable and competent way. You will also have much less to be anxious about when it comes to cross-examination because those are central issues for illustrating gaps and flaws in assessments and recommendations. That is not to say that clients may not have other concerns that need to be addressed by a social worker, but we advise first attending to the factors we have laid out if there is a protective legal case for your client.

VULNERABLE ADULT PROTECTION

The government as well as individuals can bring cases to protect vulnerable adults, including the elderly, individuals with developmental disabilities, or those living with mental illness. Vulnerable adult cases generally fall into one of three categories: (1) protecting an adult from abuse or neglect; (2) protecting an adult who is found to be incapacitated through guardianship proceedings; and (3) protecting an adult through involuntary commitment proceedings when their mental illness presents a severe danger to themselves or others. Guardianship and involuntary commitment involve the removal of significant individual rights from a person and should be considered as a last resort after alternative options have been identified and tried. We discuss these cases in greater length in later sections of this chapter.

The critical social work and legal intersections of these particular kinds of matters involve providing information that will allow the judge to make an informed decision about whether or not the person has the ability to provide informed consent; whether the person has the capacity to make decisions about themselves and their financial, medical, or other personal matters and their treatment; information and exploration of alternative, less restrictive options to commitment or guardianship; or providing information that assists others in evaluating whether or not a person's refusal to access treatment and services for mental illness, substance abuse; or abuse is causing them to be a serious danger to themselves or others.

For a rights based social worker, the overarching social work task in this situation is to protect the client's right to self-determination to the fullest extent possible and to assume competence unless proven otherwise. At this point, it would be a good idea to review the information presented in Chapter 3 on client self-determination, conflicts, confidentiality, and informed consent as it is very relevant to these types of proceedings and social workers may be working with clients and their family members who may all have different interests and points of view.

It is important for social workers working with vulnerable adults who are the subject of protective or proceedings to review the material presented in Chapter 8 regarding interviewing and witness preparation with special populations such as elders, developmentally disabled, and victims of violence. Often, because of poorly conducted interviews, important information regarding a client's functioning and ability to understand and comprehend may be misrepresented or missed and or ignored. It is important to also identify in these types of cases if a client has a Power of Attorney (POA) that may limit or constrain their decision-making ability. You may also be asked to evaluate the reports submitted by other professionals as well as prepare and give testimony yourself. Again, we encourage those social workers working in the implicit context to be proactive in offering your client's attorney your assistance when your client wishes or when you can provide information or testimony that allows you to better safeguard the rights and interests of clients you are working with who may be lacking capacity.

Initiating Legal Proceedings in Vulnerable Adult Abuse Cases

As you learned in Chapter 6, most states have mandated reporting laws that require the reporting of elder and vulnerable adult abuse. As you remember, vulnerable adult abuse refers to a range of conduct that places the emotional, financial, or physical stability of a vulnerable individual at risk. The Adult Protective Services agency is responsible for investigating allegations of vulnerable adult abuse, whether in private homes, nursing homes, group homes, institutions, or assisted living facilities. During the investigation the social worker or caseworker determines both the level of risk and the vulnerable adult's capacity to understand the risk, as well as their ability to give an informed consent for corrective services (Donovan & Regehr, 2010). The Adult Protective Services worker would also be responsible for filing a petition to the court if one is needed. In addition, it is important to remember that cases involving vulnerable adult abuse can be brought in criminal, civil, family, or probate courts depending on the legal relief that is sought and the party initiating the proceeding. In most states, once the caseworker has completed their investigation and has indicated abuse or neglect, there are provisions for initiating both civil and criminal action. In some states, once a finding of vulnerable adult abuse occurs, adult protective staff is also mandated to report the abuse to local law enforcement agencies.

Legal Standards: Endangered Adult and Abuse

The first legal decision that needs to be made is whether this person meets the criteria for vulnerable or endangered adult and whether or not abuse and neglect has occurred, similar to a child protection matter. A definition of what constitutes vulnerable adult abuse and who are considered vulnerable or endangered adults are contained in state statutes that address adult protection. Again we encourage you to pull up your state statute to identify the criteria for who may be considered a vulnerable adult and what the definition of abuse and neglect is for vulnerable adults. Some states, such as Oregon, provide very explicit circumstances about who is considered to be vulnerable and what is considered abuse and neglect by individuals as well as by institutional providers detailing what constitutes neglect, financial exploitation, physical abuse, and verbal abuse (Or. Rev. Stat. § 124.050, 2022). Other statutes offer more room for discretion; for example, Chapter 3, Section 12-10-3-2(a) of the Ind. Code (2016) clearly defines what is required to be considered an endangered adult but provides less guidance on the definition of neglect:

> "[E]ndangered adult" means an individual who is: (1) at least eighteen (18) years of age; (2) incapable by reason of mental illness, intellectual disability, dementia, habitual drunkenness, excessive use of drugs, or other physical or mental incapacity of managing or directing the management of the individual's property or providing or directing the provision of self-care; (3) harmed or threatened with harm as a result of: (A) neglect; or (B) battery.

The court may be asked to make a number of other decisions depending on the ability or willingness of the client to consent to services or the level of emergency perceived by those involved in the case. For example, in many jurisdictions if a client consents to services and a spouse or other family member or person attempts to interfere, the court can issue an order preventing them from doing so and requiring the services to be provided. Social workers who are assisting with or are preparing the petition themselves will need to identify and collect factual and clinical data that can give the court information that can satisfy these three circumstances.

In the event that the client will not consent, or lacks the capacity to consent to services, most states allow Adult Protective Services to petition the court to require the endangered client to receive services. We will be addressing the issue of capacity in more detail under the section on guardianship. In order for the court to compel the individual to receive services, there must be a court hearing and judicial finding before an order compelling services is permitted. In Indiana, the court must find that the person: (a) is an endangered adult; (b) is in need of protective services; and (c) lacks the ability to make an informed decision concerning the endangered adult's need for protective services (Ind. Code § 12-10-3-2, 2010). Adult Protective Service workers can also request emergency orders for services such as out-of-home placement when they can demonstrate the individual is involved in a life-threatening emergency and is in need of emergency protective services.

Legal Standard "Capacity to Consent"

Some states specifically identify what they mean by lack of the ability, or incapacity to make an informed decision regarding the need for protective services. Some states also provide a definition of what having capacity to make a decision means. An example is Florida's statutory provision:

> "Capacity to consent" means that a vulnerable adult has sufficient understanding to make and communicate responsible decisions regarding the vulnerable adults person or property, including whether or not to accept protective services offered by the department. (Fla. Stat. § 415.102[3], 2010)
>
> "Lacks capacity to consent" means a mental impairment that causes a vulnerable adult to lack sufficient understanding or capacity to make or communicate responsible decisions concerning person or property including whether or not to accept protective services. (Fla. Stat. § 415.102[15], 2010)

Other states include in their definitions of capacity and incapacity the ability of the vulnerable adult to make provisions for healthcare, food, clothing, and shelter specifically. It is important for social workers to know that there are specific elements needed to satisfy a legal standard so they can collect assessment data to address each element. During a trial, testimony and evidence will be presented to show whether each element was met.

Outcomes of Adult Protective Services Cases: Service Orders and Orders of Protection

If the court finds that the conditions in the law for adult abuse have been met, the court has the authority to order protective services both on an emergency and a nonemergency basis. Many states have statutes that place time limits on how long an order may be in effect and the processes for reviewing orders. For example, in Ohio the petitioner may request a number of orders including an evaluation, emergency services order, orders requiring a party to leave the elder's home, restraining orders, and freezing of the adult's financial assets (Ohio Rev. Code § 5101:2-20-12, 2021). Many states also require that orders stipulate that the "least restrictive" measures be taken to protect the individual. An example of this requirement is that every effort to keep the individual in their home rather than place them in a nursing home must be made by the worker. In addition many states also allow the client, a family member, service provider, guardian, or other interested person to petition the court any time there is a change in the conditions that caused the order to be made.

Another possible outcome is that the court can issue temporary or longer term restraining orders against the abuser in order to ensure the least restrictive environment for the client. In California, an elderly client who has been abused can initiate legal proceedings by petitioning the Civil Court for an order of protection. The process for obtaining a restraining or protective order is presented in more detail in the following section. Vulnerable adult abuse can also be a factor in legal cases brought in probate court when there has been financial abuse, including interference with a will, estate, or conservatorship.

Some states specifically allow vulnerable adults who have been found by a court to be abused and neglected, to file as an individual for damages. For example, in Fla. Stat. § 415.1111 (2010): "A vulnerable adult who has been abused, neglected, or exploited as specified in this chapter has a cause of action against any perpetrator and may recover actual and punitive damages for such abuse, neglect, or exploitation."

FAMILY OFFENSE CASES

Victims of domestic violence can petition a Civil Court for legal remedies including orders of protection on behalf of themselves or other members of their family including children. It is important to remember that while Criminal Courts can also issue orders of protection for victims of violence, the order of protection has to be part of an ongoing legal case in Criminal Court brought by the District Attorney or prosecutor. Civil Courts are available for any victim who believes that they need protection, regardless of whether there is a current Criminal Court case about the domestic violence.

Initiating a Family Offense Proceeding

In each instance, the victim of the domestic violence files a petition in Civil Court alleging the specific abuse that occurred and requesting an order of protection, on behalf of themselves and any minor children. The petition is filed against the abuser, who is the respondent in the matter. In most states, in order to qualify for a protective order certain conditions must be met. These include the type and nature of the relationship with the abuser, the type of abuse, or age. For example, some states require that there be a familial relationship between the petitioner and the respondent, including having children in common, or being related by blood or marriage.

Legal Standards for Decision-Making

The first step is to see how the state statute defines a family offense or "abuse." We use the example of the Tennessee statute to identify the decision-making points throughout the process of obtaining an order of protection. The first step is to understand what is considered domestic abuse. In Tennessee, abuse is defined as:

> "Abuse" means: (A) Inflicting, or attempting to inflict, physical injury on an adult or minor by other than accidental means; (B) Placing an adult or minor in fear of, or in, physical harm or physical restraint; (C) Causing malicious damage to the personal property of the abused party; or (D) Intentionally engaging in behavior that amounts to financial abuse. (Tenn. Code § 36-3-601[1], 2023)

The next requirement of the statute addresses who is considered to be a "domestic abuse victim" and the type of relationship the victim must have with the abuser in order to file for an order of protection.

> "Domestic abuse victim" means any person who falls within the following categories (A) adults or minors who are current or former spouses; (B) Adults or minors who live together or who have lived together; (C) Adults or minors who are dating or who have dated or who have or had a sexual relationship. As used herein, "dating" and "dated" do not include fraternization between two (2) individuals in a business or social context; (D) Adults or minors related by blood or adoption; (E) Adults or minors who are related or were formerly related by marriage; or (F) Adult or minor children of a person in a relationship that is described in subdivisions (5)(A)-(E). (Tenn. Code § 36-3-601[5], 2023)

In Tennessee and in some other states, teenagers who are impacted by dating violence can file for an order of protection but the petition may have to be signed by one of their parents or a guardian. Tennessee allows a caseworker who is working in an agency that receives funding to do domestic violence and child abuse prevention and intervention to sign a minor's petition. In cases where the minor may have another case in Family Court, a guardian ad litem may also sign the petition (Tenn. Code § 36-3-602[b], 2023).

A victim is able to ask for a temporary or interim order of protection immediately upon filing the petition even if the respondent has not been provided with notice or served with the petition and a full hearing on the matter has not happened under certain circumstances usually called "good cause." This is generally referred to as an *ex parte* (i.e., for one side only) proceeding, because the judge makes the determination with only one of the parties present, in this instance the petitioner. Consequently, the judge cannot make a final order of protection because the respondent has not been notified of the proceedings and given the opportunity to contest the allegations. In Tennessee, a temporary ex parte order can be given when:

> Upon the filing of a petition under this part, the courts may immediately, for good cause shown, issue an ex parte order of protection. An immediate

> and present danger of abuse to the petitioner shall constitute good cause for purposes of this section. (Tenn. Code § 36-3-605[a], 2023)

In order to satisfy this standard of an immediate and present danger, a judge must be convinced that unless the abuser is stopped, the petitioner will be in immediate danger. A legally informed social worker could surmise that a client seeking to show an immediate and present danger would need to present facts such as describing any recent events or threats of violence, the frequency and severity of the violence, the degree of injury in the past and present, whether the abuser has been convicted of or plead guilty to domestic violence in the past, the use or threatened use of a weapon, the abuser's use of drugs or alcohol, and whether the abuser has threatened suicide. It is critical that social workers are familiar with the techniques presented in Chapter 8 about interviewing victims of abuse because victims sometimes describe the abuse in vague and general terms that may not meet the legal standards. Additionally, victims of abuse may have considerable difficulty providing coherent histories and timelines for the abuse because of the trauma. Cognitive interviewing can elicit details that can make client narratives very compelling and legally sufficient.

Once a judge issues an ex parte order there must be a hearing held within a certain number of days: in Tennessee, it is 15 days from the time the order is issued. Both sides have an opportunity to present evidence to prove or disprove the allegations and the burden of proof for the petitioner in this state is by a preponderance of the evidence.

Legal Decisions and Outcomes

Once there is a hearing on the petition for an order, the judge can discontinue the ex parte order if the allegations are not proven or, if they are proven, extend the order of protection for a period generally not to exceed 1 year although duration of final orders varies from state to state. During this time, either party can ask that the order be continued or discontinued; after the prescribed period for the order, another hearing will be required to continue the order for longer or it will expire. Orders of protection can also include provisions that evict the abuser and grant possession of the residence to the person who received the order or find suitable housing for the victim if the abuser is the owner or lease holder. Orders of protection can also award temporary custody and financial support to the victim. In some states, orders of protection can also mandate batterers treatment or treatment for substance abuse. Understanding what outcomes are possible and what the court is able to order as part of a family offense case will be critical in helping your client obtain their goal, understand their options, and participate fully in the proceeding. In domestic violence cases, it is also imperative for a social worker and lawyer to understand the risks associated with their client leaving their abusive partner because of the increased risks for harm and retaliation. Many other barriers can also impact a client's willingness to file a protective order, particularly when there are children involved or a lack of resources.

Violation of the Order of Protection

Violations of orders of protection can have both civil and criminal penalties, including that a person may be arrested for violating the order. The Civil Court would conduct a hearing to determine whether the order of protection was violated and, in many states, the respondent can receive a term of civil confinement. In states that permit civil confinement, the amount of time is generally limited to 3 or 6 months. To continue with our example of Tennessee, if a judge finds an order of protection was violated, they may order a contempt hearing and can issue a bond for the offender. A judge can, after the contempt hearing, levy a fine against the offender or order a bond that will remain in place until the order of protection has expired or is terminated by the court (Tenn. Code § 36-3-610, 2010).

GUARDIANSHIP CASES FOR CHILDREN AND ADULTS

Guardianship is a legal relationship under which a person, or in some cases a public agency, is appointed by a court to make decisions for, and advance the interests of, an incapacitated adult or a minor child. Guardians can be appointed in Probate Court for adults with diminished capacity, including mental retardation, developmental delays, medical conditions, or mental illness and for children. Legal guardians can be appointed to make decisions about an individual's personal, medical, and financial affairs, including estates and property, if the court finds that the individual lacks mental capacity to make those decisions. Many important rights of a person can be removed during this type of civil proceeding. Some of these may include consent to medical treatment, determining where the person may live, make contracts, marry, vote, or have a driver's license.

Family and Dependency Courts can appoint guardian ad litems (GALs) for children who are the subjects of court proceedings involving abuse and neglect, termination of parental rights, adoption, custody, and visitation matters. As you learned in a previous section addressing child protection, in some cases the courts are required to appoint a guardian ad litem. The issue here is that sometimes the only guideline for making critical decisions on behalf of a minor or adult is that of the "best interest" standard. As you will learn in the case example for child protection and the discussion of custody, guardianship, and visitation cases later in this chapter, there is wide variance in the definition of the best interest standard. Therefore, under a standard with a potentially ambiguous definition, the guardian or GAL has considerable discretion unless the statute in your state is very clear about the limitations of this power and definition of what criteria must be considered to determine best interests.

Initiating Legal Proceedings in Guardianship

In most states, a family member or other individual who has an interest in the matter can bring a guardianship petition for an adult. A public guardianship can also be established if the adult in question does not have any family members that are able to assist. In those cases, a public guardian can be appointed through the court and may include staff of a social service agency charged with caring for diminished capacity or incapacitated adults (Teaster et al., 2007). Once the petition is filed, the individual who is the subject of the petition has to be notified of the proceeding, and in some states other family members must be notified as well.

Legal Standard: "Incapacitated Adult or Person"

The primary legal decision in a guardianship case involving an adult is determining whether the individual meets the statutory definition of an "incapacitated adult" or in some states an "incompetent adult." An example of one state's definition is Pennsylvania:

> "Incapacitated person" means an adult whose ability to receive and evaluate information effectively and communicate decisions in any way is impaired to such a significant extent that he is partially or totally unable to manage his financial resources or to meet essential requirements for his physical health and safety. (20 Pa. Cons. Stat. § 5501)

There are many concepts that are important to highlight prior to undertaking an assessment of capacity. The first is that personal autonomy and client self-determination hold that, absent proof determining otherwise, all competent adults have the right to make their own decisions. The second important concept is that there should always be the presumption of capacity as the starting point of an evaluation. Many states preface statutes and legislation with a policy statement that lays out the intention of the law. The legislative intent is also useful for social workers to read as it frequently includes key values that informed the law but may not be clear in the actual text of the law. Staying with our example of Pennsylvania, the beginning of the statute's chapter lays out the intent and purpose of the law:

> Recognizing that every individual has unique needs and differing abilities, it is the purpose of this chapter to promote the general welfare of all citizens by establishing a system which permits incapacitated persons to participate as fully as possible in all decisions which affect them, which assists these persons in meeting the essential requirements for their physical health and safety, protecting their rights, managing their financial resources and developing or regaining their abilities to the maximum extent possible and which accomplishes these objectives through the use of the least restrictive alternative; and recognizing further that when guardianship services are necessary, it is important to facilitate the finding of suitable individuals or entities willing to serve as guardians. (20 Pa. Cons. Stat. § 5502)

It is very important that you consult your state's statutes because states have different standards that are used by the court to determine when someone is incapacitated, the procedures required to make that determination, and the procedures and protections granted to the person who is being evaluated by the court. Rights lost by the person may also vary from state to state (Saltzman & Furman, 1999). Some states specifically identify rights that are not lost during guardianship and these may include consent for abortion, sterilization, electroconvulsive shock therapy; consent to marry or divorce; and consent for the performance of any experimental medical or behavioral health procedures or participation in research experiments.

During a hearing or trial on the adult's capacity, the court may seek testimony from doctors, mental health professionals, social workers, and family members. Some state statutes identify what must be included in an evaluation and that usually relates to providing information that allows the court to assess if the statutory criterion has been met. In Pennsylvania, an evaluator would have to provide the following: description of the functional limitations and physical and mental condition of the alleged incapacitated person, the step taken to find less restrictive alternatives, the specific area of incapacity over which it is requested that the guardian has assigned powers, and the qualifications of the proposed guardian. In Pennsylvania, efforts to accommodate the testimony and reports of expert witnesses have resulted in a court form for the expert report on the basis of incapacity and can be helpful for social workers to review if they are working with a client involved in a guardianship matter. As you might imagine, social workers, because they use a biopsychosocial model of assessment, are the professionals most likely to collect information during the assessment process that identifies a person's strengths and abilities. The assessment also identifies what aspects of the client environment may be contributing to a client's individual concern and need to be modified with the goal of enhancing a client's functioning or expanding their decision-making capacity. This information would be potentially relevant both to the expert report which must be submitted with the petition for guardianship and testimony at the hearing.

Some states also have different standards for competency or capacity for different decisions a person may be called upon to make. This requires a court to consider why the petition is being brought and what types of decisions are being questioned. This means that a court may find a person incompetent to make some decisions, such as those related to financial dealings, but competent to make other decisions, such as medical care. This is usually called "limited guardianship." Capacity, both in the law and in social science, is viewed as a very fluid and changeable situation and this calls for the constant reevaluation of the competence decision on the part of legal rights-based social workers.

Possible Outcomes of a Guardianship Case

Guardianship laws and decisions should attempt to strike a balance between protecting the legal rights and self-determination of an individual and the state's responsibility to protect incapacitated individuals from harm. States vary on the way they attempt to balance these competing imperatives. At the end of a hearing or trial, the judge can appoint a guardian to make all or a specific set of decisions on behalf of the adult. The range of decisions can include medical treatment, property management, financial management, and the ability to marry and to vote. Based on the determination of the competency hearing the guardian may be authorized to have decision-making power about one very specific and discrete aspect of the client's life or a wide range of decisions that impact the individual's daily life and well-being.

Individual states also differ in the procedures used to appoint a guardian as well as in the statutes that lay out the power, authority, and responsibilities of the guardian, reporting requirements, who may be the guardian, and whether the guardian is paid or not. In many jurisdictions, if a family member is not appropriate, social workers are appointed by the court to function in this role. The social worker may also be in a situation where they are required to investigate potential guardians, such as a family member.

In Chapter 2, you learned that many courts have created alternative programs, such as mediation that aims to identify the interests and rights of parties to a legal proceeding and to avoid a trial, which in situations of vulnerable adult abuse can be emotionally difficult for both the victim and the nonoffending family members. Alternative venues as forums that can support and advance social work practice are covered extensively in Chapter 11. One way that social workers can be effective advocates for their clients is to be knowledgeable about alternatives to guardianship such as POA, representatives for receipt of benefits, trusts, medical decision-making authority, and living wills or case management services. These alternatives can be part of a mediation agreement or a plan to avoid the need for filing for guardianship altogether. Social workers should also be familiar with evidence-based practices (EBPs) that improve and provide remediation for the social and cognitive functioning of elders and persons with mental illness (Bartels et al., 2003).

Responsibilities and Duties of a Guardian

The National Association of Social Workers (NASW) Code of Ethics (2021) makes it very clear that social workers have extra duties when working with those who have been found to lack capacity. Section 1.4 states, "When social workers act on behalf of clients who lack the capacity to make informed decisions, social workers should take reasonable steps to safeguard the interests and rights of those clients." In our view, those reasonable steps cannot be taken if there is no understanding of the rights and decisions that have been limited by the court and the roles, powers, and duties of the court-appointed guardian which can be found in state statutes.

Broadly defined, guardians are usually required to make decisions in the "best interest" of the client (National Guardianship Association, 2022). They identify and arrange for needed services to support the client and enhance capacity and to encourage the person to participate to the maximum extent of their ability in making decisions and taking actions on their own behalf. An excellent resource for social work advocates is the National Guardianship Association that has published very detailed standards for best practice and ethical behavior of guardians (National Guardianship Association, 2022).

A legal guardian of an incapacitated adult may be required by law to make decisions in the best interest of their client or to use substituted judgment. The first standard, best interest, means that the guardian can make a decision based on what they believe is best for the client and the least intrusive and least restrictive course of action available given the capacity of the client. With substituted judgment, the guardian must try to implement a decision that would be the course of action that the person, if they still had capacity, would want. The guardian would attempt in this instance to see if any wishes about the matter at hand were expressed in writing or verbally. In either situation, it is critical for the social worker to understand the legal standard applied in their particular state in order to understand the responsibilities of the guardian and the basis for decision-making on behalf of the incapacitated individual. Additionally, guardians are typically required to file annual reports with the court which detail the continuing need for the guardianship; names and roles of other medical, mental health and social work providers; and the activities of the guardians with regard to medical, daily, and financial decision making.

INVOLUNTARY COMMITMENT

Civil Courts also hear cases involving requests for the involuntary commitment of individuals with mental illnesses to both inpatient and outpatient settings for treatment and medication. As you might imagine, civil commitment cases raise significant issues given the involuntary hospitalization, institutionalized care, and conflicts with ethical mandates to value patient autonomy and care (Testa & West, 2010). States allow for civil commitment for persons with substance abuse and those who have a developmental disability. States also have statutes authorizing the involuntary commitment of minors for mental health and substance abuse treatment. In these cases, social workers in the explicit and implicit legal context need to understand the standards used by a court to determine whether or not an individual can be ordered to a psychiatric hospital, go to a clinic, or take medication and be treated against their will. Many of the procedures and processes are the same, but the definitions of mental illness and dangerousness may be slightly different to adapt to the developmental differences between mentally ill adults and minors.

In general, state statutes regarding involuntary civil commitment to both inpatient and outpatient facilities contain information about the following: how to begin an action including petitions and notice, screening requirements and required information, requirements and circumstances that would result in temporary commitment prior to a hearing, rules about discovery, testimony, right to counsel, timing and location of hearings, procedural aspects of hearings, standards of proof, burden of proof, standards of commitment that must be legally met, discharge, conditional discharge, duration of the commitment, review hearings, patients rights, and procedures to raise treatment issues. For social workers who may be interacting with or working on behalf of individuals who may be facing the possibility of an involuntary commitment, it is critical to understand the legal requirements and rights of the individual in that process and to ensure to the best of their capacity that the individual is also made aware of their rights and limitations when involuntarily committed.

Initiating an Involuntary Commitment Proceeding

Most states authorize any person to file a petition for involuntary commitment or treatment if they have knowledge of a person who is mentally ill, lacks capacity to make an informed judgment about treatment, presents a danger to self or others, or is in need of treatment that would prevent further disability that would predictably result in dangerousness. For substance use, a petition may allege that a person lacks control over their substance or alcohol use, that they lack the capacity to consent or understand the need for treatment, and that they pose a danger to self or others. Depending on your locality, petitions might be filed through a district attorney's office or a local court clerk. Many states require some kind of initial screening of the petition to ensure that it meets the statutory criteria for involuntary commitment.

Usually the petition will need to be accompanied by a certification by an authorized mental health provider in support of the petition as defined in the statute or if that is impossible, a certification that the client was asked to go for an evaluation and refused. In some localities, the petition requires that the mental health provider also certifies that there is a bed available in a facility. There is usually a requirement that two mental health professionals provide the certification, one of whom must be a psychiatrist. Some states also require a sworn affidavit from the person petitioning the court that lays out the underlying facts that support the petition, including that the person is mentally ill, is a danger to self or others, and has been requested to go to treatment and refuses. Again, it is important to make a distinction between facts and inferences, and knowing the standards will help you or a family member understand what to write and how to protect an individual's rights. If a person has not been evaluated and a judge finds that there is reasonable cause to believe the facts in the petition are true, the judge can issue an order to transport the person for an emergency evaluation. After an evaluation, if the mental health professionals provide evidence that shows there is "probable cause" to believe that the statutory requirement for an involuntary commitment can be met, the judge can order a temporary commitment. A mental health professional will need to make sure that they can provide evidence in their certification that addresses the statutory requirements.

In some states, such as Connecticut and West Virginia, an licensed clinical social worker (LCSW) with appropriate training can complete emergency certificates. As a practitioner in this area, you would want to know the definition for who is considered under the law to be what is often referred to as a qualified mental health professional. It is important to remember that mental health professionals cannot decide, or say in their report, that the criteria are met; only a judge can do that as part of their legal authority by having jurisdiction over these matters. A judge may also issue a temporary commitment order for a voluntarily committed patient to stop them from leaving the hospital if there is a reasonable cause to detain them.

States have strict time limits within which a hearing must occur after a temporary commitment order is issued, such as within 20 days after the admission as is the case in New Jersey for adults (N.J. Rev. Stat. § 30:4-27.12, 1987). Individuals who are the subject of involuntary commitment and treatment proceedings often have the right to counsel and to have an independent mental health and medical evaluation to counter the evaluation completed by the petitioner. Additionally, the individual often has the right to be present at the hearing and to participate in the hearing. Each state determines the standard of proof needed to support an order of commitment but generally it is at the level of "clear and convincing evidence" and the burden of proof is on the government to show that the individual meets the legal criteria for commitment or mandated treatment in that state. As we discussed in other chapters, the higher standard reflects the significant freedoms that can be impacted as a result of the proceedings.

Legal Definitions and Standards for Involuntary Commitments

The first inquiry in these types of cases is whether the individual meets the criteria in their state to be considered a mentally ill person, substance using, or developmentally disabled person or youth under the law. In many states this finding must be made prior to issuing an involuntary order of commitment. An additional finding must be made that the mental illness results in an inability to make an informed decision about treatment. As you learned, state statutes will define what is meant by "mentally ill" or "substance" using person. It is important to understand that a diagnosis or medical language cannot substitute for the statutory standard and legal determination. An example of one statutory definition for mental illness is found in New Jersey:

> "Mental illness" means a current, substantial disturbance of thought, mood, perception, or orientation which significantly impairs judgment, capacity to control behavior, or capacity to recognize reality, but does not include simple alcohol intoxication, transitory reaction to drug ingestion, organic brain syndrome, or developmental disability unless it results in the severity of impairment described herein. The term mental illness is not limited to "psychosis" or "active psychosis," but shall include all conditions that result in the severity of impairment described herein (N.J. Rev. Stat. § 30:4-27.2[r], 2024).

It is important to note that the statute lays out that the mental illness must not only be current but must also be substantial enough to "significantly" impair or hinder the individual's ability to control themselves.

Then the court must determine whether the mental illness renders the individual in question a danger to themselves or others, or incapable of meeting their basic needs, including the need for ongoing medical treatment to control their mental illness. For example in Illinois, the court can only involuntarily admit someone to a psychiatric hospital if, as a result of a mental illness, they are "reasonably expected, unless treated on an inpatient basis, to engage in conduct placing such person or another in physical harm or in reasonable expectation of being physically harmed" or "unable to provide for his or her basic physical needs so as to guard himself or herself from serious harm without the assistance of family or others, unless treated on an inpatient basis;" or "because of the nature of his or her illness, is unable to understand his or her need for treatment" (405 ILCS § 1-119, 2010).

As you can see from the grounds stated in the law, it is not enough for the court to find that an individual has a mental illness or even that an individual with a mental illness refuses treatment. The law requires that there be a link between the mental illness of the individual and the substantial likelihood of dangerous conduct to self or others.

Therefore, in order to prove the grounds for involuntary commitment or treatment, a mental health or other medical professional must present evidence or testify before the court can determine whether or not an individual can be committed. In Illinois, an LCSW can complete a certification for involuntary commitment. If you were one of the mental health professionals presenting testimony at the hearing, you would need to show that your assessment provided facts regarding each of the preceding criteria. Social workers who work with mental health professionals may also be called to testify as to their observations and assessment of the individual given that they are considered to be part of the treatment team. Conversely, if you are an advocate for the client you may present facts and testimony that dispute that the client's behavior met the statutory criteria.

Once again, this assessment requires a social worker to balance the safety of the community with the importance of protecting an individual's freedoms and rights. It is imperative that evaluations occur right before the hearing so that the diagnosis and assessment are current, further underscoring the importance of viewing these cases as fluid. One of the most important advocacy tasks that a social worker can do in these instances is to attempt to find alternative means that can effectively reduce risk. Evidence-based alternatives should be considered such as those offered by the U.S. Department of Health and Human Services (USDHHS): Assertive Community Treatment (2008), integrated treatment for co-occurring disorders (2010a), as well as supported housing and employment. Another excellent evidence-based guide is Illness Management and Recovery (USDHHS, 2010b). Other recommended treatments and techniques for specific disorders and co-occurring disorders include behavior modification treatment (Scott et al., 2023) and dialectal behavioral therapy.

Potential Outcomes

After a hearing, the judge can find that the person does not meet the standard for involuntary commitment and can issue a discharge order usually enforceable within 48 hours. The judge may also issue an order of conditional discharge where there are conditions surrounding treatment that have been recommended by the hospital or clinic staff and developed with client participation. In this case, the discharge can happen if the conditions are met. A judge can also decide to issue an order of commitment for a period of time decided by the court, within the limits defined by state law. When a judge issues commitment and treatment orders, they will also set a date for a review hearing to evaluate the continued need for commitment. The same standards used in the initial hearing are used to make decisions in the review hearings.

Postcommitment Advocacy

Most states have standards of treatment for patients in mental health facilities. In the case of clients who have been involuntarily committed, they are entitled to receive services that are targeted to allow them to return as soon as possible to their community. In most instances, patients can challenge either administratively or during any commitment hearings whether they are receiving the services mandated by law as long as they provide notice to the court. Issues can include the effectiveness of treatment plans in addressing the conditions leading to the commitment or not addressing a medical or other issue. When committed to outpatient treatment, clients cannot be forced to take medication against their will, while inpatient clients may be forced to take medication if it is deemed an emergency situation by hospital staff. There are a range of occasions for social workers to intervene on behalf of clients postcommitment including advocating for shorter terms, visitation, and improved services.

CIVIL PROCEEDINGS INITIATED BY INDIVIDUAL ACTORS

In this section, we continue to focus on the next steps in a civil proceeding, but we will highlight those proceedings typically initiated by individuals that allow for higher levels of client self-determination and less infringement on the rights and liberties of the individual. We also focus on the kinds of civil cases we identified in Chapter 1, where there are large numbers of indigent clients who are representing themselves or appearing pro se, and where questions of access to justice and understanding their legal rights are often implicated.

DIVORCE

Any discussion of a civil proceeding to divorce must first begin with the legal basis for getting married, a prerequisite to any divorce proceeding. State law regulates legal marriages and civil unions by declaring who can marry whom and what legal steps need to be taken in order to enter into a legal marriage or civil union. The benefits from a legal marriage or civil union include tax benefits, medical insurance, the right to make medical decisions on behalf of your spouse or partner, entitlement to become a guardian or conservator for an incapacitated spouse or partner, and rights of inheritance. Common law marriages are recognized in some states and refer to the process by which a couple who have lived together for a specific amount of time are considered to be married even though they have not formally applied for a marriage license.

Initiating Divorce Proceedings

In order to dissolve or end a marriage or civil union, a couple has to petition the state. Generally, a state will require that the couple has lived in the state for some period of time ranging from 6 months to a year before entertaining a petition for divorce. A divorce is either contested, meaning that one or both parties disagree on the terms of the divorce, or uncontested, meaning that both parties agree to the divorce. The decision as to whether the two parties will contest the divorce and the final decree that the court can order as a result of the divorce is a critical legal moment in the case. Because of this, many states mandate that both parties attend a conference in the beginning of the case or mediation to determine whether there is any possibility of resolving the case without a contested trial.

Legal Decisions in Divorce Proceedings

In some states, the petition for a divorce must state the grounds for requesting the divorce. These grounds can include irreconcilable differences, adultery, cruel and inhuman punishment, or abandonment. In other states, a spouse can file for a no-fault divorce, which means that the petition for the divorce does not have to include a reason or grounds for the divorce. Many states have a waiting period of 6 months to a year before a divorce can be finalized.

There are a number of legal issues confronted when a couple decides to divorce, whether they were legally married or obtained a civil union or domestic partnership. Financial issues include the identification and division of marital and individual assets, custody and visitation of any minor children born or adopted during the marriage, and ongoing child and/or spousal support. It is important to remember that financial assets include real property such as a home and other belongings, in addition to stocks, pensions, Social Security benefits, and other investments.

Possible Outcomes

The possible outcomes from a divorce proceeding include custody and financial determinations in addition to the final order decreeing that the couple is divorced and no longer legally married. The court can make an order of custody and visitation as part of the final divorce decree, and those options mirror the options available in a custody proceeding. The order of custody can be very specific, detailing the days or holidays that one parent has access to the child or the order can be more general allowing the parties to determine the specifics of the custodial arrangement among themselves. The court can also determine the separation of assets and any maintenance or alimony for either party for their own support or the support of any minor children. Given the range of decisions that are made in a divorce proceeding and the potential impact on the daily life, family structure, and financial situation of the client, it is important for social workers to understand how the divorce case can significantly impact their clients overall well-being.

PATERNITY AND CHILD SUPPORT PROCEEDINGS

Paternity proceedings involve a determination by the court to legally recognize a man as the biological father of a child. Paternity proceedings are brought either by the mother or the father to establish paternity or to contest an assumption or claim of paternity. Often a paternity petition is brought as a corollary matter to a child support case to establish that the man does or does not owe a legal duty of support to the child in question. Paternity is established in two ways: by an acknowledgment of paternity or by submitting to genetic testing to determine paternity. In most states, a man can acknowledge paternity without undergoing any genetic testing if there is no objection from the child's mother. Child support can then be established in a separate court proceeding.

Child support proceedings can be brought by a caregiver, parent, or in some states, by the local welfare agency to obtain a court order mandating child support for any minor children. Child support, a fixed amount of money to assist the custodial parent with a child's monthly expenses, is not related to gender and can be sought from a mother if a father has custody. Child support usually lasts until a child has reached the age of majority or in some cases, such as child who has disabilities, can be required to continue past the age of majority.

Under the federal law, the Child Support Enforcement Act (1984), each state must have a child support enforcement system in place and allow district attorneys to arrest and incarcerate nonpaying parents. All clients who are collecting public assistance will automatically receive services from the child support enforcement system but any other person in the state may apply for services. This can include locating the father and establishing paternity or parentage, going to court for a support order, enforcing orders, and modifying orders if necessary. There is also a federal law that provides for the enforcement of child support orders when a parent has moved to another state.

Potential Outcomes in Child Support Matters

The potential outcomes from a child support case concern the specifics of the order of support that can be entered by the court. A child support order can range from a minimum support amount, generally dictated by state statute, to a specific amount that can be garnished involuntarily from the parent's wages. States have guidelines regarding what percent of income must be deduced from the net income of the parent. Percents differ according to how many children are involved. For example, in Connecticut courts will generally order that 22% to 24% of net income will be deducted for one child. Parents can also sue for "back child support" or support from the period before the order was issued if the person being sued has the means to pay and records and receipts were kept by the parent requesting the support to demonstrate the expenses spent to care for the child. Child support can cease if a parent enters active military duty or if a parent's rights are terminated.

An important piece of information for social workers to know is that child support orders can be modified if circumstances change for either parent. There can be both temporary and permanent modification orders. The circumstances can be found in state child support statutes or court rules. This is a significant issue for both parents, as either parent can request a modification. It is important information for social workers working with low-income, disabled, unemployed, or seasonally employed clients because the penalties for nonpayment of child support are severe and can include incarceration.

Reasons for a temporary reduction or increase in payments can be a medical illness or emergency, a financial setback such as unemployment, homelessness, an injury, or any other change resulting in financial hardship. The support order can be reduced, suspended, or increased on a temporary basis until the situation has stabilized. In many states, judges have the discretion to modify the amount as long as they can articulate their reasoning and there are facts to support it, such as a parent having to provide support for an elderly family member or already paying child support for children born during a prior marriage or relationship.

There are certain circumstances that allow a permanent modification in support payments and these include a permanent disability for either parent, a considerable change in income for either parent, changes in child expenses such as an increase in health insurance, the age of the child or any condition of the child that increases the level of care and support required by the parents.

Parentage for LGBTQ Parents

Parentage refers to the legal relationship between a parent and their child which is established either through birth recognized on the state-issued birth certificate or a court order most often through adoption proceedings. Parentage is important to establish as it determines the legal rights and responsibilities that accrue for a legally recognized parent including the right to consent to medical treatment, access records concerning the child, make educational decisions, and gain access to health insurance among other things. The Supreme Court decided in the case of *Obergefell v. Hodges* (2015) that, given the fundamental right to marry, states must issue marriage licenses and recognize marriage licenses of same-sex couples. There is no common consensus among states regarding establishing parentage for lesbian, gay, bisexual, and transgendered couples where one parent is biologically related and the other is not. Most advocates recommend that the nonbiologically related parent officially adopt the child in order to protect their legal relationship. Some states such as Oregon have what is called a parent–parent birth certificate that is issued for LGBT parents establishing parentage for both parents. When working with LGBT parents, it would be important to refer them for legal assistance if there are questions about establishing parentage and physical and legal custody of the child.

CHILD CUSTODY, VISITATION, GUARDIANSHIP, ADOPTION, AND EMANCIPATION

The common thread throughout all of the civil proceedings listed is that they involve circumstances under which a court can make an order regarding who has responsibility to support, care for, and make decisions about the person or property of a minor child. In each of these cases, an individual can request that the court change the legal relationship or responsibility for caring for a child and therefore make it critical for social workers to have a foundational understanding as these issues often arise in work with families in both the explicit and implicit legal context.

Child Custody Matters

Custody refers to the legal rights to a minor child, including everything from physical custody, medical decision-making, educational planning, and religious determinations. Legal custody refers to the range of decisions that parents make on behalf of their children including medical, educational, and religious decisions. Physical custody refers to the person responsible for providing shelter and basic necessities for the child; in other words, with whom the child lives. Both physical and legal custody can be held by one or both parents, and can be shared and limited by court orders in child custody matters. Biological parents are assumed to have legal custody of their children, if they are both listed on the child's birth certificate and a parent's rights have not been terminated or otherwise limited by a court order, including abuse and neglect cases. Civil Courts retain jurisdiction to determine custody disputes, in other words to rule on who a child should live with and who should take primary care of a child, in addition to who should make legal decisions for the child.

The court has a number of options within its authority when making the final determination of custody. The court can award sole custody to one of the parties, or order joint custody between the two parties. For example, under the Michigan Child Custody Act (1970), a court can award joint legal custody, which means that the parents share decision-making power with regard to the child's medical, educational, and religious upbringing. A Michigan court can also award joint or shared physical custody, meaning that both parties are allowed to have the child live with them on a determined schedule. A custody order after a trial is considered a final order that can only be changed or modified by coming back to court and generally requires that the person seeking the modification show that there has been a change of circumstances warranting a modification to the order. Judges also have the option of ordering supervised visitation. Supervised visitation is when there is contact between a noncustodial parent and the child in a setting where there is a third party who oversees the contact and makes sure there are no risks to a child's safety.

In order to request custody of a child from a court, an individual has to show that there is a relationship to that child. In most instances, the biological or adoptive parent demonstrates the relationship to the child. If a nonparent petitions the court for custody of a child (e.g., a grandparent, cousin, sibling), most states will require the nonparent to demonstrate special circumstances that give them the ability or legal standing to ask for custody. For example, a grandparent or uncle would have to demonstrate extraordinary circumstances in New York before the court would even entertain a hearing on whether it is in the child's best interests to have custody awarded to the relative because of the Court of Appeal's decision in *Bennett v. Jeffreys* (1976). The court in that case concluded that:

> To recapitulate: intervention by the State in the right and responsibility of a natural parent to custody of her or his child is warranted if there is first a judicial finding of surrender, abandonment, unfitness, persistent neglect, unfortunate or involuntary extended disruption of custody, or other equivalent but rare extraordinary circumstance which would drastically affect the welfare of the child. It is only on such a premise that the courts may then proceed to inquire into the best interest of the child and to order a custodial disposition on that ground. (*Bennett v. Jeffreys*, 1976, p. 548)

Extraordinary circumstances have been found in cases where a parent abandoned a child for a period of time, abused a child, or otherwise demonstrated a willingness to relinquish their rights to custody of the child.

While the specific legal standard will differ from state to state, most custody acts require the court to consider a number of factors in determining what will be in the child's best interest in terms of which parent or caregiver is granted full or partial legal or physical custody. In many states there are a numbered list of factors that require a court to consider the physical and educational needs of the child, specific medical or emotional needs of the child that require special parenting arrangements, the child's preference depending on the child's age, the history of each parent or caregiver's participation in raising the child, prior abuse or neglect by either of the parents or caregivers, and the impact of a parent's physical, mental, or substance abuse issue on the child's development and well-being. Social workers can support attorneys and clients with custody cases by helping to identify and gather evidence including school reports, medical records and receipts detailing the parent's financial support of the child.

Additionally, most states have provisions in their state custody laws that require judges to consider the impact of domestic violence or any findings of domestic violence when making a final custodial determination. For example, under Minn. Stat. ch. 518, § 518.17 (a)(4) (2023), before making a decision on which parent is granted custody, the judge has to consider "(4) whether domestic abuse, as defined in [the law] has occurred in the parents' or either parent's household or relationship; the nature and context of the domestic abuse; and the implications of the domestic abuse for parenting and for the child's safety, well-being, and developmental needs." Here is another example of where social work practice is implicated in the law because social workers are often working with clients who are victims of domestic violence and are privy to information concerning the impact on the victim and their children. One can imagine that it would be critical for social workers working with victims of domestic violence to provide this information to attorneys representing clients in custody proceedings.

Guardianship

Guardianship of minor children, which is similar to custody, includes establishing a legal relationship between a nonparent and a minor child but only to the extent that the kind of guardianship sought from a court permits. There are several types of guardianship and some types involve sharing decision-making with the parents of the child. Guardians of children, similar to adults, can be appointed to make decisions about property or financial affairs and about the person such as those relating to medical care. That decision-making power for a guardian can be on an emergency or interim basis, such as is the case in child abuse proceedings or an illness to decide about one very specific decision such as a medical procedure. Stand-by guardianship is when a parent may have a medical or mental illness that can incapacitate them and in advance of the incapacitating event, they have a court appoint a legal guardian for their children that will automatically activate when the incapacitating event, including death, occurs. When guardianship is limited in any way, it is important to remember that parents retain their decision-making rights about all other matters and in cases such as temporary and stand-by guardianship are considered to be co-decision-makers with the appointed guardian.

In most states anyone seeking to become the guardian of a minor child has to petition the court and must notify the biological parents of the child in addition to any other adult that the child is living with at the time of the filing and, in some states, must notify the child if over a certain age. Guardians can be anyone who knows the young person including grandparents, siblings, other relatives, and friends of the family. Parents must still continue to support their children during the course of the guardianship and the children are legally entitled to the parents' benefits or estate in the event of their death. In some cases such as in child welfare cases, guardians are eligible for financial assistance including public assistance for the child (in some states, even if they would not otherwise qualify) as well as foster care payments. Most states also have procedures to remove a guardian when there is concern about how they may be performing their duties.

Adoption

An adoption is the legal process of assigning the rights associated with being the biological parent of a child to a nonbiological parent. An adoption can only proceed with the consent of the biological parents who voluntarily surrender their parental rights or when there has been an involuntary termination of the parent's rights. Adoption involves the termination of the legal relationship between the biological parent and the child. The biological parent ceases to have any legal rights regarding the child, including custody, visitation, and financial responsibility.

Unlike guardianship, which is considered to be temporary, adoption is permanent. State statutes regarding adoption will generally address the following issues: who may be adopted, who may adopt, who may not adopt, who may place an adoptee, the types of adoption, who must consent, who need not consent, under what circumstances consent is not required, withdrawal of consent, legal representation, notice requirements, investigation of the adoptive home, hearing procedures, contested adoptions, the legal effects of the adoption, appeals, rights of involved parties such as biological and foster parents, access to records, recognition of foreign adoptions, and other financial issues such as adoption subsidies for children adopted from foster care.

There are several different types of adoption: agency, private or independent, kinship/relative, stepparent, and international. State laws and statutes will address any specific requirements or procedures instituted for each kind of adoption. For example, in Alabama, in the case of independent adoptions, the statute states that no fees or money can be exchanged for bringing together an adoptee, adoptive, or natural parents. There are many states that allow what is called "open adoption" where birthparents and extended family may be able to have continued contact with a child or semi-open adoption where there is a way for information, greeting cards, or letters to be exchanged between birth parents and adoptive children and families.

Visitation

Issues around visitation with children are also heard in Civil Court where a judge can make a formal order determining visitation with a child. Often, visitation issues are handled as a part of a larger custody matter or if one parent or caregiver has physical or legal custody, visitation may the only remaining issue that is being litigated. Visitation orders can vary from very general, authorizing visitation as determined by the two parties on their own, to very specific, setting out the duration, dates, level of supervision, and drop off location of the visits. In some instances, you will see references to detailed parenting plans which can be incorporated into the court's order and dictate the specific terms of visitation between parents. Each state will differ as well on whether a nonparent can request visitation and what circumstances need to be shown to allow the court to order that a nonparent has visitation in a custody matter. The U.S. Supreme Court held in *Troxel v. Granville* (2000) that Oregon's visitation law was in violation of a parent's rights under the Fourteenth Amendment to raise their children free from state interference because it did not give any deference to fit parent's determination about the nature and extent of visitation with a nonparent. Also, depending on the state and laws related to civil unions and domestic partnerships, LGBT individuals can be awarded both custody and a visitation right after a relationship has ended.

Emancipation of Minors

Social workers that work with adolescents may be familiar with the term "emancipation of a minor." This is a Civil Court process that releases a minor from parental control and any legal rights and responsibility over the child. A parent and child may consent to an order or after a hearing the judge may issue an order. Again, state statutes differ but in general a minor must show that they are in the U.S. military, are living on their own and able to care for their financial needs, are married, or satisfy other conditions that are under the court's discretion to decide but generally concern the minor's ability to care for themselves in the same way as an adult.

Emancipation for a minor means they will receive rights such as the right to marry, join the military, enter into contracts with other parties, or sue someone on their own. Responsibilities mean that the minor could be sued as an adult and will be responsible for, managing their finances, earning their own living and any contracts that they may enter into, including leases. Emancipated minors may also collect public assistance in the same manner as an adult and make educational determinations on their own including establishing their own residence for purposes of school enrollment. Some states have statutes that authorize partial emancipation such as giving the minor the power to make decisions in a limited and specific area such as the right to choose their own school while parents retain control in all other areas. Other states do not recognize emancipation at all, and social workers in settings with adolescent clients will want to understand the specific laws of their state before advising adolescents about the possibility of emancipation.

Initiating Custody, Guardianship, Adoption, Visitation, and Emancipation Proceedings

What all of these issues have in common is that they all involve the necessity of obtaining the consent of the biological and legal parents of the child to the proposed change. Much of what happens initially in court once a petition is filed is to ensure that notice was properly given, that good faith attempts were made to locate and serve both of the biological parents, and that any consents to give up some or all parental rights was voluntarily made. After the filing of a case concerning a minor, the Civil Court is required to determine that the other party is notified or served meaning that they have knowledge of the allegations against them, the opportunity to respond, and the ability to have a hearing or trial on the matter.

In the event biological parents do not consent or contest the custody, guardianship, visitation, adoption, or emancipation, they have a right to a Civil Court hearing. Generally, the parties to these proceedings have a right to be represented by counsel, but unless there is a state guarantee of counsel, there is no right to have counsel appointed if the party cannot afford to hire private counsel. The judge will hear testimony from both parties and other witnesses that could include relatives, service providers, or experts. In most jurisdictions, the judge has the authority, or in the case of adoption is required to order, a forensic evaluation or investigation to be conducted by a neutral third-party evaluator such as a psychologist or social worker. Social workers have long functioned as evaluators in these contexts utilizing their expertise to investigate and research the issue at hand, and provide a report with recommendations. The evaluator has to be agreed upon by all of the parties, and the cost of the evaluator is generally split among the parties. Organizations such as the American Psychological Association (APA) have established both ethical and clinical guidelines for conducting custody and visitation evaluations for the court (APA, 2010). Studies have found that judges rely positively on the child custody evaluations in their decision-making (Axelson & Gentile, 2024).

One type of evaluation that is part of an adoption proceeding is usually called a "home study" and is most often conducted by social workers. Home studies usually involve investigating the suitability of the adoptive parents, investigating the circumstances that led the biological parents to desire to surrender their child if this is a voluntary adoption, medical histories, criminal background checks, and other relevant factors that may come up in each case.

As mentioned earlier, the common standard in each of these cases is that the judge will be making a determination of whether or not the change in circumstances or custody that the parties are asking for on behalf of the child is in the child's best interest. Individual states may include additional guidelines, such as ability of the prospective custodian or guardian to meet the physical, emotional, moral, and educational needs of the child, the existence of a relationship between the child and the applicant, any history of domestic violence between the parties, and if the child is over a certain age (usually 12 years old or in some cases, any age where the child shows sufficient capacity), the wishes of the child.

The "best interests of the child" is a multifactored standard that includes an assessment of the parents' attachment to the child in question, financial security, emotional well-being, and physical well-being. Under Michigan's Child Custody Act (1970), a judge has to review the following factors before deciding what is in the child's best interest and making a final order of custody:

- **a.** The love, affection, and other emotional ties existing between the parties involved and the child.
- **b.** The capacity and disposition of the parties involved to give the child love, affection, and guidance and to continue the education and raising of the child in his or her religion or creed, if any.
- **c.** The capacity and disposition of the parties involved to provide the child with food, clothing, medical care or other remedial care recognized and permitted under the laws of this state in place of medical care, and other material needs.
- **d.** The length of time the child has lived in a stable, satisfactory environment, and the desirability of maintaining continuity.
- **e.** The permanence, as a family unit, of the existing or proposed custodial home or homes.
- **f.** The moral fitness of the parties involved.
- **g.** The mental and physical health of the parties involved.
- **h.** The home, school, and community record of the child.
- **i.** The reasonable preference of the child, if the court considers the child to be of sufficient age to express preference.

j. The willingness and ability of each of the parties to facilitate and encourage a close and continuing parent–child relationship between the child and the other parent or the child and the parents. A court may not consider negatively for the purposes of this factor any reasonable action taken by a parent to protect a child or that parent from sexual assault or domestic violence by the child's other parent.
k. Domestic violence, regardless of whether the violence was directed against or witnessed by the child.
l. Any other factor considered by the court to be relevant to a particular child custody dispute.
(Mich. Comp. Laws ch. 722, § 722.23, 2010)

As you can see from the statute, the law is complex and multifaceted with a number of different criteria but less guidance as to the relative importance or weight of each of the considerations. However, it will be important that any custody evaluation done by a social worker or other mental health professional collects facts and data on each factor that will allow the judge to make an informed decision based in part on the evaluation.

The court will consider all of the testimony at trial, both from witnesses and documents, in addition to any court-ordered investigations or reports when determining what is in the child's best interest. Indeed, the court should look to a number of different sources in order to determine the best interests of a child. The New York Court of Appeals, in the case mentioned earlier of *Bennett v. Jeffreys* (1976), specifically noted the importance of this evidence, noting that "[i]n custody matters parties and courts may be very dependent on the auxiliary services of psychiatrists, psychologists, and trained social workers" (*Bennett v. Jeffreys*, 1976, p. 548). Therefore, social workers working with clients involved in any of these matters should understand the context for the court's decision-making. For social workers working with an attorney representing a parent in one of these matters, assessment and information gathering that focuses on the factors outlined in your state's custody, guardianship, or visitation law can be invaluable in advocating for the client's desired outcome.

HOUSING AND LANDLORD–TENANT DISPUTES: PRIVATE AND PUBLIC HOUSING

All social workers know that secure and safe housing is central to individual and family stability and often a requisite condition for individuals to attain other significant goals such as the return of a child from foster care, release on bond or bail, obtaining custody and visitation rights, or securing employment. The main difference between publicly owned and private housing is that in public housing the landlord is the "government" and in private housing the landlord is an individual. The local housing authority handles the management of the housing including processing of any grievances or evictions. In either situation, the landlord and the tenant sign a lease that is considered to be a legal contract and any changes to a contract must be done through appropriate legal processes, which implicate rights and protections for both the landlord and the tenant.

It is important for clients to know that signing a lease, whether with a government or private landlord, is a legal contract and that means that the client and the landlord agree to perform duties, assume responsibilities, and at the same time obtain rights and protections. In both public and private housing if a client cosigns a lease with another person, they assume responsibility for the obligations of that person as well as their own. The federal government and states have statutes that cover the duties and responsibilities of both private and public landlords and tenants such as under what conditions a lease can be modified, changed, or terminated; repairs and housing code violation;, security deposits; procedures for rent withholding; notifying a tenant of lead paint; and eviction. As an example, the laws that govern the rental of residential property in the state of Georgia can be found in Official Code of Georgia, Title 44, Chapter 7 (2023). For some groups such as the disabled, victims of domestic violence, seniors, indigent individuals, military personnel, and tenants living in properties facing foreclosure, the federal government provides additional protections related to eviction. In every state, these statutes governing housing rentals in the private and public arena are used as the basis for initiating civil proceedings in Housing Court.

It is also important to note that all tenants are protected from discrimination in housing-related matters and that disabled persons are entitled to what is called "reasonable accommodations" by landlords. Reasonable accommodations in housing mean making the rules or provisions necessary to afford handicapped persons "equal opportunity to use and enjoy a dwelling" (Fair Housing Amendments Act, 1988). You will learn more about how to address discrimination and civil rights complaints in the following section of this chapter, Civil Rights and Civil Liberties Proceedings, and in Chapter 12 when you will learn about administrative proceedings.

Low income clients who live in public, subsidized, or Section 8 housing may need advocacy from social workers to assist with problem-solving for issues that can put housing at risk, such as managing changes in benefits; unemployment; illness; security issues such as disputes with tenants; and problems with other family members, children, and adolescents that violate conditions of leases. It is important that you investigate the specific requirements in your client's lease because additional requirements of a lease and grounds for eviction can be set by local authorities as well as by the federal government. Social workers can lower risk of eviction by acting preventively and developing plans with families that address the specific conditions creating risk for eviction.

Initiating a Housing Court Proceeding

When petitions are filed in civil matters related to housing, either the government or an individual can file a petition. Tenants in both public and private housing also have the right to file a petition in Housing Court against their landlords, as do landlords against tenants. One difference between public and private housing is that before a party can institute a civil proceeding in a public housing matter they must first go through a grievance process with their local housing authority. Therefore, tenants in public housing are required to go through the local housing authority's grievance procedures, including participating in an administrative hearing presided over by a hearing officer, before accessing a legal remedy in Housing Court.

The federal government allows that under certain conditions related to protecting the health and safety of public housing residents that the housing authority can forego the grievance procedure and proceed directly to court to initiate eviction proceedings. These conditions include any criminal or other activity that threatens the health, safety, or right to peaceful enjoyment of the premises by residents or employees; drug-related criminal activity on or off the premises; and illegal use of a controlled substance or abuse of alcohol that threatens the right to health, safety, or peaceful enjoyment.

Legal Standard: Grounds for Eviction

The bases for eviction can include not following the conditions and terms of the lease, failure to pay rent, damage to the home, becoming a nuisance to other tenants, serious and continuing health hazards, refusing to leave when a lease has expired, and illegal drug activity if it is specifically included as a provision of the lease. In some states, tenants in public housing have additional responsibilities as part of their lease including activities referred to as community service and self-sufficiency requirements. If a tenant fails to comply with those requirements, then they can place the renewal of their lease at risk.

A public housing authority can terminate a lease and move to evict a tenant if the tenant, other members of the household, or any of their guests is found to have engaged in criminal or drug-related activity. In some venues, residents who are not employed or in job training programs are required by the conditions of their lease to do community service (Housing Authority City of Los Angeles, Section VIII-A, 2017).

It is crucial for social workers to know that the person holding the lease is not only responsible for their own behavior but the behaviors of all other family members and guests. The Supreme Court in *Department of Housing and Urban Development v. Rucker* (2002) held that under federal law public housing tenants can be evicted when members of their household or other guests commit certain crimes regardless of whether the tenant knew about or could have prevented such criminal activity. This means that if your client is an out-of-control adolescent who is caught using drugs and is defiant of parental authority, the client's behavior can put their entire family at risk for eviction and homelessness. Another example of family member behavior that creates risk can be seen in the lease requirements for public housing in Norwalk, Connecticut, where one of the grounds for eviction from public housing is unexcused absences from school for a child living in the household. Social workers working in both the implicit and explicit legal context should immediately help clients target and prioritize those problems that are creating risk of eviction, whether they be income related or related to family stress or dysfunction.

For example, with our case example, we know that Ms. Jones's aunt has agreed to allow her niece to live with her until she is able to move into her own place and has more stability. Based on your review as a legally informed social worker, you would want to inquire whether the aunt lives in public housing given the nature of Ms. Jones's criminal case and the potential impact of criminal drug use or activity by her niece in her aunt's house. The legally informed social worker would know that if Ms. Jones is convicted of a drug offense in her criminal case, then not only will her own housing plan be at risk, affecting her child neglect case, but her aunt and her family may also be at risk for eviction. Without knowing the potential stakes for a family's housing, social workers who are not legally informed may unfairly judge caretakers who may seem rejecting or punitive in wanting their child or relative to leave the household. Furthermore, any counseling on options for Ms. Jones would be lacking without taking into account the potential risks of being in public housing.

Right to Notice

In eviction cases, the tenant in both public and private housing has a right to be notified by the landlord that they are seeking for the tenant to be removed by a certain date. If the tenant does not fix the alleged infraction, perhaps by paying the rent that is owed, the landlord has a basis for suing in Housing Court for an unlawful detainer. When clients are exhibiting problems that could result in eviction, as you learned in the preceding, they must receive notice or warning of eviction. In most states, each ground for eviction has a specific amount of time that must pass before a landlord can commence a civil proceeding. These time limits may differ from state to state so it is important that you check the regulations in your state that cover rental properties. It is important for social workers to understand the notice requirements because these are key intervention points for clients and with assistance may be able to avoid eviction. In California, a client will receive a 3-day notice for nonpayment of rent or a 30-day notice for other issues when termination is sought in a public housing case. Once a client receives a notice of eviction for rent arrears, a social worker can assist by having the client contact the building management or landlord to arrange for a payment plan and to assist the client to access benefits or rent assistance programs that are available to low-income residents at risk of losing their home in your locality.

Social workers can also intervene at the "30-day notice" that is a warning that there is some violating condition or behavior that must be changed. This can include serious health hazards or conditions or physical injury or damage to property. Social workers can institute problem-solving processes when the client's or family member's behavior is an issue by helping the client to identify the behavior and put in place a plan to address the behavior so a client can attest that the behavior will not happen again. Social workers, by providing written documentation of service provisions that specifically addresses the behavior in question, can provide legal proof and serve as documentation that there is a plan in place for the behavior to stop and demonstrate the client's commitment to the plan. For example, participation in a community-based dispute resolution center to settle a dispute with another tenant, helping clients to access benefits and payment plans to pay utility bills so their service will be restored, or participating in evidence-based family treatment such as multisystemic family therapy with an adolescent who may be getting into fights may be ways to address the management's concerns with client behavior and thus avoid the continuation of legal proceedings.

It goes without saying that most clients involved in eviction proceedings will be experiencing high levels of anxiety and distress. Social workers have access to a range of generalist practice models that can be employed while working with clients who are in the process of eviction including crisis intervention, task-centered, solution-focused, problem-solving, and strength-based models that can effectively engage the client in the problem-solving process with you and mobilize them to action.

Court Hearings

If an agreement is not worked out or the grounds for eviction cannot be addressed, the landlord may begin a civil proceeding also called a summary proceeding or eviction action. A complaint, similar to the notice, must be filed and include the grounds for eviction with specific details such as how much rent is due and a copy of the notice and the lease. A summons will be issued requiring the tenant to appear at the next court date. The summons is an important document because it will tell the client their rights such as the right to be represented by counsel, the right to request a jury trial, and referrals to legal aid if they cannot afford an attorney, as there is no guaranteed right to counsel in housing cases. Once a case has been filed in California Housing Court, for example, either party can request a trial by jury. While states differ in their specific guidelines, most states include rules on the required notice, trial process, settlement options, and stays. It is also illegal in most states for landlords to evict tenants by shutting off the utilities or "locking them out." This may also include a prohibition against disposing of a tenant's property as part of the eviction or before there is a formal court proceeding.

When legal issues arise for tenants in a public housing arrangement, those matters are heard in Housing Court as well and the public housing authority or landlord is responsible for bringing the case against a tenant. Even though there may be an administrative process that tenants in public housing must use before going to Housing Court, the local housing authority still has to bring a civil case in order to evict a tenant. Once the housing authority has decided to pursue an eviction, the tenant can challenge that decision in Housing Court, and the housing authority has to receive an order of eviction from Housing Court to evict the client or terminate the tenancy. Once the housing case has been filed, the tenant is entitled to all of the protections described earlier, including the right to notice of the proceeding and the right to be represented by an attorney in the matter. Tenants can also initiate civil proceedings if they feel they have been illegally evicted or a landlord has locked them out of their home, shut off utilities, or if repairs are not being made.

Defenses for the Tenant

States frequently provide defenses for tenants even when there are also grounds for the eviction. The most common ones include a presumption of retaliation if a landlord moves to evict a tenant after they have made a complaint for a health or safety violation or tried to enforce their rights in some way; a failure by the landlord to uphold their duty of providing reasonable repairs or keeping the property up to the relevant codes and standards; and if what the landlord is alleging is not true or as serious as the landlord alleges. Tenants should be able to prove that they gave written notice to the landlord of, for example, a safety violation and that a reasonable amount of time has passed for the landlord to fix the problem. Tenants may also raise defenses if the landlord did not provide them with timely or adequate notice of the eviction proceedings, or if the tenant has tried to fix the problem raised by the landlord, for example, by paying any back rent that was owed.

Potential Outcomes: Eviction, Negotiation, and Settlement

During the Housing Court case, the tenant and the landlord may reach a settlement that is ultimately approved by the court. The settlement could include a plan for the tenant to pay any back rent that is owed to the landlord within a prescribed amount of time. If there is no settlement, then the case will proceed and the tenant will either prevail or there will be a formal order of eviction from the Housing Court. As noted earlier, throughout the Housing Court case, including during settlement negotiations, tenants can be represented by attorneys or may appear pro se.

If there is a settlement, then the parties would consent to a stipulation, approved by the court, detailing the terms of the agreement. If there is no settlement, then the case proceeds to trial and a jury or judge determines the case. If the judge or jury rules in favor of the landlord, the tenant has the right to ask for a "stay" of the order of eviction in order to gain more time to find new housing or remedy the original problem. If the client does not show up for the trial, the court can issue a default judgment, meaning that the landlord can legally evict the client or order a money judgment for unpaid rent that allows the landlord to begin collection proceedings. The landlord will receive an Order of Eviction that gives legal authority to physically remove the tenant and their belongings.

Through an understanding of the legal process, grounds for eviction, and the risk and protective factors that have been found to be associated with homelessness, legally informed social workers can in many instances prevent eviction and help negotiate settlement plans so that housing stability is maintained.

CIVIL RIGHTS AND CIVIL LIBERTIES VIOLATIONS

Civil rights are those rights that all citizens have to be protected from unequal and discriminatory treatment or conversely to be treated equally because that person has a particular characteristic. Civil rights laws also extend protection from discrimination to those with disabilities, institutionalized persons, and pregnant women. Examples of civil rights violations include discrimination on the basis of race, age, ethnicity, immigration status, gender, disability, marital status, religion, or sexual orientation in employment, education, government benefits or services, housing, access to credit, access to businesses or buildings, healthcare services, transportation, disaster relief, or voting. Hate crimes are considered to be a criminal civil rights matter.

These rights stem from federal law although individual states, as well as local cities and municipalities, can extend protections that may not be covered by federal law. Under federal law, the Civil Rights Act (1964) prohibits discrimination in a number of settings including those listed. Many of the federal civil rights laws are codified in U.S. Code Title 42, Chapter 21. Civil rights laws are often reinforced and interpreted in court cases at the federal, state, and local levels as well as during administrative proceedings. Civil liberties are those rights that are guaranteed by the Constitution and the Bill of Rights of federal and state governments or have been interpreted by the courts to stem from those laws. Some of these rights include: the right to freedom from unreasonable search and seizure, the right to privacy, and right to due process. The Civil Rights Litigation Clearinghouse is an excellent resource for social workers and attorneys (www.clearinghouse.net). This site has an extensive collection of information about a wide range of civil rights cases particularly relevant to social work practice. Categories of cases include child welfare, disability rights, immigration, indigent defense, mental health, nursing home facilities, prison conditions, education, and public benefits, to name a few.

Initiating a Civil Rights or Civil Liberties Proceeding

There are two paths to addressing a civil rights or civil liberties violation: by filing a complaint with the government at the federal or local level, thereby triggering an investigation and administrative proceeding or by filing a civil lawsuit in court. Depending on the facts and the law that was violated, the agency will decide at what level the complaint will be addressed, either federal or state. This is usually dependent on the source of the law that relates to the case. In some cases, such as employment discrimination, laws require that the person file a complaint first with the government before they may file a civil lawsuit. Administrative complaints and proceedings are covered in more depth in Chapter 12.

Civil suits can be brought against a private or government entity if an individual believes that their civil rights or civil liberties have been violated. A person can sue private individuals and government bodies and officials personally when authorized by statutes. Groups of persons with a common interest can also sue for rights violations on behalf of their group, which is called a class action lawsuit. Class actions will be presented in greater depth in Chapter 13 as an important tool for social work advocacy.

The right to sue the government or persons acting on behalf of the government for violations of civil rights and civil liberties stems from Title 42 Section 1983 of the United States Code, often referred to as "Section 1983" cases. The law states:

> Every person who, under color of any statute, ordinance, regulation, custom, or usage, of any State or Territory or the District of Columbia, subjects, or causes to be subjected, any citizen of the United States or other person within the jurisdiction thereof to the deprivation of any rights, privileges, or immunities secured by the Constitution and laws, shall be liable to the party injured in an action at law, suit in equity, or other proper proceeding for redress.

It is important to remember that there are often time limits called statutes of limitations that dictate how much time can pass between the act of discrimination or rights violation and when you can make a complaint or file a lawsuit. For example, in some situations, the time limit begins when the violation occurs and in others when the person realizes that their legal right has been violated.

Legal Standard: Elements of a Section 1983 Claim

There are four parts to proving a civil rights or civil liberties claim. First, you must show that a particular right protected by the Constitution or by statute was violated and identify the specific law that guarantees the right. A violation of the Fourth Amendment's guarantee against unreasonable searches or seizures is an example of a federal constitutional right that may be violated. Second, you must identify the behavior or the conduct of the person who violated the right. Third, you must show that the person was acting under "color of law" and finally that the violation of the right and any damages that stemmed from that was caused in a foreseeable and particular way by the conduct of the person acting under "color of law." The plaintiff must prove by a preponderance of the evidence, in other words that it is more likely than not that the defendant is legally responsible for the damages claimed by the plaintiff.

The Supreme Court case, *United States v. Classic* (1941), defined color of law as: "[m]isuse of power, possessed by virtue of state law and made possible only because the wrongdoer is clothed with the authority of state law, is action taken 'under color of' state law" (*United States v. Classic*, 1941, p. 326). Even if the person commits an act that was not authorized by that person's position, when the act is committed in the course of their official duties then it is considered under color of law. Private entities and individuals that contract with the government who willingly participate with the state in joint pursuits may also meet the requirements of acting under color of law.

Courts have interpreted the causal element requiring a connection between the conduct of the official and the harm to the plaintiff by requiring a showing that the harm was the result of a government entity's action that implemented a policy, regulation, decision, or local custom that was the reason or cause for the rights violation. For example, the courts have also extended this to mean that it is "an unconstitutional policy" not to train your staff when not doing so would result in the employee making a wrong or illegal decision. Courts have also extended liability to supervisors that directly participate with the employee in any of the conditions described that create harm.

Who Can Be Sued and Absolute and Qualified Immunity

Neither a state nor a state official in their official capacity can be sued under Section 1983. The Eleventh Amendment shields a state from suit in federal court unless the state consents to suit or waives its immunity. The Supreme Court, however, in *Monell v. Department of Social Services* (1978) held that local governments may be liable for damages when the local government implements an unconstitutional policy or regulation that is the basis for the plaintiff's rights violation. Therefore, local and municipal governments are in a different position than state governments with regard to liability and potential Section 1983 claims.

Individuals, as "persons" under the law, can be sued in their personal or their official capacity. When an official is being sued in their personal capacity this means that they are being held personally liable for an action taken under color of law. When an official is being sued in their official capacity it is the same as suing the local government body itself. In this case you must also prove that there is an official rule or custom that is the cause of the violation.

When you are sued as a government actor there are two possible defenses to the suit proceeding: absolute immunity and qualified immunity. Absolute immunity means that under the law you are "immune" from being sued for any act done in your official capacity despite your intention. Some examples of absolute immunity include the following: witnesses testifying in trials, legislators, prosecutors and other investigators and judges with judicial immunity. Qualified immunity means that a government actor will have immunity from being sued unless the court can find that there was a violation of clearly established constitutional or federal statutory right and it was clear that a "reasonable official" in the same situation would have known that the conduct was unlawful.

Potential Outcomes

If the case is not settled and the court does not grant summary judgment to either of the parties, there are three types of remedies possible from a successful Section 1983 claim: compensatory damages, injunctive relief, and declaratory relief. Once the plaintiff has proven that they were deprived of their rights, the plaintiff is entitled to nominal damages unless they can further prove actual damages. A person could be entitled to special damages by providing evidence of expenses such as medical or psychiatric expenses and lost wages. General damages may be awarded if there is evidence of pain and suffering or emotional distress. A person may be entitled to punitive damages if the person can prove that the defendant's conduct was recklessly callous or indifferent to the rights of others. Injunctive relief means that the court will issue an order or injunction that requires a person or government to stop a specific action or to take a certain action. Many times injunctive relief will include court supervision and oversight. Declaratory relief refers to a court's order clarifying the rights of a party under the law but not ordering specific action.

After reading this section you may think that you are potentially one of the individuals that may be sued under a Section 1983 claim. Social workers working for the state either directly or through joint state initiatives have been sued. Particularly in child protection cases, courts have held that Child Protective Service workers have qualified rather than absolute immunity. Aside from the ethical duty you owe your client to be legally literate, this is yet another reason that throughout the course of this book we have been advocating that social workers take a proactive approach to the law. It is critical that social workers have the skills to access and read state regulations that identify the duties of a social worker and the rights of clients in whatever area of practice you are working in whether it be substance abuse services or school social work. Our position is that the best way to reduce your own risk and liability is to be aware of and to assert the rights, entitlements, services, ethical mandates, and standards of practice due to your clients.

REFERENCES

20 Pa. Cons. Stat. § 5501.

20 Pa. Cons. Stat. § 5502.

405 ILCS § 1-119 (2010).

American Psychological Association. (2010). Guidelines for child custody evaluations in family law proceedings. *American Psychologist*, *65*(9), 863–867. https://doi.org/10.1037/a0021250

Axelson, T., & Gentile, J. (2024). Are child custody evaluations beneficial to family law judges? A study from the judicial perspective. *Family Court Review*, *62*(1), 194–211. https://doi.org/10.1111/fcre.12772

Bartels, S. J., Dums, A. R., Oxman, T. E., Schneider, L. S., Arean, P. A., Alexopoulos, G. S., & Jeste, D. V. (2003). Evidence-based practices in geriatric mental health care: An overview of systematic reviews and meta-analyses. *Psychiatric Clinics of North America*, *26*(4), 971–990. https://doi.org/10.1016/s0193-953x(03)00072-8

Bennett v. Jeffreys, 387 N.Y.S.2d 821 (N.Y. 1976).

Child Support Enforcement Act, 42 U.S.C. §§ 651–669b (1984).

Civil Rights Act of 1964, 88 Pub. L. No. 352, 78 Stat. 241 (1964).

Department of Housing and Urban Development v. Rucker, 535 U.S. 125 (2002).

Donovan, K., & Regehr, C. (2010). Elder abuse: Clinical, ethical and legal considerations in social work practice. *Clinical Social Work Journal*, *38*, 174–182. https://doi.org/10.1007/s10615-010-0269-2

Fair Housing Amendments Act, 100 Pub. L. No. 430, 102 Stat. 1619 (1988).

Fla. Stat. § 415.102(15) (2010).

Fla. Stat. § 415.102(3) (2010).

Fla. Stat. § 415.1111 (2010).

Housing Authority City of Los Angeles, Section VIII-A (2017).

Ind. Code § 12-10-3-2(a) (2016).

Ind. Code Ann., § 12-10-3-2 (2010).

Michigan Child Custody Act, Mich. Comp. Laws § 722.21 et seq. (1970).

Minn. Stat. ch. 518, § 518.17 (a)(4) (2023).

Monell v. Department of Social Services, 436 U.S. 658 (1978).

National Guardianship Association. (2022). *Standards of practice.* https://www.guardianship.org/wp-content/uploads/NGA-Standards-2022.pdf

N.J. Rev. Stat. § 30:4-27.12 (1987).

N.J. Rev. Stat. § 30:4-27.2(r) (2024).

National Association of Social Workers. (2021). *Code of Ethics of the National Association of Social Workers.* Author.

National Guardianship Association. (2022). *Standards of practice.* https://www.guardianship.org/wp-content/uploads/NGA-Standards-2022.pdf

Obergefell v. Hodges, 576 U.S. 644 (2015).

Official Code of Georgia title 44, c.7 (2023).

Ohio Rev. Code § 5101:2-20-12 (2021).

Or. Rev. Stat. § 124.050, 2022.

Saltzman, A., & Furman, D. (1999). *Law in social work practice.* Nelson-Hall.

Scott, H., Ankit, J., & Cogburn, M. (2023). *Behaviour modification.* StatPearls Publishing. https://www.ncbi.nlm.nih.gov/books/NBK459285/

Teaster, P., Wood, E., Karp, N., Lawrence, S., Schmidt, W. Jr., & Mendiondo, M. (2007). *Wards of the state: A national study of public guardianship.* https://www2.stetson.edu/law-review/wp-content/uploads/2022/02/37.1.06.Teaster.pdf

Tenn. Code § 36-3-610 (2010).

Tenn. Code § 36-3-601(1) (2023).

Tenn. Code § 36-3-601(5) (2023).
Tenn. Code § 36-3-602(b) (2023).
Tenn. Code § 36-3-605(a) (2023).
Testa, M., & West, S. (2010). Civil commitment in the United States. *Psychiatry* 7(10), 30–40. https://pubmed.ncbi.nlm.nih.gov/22778709/
Troxel v. Granville, 530 U.S. 57 (2000).
U.S. Department of Health and Human Services, Substance Abuse and Mental Health Administration. (2008). *Assertive community treatment evidence-based practice kit.* (SAMSHA Publication No. SMA08-4345). http://store.samhsa.gov/product/SMA08-4345
U.S. Department of Health and Human Services, Substance Abuse and Mental Health Administration. (2010a). *Integrated treatment for co-occurring disorders evidence-based practice kit.* (SAMSHA Publication No. SMA08-4367). http://store.samhsa.gov/product/SMA08-4367
U.S. Department of Health and Human Services, Substance Abuse and Mental Health Administration. (2010b). *Illness management and recovery evidence-based practice kit.* (SAMSHA Publication No. MA09-4463). http://store.samhsa.gov/product/SMA09-4463
United States v. Classic, 313 U.S. 299 (1941).

CHAPTER 10

The Intersection of Social Work and the Law in Criminal Proceedings

INTRODUCTION

In this chapter, we discuss what occurs during a criminal proceeding after an individual has been arraigned. You will learn about the issues that are decided at pretrial hearings, the trial itself, sentencing, and the rights of victims and defendants. You will also learn about working with clients postsentencing while they may be incarcerated, on probation or parole, or in a reentry program. You will also learn about the issues that are specific to victims of crimes and may arise during these phases of criminal proceedings. Finally, you will learn about the process for juvenile defendants in the juvenile justice system. Throughout this chapter, you will be introduced to some of the introductory knowledge and skills that will assist you as a social worker in understanding key decisions being made in the case, the legal context of those decisions, and how social work knowledge and practice can assist decision-makers and clients during the course of and after resolution of criminal and juvenile justice proceedings.

SOCIAL WORK AND CRIMINAL JUSTICE PROCEEDINGS

Throughout criminal justice proceedings, there are a number of ways social workers are involved in both the implicit and explicit contexts of practice. Forensic social workers working in the explicit context can be asked to do various assessments by lawyers and the court such as evaluations of competence to stand trial, risk assessment, mental health assessment, substance use assessment, assessment of the impact of the crime on the victim, preparation of a victim impact statement, and assessment at the time of sentencing of any factors that should be weighed when deciding on the severity of a sentence. Social workers can also assist attorneys in selecting jurors, preparing clients and witnesses to testify, developing evidence, supporting victims, and testifying in court.

As you learned in Chapter 1, the social work profession and those working in the implicit context should have serious concerns about the number of persons incarcerated in the United States, the effects of incarceration on large numbers of children and other family members, the quality and availability of criminal defense representation for indigent clients, and, most importantly, the research documenting the racial disparities that exist at every phase of criminal justice decision-making for both adults and juveniles.

Incarceration has been increasingly relied on to address a number of social and behavioral health problems, which has had a disparate impact on low-income people of color and individuals with disabilities as evidenced by the large numbers of individuals incarcerated for drug-related offenses, often with co-occurring mental health issues. The majority of people who are incarcerated are underemployed or unemployed and have low levels of educational attainment, many coming from and returning to neighborhoods and communities that are underresourced and underserved. Research has indicated strong connections with truancy, suspension, drop-out rates, expulsions, and juvenile delinquency. In a study conducted by the National Association for the Advancement of Colored People (NAACP), researchers collected data and profiled six cities showing how increases in prison costs have undermined educational opportunities for low-income individuals (NAACP, 2011). Indeed, the link between economic inequality and mass incarceration has been documented repeatedly even with the overall decrease in the prison population, especially since Black individuals in the United States are imprisoned at five times the rate of White individuals (Ghandnoosh, 2023). The link between criminal justice policies and the perpetuation of poverty should be of great concern for rights-based social workers whether they are working in the implicit or explicit context.

In response to overcrowded prison conditions, a struggling economic environment, the restorative justice movement, concern about low-income individual's access to justice, and high rates of rearrest and recidivism, federal and state governments have pivoted to identify and implement interprofessional, collaborative, evidence-based interventions that address the underlying conditions that increase the risk of crime and delinquency. These assessments allow decision-makers to identify risk, increasing the ability of criminal justice systems to provide alternatives to detention and incarceration and to expand the community-based options available at the plea bargaining, sentencing, and reentry phases of the process. Other scholars and advocates have promoted prison abolition as the only means to address the systemic issues plaguing the carceral system (Cho, 2023).

Collaborative Opportunities

Currently, there are many collaborative opportunities in both the implicit and explicit legal contexts for social workers to work in a strength-based and preventive way to disrupt the trajectory of criminal justice system involvement and corresponding links to poverty for both adults and juveniles. Problem-solving courts that have a focus on treatment for substance abuse and mental health are another example of social work knowledge and expertise driving innovation. These courts use social workers to conduct assessments and provide case management. You will learn much more about the ways these alternative venues work and the role of social workers in Chapter 11. As we hope you can see by now, social work knowledge and skills you already possess can be effectively applied in any legal context if you understand what legal decisions are being made and what legal standards will be used for decision-making.

Social workers, who are experts in conducting assessments and developing individualized intervention plans, can collect data about each of the risk and protective factors that may exist on all system levels and can develop evidence-based plans to decrease risk and promote resilience. Effective social work–intervention plans allow for clients to take personal responsibility for their criminal or delinquent behavior while simultaneously identifying and addressing the environmental and systemic factors that led to their entry into the system in the first place, negatively influencing outcomes, and mitigating against successful rehabilitation. Plans that proactively identify and address these external obstacles, including the issue of racial disparity, increase the possibility of engagement and motivation to change on the part of the client and address concerns about community safety.

This approach can also be activated preventively in many implicit social work settings in communities where there are high rates of incarceration. As an example, social workers working in underresourced and low-performing schools in low-income communities can research and identify the risk and protective factors in their community and implement preventive interventions relating to gang involvement, violence, knowledge of the law, and respect for person and property. Social workers working in employment programs should understand and be able to proactively address the special needs and concerns of those convicted of a crime when seeking to reenter the workforce and obtain economic security.

Social workers working in child welfare agencies should be aware of the concerns and implications for incarcerated parents. In practice, this could include informing parents who are incarcerated of their right to visit with their child. If Ms. Jones were incarcerated after the birth of her son or if her child were older, a social worker would ensure that she knew of her right to visit with her child, maintain communication, and participate in any meetings or court appearances concerning his care. Proactive social workers working with incarcerated parents, particularly when a crime involves substance abuse, should communicate with correctional staff to ensure the parent's right to mental health and substance abuse treatment is met, as well as participation in education and training programs that enhance their capacity to resume parenting when released. These are only a few examples of what social workers can do if they are aware of the implicit legal context that comprises an important part of the world of their clients.

Across the country, public defender offices have embraced the model of holistic advocacy and reframed their advocacy efforts to address the collateral consequences of the criminal justice system and to prevent recidivism. As we discussed in earlier chapters, holistic defense is defined as an interdisciplinary team that prioritizes meeting the legal and social service needs of clients through client-centered advocacy, frequent communication and collaboration, and awareness and connection to the local community. In support of this model, many public defender offices have fully integrated social workers into the legal office and developed programs with social workers that address the underlying conditions and causes of criminal behavior, as well as the emotional and social concerns of clients—things that attorneys cannot address while trying to ensure the protection of client rights and to craft an effective and zealous defense.

The use of social workers supports public defenders in their desire and ethical mandate as attorneys to ensure more effective representation during the investigation, trial, sentencing, and postconviction phases. Social workers in these roles do not just provide individual services to clients but also set up relationships and linkages with community-based service and treatment providers, developing a network of services that can be accessed at various points of the advocacy process for clients. Social workers in the community who are aware that their client may have a public defender can and should offer themselves as a resource and in this way increase the opportunity for clients to access real justice.

Studies of social work services in public defender offices demonstrate that social work intervention expands the options available for clients, attorneys, and other legal decision-makers and improves the quality of legal representation (Anderson et al., 2019; Matei et al., 2021). In public defender offices, the state and local legislators that provide funding for these services have acknowledged the invaluable contribution of social workers. Many of these offices have conducted evaluation research that utilizes a cost–benefit analysis to show state and local officials how much money can be saved through social work intervention in public defender offices. An evaluation of a pilot social work program in Kentucky that placed four social workers in public defender offices showed significant cost savings to the state through social workers developing plans that prevented the incarceration of nonviolent offenders and facilitated substance abuse and mental health treatment (Walker et al., 2016).

Finally, many of the evidence-based interventions being promoted in both prisons and community corrections are based on models of risk and protective factors that have been identified in the research as contributing to criminal and delinquent behaviors (Warren, 2007). "Strength-based practice" is being promoted as a means to engage family support during incarceration as a behavioral management tool for correctional personnel. For example, programs may use ecomaps and genograms to provide case management and develop plans for reentry. Motivational interviewing is considered to be an evidence-based tool for use by probation and parole officers. Each of these interventions is firmly based in social work practice and in some cases foundational to social work education and training.

When learning about the path of a criminal case, it can be helpful for social workers, regardless of whether they are working in the implicit or explicit legal context, to consider how a social worker who is fully embedded in a public defender office would collaborate on the legal team and support the client in achieving their goals, not only in the context of their immediate criminal matter but also in more long-term aspects of their well-being and stability. With this framework, you will be able to expand your notions of social work practice for clients impacted by the criminal justice system and identify new areas for collaboration, intervention, and advocacy.

THE PATH OF A CRIMINAL CASE IN STATE COURT

The body of statutes and laws regarding criminal proceedings, definitions of crimes, penalties for crimes, the rights of victims and defendants, and court procedures can be found in state statutes, tribal codes, court rules, and the caselaw of your state. Again, we recommend that as you are reading this chapter, you refer to your state and tribal court website and access the court rules for criminal and juvenile proceedings and the state's criminal codes found in state statutes. State statutes and criminal codes define crimes and lay out the elements of a specific crime that must be met for the prosecution to prove its case, what defenses are allowed and when they must be presented, sentencing rules and guidelines, definitions for conditions such as mental illness or intoxication that may or may not be used as defenses, and the rights of victims and offenders. This section also covers such topics as how and what evidence can be presented, the burden of proof in criminal matters, procedures in the event of certain sentences such as the death penalty, and the rights of defendants throughout the criminal court process.

With regard to tribal justice systems, it is important to remember that the structure of many tribal justice systems is similar to that of the criminal justice system that you may be familiar with in your county or city. However, some tribes implement a blend of procedures that incorporate the tribal community's worldview, traditions, and perspective. Tribal systems include a law enforcement component, prosecution, judiciary, and corrections. Rules and procedures are similar and follow laws or codes enacted by a tribe. Many tribes do not have public defenders, but defendants have a right to an attorney or a lay advocate. In the tribal justice system, judges and advocates are often tribe members and not attorneys. Increasingly, the federal government has sought to limit tribal control of their criminal justice systems by imposing sentencing restrictions. The tribal justice system is very complex because of questions regarding whether the tribe, the state, or the federal government has jurisdiction; whether or not there is shared jurisdiction; whether all the persons involved in the crime are Native Americans and thus treated differently; and the nature of the offense. For example, the federal government has retained authority to prosecute certain felony crimes. The tribal justice system is a complex topic that cannot be addressed in full in the confines of this chapter or textbook. If you are working with or within tribal communities, we encourage you to seek out additional resources and research available at both the Tribal Law and Policy Institute's Tribal Justice Clearinghouse and the Bureau of Indian Affairs.

INVESTIGATION AND DISCOVERY

Regardless of the charges, an investigation is an integral part of the Criminal Court process. The police generally conduct an investigation prior to arresting an individual, and the district attorney or prosecutor will generally continue that investigation throughout the pendency of the case as part of their preparation of the criminal case for trial or for plea negotiation. The prosecution's investigation will include speaking with witnesses and collateral sources, including any victims, family members, and experts that may contribute to their understanding of a particular issue in the case. The prosecution has an obligation to provide the defense attorney with any and all evidence that they have obtained. This could include the reports filed by the police when Ms. Jones was arrested, lab tests conducted on any alleged drugs recovered from the scene, and the statements of any witnesses or victims.

As a result of the Supreme Court case *Brady v. Maryland* (1963), the prosecution also has the obligation to provide defense counsel with any evidence that tends toward the innocence of the defendant or could reduce the punishment for the defendant at the sentencing phase. Evidence that suggests the innocence of the defendant is also referred to as exculpatory evidence; evidence that might reduce the severity or duration of sentencing is referred to as mitigating evidence. Examples of these types of evidence could include when the prosecution has made a deal with a witness not to prosecute the witness for criminal behavior in exchange for their testimony or when there is evidence that the victim's description of the defendant does not match the physical features of the defendant. In short, any material evidence that would tend to show the innocence of the defendant, even if only the prosecution or the police know it, must be turned over to the defense attorney in order to ensure that the defendant receives due process under the law.

The defense attorney will conduct their own investigation as well by speaking with witnesses, victims, and the client to determine what the possible defenses to the charges may be. The defense attorney will try to gather as much information early on from the prosecutor so that they know what evidence will be presented at trial to prove the defendant's guilt. Based on that review of the discovery, the defense attorney will investigate other theories of defense and often talk to collateral sources including other witnesses and family members. Often, defense attorneys and public defender officers will employ investigators responsible for further investigating the alleged criminal activity and assisting the defense attorney with trial strategy and preparation.

Social workers may be contacted throughout an investigation by either the defense or the prosecution if they work in a hospital or clinic setting and interacted with the victim after the alleged criminal activity. The defense attorney may also contact social workers that have been working regularly with the defendant, such as Ms. Jones's substance abuse counselor, with the goal of gathering evidence that supports their theory of the case and portrays the defendant in a different light than the prosecution. This initial contact may be by phone or e-mail correspondence or by a legal subpoena. A social worker in this situation would want to discuss the potential contact with their client and ensure that they are maintaining confidentiality and seeking explicit permission from their client before any disclosures not court ordered.

A defense attorney or their investigator can speak to the complainant or the victim about what happened and whether or not they wish to pursue charges against the defendant. A defense attorney may also contact the complainant or victim of the alleged crime as part of the ongoing investigation to assess whether there may have been possible defenses that could potentially result in a charge of a lesser crime or no charge at all. A prosecutor may continue to speak with witnesses to determine whether their testimony will be credible and helpful for the prosecution. You should note that this is different from a civil proceeding, because the prosecutor is not the lawyer for the individual victim or victims, but rather represents the state or local municipality. Therefore, there is no ethical bar to the defense attorney speaking with the victim or complaining witness because they are not, by definition, a represented party. An ethical attorney and any other employees working on behalf of the attorney including social workers and investigators would need to clearly identify themselves and their position in the defense attorney's office.

A social worker in the explicit legal context could work with either the prosecution or the defense attorney as an employee of those offices. When working with the prosecution, social workers are sometimes called to assist with interviewing and providing services to victims of crimes. Whether this role is for the defense or the prosecution, social workers can assess a client's level of cognitive understanding, memory, and ability to read and write to help the assigned attorney determine the best way to include the defendant or victim in their representation and potentially to elicit testimony from them as witnesses. A social worker can also begin to gather information about the person's circumstances that not only can shed light on the circumstances surrounding the person's arrest or victimization, but can later be useful during plea bargaining or in the event of a conviction, the sentencing phase of a trial.

As you learned in Chapter 8, social workers working with either the prosecution or the defense can also use cognitive interviewing techniques and can teach clients to use cognitive behavioral techniques to calm themselves when they are triggered or stressed and traumatized by their experience during legal proceedings. These techniques can be utilized prior to being interviewed by an attorney or the police in order to increase the eliciting of details during the interview. A client can also utilize these skills of self-regulation, such as deep breathing, during an interview if they become upset. Finally, these relaxation skills can also be used after an interview to center and calm the client before they leave and go back to their home or workplace.

MOTION PRACTICE

It is important for social workers working in the implicit context to listen to clients' narratives about their experiences throughout the criminal justice process and to direct a client to speak to their attorney about an incident or event that may give rise to a concern about that client's rights. Defense attorneys can file a number of legal motions in the beginning of a case that can ultimately protect clients' rights, and social workers may learn of the rights violation from the client or from their practice with the individual.

As one example, the client has the legal right not to have any evidence that was illegally obtained by the police or prosecution presented against them at trial. This evidence should be suppressed or kept out of the trial or plea negotiation process. In many cases, the prosecution may not be able to prove their case at trial if the illegally obtained evidence is not presented to the judge or jury. Keep in mind that the illegal evidence could include statements or admissions from the defendant or property seized from the crime scene such as weapons, money, or drugs. A motion to suppress evidence would be filed if there were an argument that the evidence was obtained illegally. The attorney would make a legal determination about which evidence may have been illegally obtained and then raise that claim through motion practice in the trial. As we have mentioned throughout, this part of the criminal case process—drafting legal motions and determining legal case strategy before trial—is legal and squarely within the purview of the attorney and their training. It is important for social workers to understand that motion practice is a critical piece of the representation for a defendant as well as for the prosecution.

PLEA NEGOTIATION

A *plea* is the legal term for the answer that the defendant makes to the criminal complaint charges. The pleas available in Criminal Court include not guilty, guilty, not guilty by reason of insanity, and in some jurisdictions, a no contest or nolo contendere plea which means that the defendant is not contesting the charges but is also not admitting guilt. Generally, clients are advised to plead not guilty when the case is first arraigned. As you might have surmised from the initial overview of the process, a defense attorney has limited information at the inception of a case and therefore a limited sense of the sufficiency of the prosecution's case and the relative strength of any potential defenses. A defendant can always change their plea to guilty to the criminal charges in the complaint at any point in a criminal case to avoid going to trial. The plea negotiation phase of a criminal case refers to the discussions between the prosecution and the defense about charges the defendant would plead guilty to resolve the case without going to trial. For example, Ms. Jones's attorney may attempt to negotiate for a plea agreement that would have her plead guilty to the lesser misdemeanor charge in exchange for having the more serious felony charge dismissed.

The decision to offer a plea agreement rests solely with the prosecutor although defense counsel can negotiate and suggest certain resolutions based on their assessment of the strength of the prosecution's case. Social workers for the defendant can use much of the information that they have already collected prior to arraignment (discussed in Chapter 7), to assist the defense attorney in their discussions with the prosecutor for a particular plea. If this were Ms. Jones's first criminal offense, the social worker would provide proof that Ms. Jones has been participating in substance use treatment and is pregnant. In many cases, a report from the social worker about the defendant's prior history and current activities or level of functioning related to the concerns of the prosecution or the victim can be instrumental in negotiating the best legal outcome for a client.

The vast majority of criminal cases are resolved without going to trial because defendants accept plea agreements at any point in the proceeding prior to trial. This is due in part to the overburdened nature of the Criminal Court in most jurisdictions, where the system would not have the resources for the majority of cases to proceed to a full criminal trial. This creates a tension that social workers should be mindful of when working on either side of the criminal justice system. Increasing caseloads and pressure to resolve cases without going to trial can certainly play a role in how and when clients are counseled to accept pleas. Clients will also have a number of factors that will play into their decision-making about whether to accept a plea including the impact of the criminal case on their family, employment, or education and their development if they are minors. Social workers working with criminal defendants should bear those additional considerations in mind in their assessment and advocacy. A social worker can play a critical role in this process by helping the client identify the collateral consequences of any plea and the impact that might have on their goals.

The plea negotiation process removes the ultimate decision about a defendant's sentence from the judge, who is presumed to be impartial. As we have covered before, the judge is supposed to be an impartial actor in this system and is responsible for overseeing the proceedings and ensuring that the laws and procedures of their particular court are followed. In contrast, neither the prosecutor nor the defense attorney is impartial because they are representing the interests of their client, either the defendant or the government. During plea negotiations, the prosecution proposes not only the specific charges that the defendant would plead guilty to but also the potential sentence that would be imposed as a result of that plea. In some cases, the judge may also suggest a possible resolution to the parties and would ultimately be responsible for accepting the terms of any plea agreement.

Social workers can assist defendants and victims with raising concerns with the plea negotiation process to their attorney. What is important to remember is that accepting a plea means that an individual is also waiving significant constitutional rights such as the right to a trial where allegations must be proven beyond a reasonable doubt. One concern raised by scholars and critics of plea bargaining is that because it is used so frequently and that everyone, such as the police, prosecutors, and defense attorneys, know that this is the practice, it can result in less than thorough investigations (Lynch, 2003). Indeed, a report from the American Bar Association's Plea Bargain Task Force found that 98% of cases resolve by plea bargains in the federal criminal court system and refers to trials as legal artifacts (Johnson, 2023). Another argument is that plea bargaining is coercive because the state has much more bargaining power than the individual and can lead to innocent individuals pleading guilty (O'Hear, 2008). In this instance, the amount and quality of information gathered during discovery and investigation is significant currency that social workers may be able to provide to support their clients and ensure the fairness of the process. Advocates have called for a more robust and transparent process for plea bargains and additional data on racial and ethnic disparities during the plea bargaining process. A study conducted by the Equal Justice Initiative in 2017 examined over 30,000 cases in Wisconsin over several years and found significant racial bias in plea deals. Data specifically showed that Black clients in comparison to White clients were much more likely to be convicted of the highest charge, and less likely than Whites to have a crime reduced or dropped (Berdejó, 2018).

Successful plea bargaining depends in part on both the advocacy of the defense attorney and the access to resources including investigators and expert witnesses for the defense team. At the misdemeanor level, the volume of cases is so large that fewer resources at this level are available to create alternative plans for clients and prevent criminal convictions. As we learned in Chapter 7, the number of prior convictions is related to later sentencing severity, particularly for defendants who may be disproportionately represented in the criminal justice system. Intervention and assistance to defense counsel by social workers at this level can interrupt the cycle of racial disparity.

Felonies as we know are more serious charges, and as we have learned most felony cases are resolved through plea bargaining. Plea bargaining for felonies is also a key intervention point when addressing racial disparity because the majority of felons are low-income persons represented by public defenders who, similar to misdemeanor cases, do not always have significant access to expert witnesses, treatment and service providers, or community resources. Social workers in both the implicit and explicit context can assist in leveling the playing field by providing the defense attorney with information about referrals and services, alternatives to incarceration programs, and provide case management that can assist in the negotiation of a more fair sentence for the defendant that is designed to target the environmental and risk factors that brought the person into contact with the system in the first place.

When determining whether or not to counsel a client about accepting a plea bargain, the defense attorney will consider the results of the investigation and the evidence that the prosecution provided and plans to present at trial. The defense attorney would also weigh the various defenses available at trial to determine the probability of having a jury or judge find the defendant not guilty of the alleged crimes. A social worker with the defense team can assess the defendant's ability to handle the stress of a trial, as well as the impact of a trial on their relationships, responsibilities, and commitments in other areas of their life. The social worker and the defense attorney can also counsel the defendant about the long-term consequences of deciding to accept a plea or to go to trial.

It is important for both the attorney and social worker to understand that clients have very unique and individualized reasons for taking a plea or not, particularly if they believe that they have done nothing wrong and may be frightened about being more severely punished if they go through a trial. It is also significant to remember in some instances that a client may want to take responsibility for a crime they may have committed and plead guilty for that reason. The key point here is that it is essential that a client's motivation and decision regarding a plea is fully explored and that they are fully informed and know what rights are being waived and what risks or benefits may come from their decision. As you might imagine, it is especially important for the social worker to foster a trusting relationship with the client and provide multiple opportunities for the client to discuss their options. As you learned in Chapter 3, the attorney is ethically bound to accept the client's ultimate decision on whether to proceed to trial or accept a settlement offer. Therefore, this decision is squarely within the purview of the client to make and as such, rights-based social workers will want to ensure that clients have full information and a meaningful process to inform that decision-making.

Generally, during plea negotiations, the defendant would be offered a lower sentence or lesser charge than the defendant was originally charged with in the complaint. In many cases, the defendant may be offered a violation, for example, of disorderly conduct, when they are charged with a relatively minor misdemeanor offense. A violation is not considered to be a criminal conviction, and cannot result in any extended period of incarceration. In some instances, the violation requires that the defendant pay a fine of some amount.

If Ms. Jones were offered a plea to the lesser misdemeanor charge of possession, as opposed to the felony, her attorney would likely counsel her on the collateral consequences of this conviction. You will learn more about the collateral consequences of involvement in the criminal justice system later in this chapter, but this essentially means the impact of a criminal conviction on other aspects of an individual's life including employment, housing, family unity, and education. If Ms. Jones makes an admission in Criminal Court that she possessed illegal drugs, she may be negatively impacting her Family Court case where the ultimate issue is whether her substance abuse caused her to neglect her son placing him at risk of harm. Her statements made in open Criminal Court would be admissible as sworn statements in Family Court. Furthermore, the conviction for a drug offense may cause problems with her receipt of public housing as you learned in Chapter 9, and may also have negative consequences for her ability to secure employment, maintain any employment licenses, or receive public benefits. Many employers request information about an applicant's criminal conviction history, and Ms. Jones would have to report that she was convicted of a misdemeanor charge. Finally, if Ms. Jones was not a citizen, regardless of whether she had legal documentation to reside in the United States, her plea, even to the lesser misdemeanor charge that might allow her to avoid any incarceration, may also make her subject to deportation proceedings or immigration detention. It is critical that clients are made aware of all the collateral consequences of accepting a plea agreement as part of the counseling process.

Another possible resolution is an adjournment in contemplation of dismissal (ACD) rather than proceeding to trial. With this option, the case is adjourned for a set period of time usually between 6 and 12 months. During that period of time, the client has to follow the order of the court to refrain from any illegal activity or further arrests. Once the time period has passed, the case is dismissed in its entirety. Social workers can assist defense attorneys in understanding whether this is a realistic option for clients and counseling clients on the benefits and disadvantages of accepting the ACD.

When determining a position in plea negotiations, the prosecutor also considers the results of the investigation and evidence gathering, in addition to the strength of their witness's testimony including the testimony of police officers or victim. Victims in many states have rights to be informed and give feedback to the prosecutor during this process and in some states, address the court either orally or in writing before the entry of the plea. A social worker can play an important role in plea negotiations when working with the prosecutor by advising on the victim's ability to testify in front of a jury or judge. In California, the state constitution provides victims with a number of enumerated rights including the right for notice from the prosecutor of certain events, to be treated with fairness and respect, and "to be heard, upon request, at any proceeding, including any delinquency proceeding, involving a post-arrest release decision, plea, sentencing, post-conviction release decision, or any proceeding in which a right of the victim is at issue" (Cal. Const. Art. 1 § 28 [b][8]). It is important for the prosecutor and the victim's social worker to understand that the victim may not have a clear understanding of the plea negotiation process or their role in it. The victim should be informed by the prosecutor and social worker of the pros and cons from their perspective of offering this plea, and be given an opportunity to voice their concerns or disagreements with the prosecution's proposal.

In order to be an effective victim advocate, it is crucial to research whether or not it is up to the victim to initiate action or input in your state, or whether the state statute requires that the victim's statement be attached to the court records and be considered by the court when approving the plea. For example, while California has a victim's bill of rights which states that the victim has a right to receive notice of a sentencing hearing, the victim must notify the Board of Prisons if they wish to speak at a parole hearing. In addition, a social worker working with a victim of crime would want to know whether a victim is entitled to any compensation and the process for applying for victim compensation. The federal Office of Victims of Crime (www.ovc.ojp.gov) provides an overview of each state's victim services including compensation programs.

TRIAL

If a defendant does not accept a plea offer or plead guilty, then the case proceeds to trial before a judge or a jury of their peers. As you remember from Chapter 8, the trial will include evidence presented by both the prosecution and the defense through live witnesses, records, and physical evidence. Those witnesses are subject to cross-examination by the opposing side and throughout the trial. Throughout the trial, the attorneys on both sides make legal arguments about what evidence is properly admissible through objections and written motions to the oral testimony and submitted documentary evidence. The trial begins with opening statement by both the prosecution and the defense to introduce what evidence will be presented and why the defendant is or is not guilty. At the end of the trial, both sides will make closing arguments as to why the prosecution has or has not met its burden of proving that the defendant is guilty beyond a reasonable doubt.

All criminal trials, whether they are before a jury or a judge, have the same standard of proof. The prosecution, who bears the burden of proof in a criminal trial, must prove the allegations in the complaint beyond a reasonable doubt. This is the highest standard of proof, because any reasonable doubt as to the defendant's guilt means that the prosecution has not met their burden. If the prosecution is not able to prove a charge beyond a reasonable doubt, then the charge must be dismissed. The standard is higher than in civil proceedings precisely because the result of a conviction could be incarceration, or the deprivation of the individual's liberty.

It is not unusual for a judge or jury to determine that the prosecution has proven one charge but not others enumerated in the complaint. When proving that the defendant committed the alleged crime, the prosecution must establish all of the elements of the offense that are defined in the text of the statute. For social work practitioners, the most important aspect of elements of a crime is the idea that many crimes have an element that requires that the person committing the crime has the ability or capacity to possess a particular state of mind that is required for the commission of that crime. This is important because in the next section a person's capacity at the time they committed the crime is important to several defenses that, under the law, a defendant can use to mitigate their culpability for committing a particular crime. Social workers should be aware of these defenses as they are frequently in possession of information that can speak to a person's state of mind and various internal and external conditions that may have an impact on how a person is thinking and feeling.

DEFENSES

When preparing for a trial, one of the most important decisions for the defense attorney is what defense will be presented to the criminal charges at trial. In criminal trials, the defense is usually the "theory" of the criminal case for the defense. A social worker can be particularly helpful in determining the defense strategy by providing information from their assessment and work with the client, as well as information gathering from collateral sources. Some potential defenses include innocence, misidentification, self-defense, duress, and not guilty by reason of insanity. Social workers may be called to testify as both an expert and a fact witness during trials where some defenses are being argued.

An innocence defense could include presenting evidence that the defendant was not at the scene of the crime or was misidentified by the victim or complaining witness. A self-defense strategy would include evidence that the defendant was not acting criminally with intent to hurt the victim, but rather was defending themselves against criminal or violent behavior on the part of the victim. For example, in many cases involving domestic violence, the defense strategy may be that the defendant was actually the victim in the situation and was fighting back in order to protect themselves. Many states allow expert testimony explaining "battered woman's syndrome" and how it can provide a reason or show cause for the victim to behave in this way.

An Example of a Legal Defense: Duress

In some cases of interpersonal violence, the defense of duress may be used. This defense means that the person only committed the crime because they were under threat of physical harm or injury by another person if they did not commit the crime. As with all criminal codes and laws, certain defenses are also defined in state criminal codes. As an example, in Colorado the legal standard for duress is:

> A person may not be convicted of an offense, other than a Class 1 felony, based upon conduct in which he engaged at the direction of another person because of the use or threatened use of unlawful force upon him or upon another person, which force or threatened force thereof a reasonable person in his situation would have been unable to resist. (Colo. Rev. Stat. § 18-1-708, 2010)

Consider that, in the case of Ms. Jones, the social worker discovers during assessment that Ms. Jones's boyfriend and Matthew's father was physically and emotionally abusive to her. The social worker further learns that her boyfriend would frequently ask Ms. Jones to make deliveries of packages for him and one time when she refused, twisted her wrist causing a fracture. As part of this disclosure, she relates that if she refused again he told her that he would punch her in the stomach and kill the baby. In this instance, the attorney would consider a potential defense that Ms. Jones was acting under duress and therefore should not be found guilty of the alleged criminal activity. At trial, the attorney might offer testimony to show that Ms. Jones did not have the capacity to form intent to sell the drugs because she was acting under duress from her boyfriend. The duress could be evidenced by any medical or police reports and testimony from the community-based social worker to whom Ms. Jones disclosed the domestic abuse. Based on her history of interpersonal violence and her previous physical injury, it would be reasonable for Ms. Jones to be unable to refuse the request.

There are other defenses related to a client's capacity or mental health that social workers should familiarize themselves with in the event that they are working with someone who has been arrested for a crime. Social workers may be called upon particularly when the defense involves an issue of the client's competence or mental health. A defendant may raise the defense of not guilty by reason of insanity, meaning that at the time of the crime the defendant was severely mentally ill and therefore cannot be held criminally liable for their conduct. Another defense that that might be raised depending on the state is diminished mental capacity. In some states, voluntary intoxication, although not a defense to a crime, may be allowed when it is relevant to negate the evidence of a specific intent if the specific intent is an element of the crime the person is charged with as stated in California's penal code which allows "evidence of voluntary intoxication ... solely on the issue of whether or not the defendant actually formed a required specific intent" (Cal. Penal Code, § 22, 2024).

In these situations, the court would require a forensic evaluation to determine the mental status and degree of illness at the time of the alleged criminal activity. As we saw in Chapter 9, state statutes, in this case the state criminal codes, include definitions and standards that can assist a social worker in knowing what to look for, what information is particularly important to collect, and what needs to be proven in order to meet a legal standard regarding the definition of mental state.

The Insanity Defense: Evolving Legal Standard

It is important to know that despite the enormous attention to the insanity defense, it is also the least frequently used and least successful defense. The legal standard used to define and prove insanity has evolved over time because both "insanity" and the circumstances under which it can be used as a defense are very difficult to define. States vary in the standards that they apply but there are generally four tests or some combination of the four that form the basis for the state statutes.

The M'Naghten rule, first defined in 1834 in England, refers to the test to prove insanity where a person must have some defect of the mind that results in a defect of reason that makes them unable to appreciate that what they were doing was wrong. The criticism of this test was that it focused only on cognitive ability thus excluding those persons who have a mental illness characterized by severe compulsions and inability to control their impulses. The "Irresistible Impulse" test expanded the standard to include those conditions when a defendant could tell right from wrong but the mental condition made it impossible for the person to control their impulses and behaviors. The American Law Institute (ALI) developed a new test when it was also developing a model penal code. This test encompasses the features of the previous tests and requires that the diagnosis of the mental disease or defect be a medical diagnosis. All of the federal courts and many of the state courts have adopted this rule (Rottman & Strickland, 2004).

Under the ALI test a person is not responsible for their criminal offense if, at the time of the crime as a result of a mental illness or mental defect, the person lacks capacity to appreciate the criminal nature of the behavior or to make the behavior conform to following the law. Although many states are using the ALI test, it is important to check your state's criminal code regarding the insanity defense. In fact, some states, such as Montana, have dropped the insanity defense entirely. In Montana, evidence of mental illness can only be used to show that the requisite intent to commit the crime was not present, with the code stating that "[e]vidence that the defendant suffered from a mental disease or disorder or developmental disability is admissible to prove that the defendant did or did not have a state of mind that is an element of the offense" (Mont. Code 46-14-102, 2023). As you can see, some states make a finding of criminal liability and mental illness. This means that in those states, persons can be incarcerated and receive mental health treatment in prison or they may be involuntarily committed to a psychiatric facility and when improved, are then sent moved to prison. State statutes also identify tests that must be met in order for the offender to be released when they have been committed to a psychiatric facility.

An Example of a Legal Standard: Insanity and Diminished Capacity

Using Colorado's laws as our example, we can see that the statute uses a combination of the M'Naughten and Irresistible Impulse rules. The statute also makes a clear distinction between extreme feeling states and impulses directly related to a mental illness. In Colorado, the same definition is used to determine a state of "diminished capacity," which in Colorado could be used to provide evidence not about guilt or innocence but that the person did not have the capacity to form the mental intent that is required as an element in various criminal charges (Colo. Rev. Stat. § 18-1-803, 2010). The following is the statutory definition of the test that must be met for an insanity defense and evidence for diminished capacity (Colo. Rev. Stat. § 16-8-101.5, 2010):

a. A person who is so diseased or defective in mind at the time of the commission of the act as to be incapable of distinguishing right from wrong with respect to that act is not accountable; except that care should be taken not to confuse such mental disease or defect with moral obliquity, mental depravity, or passion growing out of anger, revenge, hatred, or other motives and kindred evil conditions, for, when the act is induced by any of these causes, the person is accountable to the law. Or

b. A person who suffered from a condition of mind caused by mental disease or defect that prevented the person from forming a culpable mental state that is an essential element of a crime charged, but care should be taken not to confuse such mental disease or defect with moral obliquity, mental depravity, or passion growing out of anger, revenge, hatred, or other motives and kindred evil conditions because, when the act is induced by any of these (1) The applicable test of insanity shall because, the person is accountable to the law.

The statute goes on to define what may not be considered and rules out voluntary intoxication due to the use of substances (Colo. Rev. Stat. § 16-8-101.5, 2010):

a. "Diseased or defective in mind" does not refer to an abnormality manifested only by repeated criminal or otherwise antisocial conduct.

b. "Mental disease or defect" includes only those severely abnormal mental conditions that grossly and demonstrably impair a person's perception or understanding of reality and that are not attributable to the voluntary ingestion of alcohol or any other psychoactive substance but does not include an abnormality manifested only by repeated criminal or otherwise antisocial conduct.

In Colorado, psychiatrists and psychologists are authorized to conduct evaluations regarding the mental status of a defendant. Again it is important to remember that a diagnosis of mental illness alone is not enough; there must be evidence that the mental disorder is causally connected to the lack of a specific intent, not just an overreaction or misperception. The job of the witness is to explain the causal connection. Although in this state social workers may not be evaluators, the statute allows that both the prosecution and the defense can call lay witnesses, opening the door for testimony by social workers. The law allows, "witnesses not specially trained in psychiatry or psychology may testify as to their observations of a of the defendant's actions and conduct and as to conversations that they have had with him bearing upon his mental condition and shall be permitted to give their opinions or conclusions regarding the mental condition of the defendant" (Colo. Rev. Stat. § 16-8-109, 2016). Under this provision, social workers would be allowed to testify about facts they have that relate to the client's condition.

Competence to Stand Trial

In contrast, the issue of a defendant's competence may arise if there is a concern on the part of any of the parties or the judge, that the defendant is not competent to stand trial. In this scenario, the defendant would have to demonstrate that they are unable to understand the criminal court process; for example, the charges that are being brought against them and that they are unable to assist their attorney in the representation. The Supreme Court laid the foundation for evaluating competence stating that the defendant must have "sufficient present ability to consult with his lawyer with a reasonable degree of rational understanding—and ... has a rational as well as factual understanding of the proceedings against him" (*Dusky v. United States,* 1960, p. 402).

This standard for competence reflects back to the requirement of due process for every defendant in order to ensure a fair and just trial. It would be difficult to imagine how an individual not competent to stand trial could understand the consequences of accepting a plea agreement, proceeding to trial, testifying in their own defense, refusing to testify in their own defense, and assisting with the cross-examination of witnesses. Each of these decisions has a profound impact on the criminal justice process, especially in light of the severe consequences possible in a criminal trial. As a result, every state has developed its own rules for competency evaluations detailing what needs to be included in an evaluation and who is able to conduct the evaluations. As you learned in Chapter 8, there has been increasing acceptance of the admissibility of social work testimony regarding competence to stand trial and the use of social workers to perform competency evaluations (Siegel, 2008).

As mentioned, individual states have different rules and laws related to who may conduct competency evaluations, who may raise the issue of competency, procedures for hearings that make a determination about competency, what happens when someone is found incompetent, and procedures for what are referred to as *restoration hearings* or the process for determining whether someone who was determined incompetent has returned to a state of competency. Staying with our example of Colorado, we discover by reading the definitions that only a licensed psychologist or psychiatrist with specific forensic training can perform a competency evaluation (Colo. Rev. Stat. § 16-8.5-101, 2010). A judge, defense attorney, or prosecutor may all raise the question of competency, and an evaluation will be ordered and a preliminary hearing will be held. The judge in this state will make a finding that the defendant is either competent or incompetent to proceed. If no one disagrees with the finding at this hearing, a final determination will be made. If one of the parties disagrees, a second evaluation and hearing may be held (Colo. Rev. Stat. § 16-8.5-103, 2010).

The important statutory definitions relevant to social workers who do competency hearings or social workers working in the implicit context who have real concerns about their client's ability to fully comprehend what is happening to them include: the meaning of competence to proceed, incompetence to proceed, mental disability, and developmental disability, all of which are located at Colo. Rev. Stat. § 16-8.5-101 (2010). Although social workers are not evaluators in Colorado's statutory scheme, since they can be evaluators in other states; an example of one state's legal standard defining "incompetent to proceed" will be instructive. You will note that there are ways that the determination of competency is similar and different from the standards related to competence and capacity in civil proceedings. For social workers, the same causal connections must be made as in civil proceedings: The mental illness or disability impairs the person's ability to safeguard and protect their own interests and thus to make informed decisions. In this instance, you are being asked to very specifically evaluate the ability of a person to actively participate, understand, and comprehend the nature of the proceedings and thus give their attorney direction or make informed decisions about their defense:

> Incompetent to proceed means that as a result of a mental disability or developmental disability, the defendant does not have sufficient present ability to consult with the defendant's lawyer with a reasonable degree of rational understanding in order to assist in the defense or that as a result of a mental disability or developmental disability the defendant does not have a rational or factual understanding of the criminal proceedings (Colo. Rev. Stat. § 16-8.5-101, 2010).

After a person has been found incompetent to proceed in Colorado, the statute also lays out what options are available to the judge once this finding has been made. This is another point where social work advocacy can be important for the defendant. Under Colo. Rev. Stat. § 16-8.5-111 (2010), a judge may order a release on bond with an order to receive mental health treatment at a community-based mental health or rehabilitation facility. If the court finds the defendant is not eligible and must remain in custody, a defendant can be involuntarily committed to a psychiatric facility. Again, determining the level of understanding and insight a person has about their condition and assessing their ability and desire to change would be important information for decision-makers at this juncture. Under the statute, the mental health provider will notify the court whenever the person is restored to a state of competence and the case would proceed.

VERDICT

Once a jury trial has finished, the judge will instruct the jury on the law that has to be applied in the case. These jury instructions are specific to the case at hand and can include instructions about the particular charge or how to consider evidence that was presented at trial. The jury has a period of time during which they can deliberate and come to a decision. In a jury trial, the verdict has to be unanimous in order to convict a defendant of a crime. As mentioned earlier, a jury may decide to convict a defendant on one charge but not on other charges. If the defendant is found not guilty, then the case is dismissed and the defendant is free if they were incarcerated during the trial. The judge can also declare a mistrial, which means that there was a procedural error in the case including misconduct on the part of an attorney or juror or improperly admitted evidence. A mistrial can also happen if the jury is not able to reach a unanimous decision, often referred to as a hung jury, thereby requiring the trial to be ended before reaching a verdict. If the judge declares a mistrial, then the trial has to start from the beginning with a new pool of jurors and a new trial. If the defendant is found guilty either by the jury or by a judge at a bench trial, then the case proceeds to the sentencing phase.

Sentencing

Once the judge or jury has found the defendant guilty, the trial is over and the case proceeds to the sentencing phase. During this phase of the criminal process, the judge makes the decision about what sentence will be imposed on the defendant as a result of the conviction. The sentence could include a period of incarceration, community service, or other alternative to incarceration and probation.

While there are some states such as Texas that permit a jury to determine the sentence, most states have laws requiring that the judge determine the sentence for the defendant. Often the judge will have to use the state or federal sentencing guidelines when determining what the sentence will be for the defendant. In these instances, the judge does not have discretion to impose a shorter or longer sentence for the defendant, but must stay within the range set by the sentencing guidelines passed into law by the legislature and often include a mandatory minimum. The sentencing guidelines generally consider a number of factors including whether it was a violent or nonviolent offense; whether it was a misdemeanor or felony; whether the crime included drugs, weapons, or a child victim; and whether the defendant has a previous criminal record or was on probation or parole when this crime occurred. These are also known as aggravating factors. In addition to determining the amount of time that a defendant can be incarcerated, the sentencing phase will also determine the time period for probation, either upon release from incarceration or as the sentence imposed by the judge.

Other options at the sentencing phase include fine, community service, and victim restitution. For example, in Arizona, if a defendant is convicted of a violent crime while under the influence of a drug then they are not eligible for early release from prison or probation until their entire sentence has been served pursuant to Ariz. Rev. Stat. ch. 11, § 41-1604.15 (2010). Most states and the federal government make their sentencing guidelines available online, either through the local court website or the U.S. Sentencing Commission, available at www.ussc.gov.

As part of the sentencing phase both the prosecution and the defense can offer evidence to advocate for either a more severe penalty or a reduced sentence. The prosecution can present what is called aggravating factors or conditions that made the impact of the crime more severe. The defendant can present what is called mitigation evidence in order to provide the court with a more historical context for the defendant's actions and to advocate for a reduced sentence. This may be something that social workers are already familiar with as this is usually the case in trials that involve the death penalty or imposition of a life sentence. Social workers have been and continue to be critical players on death penalty mitigation teams.

Social workers can play an integral role in gathering mitigating information and writing mitigation reports if they are aware of what their state statutes identify as both aggravating and mitigating factors (Schroeder et al., 2006). Social workers who are working with victims of crime may also be in a position to give prosecutors information relating to aggravating factors or circumstances that dramatically increased the impact of the crime on the victim or their families. Staying with our example of Colorado, the court, after finding a person guilty of a Class 1 felony, will conduct a separate hearing to determine the sentence. Historically, Colorado law allowed for the convicted defendant to be sentenced to death or life imprisonment unless the defendant was younger than the age of 18 or, as detailed in the former statute, incapacitated. In 2020, Colorado abolished the death penalty and therefore the only possible sentence for a Class 1 felony is life imprisonment. The state statutes also identify what evidence may be presented including information about the defendant's character and circumstances, evidence presented in the guilt phase of the trial, evidence on the mitigating or aggravating circumstances presented in the statute, and any characteristics of the victim and the impact of the crime on the victim and the victim's family.

In Colorado, the following mitigating factors have been identified by the statute: the age of the defendant at the time of the crime, the defendant's capacity to appreciate the nature of the crime was diminished but not to the extent required for a defense, the defendant's participation was not as great as other principals who committed the crime with them, the defendant could not have known that what they were doing could have resulted in a risk of death, the emotional condition of the defendant at the time the crime was committed, the absence of prior convictions, the level of cooperation with the police and prosecutor, the influence of alcohol and/or drugs, or the defendant is not a continuing threat to society (Colo. Rev. Stat. § 18-1.4-102, 2010).

Aggravating factors related to Class 1 felonies can include killing certain officials such as judges, police officers, and elected officials; the murder of a child or pregnant woman; homicide committed as part of a hate crime; being part of an agreement or contract to kill a person; killing someone during the commission of another felony; and using explosives to cause a death (Colo. Rev. Stat. § 18-1.4-102, 2010). This list is not all inclusive and again we advise you to check the criminal code in your state for more details about what are considered aggravating and mitigating circumstances in your jurisdiction.

While Class 1 felonies are the most serious and therefore carry the most serious sentencing option, other felonies including felony drug charges often have more options in terms of sentencing beyond incarceration. As an example, a convicted felon in Colorado may be able to access community corrections, deferred sentencing, and probation.

Legal Evidence-Based Practice at Sentencing

Working with aggravating and mitigating factors is similar to working with and balancing risk and protective factors. The judge and jury will have to do that kind of balancing in order to decide a sentence that is fair and just for both the offender and the victim. As we mentioned in Chapter 7, many jurisdictions are not only using evidence-based risk assessment and screening tools at the point of pretrial decision-making, but increasingly also when making decisions during the sentencing, prison intake, and parole phases of the process.

There has been much research conducted over the years identifying what risk factors and interventive responses to them are related to criminal recidivism. Overviews of the research, or meta-analyses, have identified a set of factors that appear repeatedly throughout the research and are correlated with risk of recidivism. These have been referred to as criminogenic risk factors (Andrews, 2006). Some of these factors are static and cannot be changed and some are dynamic and thus open to change. The dynamic factors are also called criminogenic needs. In this model, interventions would be targeted toward those risk factors that are dynamic and can be changed and, in this way, risk of recidivism is lowered (Latessa & Lovins, 2010). Assessments should then focus on these crime-producing needs and identify clearly how to target and treat them according to the level of risk presented. It is important to realize in this situation that risk is associated with reoffending, not the seriousness of the crime.

There have been a number of risk assessments, many computerized, developed as a result of this research. All of these assessments include some configuration of the following risk or criminogenic needs factors: antisocial values, attitudes, and beliefs; pro-criminal family members and associates; antisocial personality and behaviors; family and/or marital discord; substance abuse; poor school or work performance; and excessive leisure/recreation. Some of the software will not only identify risk but will then identify the level of service need, including alternatives to incarceration as well as case management plans. Some of the more frequently used programs are: Correctional Offender Management Profiling for Alternative Sanction (COMPAS), Level of Service Case Management Inventory (LS/CMI), Level of Service Inventory (LS-R), Community Supervision Screening Tool (ORAS-CSST), Community Supervision Tool (ORAS-CST), and Prison Intake Tool (ORAS-PIT). Some of the tools, such as ORAS-CSST, perform a screening function that identifies moderate to high-risk offenders before doing a full assessment to conserve resources. Others, such as the ORAS-PIT, prioritize who will get treatment resources in prison based on risk (Center on Sentencing and Corrections, 2010).

As with other risk-assessment tools, there are a number of important criticisms of the tools that must be identified. One concern is that the accuracy of any information obtained to enter into the assessment is highly dependent on the skill of the interviewer. Another concern is that standardized tools may not be gender or ethnicity sensitive (Center on Sentencing and Corrections, 2010). Another critique after a meta-review of the analysis on criminogenic risk assessments is the overreach of the tools and lack of transparency around models (Prins & Reich, 2021). Instruments also do not rule out bias. Given what we know about the significant racial bias that exists at every stage of the justice system and decision-making, it is always important to take a critical eye to risk assessments and the potential for bias. Social workers should read about the samples that were included in the validation studies of an instrument that you consider using to see if there are findings related to the relevant population of your work. Social workers may become concerned about offenders only receiving services based on risk but should realize that those who do not need treatment are also screened out, lowering the risk of mandating treatment for individuals who may not require it and who have a problem that is more structurally related such as a lack of education. Also, some research has shown that targeting factors that are identified as noncriminogenic needs such as anxiety or poor self-esteem can result in increased risk of recidivism. Focused and standardized assessment can also result in more offenders receiving community supervision and avoiding incarceration. Assessment instruments can also be administered at various points to assess the efficacy of the service plans.

After identifying the dynamic factors or those factors that can be changed, the next step in the process is to identify interventions that target the needs. For example, as part of a social work assessment to be used during sentencing, a social worker may assess that the client has a risk factor of family and marital discord. If you want to target and lower risk, then your plan would include a recommendation and referral for an intervention that will improve communication, reduce conflict, and build relationships in a way that will assist the family with the development of self-monitoring. Some action-based models that could achieve these outcomes would be: functional family therapy, multisystemic family therapy, and the family teaching model.

It is important that a social worker provides an attorney with an updated view of what has happened during the period of time since the pretrial proceedings and the actual completion of the trial. Identifying any change in circumstances related to the level of risk from the time the client was arrested to the time of sentencing will be critical information for the social worker and attorney to discuss as part of the strategy for the sentencing phase of the case.

Consideration of the Victim During Sentencing

Finally, as part of the judge's consideration of the sentence, a victim or a relative on behalf of a deceased victim is generally able to prepare and submit a victim impact statement or present one in court. It is important for social workers working with victims to assist clients during this process because often the victim impact statements are presented orally to the judge in open court. Returning to our example of Colorado, a victim in that state has a right to be present at the sentencing hearing "to inform the district attorney and the court, in writing by a victim impact statement, and by an oral statement of the harm that a victim has sustained as a result of a crime, with the determination of whether the victim makes written input or oral input or both to be made at the sole discretion of the victim" (Colo. Rev. Stat. tit. 24, § 24-4.1-302.5 [g][1], 2023).

The court has the authority to order restitution as well as the obligation to advise the victim that they may pursue civil damages against the person convicted for the actual money damages that resulted from the commission of the crime. The victim impact statement can have a significant effect on the judge's decision about what sentence to impose. Victim impact statements are designed to highlight the emotional, physical, and financial harm that the victim underwent or is still undergoing as a result of the crime (National Center for Victims of Crime, 2008). Often the statements will highlight any medical or psychological treatment that was necessary after the crime. Under the Violent Crime Control and Law Enforcement Act of 1994, victims of violent or sexual crimes have the right to provide testimony about the impact of the crime at sentencing. Social workers can elicit narratives that show the judge and jury what the victim's life was like before the crime and how their life has changed because of the crime. Giving details of physical and emotional injuries and how they limit many activities such as work or recreation that the victim enjoyed prior to the crime are important to include in an impact statement. If a family member is relaying information about a person who died, letting the judge and jury know personal details about the person and their life and how they touched others can let the decision-makers know the extent of the pain caused by the loss of that person. It is not appropriate to include in a victim impact the sentence the victim hopes the offender will get or anything that a jury may find offensive. A victim impact statement at sentencing may provide some degree of closure for the victim, allowing them to feel heard regarding the life changing experience of becoming a victim of crime and to move forward with their life.

Incarceration

Once a defendant is convicted and sentenced to any period of incarceration there are a number of important issues and decisions that the person and their family members will need to address. Social work advocacy and intervention can be critical in minimizing the risk to children and families associated with incarceration and to assist the family member who is incarcerated with the adjustment to their new and more restrictive situation (Strickman et al., 2010). Social workers who are working directly with incarcerated persons and their families can be proactive and begin the process of reentry planning well before the scheduled release date of the incarcerated family member. In fact, it is suggested that reentry planning begin the moment the person is incarcerated.

However, what frequently happens because of institutional barriers such as placement in prisons that are far from the residential community of the offender, restrictive visitation policies, financial barriers related to the cost of telephone calls, and the lack of privacy, is that relationships that could serve as a powerful source of support, motivation, and hope for offenders and their children and families are very difficult to maintain. Reentry planning that begins during incarceration should identify risk factors that may increase safe risks, and the probability of recidivism for the person you are working with, and to advocate with and for the client and their family to obtain access to services that will address these factors during the period of incarceration. It is also important to discuss with clients and families the impact of incarceration on the individual and if a recommendation for trauma informed therapy or family based therapy to assist in the reentry process for both the defendant and the family is warranted. As you have learned, some correctional facilities are using the ORAS-PIT to screen at prison intake for the purpose of providing treatment. Social workers in the implicit context can assist family members in becoming proactive advocates in setting up postrelease plans that immediately engage the client with their family and children, and elicit and connect to community supports.

State departments of correction and prison administrators are beginning to develop, incorporate, and evaluate prison-based evidence-based practices that are tied to the assessment of criminogenic need and risk. Using information obtained from risk assessment allows administrators to make placement decisions based on level of risk and improve the safety and treatment of offenders. Proponents of these risk-assessment models also make the case that they reduce bias in decision-making and may effectively reduce racial disparity in decision-making. Correctional programming should focus on the risk factors that are dynamic and can be changed. Therefore, effective interventions are those that match the level of risk with the highest risk receiving the highest intensity of treatment, matched to an individual's criminogenic needs, and delivered in a manner that is effective in meeting those needs (Andrews & Bonta, 2003). Evidence-based treatments implemented in prison and aftercare programs found to reduce recidivism by providing drug treatment include in-prison therapeutic communities that are special drug-free units that follow group-run principles in organizing and running the unit (Washington State Institute for Public Policy, 2006). In regard to individual counseling, the most effective treatment identified was some form of cognitive behavioral treatment that addresses the antisocial values, attitudes, and beliefs related to criminogenic need and that provide opportunities to model and practice problem-solving and pro-social skills. In regard to sex offenders, cognitive behavioral interventions have been found to reduce risk significantly in low-risk sex offenders who are placed on probation (Washington State Institute for Public Policy, 2006). Adult education, prison industry work opportunities and employment training, and job assistance also led to modest results in reducing recidivism. For minors involved in the juvenile or criminal system, family functional therapy (FFT) is an evidence-based family intervention model that works with both the child and family to identify protective factors and reduce risks that are associated with recidivism, as well as other risk factors that may have contributed to the child entering into the justice system (Alexander & Sexton, 2000).

A Note on the Detention of Immigrants

We cannot leave our discussion of incarceration without noting that the detention of illegal immigrants is the largest growing prison expansion in the United States. In 2023 the federal agency, Immigration and Citizenship Enforcement

(ICE), held approximately 30,000 immigrants with the vast majority being detained in private facilities run by for-profit companies. Immigrants in these facilities are facing civil proceedings related to their immigration status. Detained immigrants do not have the right to be released on bond if they are not considered to be dangerous or a flight risk. The circumstances of detained immigrants include asylum seekers waiting for a hearing, those convicted of a crime who are being deported, lawful permanent residents who have been convicted of a minor offense, those legal immigrants who left the country but have overstayed a temporary visa and cannot reenter, and those caught at the border trying to enter the country without documentation. Many human and civil rights organizations have documented the inhumane conditions and treatment that immigrant families and children suffer while detained, particularly after the devastating family separation policy in 2017.

Parole and Probation

Community supervision in the form of parole or probation is another area where social workers can provide critical advocacy and support to clients. At the end of 2022, over 3 million individuals were on some form of community supervision in the United States (Kaebe, 2024). Parole refers to period of supervision that is required when an inmate is released early from their prison sentence into the community to serve the remaining duration of their sentence; in other words, postrelease supervision. The decision whether or not an inmate is granted parole can be mandatory or discretionary meaning it is within the purview of the parole board, which in most states is an agency connected with the executive branch or corrections department. Generally states have guidelines for when an inmate, based on their sentence and the conviction, is eligible for parole. The parole board can decide not only whether an inmate is granted parole but also the conditions that are attached to the parole. If an individual violates any of the conditions of the parole (e.g., by being arrested again), then they can be sent back to prison.

Usually, states have parole boards that conduct various hearings on all matters relating to parole. For example, in California the Board of Parole Hearings conducts parole consideration hearings, parole revocation hearings, and parole review hearings. Parolees are guaranteed the right to a hearing and notice when they are taken into custody for a parole violation. The state must establish that there has been probable cause to believe the person violated a condition of parole. If there is a finding of probable cause, the offender has the right to a revocation hearing. In most states a person has the right to an attorney for a revocation hearing. Parole hearings, like probation violation hearings, are an important moment for advocates because alternative options to incarceration can be suggested. Changing some of the conditions of parole to better meet the offender's level of risk when tied to an assessment of risk and a clearly articulated plan to address it can be incorporated as conditions of parole.

PRISONERS' RIGHTS

Defendants and victims face continuing legal issues postsentencing and do not have a right to an attorney to assist them with these postsentencing legal needs. During the period of incarceration, there are a number of rights to protect an incarcerated person (Cnaan et al., 2008). Social workers can play an important role in making sure that clients are aware of these rights and know the processes and procedures involved in appealing cases, obtaining appropriate medical or psychological care, and child visitation and custody issues. It is important for social workers to understand the rights of incarcerated clients so that they do not miss opportunities to advocate for clients and to provide a stronger foundation for the inmate's eventual reentry to society.

During their period of incarceration, an inmate has various rights that the courts have considered to stem from constitutional rights. As you remember from Chapter 9, when a person claims that the government has violated civil rights or liberties under Section 1983, the person may sue the government. Many claims filed by prisoners are filed under Section 1983 and thus are actually civil proceedings. However, in this section we identify rights as they have been specifically applied to prisoners when they have been incarcerated. All claims, even if they happen in prison, still have to meet the legal standards you read about in Chapter 9 under a Section 1983 claim.

Some constitutional rights that prisoners have while incarcerated are: due process during disciplinary proceedings, discrimination claims, right to mental health and medical treatment, communication with outside counsel and family members, freedom from unclean or crowded prison conditions, access to law libraries and legal assistance, freedom from abuse, certain privacy matters such as HIV status, and meaningful participation in any ongoing Family Court or other civil matters. A wonderful resource for social workers working with incarcerated individuals is *A Jailhouse Lawyer's Manual* written by the Columbia Human Rights Law Review (2009). This treatise, written for individuals who are incarcerated, covers all of the rights of prisoners and obligations of corrections facilities. Although it covers the specific laws for New York State inmates, it also reviews the federal laws relating to prisoners' rights.

While prisoners have rights while incarcerated, the enforcement of those rights through litigation has been seriously curtailed by the Prisoner's Litigation Reform Act (1997). This federal law requires prisoners to exhaust, meaning to pursue until completion, any administrative hearings or internal grievance procedures set up by the prison or agency responsible for the prison. Therefore, it is important for social workers to understand that a prisoner's first avenue for challenging a violation of their rights may be in the administrative forum or by filing an internal grievance or complaint.

While in prison, inmates have the right to receive medical and mental healthcare. The Supreme Court held in *Estelle v. Gamble* (1976) that withholding medical treatment to inmates in serious need of treatment was a violation of the Eighth Amendment's prohibition against cruel and unusual punishment. In order for the inmate to have a legal claim for a violation of their constitutional right, they would have to demonstrate that the harm was sufficiently serious and also that the prison official was aware of the medical condition and demonstrated deliberate indifference. Most federal and state courts include the right to psychiatric care for a mental health illness and have extended this right to adequate medical care. It is important to note what is considered to be a mental illness under your state's specific law or the law of the federal appellate court where you are practicing. Additionally, the law does not protect an inmate's right to unreasonably expensive or the best medical care, but simply adequate medical care.

Individuals who are incarcerated also have the right to be free from abuse, either from other inmates or from corrections officers. These rights are contained in federal and state law, including the right to be free from cruel and unusual punishment under the Eighth Amendment to the U.S. Constitution. If you are working with an inmate who has been assaulted and believes that their rights were violated, it is important to check your local regulations and laws because the state agency responsible for the prison may have its own internal grievance procedure, similar to what is described in Chapter 12 on Administrative Proceedings. An inmate may be required to complete the internal administrative procedures before filing any lawsuit in state or federal court to address the assault. Under state law, the inmate may have a civil claim against a prison officer, if the inmate can demonstrate that there was intent to harm.

Incarcerated parents have specific issues that can significantly impact their ability to parent or comply with a court's order, for example, for child support (Strickman et al., 2010). The period of incarceration does not automatically modify or terminate an order of child support, and if the support is not being paid, then the client may be accruing substantial amounts of child support arrears that will be due upon release. As you learned in Chapter 9, this can be avoided by seeking a modification of the child support order in light of the period of incarceration.

Visitation and custody issues are critical for incarcerated parents, especially when those issues arise in the context of an abuse or neglect proceeding in Family Court. All of what you learned in Chapter 9 regarding custody, visitation, and guardianship can be applied in this context if you are working with a family where a caregiver has been incarcerated. If Ms. Jones had still been incarcerated when her son was born and the neglect case was filed in Family Court, she would have to be produced by the local corrections department to the Family Court so that she could actively participate in the proceedings. Additionally, Ms. Jones would only be able to access services such as parenting or substance abuse treatment if they were available in the detention facility. Furthermore, she may not have been able to visit with Matthew depending on whether the Family Court ordered visits at the detention facility, and certainly those visits would not have been as frequent or long as they would have been if she were in the community.

As you remember from the case exemplar in Chapter 9, the Adoption and Safe Families Act (ASFA, 1997) requires that a termination of parental rights proceeding be explored if a child remains in foster care for 18 of the last 24 months. For parents who are incarcerated, this mandate may not allow enough time for their periods of incarceration to end or for them to engage in the services identified by the child welfare agency for reunification with their child. Furthermore, as discussed earlier, many parents are incarcerated in prisons far away from their family, making meaningful visitation and service planning more difficult.

In light of these barriers, some states, including New York, have provided for expanded discretion under ASFA when working with incarcerated parents, requiring that the foster care agencies recognize and accommodate the special circumstances of incarcerated parents when planning for their family's reunification. For example, a social worker working at a foster care agency may be required to facilitate visitation at a prison or, as an alternative, video-conferencing or a telephone visit between children and their parents when the correctional facility is far away. The social worker should be in contact with any social work staff from the prison to determine what services are available while the parent is still incarcerated and what if any reentry services are provided. Finally, the social worker would need to find alternate means of including the incarcerated parent in the planning that occurs in service plan reviews and family team conferences, either by video- or teleconferencing or in writing.

Victim's Rights After Sentencing

Once an offender has been sentenced to incarceration, the victims have the right to be notified of any hearings or proceedings, or that a postconviction release is being considered about the person who was convicted of the crime against them. In some states, again using our example of Colorado, the victim has the right to be heard or to provide written information at any such proceeding, which is defined as reconsideration of a sentence, a parole hearing, or commutation of a sentence (Colo. Rev. Stat. § 24-4.1-302.5, 2010). The victim also has the right to be notified if the person is paroled to the community and can provide an impact statement to be included with any referral to a community-based correction program. They also have the right to be notified if the offender escapes, or transferred to a less secure correctional facility, or released from any state, public, or private hospital. Again it is critical to identify whether or not the burden of triggering the right is on the victim or the state. In Colorado, the victim triggers the postconviction rights by submitting a written request (Colo. Rev. Stat. § 24-4.1-302.5, 2010).

REENTRY ISSUES

When an individual is released from jail, regardless of the amount of time that may have been spent incarcerated, they face a number of hurdles as a result of their sentence. Indeed even if a defendant receives a nonjail sentence; they are often subject to the collateral consequences of their involvement with the criminal justice system. As we identified earlier when discussing plea bargaining, social workers should be attuned to the collateral consequences of the criminal conviction because the conviction can have a significant impact on the client's ability to access housing, to access employment, and to vote. Indeed, the collateral consequences often have a more profound effect on a client's stability than the original criminal conviction itself.

As you learned in Chapter 9, a client in public housing may face considerable consequences as a result of criminal justice involvement. Having a conviction for possession of drugs can render an individual ineligible for public housing programs and may also put relatives who live in the same public housing unit at risk of being evicted. Employment is also a significant barrier for many individuals returning from a period of incarceration. Most states have regulations that prohibit providing an employment license for certain jobs depending on the nature of the conviction. The regulations are set by the particular state or local agency that provides the licenses; the determination of whether an individual with a conviction can obtain a license can be mandatory or discretionary on the part of the agency. Jobs that require licenses from the state or local municipality include barbers, drivers, sanitation workers, cosmetologists, and security guards.

A criminal conviction can also place your welfare benefits at risk. Some states have adopted a ban on welfare, including cash assistance and food stamps, for any person convicted of a drug-related crime, while other states have opted out of this provision. As of 2023, 25 states have opted out of the ban on accessing benefits if the recipient has a drug-related conviction (Love and Sibilla, 2023). The ban on welfare for any felony drug conviction was created as part of welfare reform in 1996, and allows states to opt out or use a discretionary approach. It is important to learn what the rules are in your specific state so that you know whether your state has opted out of the ban on welfare benefits entirely or has modified the terms of the ban, potentially allowing for benefits if the conviction was for possession instead of sale or the defendant is part of a substance abuse program.

In 48 states, you are not allowed to vote if you have been convicted of a felony, which is often referred to as felon disenfranchisement. The Sentencing Project estimates that 4 million Americans were barred from voting in the 2024 elections because of state laws that prohibit individuals with a felony conviction from this form of civic participation (Uggen et al., 2024). Again, there is a disparate impact on Black individuals who would otherwise be eligible to vote given one in 22 Black individuals are disenfranchised as a result of felony convictions. For example, in New York, Ms. Jones would not be able to vote if she were incarcerated at the time. However, as a result of reforms in 2021, she would be able to vote even if she had been convicted of a felony, once she was released from prison regardless of whether she is on parole.

Social workers should check their local regulations to see whether their particular state provides for any relief from a criminal conviction, sometimes referred to as a *certificate of relief from disabilities*. While this is not a pardon of the criminal case, which would result in the case being effectively dismissed, the process can be particularly helpful for convicted defendants in accessing employment.

JUVENILE JUSTICE

As you learned in Chapter 7, the juvenile justice system functions in a quasicriminal manner when adjudicating cases involving juveniles accused of illegal activity. To understand the scope of the juvenile justice system, you only need to know that in 2007, 31 million youth were under the jurisdiction of a Juvenile Court and from 1960 to 2007, juvenile delinquency cases across the United States increased by 300% (Puzzanchera & Robson, 2014). In 2019, juvenile courts across the country handled 722,600 cases which represents a significant reduction in the number of cases (Hockenberry, 2022). While each state has its own laws for the upper-level age to be considered a juvenile versus an adult subject to Criminal Court proceedings, most states follow a similar process for processing juvenile delinquency cases in their Family or Dependency Courts. You can find information on each state's juvenile justice system by referencing the state profiles on the National Center for Juvenile Justice's website. You can also go to your state court websites to access the court rules for Juvenile Courts. As always, it is important to access the local laws and processes in order to understand the different opportunities for advocacy and involvement when working with young people involved in the juvenile justice system.

Court rules and statutes will, as in other areas of the law, provide important definitions of terms and standards and describe the process that occurs when a juvenile is arrested, the processes for determining whether a juvenile case will be heard in dependency or adult Criminal Court, the procedures for placing a youth in detention and the time limits during which they may be held, the kinds of notices required and who must receive them, what must be contained in a petition, a juvenile's rights including that of legal representation, penalties that may be imposed by Family Court, standards for the operation of juvenile facilities, standards for release to aftercare supervision and what happens when a youth violates the conditions of probation or aftercare supervision.

Intake: Diversion or Filing

Before a state juvenile delinquency court hears any case, most have an intake or screening department that determines whether or not the case will be filed. As you learned in Chapter 7, there is a movement to use evidence-based risk-assessment protocols to assist a number of decisions that will be made during the processing of a juvenile justice case, including at the pretrial phase and especially the decision whether to detain the juvenile. This department determines whether there is enough evidence to file a petition alleging delinquency or to resolve the matter informally. In some instances, depending on jurisdiction and type of offense, parents and the juvenile will be provided with a voluntary referral to a social service program or the opportunity to pay a fine and avoid a formal court filing. If the intake department determines that there is enough evidence or the alleged criminal behavior is of a serious enough nature, then a petition is filed in court. Most of the cases will be heard in a Family Court or Dependency Court.

Additionally, a juvenile may be detained temporarily as part of the juvenile delinquency case. In this situation, the juvenile remains in a detention center pending the outcome of the delinquency trial or a hearing on the juvenile's continued detention. In Colorado, a juvenile can be temporarily detained, but the juvenile can also be released to their parent, released with services, provided with a temporary shelter, or placed in a more supervised setting that does not rise to the level of formal detention. The criteria for determining whether or not the juvenile is detained and what setting is required include an assessment of the juvenile's need for supervision, services, and physical restriction which are determined by a working group of practitioners from the court, district attorney's office, and local community groups (Colo. Rev. Stat. § 19-2-212).

Juvenile Transfers

It is important to remember that every state has provisions for transferring cases of the most serious level to the Criminal Court so that a juvenile can be tried as an adult. In general, a state will have a guideline for the minimum age possible for a young person to be transferred to Criminal Court. For example, in Illinois, a young person can only be transferred to Criminal Court to be tried as an adult if they are at least 13 years of age. This is despite Illinois's law defining the jurisdiction of the Juvenile Court to include all young people aged 7 to 16 years. In order for the transfer to happen, the Juvenile Court would hold a hearing to determine whether it is appropriate for the case to be transferred to adult Criminal Court and the prosecution would bear the burden of proving that the case is more appropriately heard in Criminal Court instead of Family Court. It should be noted though that some states have laws mandating that a juvenile be charged in Criminal Court if they are of a certain age and are accused of committing a set of specific, generally more serious, crimes. In these instances, often referred to as designated crimes or felonies, the juvenile's case would never be heard in Juvenile or Family Court but proceed directly to Criminal Court.

States may have different mechanisms to provide for transfer. The most common mechanism is judicial waiver, which gives Juvenile Court judges discretion to waive juvenile cases to adult Criminal Court. Other transfer mechanisms include direct file, which provides prosecutorial discretion to file criminal charges against juveniles directly in Criminal Court, and statutory exclusion, which mandates juvenile prosecution in adult court. Usually the burden is on the prosecution to prove the juvenile should be transferred to adult court. There is a mechanism called presumptive waiver that advocates should be aware of. This mechanism allows the juvenile to make the case that they are more suited to the rehabilitation that occurs in the juvenile justice system. In this instance the burden of proof is on the juvenile to prove that they should not be transferred.

A report sponsored by the Office of Juvenile Justice and Delinquency Prevention (Redding, 2010) reviewed the research that addressed whether transfers result in a decrease in recidivism for those juveniles and found that transferred juveniles, particularly those with crimes involving violence, were more likely to reoffend and to be rearrested. All of the findings of the six large-scale studies presented in the report showed a much higher rate of recidivism for juveniles transferred to the criminal system than those that remained in the juvenile system. This was true even for juvenile offenders who had received probation in Criminal Court (Redding, 2010).

Adjudication or Trial Phase

Once the case is formally filed, the juvenile has the right to a trial to determine whether the prosecution can prove that guilt of the alleged delinquent conduct. The juvenile has a right to an attorney in these proceedings, because the outcome of the case could result in their detention or deprivation of their liberty. The same process as in a criminal trial applies in a juvenile justice adjudication. Therefore, the prosecutor has the burden of proving the delinquent conduct and the juvenile defendant has the right to cross-examine any witnesses brought against them and to testify or provide evidence on their own behalf. As we discussed earlier, the standard of proof, which is the same in a criminal matter, is beyond a reasonable doubt.

Disposition

Once the juvenile has been found to be delinquent, sometimes called a status offense, then the judge proceeds to the dispositional phase of the case. In many cases, the judge will request a report from probation prior to the disposition hearing in order to assess the needs of the juvenile. In Colorado, a presentence investigation and report focusing on the offense, victim's needs, psychosocial history, education, employment, and family supports are required for all juveniles with felonies under the Colo. Rev. Stat. § 19-2-905 (2010). During this phase, because there has been a finding, the judge has the authority to mandate the juvenile to services or placement, including nonsecure detention and secure detention. The judge may also require the juvenile to be supervised for an amount of time by probation, to conduct community service, to pay a fine, or to provide some form of restitution. Of course the judge can fashion a dispositional order that includes a number of these options. For example, a young person could be ordered to reside in a nonsecure detention placement, while also undergoing counseling and drug treatment and completing 50 hours of community service.

If a juvenile is found to be a delinquent, or guilty of the criminal activity charged, then the judge may also order a disposition of an alternative to detention program or probation. These alternatives to detention (ATD) programs generally involve a high level of case management and supervision for the young person and their family and are much more effective in reducing recidivism than placing a youth in secure confinement (Justice Policy Institute, 2009). To return to our example in Colorado, the court can sentence a juvenile to a juvenile justice facility, detention, jail, placement with a relative, probation, a community program, placement in a hospital, a fine, restitution, and mandated services including anger management (Colo. Rev. Stat. § 19-2-907–19-2-926, 2010).

Legal Evidence-Based Disposition

Similar to the adult system, juvenile justice systems are also conducting a reviewing meta-analysis to determine what factors are related to recidivism among juveniles. Various states are designing and requiring structured risk and needs assessment tools to assist decision-makers in identifying which juveniles may be at the greatest risk of reoffending and toward whom, and what resources must be targeted. These protocols also assist decision-makers to better identify youth that can be successfully treated and supervised in the community.

Results from the largest and most comprehensive meta-analyses of juvenile justice interventions mirror the findings in adult studies: Interventions directed at high-risk offenders were more effective at reducing recidivism than when directed at low-risk offenders. High risk was most significantly related to the nature and extent of prior offenses (Lipsey, 2009). Regardless of the setting of the —intervention—probation, parole, or secure facilities—it was more successful when applied to those at higher risk (Lipsey, 2009). Programs found to be most successful for juveniles were those that were restorative in nature such as victim–offender mediation, those that used cognitive behavioral techniques that focus on skill building (social, academic, and vocational), counseling such as multisystemic family therapy and cognitive behavioral treatment, and case management and service brokering (Lipsey, 2009).

As with adults, the identification of criminogenic needs is key to identifying both the level of risk and the interventions that should be part of the treatment plan. Adult criminogenic need categories that should be explored for juveniles are prior and current offenses, substance abuse, education, family, peers, leisure, attitudes, and criminal orientation. One challenge in adapting adult models of structured risk assessment is the level of variability and change related to adolescence. There can be wide variability relative to one adolescent over time. It is important that the assessment be ongoing to determine when and if there are changes to the level of risk. One instrument that has been found to have good reliability and gender and ethnic sensitivity is the Youth Level of Service Case Management Inventory (YLS-CMI). This tool allows a wide range of juvenile justice professionals, including social workers, to collect information about risks and strengths, to develop goals related to risk and strengths, to identify interventions, and to develop an effective case management plan. The program also allows the user to monitor and evaluate the case plan.

Structured decision-making has been advocated for use during all the phases of a juvenile proceeding: intake and the decision to detain, disposition, and review hearings. Structured decision-making for juveniles has also been found to be effective in reducing racial disparities in detention and aftercare supervision (Mulvey & Iselin, 2008).

Detention and Confinement

Rights-based social workers should be aware that historically "cases involving black youth were more likely to be detained than cases involving white youth in each year between 1985 and 2009 across offense categories" (Puzzanchera et al., 2012, p. 35). As you learned earlier, even though juvenile detention has significantly declined over the years, Black youth are 4.7 times more likely to be detained or committed than their White peers according to data from 2021 (Rovner, 2023). It is important to make a distinction between the terms "secure detention" and "secure confinement." Secure detention refers to a youth being detained after arrest and prior to the hearing or trial (discussed extensively in Chapter 7). Secure confinement is placement when youth are found guilty and is the outcome of a dispositional hearing. Youth can be placed in secure confinement anywhere from a few months to several years (Sickmund, 2010).

Juveniles also have rights when they are placed in secure facilities or otherwise placed in confinement. In the same manner as adults, the U.S. Constitution gives a juvenile who has been placed in confinement the right to safe conditions, the right to medical care, and the right to be free from unreasonable restraint (Justice for Youth, p. 9). Juveniles cannot be placed in solitary or room confinement for extended periods of time, and most states have very specific laws and regulations covering when room confinement or solitary confinement is permitted. For example, in Massachusetts, staff cannot place a juvenile in room confinement where they are not able to leave on their own, unless the youth is exhibiting "seriously disruptive or dangerous behavior" (Mental Health Legal Advisors Committee, 2012, https://mhlac.org/wp-content/uploads/2018/11/JustForYouth.pdf). Juveniles are also protected from unreasonable restraint by staff, and Massachusetts is an example of the specific circumstances required to authorize the use of physical or mechanical restraint. In a Massachusetts facility, staff may only use restraint in the following situations:

> For restraint to be used, the youth must be demonstrating by his actions that he is dangerous to himself or others and staff must have concluded that no other intervention has been or is likely to be effective in averting the danger. Staff must try verbal counseling, point-system sanctions, room confinement, and direct warnings before using restraint. An exception to this rule is if a youth attacks another person suddenly or without warning or presents an imminent danger to himself or others. Staff may not restrain youth as punishment or for convenience. Staff may not restrain for noncompliance with a program rule, staff directive or expectation alone. Staff

> may restrain to protect program property, but only when staff reasonably believes that the safety of the youth or others is threatened. (Mental Health Legal Advisors Committee, 2010, 10.14)

Additionally, youth in secure juvenile justice facilities have the right to communicate with their family and legal counsel, participate in religious services of their choice, retain their personal property, receive adequate medical and mental healthcare, and have their records treated confidentially. Each state has specific regulations and policies on the use of searches, including pat down searches and strip searches. It is important to access the relevant regulation or policy for your state with regard to searches if a young person or their family member raises a complaint. Finally, parents of juveniles in secure and nonsecure facilities also have rights to communicate with their child and be updated by the facility staff on their child's medical, educational, and behavioral plan and progress while in the facility.

There is a large and convincing body of research documenting that secure detention and confinement are not effective in preventing rearrest and recidivism. Some studies show that anywhere from 50% to 70% of juveniles held in secure confinement reoffend and in fact go on to become involved with more serious offenses (Mulvey, 2011). Rights-based social workers should be aware that statistically "cases involving black youth were more likely to be detained than cases involving white youth in each year between 1985 and 2009 across offense categories" (Puzzanchera et al., 2012, p. 35). Currently, states spend about $5.7 million confining youth, many for nonviolent crimes (Justice Policy Institute, 2009). There is no compelling evidence that placing juveniles in secure confinement improves public safety. States that used more community-based, alternative programs were able to demonstrate a drop in crime and rates of rearrest (Justice Policy Institute, 2009). Studies have also found that it is the experience of the incarceration itself that creates the highest risk factor for future offending, particularly in large training schools (Benda & Tollett, 1999).

Conditions that have been reported in secure juvenile confinement demand that social workers working in the implicit context assist families in advocating for the needs and safety of their children. They should also advocate for and create more community level evidence-based programs that identify and respond to criminogenic needs with evidence-based interventions. Severe overcrowding results in stressful and harsh conditions that produce violence, abuse, increased risk of suicide, and the development of psychiatric symptoms. Class action lawsuits have addressed the failure of secure facilities to both screen and address the mental health needs of detained youth. Youth who have been confined are also less likely to have their educational and vocational needs met and thus more likely to recidivate (Justice Policy Institute, 2009).

Probation and Parole in Juvenile Cases

The judge can sentence a juvenile to probation similar to the adult criminal justice system. In the case of juveniles, a young person would still be required to adhere to the conditions of the probation, which can be set by the judge but amended by the probation officer in certain situations. The conditions for a juvenile on probation could include school attendance, an order of protection, curfews, obeying rules at home, refraining from disciplinary incidents or suspension at school, restitution, and drug tests. For example, under Colo. Rev. Stat. § 19-2-913, 925–926 (2010), a juvenile on probation can also be required to attend school, participate in a work-readiness program, and comply with ongoing supervision and monitoring. If the probation officer believes that a juvenile has violated a term of their probation then, similar to the adult system, the juvenile has a right to a hearing on the violation as the possible consequence of being found in violation of a court's probation order is confinement. At the end of a hearing on an alleged violation of a probation order, the court can extend a period of probation, modify the terms of the juvenile's probation, or order confinement for the juvenile for a set period of time.

For juveniles who were committed or placed in a secure facility, parole and other transitional reentry services are provided. Under Colo. Rev. Stat. § 19-2-909(1)(b) (2010), the Juvenile Parole Board has authority over all juveniles on parole and the decisions regarding the terms and conditions of their parole, including the decision to extend a juvenile's parole period. Some states, including Colorado, mandate parole for juveniles who have been adjudicated delinquent for more serious acts. As is the case for adults on parole, the terms and conditions of the parole can be very specific and include ongoing supervision, drug testing, school attendance, and mandated services.

Rights of Victims in Juvenile Cases

States also afford victims' rights at various points throughout the juvenile justice process. In Missouri, for example, victims have the right to be present at all juvenile proceedings where the charge would be a felony if the juvenile were charged as an adult. Victims have a right to be informed of court dates, continuances and dispositions, and to confer with the prosecuting attorney regarding pleas and dispositions. Many of the same rights afforded to victims in adult proceedings are afforded during juvenile proceedings, including but not limited to notice of any release or change in disposition, the right of providing a written statement, and the right to restitution.

REFERENCES

Alexander, J., & Sexton, T. (2000, December). *Functional family therapy.* The Office of Juvenile Justice and Delinquency Prevention (OJJDP), Juvenile Justice Bulletin.

Adoption and Safe Families Act of 1997, 42 U.S.C. § 1305 (1997).

Anderson, J., Buenaventura, M., & Heaton, P. (2019). The effects of holistic defense on criminal justice outcomes. *Faculty Scholarship at Penn Law, 132*(3), 819–893.

Andrews, D. A., & Bonta, J. (2003). *The psychology of criminal conduct* (3rd ed.). Anderson Publishing Co.

Andrews, D. A. (2006). Enhancing adherence to risk-need-responsivity: Making quality a matter of policy. *Criminology and Public Policy*, 5, 595–602.

Ariz. Rev. Stat. c.11, § 41-1604.15 (2010).

Benda, B. B., & Tollett, C. L. (1999). A study of recidivism of serious and persistent offenders among adolescents. *Journal of Criminal Justice, 27*, 111–126. https://doi.org/10.1016/S0047-2352(98)00051-8

Berdejó, C. (2018). Criminalizing race: Racial disparities in plea bargaining. *Boston College Law Review, 59*(4), 1187–1250. https://www.project-scope.org/wp-content/uploads/2020/08/Criminalizing-Race.pdf

Brady v. Maryland, 373 U.S. 83 (1963).

Cal. Const. Art. 1, § 28(b)(8).

Cal. Penal Code § 22 (2024).
Center on Sentencing and Corrections. (2010). *Illinois risk, assets and needs task force: National information on offender assessments, Part* II. Vera Institute of Justice. https://idoc.illinois.gov/content/dam/soi/en/web/idoc/documents/national-information-offender-assessments-partii-memo.pdf
Cho, E. H. (2023). *Unchecked growth: Private prison corporations and immigration detention, three years into the Biden administration.* https://www.aclu.org/news/immigrants-rights/unchecked-growth-private-prison-corporations-and-immigration-detention-three-years-into-the-biden-administration
Cnaan, R. A., Draine, J. N., Frazier, B., & Sinha, J. W. (2008). The limits of citizenship: Rights of prisoners and ex-prisoners in USA. *Journal of Policy Practice*, *7*(2–3), 178–198. https://repository.upenn.edu/handle/20.500.14332/47253
Colo. Rev. Stat. § 19-2-212.
Colo. Rev. Stat. § 18-1-708 (2010).
Colo. Rev. Stat. § 18-1-803 (2010).
Colo. Rev. Stat. § 16-8.5-101 (2010).
Colo. Rev. Stat. § 16-8-101.5 (2010).
Colo. Rev. Stat. § 18-1.4-102 (2010).
Colo. Rev. Stat. § 16-8.5-103 (2010).
Colo. Rev. Stat. § 16-8-109 (2016).
Colo. Rev. Stat. § 16-8.5-111 (2010).
Colo. Rev. Stat. § 24-4.1-302.5 (2010).
Colo. Rev. Stat. § 19-2-905 (2010).
Colo. Rev. Stat. § 19-2-907–19-2-926 (2010).
Colo. Rev. Stat. § 19-2-913, 925–926 (2010).
Colo. Rev. Stat. § 19-2-909(1)(b) (2010).
Colo. Rev. Stat. tit. 24, § 24-4.1-302.5 (g)(1) (2023).
Columbia Human Rights Law Review. (2009). *A jailhouse lawyer's manual.* https://jlm.law.columbia.edu/a-jailhouse-lawyers-manual-12th-edition/
Dusky v. United States, 362 U.S. 402 (1960).
Estelle v. Gamble, 378 U.S. 546 (1976).
Ghandnoosh, N. (2023). *Ending 50 years of mass incarceration: Urgent reform needed to protect future generations.* https://www.sentencingproject.org/policy-brief/ending-50-years-of-mass-incarceration-urgent-reform-needed-to-protect-future-generations/
Hockenberry, S. (2022). *Delinquency cases in juvenile court, 2019.* https://ojjdp.ojp.gov/publications/delinquency-cases-2019.pdf
Johnson, T. (2023). *Plea bargain task force report.* https://www.americanbar.org/content/dam/aba/publications/criminaljustice/plea-bargain-tf-report.pdf
Justice Policy Institute. (2009). *The costs of confinement: Why good juvenile justice policies make good fiscal sense.* https://justicepolicy.org/wp-content/uploads/2022/02/09_05_rep_costsofconfinement_jj_pS.pdf
Kaebe, D. (2024). *Probation and parole in the United States, 2022.* https://bjs.ojp.gov/library/publications/probation-and-parole-united-states-2022
Latessa, E. J., & Lovins, B. (2010). The role of offender risk assessment: A policy maker guide. *Victims and Offenders*, *5*(3), 203–219. https://doi.org/10.1080/15564886.2010.485900
Lipsey, M. W. (2009). The primary factors that characterize effective interventions with juvenile offenders: A meta-analytic overview. *Victims and Offenders*, *4*, 124–147. https://doi.org/10.1080/15564880802612573
Love, M., & Sibilla, N. (2023). *Access to SNAP and TANF benefits after a drug conviction: A survey of state laws.* Collateral Consequences Resource Center. https://i0.wp.com/ccresourcecenter.org/wp-content/uploads/2023/11/Cover-from-SNAP-TANF-scaled.jpg?ssl=1
Matei, A., Hussemann, J., & Siegel, J. (2021). *Assessing a social worker model of public defense.* https://www.urban.org/sites/default/files/publication/103811/assessing-a-social-work-model-of-public-defense_1.pdf

Mental Health Legal Advisors Committee. (2012). *Just for youth: Advocating for youths in the Massachusetts Department of Youth Services.* https://mhlac.org/wp-content/uploads/2018/11/JustForYouth.pdf

Mont. Code 46-14-102 (2023).

Mulvey, E. P. (2011, March). *OJJDP juvenile justice fact sheet: Highlights from pathways to desistence: A longitudinal study of serious adolescent offenders (NCJ2310971).* U.S. Department of Justice. https://www.pathwaysstudy.pitt.edu/documents/OJJDP%20Fact%20Sheet_Pathways.pdf

National Association for the Advancement of Colored People. (2011). *Misplaced priorities: Over incarcerate, under educate.* https://www.prisonpolicy.org/scans/naacp/misplaced_priorities.pdf

National Center for Victims of Crime. (2008). *Victim impact statements.* Retrieved from https://victimsofcrime.org/

O'Hear, M. M. (2008). Plea bargaining and procedural justice. *Georgia Law Review, 42*(407), 407–469. https://doi.org/10.2139/ssrn.982220

Prins, S. J., & Reich, A. (2021). Criminogenic risk assessment: A meta-review and critical analysis. *Punishment & Society, 23*(4), 578–604. https://doi.org/10.1177/14624745211025751

Prisoner's Litigation Reform Act of 1997, 42 U.S.C. § 1997e (1997).

Puzzanchera, C., Adams, B., & Hockenberry, S. et al. (2012). *Juvenile court statistics 2009.* https://ojjdp.ojp.gov/sites/g/files/xyckuh176/files/pubs/239114.pdf

Puzzanchera, C., & Robson, C. (2014). *Delinquency cases in juvenile court*, 2010. https://ojjdp.ojp.gov/sites/g/files/xyckuh176/files/pubs/243041.pdf

Redding, R. (2010). Juvenile transfer laws: An effective deterrent to delinquency? *ODJJDP Juvenile Justice Bulletin* (NCJ220595). Washington DC: U.S. Department of Justice, Bureau of Justice Programs, Office of Juvenile Justice and Delinquency Prevention. National Criminal Justice Resource Center, http://www.ncjrs.gov/pdffiles1/ojjdp/220595.pdf

Rottman, D., & Strickland, S. M. (2004). *State court organization 2004 (NCJ 212351).* U.S. Department of Justice. https://static.prisonpolicy.org/scans/bjs/sco04.pdf

Rovner, J. (2023). *Black disparities in youth incarceration.* https://www.sentencingproject.org/fact-sheet/black-disparities-in-youth-incarceration/

Schroeder, J., Guin, C. C., Pogue, R., & Bordelon, D. (2006). Mitigating circumstances in death penalty decisions: Using evidence-based research to inform social work practice in capital trials. *Social Work, 51*(4), 355–364. https://doi.org/10.1093/sw/51.4.355

Sickmund, M. (2010). *Juveniles in residential placements 1997–2008. OJJDP fact sheet (NCJ 229397).* U.S. Department of Justice, Office of Justice Programs, Office of Juvenile Justice and Delinquency Prevention. http://www.ncjrs.gov/pdffiles1/ojjdp/229379.pdf

Siegel, D. M. (2008). The growing admissibility of expert testimony by clinical social workers on competence to stand trial. *Social Work, 53*(2), 153–163. https://doi.org/10.1093/sw/53.2.153

Strickman, C., Alioto, J., & Clarke, J. (2010). *Incarcerated parents manual: Your legal rights and responsibilities.* Legal Services for Prisoners with Children. http://www.prisonerswithchildren.org/pubs/ipm.pdf

Uggen, C., Larson, R., Shannon, S., Stewart, R., & Hauf, M. (2024). *Locked out 2024: Four million denied voting rights due to a felony conviction.* https://www.sentencingproject.org/reports/locked-out-2024-four-million-denied-voting-rights-due-to-a-felony-conviction/

Violent Crime Control and Law Enforcement Act of 1994, Pub. L. No. 103-322, 108 Stat. 1796.

Walker, R. and Miller, J. (2016). *SFY 2014 evaluation report.* Kentucky Department of Public Advocacy Alternative Sentencing Worker Program. https://dpa.ky.gov/wp-content/uploads/2019/10/DPA-ASW-UK-Outcome-Study-FY-2014.pdf

Warren, R. K. (2007). *Evidence-based practice to reduce recidivism: Implications for state judiciaries.* Crime and Justice Institute & National Institute of Corrections.

Washington State Institute for Public Policy. (2006). *Evidence-based adult corrections programs: What works and what does not.* http://www.wsipp.wa.gov/rptfiles/06-01-1201.pdf

CHAPTER 11

Alternatives to Traditional Methods of Addressing Legal and Social Problems

INTRODUCTION

This chapter introduces you to some of the alternative forums, both judicial and quasijudicial, that have evolved as part of the preventive, therapeutic jurisprudence, and restorative justice movements. You are introduced to conferencing, mediation, and problem-solving courts as forums for explicit legal context practice and as adjuncts to your work in the implicit legal context. You will understand the benefits and disadvantages of these alternative venues and the implications for issues of access to justice. Finally, you will be briefly introduced to theories about approaches to mediation, the process of mediation, and alternative dispute resolution, plus some important skills needed to become a collaborative and critically competent social worker when interfacing with alternative venues.

WHAT ARE ALTERNATIVE VENUES?

In the previous chapters, you learned about the different processes and procedures used to address problems between individuals and the government and between individuals and other individuals in the courts of the U.S. justice system. As you learned in Chapter 2, legal theories of preventive law, restorative justice, and procedural justice have influenced changes in the way that the U.S. legal system makes decisions before, during, and after a court case, and interactions with clients who may appear as litigants, defendants, witnesses, and victims in court cases.

In response to the increasingly punitive nature of the U.S. justice system, restorative justice initiatives seek a more balanced approach that includes a focus on protection of the community, accountability for violations against the law, and resources and skills offenders need to live responsibly and productively. The ultimate goal is to "restore" the relationship of the community and the victim to a state of well-being and to provide the offender with training and treatment (Smith, 2001). This has resulted in the development of conferencing and mediation programs in child protection, juvenile justice, and criminal justice (Connolly, 2009). These initiatives were discussed in Chapter 7 with survivors of trafficking, the debates around how victims and offenders are defined, how victims can also be offenders, and the complexity that arises in assessing and recommending treatment in those cases.

Procedural justice concerns have led to a focus on the inclusion of voice and attention to culture, and the power of informal and nonprofessional help-giving systems within families and communities. It has also called attention to perceptions of fairness and who has decision control. The underlying theory is that when individuals' and families' perspectives are elicited, and the problem is solved in a manner that integrates those perspectives, the result will be the promotion of active responsibility in solving the problems. Under the theory of responsive regulation, individuals should be given the opportunity to self-correct before the state moves into regulatory control (Neff, 2004; Pennell, 2004). An individual or family retains their decision-making power to the extent that they can behave responsibly. It is important for social workers participating in conferencing and mediation to ensure that these theoretical orientations underpin the alternative venue. A lack of attention to these principles can result in conferences and mediation sessions becoming routinized, professional-led, and "rubber stamps" for service plans and families as individuals may admit to behaviors without due process and knowledge of their legal rights (Nixon et al., 2005).

Increasingly the public and other branches of government have been looking to the judicial system to identify and craft interdisciplinary and nonadversarial solutions to the behaviors and problems that may bring individuals into Civil or Criminal Court. It is believed that in certain matters the adversarial approach can intensify conflict and differences in ways that are not effective or helpful for many constituents. The therapeutic jurisprudence movement and the subsequent proliferation of research using that theoretical perspective have identified the adverse effects that adversarial proceedings can have on the emotional and psychological life of those interacting with the justice system. Additionally, the movement generated research evaluating alternative methods with the goals of prevention and more long-lasting solutions that have the objective of reducing recidivism and addressing the underlying issue that led to court involvement.

This research has supported the preventive law movement and has resulted in some changes in the role of courts and justice systems from framing themselves as adversarial to problem-solvers. As we have seen, many of the issues addressed in legal forums such as child abuse or juvenile delinquency often involve racial and economic inequities, psychosocial problems as well as legal issues and it is believed that specialized problem-solving courts that integrate treatment services with court processes will provide more effective outcomes for victims, offenders, and members of the community. You are also now aware that many participants in the justice system do not believe that their voices are heard and that there is disparate and discriminatory treatment. As you learned in Chapter 2, if you view this condition through a procedural justice framework, beliefs in the unfairness of treatment, and justice decision-making processes makes it more likely that citizens will become involved in rule-breaking behavior and not respect the authority of the law (Tyler, 2003).

All of the justice forums that we have introduced in this book thus far: civil, criminal, and administrative incorporate some form of conferencing and mediation. Civil and Criminal Courts continue to develop a range of specialized problem-solving courts. In the following section you will be introduced to the wide range of options that may exist for your client in each of these forums if your client does not want to engage in extensive litigation or adversarial proceedings. In many of these venues, social workers are recognized as the preferred facilitative professional because they already possess many of the skills and knowledge needed to implement and facilitate these alternative methods of problem solving such as brokering, conflict resolution, problem solving, negotiation, and mediation.

It is also important to note that in the interests of our focus on racial and ethnic justice, alternatives venues have been suggested as mechanisms that can begin to address issues such as over representation and institutionalized practices of discriminatory and disparate treatment. Research has found that for many cultural groups the collaborative decision-making processes involved in many of these alternative methods are more culturally coherent and are actually an acknowledgment of the problem-solving and peace-making methods used for centuries within many ethnic groups and Indigenous populations.

SOCIAL WORK ROLES IN ALTERNATIVE VENUES

The field of alternative venues explicitly and clearly acknowledges that the generalist and ecological orientation of social work practice and social workers' clinical expertise, knowledge of service systems and referral processes, and skill and value set that includes administration, collaboration, consensus, problem-solving, and community organizing, make them the preferred employee for a range of positions within this field. Employment possibilities range from statewide coordinators of problem-solving courts, to intake and screening of individual participants in a local problem-solving court, to conference facilitators and mediators.

Social Worker as Conference Facilitator

In this role the social worker functions as the facilitator of the conference, referring to a meeting of stakeholders and parties which, depending on the type of case, may include victims and offenders. Social workers are frequently facilitators of restorative justice conferencing initiatives in both Family and Criminal Courts. In many of the evaluation studies that have been conducted on family conferencing models, one of the most important variables leading to the success or failure of conferencing is the role played by and the competence of the facilitator. The social worker should be trained in whatever model of conferencing is being used but should recognize that essentially conference facilitation is culturally competent group work. Many of the skills that social workers learn in their foundation year such as pregroup planning, the difference between casework and group work, addressing power imbalances in groups, developing mutual aid and social responsibility in all group members, implementing the "seven step progression" of group problem-solving (Kurland & Salmon, 1992), and process and outcome evaluation can all be employed to facilitate an effective conference.

Social Worker as Mediator

Social workers have successfully established mediation practices across several venues such as divorce and postdivorce disputes, parent–child conflicts, child welfare issues, community conflicts, conflicts over the care of those lacking capacity, and personnel issues as members of organizations. As you will learn later in the chapter, the specific role of the social work mediator will depend on the type of mediation utilized, your local state statutes, and court rules. No matter what model of mediation is employed, the role of the mediator is essentially a neutral, impartial party who assists individuals in conflict to come to a mutually agreeable solution. The standards of practice for social workers promulgated by the National Association of Social Workers (NASW) are meant to apply to mediators as well.

Social Worker as Client Advocate

Social workers working with individual or family clients in the implicit legal context of social work practice may become involved in alternative venues when in the role of advocate for the client. In this role you would ensure that your client is aware of any legal or due process rights they may be waiving by agreeing to participate in an alternative venue. Collaborating with client attorneys or providing a resource for a client to obtain legal counseling about this decision is a key advocacy task. You may be asked to accompany a client who has a disability or mental health issue who needs support to effectively participate in an alternative venue. In this role you can assist clients to effectively prepare to participate in a meaningful way, to exercise self-determination, and to collaborate with other service providers to ensure effective and positive outcomes. Social workers can also play a critical role as an advocate that fall outside of the traditional context of working directly with an attorney representing a client. Social workers can volunteer or may be asked by legal representatives to participate in preparing a client for court, attending court with a client as support, or drafting and identifying letters of support as a part of the client's mitigation packet. These roles may arise whether the social worker has a history working with the client, or partners with law offices and communities to engage in community defense and or "participatory defense." Participatory defense is another movement defined by one organization as "a community organizing model for people facing charges, their families, and their communities to impact the outcome of cases and transform the landscape of power in the court system" (Participatory Defense, 2024). Social workers can play key roles in clients and individuals lives facing systemic involvement.

Social Worker as Lay Representative

If you are functioning as a lay representative for a client who has a conflict regarding an administrative matter such as benefits or special education and is requesting a hearing, you will most likely be asked to participate in mediation to attempt to resolve the conflict prior to having a hearing. In this role you would help identify the client's interests and needs and if your client does not feel comfortable negotiating, you would represent your client's position during the mediation process. As with any direct service role for a social worker in the explicit legal context, you would also prepare the client for their role in the administrative matter which could include testifying, identifying goals, and gathering evidence. Social workers can also partner with legal aid and other law offices that offer collateral services to assist in fighting for clients' rights in other matters including benefits or special education. The legal agency may have the ability to represent the client on the collateral matter and work in collaboration with the social worker in an outside organization to support the client with their case.

Social Worker as Problem-Solving Court Administrator

Social workers can be administrators of problem-solving courts at both the state and local levels. At the state level, social workers plan and develop statewide initiatives for problem-solving courts. The administrator would typically conduct tasks and activities that social workers are very familiar with such as identify service needs and plan responses; work closely with judges and problem-solving court personnel; make sure that data are being compiled, analyzed, and reported to inform practice; evaluate programming; make personnel decisions; develop and monitor budgets; assess training needs and develop educational programming for court personnel; coordinate grant applications, data collection, evaluation, and distribution of funds.

Social workers also coordinate and administer local problem-solving courts and in this role function much like a program director. Familiar tasks include recruiting, hiring, training and supervising staff; managing daily activities and projects; preparing budgets and authorizing and monitoring expenditures; developing collaborative partnerships with service agencies to meet the needs of the population that the particular court is serving; developing and assessing policies and procedures and recommending and making necessary changes; collecting, analyzing, and sharing court data; and serving a public relations function with the government, community, and media.

Social Worker as Evaluator and Case Manager

In this role the social worker will conduct screening and assessment related to the presenting problem that is being addressed by the particular court. The assessment might generally include the level of motivation for change, the type of intervention required, and the identification of programs that will be appropriate for the treatment of the client. In this role you might also provide case management services such as monitoring the client treatment plan and participating in team meetings to assess progress, and also providing a recommendation to the court if the client is able to be discharged from treatment, services, and or from court supervision. You will also provide reports to the court and possibly collect and compile data to evaluate the progress of the court in reaching its purpose and goals.

Social Worker as Probation Officer

Social workers may be assigned to or manage the units of the probation department to provide supervision of those in Juvenile and Criminal Courts' problem-solving courts. Managers may supervise and provide training to the teams attached to the court, make sure that the rules, regulations, and policies of the court are complied with and oversee data collection, compilation of statistics, and evaluation of the problem-solving court. A probation officer at the case level provides case screening, intake, case management of the services ordered by the court, preparation of assessments, and progress and discharge reports.

Social Worker as Treatment Provider, Educator, and Evaluator

Social workers may also be employed with many of the community-based mental health, substance abuse, and social service programs that support the treatment plans of those participating in alternative venues. Many of the alternative venues designed for youth participation include both educative and/or treatment components, most usually group-level interventions. Social workers can play a part in researching, developing, implementing, and evaluating interventions that support the processes of alternative venues and are designed to reduce recidivism. An example is the collaboration between the Teen Court of Greater Baton Rouge and Louisiana State University School of Social Work where social work interns have designed, run, and evaluated a group-level intervention with at-risk teens ages 10 to 17 who are processed through the Teen Court. The group work intervention consists of social work interns functioning as mentors and facilitators and addresses such issues as peer pressure, goal setting, problem-solving, communication, and anger management.

CONFERENCING

History and Theoretical Background

The procedural justice movement has highlighted issues of fairness and inclusion during processes and proceedings of professional decision-making. This trend has led to the development of conferencing as a way of redistributing the power and responsibility of solving and addressing social problems such as child abuse and neglect, domestic and community violence, and juvenile and adult crime. A major goal of conferencing is to leverage the power of the family and community toward the solution of family problems.

Conferencing originally started in New Zealand as a way to return decision-making on behalf of Indigenous children and families to the native communities to which they belonged. Initiated by the Maori people, family group conferencing was an acknowledgment that as a group they were being overrepresented in foster care and that the strengths of their families and cultures were being overlooked. In the United States, as child welfare decisions became increasingly monitored and decided by courts and judges, family group conferencing was seen as a way to move away from adjudication and return the focus of decision-making to a more voluntary, collaborative relationship between the social worker and family. Conferencing has been extended and developed as a way of returning voice and decision-making to groups such as parents in the child welfare system, victims of crime, juveniles, and native peoples (Gibbs, 2009). Conferencing highlights the important social work value of self-determination, especially with mandated clients and the right that individuals have to be informed about, and participate in, making decisions that greatly affect their lives. While the goals of conferencing are in line with procedural and community justice, many researchers have noted that conferencing in practice can become formulaic and standardized and antithetical to the goal of empowerment espoused in the theory and policy of conferencing (Moyle & Tauri, 2016; Nygård & Saus, 2018).

Conferencing assumes that given the right information, personal and community support networks, and professional support and resource provision that families and individuals can develop plans that are protective and restore the relationship between family and child or victim and offender, and help access the community as playing a part in the care and protection of its members. It is also hoped under the procedural justice formulation that conferencing will change the relationship and increase the trust between members of oppressed communities and the state. Conferencing is also used as an adjunct and support to Civil and Criminal Court processes. Under the restorative justice formulation and in the juvenile justice and Criminal Court arena, conferencing is used as a method to rehabilitate the offender and reintegrate them back into the community. It is believed that this is a move away from retribution and toward rehabilitation and is a more effective way to address recidivism.

Conferencing in Civil, Criminal, and Juvenile Justice Forums

Perhaps the most familiar form of conferencing is the Family Group Conference (FGC) being used as a forum for decision-making in child protection and juvenile justice planning. FGC is a decision-making process that can be used to explore many different child protective decisions at different phases of the process. Decisions such as the best plan to ensure child safety, coordination of services, permanency planning, visitation planning, and family reunification can be the topic of an FGC (Sandau-Beckler et al., 2005).

To return to our case example, it is likely that within several days of her infant's removal Ms. Jones would have been invited to some form of FGC by the child welfare agency caseworker. The most pressing issues would be to make sure that Matthew is safe and to determine what resources or services might be needed to enhance the protective capacity of Ms. Jones. Ms. Jones would be instructed to identify family members or other community supports such as her aunt, her pastor, or her community-based social service worker who would be invited to attend. Depending on the jurisdiction, the conference might be held prior to the child welfare agency seeking an emergency removal order from the Family Court judge or after the removal order has been granted but prior to the adjudication of dependency.

Social workers who are working in either the implicit or explicit context may be in a position to refer clients for or participate in family group decision-making conferences. There are several different forms of FGC and therefore it is important that you check with your local child protective service agency to see what format or type is being used in your jurisdiction. There are some important variations in regard to who facilitates, confidentiality, structure, who refers, decision-making responsibility when consensus cannot be reached, and whether the option of offering an FGC by child protective services is required and under what circumstances (Casey Family Services, 2009). Some states have notice requirements and will not have a conference without the presence of the parent; in other venues the conference may proceed without the parent being present. Furthermore, each jurisdiction may have different procedures and rules for whether clients are able to attend FGCs with their attorney or representatives from their attorney's office. The various forms of FGC that are being used in the United States are called Family Group Decision-Making, Family Unity Meetings, Family Team Conferencing, Permanency Teaming Process, and Team Decision-Making (Casey Family Services, 2009).

Based on the principles of restorative justice, this intervention also appears on policy and legislative agendas in the juvenile justice system. This approach has been used as a method of diverting juvenile offenders out of the system prior to adjudication (Edwards & Parkinson, 2018; McGarrell & Hipple, 2007). FGC in juvenile justice employs a neutral facilitator to assist victims, offenders and their families, and other concerned parties such as clergy, juvenile justice personnel, police, and community leaders to have a dialogue about the crime and its impact. Cases can be referred by judges, police, schools, and probation officers and usually involve offenses such as theft, arson, minor assaults, and vandalism. The FGC process has been implemented in schools, police departments, probation offices, residential programs, community mediation programs, and neighborhood groups. Conferencing is most often used as diversion from the court process for juveniles but can also be used after adjudication and disposition to address unresolved issues or determine specific terms of restitution Walker (2002).

Conferences in this venue have been referred to as FGC, community conferencing, real justice conferencing, and restorative group conferencing (RGC). RGC has been designed as an intervention for youth who are involved in both child welfare and juvenile justice systems. In Minnesota under the Restorative Justice law, restorative justice programs are authorized by statute to: "discuss the impact of the offense on the victim and the community; provide support to the victim and methods for reintegrating the victim into community life; assign an appropriate sanction to the offender; and provide methods for reintegrating the offender into community life" (Minn. Stat, c.609, § 611A.775, 1998). The restorative justice program would be responsible for holding conferences with the offender and a range of impacted individuals including the victim, victim's family, offender's family, and members of the community if deemed appropriate.

Legal Framework of Conferencing

In addition to Minnesota, other states specifically authorize the use of FGC through statutes and laws. It is critical for legal evidence-based practitioners to be familiar with both the laws or regulations in your state or locality as well as the evaluation research that identifies the conditions under which FGC has been found to be satisfactory and effective for the families participating in them and even when they do not. If you are working in the implicit context you may be in a position to assist your client in making a decision to request an FGC or, in the absence of preparation by an FGC facilitator, assist a family in the tasks of preparation such as deciding who to invite, how best to present a family's strengths and resources, and suggest a consultation with their attorney to make sure they understand the legal and confidentiality implications of participating. For example, in our case example, a social worker who is Ms. Jones's substance abuse treatment worker would want to know if anything Ms. Jones or they say at an FGC could be used against her in both her civil and criminal trial. Additionally, given the personal nature of the information the substance abuse counselor is privy, it would be important for both the counselor and Ms. Jones to know if what is discussed is confidential and what limits on confidentiality might apply depending on the role of other participants in the FGC. Later in the chapter you will learn more about the steps involved in implementing an FGC and the justice and due process concerns relevant to alternative venues such as conferencing.

An example of a statute related to FGC in child protection and juvenile justice, is Nebraska's statute on conferencing entitled "Restorative Justice Practices." The statute gives the court discretion about whether or not they will provide the opportunity for the family to participate and defines some of the issues that may be addressed:

> (1) In any juvenile case, the court may provide the parties the opportunity to address issues involving the child's care and placement, services to the family, and other concerns through restorative justice practices. Restorative justice practices may include, but are not limited to, prehearing conferences, FGCs, expedited family group conferences, child welfare mediation, permanency prehearing conferences, termination of parental rights prehearing conferences, juvenile victim-offender dialogue, victim youth conferencing, victim-offender mediation, youth or community dialogue, panels, circles, and truancy mediation.
> (Neb. Rev. Stat. c.43, § 43-247.01, 2010)

As mentioned previously, FGC was initiated by Indigenous peoples and has been embraced by many tribes in the United States. Many tribal nations have incorporated the option or requirement of FGC into their legal codes (www.tribal-institute.org/lists/codes.htm). An example of an FGC mandated by statute can be found in the Navajo Nation Code, Chapter 9, Section 1101, which defines family group conferencing as the following:

a. The goal of family group conferencing is to ensure families reassume primary responsibility, *t'áá hwó ájít'eego*, with guidance from the Division, regarding children's safety and well-being to eliminate the need for Court intervention.

b. The division is required to refer every reported and substantiated case of child abuse and neglect to a FGC when the abuse or neglect does not require removal.

c. The division may refer to cases involving family disputes or neglect where the child has not been removed to family group conferencing through the Peacemaking Program.

d. Concerned family members and professionals may refer any matter concerning a child to family group conferencing either through the Division or Peacemaking Program. Such a referral shall not preclude removal if reasonable grounds exist to believe that the child is abused and/or neglected, and removal is necessary.

The Navajo Nation Code clearly states the goal of the FGC is to have the family take primary responsibility for the child and the child's well-being in every case where there is not a removal, and envisions that family and community members, including professionals, would be included in the conferencing.

Oregon provides us with another example of statutes defining family group decision-making as "a family-focused intervention facilitated by professional staff that is designed to build and strengthen the natural caregiving system for the child [and] may include FGCs, family unity meetings, family mediation or other professionally recognized interventions that include extended family and rely upon the family to make decisions about planning for its children" (Or. Rev. Stat., c.417, §§ 417.365-413.75). However, the Oregon law clarifies that the opportunity to participate in an FGC is at the discretion of the Department of Human Services. The Oregon Revised Statutes, Chapter 417, Section 417.368 notes that "[1] [t]he Department of Human Services shall consider the use of a family decision-making meeting in each case in which a child is placed in substitute care for more than 30 days . . . [3] If the department elects not to conduct a family decision-making meeting, the reasons for that decision shall be clearly documented in the written service plan of the child developed by the department." The due process protections for parents and children include the requirement of written documentation in the case record of any decision made not to offer a family the opportunity to participate. In addition, the statute lays out the time frames within which the conference must occur if it is offered, the notice requirements to any parents or relatives who had direct contact with the child within the year prior to placement, and if a potential participant is deemed a safety risk. The law makes provisions for the participants to provide written statements and documents, allows children age 12 and older to attend, reviews what must be covered in the plan, and states the requirement that participants must receive a written copy of the plan within 21 days.

A number of states are beginning to articulate and memorialize principles of restorative justice through statutes and codes as part of the values and focus for juvenile justice reform efforts. The state of Montana under Montana Code, Chapter 15, Section 2-15-2013 (2007) established an Office of Restorative Justice that promotes restorative justice programming, training, and implementation. The law defines the office's purpose as promoting "the use of restorative justice throughout the state by balancing the needs of victims, communities, and juvenile and adult offenders; [and] provide technical assistance to jurisdictions and organizations interested in implementing the principles of restorative justice; [and] bring additional resources to Montana communities for restorative justice programs." Programming includes victim/offender meetings, family group conferencing, sentencing circles, and school expulsion alternatives (Pavelka, 2008). Pennsylvania has integrated a restorative justice approach for reform under the Juvenile Act, located at 42 Pa. C.S. Section 6301, when it required that the system provide balanced attention "to the protection of the community, the imposition of accountability for offenses committed and the development of competencies that will enable youth to become responsible and productive members of society."

Another important resource for you to access is the administrative regulations and procedures that every state agency develops to define how the department implements any laws or statutes that affect them. Many state human, health and social service agencies post policies and procedures on their websites that give very detailed information about how family group conferencing is being implemented in their jurisdiction, including identifying what model of conferencing may be used. For example, if you were to access the Department of Social and Health Service website in the state of Washington, you would find a number of procedure and policy manuals relevant to FGC: Family-Centered Practice Model, Case Services Policy Manual and Indian Child Welfare Manual (Washington State Department of Social and Health Services, 2024). These are excellent educational and advocacy resources for yourself and your clients.

THE PROCESS OF CONFERENCING

Role of Facilitator

The role of the facilitator in the different conferencing models can vary and is dependent on what model of conferencing is being used as well as the statutory and procedural requirements of the jurisdiction. In the original family group conferencing model, the facilitator must be someone who has no case-related responsibilities. In the Family Team Conferencing and Permanency Teaming Process, the facilitator is usually the assigned social worker or in the event of a conflict another agency worker. In Team Decision-Making, the facilitator is an agency worker assigned to a different unit with no case responsibility (Casey Family Services, 2009). Despite these various models the overall research supports the idea that the facilitator of conferences should not have service responsibility for the participants. Some jurisdictions have addressed this by having separate units within the agency for facilitators, contracting out with a private agency, or developing panels of trained citizen volunteers.

Planning and Preparation

The tasks involved in the planning and preparation phase include defining the purpose of the meeting, identifying the issues to be addressed, assessing the participants capacity to meaningfully participate, making decisions about who to invite to the conference, inviting participants, assessing issues of safety and risk, and meaningfully preparing participants.

Again, your foundational social work skills are especially significant at this stage. For example, participants such as parents, juveniles, and victims should be screened in order to determine if there is a mental illness or disability that may impact their ability to participate. In this instance, the facilitator should ensure the presence of an advocate to make sure the person's interests are articulated and represented. Asking participants to write questions and notes before the conference and to identify and bring important documents can help participants become more reflective. Having prepared questions for the Child Protective Services worker or other service providers will make clients participate more as an equal rather than being the sole focus of service providers. As part of your preparation, you can also ask the family how they would like to open the meeting. Sometimes sharing a picture of the family or providing a description of a family ritual can individualize a family, youth, or victim and highlight their unique characteristics for participants in the conference.

In victim/offender conferencing involving domestic violence and involving child abuse if the child is participating, special attention and preparation must be paid to ensure the victim's feelings and concerns are expressed and addressed. Ideally the meeting should be held in a neutral location in the community and during times that encourage the greatest amount of individual and community participation. Location is repeatedly cited in the literature as an important factor in determining family comfort and thereby facilitating their participation (Merkel-Holguin, 1998).

Convening the Conference

The primary tasks at this part of the process include introducing all of the participants, reviewing the purpose of the meeting, and reviewing rules including confidentiality. As mentioned it is very important to check the confidentiality rules for your jurisdiction as they are different depending on locale and type of conferencing employed. Being clear about confidentiality and what information can be shared with the court or used in court are essential for the development of trust and attention to the protection of client rights necessary for a candid discussion of the issues in the conference. This includes clarifying for all participants what information will be recorded and which parties or persons will receive copies of any documentation from the conference. Furthermore, the facilitator will be responsible for making sure that any issues of language access and interpretation are addressed before the conference so that all parties can participate fully.

The tension for legal evidence-based practitioners is that although the primary intent of this intervention is to return decision-making to family, the conferences take place within regulatory and legally monitored systems. As an example of this, consider that a decision reached in the FGC to reunify a family would still have to be approved by the judge. There is always a balance between empowering the individual or family and keeping children, the victim, or the community safe. It is important for practitioners of Legal and Evidence-based Practices (LEBP) to be aware that, because the plans must be approved before they are implemented, the mandatory authorities retain their legal role while responding to the family group and regulatory requirements of the case. We will address justice concerns later in the chapter as the themes of voluntariness, confidentiality, balancing power, and client capacity emerge in critiques of these venues as access to justice issues and so will be explored in more depth.

Facilitators should always be aware of the historical and current context of institutionalized racism and discrimination to understand and respond appropriately to some of the emotional and behavioral triggers and reactions toward the child welfare or juvenile justice system that participants may exhibit when discussing issues at the meeting. Acknowledging the context and being clear and transparent about what power of decision-making families do or do not have is crucial to ensuring an effective and transparent process.

Information Sharing

In this phase of the process, the facilitators ask all of the participants to identify the family's or individuals' strengths. After sharing strengths and using the same process, the facilitators ask all the participants to identify the issues of concern or challenges faced by the family or individual. The facilitators will then identify groups and categories of strengths and issues of concern. To the extent possible, issues of concern should be elicited from the family first before caseworkers or other service providers provide their input. Issues of concern and strengths should be actual observable behaviors that can be addressed or enhanced, and not opinions or intuitions. It is critical that facilitators ensure that the individual or family is aware of the agency or the court's purpose or legal goal. For example, in an FGC involving child protection the central issue, regardless of what the family identifies, will always be "Is this child safe?" and this should be very clear to the family. The facilitator should have a clear understanding of risk and protective factors for child abuse and neglect, domestic violence, and juvenile offending and use that conceptual framework to think through the behaviors of concern and family strengths as a way of ensuring that the primary goal is not lost.

Facilitators should also attempt to make this stage interactive by giving participants time to ask questions or to clarify information, rather than having caseworkers or service providers give formal presentations as "experts" about the family or individual and by directly asking family members for their feedback to the professionals. Again, your social work skills of facilitating discussion, reflection, and space for all participants to share their thoughts will be invaluable toward a successful conference.

Family Private Time

This is phase of the process when professionals leave the room and families are given a private opportunity to develop a plan. Families may become upset or disagree during this time and a facilitator may be asked to join as moderator. At times the facilitator may be asked by the family to shift roles and become a consultant as they are working out the plans or have a disagreement. It is important that facilitators do not direct the family or give recommendations during this phase even if the family or individual is directly asking. While it can be tempting to provide your opinion or conclusion at this stage of the proceeding, it is critical to the model to allow the family to create a plan that is based on their needs, culture, and community.

Reconvening

At this phase of the process, the facilitator invites the family to share their plan. After the family presents their plan, the participants discuss the proposed plan and begin to develop a concrete plan. The plan should focus on addressing the observable behaviors identified as concerns and enhancing the behaviors identified as protective during the information-sharing phase, not forgetting to address the central questions of safety and sustainability for the family. The plan must then be agreed to and approved. The responsibilities and roles of every participant—individual or family, service providers, advocates, and community members—should be clearly identified and put in writing. As mentioned, the plan should be clear to all participants who will be allowed to view that document.

Ending

In this phase the conference is brought to end. Summarizing the key points of the conference and important agreements and issues provides closure. Pennell and Burford (1997) suggest ways to enhance outcomes are to ensure that participants have written copies of the plan. Part of writing up the plan should include who will have the responsibility for monitoring and evaluating the plan. We suggest that both the family and a professional be given the dual responsibility for monitoring and overseeing that the plan is carried out and implemented to continue the focus on the family or individual assuming responsibility for their own regulation.

After the Meeting

There should be follow up with the family or individual who is responsible for monitoring the plan. If needed the FGC can be reconvened to evaluate or assess why some aspect of the plan is not being implemented or is no longer necessary. It is crucial to make sure that the family or individual has access to the resources and services to carry out the plan. Often, this is where gaps between the aspirational model of FGC and the realities of implementation occur. Not all communities and families have access to the kinds of resources that may be needed to effectively carry out the plan. Social workers should use macro-level skills to identify and advocate for funding that allows community-based agencies to implement and provide evidence-informed services to child welfare system participants. Furthermore, social work advocates and facilitators should ensure that plans developed in the FGC are realistic in terms of accessing services not only in the community but also within the time frame proposed by the court or the FGC agreement.

ALTERNATIVE DISPUTE RESOLUTION AND THE COURTS

History and Theory

Mediation and alternative dispute resolution programs have proliferated during the last three decades in civil, criminal, and administrative forums in response to large caseloads, litigation expenses, delays in court processing, participant dissatisfaction, and the increasing needs of pro se litigants. Federal legislation such as the Civil Justice Reform Act of 1990 and the Alternative Dispute Act of 1998 encouraged and, in some cases, mandated, federal and state courts to develop mediation and alternative dispute resolution programs and offer all litigants the option of mediation prior to trial as one of several ways to reform the courts and reduce caseloads.

There are several different kinds of alternative dispute resolution mechanisms attached to courts that social workers may be exposed to when they are interacting with the justice system. The first of these is called a settlement conference that is conducted by a judge to try and get the parties to evaluate their case and "settle" as a way of avoiding a trial. This type of mediation is also called evaluative mediation where the mediator takes a more active role, identifies the weaknesses and strengths of the case, makes informal or formal recommendations, and focuses on the legal rights rather than needs of the party. Arbitration is when the parties agree on an arbitrator who will render a decision that the parties must go along with. The mediator under an evaluative model has some kind of legal or topical expertise.

Another type of alternative dispute resolution process is mediation. Simply put mediation has the goal of resolving issues in a less formal, more comfortable setting than a courtroom with the assistance of impartial facilitators. The process of mediation can usually begin one of two ways: one or both of the parties can request it, or the judge in some situations can or must order it. The facilitator assists the participants to identify their needs and interests and negotiate a resolution acceptable to everyone that can be presented to and authorized by the court. In what is known as facilitative mediation, the mediator assists the parties in coming to an agreement without offering an opinion or an assessment. In this method the parties are empowered to be in charge of the outcome.

When relationships will continue after the legal dispute such as between a landlord and tenant, a juvenile and a victim that attend the same school, a divorcing couple, a child welfare worker and a parent, or a parent and a child, mediation can be employed to reconcile relationships, teach problem-solving skills, and help participants identify what is important to them. Mediation that is focused on empowering parties and preserving and enhancing relationships is also known as *transformative* mediation. The goal of mediation is to resolve the dispute but in a way that changes or repairs relationships. In a review of the research on mediation during divorce proceedings it was reported that participation in divorce mediation had a more positive effect than litigation on the relationships between the divorcing couple and increased the parents understanding of the needs and psychological effects of divorce on their children (Shaw, 2010; Thoennes, 2009). Research conducted to explore the effects of victim–offender mediation on victims found that one of the most important outcomes for the victim was receiving an apology from the offender. Later in this chapter you will learn about the steps involved during mediation in more detail.

The administration of mediation can be different depending on the model used by your state. There are various structures of mediation across different states and can include mediation as part of the court itself and staffed by court employees; mediation taking place in the court but facilitated by a panel of neutral, independent contractors paid by the court or, at times, by the parties themselves; or mediation taking place completely outside the court when the court contracts with an agency or organization to provide the mediation services using volunteers or paid staff.

Although mediation was first introduced, and remains in many cases, a voluntary choice for participants, some states are mandating that disagreeing parties participate in mediation prior to the initiation of court proceedings. For example, some states mandate that parents participate in mediation prior to proceeding to a custody trial. There are also different levels of confidentiality throughout state statutes and individual court rules that may be confusing. It is important that both you and your client understand that a legal consultation may be needed to make sure your client is fully informed of their rights and potential consequences before deciding to participate in mediation. If you are working with immigrant populations, admissions of crimes or other behaviors may unintentionally create grounds for deportation.

Research informed by the theories of therapeutic jurisprudence began to illuminate the effects of contentious and protracted legal proceedings on the development and well-being of children. Therefore, the use of mediation and other nonadversarial techniques and structures is widely used in the context of divorce, custody, child protection allegations, termination of parental rights, domestic violence, same-sex partnerships, and permanency proceedings. The objective continues to develop and use nonadversarial structures in the family law, juvenile justice, and child protection arenas to address the complexity and diversity of family issues and conflicts, address restorative justice concerns, speed up the processing of matters to ensure faster permanency for children, and place responsibility for problem-solving on the individual, the family, and the community (Edwards, 2004).

As you discovered in Chapter 5, the ecological and generalist approaches that are the cornerstone of social work practice uniquely prepare social workers to function effectively in alternative venues. For many clients going through the process of mediation it is often experienced as an effective intervention in and of itself and one that social workers "informally" engage in all the time: Social workers facilitate processes where clients are heard and are recognized as a unique individual who may have different interests and needs than the next person even if they have a similar issue or problem. Mediation practice is particularly well suited to the knowledge, skill, and value base of social work. Formal mediation can occur between a range of micro, mezzo, and macro systems that social workers are "mediating" informally every day in the course of regular practice: two individuals, couples, parent and child, family members, youth and police, offender and victim, parent and child welfare agency, parent and school system, business and consumer, and individual and government agency.

Some social work authors maintain that mediation is simultaneously a social justice intervention as it gives clients access to information, educates them by teaching problem-solving skills, promotes access to justice for those who cannot afford attorneys or litigation, preserves ongoing relationships, and evidences a belief in the capacity of the client to examine facts and use them to make responsible decisions (Connaway & Gentry, 1988; Parsons, 1991; Parsons & Cox, 1989). One of the benefits of mediation is that it requires participants to directly communicate with each other, identify the real problems and issues, and retain the power of decision-making.

Using a procedural justice framework and applying it to mediation practice it is important to identify for clients, particularly clients who feel powerless in the face of legal and other professionals: When you communicate effectively, take ownership of the attempt to solve the problem, come to a resolution that both you and the other participant perceive as fair, and use your community to support you then you are shifting the decision-making power away from authorities and back to yourself. Under a responsive regulation model this amplification of voice, taking responsibility for problem solutions, and therefore increasing motivation to commit to and implement a solution, decrease or eliminates the need for outside regulation (Braithwaite, 2002).

Mediation in Civil, Criminal, Juvenile Justice, and Administrative Venues

The use of mediation is now available in many Civil and Criminal Courts and administrative hearings in a wide variety of matters that include many of the unmet legal needs of clients you read about in Chapter 1. Most state court websites have a section on alternative dispute resolution and mediation services that are attached to various courts, as well as the kinds of matters that can be referred or requested. For example, if you access the website for Utah state courts, you will see that in Utah the Juvenile Court, the District Court, and the Appellate Court all offer mediation programs. Under Juvenile Court, families and youth can participate in Child Welfare Mediation, Truancy Mediation, and Victim–Offender Mediation. In District Court, Utah requires mandatory divorce mediation, and offers voluntary Co-Parenting Mediation, Landlord/Tenant Mediation, and Small Claims Mediation (Utah State Courts, 2024).

In Civil Court mediation is available for child protection cases both before and after adjudication, divorce and custody proceedings, guardianship, probate or disputes about wills and estates, some wrongful injury cases such as elder abuse that occurs in nursing homes, and for some juvenile offenses. Additional Civil Court matters where mediation is available depending on your city or state are employment; housing; discrimination; education and special education; child support; open adoption; permanency and termination of parental rights; small claims; business and contracts; insurance; malpractice; foreclosure and bankruptcy; and insurance cases. In Criminal Courts mediation is available for misdemeanors and some felonies. In administrative venues, conferencing and mediation is usually available instead of hearings. Mediation is frequently used in special education and other benefits and entitlements disputes.

In addition, there are organizations usually referred to as "community justice centers" where mediators are available to assist community members in the resolution of disputes. There is an increasing trend for the development of partnerships with the judiciary and community-based mediation centers to provide mediation services as a means of pretrial diversion for both civil and criminal cases. For example, the New York Unified Court System has partnered with community-based mediation centers throughout the state to offer citizens an alternative to using the courts to settle disputes. The mediation centers address issues that emerge between consumers and businesses, families and schools, planning for elders, conflicts between neighbors, and victim and offender restitution (New York Courts, 2024).

Legal Framework of Mediation

The authorization for and the procedures pertaining to the practice of mediation in each state comes from federal laws, state statutes, and individual court rules. Statutes and rules discuss important issues such as the purpose, goals, and function of mediation, the kinds of issues the state allows to be mediated, confidentiality rules, qualifications and standards for mediators, who may refer, whether mediation is voluntary or mandatory, rules of how mediation is conducted, options if mediation is not successful, attendance, and the power and duties of the mediators. Some state law provides for centers for alternative dispute resolution within the state judiciary. One example is in Hawaii where, under Chapter 613-2 of the Haw. Rev. Stat. (1989), the legislature authorized the creation of the Center for Alternative Dispute Resolution within the court system. According to the statute, the goal is to "facilitate the effective, timely, and voluntary resolution of disputes. Through these resolutions, it shall help reduce public and private costs of litigation and increase satisfaction with the justice system" (Haw. Rev. Stat. c613-2[a], 1989).

A source of information regarding mediation and alternative dispute is the Resolution Systems Institute's website, which has a Court ADR Resource Center that allows you to look up your individual state (Resolution Systems Institute, 2024). You can then access information about where the authority for mediation comes from; the mediation or alternative dispute processes available; the statutes, laws, and rules in your state that are relevant; research; statistics and evaluation studies of mediation processes and manuals; and other guidelines your state has developed. As mentioned in previous chapters it is well worth your while to go directly to your state statutes, laws, and court rules and make sure information you find on other sites is up to date. Here you can also find who may be qualified as a mediator (note that, in many states, to participate in family law mediation, a master's level social work degree is a requirement). If you have expertise in a certain area of practice such as healthcare or child welfare, you may be eligible with some training to become a court-appointed mediator.

Continuing with our earlier example of Hawaii, the authority for court ADR comes both from the federal law and courts (Alternative Dispute Resolution Act of 1998) and state courts (Hawaii Fam. Crt Rule 53.1, 1999). Checking the state Family Court Rules, we see that Rule 53.1 and allows "[t]he court, in its discretion or upon motion by a party, may order the parties to participate in an alternative dispute resolution process subject to conditions imposed by the court." As written in the law, this rule is very general and gives the court a great amount of discretion about whether to order a party to participate and under what conditions. From an advocacy point of view, it is important to know that your client can request mediation if they desire even though the judge will ultimately decide whether to order it. We can also determine that in Hawaii mediation is available for appellate court matters, bankruptcy, child custody and visitation, child protection and dependency, civil, criminal, family, foreclosure, landlord/tenant, personal injury, probate, small claims, and victim–offender. Hawaii has also published nonbinding aspirational guidelines for mediators.

Some court rules and statutes are more explicit and detailed than others. For example, the state of North Carolina has authorizing legislation for mediation in Criminal Court matters N.C.G.S. § 7A-38.3D (2008). The legislation further required the Supreme Court of North Carolina to develop the rules for mediation. The Supreme Court of North Carolina subsequently developed very detailed rules pertaining to mediation in matters that are pending in Criminal Court and the full text of the rules can be found on the state judicial website (North Carolina Office of Administrative Hearings, 2009). The rules cover the purpose of mediation, the factors judges should consider in determining whether to encourage mediation, the timing of the suggestion that the parties mediate, the kind of notice and what must be in it, intake and screening procedures, who may be a mediator, how to schedule the mediation, where the mediation is to be held, attendance requirements, who may attend and participate, the procedures for finalizing agreements, the duties and authority of the mediator, confidentiality, the process for reporting the results of the mediation, and certification requirements of those who may be appointed as mediators.

THE PROCESS OF MEDIATION

Role of Mediator

The role of the mediator most essentially is that of a neutral and impartial party. The mediator promotes settlement, compromise, or understanding among two or more conflicting parties (Parsons, 1991; Smith & Smock, 2008). The role of the mediator is very dependent on what approach to mediation is being used (evaluative, facilitative, or transformative) as well as the guidelines and rules for mediators in your locality as promulgated in your state's statutes and court rules. Therefore, the following is a very general overview of the process of mediation and may vary depending on where you live. Again, the following information is not intended to teach you how to be a mediator but rather to expose you to legal practices you may come across in your day-to-day social work practice.

Intake

Intake is generally the process that occurs in order to assess the appropriateness of the parties to participate in mediation. As you have learned in some states, some kinds of mediation are mandatory so there is no discretion involved by a judge or the parties. In other kinds of mediation, a judge has discretion to order mediation even when the parties do not request it. The judge may also order mediation over any party's objection. Often any of the parties may request mediation in writing or through the use of a motion; however, the judge may either grant or deny the request. In administrative venues clients can request mediation by contacting the administrative agency; for example, the local special education department. When conducting any mediation where there has been the suggestion of violence it is an important aspect of intake to meet the parties in advance and screen for issues of risk and safety. Again, many court rules or statutes will lay out the procedures for requesting mediation and the circumstances under which it may happen as well as who is eligible.

In some instances, the attorneys for the parties and the mediator will have a series of conference calls, or premediation meetings, to design the process and to identify the conditions or events that need to happen to facilitate a settlement. In the case of divorce, particular financial documents might be necessary. Rules about the informal and formal sharing of documents will be addressed. The key question to be addressed at the preliminary conference is what steps must take place before negotiation to maximize the potential for settlement?

Preparation

Preparation usually involves contacting the parties and arranging for the dates, times, and location of the mediation sessions. When victims are involved, it is always important to consult with them first about location and issues regarding their immediate safety. Sometimes the attorneys for the parties will explain and prepare their clients for mediation sessions and in other situations it may be the role of the mediator. Most mediators conduct a meeting with both parties to explain the "ground rules" on how the mediation will proceed and the agenda for the meeting, and will have each participant sign an agreement to mediate the issue and a confidentiality agreement.

In situations involving high emotions or complex issues the parties should plan to conduct the mediation in several sessions. This can be critical in elder, child abuse, domestic violence, and victim offender mediation to allow time to address the significant emotional issues that may emerge and act as barriers to the taking in and processing of information. In some cases, the first session may lay out the facts and introduce participants to the process. This allows for the development of trust and familiarity before moving to the negotiation phase.

Beginning

Mediation sessions usually begin with an orientation to the process followed by opening statements by each of the participants. The mediator will document the meeting process. When facilitating mediation sessions that involve victims, it is important to offer victims the opportunity to speak first in the session and to ask questions. After the opening statements that should identify the needs of the parties, the mediator will facilitate the setting of an agenda. The key issues to be resolved should be identified, for example, how restitution may be made to a victim of a crime. This is the most important and critical part of the mediation. The areas of disagreement should be clearly identified and then discussed.

Discussion and Negotiation

It is best to take one issue at a time and discuss each one before proceeding to the next. At times the mediator may need to meet or consult with the parties individually to aid in clarifying a point or addressing a concern. As said, negotiating resolutions to the issues is best done one at a time, although there may be issues that are related to each other such as what kind of restitution and how much money that may entail. This really is the problem-solving phase, and participants are encouraged to generate multiple resolutions to the disagreement. Social work mediators will find that many of the skills they have learned in carrying out task-centered or solution-based practice models can be effectively employed during mediation sessions. Parties may need space and opportunity to research some of the solutions as well as to learn more about their legal rights and duties. Identifying areas or places where the parties can come together is an important skill at this phase.

Settlement

At the conclusion of the mediation sessions, hopefully there will be a voluntary and acceptable agreement. The mediator or the clients' attorneys will write up all the points of initial disagreement and identify the resolution for each of the issues.

Court Review

Once agreed to and signed, the agreement is presented to the court for review and approval. If the mediation session has failed, the court will be informed, and the parties will use more formal proceedings such as a trial or an administrative hearing to settle their dispute. In some circumstances such as child protection mediation, the court has the authority to accept, reject, or modify agreements.

PROBLEM-SOLVING COURTS

In 1989, the first problem-solving court was initiated in Miami as a response to the increasing number of felony drug cases resulting in large court caseloads, increasing numbers of drug-involved individuals being sent to prison and jail, and high rates of recidivism for this population. The objective of drug court is to use the rule of law to help motivate offenders to address their substance dependence, be diverted from incarceration, and change their behavior to prevent future court involvement. As of 2023, according to the National Treatment Court Resource Center, there are 4,255 problem-solving courts in the United States addressing a range of populations and issues such as prostitution, truancy, gambling, and parole violations with over 350 problem-solving courts aimed at juveniles (National Treatment Court Resource Center, 2024). All 50 states have appointed a statewide drug or problem-solving court coordinator.

Problem-solving courts aim to change the relationship between the community and the court by encouraging collaboration among judges, attorneys, social service agencies, community groups, and schools. The goals of this collaboration are improving public trust in the justice systems, creating more solutions and responses to social problems, and working toward a more individualized experience of justice by tailoring individual plans for participants that address the underlying conditions and issues that bring individuals into the justice system.

A number of researchers and organizations have attempted to identify common elements or components of problem-solving courts. First applied to drug courts, developers have identified Ten Key Components of Drug Courts (U.S. Department of Justice, 2004). Other courts such as DUI courts, Mental Health, and Tribal Wellness courts have adapted these 10 key components to meet the needs of the specific populations in their programs. Critical components of most problem-solving courts include a team approach, early identification and screening of participants, ongoing judicial interaction with the participant, ongoing case management and reporting to the court supported by the use of incentives and sanctions and integration of a wide range of community-based services along with court processing of the problem, education of the public and professionals about various conditions such as substance abuse and mental illness to achieve system change, and use of data collection to track individual outcomes (Porter et al., 2010).

Although most problem-solving courts contain these components there are some important distinctions at the point of referral. Some participants are diverted to the problem-solving court prior to conviction or a finding in the case of Civil Court, and some courts, such as reentry courts, receive participants postconviction or after a court has adjudicated the issue at hand. As you will see later in the chapter diverting to a problem-solving court prior to or postconviction raises significant justice and due process issues including the requirement that in order to participate, a client must agree to waive certain rights and subject themselves to a much higher level of supervision than if they made the decision to go through usual system processes. Social workers should be aware of these due process issues before they participate or encourage participation in alternative venues.

Types of Problem-Solving Courts

The most common kind of preconviction problem-solving courts are drug courts. Individuals are referred to drug courts when it is believed that an underlying substance abuse problem is the root cause of what brings an individual into contact with the justice system. Drug courts are currently found in Civil Court for juveniles who are identified as having problems with alcohol or other drugs and parents with a child protection matter that is related to substance abuse. In Criminal Court there are drug courts for nonviolent substance-abusing offenders at both the misdemeanor and felony levels. Adult Drug Court is a specially designed court that aims to achieve a reduction in recidivism and substance abuse, as well as increase the offender's likelihood of successful rehabilitation through early, continuous, and intense judicially supervised treatment, mandatory periodic drug testing, community supervision, and use of appropriate sanctions and other community-based social and human services (U.S. Department of Justice, 2004).

A Tribal Healing to Wellness Court is a component of the tribal justice system that incorporates and uses principles of spiritual and physical healing and a return to a state of balance or harmony to meet the specific substance abuse needs of each tribal community (Tribal Law and Policy Institute, 2005). The Tribal Healing to Wellness Court team includes tribal judges, advocates, prosecutors, police officers, educators, and substance abuse and mental health professionals, and also tribal elders and traditional healers and as such tries to retain and emphasize the unique elements and strengths of Indigenous justice systems.

Mental Health Court is modeled after Drug Courts and was developed in response to the overrepresentation of people with mental illnesses in the criminal justice system. Mental Health Courts divert select defendants with mental illnesses into judicially supervised, community-based treatment and attempt to strengthen the criminal justice and mental health system collaboration within a community. Currently, all Mental Health Courts are voluntary. Defendants are invited to participate in the court following a specialized screening and assessment that will also determine the degree of risk in terms of public safety if the individual is not incarcerated. For those who agree to the terms and conditions of community-based supervision, a team of court staff and mental health professionals work together to develop treatment plans and supervise participants in the community.

There are a number of variations of the Drug and Mental Health Courts that focus on specialized populations and problems: Homeless Court, for those homeless individuals who have outstanding warrants, fines, and are arrested for misdemeanors; Veterans Court for misdemeanors and felonies that occur due to combat-related PTSD and substance abuse; and Gambling Court for those individuals with pending criminal charges who are suffering from pathological or compulsive gambling. Domestic Violence Courts have been designed to address some of the chronic problems associated with domestic violence cases such as low reporting, withdrawn charges, threats to victim, lack of defendant accountability, and high recidivism, accomplished through intense judicial monitoring of the defendant, significant attention to the victim, and close cooperation between the court, police, and social services.

Postconviction courts include DWI Court, which is a postconviction court dedicated to changing the behavior of the repeat offender arrested for driving while impaired (DWI) who has an alcohol use problem, and Reentry Courts, designed to facilitate the reentry and reintegration of incarcerated offenders back into the community by providing a system of accountability through court monitoring and support services in the community in lieu of the offenders last year of a sentence of incarceration. Using a program similar to that of the other problems-solving courts, a series of sanctions and rewards are used to influence the behavior of parolees without resorting to incarceration when there is a parole violation. This voluntary court usually provides supervision from 12 to 18 months postprison discharge.

Community-Based Problem-Solving Courts

Community-based courts attempt to promote joint responsibility of the justice system and community for local quality-of-life crimes by locating the court within the community where the actual crimes are committed and directly affect the members of that community such as petty theft and vandalism. Members of individual neighborhoods and communities, through participation on Citizen Advisory Boards, identify the issues of concern for their particular neighborhood and assist court officials in developing sentences that may involve offenders repaying the community by providing community service. Community courts may also mandate and monitor the completion of participation in social services and may serve as a gateway to social services for a particular community (Lee, 2000).

Problem-solving courts, frequently based in community locations, are increasingly being used to divert juveniles accused of status and delinquency offenses out of the juvenile justice system. Truancy Court attempts to identify and overcome the underlying factors in a youth's life that result in truancy and through the collaborative efforts of parents, teachers, police, community members, and social service providers, attempts to address the issues undermining academic success. Truancy Court offers the youth an opportunity to have petitions against them dropped if they participate in the court and improve their attendance in school.

Youth Courts also known, as Teen Courts or Peer Courts, are community-based programs in which youth are judged by their peers for minor delinquency, status offenses, and problem behaviors. Youth court programs are popular, with a reported 1,050 youth court programs in 49 states and the District of Columbia (www.youthcourt.net). The philosophy guiding the Youth Court is similar to most problem-solving courts: to hold individuals accountable, to repair the relationship between the community and the justice system through education, to empower and involve community members, and to promote skills and behaviors that facilitate community reintegration and civic participation. Sentences are determined by peers and can include community service; mandated class attendance; attending victim impact panels (e.g., for those impacted by drunk driving); restitution; writing and artwork assignments; mentoring and attendance at groups; and skills workshops like the program developed by social work interns in Louisiana (National Youth Court, 2004).

Legal Framework of Problem-Solving Courts

Like the other alternative venues, Problem-Solving Courts are created through federal and state law and court rules promulgated by individual state and local judicial systems. Laws and statutes can authorize both the existence of and the funding for problem-solving courts. For example, the federal law, Second Chance Act of 2007, was designed to improve outcomes for incarcerated individuals returning to communities from prisons and jails. This legislation authorizes federal grants to government agencies and social and human service organizations to provide employment assistance, substance abuse treatment, fathering programs, housing, family programming, mentoring, victims support, and legal services that can help reduce recidivism. Many reentry courts have made use of the funding from this Act to create and administer their programs.

As is the case with mediation programs, most state judicial websites will also have a section that identifies and describes any problem-solving courts that may be available for that particular state. Using the state of Illinois as an example, by accessing the state judicial website for problem-solving courts through the Illinois Probation, you can access a map of the problem-solving courts in all of the counties in Illinois and the types of courts (Administrative Office of Illinois Courts, 2024). You can quickly ascertain that there are drug courts, mental health courts, veterans courts, and DUI courts for cases involving driving under the influence. Additionally, there are training materials and checklists for all of the participants in the problem-solving court including the coordinator, defense attorney, judge, prosecutor and treatment providers. If our case example of Ms. Jones moved to Illinois, the substance abuse counselor working with her would access the education tools and checklist to understand the underlying law, processes, and goals if Ms. Jones participated in a drug treatment program assigned by Drug Court.

Using the example of Drug Court and continuing with our example of Illinois, we find that drug treatment courts were authorized by state law in the

Illinois Code. The purpose of the state law creating the drug treatment court is laid out in the first section declaring that the legislature

> recognizes that substance use disorders and mental illness co-occur in a substantial percentage of criminal defendants. There is a critical need for the criminal justice system to recognize individuals struggling with these issues, provide alternatives to incarceration to address substance use disorders when possible, and provide appropriate access to treatment and support to such individuals. (730 Ill. C.S. § 5)

The statute proceeds to define key terms in the drug court program including drug court professional, peer recovery coach, validated clinical assessment, and clinical treatment plan. The law also details which defendants may be eligible for the drug court program and at which stage in the criminal case process, defining a combination drug court program as "allow[ing] an individual to enter a problem-solving court before a plea, conviction, or disposition while also permitting an individual who has admitted guilt, or been found guilty, to enter a problem-solving court as a part of the individual's sentence or disposition" (730 Ill. C.S. § 10). The statute clarifies that a defendant must consent to a drug court program and must be approved by the judge for admission into the program (730 Ill. C.S. § 20[a]). Defendants who are excluded from the program include defendants with a crime of violence in the past 5 years, a defendant who does not wish to enter a treatment program, and a defendant who denies use of drugs. (730 Ill. C.S. § 20[b]).

Social workers would want to pay close attention to the procedure for admission to the drug court program because it involves a screening, clinical needs assessment, and risk assessment (730 Ill. C.S. § 25[a]). The clinical needs assessment has to include an assessment of "substance use and mental and behavioral health needs" and be administered by approved professional staff. The risk assessment needs to use a risk assessment tool that has been approved by the courts. Additionally, social workers would notice that the procedural rules recognize the role of trauma in substance abuse and direct drug court programs to "partner with advocates, survivors, and service providers in the development of the programs" (730 Ill. C.S. § 25[f]).

Finally, a review of the Drug Court Act would educate a social worker about the reasons for being terminated from the program including a voluntary withdrawal and violation of the terms of the program which would reinstate the criminal proceeding. (730 Ill. C.S. § 35[a]). Upon successful completion of the drug court program, however, either the prosecution or the defense attorney can motion the court to vacate the criminal case and expunge the vacated conviction (730 Ill. C.S. § 35[b]).

THE PATH OF A PROBLEM-SOLVING COURT

Returning to our case example, you remember that Ms. Jones has cases in both Criminal Court and Family Court. Therefore, Ms. Jones would be potentially eligible for an alternative venue in both matters. In Criminal Court, Ms. Jones might be able to participate in a Drug Court, rather than having her criminal case proceed along the path outlined in Chapter 10. In Family Court, Ms. Jones might be eligible to participate in a Family Treatment Court, a civil Drug Court, or Child Protection Mediation rather than having her child welfare case alleging neglect as a result of substance abuse proceed along the path detailed in Chapter 9. Whether you are working with Ms. Jones as a social worker employed by the alternative venue or with an attorney representing Ms. Jones in either forum, it is important to understand the process that Ms. Jones will undergo when making a decision about participating in the problem-solving court and subsequent interactions with the problem-solving court and treatment providers.

Intake

Motivational interviewing is an evidence-based intervention that is becoming widely used in the community corrections community. Social workers learn about the stages of change models and the skills to conduct motivational interviewing during their courses and in their field placements. It is critical that clients participating in alternative venues, particularly problem-solving court, are ready and motivated for change because, as we will discuss in the final section of this chapter, there are justice issues in regard to the waiving of rights and the application of sanctions. As discussed, court rules as well as ethical practice may require the use of empirically validated screening instruments and that the professional administering the instrument is trained and capable of administering it.

Ms. Jones in this instance would be screened both for her legal eligibility to be considered for the Drug Court as well as her clinical eligibility and level of motivation to participate in the program. During the screening process Ms. Jones would meet with a Drug Court employee, often a social worker, who would conduct a social history that would include a statement of the presenting problem; social, peer, and environmental information; financial status; family history including other members who may be alcohol or drug dependent; educational and occupational status; medical or mental health issues; other legal issues; and current thoughts of suicide or homicide. The screening would also include a detailed history of type of and history of substance use and prior treatment. In many states the information to be gathered during the intake and screening process is prescribed by court rule as we discussed earlier in the review of Illinois's Drug Court Act and the requirement of a clinical needs assessment and risk assessment.

Counseling

Ms. Jones's attorneys in both Criminal Court and Family Court will counsel her on the benefits, disadvantages, and potential consequences of participating in a problem-solving court versus a nonspecialized court process. Ideally, a social worker working with the attorney in Criminal Court or Family Court would be present when the attorney is meeting with Ms. Jones and would have discussed with the attorney their assessment of Ms. Jones to engage in mandated treatment through the courts. You can imagine how important it would be for

Ms. Jones to be able to discuss any concerns that she may have about participating in a problem-solving court knowing both that all the information that she shares with her attorney and the social worker is confidential and the social worker is able to answer questions regarding the treatment program and monitoring.

The criminal defense attorney counsels Ms. Jones that she will have to make an admission to the criminal drug charges in order to participate in the Drug Court. By making this admission, Ms. Jones gives up her right to have a trial in her case and have a jury of her peers determine whether or not she is guilty. The attorney may inform Ms. Jones that she does not have full discovery from the prosecution to determine the strength of their case and has not had time to conduct an independent investigation of the allegations against her. Therefore, it is possible that Ms. Jones could receive a better legal outcome if she does not participate in the Drug Court or waits until they are further along in the process to request admission to the program. Finally, the attorney informs Ms. Jones that any admission in Criminal Court will mean that she has a criminal conviction record, unless the particular Drug Court allows for a defendant to receive a nonconviction disposition, such as an adjournment in contemplation of dismissal or to have the conviction vacated as detailed in the Illinois statute. For example, if Ms. Jones made an admission to drug possession or sale in Criminal Court, that admission could be used against her in a Family Court case alleging that she neglected her child.

Knowing that Ms. Jones was previously involved in a drug treatment program, the attorney makes certain that she understands the consequences of failing to participate in the drug program once in Drug Court. The consequences could include increased court monitoring, loss of any favorable resolution such as an adjournment in contemplation of dismissal, and potentially jail. A social worker working with the defense attorney could be particularly helpful in this situation by describing the types of behavior or relapse that might result in a sanction from the Drug Court such as losing accumulated clean time or being incarcerated.

The attorney in Family Court would raise similar issues when counseling Ms. Jones about participating in Family Treatment Court. If an admission is required, the attorney informs Ms. Jones that she may have a better legal outcome from proceeding along the traditional path of a Family Court case, especially if the attorney suspects that the petitioning child welfare agency may not be able to prove the allegations. Additionally, the attorney counsels Ms. Jones that the Family Treatment Court model may be a longer process and therefore court oversight and continued supervision of her family would be longer than in the traditional forum. The attorney tells Ms. Jones that she will have to come for more court dates over a shorter period, given that the Family Treatment Court will be monitoring her progress in the program and reporting regularly on her progress to the court. However, the attorney notes that often in Family Treatment Courts, because of the closer oversight and monitoring, judges are more amenable to returning children to their parents' care or increasing the level of visitation and decreasing the level of supervision of that visitation. Finally, the attorney would discuss the collateral consequences of admitting to the allegations in Family Court including having her record include a finding of neglect. This finding could impact Ms. Jones's ability to gain employment in certain fields or to become a foster parent. As you can see throughout this overview of counseling topics, a social worker working with Ms. Jones's Family Court attorney would have multiple opportunities to use trauma-informed interviewing and expertise in treatment programs to inform the counseling and discussion with Ms. Jones.

Program Admission

Both the Family Treatment Court and Drug Court assess Ms. Jones to determine whether she is legally and clinically eligible to participate in their program. In Family Court, Ms. Jones cannot have any prior abuse or neglect cases and must not present with any mental health or domestic violence issues that would rule her out from participating. In Criminal Court, Ms. Jones cannot be charged with any violent offenses and may not be able to present with any mental health issues, which would bar her admission into the participating drug treatment programs. Ms. Jones must also express her willingness to enter treatment and cannot deny substance use if she is seeking admission to the program. If Ms. Jones agrees to either specialized court, she will have to sign a contract agreeing to participate fully in the treatment and to abide by the rules of the treatment court program. In most states, participants are required to receive an orientation manual that clearly lays out all the requirements of the court.

Court Admission

Once Ms. Jones decides to enter problem-solving court, she will be required to make an admission to the allegations. Often, attorneys can negotiate the specifics of the admission that the client has to make, but with problem-solving courts, the admission would have to relate, in this case, to the allegations of drug use. Therefore, Ms. Jones would have to say in Criminal Court that she possessed drugs on the day in question. In Family Court, if the judge asks Ms. Jones whether she used drugs while pregnant and was not regularly in a program, Ms. Jones would have to answer yes or state the same on her own. In both forums, Ms. Jones will have to stand in open court and admit to the allegations in the petition by stating what she did. The court has an obligation to explain to Ms. Jones, in both forums, that she has the right to go to trial, to present evidence, and to cross-examine any witnesses that testify against her. The court also must make a record that Ms. Jones understands that she is giving up her right to a trial and to appeal any decision of the court by making this admission and that she is doing so voluntarily and with full information. Once the admission has been made, the court begins the process of monitoring, testing, and reporting on Ms. Jones's compliance.

Treatment

In both Family Court and Criminal Drug Court, Ms. Jones will be referred to a community-based treatment provider with which the court has contracted to address her substance use. Ms. Jones may also be referred to other services to address concerns that may have come up during the social history such as employment and education. In the civil Drug Court, there will also be services related to any risk factors for child abuse and neglect that have been identified by the local Child Protective Services (CPS). Ms. Jones will most likely have a court-based case manager who will monitor her compliance with the treatment plan and make reports to the court. As a legal- and evidence-based practitioner who may be working on this case in either the implicit or explicit context, it would be important to access the earlier research conducted about the kind of substance use treatment that research has shown to be effective with mothers who have young children. In addition, throughout the case we have learned of Ms. Jones trauma history and know that trauma is frequently associated with substance use in women. This too has implications for the kind of treatment Ms. Jones is referred to. Accessing treatment that is evidence-based and effective is crucial as there are serious repercussions involved if Ms. Jones falls out of compliance or relapses.

Monitoring and Drug Testing

Drug testing will occur on a regular basis through the court and the type of test (urine, blood, sweat, hair, and saliva) will depend on the type of substance used. Ms. Jones will most likely be regularly tested for marijuana and cocaine use. Procedures for scheduling and conducting drug testing are often required by statute or court rule and are usually written in the court's policy and procedure manual. The case manager assigned to the court will collect reports from service providers, monitor the client's progress with both the treatment plan and any court regulations and agreements laid out in the participation agreement and orientation manual. The case manager will also regularly schedule team conferences with the judge, the probation officer or CPS worker, service providers if appropriate, and the prosecuting and defense attorneys.

Court Appearance and Report

The Family Treatment Court holds regular court appearances (often once a month) to update the court on Ms. Jones's progress in treatment. Before each appearance, Ms. Jones is required to submit to a supervised drug test and the results are submitted immediately to the court. The family treatment court staff provides the court with an update including progress in individual and group programs, information provided by treating counselors at the program, drug tests results, and the total number of clean days. The reports include accounts of Ms. Jones's participation in group counseling, and her work with her counselor in trying to have her son returned to her care. Ms. Jones will have to complete the entire treatment program and aftercare program before she will graduate from treatment court and no longer be required to attend court. As you can see throughout the process of the problem-solving court, there are multiple opportunities for social workers to use their training, skills, and expertise.

JUSTICE CONCERNS THAT MAY ARISE IN ALTERNATIVE VENUES

While there are many benefits to alternative venues, critics have also raised concerns about the fairness and justice of problem-solving courts and other alternative venues. At first glance, social workers may be very enthusiastic about the opportunity for clients to have access to treatment rather than be incarcerated or suffer other significant and destabilizing consequence such as child removal. However, thoughtful critics have raised the question about whether social and mental health services are best delivered through a court. Questions are also raised about the implications of situating solutions to social problems such as homelessness and prostitution via the courts rather than community-based service programs. Problem-solving courts and the use of mediation have evolved as alternatives to the widespread criminalizing and prosecution of certain behaviors that disproportionately target some groups such as African American males. Alternative venues are suggested as ways to reduce disparity in the justice system.

As social workers with our focus on the larger society we should be suggesting that in order for problem-solving approaches in the justice system to be truly just, they need to extend beyond the individuals who are being processed in these courts and take a problem-solving approach to some of the larger structural issues such as discrimination, poverty, and racism that also underlie the genesis of the social problems and highlight government rather than focus on individual failures.

Spinak (2010) suggests that the shifting of power, planning, and resources for problem-solving away from the local community and into the courts may result in disparate outcomes for families of color, some of whom are living in communities having many of the structural conditions already mentioned, thus more likely to come under the surveillance of the court and to have the entire burden and responsibility shifted onto the individual or family.

The question is posed as to whether problem-solving courts by singling out certain populations such as veterans, substance abusers, and the mentally disabled and by addressing "quality of life" issues in certain communities, are not also "criminalizing" behavior that might be more expertly and effectively addressed in other community-based systems rather than the courts. In regard to the rapid proliferation of alternative venues we as a profession should be thoughtful and critical consumers.

Another issue of concern for social workers is the lack of importance attached to the kind of and efficacy of the treatment provided through participation in alternative venues. As social workers we should be noting the lack of attention in many alternative venues to the knowledge our profession has about how and when individuals change and the importance of self-motivation, self-determination, and participation in the development of plans for change. What kind of treatment is provided, for whom, for how long, and whether it is evidence-based, empirically validated, or culturally appropriate does not appear in the evaluation research studies of problems-solving courts or service agreements that result from conferencing and mediation. As noted by one author (Bozza, 2007), the quality or effectiveness of the treatment ordered appears secondary:

> The low priority given to the efficacy of treatment modalities as a sine qua non of the continuing problem-solving mission strongly implies that while advocates of problem-solving courts believe there is something important about the role of treatment they facilitate, they do not know exactly how it works and are not really concerned about it (Bozza, 2007, p. 110).

Without attention paid to the development of individualized, collaborative, culturally coherent, and evidence-informed treatment plans, alternative venues lose their potential to effect longer-lasting change that addresses the unique issues for that particular individual. The alternative venue then becomes just another method of coercive control with the power to apply aversive sanctions such as incarceration.

Many of the concerns regarding alternative venues relate to the procedural requirements for participating in an alternative venue including mandating an admission to a specific conviction, mandating treatment at a particular program, sanctions for failure to engage in the program, and waiving a client's right to a trial on the merits. As you have learned, clients may access alternative venues whether they are involved in a case brought by the government, such as an arrest for drug possession with a referral to drug court, or an individual actor, such as mediation for a custody dispute between parents. In each instance, the alternative venue is supposed to be a choice that is voluntarily entered into by all parties. Critics of alternative venues have noted the potential lack of voluntariness and self-determination of clients when the case involves a mandate of services that is tied with a favorable resolution in Criminal Court or child welfare proceedings. For example, the voluntariness of participation could be reasonably questioned when the proceeding determines whether your child returns home to your care or whether you are incarcerated. In some cases, the only nonjail alternative for clients in Criminal Court is participation in a problem-solving court. Both legal and social work practitioners have noted the inherent tension in "sentencing" clients to treatment, when it is otherwise believed that the successful completion of a treatment program is directly tied to the client's voluntary acceptance of the treatment and its guidelines.

Many drug treatment programs will impose internal sanctions such as a loss of privileges or passes for a failure to comply with the program's regulations, including testing positive for drugs or breaking a program rule. However, alternative venues such as drug treatment court may include incarceration as a sanction for failure to complete a treatment program or a relapse. The sanction of incarceration is not one that would otherwise be employed by a treatment program and underscores not only the questions of voluntariness but also the efficacy of using jail instead of ongoing treatment and counseling as a sanction for relapse.

The timing of alternative venues can also raise due process and fairness concerns because the intake process is generally conducted very soon after or immediately after the client enters court. In this sense, attorneys are often in a position of having to counsel clients about the relative benefits of participating in the alternative venue without a full understanding of the client's history, ability to complete a mandated program, or the strength of the prosecuting agency's case against the client. Because most alternative venues such as drug court in the Criminal Court and Family Court contexts require an admission, an attorney may not have been provided with any discovery or evidence that the other side intends to raise at a trial. In this manner, the attorney is potentially at a disadvantage in counseling a client about their right to go to trial, the potential consequences of waiving their right to go to trial, and the relative merits of the other side's case.

For some clients, particularly clients with immigration issues, this presents a particularly difficult problem. A client who is undocumented may face immigration consequences including deportation as a result of any admissions or convictions, even if they were made in order to access an alternative venue. This is because the definition of a conviction in federal immigration law is more expansive than a conviction defined under state criminal law. If an immigration judge determines that the admission and participation in a problem-solving court is a conviction under immigration law, then the client may be rendered ineligible for legal status or citizenship or even result in deportation.

Finally, an attorney is placed in the position of having to diagnose or assess a client's ability to participate in the mandated treatment program early in the stages of their legal representation. Without the benefit of working with a social worker, an attorney has to counsel their client about the potential consequences of failing to participate or complete in any mandated program as part of admission to an alternative venue. For example, with a drug treatment court, the attorney may face questions from a client regarding the type of treatment, mandates, and consequences of relapse. While the staff of the treatment court would have provided this information to clients during the intake process, clients will often ask attorneys for advice when deciding whether to participate, which may ultimately mean making an admission and having a conviction. Without the assistance of a social worker trained in assessing a client's history with treatment, the attorney may be lacking critical information to advise the client properly. One can imagine the difficulties raised in this context when advising clients about participating particularly in drug treatment courts and mental health courts.

Along the same lines, the problem-solving court model has been criticized for expanding the role of the judges, prosecutors, and defense attorneys beyond adjudication and legal representation to assessment and the provision of social services. This also includes the issue of court supervision over the treatment plan exceeding the supervision that would normally occur during a regular tracked criminal case. In other words, clients may continue to have court involvement for many months after a traditionally tracked Criminal or Civil Court case would have ended.

Balancing Power

Two of the dichotomies or tensions at the heart of alternative venues that are especially important are the relation between formal and informal helping and between care and control, or empowerment and coercion. Conferencing and mediation can easily become a forum for professionals who want to quickly produce a plan for court rather than an opportunity for families to meaningfully participate. As Firestone points out, "the state has a great advantage over the individual" (Firestone, 2009, p. 102), particularly in regard to access to resources. Frequently the same group of professionals who participate in mediation, conferencing, and problem-solving courts have familiarity and experience with the process and with each other. Individuals and families may have little experience in these techniques and in identifying their needs and interests and advocating on their own behalf. Frequently, clients have been socialized into deferring to professionals and are at a disadvantage in a venue that requires the exertion of self-determination and mediation skills (Firestone, 2009). When the power imbalance is so large that clients' rights cannot be protected, it may be best to use more traditional court processes where power imbalances certainly exist but alongside the traditional checks from the adversarial system.

Confidentiality

The issue of confidentiality in alternative venues is another area for rights-based social workers to bring increased scrutiny. In family group conferencing, there are a variety of different models and consequently different degrees of confidentiality that attach to the information shared during the conference. For example, in some family group conferencing models, participants are asked to sign a confidentiality agreement. This agreement details what information will remain confidential and what information may be released to the court or other parties.

However, in other states that use a permanency teaming model, the participants must be informed of state-specific laws and limitations on confidentiality including mandating reporting of child abuse and neglect. In this model, the information shared by a parent during a conference could be revealed in court documents and be the basis for making a report to the local child welfare agency of suspected maltreatment. In either instance, the discussion of confidentiality is a critical aspect of the conference and a client's ability to understand and to engage in the process by being fully aware of what information is confidential and what information might be shared with other agency workers, the court, or other players.

Many states have their own mediation confidentiality statutes, which are quite diverse. The National Conference of Commissioners on Uniform State Laws and the American Bar Association have jointly drafted a Uniform Mediation Act that would generally establish a privilege for mediation communications. These statutes generally provide that mediation communications cannot be used as evidence in court or be subject to discovery. However, information otherwise admissible or subject to discovery does not become inadmissible or protected from discovery solely because it is used in mediation.

Many mediation confidentiality statutes provide an exception to confidentiality for mediation communications providing reasonable suspicion of child abuse or neglect. Because, by definition, child protection cases deal with child abuse or neglect, the exception to confidentiality is typically interpreted to refer only to previously unreported allegations of child abuse or neglect. Confidentiality is especially an issue in child protection mediation. Mediation is often just one event in an ongoing child protection case in which many of the participants frequently communicate with each other. In particular, the adverse legal parties, typically the parents and child welfare agency, are usually required to work together on a regular basis. Thus, it may be hard to separate communications made in mediation from those made elsewhere.

Moreover, one of the purposes of mediation is to share information to help prepare for court hearings, and hearings may be necessary even if the parties reach agreement. Even if information is not used directly in discovery or court hearings to impeach testimony, interactions in mediation may have a significant effect on the attitudes, behavior, and recommendations of the parties as well as help to shape questions in court hearings. Understanding the intricacies of confidentiality rules is difficult for most people and may be especially difficult for the often less-educated family members who are involved in child protection cases. Therefore, rights-based social work practitioners will focus on the particular laws and rules surrounding confidentiality in alternative venues to guide their own practice working in the explicit and implicit legal context and to educate their clients who may be considering or involved in an alternative venue.

The Importance of Emotion and the Determination of Capacity to Meaningfully Participate

Finally, alternative venues and conferencing must consider that in most instances the cases selected involve highly emotional issues and various levels of client capacity (Firestone, 2009). Clients entering into the decision to participate in the use of alternative venues frequently are in the midst of crisis and highly charged events such as child removal or the arrest of an adult or juvenile. Additionally, many potential participants have mental health and substance use issues that qualify them for participation in problem-solving courts but may also impact their capacity to freely choose and participate meaningfully in alternative venues (Firestone, 2009). Clients need to be able to understand the facts, the issues, and all the alternatives available to them as well as the pros and cons of each and the relevant consequences. For legally informed evidence-based practitioners this means sharing the evaluation research regarding the effectiveness of conferencing, mediation, and problem-solving courts with your client as part of an informed consent. Clients whose capacity to participate may be impaired should in all instances have an advocate, and social workers, regardless of role, should use the skills they learned in Chapter 9 to enhance capacity, competence, and ensure client self-determination.

Social workers should be familiar with laws and regulations requiring accommodations for individuals with disabilities and make sure the conference, mediation session, or the court provides accommodations to enhance client participation such as interpreters and the provision of relevant materials both in writing and verbally, minimizing distractions and offering frequent breaks. Professionals should also try to adjust their behavior by speaking slowly, not using technical jargon, asking clarifying questions, and consistently reaching for feedback about client understanding (Firestone, 2009). Also if it is determined that the client is incapacitated in such a way that there cannot be meaningful participation the facilitator/mediator/judge should terminate the alternative venue.

Ethical Codes and Guidance

As we discussed, a number of commentators have identified significant ethical and legal issues that are associated with the use of alternative venues. Professionals should always use their own professional codes as a starting point when determining ethical practice and resolving questions that implicate ethics. A number of national organizations, including NASW, Victim Offender

Mediation Association, Association of Family and Conciliatory Courts, American Bar Association, and the Center for Dispute Settlement, all have developed and published practice standards and ethical principles for mediators. Common areas addressed include role, competence, conflicts of interest, impartiality, confidentiality, voluntariness, self-determination, informed consent, termination of mediation, fee structures, and collaboration with other professionals.

In addition, various states have associations and councils that publish guidelines and standards for mediators. Some states such as Arkansas, promulgate standards for mediators through court rules (Arkansas Judiciary, 2024). We recommend that you check your state to see if the guidelines for practice are contained in court rules or if local voluntary and professional organizations provide aspirational guidelines.

REFERENCES

42 Pa. C.S. Section 6301.

730 Ill. C.S. § 25(a).

730 Ill. C.S. § 25(f).

730 Ill. C.S. § 35(a).

730 Ill. C.S. § 35(b).

730 Ill. C.S. §10.

730 Ill. C.S. §5.

730 Ill. C.S. §20(a).

730 Ill. C.S. §20(b).

Administrative Office of Illinois Courts. (2024). *Problem solving courts.* https://www.probation.illinoiscourts.gov/psc

Alternative Dispute Act of 1998, Pub. L. No. 105–315, 112 Stat. 2998 (1998).

Arkansas Judiciary. (2024). *ADR statutes.* https://arcourts.gov/administration/adr/adr-statutes

Bozza, J. A. (2007). Benevolent behavior modification: Understanding the nature and limitations of problem-solving courts. *Widener Law Review, 17,* 97–144.

Braithwaite, J. (2002). *Restorative justice and responsive regulation.* Oxford University Press.

Casey Family Services. (2009). *Family teaming: Comparing approaches.* https://www.pdx.edu/center-child-family/sites/centerchildfamily.web.wdt.pdx.edu/files/2020-07/FGC-family-teaming.pdf

Civil Justice Reform Act of 1990, 28 U.S.C. §§ 471–482 (1990).

Connaway, R. S., & Gentry, M. E. (1988). *Social work practice.* Prentice Hall.

Connolly, M. (2009). Family group conferencing in child welfare: The fit with restorative justice. *Contemporary Justice Review, 12*(3), 309–319. https://doi.org/10.1080/10282580903105822

Edwards, D., & Parkinson, K. (2018). *Family group conferences and social work in social care.* Policy Press.

Edwards, L. P. (2004). Mediation in child protection cases. *Journal of the Center for Families, Children and the Courts, 5,* 57–69. http://www.judgeleonardedwards.com/docs/057_Edwards.pdf

Firestone, G. (2009). Empowering parents in child protection mediation: Challenges and opportunities. *Family Court Review, 47*(1), 98–115. https://doi.org/10.1111/j.1744-1617.2009.00243.x

Gibbs, M. (2009). Using restorative justice to resolve historical injustices of indigenous peoples. *Contemporary Justice Review*, *12*(1), 47–57. https://doi.org/10.1080/10282580802681725

Haw. Rev. Stat. c.613-2, 1989.

Haw. Rev. Stat. c.613-2(a) (1989).

Hawaii Fam. Crt Rule 53.1, 19 (1999).

Kurland, R., & Salmon, R. (1992). Group work vs. casework in a group: Principles and implications for teaching and practice. *Social Work with Groups*, *15*(4), 3–14. https://doi.org/10.1300/J009v15n04_02

Lee, T. (2000). *Community courts: An evolving model.* Community Justice Series No. 2 (NCJ183452). U.S. Department of Justice, Office of Justice Programs. http://www.ncjrs.gov/pdffiles1/bja/183452.pdf

McGarrell, E., & Hipple, N. K. (2007). Family group conferencing and re-offending among first time juvenile offenders: The Indianapolis experiment. *Justice Quarterly*, *24*(2), 221–246. https://doi.org/10.1080/07418820701294789

Merkel-Holguin, L. (1998). Implementation of family group decision making in the U.S.: Policies and practices in transition. *Protecting Children, 14*(4), 4–10.

Minn. Stat. c.609, § 611A.775 (1998).

Mont. Code c.15, § 2-15-2013 (2007).

Moyle, P., & Tauri, J. (2016). Family group conferencing and the mystifications of restorative justice. *Victims & Offenders*, *11*(1), 87–106. https://doi.org/10.1080/15564886.2015.1135496

N.C.G.S. § 7A-38.3D (2008).

National Treatment Court Resource Center. (2024). *Treatment courts across U.S. states/territories.* https://ntcrc.org/wp-content/uploads/2024/06/2023_NTCRC_TreatmentCourt_Count_Table.pdf

National Youth Court Center. (2004). *Selected topics on youth courts: A monograph.* https://www.ojp.gov/pdffiles1/ojjdp/208164-208170.pdf

Navajo Nation Code c.9, § 1101.

Neb. Rev. Stat. c.43, § 43-247.01 (2010).

Neff, R. (2004). Achieving justice in child protection. *Journal of Sociology and Social Welfare*, *31*(1), 137–154. https://doi.org/10.15453/0191-5096.2964

Nixon, P., Burford, G., & Quinn, A. (2005). *A survey of international practices, policy & research on family group conferencing and related practices.* American Humane Association No Child Left Behind Act of 2001, 20 U.S.C. § 6301 (2002).

North Carolina Office of Administrative Hearings. (2009). *Procedural rules that apply to contested cases in county courthouses.* https://www.oah.nc.gov

Nygård, R., & Saus, M. (2018). Is family group conferencing a culturally adequate method outside the origin of New Zealand? A systematic review. *Social Work & Social Sciences Review*, *20*(1), 78–108. https://doi.org/10.1921/swssr.v20i1.1164

Or. Rev. Stat. c.417, § 417.368.

Or. Rev. Stat. c.417, §§ 417.365-413.75.

Parsons, R. (1991). Empowerment: Purpose and practice principle in social work. *Social Work With Groups*, *14*(2), 7–21. https://doi.org/10.1300/J009v14n02_02

Parsons, R. J., & Cox, E. (1989). Family mediation in elder care decisions: An empowerment intervention. *Social Work*, *34*, 122–127. https://www.jstor.org/stable/23715783

Participatory Defense. (2024). *A community organizing model.* https://www.participatorydefense.org/about

Pavelka, S. (2008). Restorative juvenile justice legislation and policy: A national assessment. *International Journal of Restorative Justice*, *4*(2), 100–118. https://www.slideshare.net/slideshow/restorative-juvenilejusticelegislationandpolicyanationalassessement/11860970

Pennell, J. (2004). Family group conferencing in child welfare: Responsive and regulatory interfaces. *Journal of Sociology and Social Welfare*, *31*(1), 117–135. https://doi.org/10.15453/0191-5096.2963

Pennell, J., & Burford, G. (1997). *Family group decision-making: After the conference—progress in resolving violence and promoting well-being: Outcome report summary*. American Humane Association.

Porter, R., Remple, M. A., & Mansky, A. (2010). *What makes a court problem-solving: Universal performance indicators for problem-solving justice*. Center for Court Innovation. http://www.courtinnovation.org/sites/default/files/What_Makes_A_Court_P_S.pdf

Resolution Systems Institute. (2024). *Court ADR basics*. https://www.aboutrsi.org/resource-center/court-adr-basics

Sandau-Beckler, P., Reya, S., & Terrazas, A. (2005). Familias primero: Family group decision making in El Paso County, Texas. *Protecting Children, 19*, 4. Englewood, Colorado: American Humane Association.

Shaw, L. (2010). Divorce mediation outcome results. *Conflict Resolution Quarterly*, *27*(4), 447–467. https://doi.org/10.1002/crq.20006

Smith, A. L., & Smock, D. R. (2008). *Managing a mediation process*. U.S. Institute of Peace.

Smith, M. (2001). *What future for "public safety" and "restorative justice" in community corrections? Sentencing and corrections: Issues for the 21st century, 11*. National Institute of Justice. http://www.ncjrs.gov/pdffiles1/nij/187773.pdf

Spinak, J. M. (2010). A conversation about problem-solving courts: Take 2. *University of Maryland Law Journal on Race, Religion, Gender and Class*, *10*, 113. http://digitalcommons.law.umaryland.edu/rrgc/vol10/iss1/7

Thoennes, N. (2009). What we know now: Findings from dependency mediation research. *Family Court Review*, *47*(1), 21–37. https://doi.org/10.1111/j.1744-1617.2009.00237.x

Tribal Law and Policy Institute. (2005). *Process and outcome evaluations in four tribal wellness courts*. http://www.tribal-institute.org/download/IntroductionFINAL.pdf

Tyler, T. R. (2003). Procedural justice, legitimacy, and the effective rule of law. In M. Tonry (Ed.), *Crime and justice* (Vol. 30, pp. 431–505). University of Chicago Press.

U.S. Department of Justice. (2004). *Defining drug courts: The key components* (NCJ205621). Office of Justice Programs, Bureau of Justice Assistance and National Association of Drug Court Professionals Drug Court Standards Committee. http://www.ojp.usdoj.gov/BJA/grant/DrugCourts/DefiningDC.pdf

Utah State Courts. (2024). *Alternative dispute resolution programs*. https://www.utcourts.gov/content/dam/mediation/docs/ADR_flowchart.pdf

Walker, L. (2002). Conferencing: a new approach for juvenile justice in Honolulu. *Federal Probation Journal, 66*(1), 1–7.

Washington State Office of Children, Youth & Families. (2024). *Policies and procedures*. https://www.dcyf.wa.gov/practices-and-procedures

CHAPTER 12

Administrative Proceedings, Players, and Advocacy Roles

INTRODUCTION

The scope of administrative law is as varied and far reaching as the multiple government agencies that clients, social workers, and lawyers interact with on a daily basis. It is critical that social workers understand the parameters of administrative law and how it can be used to advocate for your client. In this chapter you will learn how knowledge and understanding of administrative law can be an effective tool in the achievement of service and treatment goals developed for and with your client and in achieving the social work values of empowerment and social justice. Key aspects of administrative law, such as the concepts of procedural fairness and due process, can support and assist the social worker in implementing important social work values such as social justice and meaningful realization of clients' rights. You will also learn what processes exist to challenge decision-making that is not in the interests of your client and learn about the stakeholders in that system. This includes learning about the impartial hearing process, the relationship between administrative law and civil rights, and how to advocate for and support your clients when they believe that an agency has behaved in a discriminatory manner.

WHAT IS ADMINISTRATIVE LAW?

Administrative law encompasses the functions, responsibilities, and boundaries of any government agency at the federal, state, or local level. Government agencies work on a broad variety of issues, but can generally be classified as falling into one of the following four categories: developmental, promoting social welfare, regulating economic activities, and protecting health and safety (Mashaw et al., 1998). Developmental agencies deal with the infrastructure and maintenance of government systems such as the National Parks Service's responsibility for overseeing the national parks system. Economic agencies regulate the economy and include the Federal Reserve and the Department of the Treasury.

Clearly, the two most important categories for social workers and their clients are government agencies that regulate the provision of social welfare services and health and safety including education, services for special populations such as the developmentally disabled, elders, mental health services, substance abuse treatment, and the administration of justice, including the protection of civil rights. Agencies at the federal, state, and local levels regulate social welfare services including programs for public assistance, food stamps, and Medicaid. Government agencies also regulate programs that provide services for mental health, developmental disabilities, criminal justice, juvenile justice, immigration, substance abuse, child welfare, and child protection services. Health and safety agencies include the federal Food and Drug Administration and state-based Workers' Compensation Boards, which administer claims relating to workplace injuries. The federal Department of Education oversees general and special education, as well as higher education services such as the administration of student loans. The Office of Civil Rights, as part of the Department of Justice, investigates and addresses civil rights violations in programs that receive federal funds. There are also State Offices and Commissions on Civil Rights that investigate discrimination in their jurisdictions.

The most important piece of legislation governing federal administrative agencies is the Administrative Procedures Act (APA) (1946). While other laws govern specific agencies or policies, the APA sets forth the general guidelines and rules for all federal agencies regardless of their subject area or mission. Passed in 1946, the APA established uniform guidelines for the most important of federal agency actions—rulemaking and adjudication. The lengthy statute defines what constitutes an agency, its obligation for public disclosure, and the minimal procedures an agency has to follow to make a rule and to enforce or review that rule. In this sense, the APA impacts every client who interacts with a federal agency either through the process by which a regulation was determined or their rights to challenge an agency's decision (Mashaw et al., 1998).

It is important not only to identify whether you are working with a federal, state, or local agency but also to understand the overlap among federal, state, and local agencies dealing with the same benefits or subject matters. For example, if you are working with a youth who has a learning disability and they are suspended from school, federal, state, and local regulations are all implicated. In order to identify what rights your client has, what procedural safeguards the school must implement, and what the process will be you must start with the federal law, in this case the Individuals with Disabilities Education Act (IDEA) (2004). Part of the IDEA requires that "within 10 school days of any decision to change the placement of a child with a disability because of a violation of a code of student conduct," the local education agency, the parent, and relevant members of the child's individualized education plan (IEP) team must conduct a manifestation determination (34 CFR § 300.530(e). This hearing will determine whether or not the conduct was directly related to or a manifestation of the child's disability. If that is the case, this places more duties and responsibilities on the school and gives the student more protections.

Additionally, you would want to reference the individual state agency responsible for the service so that you can understand the specific regulations and processes of the state agency. This is because each state will then develop regulations that allow them to be in compliance with the federal law. So, for example, the Connecticut State Department of Education, which oversees the local town or city boards of education, sets the processes and regulations for parents to contest school decisions such as a change in placement or when a child enrolled in special education is suspended for more than 10 days. The school district is required to hold a manifestation determination meeting within 10 days of the change in placement, as that is required by federal law.

This meeting, similar to an IEP meeting, includes the parents, teacher, and other relevant school personnel. Parents may bring an advocate or friend to this meeting. If there is a finding that the behavior is directly connected to the disability the child cannot be replaced without parental agreement. The school will be required to complete a "functional behavioral assessment" which then results in a "behavioral intervention plan." If the child already has a behavioral intervention plan, then it must be reevaluated and modified. If you are a resident of the cities of New Haven or Hartford the local school district will also have specific policies about where and how these meetings are conducted. A helpful starting point in working with clients with education issues can be the school district's website and parent's guides to the special education process in your jurisdiction, often compiled by local legal services and advocacy organizations.

AGENCY RULES AND REGULATIONS

Agencies are responsible for creating their own governing policies and procedures, which are generally referred to as *regulations* or *rules*. While the Executive Branch creates the agency and details its purpose, the day-to-day governing procedures are determined by the agency itself. Regulations or rules are the "laws" that govern how an agency acts, what it is able to do, and how it resolves problems. The regulations are specific to the agency and are often incredibly lengthy and complex. Some social work agencies orient social workers to policies and procedures, but often social workers do not realize that agency policies and procedures are fundamentally based on ensuring compliance with local, state, and federal regulations. It is important as a social worker to identify and read the regulations governing the agency or organization you work for as well as those related to the services you are providing. Multiservice agencies may involve several different federal, state, and local agencies.

For example in *The Case of Michelle Jones* regulations and rules relevant to agencies receiving federal funding to provide for the treatment of substance use disorders are determined at the federal level by the Substance Abuse and Mental Health Services Administration (SAMHSA; 2024). On their website, the agency lists and provides a summary of the federal laws and regulations that impact substance abuse and mental health issues including the Affordable Care Act (ACA; 2010), Americans with Disabilities Act (ADA; 2008) and regulations pertaining to patient confidentiality and disclosure of medical information pertaining to substance abuse. For example, Ms. Jones would be entitled under federal law to parity with medical and surgical benefits in her insurance coverage for any addiction and mental health treatment.

If Ms. Jones were a resident of Montana, the next level of regulation would be at the state level and overseen by the Department of Public Health and Human Services—The Addictive and Mental Disorders Division. Rules and regulations relevant to that division can be found in Chapter 24 of the Montana Code (2023), which specifically addresses the treatment of chemical dependency. Various sections of the Code identify what services must be provided by the state (Mont. Code Ann., c.24, § 53-24-204, 2023), rules for acceptance into treatment (Mont. Code Ann., c.24, § 53-24-209, 2023) and even visitation and communication rules while in inpatient treatment (Mont. Code Ann., c.24, § 53-24-305, 2023).

A review of the laws around visitation would show that Ms. Jones was entitled to "opportunities for adequate consultation with counsel and for continuing contact with family and friends consistent with an effective treatment program" (Mont. Code Ann., c.24, § 53-24-305, 2023).

As you can see, clients must understand complex policies and rules of agencies derived from three levels of government in order to receive critical benefits or services or to challenge unjust or discriminatory decision-making. Because of these complexities, clients may waive their rights or not understand what they are being asked to do or comply with, thus placing them at risk of losing benefits and services. Absent a lawyer to advise a client at each instance, which as we know from earlier chapters may not be financially feasible or accessible, the client may not have access to information about their rights and therefore a rights-based social worker could play a critical role in helping the client identify their rights. If needed, the social work could ultimately refer them to or work collaboratively with a lawyer to enforce those rights.

Most federal and state agencies distribute and post guides for clients that summarize or highlight the most important regulations and procedures for challenging agency decisions and policies but we recommend that when you can, you read the regulations yourself and share them with your client as part of informed consent. Not only should you be referencing the regulations in order to advocate for your client, but also to ensure that you as a social worker are providing or offering all the services a client is entitled to, are in compliance with the regulations, and that you are upholding and respecting the rights of your clients.

Federal, state, and local government websites will have a list of all state agencies and departments, many linking to the individual agency or department website. Frequently included on the websites are listings of the services the departments are charged with providing; relevant regulations and statutes they are charged with implementing; and procedures, processes, and forms for requesting services as well as for filing formal complaints and requesting fair hearings. Another source for state codes and regulations is the website for the judicial branch of each state.

Creating Rules and Regulations

At times, social workers in supervisory or managerial positions in government agencies may be responsible for drafting legal regulations (Saltzman & Furman, 1999). During this process social workers may also work in partnership with agency legal staff and can use many of the skills and knowledge identified in this book to facilitate productive communication and collaboration around this task. In many instances, social workers and other advocates can have a profound impact on the creation of these regulations by participating in the public comment period that precedes a regulation being enacted.

While the agency will initially draft their own version of a regulation, both federal and state statutes require that the agency institute some form of *public review* whether it is through a public hearing on the proposed regulations or time period for submitting comments. It is important for you to know that as an individual social worker you can submit comments in writing, attend and testify at public hearings, or join with other advocacy groups to propose changes in the regulations. Line social workers and case managers are in the best position to comment on how regulations are implemented because they are the ones who address the everyday practical realities of implementation. Additionally, social workers are often dealing with the crisis that occurs for clients when benefits are suddenly cut off or a regulation has an arbitrary time limit within which service can be provided that does not comport with what research demonstrates is the time needed to recover from the condition the service is supposed to ameliorate. Being a legally informed evidence-based practitioner will help you to understand the importance of having regulations and rules based on research and the importance of social scientists having a voice in rule making.

Although many regulations and rules directly impact social work practice and clients, social workers may not be aware that regulations are being proposed or where they can obtain copies of the proposed regulations. Social workers can stay abreast of proposed rule changes by looking at the websites for federal, state, and local agencies and joining listers that monitor pending regulations and law reforms. Many legislative sites also have functions that allow you to get alerts when changes in regulations are being proposed. You can always bookmark sites particularly relevant to your field of practice to stay abreast of updates. Social workers can also join organizations and associations relevant to their work that may track and publish proposed regulations. You will learn more about the public comment period and your role in advocating for socially just and evidence-based rules and regulations in Chapter 13.

When you make a commitment to being a rights-based social worker, it is critical to become familiar with laws and regulations and begin to see how profoundly they impact your client and your practice as a social worker. Hopefully, through this information gathering, you will feel more passionate and motivated about participating in the passage of proposed regulations that impact your clients and the way you are allowed to practice social work.

Due Process and Procedural Fairness Aspects of Administrative Law

The process during which agency and government decisions are reviewed or contested is called the *impartial hearing process* or a *fair hearing*. While the decision-making process can and most likely will vary from agency to agency and state to state, there are basic tenets of administrative law that will help you navigate these agency systems on behalf of your client. The first basic tenets of administrative law are the concepts of *due process* and *procedural fairness*.

As you learned in previous chapters on the civil and criminal forums, due process under the law relates to the concept of fundamental fairness for all actors in a legal proceeding. This is no different for individuals interacting with administrative law. The Supreme Court declared in *Goldberg v. Kelly* (1970) that welfare recipients were entitled to an evidentiary hearing to challenge the termination of their benefits. An *evidentiary hearing* requires not only that the agency and the individual challenging the decision be allowed to present evidence, but also that the individual challenging the agency decision be allowed to cross-examine any witnesses against them. The Supreme Court noted that "the same governmental interests that counsel the provision of welfare, counsel as well its uninterrupted provision to those eligible to receive it; pre-termination evidentiary hearings are indispensable to that end" (*Goldberg v. Kelly*, 1970).

You will notice throughout the discussion of administrative hearings that there are many procedural safeguards in place to protect due process for individuals. While clients may not be aware of these procedural safeguards, social workers in the implicit or explicit legal context can play a vital role in informing clients of their rights in these forums. Two of the most well-known safeguards are *notice* and the *right to be heard*. Notice refers to the requirement that an individual be notified formally in writing of any agency decision whether it is to grant, terminate, or modify a benefit or service. In most cases, notice will be in the form of a letter from the government agency and should describe clearly the rights and procedures for challenging any decision. This notice must be timely and allow a recipient to challenge the decision.

The *right to be heard* refers to an individual's right to challenge the government agency's decision and present their own arguments for why that agency's decision was improper. Generally, this happens at a fair hearing or administrative hearing before a *hearing officer* or an *administrative law judge* (ALJ). These safeguards apply across federal, state, and local agencies and are important to identify on behalf of clients.

Due process safeguards and processes can and should be thought about as a way to evaluate agency practice and identify errors in the way the law is being implemented or the need for a change in the law. Due process can serve as a model for responsible and legal practice, and provision of services can be evaluated against these standards. Dickson (1976) advocates that agencies should develop a system of procedures that anticipate demands for fair treatment and accountability, and in this way provide procedural safeguards rather than perceive them as being imposed by outside forces. This is consistent with the view of the social work scholars we introduced in Chapter 2 that maintain social workers must become more proactive in their relationship to the law and not just passively respond to rules and laws, particularly when they are not in the interest of the client or the profession.

Returning to *The Case of Michelle Jones*, consider if Ms. Jones needed to apply for public assistance in order to reunite with her son so that she could arguably demonstrate to the Family Court judge that she was able to provide him with his basic needs. In some jurisdictions, the family service plan determined by the agency and Ms. Jones would include securing benefits or employment as a goal which will be monitored by the child welfare agency and presented as evidence to the court of Ms. Jones's ability to care for her son. Consider that, when Ms. Jones told her child welfare caseworker that she did not have the proper identification in order to start the application process for benefits and that she needed help with securing identification documents, the caseworker replied that getting such identification is not what the agency does. In this instance, the agency does not perceive that they are in fact denying Ms. Jones a service and therefore she would not receive a notice that a service is being denied. She may or may not have been advised of her rights or the services she is entitled to when she first began working with the child welfare agency and therefore may not be aware of whether or not the agency has an obligation to provide assistance. Additionally, given that Ms. Jones most likely engaged with the agency right after her child was removed, she may not have been in a position to comprehend fully her rights even if she received a copy of her rights with relation to the child welfare agency.

Unless she is working with a rights-based and legally informed social worker in some other setting or as part of her legal team, she will not even know that she has the ability to make a complaint, advocate for herself, make demands, or contest this issue that so profoundly affects her reunification with her son.

A rights-based, legally informed social worker would know to access the federal agency, Administration for Children and Families and check the website (www.acf.hhs.gov) in order to review the U.S. Department of Health and Human Services, Child Welfare Policy Manual (Children's Bureau, 2024). The manual details for any program funded under the Title IV-E and B of the Social Security Act, including tribal child welfare programs, that fair hearings are required for appeals that involve the right to challenge the denial of services as well as denial of financial claims. The manual cites examples of issues that might result in a grievance and request for a hearing, including the following: "[A]gency failure to offer or provide appropriate pre-placement preventive services or reunification services; Agency may not have placed child in the most family-like setting in close proximity to his parents; Parents were not informed of their rights to participate in periodic administrative reviews; Agency failed to provide services agreed to in case plan; A request for a specific service is denied or not acted upon; and Agency failure to carry out terms of adoption assistance agreements" (Child Welfare Policy Manual, 8.4G).

The legally informed social worker would then check their state department of child and family services or a tribal agency if the social worker is working with Native American children living on a reservation and receiving services from the tribe, to access the specific administrative due process procedures to address these issues for their state or tribe. The evidence-informed social worker would also know that ensuring a reliable source of income and future employment would minimize risk of child neglect. In this way, the knowledge of the law informs the social worker's practice and advocacy for their client to ensure the full realization of the client's rights and goals.

IMPLICATIONS FOR SOCIAL WORK PRACTICE

As pointed out by Stein (2004), knowledge and understanding of administrative law is crucial to effective social work practice, yet very little attention is paid to it in survey courses of social work and the law or even in many textbooks. As we have presented, rules that often guide or circumvent social work practice, such as who is eligible for services, how long services can be provided, and even a social worker's responsibilities to their clients during practice, are the result of regulations and statutes. It is important to remember that by advocating for clients to know about and use the processes set up by administrative law to challenge government actors' decisions, social workers are ensuring that the law is applied fairly and consistently and as intended by policymakers (Lens, 2007).

During courses on social policy, many social workers learn how to influence the promulgation of administrative law on federal, state, and local levels but often do not understand how to use administrative law to enhance micro or individual practice. Because social workers usually mediate between the individual and the state or federal governments, every aspect of working with clients intersects with administrative law. When working with clients, social workers identify protective and risk factors for their clients that have been identified in the literature relevant to the condition or problem the client and worker are collaborating together to change. The prevention and decreasing of risk factors for many social problems always includes the provision of services such as educational opportunities, mental healthcare, or housing. Accessing the right services are an essential part of treatment and case planning and consequently all social workers should be familiar with administrative law and due process safeguards. Often case plans fail because a service is not being provided or it is inappropriately denied and this can be avoided if social workers know the principles and procedures of administrative law.

Some agency decisions that are relevant to clients of social workers and can be contested are those that involve termination; reduction or denial of financial assistance such as public assistance, food stamps, Social Security disability insurance, unemployment insurance, Medicaid, Medicare, veteran's benefits, child support, foster care, and adoption subsidies; child care assistance; and workers' compensation.

Clients can also challenge agency decision-making if they are not receiving the services they are entitled to under the law, if they are being discriminated against in receiving services, or when services have been reduced or terminated. Examples of these services include housing, social services, education, special education services, services to assist those with developmental disabilities, child care, home healthcare, mental health, nursing homes and substance abuse services, vocational and employment training, and assistance to name a few.

Clients involved with the criminal and juvenile justice systems can also bring complaints that result in administrative hearings. Indeed, in some states, a prisoner must first file an administrative complaint before pursuing any other legal case, a process generally referred to as "exhausting" all legal remedies. With adult clients, administrative hearings can be requested to challenge agency practices in jails and prisons. For example, in California inmates can file an administrative appeal when they are denied a variety of services including medical care, visits, or an accommodation for their disability. Prisoners are also able to file administrative complaints against staff or corrections officers for misconduct including discrimination, harassment, or brutality.

Juvenile clients who are detained as a result of a juvenile delinquency case are also entitled to administrative review regarding the conditions of their confinement, including access to healthcare and mental health needs. In Georgia, a juvenile can request an administrative revocation hearing, the internal process created by the Department of Juvenile Justice to determine whether or not a young person has violated the conditions of their placement or aftercare service (Ga. Rules and Reg. c.97-2, Rule 97-2-01).

Other kinds of administrative hearings that affect social workers include those cases that are related to regulatory bodies or commissions that govern professional standards, licensure, and practice. Many of these cases require the judge to determine whether a sanction such as suspension or revocation of a license should be imposed upon the holder of an occupational or professional license, such as doctors, dentists, nurses, accountants, social workers, psychologists, and securities dealers. These cases also include matters involving the denial or revocation of day care licenses and appeals regarding whether an individual's name should be placed on the Central Registry for Child Protection if they are named in a report of child maltreatment.

PROCEDURAL JUSTICE AND FAIRNESS

Studies of citizen interaction with government agencies indicate that individuals distinguish between a fair outcome and a fair process. People are concerned both with how a decision is made and the content of the final decision. Some studies argue that procedural fairness is more important to people than the actual outcome itself. Many times government bureaucracies are experienced by social work clients as harsh and punitive, yet research tells us that most often clients do not use the legal mechanisms in place or challenge what they perceive as unfair or punitive decisions (Lens, 2007). Indeed, scholars have noted the critical importance of government agencies focusing their processes on the foundational values for procedural justice of respect, voice, neutrality and trust (Lens, 2010).

Clients have a strong incentive not to complain about or antagonize workers who can deny basic needs and services or who have the power to report behavior of mandated clients to judges or other officials. This means it is critical for social workers to give clients the information they need to act on their own behalf or, in cases where clients believe they are powerless or afraid of retaliation, to explore their concerns and if needed to represent them or to advocate for them during complaint processes.

Let us return for a moment to our case study of Michelle Jones to illustrate this perspective. Let us say that, as a result of evidence-informed counseling by her social worker and lawyer during her civil neglect hearing in Family Court, Ms. Jones knows that her son may have some neurological vulnerabilities. Being proactive she decides to seek special education services when he enters preschool. Ms. Jones is a little concerned, as is his daycare provider, that Matthew is somewhat hyperactive and not meeting developmental milestones at the same rate as other children in the class. She wants to obtain services to evaluate and support him now and potentially avoid him having to go to special education when he starts elementary school. After a brief evaluation that does not include any observations of Matthew except for a few minutes while the psychologist was talking with Ms. Jones, the local committee on preschool education denies Ms. Jones's request to provide special education services to her son. Ms. Jones stops by the community-based social service agency to discuss her concerns and she expresses disappointment about the decision to deny services that she believes are necessary for her son. Ultimately, Ms. Jones communicates that she is resigned to the denial and does not think that there is anything else she can do to get her son the services he needs.

When you explore this issue more fully with her, you discover that Ms. Jones feels guilty and believes that any difficulty Matthew faces is her fault because of her pregnancy and that is why she believes she does not deserve services. She is also a little afraid that if she challenges the decision she may get in trouble with the child protection agency again because they may ask about his birth and her substance abuse. A rights-based and evidence-informed social worker would reassure Ms. Jones that Matthew has a right to special education services if he has a need, and that rights are not about "deserving." Additionally, the social worker could remind Ms. Jones that according to the research on prenatal substance use, Ms. Jones is acting responsibly and proactively and that she can request an outside evaluation that will more thoroughly explore her concerns about her son's development. You can also explain again that the law defines child neglect as failing to provide the minimal degree of care and not addressing medical and educational needs of the child. With this foundation, a rights-based social worker can articulate to Ms. Jones how she is going over and above "a minimal degree of care" by advocating for and anticipating the medical and educational needs of her son. You can offer to help her request and plan for a fair hearing, as well as with Ms. Jones's permission, collaborate with the day care staff and refer her to the local legal aid office for a legal consultation and intake. In this manner, your social work practice can incorporate the legal information to assess, counsel and advocate for Ms. Jones more holistically.

If you are working in the implicit context providing individual treatment for a client, issues of procedural fairness and access to justice will often emerge. In a study of clinical social work practice with low-income single mothers at risk for child abuse and neglect, Tempel (2009) found a positive association between case advocacy and engagement in a working alliance with the clinical social worker. Frequently, the author maintains, case advocacy is undervalued and needs to recognized as an important therapeutic intervention. Opportunities for partnership in case advocacy, including accompanying the client to an appointment with the welfare caseworker or a special education meeting, resulted in shifts in affect and perception in both the clinical social worker and client. When the social workers participated alongside clients in experiences where other service providers told the client what to do rather than asking as to their preferences, where the client received insulting and demeaning treatment, and where they witnessed clients being pressured to agree to plans they did not agree with, clinical social workers enhanced their capacity to both feel and communicate empathy to their client and created opportunities for client–worker mutuality.

Social workers in this study demonstrated affective and physiological responses to this witnessed treatment of their clients such as shock, anger, disbelief, tears, flushing, and sweating and resulted in the clinician changing cognitive schemas and biased formulations such as "she is uncooperative" or "she is paranoid" that had been negatively impacting the therapist–client relationship (Tempel, 2009, p. 132). By witnessing the visible reactions of the therapists to unjust treatment, the clinicians reported that clients also saw their therapists in new ways that brought them closer and advanced the therapeutic work (Tempel, 2009). Even in the implicit context of social work, understanding the role of due process and procedural fairness can be critical in enhancing the client–social worker relationship and advancing your practice with the client.

RACIAL AND SOCIAL JUSTICE IN ADMINISTRATIVE VENUES

Many of the administrative contexts that social workers interact with are systems that have high rates of disproportionality and disparity for people of color, their families, and children. Examples of these systems that we have already discussed include the public education system, healthcare, juvenile justice system, and child welfare system. Legal and evidence-informed social workers who are committed to achieving racial and social justice must always focus first and foremost on accessing information and data related to national outcomes for the services they provide and where and when there may be disparate outcomes for certain groups of their clients. Social workers must educate themselves and their clients about the larger context that is shaping the decision-making and outcomes of administrative agencies. Knowing the regulations and the services clients are entitled to by law, and knowing when and how clients have the right to advocate or challenge decisions on their behalf is a critical tool in the fight against social exclusion, disparity, and racial injustice. Many of the studies that address disparity in service system outcomes have found that disproportionality and disparity exist at every decision-making point within administrative systems from intake to disposition (Hill, 2004, 2007). Additionally, studies have found that individuals accessing government systems observe the impact of racial disparities in a multitude of ways including failing to enforce their rights to benefits (Lens & Katz, 2010).

As we presented in Chapter 8 regarding the juvenile and criminal justice systems, initial decisions during the pretrial phase can play a part in subsequent unfair and discriminatory decision-making at the point of sentencing. We maintain that if every social worker and their clients know their rights, the services and benefits they are entitled to receive, and how to activate procedural safeguards and processes, the decision-making in systems would be more transparent and accountable. In this way, legally informed and rights-based social workers can ensure the enforcement of rights that clients already have in place, and could begin to make inroads in racial disproportionality at the practice level.

If you envision a situation where a student with developmental disabilities is suspended, the social worker would have potentially a number of roles in working with the student, student's family, school district, or evaluator. It is important for any social worker working with families and children of color to know that in multiple state and federal investigations, children of color including Black, Hispanic, and Native American, are more than twice as likely to receive out of school suspensions and be expelled than White children for the same behavior (Losen & Skiba, 2010). In some states the percentages are even higher for African American youth (American Civil Liberties Union [ACLU] Oregon Report, 2010). A 2011 report analyzing suspension data in New York City found that students with disabilities were four times more likely to be suspended than those without a disability and that Black students represent more than 50% of those students with disabilities who were suspended. Black students were also suspended for longer periods of time, for more subjective incidents such as insubordination, and more frequently during periods where standardized tests were taking place (ACLU, 2010). While there has been an overall decline in the number of suspensions, research demonstrates that Black students and students with disabilities are still suspended at disproportionate rates (Ryberg et al., 2021).

Further, there is a substantial body of research that links school suspension and expulsion to entrance into the juvenile justice and criminal justice system (Kim et al., 2010; Morris, 2016; Nicholson-Crotty et al., 2009). We have already presented research documenting the disparate treatment that occurs for youth of color once they enter into that system in Chapter 7. This is another powerful illustration of how systems often intersect and interact in invisible ways to create negative outcomes for our clients and highlights the need to scrutinize our own decision-making and the decision-making of others for cognitive schema and bias that can lead to disparate treatment and compromises to the achievement of social justice for our clients.

SOCIAL WORK ROLES

Social workers can take on a number of roles within the administrative legal forum. You may assist the client in accessing less formal advocacy opportunities such as filing a complaint or attempting to mediate a concern. You can be working with a client or an attorney to challenge an agency decision. You can function as a lay representative and advocate for a client during a fair hearing, or you might be working in a government agency and represent the agency's position at a fair hearing. You may be in an administrative or managerial position in an agency and actually helping to create regulations and rules. At times, a social worker may unfortunately be in the role of respondent when a social worker's practice is the subject of a complaint. Complaints can charge discrimination, malpractice, or some other violation of a state professional license. As we emphasized in Chapter 3, it is critical that you read the conditions and regulations attached to your state license as well as ensuring that you are in compliance with all of the regulations attached to your area of practice. Regardless of role, the skills presented in this chapter will assist you in becoming an effective advocate, communicator, collaborator, and self-advocate.

Where Administrative Law and Civil Rights Intersect

Many state agencies, commissions, and all federal departments will take complaints when clients feel they have been discriminated against when they are seeking employment, housing, or credit, or in the provision of services to which they are entitled to by that particular local, state, or federal department. Under the Civil Rights Act of 1964, discrimination on the basis of race or sex was prohibited in employment decisions such as hiring, promoting, and firing. The U.S. Equal Employment Opportunity Commission (EEOC) was created by the legislature to serve as the agency responsible for implementing the law and you can find an overview of their responsibilities, laws, and regulations at www.eeoc.gov. Currently the EEOC brings lawsuits against employers accused of discrimination and enforces laws prohibiting discrimination on the basis of race, sex, religion, pregnancy, national origin, age when 40 years or older, genetic information, or disability.

Most federal departments have Offices of Civil Rights that enforce civil rights laws that prohibit discrimination by any of the entities that they oversee. For example, the federal Department of Health and Human Services is charged with ensuring that all persons in the United States have the right to receive health and human services in a nondiscriminatory way. As an example, you cannot be denied services or benefits simply because of your race, age, national origin, or disability.

The Office of Civil Rights has jurisdiction over entities that receive federal monies or that provide government services such as local social and health services agencies, clinics, hospitals, juvenile detention facilities, and nursing homes to name a few. A complaint with the Office of Civil Rights must be filed within 180 days of when the act or omission occurred. The Office of Civil Rights enforces federal antidiscrimination laws prohibiting discrimination on the basis of age, race, sex, national origin, or disability in programs that receive federal funding through the Department of Education. This would include any state colleges or secondary schools, libraries, and museums. You can file a formal complaint with the Office of Civil Rights if you believe that an educational institution, which receives federal money, has discriminated against an individual or a group of individuals. The discrimination could occur at various stages in the educational process including admission to school, student services, counseling, grading, and discipline. Legally informed social workers should note that you do not have to be the victim of the alleged discrimination in order to file a complaint, as you can file a complaint on behalf of an individual or group of individuals. The details of the complaint process are easily accessible on the Office for Civil Rights of the Department of Education's website.

If you are unsure of what kinds of complaints that you or your client can make, the Office of Civil Rights section of the Department of Justice website also lists case law and opinions by topic including immigrant and employee rights, voting, hate crimes, education, housing and civil enforcement, and disability to name a few. In addition, under the section on Special Litigation, the Office of Civil Rights posts the results of investigations conducted by the Department of Justice (DOJ) when there have been complaints of civil rights violations in institutions including prisons and jails, juvenile justice facilities, nursing homes, mental health facilities, facilities for the developmentally disabled, and the conduct of law enforcement officials. The special litigation investigations are listed by topic according to the state.

Most states also have Offices of Civil Rights and many post the reports of hearings and recommendations that are made by the state office on government websites. For example, if you live in Indiana, you can access the Indiana Civil Rights Commission (ICRC) online which contains hearing reports of civil rights claims and decisions from the ICRC Administrative Law Judge. Some state offices of civil rights also have projects that seek to inform residents of their legal and civil rights and could provide trainings in your agency or for groups of your clients. Local law schools are also a good resource for social workers when you want to arrange legal trainings, as many law student groups are organized to improve access to legal information and services. Later in the chapter, we will learn more about the complaint and the hearing processes and the filing of both formal and informal complaints and hearing requests with federal, state, and local agencies. It is important to consult the agencies' websites because there are time frames within which a complaint must be filed.

ADMINISTRATIVE HEARINGS: WHO ARE THE PLAYERS?

As discussed in previous chapters, it is critical for social workers to know for themselves, and to be able to explain to a client, the various professionals that will be encountered in the legal forum within which the worker and client are operating. In administrative law proceedings, it is important not only to understand the roles of the various professionals but the limits as well as the power and discretion that key decision-makers have.

The Role of the Administrative Law Judge or Hearing Officer

The person who conducts the hearing is usually called the *administrative law judge* or an ALJ, sometimes also called a hearing examiner or hearing officer. An ALJ in is an official who presides at an administrative evidentiary hearing to resolve a disagreement between an agency and someone affected by a decision of that agency. The ALJ is the initial trier of fact and decision-maker. ALJs have some of the powers of judges such as administering oaths to witnesses, hearing testimony, ruling on whether evidence can be admitted or not, and making factual and legal determinations. ALJs are appointed at the federal and state levels, and in some county jurisdictions at the local level of government.

Party

A *party* in a case refers to a person or agency entitled to be heard in the case, meaning that they can present evidence and make legal arguments. Generally, the party either asks for the hearing or is requested to participate. You are always considered a party if a complaint is filed against you, or you appeal an agency decision and your request for hearing is granted. When you are challenging or appealing the government's decision, you are called the appellant.

Attorney for the Appellant

An *appellant* or other party is entitled to bring an attorney to a fair hearing to represent their interests and advocate on their behalf. Like other evidentiary hearings, this means that the attorney can present evidence, examine witnesses called to testify for their client, and cross-examine witnesses who are called to testify against their client. Unlike criminal proceedings, there is no right to an attorney in fair hearings under the law. However, there are many state and local legal services offices with attorneys focusing on fair hearings. If an attorney represents your client, it is important to understand that as the client's social worker you may have important information, documents, and evidence that can assist in preparing the case. With your client's permission, it may be helpful to set up a consultation with the attorney so that you can discuss your work with the client and present corresponding documentation. As the client's social worker, you may also be called upon to testify on behalf of your client during the hearing.

Lay Representative

A *lay representative* is an advocate who is not an attorney, but is permitted by federal and state law to represent a client at an administrative or fair hearing. The lay representative is entitled to present evidence on behalf of their client, including questioning witnesses and the government agency caseworkers. As you will learn later in the chapter, states are divided as to whether lay representatives can represent individuals in certain fair hearings, most notably hearings for special education services under the federal IDEA. In some states including Florida, a lay representative is prohibited from representing a client in an administrative hearing because it is considered to be the unauthorized practice of law.

Agency Representative

Social workers working in government agencies can and do at times represent the government agency during the hearing process. Social workers who are government employees may also be called as a witness and required to testify during impartial hearings. As we discussed in earlier chapters, the social worker's testimony could cover a range of topics including their professional assessment, documentation of services provided to the client, and justification for the agency's ultimate decision.

THE PATH OF A FAIR HEARING

Models of Administrative Hearings

There are generally two models of "who" conducts administrative hearings at the state level. The first, which follows the model used in federal agencies, has a group of hearing officers, or ALJs attached to each agency that conducts hearings. The power and duties of these judicial officers vary from state to state. States having this model include New York and Ohio. The second model, which was developed in response to concerns about the fairness and impartiality of decision-makers employed by the agency, is the *central panel model.* This model is an independent state agency made up of ALJs who conduct impartial administrative hearings on behalf of citizens and governmental agencies. States having this model include Washington, North Carolina, and New Jersey. It is important to find out which model is being used in your state as this may implicate where the client might file a claim and small differences in process and procedures.

Filing a Hearing Request

When your client believes they have been unfairly denied a service by a government agency or believes an administrative agency has made a wrong or unfair decision, the first step to be taken is to file a *complaint.* Whether or not your state has a central panel model, the client must file a written request for a hearing. Some agencies have forms specifically to request a hearing; for others the complaint may be in the form of a letter. Check your state's website to see if there is a central panel or you must go through the individual agency. Many of the websites have important information such as forms to request a hearing, applicable regulations, specific procedures for your jurisdiction, and information about whether or not you are authorized to function as a lay representative. Often the state administrative website posts fair hearing decisions on the site, searchable by topic. This is a good resource to help you determine what kinds of claims were heard and what kinds of evidence and arguments were persuasive, and can be of real assistance in helping your client develop and prepare their case.

Most often when there is going to be a decision in regard to financial assistance or service delivery, your client will receive a notice telling them what the decision is, what the hearing process is, and the time frame in which the complaint or request for a hearing must be filed. This form, also called *notice*, will usually include the regulation or law the agency is using to reach their decision. This will tell the client what "theory" the agency will be using to argue their case. This gives your client important direction and information about what argument and evidence to collect to dispute the agency's "theory."

Very often, the agency will offer the option of a conference or a review by a third party. This does not preclude your client's right to a fair hearing. If benefits or services are being reduced or discontinued, it is important that your client specifically asks that these entitlements continue until the fair hearing decision is made. It is often helpful to participate in the conference to see whether or not the decision can be changed, but it does not waive your client's right to a fair hearing. You can make use of many of the important skills and strategies you learned in Chapter 11 that make you more successful during conferencing and mediation and that will help your client to avoid having to go to hearings and trials without compromising their rights.

Most complaints will need to include information about your client, the state agency, the reason you are requesting the hearing, a brief statement of what evidence or facts support your request, and what "remedy" or solution to the problem your client is requesting. Some reasons for fair hearings may include the belief that the state actor exceeded authority or jurisdiction, acted arbitrarily or capriciously, failed to act as required by law, or failed to follow procedure.

When starting your preparation with your client for writing the complaint or request for a hearing, you need to identify what decision of the agency is at issue in the impartial hearing. In other words, are you challenging a denial of benefits, a reduction in the amount of a benefit, a sanction, or to suspend a child from school? Once the issue has been identified, it is important to research the regulations regarding the procedures for making that decision so that you know exactly what was required of the agency and of your client. State regulations for each agency will have detailed information about due process procedures. In many cases, the regulations or statutes at issue will be listed in the notice received by the client about a change to their benefits or entitlements. Those notices are always a good starting point for researching your client's rights and remedies. For example, the first step in that process would be to review carefully the notice provided by the agency denying a benefit or the facts that support that decision that your client wishes to challenge, such as a classification decision in special education.

Your client generally has to request the fair hearing during a certain time period once the notice of change in benefits has been received. It is critical for you to impress upon your client that anytime they receive a document relating to their services that they should read it carefully, and if they have any doubt or question about what is being said to bring it to a trusted advocate for review. Many clients miss the time period within which they might appeal the decision, and even when they have a very strong case, may not be able to obtain an exception or extension. The time period for requesting the fair hearing should be clearly stated on the notice from the agency and is generally 60 to 90 days. Even if a client has passed that time line—from the date of the denial of benefits—you can still request a fair hearing and contest the adequacy and timeliness of the notice provided to the client. Some examples may be that the client is a non-English speaker and the notice was not written in a language they could understand or translate, or that your client has a reading disorder and did not receive notice verbally as well as in writing.

Burden of Proof

The *burden of proof* in fair hearings generally falls on the party that is trying to change the current status of the benefit. In most instances, that will be the government agency that has taken steps to reduce, eliminate, or sanction the current benefit. In some instances, the burden of proof will be on your client if they are attempting to show that a benefit amount is inadequate or they are challenging a decision. In either situation, the standard is generally referred to as substantial evidence or preponderance of the evidence. So the party trying to change the benefit has to show with substantial evidence that the change is justified under the regulations or statutes. In Ms. Jones's case, the agency would have the burden of proving that terminating her Medicaid or other public benefits was legal.

Right to Present a Defense and Possible Defenses

Your client has the right to present a defense at the fair hearing, including live witnesses and documentation, and also has the right to cross-examine any of the witnesses put forward by the agency. Furthermore, your client can object to evidence that is not properly before the ALJ. An example of improper evidence would be anything that is not relevant to the issue in the fair hearing, was not provided prior to the fair hearing, or is based on hearsay (i.e., third-party statements) or knowledge of another witness. The ALJ will rule on any objections to evidence and either allow the evidence to be presented or determine that it is inadmissible.

Prehearing Processes

Some ALJs will conduct at least one prehearing conference, often by telephone. Your client is required to appear at the conference and if for some reason they cannot, you should contact the ALJ and reschedule. Prehearing conferences are meant to clarify any confusion for the client about the process, to identify the real disagreements to be addressed, and to set a realistic timetable to prepare for and schedule the hearing.

In many jurisdictions, you may be required to attend a prehearing conference or mandatory dispute resolution process such as mediation. As you already know, this is a process where the parties sit with a neutral third party and try to resolve the issue. In these instances, the agency attempts to settle the disagreement without going to a full fair hearing. The purpose of mediation, unlike the hearing, is not to focus on who is right or wrong but rather how to resolve the conflict in a way that meets the interest of both parties. As was discussed in

Chapter 11, because social workers are frequently balancing multiple interests they are especially equipped to make use of mediation. Social workers are also trained to reach decisions based on collaboration and consensus and these skills will assist them during the negotiation process. If mediation does not result in an agreement, the client still has the right to proceed to a fair hearing.

You should be prepared to argue all of the issues on behalf of your client and should have determined prior to the conference with your client what they would be willing, if at all, to settle. For example, if the client is attempting to gain an increase in the benefit amount, there may be an amount in between the requested benefit and the current amount that would be approved by the client. This could be one of the proposed settlements brought to the prehearing conference, increasing the possibility of settling the case without a hearing.

You and the client should come prepared to tell your side of the story, to hear the other side, and to clearly and specifically say how you want to resolve the problem (i.e., "I want a home health aide three times a week"). The client should always be clear about what rights they have and the interests at play. Interests can be tangible like a bottom line dollar amount, or intangible such as a worker offering an apology for a mistake or the client feeling they are being listened to and taken seriously. Social workers should work with the client before the meeting to identify what bottom line tangible and intangible interests are at stake and where they might be willing to compromise. Many times alternative dispute resolution or mediation may fail because the intangible interests of the clients are not identified or addressed. As we presented in Chapter 2, the literature that explores issues of procedural justice tells us that many times a fair process is more important to clients than actual outcomes.

Many cases are settled by agreement without a hearing. Most agencies encourage parties to settle their disagreements, if possible. This means that at anytime you are free to respond to or contact the other party or that person's attorney to discuss the possibility of settlement. If you are reaching an agreement as the hearing approaches and need some more time, you should ask the ALJ to postpone the hearing so you can work on settling the case. Settlement discussions are usually not disclosed to the ALJ. If the case goes to hearing, settlement discussions cannot be mentioned at the hearing. If you settle the matter, you should sign an agreement (called a "stipulation" or "settlement agreement") setting forth the terms of settlement. An *order*, which is a command to the parties, may then be issued by the ALJ accepting and implementing the stipulation.

Once you receive a date for the fair hearing, your client is entitled to access information through prehearing motions. As you learned in Chapter 8, motions are written legal documents filed in court and presented to the judge, arguing for a specific remedy or outcome. An example of a prehearing motion is for benefits to continue during the time period that it takes to schedule and conduct the fair hearing. Often a client's benefits are terminated regardless of whether a fair hearing is requested or not. Therefore in cases where a client may be eligible to receive benefits while the fair hearing is pending, you should immediately request in writing that the benefits continue. It is important to note in that request why your client requires the continuing benefits.

You can also request in writing any special accommodations or interpreters that your client requires during the hearing. Your client has the right to have an interpreter present during the hearing so that they can fully participate in the questioning and cross-examination of witnesses. It is important to ensure that your client has an interpreter available for all aspects of the fair hearing. If you believe that the fair hearing officer may have a difficult time securing an interpreter for your client, make sure to follow up on the request prior to the hearing.

Gathering and Preparing Evidence

Once the issues for your fair hearing have been identified and a settlement has not been offered or accepted, you and your client can begin to strategize about what evidence should be presented to defend their case. The agency has the burden of providing your client with copies of any documents that the agency will use at a fair hearing to prove their case. In addition, your client can request copies of any other documents that the agency has in its possession including notices or letters to your client. Indeed, your client can generally request the entire record from the agency even if it is not provided in the evidence packet from the agency.

The evidence can be presented in two manners: *testimonial evidence* meaning that a live witness testifies and *documentary evidence* meaning reports, letters, and records. Ideally, you would have a combination of live witnesses and documentary evidence to present on behalf of your client. Many of the trial preparation skills you learned in Chapter 8 are relevant here. Remember that you may need to seek releases from your client to obtain certain records and documents. Some of the agency rationale for what social workers often perceive as onerous reporting requirements can be traced back to the agencies need to be prepared for any legal challenges such as fair hearings or civil rights complaints. At this moment, if the agency worker did not have it in the record, then it did not happen.

One of the first decisions to consider is whether or not your client will testify on their own behalf at the fair hearing. Unlike in other civil or criminal proceedings, there are defenses that may render the client's testimony unnecessary. For example, in many jurisdictions, the agency will lose the fair hearing automatically if it fails to provide your client with their full record, often referred to as an evidence packet, once the agency is notified of your client's fair hearing request. Also, the agency will lose the fair hearing automatically if it is not able to provide proof of adequate and timely notice to your client in writing of its decisions. As stated earlier, these protections harken back to the fundamental decision in *Goldberg v. Kelly* (1970) that fair hearings for benefits must protect a client's due process rights and are known in legal terms as *absolute defenses.*

When preparing a client to testify at a fair hearing, the first step is to draft the questions that you or another representative would ask the client. The questions should be straightforward, open-ended, and simply written so that the client is able to tell their story. The questions should be limited to the specific issue in the fair hearing. It is important for clients to practice answering questions and telling their story to the ALJ. Additionally, you should prepare your client for cross-examination by pretending to be the agency representative and asking questions that possibly show your client's failure to follow the rules or procedures set by the agency. Even if your client has an attorney, as we addressed in Chapter 1, caseloads particularly for low-income clients who depend on government and agency benefits and services are high, and having the client well prepared and informed before meeting with their attorney will decrease the amount of preparation time needed.

One method of preparing for the fair hearing is to create with your client an evidentiary checklist and hearing notebook. The checklist should contain all of the information that is required from the agency including any denial letters, notices, statements, or appointment slips. It should also contain any information that your client may be seeking to defend their position including proof of absence from an appointment, documentation of a disability, or evidence of the need for a higher benefit amount. The hearing notebook should include all notes from any prehearing motions or conversations with the agency.

It should also include a timeline of your client's interactions with the agency and any requirements that the agency failed to meet. Additionally, the hearing notebook should include notes on all of the evidence and testimony presented by the agency at the fair hearing. This will help you to assist the client and yourself if you are acting as representative to determine what questions to ask of your witnesses, including your client, and what additional information should be provided to the ALJ. Finally, the hearing notebook allows you and the client to remember all of the arguments made by the agency so that you can present defenses to each argument at the end of the hearing.

Continuances or Adjournments

In many instances, you will discover information that requires you to conduct further investigation. For example, you may discover in the evidence packet or discovery provided by the agency that the benefits were denied because a client missed an appointment. If your client had a reasonable excuse for missing that appointment, it would be important to gather documentation. Your client may ask the hearing officer in writing, copied to all parties, at the conference or at the hearing for a continuance or adjournment before a final decision is made so that the additional evidence can be gathered. Clients who already scheduled hearings but wish to have an attorney or lay advocate present with them at the hearing can also request an adjournment to consult with counsel or have an advocate present. Certainly if new information or evidence were to be raised at the hearing, you can ask for an adjournment to prepare a defense. Finally, your client can request an adjournment if there is a reasonable excuse for their failure to appear such as illness or childcare issues. In most cases, the hearing will be *concluded on default* if your client fails to appear at a hearing. This means that your client will lose the right to appeal the agency's decision unless the client can show a reason for the absence. In these situations, it is especially important for an advocate to appear at the fair hearing to communicate the reason for the client's absence and request an adjournment.

Length of Hearing

The length of a fair hearing depends entirely on the specific issues, volume of the evidence packet, and number of live witnesses. In some cases, fair hearings are very short because the agency has not provided the evidence packet or notice of the denial properly. The fair hearings often feel very informal because all parties are generally at the same table in a small room, very close to the ALJ and other parties. While the fair hearings are generally conducted in an informal manner, the rules of the hearing are formal and should be followed throughout the hearing by all parties.

Decisions

After hearing all of the evidence at the fair hearing, the ALJ will render a decision in writing. This process can often take a month or longer. The written decision should be sent to your client, the advocate, and the agency. If your client does not agree with the decision or you believe that your client's rights were violated during the fair hearing process, then you will need to research whether your client can reopen the hearing or appeal to a different court. One example of this violation would be if the client was not allowed to present any evidence in their defense or was not provided with an interpreter for their native language. It is important to remember that there are still remedies available for clients after the fair hearing process given that many clients may reach out to you after receiving a denial from a fair hearing.

AN EXAMPLE OF A FAIR HEARING FACILITATED BY A SOCIAL WORKER

Ms. Jones and her son have been receiving cash assistance ever since she was 6 months pregnant. As part of her eligibility for this assistance, she would be required to participate in a work-related activity while receiving benefits, which she was entitled to receive beginning the last 3 months of her pregnancy. The federal program, Temporary Assistance for Needy Families (TANF), provides funding for states to administer cash assistance to families and individuals. Individual states are responsible for setting the eligibility guidelines, in accordance with federal regulations, and state-specific guidelines include the requirements for participants in the program to engage in work activities and timelines for the receipt of benefits.

Ms. Jones comes to your office, visibly upset, and hands you a notice that states she is being sanctioned for not completing her assigned work activity within the required time frame. A *sanction* is imposed when the agency believes that the participant has not met the requirements for continued eligibility, and as a result either decreases or terminates the benefits (Lens, 2008). Therefore, Ms. Jones may be facing a significant decrease in her benefits or an end to her benefits entirely.

Ms. Jones tells the social worker that she has been having serious trouble understanding directions given to her at work as well as not being able to repeat back to the teacher and her supervisor what they have told her. She has had trouble retaining the information she hears in class and is behind in completing tasks because she cannot always remember all the steps involved in completing them. Her supervisor told Ms. Jones that she has not successfully completed the program and will not graduate with the other participants. Ms. Jones tells you that she expressed her concerns to her caseworker who said that clearly Ms. Jones was smart and just needed to get used to working regularly. Ms. Jones did not feel like her worker was being rude; in fact, she believes the caseworker likes her. The caseworker had told Ms. Jones she did not want to sanction her but the supervisor told her it was required.

Ms. Jones says that these difficulties in hearing and remembering have been problems throughout her life and not being able to understand or remember what was being said in class was one of the reasons she never completed high school and dropped out. Ms. Jones said, "I just gave up." Ms. Jones further reveals that when she was in foster care, her foster mother attempted to have her evaluated for special education but did not have the legal authority to make the request and the agency did not follow through because her biological mother was not responding to phone calls. You have also begun to notice that Ms. Jones would frequently seem to not remember what you told her but you believed it was due to all the stress she was experiencing. You realize that you should have identified your assumptions and explanations for Ms. Jones's behavior and do more exploration of alternative explanations. You observe that Ms. Jones seems to compensate by being very friendly and cooperative, perhaps agreeing when she does not quite understand. Now, with this new information you suspect that Ms. Jones may need to be evaluated for a learning disability.

In beginning to think about this issue and how to respond, you conduct brief research about the larger context for TANF recipients and disabilities. One federal study found that 44% of TANF recipients report having a parent or a child with a disability, including a learning disability (U.S. General Accounting Office, 2002). Other studies suggest that anywhere from 10% to 40% of recipients present with disabilities (Loprest & Maag, 2001). Because of these limitations TANF recipients who have disabilities are at higher risk for being sanctioned (Meyers et al., 2006). Research has found that, on average, TANF clients who leave due to sanctions are less successful in obtaining employment than those who leave for other reasons. A large proportion of all welfare recipients who leave report experiencing material hardships and there is evidence that sanctioned respondents face more hardship than recipients who are not sanctioned (Reichman et al., 2005).

Meyers et al. (2006) report on seven studies that have found that Black recipients are more likely to be sanctioned than their White counterparts. In some studies, estimated racial disparities in sanctions are modest but in one study conducted in Florida, Fording et al. (2006) estimate that by the ninth month of TANF receipt, Black recipients were sanctioned at rates that were 22% to 35% higher than White recipients. Meyers et al. (2006) suggest that Black clients may be at greater risk for sanctioning because they have disproportionately high rates of other characteristics that are barriers to employment including health and disability problems. There is some evidence to suggest that White and non-White clients may experience differential treatment in TANF programs, including assignment to different activities and different treatment by front-line workers (Meyers et al., 2006). Furthermore, scholars have noted the racist and ableist underpinnings of work requirements and sanctions in benefits programs (Burnside et. al, 2022).

Various studies have also reported high error rates in the application of sanctions. An analysis of administrative appeals of sanction decisions in Texas,

Wisconsin, and New York found that sanctions were reversed in 52% of the Wisconsin appeals, 53% of the Texas appeals, 77% of the appeals in New York City, and 42% of the appeals in New York State exclusive of New York City (Lens, 2005). This overview of the larger context should raise enough concerns for the social worker that instituting a process to more closely examine the decision-making that has occurred in Ms. Jones's case would be an important aspect of socially just case advocacy.

Determining If There Might Be a Claim

After consulting the state regulations as well as the federal TANF regulations, you find that as part of implementing the ADA and the Rehabilitation Act Section 504, policy guidance from both the Department of Health and Human Services and the Department of Justice states applicants for TANF should be voluntarily screened for the presence of disabilities. For the purposes of our discussion of the path of the fair hearing, we will switch our focus to Massachusetts as a case study for Ms. Jones's attempt to fight the denial of benefits. In Massachusetts under 106 CMR § 701.395 (2016) entitled *Learning Disabilities: Screening, Assessment, Sanction Relief and Extensions*, Ms. Jones should have been offered the opportunity, both orally and in writing, to be screened for learning disabilities. Further research reveals that Massachusetts agencies must reasonably modify policies, practices, and procedures for people who have a disability and provide reasonable modifications to programs such as granting extensions to time limits for the completion of programs (106 CMR § 701.390[2], 2016).

With this research, a social worker might inquire further from Ms. Jones about whether she was offered a screening or provided with any information about learning disabilities. In response, Ms. Jones says she cannot remember anyone saying that and she does not have a paper about that. She was not aware that this problem could be a learning disability because in school she was often yelled at for "not paying attention" and nobody ever said anything about a learning disability. As a result of this research and questioning, you want to have Ms. Jones evaluated by a neuropsychologist and audiologist and are worried that because she has been sanctioned her Medicaid benefits will be cut off as well.

You also check with the state regulations and discover that with Ms. Jones's written authorization you can function as her lay representative (106 CMR § 343.150, 2016). At this point it is important for you to consult the section entitled *Rights of the Appellant* in order for you and Ms. Jones to ascertain what you can do during a hearing (106 CMR § 343.410, 2024). Some of the activities the regulation allows Ms. Jones to do are present witnesses, present evidence (both documents and testimony), and question or cross-examine any adverse witnesses. The regulations also lay out the rights and responsibilities of the department and the caseworker during the course of the hearing.

Filing a Request for a Hearing

There are a number of ways that Ms. Jones may realize a change in her benefits or a termination of her benefits. Ms. Jones may have received a letter informing her of the agency's decision, as the agency is required to notify recipients of any change in benefits in writing. The letter detailing the change or termination is often called the *notice of intent* or *notice of decision.* In that letter, Ms. Jones is informed of how the benefits are going to be altered, the basis for making the change to the alteration, and when the change becomes effective. Additionally, Ms. Jones may notice that the cash assistance amount is reduced or that her benefits have stopped altogether. There are many states where not only would Ms. Jones benefits be cut off through being sanctioned but those of her children as well. By reviewing regulations in *Continuation of Benefits Pending Appeal*, you will see that as long as Ms. Jones has filed her complaint within the proscribed time frame that her benefits will be retained or reactivated if they were cut off (106 CMR § 343.250, 2024).

Because of the importance of maintaining benefits, you would want to ensure that Ms. Jones requests the fair hearing as soon as there is a problem with the benefit, whether there is formal notice from the agency or simply a problem with the benefits. Additionally, you should review the letter from the agency with Ms. Jones to determine the basis for the change or termination and the time frame. The regulations at 106 CMR § 343.200 (2024) *Adequate Notice Requirements* will allow you to assess whether or not the agency met the requirements for notice, and 106 CMR § 343.230 (2024) *Grounds for Appeal* will help you determine if Ms. Jones has a claim.

Interestingly, Massachusetts allows a client to file a complaint on the basis of *Coercive or Otherwise Improper Conduct* by department employees (106 CMR, § 343.110, 2016). Some of the ways that the regulation defines this behavior are important in light of some of the research we have presented on the experience of clients as they negotiate benefit systems. Definitions include: "d. The worker recklessly and unreasonably fails to treat the applicant, recipient or former recipient with dignity and respect to which he or she is reasonably entitled" or "e. The worker recklessly and unreasonably discourages the applicant, recipient or former recipient from applying for assistance or discourages the applicant, recipient or former recipient from inquiring concerning their rights or appealing" (106 CMR § 343.235, 2016). One of the remedies for this claim can be the worker offering a written apology to the client or assignment of a new worker. This ground would not be relevant to *The Case of Michelle Jones* because she reports a good relationship with her worker.

It would also be important to remind Ms. Jones to keep all of her paperwork as well as the full names of any workers she is interacting with because the letter is an important piece of evidence in the fair hearing. Additionally, you should advise Ms. Jones to keep the envelope that the letter was mailed in to document any issues of timeliness with the agency's notification.

Prehearing Processes

Armed with Ms. Jones's history of a learning disability and current functioning, you can begin gathering information and records. You may first want to consult the regulations about where and how the hearing is conducted. You discover in the regulations entitled *Methods of Conducting a Fair Hearing* that hearings in Massachusetts can be conducted face-to-face, by videoconferencing, or by telephone conferencing (106 CMR § 343.120, 2016). You can also assist Ms. Jones in writing the agency to request any records or documents that the agency plans to present at a fair hearing. You can also access information in the regulations concerning scheduling, procedures for rescheduling, under what conditions your case may be dismissed, as well as powers and duties of the administrative hearing officer. An important duty of the hearing officer is to create a "record" of the proceeding. In the regulations subtitled *The Record*, it explains that the hearing officer must ensure tapes or transcripts are made of the proceedings and all documents introduced during the hearing are kept as evidence (106 CMR § 343.550, 2016).

The section entitled *Right to Examine Case File and Documents, or "Discovery,"* informs you that Ms. Jones has the right to examine her entire case file and any documents the agency will be using to present their case (106 CMR § 343.340, 2016). You further learn that you must make an appointment in advance to meet with the worker to review the file. You may also as a party request subpoenas to be issued by the Department of Hearings as authorized by *Subpoenas* within 2 days of your request (106 CMR § 343.360, 2016).

Finally, you can accompany Ms. Jones to the welfare agency for a conference with the welfare caseworker to determine whether there was an error in the decision that can be remedied without a fair hearing. Under 106 CMR § 701.395(C)(1)(c), *Sanction Relief*, if Ms. Jones agrees to participate in and complete a learning disability assessment, the sanction may be held in abeyance until the assessment is completed. This may resolve the problem immediately. However, if there were no resolution, then you would inform Ms. Jones that she should pursue the fair hearing process in order to challenge the denial of benefits.

At this juncture, you and Ms. Jones might decide to consult with an attorney about the merits of her case and any possible defenses or "theories" that could be raised in the fair hearing. There are many legal services offices and legal clinics operating from community-based organizations that provide brief legal advice to clients on fair hearings. When the attorney reviews Ms. Jones's files, he realizes that the agency did not provide Ms. Jones with timely notice when terminating her benefits, and suggests an assessment whether Ms. Jones's case meets any of the criteria where the agency does not have to give adequate notice. This is the first defense that the attorney suggests to you and Ms. Jones. In order to prove the lack of timely notice, Ms. Jones could present evidence including the denial letter and last cash assistance notice to prove that the assistance was terminated before providing notice.

When you raise the issues surrounding Ms. Jones's learning disability, the attorney suggests that another possible defense would be that Ms. Jones was not provided with reasonable accommodations for her disability as required under the law (106 CMR § 701.390[2], 2016). This includes the provision in Massachusetts's law that welfare caseworkers are required to screen participants for learning disability as referenced earlier. In order to prove this defense, the attorney might suggest that you gather records and witnesses to demonstrate not only that Ms. Jones has a recognized learning disability that directly impacted her ability to fulfill the work requirements, but also that no accommodations were made by the agency. Additionally, the attorney would note that the agency is required to make an exemption for individuals with physical or mental health disabilities including the provision that an individual with disabilities may request an extension on time limits for completing programs or work requirements. Finally, the attorney suggests that Ms. Jones might want to pursue a complaint with the Office for Civil Rights for the agency's discrimination against her because of her learning disability.

Gathering and Preparing Evidence

After the consultation with the attorney, you can assist Ms. Jones in gathering records, documents, and witnesses to testify on her behalf. You and Ms. Jones can refer to *Evidence* (106 CMR § 343.500, 2016), which tells you that oral testimony is taken under oath, and that copies of any regulations you are using can be put into evidence. Keeping in mind the theory of Ms. Jones's case, you might reach out to the social worker at the drug treatment agency to discuss any records that could support the case or whether their testimony would be helpful. You could also reach out to Ms. Jones's former foster mother to determine whether she would be willing to testify about her efforts to obtain special education services when Ms. Jones was in high school. Since you have already had Ms. Jones evaluated by a neuropsychologist and audiologist, you will have a sense of the evidence that could be presented by the evaluators including the conclusions from the report supporting your theory that Ms. Jones has a learning disability that was not properly screened by the agency.

It is very important for you to consult the regulations to make sure your evaluators are providing the kinds of documentation required by the law. In this case, the audiologist reports that Ms. Jones has an auditory processing disorder. In addition the neuropsychologist finds evidence of a receptive language disorder. It is not enough that the evaluators just provide a diagnosis; an evaluator must show that they adequately established a diagnosis of a learning disability and that they have provided enough information upon which to determine appropriate and reasonable accommodations. This means that articulating how and what methods and instruments they used in assessment should be included in the report as well as specific information that links the kind of disability to recommended accommodations.

After Ms. Jones gathers her evidence including the packet of documents from the agency, you can assist her in organizing and reviewing the evidence. It is important to keep track of dates and notices. Additionally, you can help Ms. Jones organize a timeline of what happened with the agency, including dates and the names of workers that Ms. Jones spoke to about her benefits. Once Ms. Jones has determined which witnesses will testify on her behalf, you can assist her in drafting questions for the witnesses. Ms. Jones or her lay representative, potentially a social worker, will have the opportunity to ask questions of the witnesses. It is important to prepare these questions in advance and ensure that the witnesses know what will be asked of them so that they are prepared to testify.

The following are some sample questions that Ms. Jones or her lay representative could ask the agency caseworker on cross-examination:

- For the entirety of her case, you were assigned to Ms. Jones?
- Your responsibilities as her assigned caseworker included processing her application for benefits?

- When you process applications as the assigned caseworker, you are required to screen for learning disabilities on all applicants?
- The screening process that you are required to conduct as the assigned caseworker includes considering learning disabilities, correct?
- You were also responsible for monitoring her case after the application phase?
- As part of this responsibility as the assigned caseworker, you were aware that she was at risk of not completing her work program?
- As part of your meetings as the assigned caseworker with Ms. Jones, she told you that she had difficulty hearing the instructions from teachers?
- Ms. Jones also told you that it was hard for her to remember what instructors said?
- However, as the assigned caseworker, you never asked Ms. Jones whether she had a learning disability that made it difficult for her to participate in the work program?
- And as the assigned caseworker you never screened Ms. Jones for a learning disability at any point?

When developing questions for the direct examination of the neuropsychologist and audiologist, Ms. Jones would want to focus on the qualifications of the witness and the results of her evaluation. Some sample questions could include:

- What is your current profession?
- What was your training for this position?
- How long have you been a neuropsychologist/audiologist?
- How many adults have you evaluated?
- When did you evaluate Ms. Jones?
- What did the evaluation consist of?
- What tools did you use in your evaluation?
- Why are those tools used in evaluations?
- What were the results of the evaluation?
- What does that diagnosis mean?
- What was the basis for your conclusion that Ms. Jones has a learning disability?
- What modifications would support Ms. Jones in participating in a vocational or educational program?

At the fair hearing, Ms. Jones would present evidence that she was not notified of her benefits termination within the statutory time period. She would also present evidence from the neuropsychologist and audiologist that she has learning disabilities that make it difficult for her to hear and remember instructions. The ALJ might question the caseworker about her efforts to respond to Ms. Jones's concerns about the work program and to screen for any disability. The ALJ would also question the neuropsychologist and the audiologist about the basis for their conclusions. Some accommodations recommended by the professionals might include the supervisor making sure verbal instructions are given slowly and clearly in a quiet location, that the supervisor and teacher give

Ms. Jones written instructions and written class notes, that Ms. Jones should write notes about what she believed she heard about instructions and should review the notes with her supervisor for clarification, and that Ms. Jones should use pictures and diagrams as aids to remember work procedures.

The Decision

The ALJ bases the decision in part on precedent from the federal Office of Civil Rights of Health and Human Services, which stated that the ADA and Section 504 were violated when the local Massachusetts welfare agency failed to conduct screenings for disabilities and to provide modifications, and referred participants to inappropriate education and training programs (*Ramos v. McIntire*, 2000). The hearing officer according to 106 CMR § 343.610 (2016), will base the decision on a "preponderance of the evidence." As you learned in Chapter 8 this means that the facts presented by Ms. Jones were "more likely true than not." You can also find out what specific information should be in the decision and who should get a copy by consulting the regulation. You also find out that the hearing officer must make a decision within 90 days (106 CMR § 343.140[D], 2016).

Ultimately, the hearing officer determines that Ms. Jones's benefits were illegally terminated and orders that she receive retroactive benefits, in addition to reinstating her benefits with the accommodations and modifications recommended by the neuropsychologist and audiologist to be implemented at the job readiness program attended by Ms. Jones. You and the client will receive notice of the decision which will include the order to the department that they screen for disabilities, grant an extension, and provide accommodations at the work readiness program your client attends and the retroactive payment of benefits. According to the regulations, the department must notify Ms. Jones that she has the right to full and prompt implementation of any orders within 30 days of the decision (106 CMR § 343.640, 2016). If your client disagrees with the final decision, your client may request a judicial review under the provisions of *Judicial Review*, which states that Ms. Jones could file an appeal in the Superior Court in the district where she resides (106 CMR § 343.720, 2016).

As you see from the case study, a social worker can play a significant advocacy role in a fair hearing sought by Ms. Jones at all stages of the process. From the initial identification of the issue to the resolution of the matter at trial, social workers can contribute their research and case management and advocacy expertise to support clients in accessing critical supports, holding agencies accountable, and enforcing client rights.

LEGAL AND ETHICAL ISSUES FOR SOCIAL WORKERS WHO FUNCTION AS LAY REPRESENTATIVES

Due process suggests that social workers have an expanded responsibility to help clients prepare and argue cases and to represent clients in hearings (Dickson, 1976). In most states social workers can participate in administrative proceedings as lay advocates on behalf of their client. For example, in New York, a social worker can help prepare and accompany a client to a fair hearing for welfare benefits. A family contesting the decision of the Department of Developmental Services in California can represent themselves or can be represented by a lay representative or attorney. Likewise, in Washington State, a worker can choose to have a lay representative or attorney represent them in an administrative hearing regarding unemployment benefits. However, in some states, lay representatives, including social workers, are not permitted to represent individuals or families in fair hearings for special education services because it has been determined to fall under the prohibited category of the unauthorized practice of law regulated by the state's bar.

For example, the federal law, Individuals with Education Disabilities Act (IDEA) (2004), allows for an individual to be represented by an attorney or lay advocate in a fair hearing, provided that the lay advocate has some basis of knowledge or training in the relevant field. So for example, a school social worker with expertise in providing services for children in special education might meet this criterion. However, the states that prohibit lay representatives from representing clients at fair hearings under IDEA have concluded that this lay representation is prohibited as the unauthorized practice of law. The basis for this determination is that the lay representative's role at the hearing is legal in nature, given that the lay representative will conduct direct and cross-examination of witnesses and make opening and closing statements.

The Supreme Court of Delaware ruled in *In Re Matter of Arons* (2000) that federal law recognizes the difference between attorneys and lay representatives, and lay representatives are not permitted to represent parents in hearings where they are performing legal functions such as direct and cross-examination and evidentiary objections. Additionally, the court believed that there were sufficient safeguards in the administrative hearing to guarantee due process for individuals even if not represented by an attorney or lay representative. In contrast, some legal scholars have taken the position that unless the federal law or regulation expressly prohibits lay representatives, individuals should have the right to have anyone of their choosing represent them at administrative hearings in order to promote due process and social justice (Asimow, M. as Amicus Curiae in Support of Petitioner, *Benninghoff v. Orange County Superior Court of State*, 2006). The argument made for lay representation in administrative hearings is that many clients, as we discussed in Chapter 1, do not have access to nor can they afford attorneys. The argument has also been made that in some instances nonlawyers may have a greater level of expertise in the issue being addressed in the administrative hearing.

Given the differences in state regulations and practices, it is crucial to ascertain whether or not you are permitted to represent a client at a fair hearing in your state. However, even if your client decides to represent themselves or you are not permitted to represent the client in a fair hearing, you can still play an active role in helping your client to prepare the case. Social workers can provide clients with important information regarding their rights to challenge an agency's decision and with support in gathering records, documentation, and witnesses to help their case.

As with any interdisciplinary representation, practitioners should be mindful of keeping within their professional expertise. In the same way that attorneys without social work training in clinical assessment should not attempt to assess or diagnosis clients, social workers should be mindful of their professional limits when advocating for clients. For example, a social worker working with a lawyer who will represent a client in a denial of Social Security disability benefits should not testify to a client's medical diagnosis, but rather suggest that the client and attorney gather evidence or testimony from the client's treating doctor.

While the rules about how the hearings are conducted are fairly relaxed, the rules about how decisions are made and what evidence those decisions rely on is very strict. Again you will want to consult your state's judicial branch website or the state office of administrative hearings if your state has that model to access information about the process and rules for administrative hearings in your jurisdiction. You must present facts and evidence that support your client's case and be familiar with regulations that are being used by your client or by the agency to develop their "theory" and argue their case.

There are no explicit rules governing a lay representative's responsibility to their client but reviewing the ethical rules that apply to both social workers and attorneys presented in Chapter 4 will give you the necessary framework to function ethically and responsibly as a lay representative. The key aspects of ethical practice include communicating with your client about every aspect of the proceeding and being clear about who is the decision-maker. Additionally, an ethical practitioner will consider whether their client has a legitimate argument which will be considered at the administrative level or at subsequent judicial review in light of the applicable regulations and statutes related to the case.

Whistleblowers' Protection and Retaliation

Of course, clients are not the only ones who may worry about or suffer retaliation as a result of their efforts to advocate and identify unjust and illegal practices. Social workers often find themselves confronted by unethical or potentially unlawful agency policies or actions and are concerned about the impact intervening may have on their livelihood. Despite this fear, some social work scholars present the idea that because social workers have an ethical duty to advance social justice, address discrimination, and protect the welfare of their clients, whistleblowing should be considered one of a number of available advocacy tools (Barsky, 2010; Greene & Latting, 2004; Mansbach & Bachner, 2008).

It is important for you to know that many states have laws in place that protect employees from retaliation, including discharge from their employment, by their supervisor or agency for disclosing information about the actions of a state agency or, in some states, a private employer. Some examples are the waste of public funds, abuse of authority or mismanagement of the agency, or violation of a regulation or law. Called "whistleblower" or antiretaliation laws, all states currently have statutes that protect public or private employees, although the scope of that protection and which employees are covered will vary from state to state. There are also numerous federal provisions that protect employees and relate to both public and private employers. As an example, the federal government's website (www.whistleblowers.gov) details the statutes that are enforced by the Occupational Safety and Health Administration and the process for filing a complaint of retaliation.

Under these laws, you are entitled to a hearing and certain remedies such as reinstatement if you were fired, back pay, and attorney's fees. Another reason to check the law in your state is because similar to most other hearing processes, there is generally a time limit from when the action you are complaining about occurs and the length of time you have to file a complaint. Also, states differ in the designated agency that will receive your complaint. In many states, employers are required to post a notice of the state's whistleblower laws so that employees are aware of the protections provided if they report illegal activity including abuse of funds, danger to public safety, and mismanagement. In Connecticut, state and quasipublic agencies are required to post this notice "in a conspicuous place that is readily available for viewing by employees" (Conn. Gen. Stat. § 4-61[dd][i], 2005).

A "whistleblower" case involving a social worker is *Clairmont v. Sound Mental Health and Wilson* (2011). The U.S. Court of Appeals for the Ninth Circuit issued an opinion holding that a social worker is protected from retaliation for their courtroom testimony about a former client. In this case, a social worker was a program manager for a domestic violence treatment program that had a contract with Seattle Municipal Court. A criminal defense attorney subpoenaed the social worker to provide expert testimony in the case. The attorney's client was discharged from another domestic violence treatment program and the probation office attached to the court was trying to revoke the probation. The social worker testified that because the client only spoke Spanish it could have impacted the client's termination from the other program. Two weeks later the social worker was fired by their program because of feedback about their performance from the Domestic Violence Probation Department Unit that also resulted in a stop referral order against the program that employed the social worker.

Claiming a violation of First Amendment rights, the social worker sued and the court found that indeed their relationship to the court was analogous to employee/employer and that a state agency cannot stifle an employee when they are providing testimony that "allows the public to evaluate the performance of public agencies" and in matters where there is "a public concern." Especially important for rights-based social workers, the court defined "public concern" as speech that "brings to light potential or actual discrimination, corruption or other wrongful conduct by government agencies or officials." Since that time, social workers have been involved as whistleblowers in cases involving the child welfare system, and it is important to understand your rights and legal protections as a social worker challenging an employer.

REFERENCES

34 CFR § 300.530(e).
106 CMR § 343.120 (2016).
106 CMR § 343.140(D) (2016).
106 CMR § 343.150, 2016.
106 CMR § 343.235 (2016).
106 CMR § 343.340 (2016).
106 CMR § 343.360 (2016).

106 CMR § 343.500 (2016).
106 CMR § 343.550 (2016).
106 CMR §343.610 (2016).
106 CMR § 343.640 (2016).
106 CMR § 343.720 (2016).
106 CMR § 343.110 (2016).
106 CMR § 343.200 (2024).
106 CMR § 343.230 (2024).
106 CMR § 343.250 (2024).
106 CMR § 343.410 (2024).
106 CMR § 701.390(2) (2016).
106 CMR § 701.395 (2016).
106 CMR § 701.395(C)(1)(c).
Administrative Procedure Act, 5 U.S.C. § 553 (1946).
American Civil Liberties Union. (2010). *Oregon* ACLU report: Oregon's school-to-prison pipeline. Oregon Affiliate ACLU. https://www.aclu-or.org/sites/default/files/ACLU_STPP_FINAL.pdf
Asimow, M. as Amicus Curiae in Support of Petitioner, Benninghoff v. Orange County Superior Court of State, 38 Cal. Rptr.3d 759 (No. 05CC00971) (Ca. App. 4th Dis. 2006).
Barsky, A. E. (2010). *Ethics and values in social work: An integrated approach for a comprehensive curriculum.* Oxford University Press.
Burnside, A., Lower-Basch, E., Dolby, T., Gilkesson, E., & McCorkell, L. (2022). *Advancing disability equity and access in TANF and SNAP for people with long COVID.* Center for the Study of Law and Social Policy. https://www.clasp.org/wp-content/uploads/2022/10/2022.10.12_Advancing-Disability-Equity-and-Access-in-TANF-and-SNAP-for-People-with-Long-COVID.pdf
Children's Bureau. (2024). *Child welfare policy manual.* https://www.acf.hhs.gov/cwpm/public_html/programs/cb/laws_policies/laws/cwpm/policy.jsp?idFlag=8
Civil Rights Act of 1964, 88 Pub. L. No. 352, 78 Stat. 241 (1964).
Clairmont v. Sound Mental Health, 632 F.3d 1091 (9th Cir. 2011).
Conn. Gen. Stat. § 4-61(dd)(i) (2005).
Dickson, D. (1976). Law in social work: Impact of due process. *Social Work, 21*, 274–278. https://doi.org/10.1093/sw/21.4.274
Fording, R., Schram, F. S., & Soss, J. (2006). *Devolution, discretion and local variation in TANF sanctioning.* Research Discussion Paper Series, DP2006-04. University of Kentucky Center for Poverty. https://uknowledge.uky.edu/ukcpr_papers/97/
Ga. Rules and Reg. c.97-2, Rule 97-2-.01.
Goldberg v. Kelly, 397 U.S. 254 (1970).
Greene, A. D., & Latting, J. K. (2004). Whistle-blowing as a form of advocacy: Guidelines for the practitioner and organization. *Social Work, 49*(2), 219–230. https://doi.org/10.1093/sw/49.2.219
Hill, R. B. (2004). Institutional racism in child welfare. *Race and Society, 7*(1), 17–33. https://doi.org/10.1016/j.racsoc.2004.11.004
Hill, R. B. (2007). *An analysis of racial/ethnic disproportionality and disparity at the national, state and county levels.* Casey-CSSP Alliance for Racial. Equity in Child Welfare. https://www.issuelab.org/resources/8256/8256.pdf
In Re Matter of Arons, 756 A.2d 867 (Del. 2000).
Individuals with Disabilities Education Act, 34 C.F.R. § 300.530(e) (2004).
Kim, C. Y., Losen, D. J., & Hewitt, D. (2010). *The school-to-prison-pipeline: Structuring legal reform.* NYU Press.
Lens, V. (2005). Bureaucratic disentitlement after welfare reform: Are fair hearings the cure? *Georgetown Journal on Poverty Law and Policy, XII*, 13–42.

Lens, V. (2007). Administrative justice in public welfare bureaucracies: When citizens (don't) complain. *Administration & Society, 39*(3), 382–408. https://doi.org/10.1177/0095399707301006

Lens, V. (2008). Welfare and work sanctions: Examining discretion on the front lines. *Social Service Review, 82*, 197–222.

Lens, V. (2010). Respect: The missing policy tool of welfare reform. *Social Work, 55*(3), 281–283. https://doi.org/10.1093/sw/55.3.281

Lens, V., & Katz, C. (2010). Negotiating the discourse of race within the United States welfare system. *Ethnic and Racial Studies, 33*, 1032–1048. https://doi.org/10.1080/01419870903259538

Loprest, P., & Maag, E. (2001). *Barriers to and supports for work among adults with disabilities: Results from the NHIS-D.* U.S. Department of Health and Human Services. http://aspe.hhs.gov/daltcp/reports/barriers.htm

Losen, D., & Skiba, R. (2010). *Suspended education: Urban middle schools in crisis.* Southern Poverty Law Center. https://civilrightsproject.ucla.edu/research/k-12-education/school-discipline/suspended-education-urban-middle-schools-in-crisis/Suspended-Education_FINAL-2.pdf

Mansbach, A., & Bachner, Y. G. (2008). On the readiness of social work students to blow the whistle to protect the client interests. *Journal of Social Work Values and Ethics, 5*(2), 31–42. https://www.jswve.org/wp-content/uploads/2008/06/10-005-207-JSWVE-2008.pdf

Mashaw, J., Merrill, R., & Shane, P. (1998). *Administrative law: The American public law system* (4th ed.). West Group.

Meyers, M., Klawitter, M., Lindhorst, T., & Harper, S. (2006). *Review of policies and procedures for implementation of workfirst sanction policies: Report to the Washington State Department of Health Services.* West Coast Poverty Center, University of Washington.

Mont. Code c.24 (2023).

Mont. Code Ann. c.24, § 53-24-204 (2023).

Mont. Code Ann. c.24, § 53-24-209 (2023).

Mont. Code Ann. c.24, § 53-24-305 (2023).

Morris, M. (2016). *Pushout: The criminalization of black girls in school.* The New Press.

Nicholson-Crotty, S., Birchmeier, Z., & Valentine, D. (2009). Exploring the impact of school discipline on racial disproportion in the juvenile justice system. *Social Science Quarterly, 90*(4), 1003–1018. https://doi.org/10.1111/j.1540-6237.2009.00674.x

Ramos v. McIntire, OCR Complaint No. 01-98-3055 (January 19, 2000).

Reichman, N., Teitler, J., & Curtis, M. (2005). TANF sanctioning and hardship. *Social Service Review, 79*(2), 215–236. https://doi.org/10.1086/428918

Ryberg, R., Her, S., Cahill, D. T., & Harper, K. (2021). *Despite reductions since 2011–12, black students and students with disabilities remain more likely to experience suspension.* Research Brief. https://www.childtrends.org/publications/despite-reductions-black-students-and-students-with-disabilities-remain-more-likely-to-experience-suspension

Saltzman, A., & Furman, D. (1999). *Law in social work practice.* Nelson-Hall.

Stein, T. J. (2004). *The role of law in social work practice and administration.* NY: Columbia University Press.

Substance Abuse and Mental Health Services Administration. (2024). *Laws and regulations.* https://www.samhsa.gov/about-us/who-we-are/laws-regulations

Tempel, L. R. (2009). The intersubjective action of case advocacy and engagement in a working alliance. *Smith College Studies in Social Work, 79*, 125–138. https://doi.org/10.1080/00377310902832276

U.S. General Accounting Office. (July, 2002). *Welfare reform: Outcomes for TANF recipients with impairments* (GAO-02-884). https://www.gao.gov/assets/gao-02-884.pdf

CHAPTER 13

Macro-Level Social Work Practice and Systemic Reform

INTRODUCTION

As you have learned in the previous chapters, the law can be a powerful tool for empowering clients and enforcing their rights. While civil and criminal cases often impact only the small number of individuals involved in the case, the law can also create widespread systemic change through class actions, amicus curiae (friend of the court) briefs, and legislative lobbying. It is critical that social workers understand the remedies available under the law to effectuate systemic reforms as they provide an opportunity to impact change locally and nationally for a larger number of individuals and groups. In this chapter, you will learn how knowledge and understanding of large-scale litigation and legislative lobbying can further the social work values of social justice and impact micro-level practice. You will learn what processes exist to challenge laws and decision-making on behalf of a larger group of clients through class action litigation, and how your expertise as a social worker can be included in legal decision-making through amicus curiae briefs in cases of particular interest and relevance to your clients. Finally, you will learn the knowledge and skills needed to advocate for better laws and regulations for your clients and others at the legislative level.

SOCIAL WORK AND LAW REFORM

A rights-based social worker should always be considering opportunities for law reform and change on a macro level, even if their daily practice focuses on individual client work. As the Preamble to the Code of Ethics states, "Social workers promote social justice and social change with and on behalf of clients" (National Association of Social Workers [NASW], 2021). Social workers are in a unique position to identify social problems and legal failings given their focus on direct practice and advocacy for clients, many of whom are already interacting with the legal and regulatory systems. Throughout this book, we have highlighted the ways in which social workers can assist in identifying potential legal issues, and this holds true in the realm of systemic law reform as well as individual cases. Levy (1991) notes, "[A]s the profession most prominently involved with social problems, social work is or ought to be particularly well positioned to identify and describe specific social problems and promote attention to them—including litigation attention" (p. 436).

As this chapter demonstrates, often the most successful tool for promoting both social justice and social change on a macro level is to focus on law reform through cases such as class actions, the shaping of legal caselaw through amicus curiae briefs and expert testimony, and advocacy for just, evidence-based, and well-reasoned laws. Social workers can play key roles in each of these strategies through interdisciplinary collaborations with lawyers, clients, community organizations, and legislators.

CLASS ACTIONS AS A MEANS TO SYSTEMIC REFORM

Defining Class Action Cases

Up until now, we have focused on cases where an individual client is involved in the civil, criminal, or administrative legal forum. However, the legal system allows for multiple individuals to raise legal claims in Civil Court. A *class action* is a specific form of litigation where a small number of individual plaintiffs can seek legal relief for themselves and on behalf of a larger group of people. The premise behind class actions is that there are common legal issues and interests among the individual plaintiffs and a larger group, but bringing each individual member of the larger group into the case would be impractical. For example, a class action would be appropriate for multiple employees who all suffered discrimination in a large corporation or on behalf of consumers who all purchased the same defective product or medicine that had undisclosed dangerous side effects. It would not be practical to ask each individual who was harmed by the medicine to participate in the litigation, given that the legal issues are common among them and a smaller number of plaintiffs can represent the larger group's interests and legal rights. Another example is litigants who all lived in the same geographic area bringing a class action against a manufacturer or company for dumping toxic chemicals in their water supply and consequently causing medical issues among the neighbors and class members. In many ways, class actions are a particularly effective way for clients to challenge practices of large-scale corporations or organizations, instead of having to rely on individual suits that may be too expensive or time-consuming on their own.

An example from the practice of the initial social work author Dr. Lyn Slater was her participation in the large class action lawsuit, *Marisol v. Giuliani* (1996) filed on behalf of 11 named plaintiffs representing a class of 100,000 children in foster care and children who were the subjects of abuse and neglect reports. The social work author worked in an interdisciplinary law firm that represented children in foster care in New York City. Socials workers and attorneys in that office and in other legal offices throughout the city representing children in foster care were identifying and documenting serious problems with the child welfare system including untimely and inadequate investigations of abuse and neglect, lack of mandated preplacement preventive services, untimely or incomplete assessments, shortage of appropriate foster care placements, long delays for children waiting for adoption or reunification, poor foster home oversight resulting in abuse of children in care, high caseloads and frequent turnover, inadequate caseworker support, inadequate training and supervision, and an inadequate information system to name several of the serious problems identified.

The decision was made to address these systemic concerns by instituting a litigation campaign and partnering with another advocacy agency to start a class action lawsuit. The social workers and attorneys identified particularly compelling cases that represented the range of concerns and some of these cases became the *named plaintiffs* or those individuals who are named as representative of the class and "stand in" for all the other members of the class. An example of a named plaintiff in the *Marisol v. Giuliani* case follows:

> Thomas C. is a 15-year-old who has been in foster care since he was seven. In those 8 years, Thomas endured numerous placements including a hospital, a diagnostic center, and a residential treatment center ("RTC"). In 1993, without adequate investigation, Child Welfare Administration of the City of New York (CWA) approved Thomas' placement with Rev. D., a minister Thomas met at the RTC, who took him to another state. There Rev. D. sexually abused Thomas who subsequently ran away. In 1994, Thomas was returned to the RTC where he now resides. He has since attempted suicide twice and has run away from the RTC only to return after facing hardship and abuse on the streets. CWA has failed to determine the appropriateness of the RTC placement, to pursue the possibility of adoption, or to provide Thomas with counseling. (*Marisol v. Giuliani*, 1996)

Historically, class actions have been successful in creating widespread systemic reform in government agencies, companies, and organizations. As the following examples of class actions demonstrate, the social work value of challenging social injustice is upheld by these class actions which address "issues of poverty, unemployment, discrimination, and other forms of social injustice" specifically identified by the Code of Ethics. One of the most successful and far-reaching class actions to address systemic injustice was undoubtedly *Brown v. Board of Education* (1954). In that case, a class of parents sued the Board of Education in Topeka, Kansas, on behalf of their children who were African American students forced by state law to attend a segregated school. When the parents attempted to enroll their children in the closer school, the Board of Education refused to enroll them in the closer school, which was segregated for White children. When the case reached the Supreme Court, the unanimous opinion held that segregated schools were unconstitutional declaring that "we conclude that in the field of public education, the doctrine of 'separate but equal' has no place" (p. 495). As history attests, this was one of the most significant decisions in the Supreme Court's tenure with its impact on education and civil rights nationwide.

In the field of employment discrimination, the case of *Griggs v. Duke Power Co.* (1971) was seminal for defining what constitutes discrimination against an employee on the basis of race. In that case, a class of 13 employees of a power-generating facility in North Carolina that had historically segregated employees on the basis of race sued their employer to challenge the requirement of having a high school diploma or equivalent score on an IQ test in order to work in certain departments in the company. The class plaintiffs argued that the policy acted to significantly disqualify African American employees, and to maintain what historically had been positions segregated for White employees.

As you know from previous chapters, the Civil Rights Act of 1964 prohibited employment discrimination on the basis of race, and also allows for class action lawsuits to enforce its provisions. Ultimately, the Supreme Court determined that the company could not demonstrate that the requirements were linked to the job performance. The Supreme Court in *Griggs v. Duke Power Co.* clarified that "what is required by Congress is the removal of artificial, arbitrary, and unnecessary barriers to employment when the barriers operate invidiously to discriminate on the basis of racial or other impermissible classification" (1971). The class plaintiffs were able to prove that the hiring and job transfer requirements were illegal under the antidiscrimination laws precisely because they were "fair in form, but discriminatory in operation." This notion, now more commonly referred to as disparate impact, has been codified under the federal regulations in the Civil Rights Act of 1991 to protect countless numbers of employees from discriminatory employment practices.

In 2001, the largest potential class action lawsuit at that time was brought against the Walmart Corporation alleging that the company discriminates against women with regard to pay and promotions and was seeking monetary damages for those affected by the gender discrimination. Seven female employees representing potentially over a million women who have worked at Walmart were the lead plaintiffs in *Dukes v. Walmart Stores, Inc.* (2007). The case was heard by the United States Supreme Court in March 2011 to determine whether it can properly be certified as a class action, because Walmart argued that the class is too big and has too many separate interests to proceed as a class action or representative suit as opposed to each impacted woman or small groups of women bringing individual claims. The Court ultimately determined that the class could not be certified although the justices differed in their legal reasoning why the required commonality among the class members was insufficient and therefore the case could not proceed as a class action on behalf of all women who were working for Walmart at the time of the case or had previously worked for Walmart. The size of the potential class and resulting decision highlighted the tension between class actions as mechanisms for challenging widespread corporate malfeasance, in this case an alleged pattern and practice of discrimination against female employees, and the critique that smaller groups of individual claims are more appropriate and just for determining whether or not the defendant violated antidiscrimination laws. The decision has been far-reaching in defining the types of cases that will be permissible as class actions and how commonality among plaintiffs should be discerned.

Class actions can be brought in both state and federal courts. The rules for state court class actions are governed by the specific state and must have a state law at issue. Class actions, which are brought in federal courts, must have a federal law at issue and are governed by the Federal Rules of Civil Procedure (FRCP, 2023). For example, the previously mentioned class action lawsuit, *Marisol v. Giuliani* (1996), was filed in federal district court because the plaintiffs' advocates were alleging that the child welfare administration through their actions or inactions were depriving the plaintiffs of their rights under the First, Ninth, and Fourteenth Amendments, as well as various other state and federal statutes such as the Adoption Assistance and Placement Act, the Multiethnic Placement Act, and the Child Abuse Prevention and Treatment Act.

The rules governing procedure detail the types of cases that can be brought to court and what needs to be proven before the class action will be allowed to proceed to trial. Many states have adopted the content of the Federal Rules of Civil Procedure to handle state-based class actions. However, some states have specific rules that deviate from the Federal Rules, including California. Additionally, a class action can be brought in federal court instead of state court under 28 U.S.C. § 1332(d)(2) if the amount of money at issue is over $5 million and if any member of the class is from a different state than any of the defendants or if the class members or the defendant are from a foreign state or are a foreign state.

Certifying and Determining the Type of Class Action

Under the Federal Rules, before a class can be certified or allowed to go to trial, the plaintiffs bringing the class action must demonstrate each of the following prerequisites under Rule 23(a) of the Federal Rules of Civil Procedure:

> One or more members of a class may sue or be sued as representative parties on behalf of all members only if: (1) the class is so numerous that joinder of all members is impracticable, (2) there are questions of law or fact common to the class, (3) the claims or defenses of the representative parties are typical of the claims or defenses of the class; and (4) the representative parties will fairly and adequately protect the interests of the class.

These requirements are codified under the law to ensure that the plaintiffs in the litigation are representing the rights of the other affected members of the class and there are indeed common questions of law and fact among the class. One can imagine that the purpose of the class action would be undermined by a representative party that was differently situated both in their legal argument or the facts from other members of the class.

Once the prerequisites have been satisfied, the court must determine the type of action. There are different types of class actions under Rule 23(b) of the Federal Rules of Civil Procedure. First, a class action is appropriate under Rule 23(b)(1) where having individual cases would result in "inconsistent or varying adjudications" or decisions that would impede or hinder other member's ability to protect their legal interests. Second, a class action can be certified under Rule 23(b)(2) if the defendant's alleged conduct applies generally to the whole class so that any decision would respect and remedy that whole class. Third, when the court determines that the questions of law or fact are shared by the class members and outweigh any individual differences that it is "superior to other available methods for fairly and efficiently adjudicating the controversy" under Rule 23(b)(3) of the FRCP. In *Marisol v. Giuliani*, the District Court certified the class and maintained that:

> The unique circumstances of each child do not compromise the common question of whether, as plaintiffs allege, defendants have injured all class members by failing to meet their federal and state law obligations. Indeed, as plaintiffs argue, the actions or inactions of defendants are not isolated or discrete instances but, rather, form a pattern of behavior that commonly affects all of the proposed class members. (*Marisol v. Giuliani*, 1996)

Once a class has been certified, there is an order of certification from the court that defines the class, the legal issues in disputes, any defenses, and appoints legal counsel for the class under Rule 23(c)(1)(b). It is particularly important to note that the court under Rule 23(g)(1) has to consider the experience of the proposed legal counsel in handling class actions, the resources that the proposed counsel promises to bring to the case, and the proposed counsel's investigation to ensure that all possible plaintiffs and class members have been identified. Once counsel has been appointed, the lawyers have an obligation under Rule 23(g)(4) "to fairly and adequately represent the interests of the class" as opposed to representing only the interest of the named parties. In the *Marisol v. Giuliani* case, because the named plaintiffs were children, they were assigned what is called "*next friends*" individuals who act as the representative for those individuals who are unable to participate in a lawsuit themselves because of age or incapacity and who do not have a legal guardian. Because the named plaintiffs in this case were under the custody of the defendants, the children were assigned next friends to represent their interests in the case.

Due Process in Class Actions: The Requirement of Notice

As you remember from previous chapters, due process in the law requires that the courts act with fundamental fairness to all litigants and parties. Given the particular nature of class actions, there has to be a process for notifying all members of a class that their legal rights may be at issue and providing those members with an opportunity to be heard. It is important for social workers to understand the notice requirements in class action claims, as often clients will receive written notice of a class action and have to make a decision regarding their participation in the case.

The federal rules require notice to all potential class members and in most cases the court can determine the appropriate method of communication, either by letter or publication, for example, in local newspapers. However, if a case is certified under Rule 23(b)(3) of the FRCP because there are questions of law and fact common to class members, the court must order the following specific notice under Rule 23(c)(2)(b) of FRCP:

> the best notice that is practicable under the circumstances, including individual notice to all members who can be identified through reasonable effort. The notice must clearly and concisely state in plain, easily understood language:
>
> (i) the nature of the action;
> (ii) the definition of the class certified;
> (iii) the class claims, issues, or defenses;
> (iv) that a class member may enter an appearance through an attorney if the
> (v) member so desires;
> (vi) that the court will exclude from the class any member who requests exclusion;
> (vii) the time and manner for requesting exclusion; and
> (viii) the binding effect of a class judgment on members under Rule 23(c)(3).

Finally, the court has the discretion to require notice of steps in the litigation and allow other class members to raise issues or concerns about the adequacy of their representation in order to "protect class members and fairly conduct the action" under Rule 23(d)(1)(B) of the FRCP. In the case of *Marisol v. Giuliani*, notice was distributed to all legal service organizations that represented children in foster care and their parents and were posted in foster care agencies and group and residential facilities.

Resolution of Class Action Lawsuits

Once the class has been certified and counsel has been appointed, the class action is able to proceed through the same processes of discovery and litigation preparation that you learned in Chapter 9. In the *Marisol v. Giuliani* case all of the social workers in the social work author's law firm were required to give depositions in preparation for trial. The depositions given by social workers in this case were important in detailing the evidence in support of the plaintiffs' claims and therefore providing leverage to persuade the parties to decide to come to a settlement rather than proceed to trial.

Class action lawsuits many times result in settlements where the parties agree to certain remedies that may be monetary damages and awards or changes in policies and practices. Often, the parties will enter into a consent decree, which is a judicial decree detailing the voluntary agreement that has been reached by the parties who were in dispute. For example, the remedies requested in the *Marisol v. Giuliani* case were related to ameliorating the problems and conditions in the child welfare system that had led to the lawsuit. The parties agreed upon a voluntary settlement of the lawsuit rather than moving to trial. The settlement was unprecedented in that the parties agreed that New York City would use a panel of outside experts in child welfare to evaluate, assess, monitor, and guide the reform of the child welfare system. The "Special Child Welfare Advisory Panel" had full access to all records and personnel and was charged with reporting on progress toward reform and to make recommendations based on the findings of the Panel. As part of the Panel's evaluation, Dr. Slater was extensively interviewed regarding her cases and knowledge of the system. In the event that the city did not make a good faith effort at reform, the plaintiffs could seek court-ordered relief. As a result of the lawsuit, the child welfare system in New York City undertook a number of reforms aimed at ameliorating the problems originally identified in the lawsuit. It is an example of a successful interdisciplinary reform effort as many social workers and attorneys alongside clients had a significant part in instigating this widespread reform.

In a class action lawsuit, once a settlement has been reached by the parties the court must conduct a fairness hearing prior to final approval. A fairness hearing is held by the judge prior to approval to assess the reasonableness of the settlements in achieving the outcomes identified in the suit that will provide a remedy. During the fairness hearing, the issue of attorneys' fees and monetary compensation is also addressed. After the fairness hearing the judge issues an opinion and final judgment and retains court jurisdiction for enforcement purposes. The issue of notice arises again at this point in the lawsuit as class members need to be notified and given an opportunity to comment on the settlement. Prior to the fairness hearing, the judge can also order what must be in the notice and how it may be distributed. In the case of *Marisol v. Giuliani*, the next friends of the named plaintiffs had to be notified of and agree to the settlement. In this manner, fairness hearings can also be a point of entry for social work advocacy even if social workers did not participate in the class action. As an example, in Illinois the state chapter of NASW provided written statements as part of a fairness hearing regarding the proposed resolution of the *Williams v. Quinn* (2010) class action lawsuit that sought to compel the state to allow mentally ill individuals to live in and obtain services within their local community rather than in nursing homes. NASW, based on practice experience, wrote to offer specific recommendations about the implementation of the proposed consent decree. The letter written by the local chapter is a great example of social work advocacy and the directed use of professional expertise at the later stages of the class action lawsuit process.

AMICUS CURIAE BRIEFS

Amicus curiae briefs are legal motions filed by an individual, group, or multiple organizations, who are not parties to the legal case but have an interest in the outcome of the matter. Amicus curiae briefs are most often filed in appellate courts and especially in the Supreme Court, when critical issues of law are being decided. As you remember from earlier chapters, a judge's decision at trial can be appealed or reviewed by another court for errors in the trial court's interpretation of the law or procedure. An appellate court generally hears the first appeal and the final appeal is decided by the highest court in the state, or in the case of a federal court case, the Supreme Court of the United States. The resulting decisions of the appellate courts make up the case law that we have been referring to in the previous chapters, and are used by attorneys in other cases to argue specific legal positions and interpretations of the law at issue in other cases. In the same way that class action effectuated systemic change in the law and social policy, amicus curiae briefs are powerful tools when arguing for the development of case law that supports socially just laws and policies.

The parties to the case being appealed are generally bound by the facts and evidence that were brought forth at trial when appealing a case. In this sense, an attorney cannot raise new evidence or information that was not raised at trial. However, an amicus curiae brief can bring additional information and analysis to the Court's attention, separate from the record that was developed at trial. Pursuant to Rule 37 of the Supreme Court Rules (2023), an amicus curiae brief "brings to the attention of the Court relevant matter not already brought to its attention by the parties [that] may be of considerable help to the Court." While the amicus curiae brief is ultimately written and filed by an attorney, its content can include medical and sociological data, in addition to legal interpretation and explanations regarding the potential consequences of the Court's decision. In this way, amicus curiae briefs can serve as an opportunity to educate the court on the impact of an unjust law or policy and potential consequences as a result of the Court's ruling.

As you remember from Chapter 2, social workers and social work organizations have filed amicus curiae briefs to promote social justice goals and raise issues about potential rulings that may not have been considered by the parties. In the same way that a social worker's testimony can be critical at trial, an amicus curiae brief from a social worker or social work organization can provide helpful information to the reviewing court on issues of social justice, evidence-based practice, and sociological research to name a few. Legal organizations, such as the American Civil Liberties Union and their local state chapters, also routinely file amicus curiae briefs in cases with potential far-reaching impact on specific legal issues such as civil rights, reproductive rights, prisoners' rights, and freedom of speech. Additionally, any agency of the United States is permitted to file an amicus curiae brief in any case and often the Solicitor General files briefs to present the U.S. government's position on the pending appeals.

The NASW often files amicus curiae briefs in cases of interest on the federal and state levels, all of which are available on their national website (www.nasw.org) and individual state chapter websites. In 2004, the NASW joined the American Medical Association and the American Psychiatric Association among other notable organizations to argue that the execution of a 16- or 17-year-old was cruel and unusual punishment prohibited under the Eighth Amendment of the United States Constitution in the Supreme Court case *Roper v. Simmons* (2005). Relying on scientific and social science data, the brief argued that 16- and 17-year-olds were differently situated from adult defendants given the anatomical immaturity in their brains and cognitive deficiencies, which often resulted in greater risk-taking behavior. As the brief noted, adolescents' "judgments, thought patterns, and emotions are different from adults', and their brains are physiologically underdeveloped in the areas that control impulses, foresee consequences, and temper emotions. They handle information processing and the management of emotions differently from adults" (NASW, n.d.).

Ultimately, the Court declared in *Roper v. Simmons* (2005) that the imposition of the death penalty for 16- or 17-year-old offenders was a violation of the Eighth Amendment and therefore unconstitutional. The majority opinion cited the overwhelming body of scientific and sociological evidence that demonstrated that adolescents had a developmentally different lack of maturity and sense of responsibility than adults. Justice Kennedy wrote the following:

> First, as any parent knows and as the scientific and sociological studies respondent and his amici cite tend to confirm, "[a] lack of maturity and an underdeveloped sense of responsibility are found in youth more often than in adults and are more understandable among the young. These qualities often result in impetuous and ill-considered actions and decisions." (p. 569)

In another important decision, the Supreme Court decided in the case of *Kennedy v. Louisiana* (2008) that states could not impose the death penalty on defendants convicted of raping a child under the age of 12. NASW and its local Louisiana chapter joined other organizations against sexual assault in an amicus curiae brief, describing their interest in the case as improving the quality of social work practice including the "detection, treatment and prevention of child sex abuse" (Gossett et al., 2008). The amicus curiae brief argued that the policy of seeking the death penalty for child rape would reduce the incidence of child sexual abuse being reported and increase the likelihood that offenders would kill child victims. The majority opinion cited the NASW brief's argument that the imposition of the death penalty for child rape would significantly increase the trauma experienced by child victims because they would be required to participate in a longer criminal justice process.

These two examples demonstrate the importance the court places on well-reasoned and researched amicus curiae briefs, particularly when making decisions at the Supreme Court level, which have a profound impact on laws across the country. More recently, NASW and other social work organizations have submitted amicus curiae briefs in significant Supreme Court cases on issues ranging from healthcare and reproductive rights to affirmative action. As you can see, amicus curiae briefs are another means of bringing social work values and the experience of evidence-based practice into the discussion of law reform and systemic change. They are carefully considered and can carry significant weight in the court's ultimate decision, even being cited by the majority opinion in their decision. While a social worker can have tremendous impact testifying as a lay or expert witness in an individual case, the amicus curiae brief provides another opportunity for social workers to include their experience and practice in the discussion and decision-making process of cases that implicate macro-level practice.

LEGISLATIVE LOBBYING

Legislative lobbying is the process of advocating for new or revised legislation with state and federal legislators and their staff. Social workers have a long history of working with legislators and other advocacy groups to promote social justice values through laws. For example, since the creation of the NASW in 1955, the organization has highlighted key legislative issues and lobbied for socially just policies in both federal and state legislatures.

Federal and state legislatures and government agencies, including courts, are empowered to propose and make new laws through a variety of processes. Advocacy by social workers, collectively and individually, for socially just and fair laws and regulations is a critical element of promoting the interests of clients and fulfilling social workers' ethical mandate to expose and to reform unjust systems. There are many opportunities for social workers to become involved with the legislative process, through advocacy campaigns, legislative testimony, drafting proposed legislation, and providing feedback during the public comment period. In each instance, social workers can advance laws and policies that benefit their clients by marshalling their experience as evidence-based practitioners.

The Basics of the Legislative Process

While anyone can write legislation to be proposed to the local, state, or federal legislator, only a legislator can sponsor or introduce a bill. In understanding the process of a proposed bill becoming law, it is helpful to view the federal system as a model for lobbying at the state level as well. Any proposed legislation or bill is first referred to a standing committee for review. Given the high volume of bills, many committees have issue-specific subcommittees that will first review the proposed bull and determine whether or not it will be recommended. Generally, a subcommittee will hold public hearings to obtain feedback on the potential legislation. These public hearings and comment phase are particularly important for advocates. Many organizations will work together to submit written or oral testimony during the public hearings. As you have learned in your courses for social policy, letter writing or e-mail campaigns to legislators can be particularly effective means of bringing other issues to the legislator's attention and providing the legislator with a better sense of the impact of the pending bill.

The notice and public comment period are critical periods for advocates to propose changes, support new regulations and rules, or oppose the rules in their entirety. For example, as we learned earlier, the Supreme Court can enact its own rules for handling the legal practice, evidence, and procedures in both the Supreme Court and all lower federal courts. This is because Congress has authorized them to do so under Section 2072 of the Rules Enabling Act (28 U.S.C. § 2072, 1934), which permits the Supreme Court to "prescribe rules for the conduct of their business." Pursuant to this rule, the Supreme Court is able to dictate how, when, and in what format amicus curiae briefs can be submitted in cases pending before the highest court in the country and all lower federal courts. However, the proposed rule first had to be submitted for notice and public comment before the Supreme Court was able to adopt it. During this notice and public comment period, organizations and individuals were able to raise any issues in favor or against the proposed rule before it was finalized.

The full committee can hold additional hearings after the bill has been amended and recommended by the subcommittee. Once the committee has voted to move forward with a bill, the bill is referred to as being ordered and a full report is provided to the legislative body. The written report on the proposed bill is comprehensive including the intent of the legislation, impact on any existing laws, and dissenting views. At this point, the bill is placed on the calendar for a vote by the full House of Representatives or Senate.

During the voting process, there is additional debate by the Representatives and Senators before a vote is taken. During this debate period, amendments and changes can be made to the bill. If the vote is to pass the bill, it is then referred to the other legislative entity. So, if the bill went through the Committee process in the Senate and was ultimately passed by the Senate, it would be referred to the House of Representatives to undergo the same process. If the bill is approved with the same terms in both the House and Senate, it is then sent to the Executive Branch to be signed into law by the president. At this juncture the president has the ability to veto the law if, thereby requiring the legislative houses to override the veto with a two-thirds majority vote.

Clearly, laws and regulations play a critical role in clients' daily lives as evidenced by the studies presented in Chapter 1 regarding the unmet legal needs of clients and in the case study of Michelle Jones, which demonstrates the numerous ways that social work clients interact with laws and the justice system. However, laws and regulations also underscore values of justice and fairness in their explicit text, application, and approach to remedying social ills. As you saw in Chapter 11 when discussing statutes authorizing various alternative venues, principles such as those related to restorative justice and procedural fairness were directly incorporated into the law. Therefore, the involvement of social workers in law reform and legislative lobbying is intrinsically linked to our ethical mandate to promote values of social justice; work to end discrimination, poverty, and systemic injustice; and support individual client practice both in the implicit and explicit contexts.

Keeping Track of Pending Bills and Regulations

The advent and widespread use of technology for enhanced communication, advocacy, and organizing purposes offer the new generation of social workers many ways to exert power and control in the legislative front and in legal arenas. Many public libraries have free computer access for clients, and social workers are now routinely equipped with up-to-date technology and web access for their research and practice. Prior to the development of the internet, busy social workers did not always have the time or money required for trips to state legislatures or to attend meetings or task forces. Technology and working platforms like Slack, Google Docs, Wikispaces, Zoom, Google Meet, Microsoft Team, Webex, and other platforms have changed the way we engage each other in the professional field. For example, social workers and clients can collaborate for meetings and drafting advocacy documents such as letters or briefs without leaving their homes or offices. Client participation in these advocacy efforts can be maximized with this technology because they would not need to leave their home and are often able to participate with just their phone. Free programs such as Survey Monkey, Google Forms, SurveySparrow, and HubSpot also offer technology for groups of social workers to create forms and surveys to collect and analyze data that can be shared about their cases and used for advocacy purposes. Collaborative applications and technology continue to evolve and provide an excellent resource for social workers interested in legislative change to invite broader participation from other social workers, experts, and community members and to coordinate group efforts to impact legislative reform. Other platforms like Change.org, MoveOn.com, and OpenPetition.org/us have allowed social workers and community activists to engage in advocacy by creating campaign materials and information documents, including petitions to influence and encourage the public to get involved in political and social movements in a variety of ways including supporting or opposing legislative bills. In the view of the authors, this is an enormous opportunity to renew the social work commitment to social change and proactive engagement with the legal system and to engage clients in the process as well.

Organizations maintain websites with information on current bills and proposed regulations that are relevant to their work and issue areas. For example, the NASW provides regular updates and advocacy opportunities on issues of particular interest to the social work profession including welfare reform, immigration, and social workers in schools (www.socialworkers.org/Advocacy). The website includes legal advocacy efforts such as amicus curiae briefs, information on pending legislation of interest to the social work profession, and copies of comments submitted by the organization as part of the legislative process. The American Civil Liberties Union provides national and state updates on pending legislation impacting civil rights and liberties including religious rights, prisoners' rights, drug law policy, and reproductive freedom among others. The School Social Worker Association of America (SSWAA) focuses on legislation impacting social workers in school settings including education financing, special education issues, and school counseling (www.sswaa.org/policy-and-advocacy). The National Association for the Advancement of Colored People (NAACP) also offers issue pages on their website that highlight key initiatives and relevant federal bills and policies that impact their policy agenda. Other organizations' websites focus on policy initiatives both locally and nationally for their particular issue ranging from racial equality to welfare reform and education.

As the family social worker for Ms. Jones and Matthew, you might be interested in tracking legislation that directly relates to infant and toddlers or to substance abuse treatment for mothers. You would also share this information with Ms. Jones to engage her in becoming an active advocate for those issues impacting her and her son. A research and advocacy organization called Zero to Three tracks public policy initiatives at the federal and state levels that relate to the education and developmental needs of infants and toddlers. The Bazelon Center for Mental Health Law focuses on the rights of individuals with mental illnesses through litigation and policy reform, including lobbying for progressive mental health laws in Congress. A rights-based social worker would research both local and national organizations focused on issues of interest to their client population and develop partnerships to stay abreast of pending legislation, recommend policy reforms, and include client participation in informing that process. We discuss the specific roles that social workers play in macro-level reform in the next section.

SOCIAL WORK ROLES IN MACRO-LEVEL REFORM

There are many different roles for social workers to play in macro-level law reform efforts, whether it is a class action, amicus curiae brief, or legislative advocacy campaign. Social work roles in law reform generally fall into three categories: identification of issues and clients, participation in law reform efforts through testimony and briefs, and development of socially just policy.

Identification of Issues and Clients

Social workers have considerable knowledge about the day-to-day application of laws and regulations through their work with clients. Whether it is helping a client navigate the welfare application process or hearing from clients about unjust employment practices, social workers are often the first line of defense in identifying a potential legal issue. Social workers are also in a position to identify patterns of concerns that may occur across cases. Social workers discuss these observations with other social workers in their organizations or in other professional meetings such as task forces or conferences, and therefore have a unique perspective and insight into the scope of an issue and its impact on clients and community.

Indeed, social workers are able to see the practical failures or injustice of a law in an individual case that might not yet be apparent on a systemic level or to legal services organizations working on a particular issue such as welfare reform or employment discrimination. This is in large part because a legally informed social worker interacts not only with their clients but, importantly for the concept of macro-level law reform, the application of laws and regulations. With this framework, social workers in the implicit legal context can leverage relationships with legal services organizations and other social workers practicing in the explicit legal context to discuss legal reform issues based on their daily practice and interactions with clients. As an example of this collaborative approach and feedback loop for macro-level reform, a social worker might identify that a number of their clients' medically complex children are being automatically denied benefits when they turn 18 years old. The social worker would discuss this pattern with a legal services office with expertise in benefits law and potentially identify areas for legal intervention and reform.

Once a legal issue has been identified, social workers can assist in identifying and referring potential clients to legal service organizations and attorneys. Especially with class actions, social workers can play a vital role in helping attorneys identify potential class members and providing support to those clients throughout the litigation process. For example, the Supreme Court case of *Wheeler v. Montgomery* (1970) dealt with elderly clients' rights to an evidentiary hearing if denied government provided old age benefits. A social worker was responsible for identifying the unconstitutional practice and linking the client with a legal services organization (Levy, 1991). In that matter, a social worker with the San Francisco Housing Authority unsuccessfully tried to have their client's benefits reinstated and ultimately referred the case to a local legal services office. The resulting Supreme Court case held that recipients were entitled to an evidentiary hearing if benefits were reduced, denied, or terminated along the same rationale of the *Goldberg v. Kelly* (1970) case holding that welfare recipients were entitled to an evidentiary hearing. While the case originally involved an individual client, the impact of the legal decision was profound for elderly recipients across the country.

Social workers in the implicit context can play a critical role in referring clients who may be eligible for legal relief, and also in ensuring that the clients are supported and educated throughout the litigation process by continuing to interact with the attorneys, forensic social workers, and others who participate in a class action. As you learned earlier, social workers can also identify clients who should be provided with notice of the potential class action litigation or settlement.

Participating in Law Reform Through Testimony and Briefs

Social workers can also participate in class actions and amicus curiae briefs in a number of ways. When law reform initiatives are initially reviewed, social workers can play a critical role in providing expertise to lawyers and organizations on any evidence-based research that may exist to support or undermine the legal claim. For example, the amicus curiae briefs filed by NASW all contained critical research and data on the legal issue at hand that otherwise might not have been presented to the court by the parties.

This research and expertise is important in helping to determine the strength of a particular legal claim at the outset and then supporting the legal argument during the litigation process. Participation in class action litigation and law reform, however, is not limited to amicus curiae briefs. Social work testimony in a class action can also be a critical component of proving a case. For example, a social worker working with Ms. Jones could testify about their individual knowledge about clients and how public assistance recipients are or are not properly processed for learning disabilities during the application and work assignment period.

Development of Socially Just Policy

Finally, social workers are positioned to provide legislative testimony and expertise when drafting new social policy legislation or advocating for or against pending legislation. Social workers in the implicit and explicit legal contexts can explain the current failings or successes of legislative policies and laws, and work with legislators and other advocates to draft more socially just laws. Often, the legislators are not aware of the impact that current or potential legislation is having and social workers, who interact with clients daily, are able to illuminate how the law functions in practice, which may be radically different than the intended purpose of the law. Social workers can be integral in providing written and oral testimony to legislators and speaking with legislators about policy issues throughout the process.

SYSTEMIC REFORM: THE CASE OF MICHELLE JONES

There are multiple issues in the case of Michelle Jones that could lead to systemic reform opportunities, including a class action, amicus curiae brief, and legislative advocacy. Regardless of whether the social worker is working in the explicit or implicit legal context, a legally informed social worker would recognize the possibility for macro-level reform from Ms. Jones's individual experience in the criminal and child welfare systems.

As you remember from previous chapters, while Ms. Jones was pregnant, she was receiving treatment in a substance abuse treatment program and was also incarcerated as a result of a criminal arrest for drugs. As her social worker at the drug treatment program, you identify two issues that impact not only Ms. Jones but also other women in her same position. When you realize that these issues may not be unique to Ms. Jones's situation, you recognize the opportunity for systemic legal reform and macro-level social work practice.

First, you learn that the State Legislature is attempting to amend the mandated reporting laws for social workers to include a pregnant mother's conduct as a basis for requiring a report of abuse or neglect to the state's child welfare agency. You learn of this legislative initiative through a review of issue-based websites and conversations with other social workers in drug treatment facilities working with women. You are particularly concerned about how this proposed legislation would impact your pregnant client's treatment, the therapeutic relationship, and the incentives for pregnant women who are using drugs to seek treatment during their pregnancy. The proposed amendment would require you, as the treatment provider and counselor, to report any pregnant women in your program who relapse. Professionally, you are concerned that your own professional and potential criminal liability is implicated and also that your client may now have potential exposure to the child welfare or criminal justice system, as opposed to the treatment community.

In order to gather more information, you conduct a review and learn that the NASW, along with other social service and medical organizations such as the National Association of Alcohol and Drug Abuse Counselors and the American College of Obstetricians and Gynecologists, filed an amicus curiae brief in 1997 on this very issue in the case of *Whitner v. South Carolina* (1997). The amicus brief lays out the argument against the proposed legislation in your state and details the medical and sociological data against such a sweeping policy including that it would deter pregnant women from seeking treatment for any drug use and seeking out prenatal care. The brief notes the potentially devastating consequences of such a law in making healthcare and substance abuse treatment counselors choose "whether to breach the patient confidentiality so essential to medical care and drug treatment services, or violate state law and be subject to imprisonment" (Daniel, 1998). With this legal information and the literature review on the effects of prenatal substance abuse and the importance of ensuring prenatal care and treatment during pregnancy to decrease the risk of harm to the infant, you are well positioned to advocate for a more socially just practice. This advocacy could include meetings with legislators, letter-writing campaigns, legislative testimony, and collaborations with other social service and legal organizations.

Second, during your treatment sessions with Ms. Jones, you learn more about her time in jail when she was arrested. Ms. Jones was pregnant at the time and had been receiving regular prenatal care from her local clinic before being temporarily incarcerated. The arrest experience was extremely traumatic for Ms. Jones, having never been arrested before and being concerned about her health. When she was in the jail, Ms. Jones was placed with other women who were pregnant during their detention and she was frightened to hear from them that they were not getting any medical care addressing their pregnancy. Ms. Jones also informs you that she heard many stories that women were shackled to their hospital bed during their active labor, and she became increasingly frightened of remaining in jail during her pregnancy.

You are concerned about the injustice of this practice and the potential medical risks to pregnant women being shackled during active labor. Because you work primarily in the implicit legal context, you decide to contact a social worker and attorney in the explicit legal context to determine whether there is any chance for reform. When you contact the attorney, the attorney requests that you accompany Ms. Jones to their office in order to discuss the case. Ms. Jones tells the attorney that all of the pregnant women at the jail were placed in the same cells. She says that whenever a pregnant woman was brought to the hospital, they were shackled to the bed even if they were only receiving a routine checkup; many women told Ms. Jones that if she ended up giving birth while at prison that she would be shackled to the hospital bed for her entire labor.

Recognizing that this practice may be widespread, the attorney begins by advising you and Ms. Jones that this practice has been challenged in other states. In a federal case in the Eighth Circuit, *Nelson v. Correctional Medical Services* (2009), which also involved shackling a woman during childbirth, an amicus curiae brief filed by numerous healthcare and social service organizations began by declaring that the "inhumane, unnecessary and dangerous practice [of shackling] should be abolished as a matter of law and policy." The brief, however, focused on the medical and sociological evidence, which demonstrated that shackling during pregnancy significantly increased medical risks to mothers and their babies.

Based on Ms. Jones's descriptions, the attorney initially suggests that there could be a claim under the Eighth Amendment of the U.S. Constitution for cruel and unusual punishment by shackling a pregnant woman's legs during childbirth. Additionally, if the practice was widespread, there could be a number of women who were impacted and could be entitled to legal relief through a class action. The next steps in the legal process would be to determine the full extent of any legal claims and arguments and to identify other women who may be willing to share their story with the attorney and potentially participate in litigation. The attorney would most likely research whether there is a difference in the legal claims depending on whether the woman is shackled during active labor or prenatal appointments. The attorney could also work with a social worker to identify research on the impact of shackling on pregnant women and the identification of medical experts.

As the social worker, you may have been in touch with other social workers or clients who tell a similar story and therefore could be referred to the attorney's office for an initial consultation. To feel comfortable in passing along information about a potential class action and to ensure that your clients are treated fairly during that process, it is important to have the lawyer clarify the next steps, exactly what information is needed from the potential class plaintiffs and the confidentiality of any conversations between the attorney and the client. Finally, you would want to understand what if any continued participation you will have in the potential class action.

REFERENCES

Brown v. Board of Education, 347 U.S. 483 (1954).

Civil Rights Act of 1964, 88 Pub. L. No. 352, 78 Stat. 241 (1964).

Civil Rights Act of 1991, Pub. L. No. 102–166, 105 Stat. 1071 (1991).

Daniel, N. (1998). Amicus curiae brief: Cornelia Whitner v. The State of South Carolina. *Hastings Women's Law Journal, 9*(2), 139–160. https://repository.uchastings.edu/hwlj/vol9/iss2/1

Federal Rules of Civil Procedure, 28 U.S.C. §§ 2071-2077 (2023).

Goldberg v. Kelly, 397 U.S. 254 (1970).

Gossett, D. M., Ranlett, K., Polowy, C. I., Morgan, S., & Thai, J. (2008). Kennedy v. Louisiana: Brief of the National Association of Social Workers and other organizations as amici curiae. *Federal Sentencing Reporter, 21*(2), 139–144. https://doi.org/10.1525/fsr.2008.21.2.139

Griggs v. Duke Power Co., 401 U.S. 424 (1971).

Kennedy v. Louisiana, 554 U.S. 407 (2008).

Levy, P. (1991). Social work roles in law reform litigation. *Social Work, 36*(5), 434–439. https://www.jstor.org/stable/23715938

Marisol v. Giuliani, 929 F. Supp 662 (SDNY 1996).

National Association of Social Workers. (2021). *Code of ethics of the national association of social workers*. Author.

National Association of Social Workers. (n.d.). *Brief in Roper v. Simmons.* https://www.socialworkers.org/assets/secured/documents/ldf/briefDocuments/roper%20v.%20simmons.pdf
Nelson v. Correctional Medical Services, 583 F.3d 522 (8th Cir. 2009).
Roper v. Simmons. 543 U.S. 551 (2005).
Rules Enabling Act, 28 U.S.C. § 2072 (1934).
Supreme Court Rules, 28 U.S.C. §§ 1-11 (2023).
Wheeler v. Montgomery, 397 U.S. 280 (1970).
Whitner v. South Carolina, 492 S.E.2d 777 (S.C. 1997).
Williams v. Quinn, 748 F. Supp. 2d 892 (N.D. Ill. 2010).

Index